Contributions to Economics

The series *Contributions to Economics* provides an outlet for innovative research in all areas of economics. Books published in the series are primarily monographs and multiple author works that present new research results on a clearly defined topic, but contributed volumes and conference proceedings are also considered. All books are published in print and ebook and disseminated and promoted globally. The series and the volumes published in it are indexed by Scopus and ISI (selected volumes).

More information about this series at http://www.springer.com/series/1262

Natalie Rauscher

The Future of Work in the United States

Discourses on Automation and the Platform Economy

Springer

Natalie Rauscher
Heidelberg Center for American Studies
Heidelberg University
Heidelberg, Baden-Württemberg, Germany

ISSN 1431-1933 ISSN 2197-7178 (electronic)
Contributions to Economics
ISBN 978-3-030-82306-1 ISBN 978-3-030-82307-8 (eBook)
https://doi.org/10.1007/978-3-030-82307-8

The following book was submitted as a dissertation at the University of Heidelberg, Germany in 2020 under the title: The Discourse on the Future of Work in the United States under the Influence of Automation and the Platform Economy.

This Springer imprint is published by the registered company Springer Nature Switzerland AG.
The registered company address is: Gewerbestrasse 11, 6330 Cham, Switzerland

Acknowledgments

I would like to thank several people without whom this book would not have been possible.

First of all, I would like to thank my supervisors at the Heidelberg Center for American Studies, PD Dr. habil. Martin Thunert and Prof. Dr. Welf Werner. With Martin Thunert I have found a superb first supervisor who has always supported and helped me move along during my journey as a PhD student, which can feel overwhelming at times. Through our many conversations and discussions which I have always cherished, I have learned a lot and was inspired to explore new avenues and topics. I have always been impressed by his interest and knowledgeable advice throughout the years. With Welf Werner I have won a second most knowledgeable supervisor through whose insights my work has certainly gained a whole new perspective. From the very beginning of co-teaching and working with Welf Werner, my own work has certainly moved into new disciplinary arenas and was only improved by it. For this, I want to thank both of them very much.

Secondly, I would like to thank my friends Maren Schäfer and Aline Schmidt. Spending several years working on a dissertation was made better by such good friends at my side who have always helped and supported me. Exchanging new ideas and working on projects together has always been a pleasure. I also cannot thank them enough for their willingness to plow through several hundred pages of text, offering invaluable advice and feedback.

Moreover, I would like to thank my parents Gerhard and Marianne who have always been interested in and supportive of my academic endeavors and who are just the best parents anyone could wish for.

Additionally, I would like to thank the rest of my close family, Linda, René, Alexander, and my aunt Bobby who has been the best host during my trips to California. And, of course, my friends Mona and Barbara who are always there to celebrate the highs and help through the lows of life.

During the last few years of working on this project, and especially in the most recent past, I have learned to cherish even more the many good friends I have around Germany and in the world, and my dearest colleagues in Heidelberg.

Contents

1 Introduction: Focus, Scope, and Structure of the Book 1
References 6

2 The Network Society, the Internet, and the Beginning of the New Economy 7
2.1 Employment and Economic Security in the Network Society 15
2.2 Automation, Digitization, and the Rise of the Platform Economy 21
2.2.1 Automation 21
2.2.2 Digitization 28
2.2.3 The Rise of the Platform Economy 36
2.2.4 Inequality in the Digital Age 41
References 66

3 A New World of Work: The Sharing Economy Platforms 71
3.1 Sharing, Gig, On-Demand: Crucial Definitions 71
3.2 The Sharing Economy Platforms 78
3.2.1 Users and Providers of the Sharing Economy Platforms . . . 83
3.2.2 Sharing Economy Platforms: An Ambiguous Trend 87
3.3 The Platform Economy and Labor 90
3.3.1 The Example of Uber 91
3.3.2 The Future of Work: Platform Work 98
3.3.3 Platforms: Labor Reform and Regulation 104
3.3.4 A Future Without Work? The Universal Basic Income 107
3.3.5 Present and Future of the Platform Economy in the World of Work 113
References 116

4 Corpus Analysis: Automation, the Future of Work, and the Platform Economy Reflected in Political and Public Discourse 121
4.1 Political and Public Discourse as Source Material 121
4.2 Corpus Linguistics as Method 127

4.3 Methodology: The Corpora on Congressional Hearings and Media Sources 129
4.3.1 Compiling the Data 130
4.3.2 Identifying Keywords 136
4.4 A First Glance at the Congressional Material 137
4.4.1 Impressions from the Congressional Hearings 154
4.4.2 Suggested Policies in Context of the Future of Work 158
References 162

5 Quantitative Analysis: Frequency Analysis 165
5.1 Future Trends 167
5.2 Platform Economy 173
5.3 Technology 183
5.4 Policies 187
5.5 Inequality 192
References 196

6 Qualitative Analysis: Collocations and Contextual Reading 197
6.1 Digitization and Automation 197
6.1.1 Digitization in the Congressional Material 198
6.1.2 Digitization in the Liberal Media Material 205
6.1.3 Digitization in the *WSJ* Material 210
6.1.4 Automation in the Congressional Material 216
6.1.5 Automation in the Liberal Media Material 227
6.1.6 Automation in the *WSJ* Material 238
6.1.7 Digitization and Automation in Political and Public Discourse 253
6.2 Future of Work 257
6.2.1 Future of Work in the Congressional Material 257
6.2.2 Future of Work in the Liberal Media Material 264
6.2.3 Future of Work in the *WSJ* Material 276
6.2.4 Future of Work in Political and Public Discourse 282
6.3 Platform Economy 285
6.3.1 Platform Economy in the Congressional Material 285
6.3.2 Platform Economy in the Liberal Media Material 314
6.3.3 Platform Economy in the *WSJ* Material 350
6.3.4 Platform Economy in Political and Public Discourse 372
References 375

7 The Discourse Around Technological Progress and the Future of Work 377
7.1 Summary of Findings 377
7.2 Outlook: Discourse on Technological Progress After 2017 386

7.3 Conclusion: A Difficult Vision for Future Participation in the Face of Disruption 394
References 398

About the Author

Natalie Rauscher is working in the field of American Studies with a focus on political science. In 2020, she successfully completed her PhD at Heidelberg University. She previously completed her B.A. in English and Political Science as well as her M.A. in American Studies at Heidelberg University. Her research interests include quantitative and qualitative analysis of discourses, for example on the future of work as well as the rise of the platform economy in the USA. She is also working on other topics like social movements, social media, American philanthropy and think tanks, and the impact of natural catastrophes in the USA. Natalie Rauscher is currently working as a research associate at the Heidelberg Center for American Studies (HCA) where she co-founded and hosts the HCA Graduate Blog.

Contact: nrauscher@hca.uni-heidelberg.de

List of Figures

Fig. 2.1 Gap in income between upper-income and middle- and lower-income households is rising, based on Pew Research Center (Pew-Research-Center 2020) 42
Fig. 2.2 Gaps in wealth between upper-income and middle- and lower-income families are rising, based on Pew Research Center (Pew-Research-Center 2020) 43
Fig. 2.3 GINI Index for the USA 1974–1979, 1991–2018 (upper line), compared to Germany 1994–2016 (middle line), and Norway 2003-2018 (lower line) (World Bank 2021) 48
Fig. 2.4 Information technology workers in the USA, 1970–2014 (Census-Bureau 2016) 55
Fig. 4.1 Public priorities according to Pew Research Center (Pew-Research-Center 2019) 122

List of Tables

Table 2.1	Changing employment shares, 1960–2015 in percent	16
Table 2.2	Median earnings by industry, 1960–2015 in constant 2015 dollars	16
Table 2.3	Determinants of feasibility of automation	23
Table 4.1	Corpora based on congressional material	133
Table 4.2	Corpora based on media material	135
Table 4.3	House and Senate hearings as basis for keywords	136
Table 4.4	Keyword list	138
Table 5.1	Example of collocation parameters notation (CPN)	166
Table 5.2	Liberal media: future trends, per 10,000 tokens	167
Table 5.3	*WSJ*: future trends, per 10,000 tokens	168
Table 5.4	House: future trends, per 10,000 tokens	168
Table 5.5	Senate: future trends, per 10,000 tokens	169
Table 5.6	Liberal media: automation, digitization, future of work, per 10,000 tokens	171
Table 5.7	WSJ: automation, digitization, future of work, per 10,000 tokens	172
Table 5.8	House: automation, digitization, future of work, per 10,000 tokens	172
Table 5.9	Senate: automation, digitization, future of work, per 10,000 tokens	173
Table 5.10	Liberal media: platform economy, per 10,000 tokens	173
Table 5.11	*WSJ*: platform economy, per 10,000 tokens	174
Table 5.12	House: platform economy, per 10,000 tokens	174
Table 5.13	Senate: platform economy, per 10,000 tokens	175
Table 5.14	House: number of hearings featuring "sharing economy"	177
Table 5.15	Senate: number of hearings featuring "sharing economy"	177
Table 5.16	Liberal media: platform economy—workers, per 10,000 tokens	178
Table 5.17	WSJ: platform economy—workers, per 10,000 tokens	178
Table 5.18	House: platform economy—workers, per 10,000 tokens	179

Table 5.19 Senate: platform economy—workers, per 10,000 tokens 179
Table 5.20 Liberal media: platform economy—platforms, per 10,000 tokens 180
Table 5.21 *WSJ*: platform economy—platforms, per 10,000 tokens 181
Table 5.22 House: platform economy—platforms, per 10,000 tokens 181
Table 5.23 Senate: platform economy—platforms, per 10,000 tokens 182
Table 5.24 Liberal media: technology, per 10,000 tokens 183
Table 5.25 *WSJ*: technology, per 10,000 tokens 184
Table 5.26 House: technology, per 10,000 tokens 184
Table 5.27 Senate: technology, per 10,000 tokens 185
Table 5.28 House: number of hearings featuring "AI" and "Internet of Things" 186
Table 5.29 Senate: number of hearings featuring "AI" and "Internet of Things" 186
Table 5.30 House: policies, per 10,000 tokens 187
Table 5.31 Senate: policies, per 10,000 tokens 188
Table 5.32 Liberal media: policies, per 10,000 tokens 188
Table 5.33 *WSJ*: policies, per 10,000 tokens 189
Table 5.34 House: number of hearings featuring 'education' 191
Table 5.35 Senate: number of hearings featuring 'education' 191
Table 5.36 Senate: number of hearings featuring "skills gap" and "infrastructure" 192
Table 5.37 House: number of hearings featuring "skills gap" and "infrastructure" 192
Table 5.38 Liberal media: inequality, per 10,000 tokens 193
Table 5.39 *WSJ*: inequality, per 10,000 tokens 193
Table 5.40 House: inequality, per 10,000 tokens 194
Table 5.41 Senate: inequality, per 10,000 tokens 194
Table 6.1 House: number of hearings featuring "automation," "digitization," "future of work" 198
Table 6.2 Senate: number of hearings featuring "automation," "digitization," "future of work" 199
Table 6.3 Senate: collocation graph of digitization MI $\geq$ 5, minimum collocate frequency 1 200
Table 6.4 Senate: collocates of digitization MI $\geq$ 5, minimum collocate frequency 1 201
Table 6.5 House: collocation graph of digitization MI $\geq$ 5, minimum collocate frequency 4 203
Table 6.6 House: collocates of digitization MI $\geq$ 5, minimum collocate frequency 4 204
Table 6.7 Liberal media: collocation graph of digitization MI $\geq$ 7, minimum collocate frequency 5 206
Table 6.8 Liberal media: collocates of digitization MI $\geq$ 7, minimum collocate frequency 5 207
Table 6.9 *WSJ*: collocation graph of digitization MI $\geq$ 7, minimum collocate frequency 5 211

Table 6.10 *WSJ*: collocates of digitization MI $\geq$ 7, minimum collocate frequency 5 212
Table 6.11 Senate: collocation graph of automation MI $\geq$ 7, minimum collocate frequency 5 217
Table 6.12 Senate: collocates of automation MI $\geq$ 7, minimum collocate frequency 5 218
Table 6.13 House: collocation graph of automation MI $\geq$ 7, minimum collocate frequency 5 222
Table 6.14 House: collocates of automation MI $\geq$ 7, minimum collocate frequency 5 223
Table 6.15 Liberal media: collocation graph of automation MI $\geq$ 7, minimum collocate frequency 7 228
Table 6.16 Liberal media: collocates of automation MI $\geq$ 7, minimum collocate frequency 7 229
Table 6.17 *WSJ*: collocation graph for automation MI $\geq$ 7, minimum collocate frequency 5 239
Table 6.18 *WSJ*: collocates of automation MI $\geq$ 7, minimum collocate frequency 5 240
Table 6.19 House: number of hearings featuring "automation," "digitization," "future of work" 258
Table 6.20 Senate: number of hearings featuring "automation," "digitization," "future of work" 258
Table 6.21 Senate: collocation graph for future of work MI $\geq$ 5, minimum collocate frequency 1 260
Table 6.22 Senate: collocates of future of work MI $\geq$ 5, minimum collocate frequency 1 261
Table 6.23 House: collocation graph of future of work MI $\geq$ 5, minimum collocate frequency 1 262
Table 6.24 House: collocates of future of work MI $\geq$ 5, minimum collocate frequency 1 263
Table 6.25 Liberal media: collocation graph of future of work MI $\geq$ 7, minimum collocate frequency 5 265
Table 6.26 Liberal media: collocates of future of work MI $\geq$ 7, minimum collocate frequency 5 266
Table 6.27 *WSJ*: collocation graph of future of work MI $\geq$ 5, minimum collocate frequency 2 277
Table 6.28 *WSJ*: collocates of future of work MI $\geq$ 5, minimum collocate frequency 2 278
Table 6.29 Senate: collocation graph of sharing economy MI $\geq$ 5, minimum collocate frequency 2 287
Table 6.30 Senate: collocates of sharing economy MI $\geq$ 5, minimum collocate frequency 2 288
Table 6.31 House: collocation graph of sharing economy MI $\geq$ 5, minimum collocate frequency 5 292
Table 6.32 House: collocates of sharing economy MI $\geq$ 5, minimum collocate frequency 5 293

Table 6.33 Senate: collocation graph of gig economy MI $\geq$ 5, minimum collocate frequency 2 ... 302
Table 6.34 Senate: collocates of gig economy MI $\geq$ 5, minimum collocate frequency 2 ... 302
Table 6.35 House: collocation network graph of sharing economy, gig economy, platform economy MI $\geq$ 5, minimum collocate frequency 5 ... 305
Table 6.36 House: collocation graph of gig economy MI $\geq$ 7, minimum collocate frequency 2 ... 306
Table 6.37 House: collocates of gig economy, MI $\geq$ 7, minimum collocate frequency 2 ... 307
Table 6.38 House: collocation graph of platform economy MI $\geq$ 7, minimum collocate frequency 2 ... 310
Table 6.39 House: collocates of platform economy MI $\geq$ 7, minimum collocate frequency 2 ... 311
Table 6.40 Liberal media: collocation graph of platform economy MI $\geq$ 7, minimum collocate frequency 2 ... 315
Table 6.41 Liberal media: collocates of platform economy MI $\geq$ 7, minimum collocate frequency 2 ... 316
Table 6.42 Liberal media: collocation graph of gig economy MI $\geq$ 7, minimum collocate frequency 5 ... 319
Table 6.43 Liberal media: collocates of gig economy MI $\geq$ 7, minimum collocate frequency 5 ... 320
Table 6.44 Liberal media: collocation graph of sharing economy MI $\geq$ 7, minimum collocate frequency 5 ... 333
Table 6.45 Liberal media: collocates of sharing economy MI $\geq$ 7, minimum collocate frequency 5 ... 334
Table 6.46 Liberal media: network collocation graph of sharing economy, gig economy, platform economy, MI $\geq$ 7, minimum collocate frequency 5 ... 349
Table 6.47 *WSJ*: collocation graph of sharing economy MI $\geq$ 5, minimum collocate frequency 5 ... 351
Table 6.48 *WSJ*: collocates of sharing economy MI $\geq$ 5, minimum collocate frequency 5 ... 352
Table 6.49 *WSJ*: collocation graph of gig economy MI $\geq$ 7, minimum collocate frequency 3 ... 364
Table 6.50 *WSJ*: collocates of gig economy, MI $\geq$ 7, minimum collocate frequency 3 ... 365
Table 6.51 *WSJ*: network collocation graph of sharing economy, gig economy, MI $\geq$ 5, minimum collocation frequency 5 ... 371

Chapter 1
Introduction: Focus, Scope, and Structure of the Book

Since the onset of large-scale industrialization, technological progress has always both inspired images of great opportunities and induced fears about large-scale job loss. The history of technological progress has seen many instances where people have channeled their insecurity and fears about the future into panics or even violent attacks. Public sentiments about the arrival of the machine age were displayed in many dystopian books and movies, always reflecting the fear that humans might become obsolete or even subject to machines. Today, we see another instance where many discussions around the future of work emerge, fed by the fast development of ever smarter machines that enter our lives in all kinds of ways. Since the introduction of the iPhone in 2007, everyone seems to have a small powerful computer in their pockets. These devices have become able to talk to us and understand what we are saying, connecting us to our cars and home appliances, to our workplaces, and to people around the globe. Powerful platforms have emerged as the winners of this ever-improving technological capacity. Is now the time that machines are becoming as smart as people? Or even smarter than us? Will they take over not only physical work but also cognitive tasks? What will the future of work look like under these circumstances?

In times like these it is not only important to know what technological progress looks like and how it is likely going to proceed, but it is crucial to know how various stakeholders, for example in the political or business sphere, as well as the public perceive and talk about these developments. Discourses around these topics influence how the public perceives technological progress and how it acts toward it, for example by rejecting or embracing new technology in their lives and workplaces. Political stakeholders' perspectives on and interaction with technological developments shape their ways of action and agendas for the future. Businesses and well-known (tech) entrepreneurs, as well as academic experts, are also part of the discourse around technological change and their perspectives are often reflected in media discourses, as well as political debates. Both public and political narratives and discourses around technological progress influence and reinforce each other,

N. Rauscher, *The Future of Work in the United States*, Contributions to Economics,
https://doi.org/10.1007/978-3-030-82307-8_1

especially today in the age of social media where our consumption of information has transformed and become ubiquitous.

To put it in simple terms, linguistically, discourses are units of language above the level of the sentence. However, there are multiple definitions of discourses, even inside of the linguistic discipline, for example, seeing discourse as not only a group of sentences but also as a practice, a way of talking and thinking about a subject by a certain community (McEnery and Hardie 2012: 133f). In a poststructuralist definition, "discourse is not studied to find out about 'the real world', but rather to find out how 'the real world' is talked about" (McEnery and Hardie 2012: 135). In other fields apart from linguistics, for example in political science, there is also a heightened interest in the role of language as a medium of understanding and even changing the world around us (Gadinger et al. 2014: 3). In the field of economics, Robert Shiller has established the idea of *economic narratives*. What this book calls "discourses" is shaped in many ways by this idea of narratives. Shiller argues in favor of including narratives in our study of the economy as they induce and influence actual economic behavior and therefore technological progress as well. Economic narratives can offer "an explanation about how things work in the economy, and affects how people think about the justification or purpose of economic actions. The narrative may imply something about the way the world works" (Shiller 2018: 87). Things like adoption of new technology, research, funding, societal acceptance, enthusiasm, or fears of technology all contribute to societal and economic changes. If we exclude narratives from our study of politics and the economy, "we remain blind to a very real, very palpable, very important mechanism for economic change, as well as a crucial element for economic forecasting. If we do not understand the epidemics of popular narratives, we do not fully understand changes in the economy and in economic behavior" (Shiller 2018: xi).

Thus, by studying the political and public discourses around technological change, this book aims to illuminate different perspectives and narratives around the future of work in the USA under the influence of increasing automation and the rise of the platform economy. These discourses will ultimately contribute to actual political and economic behavior.

But discourses do not only contribute to behavior; they *are* human behavior in itself. People "'use narrative to explain how things came to be and to tell stories.' In fact, the narrative is a uniquely human phenomenon, not shared by any other species" (Shiller 2018: 34). In order to understand a complex economy and the actions of the public and politicians,

> we have to take into account many conflicting popular narratives and ideas relevant to economic decisions, whether the ideas are valid or fallacious. (...) By incorporating an understanding of popular narratives into their explanations of economic events, economists will become more sensitive to such influences when they forecast the future. In doing so, they will give policymakers better tools for anticipating and dealing with these developments. (Shiller 2018: xv)

Fear-inducing narratives about technological change have haunted people since the Industrial Revolution. Today, it might not be the same as the fears of nineteenth-century Luddites who faced direct job replacement by a machine; it is "not that you will show up for work one day and be told that the company is purchasing a new computer that will do your job. Rather, the changes are more gradual, inevitable, and cosmic. (...) Fear about your future is more an existential fear about not being needed" (Shiller 2018: 9). As narratives in discourses can be seen as "major vectors of rapid change in culture, in zeitgeist, and in economic behavior" (Shiller 2018: xiii), narratives around technological change are an important entity to study in order to find out how this change will progress and how people perceive and will act accordingly.

Since the end of the Second World War, automation fears have focused on the ever-increasing power of machines to run without any human interference (Shiller 2018: 199), something that is similar to today's concerns. What came first? The stories of job loss through innovations or the media picking up on the public concern around technology? "The likely answer is 'a little of both'" (Shiller 2018: 187). But there have been different waves of perspectives on technological progress. Apart from the recurring theme of "labor-saving machines" that make humans obsolete in many occupations, there has also been the "opportunity" aspect of technological progress that was apparent in the 1990s and around the dot-com boom of the 2000s. This notion emphasized the "wonderful business opportunities brought by the coming new millennium" (Shiller 2018: 205) like investments in new digital startups. Variations of these two main themes seem to also dominate the current discourses around the future of work and further automation. There is a focus on the "wonderful business opportunities" coming out of Silicon Valley where small startups are able to garner huge venture capital to become the "next big thing," the next big player in the market. Powerful platforms of the more recent wave of technological progress include Amazon, Google, or Facebook and new actors like Uber or Airbnb. Many of these new platforms, but also other technological applications coming out of Silicon Valley, make use of advanced innovations like artificial intelligence fed through machine learning techniques. These developments seem to induce a new wave of concern about how the future of work will look like when machines will supposedly be able to learn and advance on their own. The new concerns are fed by "a 'growing fear of irrelevance' of ourselves and worries about falling into a 'new useless class.' If they grow into a sizable epidemic, such existential fears certainly have the potential to affect economic confidence and thus the economy" (Shiller 2018: 208).

Although fears of technology have apparently accompanied us through time, these concerns will continue to affect people's behavior. If political actors are unwilling or unable to envision solutions to these concerns and a way to convincingly offer people a positive vision of the future, pessimism and frustration will depress the American workforce and economy. No one can truly know what the future will look like with new intelligent machines entering every sphere of our lives, "but the narratives themselves have the potential to drive amplified economic booms and recessions, as well as public policy" (Shiller 2018: 211). The idea that machine learning and artificial intelligence will replace humans could also lead to instability in expenditure and entrepreneurship patterns, and could show up in the real estate and stock markets (Shiller 2018: 211).

Additionally, technological progress also paves the way toward an ever more independent workforce in the USA that has been growing for decades. This group in the labor market is even more vulnerable to shocks and often has no means to save and accumulate social benefits. All this could further lead to insecurity, pessimism, and frustration among the American workforce. The drop in labor force participation and growing income and wealth inequality in the USA in recent decades are concerning signs that the American economy is not as stable as past unemployment numbers and GDP growth might have indicated. By tracing the developments of technological progress of recent years as well as by investigating public and political discourses, this book will contribute to the understanding of how discourses around technological change are shaped and what their main elements are.

The treatment of these developments in political and public discourses ultimately contributes to economic and political behavior of Americans today. Concerns by the population and public actors about the future of the labor force under the influence of more technological restructuring processes, as well as a more narrow focus on the benefits of technological progress for consumers, workers, and businesses, seem to exist side by side. Yet, the political climate shows that economic insecurity is high among Americans, which is likely further fueled by the complex restructuring processes through technology and globalization. "Despite low unemployment and more than nine years of unbroken economic growth, the majority of Americans remain anxious about their economic conditions and futures" (Benner et al. 2018: i). Americans have faced slow job growth, stagnant wages, increasing inequality, and economic insecurity for decades, as well as a devastating economic recession after 2008 from which many households have still not recovered. Now many of these households have again been hit by the consequences of the COVID-19 pandemic that has led to a steep economic downturn in the USA. Although the US government reacted with unprecedented spending programs in response to the crisis, it remains to be seen how the recovery will progress and which long-term effect it will have on the labor market and the development of income and wealth inequality more broadly.

Many of the developments around economic insecurity and inequality are commonly associated with the developments of global trade in recent years. But what role does the introduction of information technology in many sectors play? This "combination [of globalization and technological progress] has given rise to a deep sense of economic anxiety—and a bit of nostalgia for a more secure economic past—that has fed into rising social and political polarization" (Benner et al. 2018: i).

Against the backdrop of these developments, it is vital to understand how recent technological changes including further automation, digitization, and the rise of the platform economy are reflected in public and political discourses. These discourses illuminate current notions toward technological change, from panic or fears to acceptance and enthusiasm. They also shine a light on the concepts to address the consequences of restructuring processes that can be found on both political sides. The question arises whether reforms of infrastructure or education or alternative ideas like the introduction of a universal basic income can serve as answers to the profound restructuring processes of the US economy.

Chapter 2 of this book looks at how developments since the large-scale proliferation of the Internet have shaped the US economy and society. The beginnings of the commercial Internet have led Western societies into the Internet age that is characterized by the power of networks in every aspect of society and the economy on a global scale. Technological progress in the Internet age has fundamentally influenced and changed the labor force and employment patterns. The overarching developments of automation and digitization in recent years will also be discussed in Chap. 2 of this book. Digitization can be considered as a more recent development within the overall concept of automation, altering business-making, value creation, and the structure of the workforce in many different fields simultaneously. Another aspect of recent technological progress is the rise of the platform economy, built on the "platform of platforms," the Internet. These new platform businesses are particular in their structure and mode of business-making that again shape many parts of the economy and society as a whole. All these developments in recent years have happened in the context of growing income and wealth inequality among Americans. Although there are several factors that have contributed to growing inequality in the USA, this book looks at technology in particular as one factor that is discussed in regard to inequality growth among Americans.

In Chap. 3 of this book, the sharing economy platforms will be presented as an example of the new way of digital business-making that is influencing several branches of the economy at the same time. Many of the very recent powerful actors to come out of Silicon Valley, such as Uber, are located in the area of the sharing economy platforms. Their online-to-offline approach to many fields of our everyday lives has shaped consumption patterns and has given rise to concerns about a growing independent workforce.

Chapters 4–6 of this book comprise an in-depth analysis of the political and public discourses around technological progress with a special focus on the future of work under the influence of automation, digitization, and the platform economy. By engaging in methods from the field of corpus linguistics such as frequency analysis, collocation analysis, as well as close reading techniques, the political and public discourses are analyzed using quantitative and qualitative methods.

By compiling files from congressional hearings from the US Senate and House of Representatives, as well as journalistic articles from the *New York Times* (NYT), *Washington Post*, and the *Wall Street Journal* (WSJ), different specialized corpora of textual data were compiled that aim to represent the more current political and public discourses around technological change in the USA. Although there are many more sources that are engaged in the discourse around technological progress in the USA, especially in the online community (blogs, online magazines), the chosen sources represent sentiments that can be considered politically liberal (*NYT*, *Washington Post*), as well as more conservative and business-friendly (*Wall Street Journal*). Additionally, these outlets were chosen because of their national outreach and readership in the USA and because they continue to be highly influential for political stakeholders.

Drawing from corpus linguistic methods, the different corpora were analyzed quantitatively through the use of software looking at frequency and collocation data of keywords and phrases. This quantitative analysis was followed by an in-depth qualitative analysis of the material that focuses on automation, the future of work, and the platform economy. By following this approach, this book identifies and evaluates the most important current contexts, themes, and narratives around automation, the future of work, and the platform economy in the public and political realm in the USA.

With technological progress moving fast ahead, the public will once again be concerned about the outlook of the future. Regardless of whether concerns are considered justified or not, political actors will be asked to offer the American people a positive vision for the future. Technology is not an independent entity that advances on an inevitable path, but technologies are human inventions that should enhance the future welfare of the society as a whole. Yet, this technological advancement can only be considered progress, if the opportunities to participate in this more technologically advanced future are available to a majority of the American people.

References

Benner C, Giusta G, Auerhahn L, Brownstein B, Buchanan J (2018) Still Walking the lifelong tightrope: technology, insecurity and the future of work. Everett Program, Working Partnerships, USA

Gadinger F, Jarzebski S, Yildiz T (2014) Politische Narrative: Konzepte—Analysen—Forschungspraxis. Springer, Wiesbaden

McEnery T, Hardie A (2012) Corpus linguistics: method, theory and practice. Cambridge textbooks in linguistics (Kindle edition). Cambridge University Press, Cambridge, UK

Shiller RJ (2018) Narrative economics: how stories go viral & drive major economic events. Princeton University Press, Princeton, NJ

Chapter 2
The Network Society, the Internet, and the Beginning of the New Economy

In order to evaluate discourses around technological progress and the so-called future of work in the USA in recent years and how these discourses reflect the developments in automation and the rise of the platform economy, we first need to look at the structure of the society we live in today.

In the 1990s, Manuel Castells introduced the idea of the *Network Society*, trying to put all societal changes through technology into one unifying concept. He has tried to form a comprehensive understanding of what has happened since the introduction of digital technology has started to gain traction and how it has changed and will change the way we live and work. In his now standard trilogy *The Information Age: Economy, Society, and Culture*, Manuel Castells paints a picture of our society in the beginning of the twenty-first century. In the first part of this work, *The Rise of the Network Society*, he introduces his idea of the Network Society, a society marked by networks in all key dimensions of social organization and practice. The Network Society is a global system that was enhanced by the spread of digital networking technology, the characteristic of the Information Age, overcoming the traditional limitations of networking. The Network Society is thus also the basis for the so-called *new economy*. According to Manual Castells, the new economy is informational, global, and networked. "Informational" means that "the productivity and competitiveness of units or agents in this economy (be it firms, regions, or nations) fundamentally depend upon their capacity to generate, process, and apply efficiently knowledge-based information." "Global" refers to the fact that "core activities of production, consumption, and circulation, as well as their components (capital, labor, raw materials, management, information, technology, markets) are organized on a global scale, either directly or through a network of linkages between economic agents" (Castells 2010: 77). And "networked" points to the development that "under the new historical conditions, productivity is generated through and competition is played out in a global network of interaction between business networks" (Castells 2010: 77). These developments have occurred over the last few decades through the spread of information technology, leading to the

N. Rauscher, *The Future of Work in the United States*, Contributions to Economics,
https://doi.org/10.1007/978-3-030-82307-8_2

information and information processing as the key factors in the new economy (Castells 2010: 78).

But how has the Network Society shaped the new economy? It is mainly based on the idea that in

> the new, informational mode of development the source of productivity lies in the technology of knowledge generation, information processing, and symbol communication. To be sure, knowledge and information are critical elements in all modes of development, since the process of production is always based on some level of knowledge and the processing of information. However, what is specific to the informational mode of development is the action of knowledge upon knowledge itself as the main source of productivity (. . .). Information processing is focused on improving the technology of information processing as a source of productivity (. . .) . (Castells 2010: 17)

Thus, Castells argues that knowledge (information) and information processing are the key foundations on which the new economy is built. Although previous "revolutions" in economic development were also based on knowledge, the difference today lies in the fact that knowledge and information generation and processing are themselves the basis of the new economy. As a result, the power of technology is amplified as the users and developers may become the same, taking control of the technology and developing it further. For Castells, it is crucial that, for "the first time in history, the human mind is a direct productive force, not just a decisive element of the production system" (Castells 2010: 31). The

> universality of digital code along with global telecommunications infrastructure means that technological innovations are globally integrated from their earliest stages. [And] the focus of technological innovations is not just on transforming the physical world, but on transforming digital information. Social media, transaction platforms, search engines, consumer data mining, and complex machine learning algorithms are just a few examples of the application of new information technologies to information itself. (Benner et al. 2018: 18)

Furthermore, MIT scholars Andrew McAfee and Erik Brynjolfsson argue that information and networks are the key elements of what they call the "Second Machine Age." The Second Machine Age began with the introduction of computers and other digital technology. This new generation of machines is "doing for mental power (. . .) what the steam engine and its descendants did for muscle power" (Brynjolfsson and McAfee 2014). The new machines are becoming more and more "intelligent" and increasingly able to perform cognitive tasks. In this age, information and knowledge have become even more crucial than before; it is the source of value creation in the new economy. Information is a good that is free and perfect: "Once a digital original is created, copies are every bit as good as their digital originals. In fact, a digital copy is exactly identical to the original digital version" (McAfee and Brynjolfsson 2017: Ch VI Position 2016). Yet, the information per se is not necessarily valuable. "The economic power of information goods increases once a network is available because networks add a critical third attribute: instant" (McAfee and Brynjolfsson 2017: Ch VI Position 2022). Thus, information can be distributed for free in a perfect copy in an almost immediate fashion, through a network, the Internet.

The dispersion of the Internet is at the beginning of this development toward the Information Age and the Network Society. The fast development of computer networking, open source software, and telecommunications networks led to the Internet's expansion after its privatization in the 1990s. The Internet was developed in the 1960s, yet it only became largely available decades later with regulatory changes and the availability of broader bandwidth in telecommunication, personal computers, and user-friendly software like Internet browsers. It was so successful because it managed to integrate multimedia content. When Netscape introduced its first user-friendly browser, the World Wide Web really took off (McAfee and Brynjolfsson 2017: Ch I Position 495–499). Innovation in this form,

> the development of new products, services, or processes—has been critical to economic growth and development since long before the advent of computers or mobile communications. The well-known economist Joseph Schumpeter was writing as early as the 1930s about 'creative destruction' in which the economy can only be understood as an evolutionary process of continuous innovation. (Benner et al. 2018: 17)

So, when this new innovation, the Internet, really took off, there was a growing demand for networking opportunities from businesses and the private realm that led to its broad diffusion. Through the Internet's proliferation, especially since the 1990s, and the vast growth of the mobile Internet and smart devices, the Internet has dispersed at a fast speed:

> The Internet has posted the fastest rate of penetration of any communication medium in history: in the United States, the radio took 30 years to reach 60 million people; TV reached this level of diffusion in 15 years the Internet did it in just three years after the development of the world wide web. (Castells 2010: 382)

The 1990s then saw the spread of wireless and mobile communication, which led to the fast diffusion of this technology (Castells 2010: xxv). Also in the 1990s, more and more enterprise systems emerged. These and the World Wide Web were business processes that reengineered how businesses could improve labor productivity, inventory turnover, and asset utilization. The Internet also further extended the reach and power of those enterprise systems to reach individual consumers on their PCs and later tablets and phones (McAfee and Brynjolfsson 2017: Ch I Position 492–494). Through the web, businesses were now able to directly reach customers through e-commerce, which has become widely successful (McAfee and Brynjolfsson 2017: Ch I Position 504). On the industry level, the availability of the Internet and instant communication enabled a whole new approach to production on a worldwide scale. Today's just-in-time production and global supply chains would not have been possible without the proliferation of the Internet.

Additionally, the growth of mobile communication has led to a variety of online developments and a growing interest in everything digital. The number of mobile subscribers continues to grow. In 2018, the GSMA, a worldwide association of mobile operators, announced that the number of mobile subscribers has reached over five billion people, two-thirds of the entire population on earth. Their projection for the year 2025 estimates 5.8 billion subscribers worldwide. The highest percentage of subscribers is still located in Europe with 85% of the population subscribing to a mobile service, followed by North America with 83% (GSMA 2019: 4). Yet, in China alone (the GSMA counts it with the Asia Pacific region) 78% of people have a mobile subscription (GSMA 2017). The diffusion of the Internet, as well as mobile devices (with Internet access), has become significant for the value creation of today's societies and economies. In fact, mobile Internet access is now often the first (and only) Internet access people use, especially, though not only, in developing countries.

In this regard, the network effect is highly significant: "commercial and government interests coincide in favoring the expanding use of the network: the greater the diversity of messages and participants, the higher the critical mass in the network, and the higher the value" (Castells 2010: 383). Companies like Facebook, Google, or Amazon have taken advantage of the network effect in the most successful way. "The ability to build networks and take advantage of network economics has become a defining feature of the information economy. Nobel Prize winning economist Jean Tirole has identified platforms that build networks—enabling interactions, collaborations and social connections in new and unusual ways—as a critical feature of today's economy" (Benner et al. 2018: 14).

However, the network effect can also become problematic because companies operating in networked markets have a tendency to accumulate massive market power, becoming monopolies or near-monopolies. This means that whoever is at the top of the market can reap a disproportionate market share compared to others:

> Such markets exist where there are strong network effects, including not just social media platforms and 'sharing economy' services, but also computer operating systems (Windows, Mac), smartphone operating systems (iOS, Android), financial markets (NASDAQ, New York Stock Exchange), and many other information-based platforms. (Benner et al. 2018: 15)

Although these effects already existed in the "analogue" days with markets around natural goods or public transportation (e.g. railroads), or in markets with high barriers to entry, the information economy has "increased the scale and diversity of winner-take-all markets" (Benner et al. 2018: 15).

As said before, the Internet was first developed in the 1960s. Like many later innovations in Silicon Valley, the Internet was a project financed by the US military. It was thus not an innovation that the market produced on its own, but the Internet as we know it today exists because large amounts of public funds were spent to develop it. Only later did it spread beyond the realms of national security. "The two sources of the Net, the military/science establishment and the personal computing counterculture, did have a common ground: the university world" (Castells 2010: 383). Funded by the military and developed at universities, the Internet spread further, outside of these restricted areas, into the commercial world as well as the counterculture sphere. Thus, the project of the Internet was funded by public investments, and by processes of innovation that are

> highly dependent on shared knowledge and communication networks. As an abundance of academic research has shown, processes of economic innovation rarely take place within isolated research units or labs. Rather they are rooted in complex networks of relationships that cut across company boundaries, and involve high levels of social ties and

communication that have no direct monetary value—so-called 'untraded interdependencies'—not simply market based contracts or legal joint ventures. (Benner et al. 2018: 19)

In Silicon Valley, "digital capitalism" found a perfect base to grow with the fusion of "Californian ideology" of hippie culture, a sense to improve the world, technological optimism, and a sense for business (Staab 2016: 39f). These origins of the web in counterculture are still helpful when trying to understand today's developments. Things like open access and sharing through Internet platforms were born in counterculture circles:

> The culture of first-generation users, with its utopian, communal, and libertarian undercurrents, shaped the Net in two opposite directions. On the one hand, it tended to restrict access to a minority of computer hobbyists, the only people able and willing to spend time and energy living in cyberspace. From this era there remains a pioneering spirit that looks with distrust at the commercialization of the network, and watches with apprehension how the realization of the dream of generalized communication for the people brings with it the limits and misery of humankind as it is. (Castells 2010: 385)

Today, some of the open-access ideas are still alive, for example in projects like Linux or Wikipedia. Yet, the Internet has also proven to be a place that reinforces deeply problematic and destructive behavior, displayed, for example, in communication on social media platforms today.

Yet, these early notions have shaped some digital activities that have become the commercial drivers of a whole range of Internet firms: The platform or sharing economy. Some of the platforms that will be discussed in the third chapter of this book have their origins in the early counterculture and sharing ideas of the beginning of the Internet. Projects like Wikipedia would not be possible without the participation and free sharing of knowledge of the participants. Couchsurfing, a platform where hosts offer free short-term accommodation around the world, is also an example of how the early "communal" ideas of the Internet have survived.

> There is a strong historical and global connection between the emergence of peer-to-peer platforms and a widespread feeling that the new technology-enabled practices these platforms allow for, empower people. (...) This explains why file sharing, open source software, distributed computing, crowdfunding, p2p lending, bitcoin, and sometimes even social media, are quite often put under the umbrella term of the sharing economy. (Frenken and Schor 2017: 2)

This sense of sharing as a community activity can be traced back to the beginnings of the Internet and counterculture, when the Internet was considered a means to give power to the individual and to do good. Famously, the motto of the Google founders had been: Don't be evil. Now Alphabet's motto is: Do the right thing (Mayer 2016). However, as will detailed in Chap. 3 of this book, many firms have somewhat abandoned altruistic sharing ideas and moved on to more commercial uses.

Although the new economy has led to innovation in many fields, productivity did not seem to increase at first. However, new measurement systems introduced by the US Department of Commerce suggested that productivity gains in the 1990s, when the Internet diffused more widely, were much higher than initially thought. Growth was first captured in the tech industry itself, which is common because "uses of technological innovation [gaining traction] first in the industries which are at their source, then they spread to other industries" (Castells 2010: 93). The new economy also benefitted from the broadening world trade following the economic crises of the 1970s, 1980s, and 1990s:

> To open up new markets, linking in a global network valuable market segments of each country, capital required extreme mobility, and firms needed dramatically enhanced communication capabilities. Deregulation of markets and new information technologies, in close interaction, provided such conditions. (Castells 2010: 96)

The global strategic components of the new economy include the financial markets, international trade, transnational production, and the transnational quality of science, technology, and specialty labor. The global economy is thus dependent on components on the institutional, organizational, and technological levels that work as a unit in real time on a planetary scale (Castells 2010: 101f.). The financialization and the internationalization of trade were the backdrop of the development of the new economy. Performance in the financial markets often shape the fate of the economy at large, even though they do not necessarily respond to market rules, i.e., they are not depending on supply and demand in the same way (Castells 2010: 106). The nature of this new economy made it harder to measure its impact on the economy on a national level:

> Around this hard core of new, dynamic, global capitalist firms and ancillary networks, successive layers of firms and industries were either integrated in the new technological system or phased out. Thus, the slow movement of productivity in national economies taken as a whole may hide contradictory trends of explosive productivity growth in leading industries, the decline of obsolete firms, and the persistence of low-productivity service activities. (Castells 2010: 97)

Yet, not everything about the new economy is global: Production, employment, and firms are often still regional and local. Increasingly, "small and medium firms in many countries with the US (e.g. Silicon Valley), Hong Kong, Taiwan, and northern Italy hosting the most prominent examples—have formed cooperative networks, enabling themselves to be competitive in the globalized production system" (Castells 2010: 122). The technology powerhouses of the new economy are mostly located in a few OECD countries, and in very few regions and cities inside these countries. The ascent of China is changing this to a certain extent, but the traditional centers have so far remained significant for technological progress. For new economy firms, it is crucial to be able to tap into knowledge and information pockets worldwide: "Productivity and competitiveness in informational production are based on the generation of knowledge and information processing. Knowledge generation and technological capacity are key tools for competition between firms, organizations of all kinds, and, ultimately, countries" (Castells 2010: 124). The sources of knowledge are often the big research universities or public research facilities that educate and generate information on a grand scale. These academic research networks also work on a global scale (Castells 2010: 124). In order to be successful, the global "technological development need the connection between science, technology, and the business sector, as well as with national and international policies" (Castells 2010: 126). The role of the government remains crucial as it provides education and the infrastructure for technological development (Castells 2010: 127). The USA played an essential role in the development of the new economy. In fact, the "new economy emerged in a given time, the 1990s, a given space, the United States, and around/ from specific industries, mainly information technology and finance (. . .)" (Castells 2010: 147).

What made the USA so special? It was a combination of technological, economic, cultural, and institutional factors that reinforced one another: With California, you had the region of the most revolutionary breakthroughs in information technology, where the industry around these breakthroughs developed. The US economy is huge in size and important in its international position, rewarding innovations in an investment-friendly environment. Tech-savvy talent from around the world was and is attracted to the USA. Culturally, entrepreneurialism, individualism, flexibility, and multi-ethnicity have been important factors in the development of the new economy. Institutionally, the restructuring and deregulation of the US economy of the 1980s and 1990s facilitated the growth of the new economy (Castells 2010: 148).

Because the tech industry in these parts of the USA has always depended on talent from around the world, they have been advocating for open borders and immigration-friendly policies. Their interest is to hire the best talent from around the world, and it seems that their hunger for skill could not be satisfied by the US supply of educated workers. Many tech firms were also shaped by first or later generation immigrants to the USA from around the world (Fitts 2017). As already indicated, Silicon Valley is a unique combination that came together in the USA. And a lot has to do with immigration. Estimates show that more than half of the founders of successful startups have at least one founder with immigrant background.

> Innovation is bred when diverse viewpoints intersect, and that only happens if you can get all those diverse in the room. As Silicon Valley has emerged as a beacon for the most groundbreaking companies, its ability retain to [sic] its ordination is reliant on attracting a steady supply of the best ideas—regardless of their country of origin. (Fitts 2017)

With the Trump administration's take on immigration policy, visa for highly skilled workers seemed to be in decline,[1] which could become an issue for Silicon Valley firms.

---

[1]During President Trump's time in office, more H-1B visas (specialty occupations) for tech workers were rejected. Companies in the USA can hire foreign workers with higher degrees (65,000 with B.A. degree per year, 20,000 with M.A. degree per year) if they are unable to find Americans to fill the jobs. The restrictive amount has made these visas highly competitive, and it seems that in both categories, rejections were rising under the Trump administration, despite old rules and regulations still being in place. Since the executive order "Buy American, Hire American," educational experience has been scrutinized more critically. The Trump administration saw this as a good result, stating that it is now only people with more advanced degrees who get accepted and not those workers that could be replacing American workers and are paid lower wages. However, many workers who have already spent years in the USA were also denied a visa renewal although they

Although the Internet lies at the heart of the Network Society and the new economy, the diffusion of the Internet is still not as wide and inclusive as people had hoped for. When the access to the Internet began to rise during the mid-1990s, people were excited about the potential as a new mass medium. At first, the thought prevailed that equality would be enhanced by easy access to information through the web. Soon however, observers noted that the already privileged were now again more likely to have access to the Internet than others. The idea of the "digital divide" was born (DiMaggio and Hargittai 2001: 2). Yet, as access quickly grew and the diffusion of technology in our daily lives is ongoing at a fast pace, the nature of the digital divide changed: Instead of focusing on the issue of whether people would find a place to access the Internet, the focus shifted to the question "what are people doing, and what are they able to do, when they go on-line" (DiMaggio and Hargittai 2001: 5)? Additionally, there is the question of how "patterns of inequality will reflect not just the differences in individual resources [when using the web], but also the way in which economic and political factors make such differences matter" (DiMaggio and Hargittai 2001: 5). As Internet access diffuses, the quality of use becomes the focus of inequality considerations.

Comparable to education, increased access to the Internet will not eliminate inequality but lead to new kinds of inequality among Internet users as to how "they are able to reap benefits from their use of the technology" (DiMaggio and Hargittai 2001: 9). There might be an inequality of opportunity among Internet users, dependent on different criteria: For example, the quality of the technical means people have, the extent of autonomy they have of using the web, the skill set they bring to the use of the Internet, and the varying purpose of using technology. With the diffusion of the smartphone and data plans, the question of autonomy when using the Internet seems to recede. Yet, the question of Internet competence remains a critical one. Education remains an important factor when digital inequality is addressed. If you do not know how to best use the Internet, where to look for information, or whether this information is reliable, then your use of the Internet remains incomplete, especially if you lack the social support to overcome these issues (DiMaggio and Hargittai 2001: 13).

Participating online can have different forms, but all of them need basic and more specific knowledge about the use of the technology and the Internet itself. Accessing social media platforms, typing a comment, or writing an e-mail might be one thing, but working on digital platforms with others or coding is a different matter altogether. This demands for specific skills including knowledge about the use of cloud computing, working on a project online with several others, hyperlinking your work, creating and managing accounts on platforms, or learning coding languages. For some, these skills might already be part of their professional skill set, but if people lack social support or the right education, they cannot use technology most efficiently and continue to be excluded from certain sources of work and income

---

had been issued visas before (Lapowsky 2019). Whether this practice will significantly change under the new Biden administration remains to be seen.

completely. Some of the most lucrative occupations in today's new economy demand even more than the aforementioned technical skills and knowledge.

The McKinsey Report on Digital America points out that:

> The digital divide may be narrowing, but it still has to be bridged in order to connect the Americans who remain offline and are being bypassed by the digital economy. A crucial part of this is ensuring that the United States matches leading countries in coverage, download speeds, and affordability. But encouraging participation is about more than providing access and infrastructure; it is about enhancing digital literacy, increasing awareness of digital tools, and encouraging their adoption by consumers and workers. Government can also help entrepreneurs and small business owners develop exporting capabilities to boost their participation in global platforms and flows. Just as digital capabilities shape competition at the company and sector level, they also matter for national competitiveness in an interconnected—and increasingly digital—global economy. (Manyika et al. 2015: 17)

Everyone is online nowadays in some way. But only few can really tap into the possibilities that the Internet and smart devices have to offer. There seems to be a new divide between the "digital haves" and "have-mores" and "the most advanced users pull away from everyone else" (Manyika et al. 2015: 3). In general, the

> typical person who uses a smartphone for communication, entertainment, or basic searches is not taking advantage of the full range of applications that produce real efficiencies. For workers, wage growth has been approximately twice as fast as the national average in the most highly digitized industries, such as ICT and professional services. Within these fields, too, a small group of workers at the leading edge command sharply higher compensation. Conversely, those who lack digital skills face narrowing job prospects. (Manyika et al. 2015: 4)

Digital skills can really make or break a career these days.

2.1 Employment and Economic Security in the Network Society

One key element of change in the Network Society is the transformation of work and employment. Many have commented on the influence of technology when it comes to inequality, an aspect that will further be discussed in Sect. 2.2.4. Yet, in line with historical change, technology has not destroyed employment so far. The labor force has, to a certain extent, adapted to market needs with higher skill levels and educational attainment. However, a lot of manufacturing jobs in the USA have disappeared as the economy has been shifting from manufacturing to services. In the 1950s and 1960s, over 30% of employment was located in the manufacturing industry but in the twenty-first century, this number has declined to 10.6% by 2015 (Table 2.1).

Many manufacturing jobs have moved overseas or have been automated. Yet, despite receding job numbers in branches like manufacturing, technology and further automation has led to increased productivity. Although employment in manufacturing has been stagnant, output in manufacturing has grown (Rose 2018: 1f).

Table 2.1 Changing employment shares, 1960–2015 in percent

	1960	1980	2000	2015
Agriculture	3.2%	2.5%	1.4%	1.5%
Nonmanufacturing production industries	17.7%	16.8%	16.1%	15.1%
Manufacturing	32.0%	23.0%	15.1%	10.6%
Low-end services	21.2%	22.3%	26.8%	30.5%
High-end services	25.9%	35.4%	40.6%	42.3%

Based on Rose (2018: 4)

Table 2.2 Median earnings by industry, 1960–2015 in constant 2015 dollars

	1960	1980	2000	2015
Agriculture	$7900	$21,900	$24,800	$25,000
Nonmanufacturing production industries	$30,100	$38,500	$41,300	$40,000
Manufacturing	$28,900	$35,600	$42,400	$42,000
Low-end services	$13,600	$19,200	$23,400	$20,000
High-end services	$25,000	$30,100	$41,300	$43,500

Based on Rose (2018: 4)

Although, as mentioned before, it might not have been steep, without the proliferation of new technology since the 1970s, productivity growth might have been even smaller.

Earnings in the different occupations also vary. Manufacturing still pays relatively well compared to other sectors, but not as many people are employed in this sector as in the past (Table 2.2).

In the low-end and high-end service sector, employment rose. Yet, there is a dual development in wages from this employment pattern. Earnings in the high-end service industry are rather high (they include business professionals, or employees in government, health care, education), but the low-end service jobs (retail, personal, and food services) pay rather poorly (Rose 2018: 5). Additionally, all jobs face profound changes due to technology. Even manufacturing jobs in the future will most likely not be traditional blue-collar jobs. Instead, it is more likely that "more workers will be skilled technicians who set up and repair computer-driven machines, high-end managers, sales representatives, accountants, designers, and research scientists" (Rose 2018: 7). All in all, the shift from manufacturing to services in the USA is ongoing and will not only change the jobs available, but also the nature of work and the income levels in many different sectors.

Thus, despite the rising levels of productivity through technology in industrialized countries, wages have not kept pace in many instances. For many families, the entry of women into the workforce has permitted the maintenance of their standard of living. Whereas in the past, one breadwinner was enough to cover the costs of living and social services such as health care (Castells 2010: xxii), living costs in the boom areas such as Silicon Valley are exploding. Finding affordable housing has become especially problematic, for instance. In general, many Americans are struggling to afford a basic middle-class lifestyle, despite a decade-long economic boom and high employment rates after the Great Recession. There are more and more households that are struggling to afford necessities like housing, food, child care, health care, transportation, and a cell phone plan, according to a study by the United Way ALICE Project (Luhby 2018). In this study, California, New Mexico, and Hawaii are presented as the areas where the biggest share of families are struggling. In many areas of the USA today, an annual income of over $85,000 is needed to afford basic necessities, something that is not attainable with most of the hourly wages paid in the USA (Luhby 2018).

Taking Silicon Valley as an example, one can see that the whole USA is facing economic insecurity due to the massive restructuring of the American economy as a whole. Even though Silicon Valley is an area where the economic situation and outlook is much better for the workforce than in other regions, apart from "the concentration of technology industries [that] makes it unique, in many ways the region represents just a more intense version of trends that are being experienced throughout the U.S. economy, and indeed the whole world" (Benner et al. 2018). The current debate around the future of work, often

> underpinned by a fear of massive technology-induced job loss, are presented as the result of a dramatic 'new economy' associated with intelligent machines, big-data driven algorithms and the gig economy. Yet this economy has roots that are at least 50 years old (as well as resurrecting ideas like piecework that go back centuries), and many of the most worrying trends we're experiencing today have been apparent since the early 1990s. (Benner et al. 2018: i)

Chris Benner and his colleagues argue that technology itself is not the source of today's economic and social problems but that social and public institutions failed to adapt to the changing business models and power shifts in the market. There has been a lack of institutions and policies to incentivize higher wages and transitions from low-paid to high-paid jobs. Lifelong training opportunities have also not been taken up to any large extent (Benner et al. 2018: i).

The composition of the workforce itself has not only changed through the entry of women but through globalization as well. Migration has led to a diverse workforce, mostly visible in metropolitan areas. But this was also met with resentment from certain groups that felt the economic downturn more severely. "Many Americans have experienced severe, persistent economic insecurity and displacement across the country over the last twenty years, and the anger is understandable. Yet the persistent failure of public policy to address the broad structural changes in our economy can't be blamed on immigrants or Muslims (...)" (Benner et al. 2018). Benner and his colleagues argue that these issues "cannot be fixed by platitudes asserting that 'net benefits from trade' or 'disruptive innovation' will eventually trickle down to ordinary Americans. We need intentional public policy that, rather than shaping markets in order to ensure the highest returns to investment, considers how to balance profits with fair returns to workers" (Benner et al. 2018: ii).

But not only the composition of the workforce is changing. The USA also faces a change in employment opportunities. Long-term employment is increasingly replaced by flexible labor, leading to less predictable careers. Inside of the new economy a dual structure emerges: Highly educated workers, often the talent of a company, and the low-skilled workers who are employed in occupations that cannot (yet) be automated. Middle-skilled occupations seem to disappear more and more. The two different groups naturally have very different bargaining powers at hand, which in turn leads to more inequality in society (Castells 2010: xxiii). This skill and wage polarization often leads to polarization in everyday areas as well, such as the housing market or transportation. Additionally, it is not clear which occupations and skills will really be valuable in the long run.

However, it is unclear whether the current development is going to continue with, on the one hand, workforce talent being rewarded with high salaries and, on the other hand, automating and offshoring of the core labor force, and subcontracting for a lot of other tasks. The public sector has been a refuge for good jobs, while entrepreneurship and innovation thrive on the margins of the corporate sector with technology allowing for self-employment and autonomy in the knowledge-based services. So far, technological change and the established institutional environment have interacted (Castells 2010: xxiv). Could the high-tech sector also serve as a refuge? It is a mixed picture when it comes to wages and working conditions. Often, business owners keep the gains from growth to themselves, which leads to rising corporate profits but not necessarily to higher wages for workers, not even in the tech industry. Labor's "share of total output in the region [of Santa Clara County] declined from 64% in 2001 to 60% in 2016, with striking declines in key information technology industries, including a decline from 76 to 58% in hardware manufacturing overall, and from 77 to 53% in computer and electronic products" (Benner et al. 2018: ii). For wages in the larger Silicon Valley area, the trend is also far from stellar. According to the study by Benner et al., wages are lower today than 20 years ago for about 90% of income earners in the region, despite a growing per capita economic output increase (Benner et al. 2018: ii).

The transformation of work in the new economy also includes another large trend, the fragmentation of work toward "a new social structure, characterized by the shift from goods to services, by the rise of managerial and professional occupations, by the demise of agricultural and manufacturing jobs, and by the growing information content of work in the most advanced economies" (Castells 2010: 217). Although manufacturing jobs are not disappearing entirely, they are often moving toward the service sector. Additionally, "service industry" is a very broad category which includes everything that is not agricultural or manufacturing work:

> The service economy model, represented by the United States, the United Kingdom, and Canada (...) is characterized by a decline in the share of manufacturing employment in overall employment after 1970, as the pace toward informationalism accelerated. Having already eliminated almost all agricultural employment, this model emphasizes an entirely new employment structure where the differentiation among various service activities becomes the key element to analyze social structure. This model emphasizes capital management services over producer services, and keeps expanding the social service sector because of a dramatic rise in healthcare jobs and, to a lesser extent, in education employment. It is also characterized by the expansion of the managerial category which includes a considerable number of middle managers. (Castells 2010: 245)

Among the fastest growing occupations are the FIRE (finance, insurance, real estate) sector and temporary work as well as contracting. Moreover, professionals, managers, technicians, and some semi-skilled service occupations are also growing at a higher rate. It is clear, however, that jobs in the new economy require a higher skill level and more education beyond high-school level (Castells 2010: 238f.).

Andrew McAfee and Erik Brynjolfsson also comment on the influence of digitization on the labor market, and how it is going to fundamentally change the nature of work. They focus on the rise of the *Machine, Platform, Crowd,* which is the title of their 2017 book. They see a continuous tendency toward the replacement of humans in many working processes. In fact, they claim that in many instances, better results can be achieved if the human factor is entirely eliminated from the process, something that humans would intuitively dismiss. Generally,

> almost all of us also believe that we're capable of delivering a great deal more than digital technologies can, even as they continue to profit from Moore's law—the remarkably steady, remarkably fast growth over time in the amount of computing hardware available for the same dollar of spending—and become exponentially more powerful. (...) [Yet] Getting rid of human judgments altogether—even those from highly experienced and credentialed people—and relying solely on numbers plugged into formulas, often yields better results. (McAfee and Brynjolfsson 2017: Ch II Position 519; 553)

They do not claim, however, that humans will become completely obsolete: "We will see that human intuition, judgment, and fast thinking still have critical roles to play, and that leading companies are making use of them in novel and brilliant ways—ways that point to a new and improved partnership between minds and machines" (McAfee and Brynjolfsson 2017: Ch II Position 557). McAfee and Brynjolfsson argue for a new way of thinking when it comes to human labor and machine labor. They see a new partnership for humans and machines in the future, where both work alongside each other. Nevertheless, humans will need to accept that there are things that machines can do much better than humans, especially yielding results from huge amounts of data. Humans, on the other hand, often have the common sense to judge and make use of the results the machines deliver.

A growing number of companies are using machines and data to automate decisions-making processes, for example in e-commerce when shoppers receive offers based on their previous purchases. There might emerge something like

> a 'second economy,' in which the transactions happen with no human involvement in a 'vast, silent, connected, unseen, and autonomous' fashion. Over time, this automatic second economy is encroaching into the familiar human-mediated one, with algorithms taking over from experts (...). As more and more of the world's information becomes digitized, it provides a plethora of data for improving decision making, converting intuition into data-driven decision making. (McAfee and Brynjolfsson 2017: Ch II Position 695)

Traditionally, however, machines can only be fed with the available data, and this data can be flawed. Data from the real world can reflect our biases and prejudices: The "danger 'that in some current contexts, the downsides of AI systems disproportionately affect groups that are already disadvantaged by factors such as race, gender and socioeconomic background' and highlighted the importance of considering the social impacts of these systems, both intended and unintended" (McAfee and

Brynjolfsson 2017: Ch II Position 763). The human factor is often still necessary to judge the results of a machine as machines still lack spontaneous "common sense."[2] Mostly, machines are fed with existing data and so they mirror what is happening in the world. They cannot judge or improve the circumstances that are already in place. They have also no knowledge of a society's history or socialization and cannot therefore not adjust their results. Although they can be redesigned if necessary, new machine learning techniques make the decision-making mechanisms of machines and algorithms actually even more and more opaque (Susskind 2020: 70).

A new wave of Artificial Intelligence that some machines display are not comparable to human intelligence, but they function in entirely new ways that are not easily explained. Machines draw from the huge amounts of data to "teach" themselves tasks without human intervention or a set of rules. In this way, powerful applications can become reality and can take over much more complicated and inexplicable tasks from humans that were deemed un-automatable just a few years ago (Susskind 2020: 71). In fact, much of the limitation of AI came from the attempt to instill machines with human ways of thinking or things like common sense judgment. But humans are often not capable of neatly explaining how they arrive at a certain result. Therefore, the newer applications operate entirely different and are not mimicking human intelligence. According to experts like Daniel Susskind, this is a game changer for the development of AI technology.

In the future, we will therefore see powerful but also limited applications for AI (that is based on deep learning) (Goode 2018). As McAfee and Brynjolfsson said, the future will probably bring a different kind of relationship between machine and human. Humans still provide the personal judgment power and spontaneous common sense that machines lack, whereas machines deliver powerful results through the resource of Big Data.

All in all, it is clear that the introduction of "smart machines" into all kinds of working processes will change the way we work and also our working time. Working time traditionally also structured social time, as employment has structured society as a whole. With the availability of technology "to reintegrate in a network of stored information contributions from various workers at various times induces the constant variation of the actual time of work performance, undermining the structuring capacity of working time over everyday life" (Castells 2010: 470). As the

---

[2]As of now, "common sense" in the way humans understand it is not codable and machines are notoriously bad at adjusting and judging. There are efforts to give programs and machines a more "human" way of thinking by instilling common sense and basic knowledge into them, which proves a very difficult task. If we look at what artificial intelligence (AI) means today, it is mostly based on deep learning techniques. From giving a program huge amounts of data, it independently derives a pattern, for example for recognizing a certain object on images. This work is successful, but only to a certain extent. It is not comparable to the knowledge and workings of a human brain. For once, humans do not need millions of examples to recognize a certain object. Then, humans are capable of adjusting their understanding when details change; machines often cannot. Humans are thus much more than just pattern recognizers; their thinking is based and advances from years of learning and understanding the world. Machines have, so far, no knowledge of the physical world around them and no common sense similar to what humans display (Thompson 2018).

amount of working time has been declining over the past few decades (at least outside of the USA), the new trend seems to be the blurring between working time and social time, facilitated through the dispersion of (mobile) Internet and the corresponding technology.

2.2 Automation, Digitization, and the Rise of the Platform Economy

Having already touched upon some of the challenges employment is facing in the new economy, this chapter further examines the concepts of automation, digitization, and the rise of the digital platform by tracing their development from the introduction of computers into the workplace to the appearance of digital services and the smart devices of today.

2.2.1 Automation

> Mechanization first, automation later, have been transforming human labor for decades, always triggering similar debates around issues of workers' displacement, deskilling versus reskilling, productivity versus alienation, management control versus labor autonomy. (Castells 2010: 256)

Automation is not a new phenomenon. At all times, mankind has developed innovative technology, from tools to computers, to advance their capabilities and make processes more productive. All technical progress led to the replacement of jobs as a consequence. Yet, other employment was created, demanding new and higher skills. Ultimately, this has led us to the advanced economy we have today. In general, one can say that the "balance between job conservation and technological progress (. . .), to a large extent, reflects the balance of power in society, and how gains from technological progress are being distributed" (Frey and Osborne 2017: 256). Today's automated processes include physical hardware such as industrial robots, as well as software, which plays an important role in service automation. In this regard, the push toward an ever more automated economy is also referred to as "a digital transformation" or the "fourth industrial revolution" (Schlogl and Sumner 2018: 5).

Thus, automation is an ongoing process. According to a 2015 report by the McKinsey Global Institute (MGI) on the state of automation in the USA, about 60% of all occupations could face about 30% or more of their activities being automated:

> This will affect skill requirements and the day-to-day nature of work for a large share of the labor force. As companies in many industries integrate these technologies, jobs and business processes will be redefined on a large scale. Workers of all skill levels, including highly skilled professionals, will not be immune. (Manyika et al. 2015: 14)

This means that automation can lead to new products and services in the long run, which will lead to more growth of the US economy. Yet, only if displaced workers are able to re-train and acquire new capabilities will they be able to benefit from this trend. The short-term consequences could therefore be "a wrenching shift for many workers" (Manyika et al. 2015: 14), as some technological developments of recent decades such as robotics, Artificial Intelligence, or machine learning, are out-performing humans in many instances. This could mean a "new age of automation" (Manyika et al. 2017: 4). Automation could lead to improved performances of business, by managing errors, enhancing quality and speed, and, as we have seen before, in some cases delivering results that go beyond what humans are capable of (Manyika et al. 2017: 4). Productivity will thus improve: MGI estimates that automation could raise productivity worldwide by 0.8–1.4% per year (Manyika et al. 2017: 4).

Looking at jobs, MGI estimates that most jobs will change, rather than entirely be automated. In 2017, they estimated that only five percent of jobs worldwide have the potential to be fully automated. Activities that are most prone to be automated are "physical activities in highly structured and predictable environments, as well as the collection and processing of data. In the United States, these activities make up 51 percent of activities in the economy accounting for almost $2.7 trillion in wages" (Manyika et al. 2017: 4). Most of these jobs can be found in the manufacturing field, in accommodation and food services, and in the retail sector. Some of these jobs are middle-skill jobs (Manyika et al. 2017). MGI estimates that half of today's work activities could be automated by 2055, taking a 20-year corridor of earlier or later fulfillment, depending on the broader economic conditions (Manyika et al. 2017: 4). The current shift toward more automation is comparable to the past shift from an agricultural to a manufacturing society in the USA. Many people will thus find their jobs displaced. However, according to MGI people will be moving into other jobs and sectors, some of which have not yet been created.

Economist Melanie Arntz and her colleagues from Heidelberg University have a different take on automation. They argue that most of the estimates about job loss due to robotics and AI are likely overblown. They see the substantial variation inside a job description as a way to circumvent automation. All workers fulfill a variety of tasks and the more these tasks include things like problem-solving, or influencing and working with others, the less likely they are to be automated (Arntz et al. 2017: 157). Overall, there might be higher potential of automation for jobs that are concerned with exchange of information, selling, or using your hands. Programming, presenting, training, etc., are tasks that are not likely to be automated any time soon. With this assessment, the researchers argue that only about 9% of the American workforce face a 70% chance of being replaced by automation, whereas other estimates see 38% of workers at a high risk (Arntz et al. 2017: 158). Other studies might underestimate specialization of many workers on the job, which leads to less replacement risk through automation for these workers (Arntz et al. 2017: 160).

There are technical, economic, and social factors that determine the pace and extent of automation (Manyika et al. 2017: 4). Whether certain activities and occupations are automated also involves other actors and considerations such as

Table 2.3 Determinants of feasibility of automation

Dimension	Factors
Technological	Type and complexity of task
Economic	Economic risks and returns based on capital and labor costs; competition
Legal	Labor and capital regulation; patents and their ownership
Political	Unionization level; public vs. private ownership of production and technology
Sociocultural	Corporate legitimacy and social expectations in society

Based on Schlogl and Sumner (2018: 6)

"can a task be automated in a way that reliably produces a good or service at a specified level of quality? Is it profitable to automate that task? Is it legally possible for a firm to replace workers with machines? How do relevant stakeholders such as political groupings, particularly trade unions, and society at large, particularly consumers, respond to automation (and the potentially ensuing lay-offs)?" (Schlogl and Sumner 2018: 5). So, before more automation is introduced into a given environment, there are several aspects to be taken into account, especially whether the tasks are automatable and can be dealt with in a more efficient manner. Additionally, companies will look into whether there will be an actual economic return to the risk and costs, especially because automated processes need to be in line with legal regulations (like labor laws, capital regulations, and patents). Moreover, the political willingness to support more automation and the attitude of societal actors such as political parties, unions, or the public also determine the pace of automation (Table 2.3). All these questions influence the speed and rate of automation in the future.

How do governments and political actors react to automation? First of all, because it enhances productivity, countries usually encourage investment and market incentives for innovation and progress. At the same time, policy-makers need to look out for the workers who could be worst affected by further automation. In many instances, workers will need to learn to accept machines in their workplace and acquire the skills necessary for the automation age:

> Policy makers cannot fend off automation, but they can support those who are affected and build the institutions and training pathways needed in a more digital economy. The first major area for action is skills development. Many of those already in the workforce will need access to short, concentrated training programs for acquiring new skills. (...) Another major focus area is worker protections. If digital platforms for freelancers and on-demand service workers continue to expand, policy makers will need to clarify how project-based workers are treated under the law and consider how to modernize the system for delivering benefits. (Manyika et al. 2015: 17)

MGI therefore advocates in favor of new education and training efforts for the labor force in the face of automation. The support for income and transition phases of workers by the government and a modern safety net are also among the recommendations by the MGI (Manyika et al. 2017: 4).

Yet, not only do workers face a more challenging labor market through the demand of new skills; the labor market also becomes more diverse overall through the growing group of on-demand service providers, for example. Additionally, policy-makers also need to consider legal regulations, as well as patent and ownership rules when it comes to more automated processes. Apart from that, politicians also have to take into account the public, lobbying groups from the business and unions' side, and their voters to find out how automation processes are affecting them. Often, the public as consumers supports new technological developments if they bring better service and prices. However, as workers they might find some of the developments more problematic (Schlogl and Sumner 2018: 6).

Although technological progress is inevitable and generally desirable, there might also be effects that are more undesirable. Therefore, there need to be ways to shape the impact of technology and automation. Yet, the extremely fast technological progress of recent years makes it very complicated to discuss the application of technology, its regulation, and its purpose and implications for the wider public. This is often due to a lack of understanding of the technology by stakeholders, but also due to the slow-moving democratic decision-making processes. Furthermore, the Silicon Valley strategy has long been, "Move first and ask for forgiveness later" (Singer 2018). This means that developers of technology and digital services first move into a market or niche and establish themselves, until the network effect leads to such dominance that regulation of the companies and their established behavior becomes more and more difficult.[3] Additionally, there are more and more ethical aspects that need to be considered when developing new technology, such as self-driving cars or autonomous weaponry. "Technology is not neutral (...). The choices that get made in building technology then have social ramifications" (Singer 2018).

The result of an ever more automated economy certainly is enhanced productivity and growth. But will all people benefit from this development?

> [Past] interactions between automation and employment cannot fully predict the future. At the same time, there is no fundamental economic law that guarantees every adult will be able to earn a living solely on the basis of sound mind and good character. The emergence of greatly improved computing power, artificial intelligence (AI) and robotics raises the possibility of replacing labor on a scale not previously observed. If this should occur, the primary challenge we will face is one of income distribution: How do we ensure that the largest number of people gain from the surge in productivity? (Autor 2016: 1)
>
> Again, solutions to this problem are not agreed upon. Yet, most see "reskilling and upskilling" as the best way to prevent a "worst-case scenario" of "technological change accompanied by talent shortages, mass unemployment and growing inequality (...)." (Schwab and Samans 2016: V)

Some experts like David Autor emphasize that fears raised by further automation could be exaggerated: "Too often expert commentators tend to overstate the extent of machine substitution for human labor and ignore the strong complementarities

[3]This has recently been discussed in the USA among politicians like Elizabeth Warren and others who are contemplating breaking up some of the big tech giants under anti-trust considerations, as well as under concerns about business models that track users' private data and sell it to third parties without the users consent or knowledge (Henderson 2018; Valdez 2019). These discussions are ongoing on both sides of the political spectrum in the USA.

between automation and labor that increase productivity, raise earnings and augment demand for labor" (Autor 2016: 1). The goal of automation is to "substitute mechanical power for human musculature, machine-consistency for human handiwork, and digital calculation for slow and error-prone workers. In particular, it allows computers to substitute for workers in performing routine, codifiable tasks while amplifying the comparative advantage of workers in supplying problem-solving skills, adaptability and creativity" (Autor 2016: 2). It remains a challenge to substitute a worker's flexibility, judgement, and common sense, as indicated before. "Focusing only on what is lost misses a central economic mechanism by which automation affects the demand for labor: raising the value of the tasks that workers uniquely supply" (Autor 2016: 2). Thus, automation has the ability to raise the worth of human labor and capabilities. Machines are good at replacing routine work, but they are not yet capable of replacing human skills like flexibility, common sense, or creative thinking. This could be the reason why technology has not meant the end to employment so far, despite all the fears to the contrary: "Why hasn't automation already wiped out employment for the vast majority of workers? This is due to an economic reality that is as fundamental as it is overlooked: *Tasks that cannot be substituted by automation are generally complemented by it*" (Autor 2016: 3). Workers who supply tasks that are complemented by automation benefit by further introduction of it. But, "if they primarily (or exclusively) supply tasks that are substituted" (Autor 2016: 3) by automation, they naturally do not benefit.

In addition to that, the supply of labor plays a role. If there are a lot of workers for a complementary task, wage gains will not be available and demand from this group will not grow. The "output elasticity of demand combined with income elasticity of demand can either dampen or amplify the gains from automation. As people and societies get wealthier, they tend to consume more—food, housing, transportation, entertainment—which generates additional demand. But when productivity is not rising rapidly, goods become more expensive over time (for example, education, healthcare, live performances and handmade crafts)" (Autor 2016: 3). Thus, automation needs to increase the productivity of a large group of workers in order to spur demand and growth of the economy. Moreover, while automation might not necessarily "reduce the quantity of jobs, it may greatly affect the quality of available jobs" (Autor 2016: 3). However, not only high-skilled labor will be in great demand. As some tasks require things like situational adaptability, visual and language recognition, as well as in-person interactions (manual tasks), workers might still be in demand because it remains hard for machines to perform these tasks, for now. Potentially, however, there is a large group of people able to execute these tasks, so the likelihood of wage increases in this area is small (Autor 2016: 4).

Yet, even though machines still have a hard time performing "human" tasks, this could change in the future. As indicated before, especially the availability of so-called Big Data and machine learning techniques, a whole new range of technologies could be developed. Rather "than teach machines rules that we do not understand, engineers develop machines that attempt to infer tacit rules from context, abundant data and applied statistics. This is the field of machine learning, and it is growing rapidly" (Autor 2016: 4). In order to prepare Americans for these rapid advances, the American education system will need to change and adapt rapidly to the new situation in order to give more workers the chance to benefit from the new economy. The "issue is not that middle-class workers are doomed by automation and technology, but instead that human capital investment must be at the heart of any long-term strategy for producing skills that are complemented by, rather than substituted by, technological change" (Autor 2016).

In general, there are contesting views about how automation is going to proceed. Often, there is more potential for automation than is actually ever realized:

> automatable tasks do not necessarily or instantly get automated: one can observe a set of tasks currently being carried out both by humans and machines in different contexts and places. Consider, for instance, subway drivers and autonomous subways, supermarket cashiers, and self-checkout machines, university lecturers, and online courses. (Schlogl and Sumner 2018: 6)

It is more likely that automated and non-automated services will exist side by side and that the "narrowly technologically deterministic view is insufficient. There are less tangible—economic, political, social, and cultural— reasons to be factored in" (Schlogl and Sumner 2018: 6). For once, there is often a long time lapse between an innovation and actual applications of this innovation in the real world. Society and the economy usually need time to adapt. Additionally, cultural factors might inhibit or spur automation in certain countries.

Schlogl and Sumner argue that there are two main camps when discussing automation: Automation optimists and pessimists. The optimistic "business as usual" camp emphasizes market dynamism and technological change as a normal element of modern economic growth. The other camp suggests that this time around, automation is different (Schlogl and Sumner 2018: 7f). Optimists refer to the adaptive capacities of the market economies and do not focus on the possible "losers" of these innovations. Moreover, automation optimists focus on the quality of work that is enhanced through robots and computers taking over dangerous or unhealthy tasks for humans. Optimists usually suggest skill development for the labor force and the enhancement of the relationship of human and nonhuman work (Schlogl and Sumner 2018: 8).

Automation pessimists see the current wave of automation as part of a bigger digital revolution that is not comparable to earlier forms of automation. Human brains rather than muscle power are replaced this time. Machines are capable of performing increasingly complex and skill-intensive tasks. "The relationship of human and non-human work is viewed as more and more substitutive rather than complementary" (Schlogl and Sumner 2018: 8). This trend is putting downward pressure on wages and upward pressure on the rate of profit from capital investment.

> The detachment of productivity gains and wage growth observed since the 1970s in many OECD countries is brought forward as evidence. Automation, pessimists argue, may ultimately lead to job losses as technologies create fewer jobs than they eliminate ('technological unemployment') or create jobs in sectors which are potentially less desirable and productive ('premature deindustrialization'). Politically, the recommendations of the pessimist camp range from a 'robot tax' to redistributive responses such as a universal basic

> income (. . .) and questions of public versus private ownership of production and technology. (Schlogl and Sumner 2018: 9)

The pessimistic camp might have been the more publicly visible in recent years. However, unemployment might not be the biggest issue around automation. Rather, stagnating wages and the decoupling of real-wage growth from productivity growth, as well as a hollowing out of middle-class employment, could be the main ramifications of further automation (Schlogl and Sumner 2018: 9). Lower-skilled occupations are not likely to be automated. Instead, the "in-between jobs," between low and high-skilled occupations, could become fewer in numbers. "The problem thus may not be so much that jobs are lost, rather than that other types of jobs expand in number. People are being driven into the jobs below their skill level, with either lower or slower growing wages than the middle-skill jobs that previously existed" (Schlogl and Sumner 2018: 9). It is decisive for the future of an automated economy what happens to productivity growth and "how what is captured is then distributed within the capital share (which may be distributed between reinvestment, divided payments, reserves building, or other activity e.g. rents), or within the labor share which may be distributed between employment growth, real-wage growth, or social security entitlements" (Schlogl and Sumner 2018: 9).

Automation is moving faster in countries with more agricultural-based employment, which is the case in developing countries. "This pattern is intuitive and is explained by the complexity and creativity of service-sector work and the amount of face-to-face human interaction involved in it" (Schlogl and Sumner 2018: 27). Nevertheless, automation can also be fueled by high labor costs, which are usually higher in developed countries (Manyika 2017: vi). Schlogl and Sumner both advocate for more than just skill-based development to address problems of automation. They also suggest social safety net provisions. Yet, a further increase in labor costs could also turn out to be an incentive to automate further.

With differing views on automation, the question remains what the future holds regarding automation. There is no doubt that automation is progressing fast in all sectors. There are many so-called disruptive technologies that even accelerate automation of knowledge work, for example machine learning (Manyika et al. 2013: 6).

Although it remains to be seen if machine learning and AI are really going to advance as fast as anticipated, the impact of AI, also on knowledge workers, could be vast. Additionally, there is great potential in cloud technology:

> The cloud is enabling the explosive growth of Internet-based services, from search to streaming media to offline storage of personal data (photos, books, music), as well as the background processing capabilities that enable mobile Internet devices to do things like respond to spoken commands to ask for directions. (. . .) Finally, the cloud can enable entirely new business models, including all kinds of pay-as-you-go service models. (Manyika et al. 2013: 6)

Disruptive automation will change the "nature of work (. . .), and millions of people will require new skills. (. . .). Automated knowledge work tools will almost certainly extend the powers of many types of workers (. . .), but they could also automate some jobs entirely" (Manyika et al. 2013: 15). With the impact on business and labor, it is clear that benefits

> of technologies are not going to be evenly distributed. (...) it is possible that advancing technology, such as automation of knowledge work or advanced robotics, could create disproportionate opportunities for some highly skilled workers and owners of capital while replacing the labor of some less skilled workers with machines. (Manyika et al. 2013: 16)

Therefore, the future of work will pose further challenges to policy-makers including the issue of inequality and enabling a struggling labor force to maintain an adequate standard of living.

The prospect of the new economy can be positive if it remains open for more than just a few highly educated professionals and if benefits are not distributed in a winner-take-all fashion to mostly the highest-skilled individuals and shareholders of the advanced companies. In a rather optimistic outlook, Brynjolfsson and McAfee see society possibly striving in the future:

> The economics of digital information, in short, are the economics not of scarcity but of abundance. This is a fundamental shift, and a fundamentally beneficial one. (...) The twists and disruptions will not always be easy to navigate. But we are confident that most of these changes will be beneficial ones, and that we and our world will prosper on the digital frontier. (Brynjolfsson and McAfee 2012: 8)

2.2.2 *Digitization*[4]

So far, the basis of the new economy, the Network Society, the Internet, and ongoing automation were discussed. As said before, automation is not a new phenomenon. However, recently, a new "layer" has been added by moving into the realm of the digital. In the discourse around technological progress, "automation" is often used as a general term. In this book, digitization is investigated as part of automation processes. In Chaps. 4–6, the specific use of the two terms in context will be presented in more detail through textual corpus analysis.

Digitization includes the "building of digital assets, expanding digital usage, and creating a more digital workforce," as well as integrating "digital tools into an ever-widening variety of business processes" (Manyika et al. 2015: ii, vi). Digital assets

[4]When we talk about the changes in digital business, the words digitization and digitalization are often used interchangeably. In fact, many sources point to that. Yet, they are not quite the same. SAP, one of the world's leading software firms, has tried to distinguish the two. They point to a distinction that makes "digitization" the "process of changing from analog to digital" forms, whereas digitalization means the "use of digital technologies to change a business model and provide new revenue (...); it is the process of moving to a digital business" (Prause 2016). In the article, the author implies that for customers it is often not important which term means what. Nevertheless, in recent years, the term digitization has become rather prevalent and can be found in most of the literature. In this book, the term *digitization* is therefore used throughout.

are measured by the spending on computers, software, ICT (information and communications technology) stock, robots, or data storage. Digital usages include digital payments, digital marketing, social technologies, and use of software for backoffice and customer relationships. A more digital workforce can mean that workers are directly employed in the tech sector or that their occupation includes use of technology to some extent. *Going digital* often translates to reinventing core processes, creating new business models, and putting the customer at the center of every process (Manyika et al. 2015: 6).

The different dimensions of digitization are hard to measure. Like electricity, digital services are a general-purpose technology that "underpins a huge share of economic activity beyond the sector that supplies it" (Manyika et al. 2015: 2). Traditionally, only the ICT sector that supplies the technological devices, the software, and services to use digital services was seen as "digital." Yet, this is only a small part of the wider development of digitization. Various branches and companies are building new digital assets and are connecting them in ways that foster new business practices. Increasingly, there are also new ways of doing work. In general, digitization is touching most of the population and every sector of the economy (Manyika et al. 2015: 1). This is based, as said before, on the wide availability of the Internet today, including mobile Internet, social media, or smartphone apps. At the same time, businesses have invested in analytics technology to examine vast amounts of data from consumers.

Digitization holds enormous potential of productivity growth in the USA. Only from the potential of three areas, online talent platforms, Big Data analytics, and the Internet of Things, estimates say that $2.2 trillion could be added to the US GDP by 2025. Additionally, manufacturing, energy, and heavy industries could add to productivity growth through digitization (Manyika et al. 2015: vi). Today, the US economy is not realizing the full potential of what could be possible through digitization. Some sectors have been slower to adopt digital technologies, some of which are very large in terms of contributing to the GDP and employment (Manyika et al. 2015: 6). New companies have emerged that also hold great potential for further growth (such as Amazon, Airbnb, Uber, Lyft, Pinterest, Snapchat, Dropbox, Google, and many more). It is estimated that by 2010 the Internet Economy had already contributed about 4.7% of the US GDP and that this number has been growing fast: "Using 2011 data, the Organization for Economic Cooperation and Development (OECD) estimated internet-related activities comprised between 3.2% (using conservative estimates) and up to 13.2% of US business sector value added (a component of GDP). They also estimated a 7.1% GDP dynamic contribution to the US economy in 2011 from the internet (. . .)" (Hooten 2017: 5).

However, today we see a new nature in productivity and employment growth.

> By definition, productivity growth stems either from improving efficiency (that is, reducing the inputs needed to produce a given output) or from increasing the volume and value of outputs relative to any given input. The productivity surge of the late 1990s reflected both of these factors. (. . .) [Businesses] not only became more efficient but were able to capitalize on strong GDP and demand growth as a result. (Manyika et al. 2015: 10)

After the 1990s, this trend changed: "In contrast, sectors that posted the greatest productivity growth in the 2000s substantially reduced employment. Some of these sectors, such as ICT and media, have highly digitized workforces" (Manyika et al. 2015: 10). This trend has continued throughout the 2000s.

> Total productivity growth has fallen by two-thirds since 2005, while real GDP growth has averaged about 2 percent per year—all during a period in which the digital economy has continued to grow. This new 'Solow's paradox' phenomenon has led some to posit that the revolutionary nature of digital technologies has been overhyped, (Manyika et al. 2015: 10)

at least when it comes to productivity.

Yet, indicators such as GDP might not be the best way to measure productivity in the digital age as the "digital frontier" (Manyika et al. 2015: 1) is a fuzzy border that is not easily pinned down. ICT is just one part of a now much wider phenomenon. ICT is building the devices and the software that are then used in other areas of the economy and our private lives: "Digitization now touches most of the population and every sector of the economy" (Manyika et al. 2015: 1).

But how can we measure growth from the introduction of technology? GDP remains a viable measure to look at growth on the national level. But while "GDP remains a key metric for making fiscal and monetary policy decisions, a number of shortcomings of GDP as a measure of economic health are well known" (Sundararajan 2016: Pos 2440 Ch 5). GDP does not capture all aspects of growth in the digital era. There are alternatives, including the World Bank's Human Development Index, the Better Life Indicator of OECD, or the Social Progress Index. But it remains difficult to measure, for example, consumer surplus or social capital in an economy where consumers are impacted in varying degrees (Sundararajan 2016: Pos 2457f Ch 5). Furthermore, in the sharing economy, for instance, many effects are local because services operate on a local level inside communities, which is even harder to measure (Sundararajan 2016: Pos 2624 Ch 5).

On the labor market, it is difficult to single out digitization as a sole impact. Yet, some overall trends can be seen. Instead of re-hiring after a downturn in the economy, companies are further automating certain areas of their businesses:

> Large companies in particular now respond to downturns with a push to improve productivity—not by increasing output and innovation but by cutting employment. (...) [T]his approach distinguished the productivity gains of the 1990s from those of the 2000s. Changes such as automation tend to become permanent (...). As a result, slowdowns now tend to hit employment hard even as productivity is unaffected. (Manyika et al. 2015: 12)

This development has overwhelmingly affected middle-skilled jobs among the US workforce:

> Since 2000, the United States has created eight million net new full-time equivalent positions; two-thirds of those have been in low-skill interactive work and the remaining one-third in high-skill interactive work. But some 2.5 million net production and transaction positions were lost during this period. Robots have supplanted assembly line workers, and software handles many of the tasks once performed by bookkeepers, secretaries, and file clerks. (Manyika et al. 2015: 12)

The shift toward digitization has therefore benefitted highly skilled workers, especially with new jobs that had not existed before. Low-skilled jobs were also added in recent decades.

Even in boom areas such as the Silicon Valley, job and wage growth have not been stellar. There seems to be a growing disconnect between the

> region's economic growth and compensation for labor. (...) Some might theorize that the low job growth rate is due to an attraction of 'talent' or a 'creative class', whereby leading Silicon Valley companies hired fewer, but more skilled and productive employees, and paid them higher wages. However, the data do not bear this out. Average wages also fell far behind productivity growth. Over the same 15-year period in which productivity per capita shot up 62%, average compensation only grew by 25% (in inflation adjusted dollars). (Benner et al. 2018: 3)

In general, this means that a declining share of total output is going to employees. This is especially apparent in branches like durable goods manufacturing (computer, semiconductor, related components) in the Silicon Valley area. This shows that there is an increasing disconnect between economic growth and labor, with wages having declined in nearly all sectors of the labor force in the last 20 years, while only the very highest earners have increased their share (Benner et al. 2018: 3). It is also consistent with the overall decline of manufacturing jobs in the USA. When it comes to pay, digitization has possibly accelerated the trend of a growing gap between the majority of workers and a small group at the top:

> The most digitized industries have posted the fastest wage growth, but they make up only about 19 percent of total US employment; digitized companies are able to generate more output and capture more profit with fewer employees. Meanwhile, average hourly wages have stagnated in real terms. Since 1980, labor productivity has grown 2.5 times faster than wages, breaking historical patterns. (Manyika et al. 2015: 12)

In this context, the digital divide on the company level is not about those online and those offline anymore; it is more about the gap between the "digital haves" and the digital "have-mores" (Manyika et al. 2015: 3). On the business level, this means that there are the market leaders who have stopped focusing on expanding access but are now looking for ways to deepen engagement and capabilities. These digital leaders are far ahead of everyone else in the economy, while most companies have not "gone digital" to the extent they could have and are lagging far behind the small group of sector leaders.

> The digital frontier is a high-risk, high-rewards environment. At a broad level, the industries with the fastest profit margin growth tend to be those with the fastest growth in software intensity. And within these sectors, the margin spreads between the top-performing companies and the lowest performers are two to four times those in other sectors. In other words, the most digitized industries are developing a winner-take-all dynamic. (Manyika et al. 2015: 3)

At the same time, competition is fierce and today's market leaders could be knocked off their pedestal with the next wave of innovation.

In the past, economies of scale were usually achieved by large networks of factories and equipment. In the digital economy, there are virtually no marginal costs, "digital platforms make the cost of doing one more transaction or creating one more peer-to-peer connection trivial, giving digital companies a distinct advantage" (Manyika et al. 2015: 9). This combination of "low-marginal-cost economics and platform architecture has allowed the most successful high-tech firms to achieve a scale that was once impossible—and to do so in record time" (Manyika et al. 2015). Information and knowledge-intensive products have high sunk costs and low marginal costs of production, meaning that the initial costs of developing a product are high and not recoverable (high sunk costs). But once the product is on the market, there are very low marginal costs (Benner et al. 2018: 12). Innovations in the tech sector are also prone to rent-seeking, i.e., that firms can reap disproportionate benefits for their innovation because there is no competitor (patent systems and intellectual property laws are encouraging this) (Benner et al. 2018: 13). In the long run, this can drag down productivity growth.

This specific structure of the digital market and digital products might also threaten the fundamental connection between value produced by an individual and the returns the individual receives for his or her work. In classical economic theory, the perfectly competitive market provides wages to people that are proportional to the marginal profit of their labor. Following this logic, skill demand is shifting with technological progress and therefore those workers with the desirable skills can reap much higher salaries than the rest (Benner et al. 2018: 12). Yet, there might be more to consider when looking at digital businesses:

> [Markets] in information products and services are different in a few but fundamentally important ways from markets in material products and services. High sunk costs with near zero marginal costs, technological rents, network effects, and winner-take-all dynamics are all prevalent in market dynamics for information products and services, leading to employment insecurity and inequalities in outcomes that are not distortions of perfect markets, but rather the logical structural outcomes of the way those markets work. (Benner et al. 2018: 12)

The structure of the digital market (high sunk costs, near zero marginal costs, technological rents, network effects, and winner-take-all dynamics) creates circumstances in which a handful of firms can capture enormous revenues. These revenues are not necessarily connected to the costs of production or the quality of the innovations:

> Incremental technological improvements, first-mover advantages, and slight market leads quite predictably will translate into disproportionate returns for a few firms, and failure for many. This is clearly understood in the world of venture capital and start-ups, where investors have a rule of thumb that only one out of ten investments is likely to be successful, but the returns in that one investment will be enough to outweigh the losses in all the others. (Benner et al. 2018: 16)

These dynamics prevail throughout the information market and are part of Silicon Valley's dynamic. Yet, this make-it-or-break-it attitude also leads to inequality of outcomes, together with a lot of unpredictability for the livelihoods of many. Although the structure of high sunk costs and low marginal costs of production leads to high rewards, today, the "windfall from being first to market quickly dries up as competitors emerge, and the price that the product can command drops quickly" (Benner et al. 2018: iii). Therefore, companies try to push down all costs that are not considered creative, including labor costs of production, distribution, maintenance of buildings, physical plants, etc. This results in the companies' revenues being more and more disconnected from the ongoing costs of production when the initial investment is paid back: "Investors, top executives, and shareholders can reap enormous profits without necessarily sharing that with direct employees, much less sub-contracted workers" (Benner et al. 2018: iii). Some of these companies are also prone to building monopolies or near-monopolies in the market, which means that these firms can get profits out of "monopoly rents" rather than through their relationship to worker productivity or wages (Benner et al. 2018: iii).

There are mostly two types of monopolies prevalent in the tech sector. The first one is based on a technological innovation. Although innovation is generally positive for the market, a lack of competition in innovative fields can lead to high rents just because there is no challenger. These monopolies are often patent-based or temporary, a "first-mover-effect." This can lead to the firms highly rewarding "the relatively small number of employees (and top level management) who create the rent-generating innovation, but leaves behind other workers, while the company continues to accumulate rent-generated wealth" (Benner et al. 2018: iii). The second common type of monopoly in the new economy is based on the "winner-take-all" markets that are often referred to when talking about the network economy. In these markets, wealth is not necessarily created through the activity of the firm but rather through the size of the network and how people are using it. Google and Amazon are examples of such companies taking over huge market shares due to network effects. The network effect is the source of the revenue; activities by the company itself are only secondary (Benner et al. 2018: iv). Additionally, there are virtually millions of "unpaid workers" that contribute to the success of the network companies by contributing so-called audience labor. This labor includes the voluntary review on platforms, or the production of content. Platforms like YouTube or Instagram are thriving on the content that the users create. Moreover, many of the top tech firms of today were building on decades of public spending in science and technological progress (e.g., military spending on things like GPS or the Internet itself). Private data and private networks of users are also a source of revenue. "Firms benefits from these socially produced sources of economic value in ways that are disconnected from returns to labor" (Benner et al. 2018: iv). Moreover, many local industries cannot reap the benefits of "globally integrated high-tech industries" (Benner et al. 2018: vi). Many local industries are part of the service industry and face highly competitive markets anyway.

> In this large, low-margin sector of the economy, wages and benefits lag far behind the compensation levels provided to high tech personnel. One result is rapidly expanding inequality, often compounded when high tech salaries increase the cost of living by driving up prices for goods and services with a locally constrained supply, such as housing. (Benner et al. 2018: vi)

Thus, there is indeed large potential for growth in the high-tech sector, but this growth is far from equally distributed. First of all, much of the growth is based on monopolistic tendencies, unpaid contributions of users such as their data, as well as network effects that favor big actors. Whereas some high-up management and the small group of employees responsible for innovation and creative tasks are highly rewarded, all other groups of workers in the tech sector, such as in Silicon Valley, are not benefitting from the boom to a great extent. In fact, the tech industry is trying to push down wages of all employees that are not immediately involved in the innovative process. Additionally, the boom area faces enormous increases in prices, for example for housing and other costs of living, thereby affecting all groups in the workforce. This also puts strain on other local industries such as services (other than tech).

Thus, although there are significant challenges in a more digitized economy, the whole economy is moving to become more digital eventually. However, this is happening unevenly across the board. The digital "have-mores" are "users with advanced digital capabilities (. . .) capturing disproportionate benefits" (Manyika et al. 2015: vi). This is what Andrew McAfee and Erik Brynjolfsson also allude to in their work on *The Second Machine Age*. They think that there are "superstar" employees who can boost their careers through their rare digital skills, while most of the other workers cannot keep pace. Additionally, the "companies leading the charge are winning the battle for market share and profit growth; some are reshaping entire industries to their own advantage" (Manyika et al. 2015: vi). Other businesses have a hard time keeping up with the fast pace of digitization. Yet, workers in digitized industries "enjoy wage growth that is twice the national average, while the majority of US workers face stagnant incomes and uncertain prospects" (Manyika et al. 2015: vi). However, as said above, it is only a small elite of tech workers and managers who enjoy significant income gains.

Apart from the ICT sector, the media, professional services, and financial services are digitized the most (Manyika et al. 2015: 4). Yet, as the platform economy is advancing, more and more services could be digitized. Some sectors have been digitizing faster than others. Firm size, complexity of operations, knowledge intensity, and the threat of competition are decisive factors for investing in digital technology. Larger firms, apart from smaller "digital natives," are more likely to digitize in order to manage greater complexity such as supply chains. Companies with groups of highly educated workers are also more likely to adopt digital technology sooner. Also, competition or the threat of competition makes firms adopt digital technology faster (Manyika et al. 2015: 6).

In the USA, there are certain areas that have great potential for productivity growth fueled by digitization. These fields include utilities, manufacturing, or mining. Moreover, the retail or healthcare sectors are expanding digital usage and still have great potential for further digitization, as do localized industries such as construction, leisure, or hospitality. Small businesses have an especially big gap to close in order to catch up with leading companies (Manyika et al. 2015: 4). If firms manage to close the gap, great consumer surplus is created. The "consumer-facing markets" (Manyika et al. 2015: 8) are lowering search and transactions costs, delivering better matching, and offering greater transparency, and there is potential to use digitization to advance societal benefits. Today's digitization winners are mostly concentrated in the fields that Andrew McAfee and Erik Brynjolfsson have called *Machine, Platform, Crowd*. In their 2017 book of the same name, they look beyond *The Second Machine Age* and emphasize current developments in digitization, which they prefer to call "virtualization" (McAfee and Brynjolfsson 2017: Ch IV Positon 1358). With this process, they refer to virtual processes entering our everyday life, from self-checkout at the supermarket to self-check-in at the airport or hotel. They support a new view on machines and humans, closer to a real "relationship." As said before, they also emphasize that in many instances, better results can be generated by leaving out the human factor completely. They do not argue that humans will become completely obsolete but, similar to their argument in *The Second Machine Age*, they argue that humans will only fulfill certain tasks that specifically require "human" skills such as judgment, common sense, managing and motivating human teams (McAfee and Brynjolfsson 2017: Ch II Position 791).

As we have seen already, one area that is gaining more and more traction is the area of machine and deep learning. With the explosion of available data from digital text, pictures, sounds, videos, etc., machines can be fed with Big Data. In "unsupervised" machine learning processes machines can learn without any human input. Yet, "supervised" machine learning is still more common: "Most successful systems rely instead on 'supervised learning,' where they're essentially given a paired set of questions and correct answers before they are asked to answer any new questions on their own" (McAfee and Brynjolfsson 2017: Ch III Position 1138). Businesses are already making use of it, for example in the area of speech recognition, where huge advances are taking place compared to a few years ago:

> Machine learning systems get better as they get bigger, run on faster and more specialized hardware, gain access to more data, and contain improved algorithms. All of these improvements are taking place now, so machine learning is advancing rapidly. (...) Neural networks have had their best successes with supervised learning, where the learning examples are tagged. But they have made little progress with unsupervised learning, which is the main way humans learn about the world. (McAfee and Brynjolfsson 2017: Ch III Position 1271–1273)

But technological progress is moving fast ahead and especially in the field of AI and machine learning the speed is breathtaking, in some instances. Especially because the notion that machine learning systems lack "common sense" and the human understanding of the physical world could turn out to be more irrelevant than previously thought. In many instances, it is a mistake to believe that "the only way to develop machines that perform a task at the level of human beings is to copy the way that human beings perform that task" (Susskind 2020: 71). According to Susskind, this "fallacy remains widespread to this day" (Susskind 2020: 71) as it contradicts the way humans view their own capabilities and make sense of how the world and technology functions. But this ongoing fast development of technology will lead to *virtualization*, in the words of McAfee and Brynjolfsson, arriving in a large-scale fashion and in branches that seemed out of reach for machines in the past.

Depending on the field, which of the digital products prevails will be part of self-selection processes as people can pick and choose (personalized) products and services online (McAfee and Brynjolfsson 2017: Ch IV Position 1395). The advances in virtualization will take place, according to the authors, in four main areas: data, algorithms, networks, and the cloud (McAfee and Brynjolfsson 2017: Ch IV Position 1448f). The new economy is significantly based on networks and they are vital for digital development. Especially wireless communication is improving rapidly with more powerful networks such as LTE (McAfee and Brynjolfsson 2017: Ch IV Position 1461) or 5G. Similarly, cloud technology is the basis for many of the new digital developments. An "unprecedented amount of computing power is now available to organizations and individuals. (. . .) This cloud computing infrastructure, largely less than a decade old, accelerates the robotic Cambrian Explosion (. . .)" (McAfee and Brynjolfsson 2017: Ch IV Position 1467). All these developments in data, algorithms, networks, and clouds lead to improvements in the fields of robotics, drones, autonomous cars, and many other machines (McAfee and Brynjolfsson 2017: Ch IV Position 1498). In the end, people might choose a human-to-human option if they like, but this will not stop virtualization to arrive in a grand fashion in most branches of life, especially when machines acquire more and more capabilities (McAfee and Brynjolfsson 2017: Ch IV Position 1634).

So far, the US economy is not as digitized as it could be and there are other factors to consider apart from the technological possibilities. The broader state of the economy, as well as the aforementioned cultural, social, ethical, legal, and political factors, also plays a role in the development and spread of more digitized technology.

2.2.3 *The Rise of the Platform Economy*

> Are these advantages insurmountable and universal? Are platforms, in other words, going to spread everywhere and take over everything, destroying old-line companies or reducing them to low-profit remnants of what they once were? (. . .) this is what's happened time and time again over the past twenty years. And as we've hopefully made clear, there's more to come; the changes brought by platforms are not yet finished. (McAfee and Brynjolfsson 2017: Ch IX Position 3259)

As this quotation makes clear, when talking about digitization, one key aspect are digital platforms. "Competitive dynamics are increasingly determined by who develops the right digital assets" (Manyika et al. 2015: 8). In a lot of cases, these assets are platforms that allow moving from physical to digital products (e.g., streaming platforms). Businesses are also building huge data repositories to make use of the consumer data. "The power of platform economics is reflected in the gross margins enjoyed by software companies, which can run as high as 80 percent, the highest of any industry" (Manyika et al. 2015: 9). As said before, low marginal costs and the platform architecture lead to large-scale networks that millions of users log on to. This also gives these companies huge amounts of data that are sold or used to improve the platform and the user experience.

Some of the most valuable digital firms today are platforms such as Facebook, Amazon, Airbnb, or LinkedIn. But other firms are adopting their examples of data usage, platform infrastructure, or connectivity to interact with customers or their workforce. Companies also build connectivity into their products (GPS or Bluetooth in cars, for example) (Manyika et al. 2015: 8). Many digital platforms have also displayed the ability to move into new business areas. For example, Amazon started with the sale of books. Yet today, Amazon is not only selling all kinds of products worldwide, but it created self-publishing platforms, it offers cloud-based business services, and it recently moved into the grocery market by acquiring Wholefoods.[5] Other companies such as Google (Alphabet), Apple, or Uber are also examples of companies that are diversifying their strategy in different markets (Manyika et al. 2015: 9).

Digital platforms usually strive to create an elevated consumer experience. These effects are notoriously difficult to measure. With a smartphone in your pocket, you have a powerful tool to navigate information, communicate, and consume. User reviews and the ability to compare lead to fierce price competitions, but also to better quality and service (Manyika et al. 2015: 10). Amazon is the prime example for this business model.

As said before, the general-purpose technology of digital technology and platforms leads to productivity increases. Yet, the question remains whether

> the platform economy, and the reorganization it portends, [will] catalyze economic growth and a surge in productivity driven by a new generation of entrepreneurs? Or will the algorithmically driven reorganization concentrate substantially all of the gains in the hands of those who build the platforms? Will it spark a wave of entrepreneurial possibilities, unleash unimagined creativity, free workers from oppressive work schedules, or unleash an avalanche of dispossessed workers who are trying to make a living with gigs and temporary contracts? (Kenney and Zysman 2016)

Certainly, consumers will benefit from a surge in productivity and innovation, as will the entrepreneurs who bring the innovative products to the market. The question is whether a large number of workers (not in their role as consumers) will also benefit from further digitization.

As McAfee and Brynjolfsson have emphasized, perfect and instant distribution of information over networks is the basis on which the new economy, and the platform economy, is built. In this scenario, the Internet is the "platform of platforms" (McAfee and Brynjolfsson 2017: Ch VI Position 2039). Platforms can be built on one another, for example, the World Wide Web was "built" on the foundation or building block of the Internet (McAfee and Brynjolfsson 2017: Ch VI Position 2044). Building blocks are valuable in this sense because "combinatorial innovation" (McAfee and Brynjolfsson 2017: Ch VI Position 2044) is possible, meaning that you can put together things that are already there in new and innovative ways. This is how the rise of so many well-known platforms came about. Often, they disrupt "analogue" predecessors or industry incumbents and become stronger as the network effect kicks in:

---

[5]Amazon is also active in other sectors. In 2021, it announced the acquisition of the film studio MGM.

> We see the same pattern time and time again: the free, perfect, and instant economics of platforms offer stiff competition. In 2009, Jan Koum and Brian Acton released WhatsApp, a smartphone application that let users send text messages to each other via their phones' data networks, rather than as SMS messages. This difference was important because many users, especially those outside the world's richest countries, paid their mobile phone company for each SMS they sent or received. Data networks typically have flat-rate pricing, and if the phone was connected to a Wi-Fi network, data transfers were completely free. (McAfee and Brynjolfsson 2017: Ch VI Position 2070)

Naturally, the world's mobile carriers were not happy about this, but as more and more people started using WhatsApp, even those who did not necessarily need free messaging downloaded the service. In this way, "Platform economics, Moore's law, and combinatorial innovation continue to produce developments that take industries and their incumbents by surprise" (McAfee and Brynjolfsson 2017: Ch VI Position 2096).

Another feature of digital platforms is the "unbundling" capability: "they can unbundle resources that used to be tightly clustered together, and therefore difficult to consume one by one. Platforms like iTunes turn this form of unbundled consumption from difficult into the default. This makes them very popular with consumers, which in turn makes it difficult for incumbents like music rights holders to ignore" (McAfee and Brynjolfsson 2017: Ch VI Position 2138). Taking the unbundling of music even further, streaming services like Spotify emerged, taking advantage of powerful smartphones, Wi-Fi, and data plans that were now available to consumers (McAfee and Brynjolfsson 2017: Ch VI Position 2148).

> The same business models don't work as well when goods are not digital: a massive bundle inevitably includes many components that go unused. If the marginal cost of those components is close to zero (as with online music), then there's no real waste from making them available. But if the goods are made of atoms (as with vinyl records or plastic CDs), then sending the consumer lots of never-to-be-used components is costly, and ultimately unprofitable. (McAfee and Brynjolfsson 2017: Ch VI Position 2158)

This trend is most likely going to continue in various fields. Additionally, the network effect of platforms favors the bigger networks, leading to the already mentioned monopolistic tendencies in the new economy (McAfee and Brynjolfsson 2017: Ch VI Position 2189).

But if platforms offer their products for free, why is that model profitable? Freemium businesses can, for instance, offer basic services for free and charge for more advanced services. Examples are Spotify, Dropbox, or Evernote (McAfee and Brynjolfsson 2017: Ch VII Position 2392–2396). Others make money with ads. Many companies such as banks or insurances offer free apps as a form of customer service. Governments or not-for-profit companies make services available for free to reach the public (McAfee and Brynjolfsson 2017: Ch VII Position 2401–2409). As said before, many of the most recent examples for successful platforms are built on things that are already there, often trying to bridge the offline and online world. One example McAfee and Brynjolfsson give is the platform Postmates.[6] Postmates makes use of the existing infrastructure of local shops and restaurants, giving customers the opportunity to order and pay via app and receive deliveries from couriers (McAfee and Brynjolfsson 2017 Ch VIII Position 2715–2720). There are more and more examples of such platforms. "The first generation of large, influential, and often disruptive Internet platforms covered the information industries. We're now seeing a second generation spreading throughout the rest of the economy" (McAfee and Brynjolfsson 2017: Ch VIII Position 2739). McAfee and Brynjolfsson call these platforms *O2O*, online to offline, as they spread from the online world to the actual world. Examples include Lyft and Uber (ride-hailing), Airbnb (short-term rentals), Caviar (food delivery), or Honor (in-home health care) (McAfee and Brynjolfsson 2017: Ch VIII Position 2741–2744). These platforms use reputation systems to overcome the information asymmetries existing between customer and providers, as well as strong brands that consumers identify with (McAfee and Brynjolfsson 2017: Ch IX Position 3097–3103). Most of the efforts by platforms are targeted at consumer satisfaction. But as the network usually has two sides, consumers on one side and providers/workers/drivers on the other, the provider side is often affected by decisions made by platforms such as changes in pricing. McAfee and Brynjolfsson claim that cuts in pricing benefit both sides of the network, but this remains a contested question (McAfee and Brynjolfsson 2017: Ch IX Position 3171). More on the issues surrounding platforms will follow in Chap. 3 of this book.

Although many successful platforms focus on consumers, McAfee and Brynjolfsson also see a wide range of business-to-business developments emerging via platforms (McAfee and Brynjolfsson 2017: Ch VIII Position 2771). As smartphone distribution is growing, the potential for O2O platforms is only increasing. They offer an example of "the power of complements, especially free ones, for pushing out demand curves," as well as the potential for novel combinations of "bits and the economics of atoms" (McAfee and Brynjolfsson 2017: Ch VIII Position 2829–2832). Processing and storage of information are crucial in this regard and will increase the network effects while keeping costs low (McAfee and Brynjolfsson 2017: Ch VIII Position 2835). "Mathematically sophisticated, data-rich services like these used to be out of reach for many real-world businesses, especially small ones. Thanks to the free, perfect, and instant economies of bits, they're now available everywhere O2O platforms are" (McAfee and Brynjolfsson 2017: Ch VIII Position 2847). In the past, businesses did not have the advantage of additional and affordable computing capacity, which is now available through the cloud (McAfee and Brynjolfsson 2017: Ch VIII Position 2870). The huge amount of data generated by these platforms is also fertile ground for machine learning and the development of better artificial intelligence (McAfee and Brynjolfsson 2017: Ch VIII Position 2858).

[6]Equivalents are GrubHub and DoorDash or Lieferando and Deliveroo which also operate in Europe and mainly focus on food delivery from restaurants.

The availability of the so-called crowd, the vast group of online users worldwide, is one reason why platforms have been so successful in their development of new products and services. Companies are engaging the "wisdom of the crowd" through the Internet when they want to develop new products. Especially in open-access projects, but also with the development of other new products, one can see that the "crowd is, in many ways, the opposite of the core: it's huge, diverse, largely uncontrollable, and often messy. (. . .) The core remains relevant and useful, but in an era of global networks and robust platforms the crowd has become an increasingly powerful force" (McAfee and Brynjolfsson 2017: Ch X Position 3659–3661). The crowd is diverse and can look at problems from many angles and perspectives by including people from various (educational and cultural) backgrounds, different problem-solving approaches, intellectual tool kits, genders, and race (McAfee and Brynjolfsson 2017: Ch XI Position 3800). In this way, a new generation of products created through the help of the crowd can successfully enter the market on a global scale.

As platforms become bigger and more popular, they also become more powerful. But often only a limited number of platforms survive in a given environment. An example here are mobile operating systems Android and iOS. Google bought Android and built a rival platform to Apple's iOS for mobile phones. Android has since become the most widely used mobile operating system worldwide. iOS is also established in the market, running Apple's iPhones. Yet, an attempt by Microsoft to establish a rival system failed, as did attempts to keep the Blackberry platform (RIM) going, which had been an early success story[7] (McAfee and Brynjolfsson 2017: Ch VII Position 2456–2486). The "popular platforms—the ones that best harness the economics of network effects, consumer surplus, and complements—become very influential because of the choices they make about curating content, membership, traffic, and so on. (. . .) The lesson is clear: powerful platforms can force hard choices on companies within their sphere of influence" (McAfee and Brynjolfsson 2017: Ch VII Position 2448). Consumers seem to favor some choice when it comes to platforms, yet ultimately they only seem to value a handful of options, often only two, and few consumers use more than one platform at a time (McAfee and Brynjolfsson 2017: Ch VII Position 2491).

Network effects are also important on the platform and large networks are often more attractive to users. Once the network has reached a certain size, it is easier to attract even more users (McAfee and Brynjolfsson 2017: Ch IX Position 3199). As said before, there is "a tendency toward winner-take-all markets when network effects are strong" (McAfee and Brynjolfsson 2017: Ch IX Position 3201). Yet, "even platform economics doesn't provide immunity to new competition, management mistakes, or technological shifts. None of today's platform heroes can grow

[7]During the trade conflict between the USA and China under the Trump administration, there were rumors that Huawei might establish a rival platform to Android after difficulties have arisen with Google. So far, this has not materialized.

complacent" (McAfee and Brynjolfsson 2017: Ch IX Position 3241). Many platforms have already disrupted existing incumbents and are likely to disrupt more.

> But they also won't be destructive to everything that existed before. The destructive potential of platforms is both real and large, but it's not unlimited. (. . .) Markets in which players are few and offerings are complicated will probably be some of the least amenable to platforms. (McAfee and Brynjolfsson 2017: Ch IX Position 3262–3303)

McAfee and Brynjolfsson also claim that platforms, especially O2O platforms, offer a way to monetize your assets, a room or a car, simultaneously improving your life and treading "more lightly on the planet" (McAfee and Brynjolfsson 2017: Ch VIII Position 2886). This is something that is often associated with what is referred to as the *sharing economy platforms*. Yet, if they really live up to this sustainable promise is questionable. More details on the sharing economy will follow in Chap. 3.

Different industries will be unequally affected by digitization developments and the rise of the platform economy, but almost all branches of society will be affected somehow. "At the industry level, for example, new energy supplies and technologies will have a particular impact on Energy, Basic and Infrastructure and Mobility industries. Processing power and Big Data will have an especially strong impact on Information and Communication Technology, Financial Services and Professional Services" (Schwab and Samans 2016: 10). This leads to massive changes in the employment structure of businesses, which means workers will be affected by digitization to a great extent (Schwab and Samans 2016: 13).

But not only existing businesses will be affected by digitization and the emergence of the platform economy, and the sharing economy as part of it. Klaus Schwab and Richard Samans advocate for a nuanced look at automation as it has often been too limited: "Our analysis reveals that upcoming disruptions to the employment landscape are going to be a lot more complex and multi-faceted than conveyed by a narrow focus only on automation, and that we must act within the current window offered by the varying speeds of technological transformations to prepare" (Schwab and Samans 2016: 13).

2.2.4 *Inequality in the Digital Age*

Since the broad diffusion of digital technology took off, we have been living in what can be called the Network Society. It is marked by the importance of technology and networks in almost all branches of life and in all of our economic activity. But recent decades have not only seen the rise of the Network Society but the rise of inequality at the same time. What are the reasons for the rise in inequality in the USA? The following chapter will assess the origins and state of inequality in the USA with special regard to the influence of technological progress on inequality.

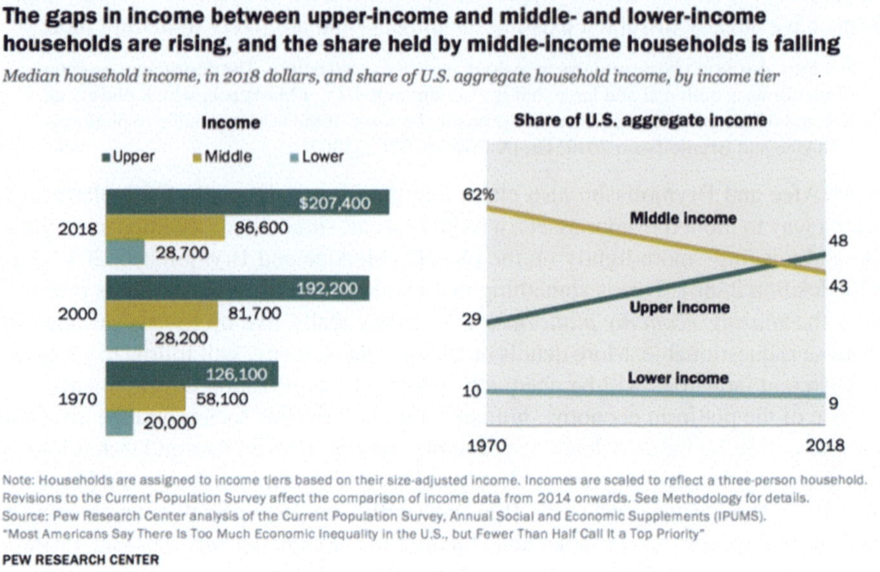

Fig. 2.1 Gap in income between upper-income and middle- and lower-income households is rising, based on Pew Research Center (Pew-Research-Center 2020)

2.2.4.1 The Origins and State of Income Inequality in the USA

Today, it has become almost universally acknowledged that inequality is more pronounced in the USA than in other Western countries. The gap between the income share of the middle and higher income groups is growing and the share of aggregate income of middle-income households in the USA has continuously fallen since the 1970s (Fig. 2.1). Looking at wealth dispersion of these income groups, the divide is even more pronounced with the upper-income group owning almost 80% of the US aggregate wealth and middle-income groups only about 17% in 2016. Lower-income groups own virtually no wealth (Fig. 2.2) (Pew-Research-Center 2020).

Globalization as well as technological progress is seen as the two main influences toward a widening gap between the upper and lower-income groups in the USA. Other influences are often seen in the decline of unionization or the financialization of the economy, both of which are also connected to globalization and technological progress. Due to both these trends, productivity of the US economy has grown since the 1970s. Yet, wages have not kept pace with this development, having grown only about 3% from 1979 to 2014. This development can be observed in many developed countries:

> This so-called wage stagnation is not unique to the United States: over the past several decades, wages for middle-income jobs have increased at an anemic pace in developed countries around the globe. Meanwhile, the wages of the highest-skilled and highest-paid individuals have continued to increase steadily. There are growing gaps in wages and

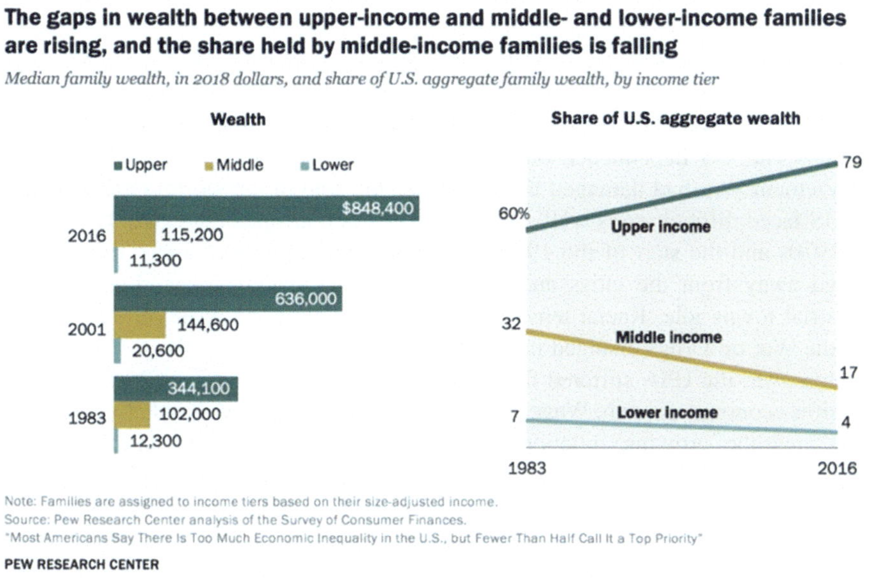

Fig. 2.2 Gaps in wealth between upper-income and middle- and lower-income families are rising, based on Pew Research Center (Pew-Research-Center 2020)

> employment opportunities between these individuals and those at the middle and bottom of the wage distribution, and there is no reason to think that these labor market trends will be reversed any time soon. (Kearney et al. 2015: 1)

How did it get to this? From 1973 until the election of Reagan in 1980, the US economy had been in a state of constant crisis. The oil shock had awoken the USA to its changing position in the world. In the post-World War II era, the USA had been the dominant power in the West, militarily, societal, and economically. The level of inequality among Americans was stable; wealth spread more evenly across all groups in society. It was the era of the so-called *Great Compression* (Goldin and Margo 1992). Beginning in the 1940s and following the period of the 1930s marked by the Great Depression, the Great Compression period saw a development of narrowing wage gaps between most Americans. "When the United States emerged from war and depression, it had not only a considerably lower rate of unemployment, it also had a wage structure more egalitarian than at any time since" (Goldin and Margo 1992: 2), which was maintained for several decades. Yet, after the 1970s, the "movement toward equality in the 1940s was reversed" (Goldin and Margo 1992: 3).

In the period right after WWII and the start of the Cold War, the political will to spread wealth more equally in order to appear as the "better system" in comparison to the socialist East was widespread. The middle class grew, almost full employment was accomplished, and strong labor unions delivered good jobs (Neckerman and Torche 2007: 336; Davidson 2013: 381). Additionally, the war had established a tax system that redistributed much more intensively than during any other period in American history. Wealthy Americans were taxed at a high rate, and the gap between the richest Americans and the middle class shrank significantly. But by 1973, other countries had caught up with the USA's economic capacity, for example Germany or Japan. The Bretton Woods system with the Dollar as the strongest currency was in decline. The US dependence on foreign oil was apparent. And the disaster of the Vietnam War had damaged the US leadership role in the world. Domestically, the US faced difficulties as well. De-industrialization gripped the USA. The end of the 1970s and the start of the 1980s saw crises in many urban areas; the affluent moved away from the cities and into the suburbs, leaving inner cities and old industrial towns idle. Racial tensions and gang violence shook the USA; policies like the War on Drugs changed inner cities further.

Moreover, the USA suffered from "stagflation," a combination of high inflation and slow economic growth. Wages stagnated, unemployment was high, interest rates grew, and the growing inflation threatened many people's standard of living (Fligstein 2010: 236). In order to tackle these problems, the Carter administration came to the conclusion that too much regulation was stifling the US economy and had to be abandoned. More competition and a deregulated market would bring down prices. Among the first projects of deregulation were the airline and trucking industry, as well as the saving and loans industry. Reagan promised to continue deregulating the economy by cutting taxes for businesses and individuals and further extracting the government from the economic sphere. With the breakup of the air traffic controllers' strike, Reagan successfully coined the unions as the "villains of the economy" (Davidson 2013: 381). Fligstein claims that "this retreat from regulation (. . .) came to dominate the way that Congress worked for the next thirty years. (. . .) From 1980 onward, the dominant policy view was that markets were always right and government was always wrong" (Fligstein 2010: 236).

These developments led to less support for Keynesian demand-side economics and into the era of supply-side economics. Keynesians were at a loss at how to tackle stagflation, something they thought was impossible. Supply-side economics focuses on the supply of labor and goods rather than on the demand side. Using tax cuts, for instance, supply-siders wanted to incentivize work and production (Supply-Side Economics 2019). Under President Reagan, many of the supply-side ideas were implemented and the economy began to grow again. However, a massive federal budget deficit ensued, as well as heightened speculation on the financial market. Inequality began to grow as well. None of these developments were fundamentally reversed under the following administrations (Komlos and Schubert 2020).

Although the 1980s saw a return of economic growth, the American economy de-industrialized further and firms began to favor so-called shareholder value capitalism. Many US companies also shifted production abroad where labor costs were much cheaper than at home. Companies claimed that due to globalization, it was the only way to remain competitive internationally. Many economists insisted that this development would, in the end, benefit everyone in society, as long as corporate profits were rising. The infamous trickle-down effect was born. Corporate profits were rising and the finance-driven economy rewarded top earners with bonuses.

However, this trend destroyed much of the unionized blue-collar workforce and much of the established corporate bureaucracies. The financial markets became the most important reference point for firms. The shareholder value had to be increased quickly or managers would find themselves without a job (Fligstein 2010: 237). During the 1980s, both "upper-tail and lower-tail inequality" increased (Neckerman and Torche 2007: 336; Davidson 2013: 381f).

With the fading away of much of the blue- and some of the white-collar working class, the value of wages declined and insecurity in the workplace increased. Education became more and more important. A rise in the return on higher education began to crystallize in the 1980s with college premiums increasing sharply (Neckerman and Torche 2007: 337). High-school graduates had more and more difficulties on the job market. On the other end of the spectrum, managerial positions were also downsized. Yet, the ones that stayed on captured huge wage gains. By then "the idea that top managers should be rewarded primarily for the financial performance of the corporation was firmly in place" (Fligstein 2010: 238). Institutional "investors, top managers, investment banks, and the financial community were the principal beneficiaries" (Fligstein 2010: 238) of this situation—not the more general labor force. In California and New York, legislation "helped Silicon Valley and Wall Street to allow managerial pay to rise as high as it could go in the name of rewarding innovation. Legislation helped the telecommunications companies and later the banks to engage in whatever activities they chose" (Fligstein 2010: 238).

Through this restructuring processes, wages and labor conditions in many densely unionized sectors came increasingly under pressure. In Europe, where unions remained stronger, restructuring of the market often led to higher unemployment, also because younger workers had a hard time entering the workforce (Castells 2010: 300). Thus, since the 1980s, business has tried to increase profits by reducing labor costs through either increasing productivity (Europe) or by lowering the cost of new jobs (USA). Labor unions were weakened, also by their inability to adapt to new workforce members and new forms of work (e.g., high tech). As Manuel Castells describes, the network enterprise developed through the availability of the Internet and was able to operate on a global scale. This posed insurmountable obstacles to most unions (Castells 2010: 301):

> The extraordinary increase in flexibility and adaptability permitted by new technologies opposed the rigidity of labor to the mobility of capital. It followed a relentless pressure to make the labor contribution as flexible as it could be. Productivity and profitability were enhanced, yet labor lost institutional protection and became increasingly dependent on individual bargaining conditions in a constantly changing labor market. (Castells 2010: 302)

In recent years, this ever-changing labor market also seems to have led to the emergence of more home and part-time work. This is a development pushed by the rise of the network enterprise and flexible work processes. Emerging technologies and the Internet push this broader development even further. Some of the new technologies further facilitated home work, part-time work, and replacement of workers in some instances (Castells 2010: 408).

In light of the developments just described, the compression period after WWII seems to be the "unusual" period in American history from today's perspective (Neckerman and Torche 2007: 336; Schor 2016). In this period, the USA redistributed wealth through the tax system. But generally, efforts for income redistribution were less extensive in the USA than in other OECD countries in recent decades. Other rich democracies have also witnessed a rising income inequality. Yet, they have done more than the USA to tackle this problem by efforts of redistribution (Bartels 2006: 40). The USA has traditionally focused more on the aspect of economic opportunity rather than redistribution efforts (Katz and Krueger 2017; Chetty et al. 2016), which could be one reason why inequality is higher in the USA today.

As mentioned above the idea of the trickle-down effect was born in the 1980s but has since faced extensive criticism. In fact, the trickle-down effect or also the claim that a "rising tide will lift all boats" goes even further back than the 1980s. In the 1960s, John F. Kennedy already claimed that this rising tide of growth benefitted everyone, the poor and the rich. Yet, today we can see that the picture is far more complex. Of course, a growing economy is good for everyone as long as employment and wages are growing. Yet, in their article *The effects of economic growth on income inequality in the US* from 2015 Amir Rubin and Dan Segal show that the top income group is much more sensitive to growth than other groups because a large portion of their income is wealth-related and their income often comes in a pay-for-performance form (often the compensation are stock options, which are highly market-sensitive). In fact, empirical evidence shows that the income of the top 1% earners is twice as sensitive to concurrent GDP per capita growth than the income of the lower 90%. The overall results by Rubin and Segal suggest that in the USA, "higher growth rates and positive shocks in future growth rates tend to increase income inequality" (Rubin and Segal 2015: 259). Additionally, wealth is even more unevenly distributed than income. "In the early 2000s, the wealthiest 1% of families held 1/3 of the total wealth, the next wealthiest 9% held another third, and the remaining 90% held the rest" (Neckerman and Torche 2007: 338). After the Great Recession, this trend has intensified and most households have still not recovered from the loss of wealth during the last recession (Pew-Research-Center 2020).

Thomas Piketty and Eammanuel Saez have offered an extensive look at inequality in the USA over the last century. In their numbers, they observe that "whereas income inequality was larger in Europe than in the United States a century ago, it is currently much larger in the United States" (Piketty and Saez 2014: 838). The USA shows that a much larger share of income goes to the top decile of earners than in Europe:

> In the United States, the top decile income share in 1910 was lower than in Europe, then rose in the 1920s, fell in the 1930s–1940s, and stabilized around 30 to 35% in the 1950s–1960s, slightly above European levels of the time. It then rose at an unprecedented pace since the 1970s–1980s, and is now close to 50%. According to this measure, primary income concentration is currently higher than it has ever been in U.S. history. It is also slightly higher than in pre-WWI Europe. (Piketty and Saez 2014: 839)

The GINI[8] Index also describes the level of inequality in countries around the world and is published by the World Bank. In Fig. 2.3, the GINI Index for the USA is displayed. Over the last 50 years, the USA displays a consistently higher GINI index than other OECD countries like Germany or Norway, meaning that in the USA, income is much more unequally distributed than in other countries.

Today, almost half of all the income of Americans goes to the top decile of the labor force. Inequality seems to be as high as in pre-WWI Europe, which can only be called an alarming trend. The period at the start of the twentieth century was marked by extreme polarization in wealth, society, and politics.

The exact consequences of rising inequality today are challenging to predict, but they will most likely not be positive for most Americans. In the long run, inequality might affect well-being, health, happiness, education, political participation, and political influence. Trust in politics can also be undermined by an unequal society. Here, the perception of inequality can be even more significant than the actual degree of inequality. Success of populist movements and leaders in the USA and elsewhere seems to point in this direction: The "effect of individuals' perceptions of excessive levels of inequality is likely to affect their democratic values regardless of how much income they have or how (in)accurate their perceptions of the actual level of national inequality" (Loveless 2013: 477). Additionally, it is unknown how future generations will succeed in reversing the effects of growing inequality (Neckerman and Torche 2007: 344). Future generations might be burdened even more if the USA does not facilitate social mobility. Although Americans tend to believe that they live in a very socially mobile society, numbers point in a different direction, especially at both ends of the distribution chain. Children of poor families tend to remain poor, and children of wealthy families are likely to remain wealthy. Race also plays an important role, which makes the USA "exceptional" in this regard compared to other wealthy countries. Huge wealth inequality usually leads to less mobility, especially if the return to capital, as Piketty describes it, will continue to grow but wages will remain stagnant (Stern and Kravitz 2016: Ch 2 Position 836f). Additionally, countries with high returns on education like the USA have relatively low mobility because educational attainments depend on family tradition and parent's earnings (Neckerman and Torche 2007: 339; Autor 2014: 848; Loveless 2013: 476ff.; Cooper et al. 2013).

This lack of mobility also threatens something that is traditionally associated with the USA: Economic opportunity and the ideal of the American Dream. The core of the American Dream is that the next generation will be better off, if one only works hard enough. Absolute income mobility is often used to assess the state of economic

[8]"Gini index measures the extent to which the distribution of income or consumption expenditure among individuals or households within an economy deviates from a perfectly equal distribution. A Lorenz curve plots the cumulative percentages of total income received against the cumulative number of recipients, starting with the poorest individual or household. The Gini index measures the area between the Lorenz curve and a hypothetical line of absolute equality, expressed as a percentage of the maximum area under the line. Thus a Gini index of 0 represents perfect equality, while an index of 100 implies perfect inequality" (World Bank 2021).

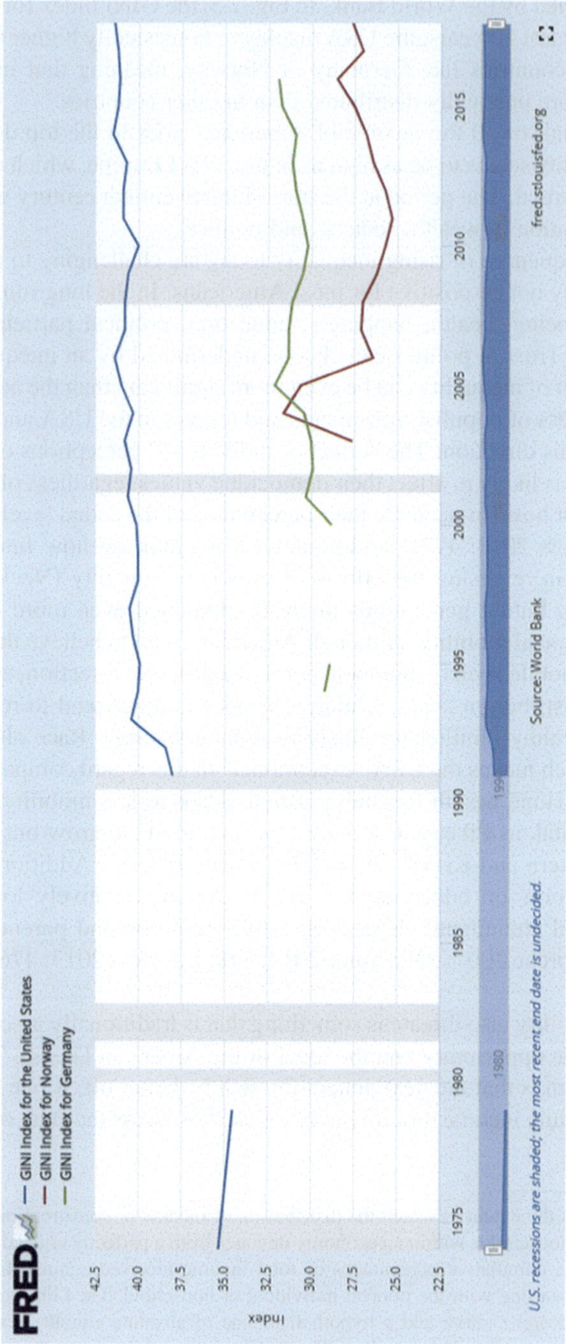

Fig. 2.3 GINI Index for the USA 1974–1979, 1991–2018 (upper line), compared to Germany 1994–2016 (middle line), and Norway 2003-2018 (lower line) (World Bank 2021)

opportunity in a country. Raj Chetty et al. find that absolute income mobility in the USA has fallen sharply since the 1940s: "the fraction of children earning more than their parents fell from 92% in the 1940 birth cohort to 50% in the 1984 birth cohort. Rates of absolute mobility fell the most for children with parents in the middle class" (Chetty et al. 2016: 2). The largest declines in income mobility could be found in former industrial centers in the Midwest such as Michigan or Illinois. Reasons for this sharp decline could be found in lower GDP growth rates since the 1970s and greater inequality in the distribution of growth (Chetty et al. 2016: 3). The authors also found a close link between the rise of inequality and the decline in absolute mobility (Chetty et al. 2016: 18). In order to reverse this trend and revive the American Dream, the USA does not only need higher GDP rates but "more broadly shared economic growth" (Chetty et al. 2016: 4) across all societal groups. Most of the economic growth in recent decades has exceedingly favored the very top.

As was described above, the origins of inequality in the USA are complex. But if the state of high inequality continues, the USA could face even more unfavorable consequences, both socially and politically with more societal unrest and political polarization that already marks the USA today. Deregulation, liberalization, and globalization of the market have changed the US economy profoundly. Additionally, changes in taxation and other government policies have led to a concentration of extreme wealth at the top. Yet, the picture is even more complex than that. The restructuring of the economy has also come about through the broad introduction of technology into businesses and the workplace, allowing for a globalized, interconnected market, which also has a role to play in the explanation of inequality in the USA.

2.2.4.2 Technology and the Polarization of the Labor Market

> Powerful digital technologies have a way of reinforcing the value of being around other highly skilled, highly productive people. (Avent 2016: 152)

Technology is often seen as one of the factors contributing to rising inequality in the USA today. Historically, there have always been winners and losers of technological progress, but over time, more jobs were created than displaced as new technology creates new demand (Kearney et al. 2015: 2). Yet, "even if technology eventually *will* increase prosperity more broadly in the long run, what kind of dislocations will there be in the interim? Many jobs that recently provided a middle-class lifestyle to workers and their families—from machinists to stock clerks—have been disappearing" (Kearney et al. 2015: 2). More and more middle-skilled jobs are being replaced by machines today. There is even more concern that through intelligent technology, many jobs might be replaced for good. Additionally, the so-called platform economy raises questions about the future of jobs, employment, and job security for American workers. All in all, new jobs, new skill sets, and new ways of working are emerging and are disrupting the American labor market and the economy.

Technology has always led to a broader restructuring of the economy and has shifted the composition of the labor force—at first from agriculture and artisans to manufacturing, then to clerking and services, as well as management positions.

> Yet the concern over technological unemployment has proven to be exaggerated. The obvious reason why this concern has not materialized relates to Ricardo's famous chapter on machinery, which suggests that labour-saving technology reduces the demand for undifferentiated labour, thus leading to technological unemployment (...). As economists have long understood, however, an invention that replaces workers by machines will have effects on all product and factor markets. An increase in the efficiency of production which reduces the price of one good, will increase real income and thus increase demand for other goods. Hence, in short, technological progress has two competing effects on employment. First, as technology substitutes for labour, there is a destruction effect, requiring workers to reallocate their labour supply; and second, there is the capitalisation effect, as more companies enter industries where productivity is relatively high, leading employment in those industries to expand. (Frey and Osborne 2017: 258)

Yet, as Keynes already said, uses of labor can be outrun by capitalization effects.

> The reason why human labour has prevailed relates to its ability to adopt and acquire new skills by means of education. Yet as computerisation enters more cognitive domains this will become increasingly challenging. Recent empirical findings are therefore particularly concerning. (...) They show that high-skilled workers have moved down the occupational ladder, taking on jobs traditionally performed by low-skilled workers, pushing low-skilled workers even further down the occupational ladder and, to some extent, even out of the labour force. This raises questions about (a) the ability of human labour to win the race against technology by means of education; and (b) the potential extent of technological unemployment, as an increasing pace of technological progress will cause higher job turnover, resulting in a higher natural rate of unemployment. (Frey and Osborne 2017: 258)

This more pessimistic view of labor's ability to adapt is countered by more optimistic views. Erik Brynjolfsson and Andrew McAfee are on the optimists' side of this development, and are not very fearful of the prospect of a digital revolution. But they also see polarization effects between the different labor groups:

> We agree with the end-of-work crowd that computerization is bringing deep changes, but we're not as pessimistic as they are. In fact, some human skills are more valuable than ever, even in an age of incredibly powerful and capable digital technologies. But other skills have become worthless, and people who hold the wrong ones now find that they have little to offer employers. They're losing the race against the machine (...). (Brynjolfsson and McAfee 2012: 3)

Brynjolfsson and McAfee are positive about the potential of the new economy, especially for entrepreneurs and innovators (Brynjolfsson and McAfee 2012: 7). They see an endless stream of innovation before us, each building on the previous one for the benefit of the individual (entrepreneur) and the whole economy. Looking at Silicon Valley firms, this idea seems to be fulfilled. Young innovators are building their ideas, backed by enormous capital, and create businesses that change the ways we consume and work. Consumers have profited from that development enormously. Yet, very few people in today's economy are those unique digital entrepreneurs. The vast majority of people are relying on traditional forms of employment to make a living.

But employment numbers are raising concerns. According to the Bureau of Labor Statistics, most of the new jobs in demand through 2028 will be low-wage and low-skill such as personal care aides, cooks, health aides, and construction labor (Stern and Kravitz 2016: Ch 2 Position 718; BLS 2020). Although they remain in high demand, high-skilled occupations such as software developers or managers will not be a career pathway for millions of workers in the future. Additionally, it is the many middle-skilled jobs that keep disappearing. Often, these occupations are replaced through automation. Many service sector jobs are created, often without paying enough for a middle-class lifestyle. A Pew research study on the middle class also emphasizes that beginning in the 1990s, "jobs increasingly have been concentrated in high-skilled and low-skilled occupations" (Pew-Research-Center 2015: 26). Moreover, as mentioned above, the share of the US aggregate household income held by the upper-income households is now almost 50%, the highest level since 1970, meaning that the share of wages for the middle and low-skilled workforce is declining (Pew-Research-Center 2015: 35; 2020). This trend has intensified in the early twenty-first century: "Overall, Americans are less well-to-do now than at the start of the 21st century. For all income tiers, median incomes in 2014 were lower than in 2000. These reversals are the result of two recessions—the downturn in 2001 and the Great Recession of 2007–09—and economic recoveries that have been too anemic to fully repair the damage (…)" (Pew-Research-Center 2015: 35). More than 10 years later, many households have still not recovered from the Great Recession.

The impact of technological progress thus occurs at a time when wages have scarcely grown over a long period of time, and when more and more income is going to business and property owners, as well as to top decile of earners. Additionally, the share of people who are actively participating in the labor market has declined dramatically over the last generation (Avent 2016: 3). It seems that for many people today, work has become a "less certain and often less remunerative contributor to material security" (Avent 2016: 4). With the introduction of more smart technology this trend is likely to continue, putting additional strain on the workforce. According to Ryan Avent, the digital revolution is bringing about "labor abundance" (Avent 2016: 4) in a grand fashion due to automation, globalization, and productivity growth of the group of the highly skilled few (Avent 2016: 5). Automation will replace more and more workers as machines become better at cognitive work. Globalization leads to even more global trade and supply chains that are impossible to manage without advanced technology, and employment in the emerging economies will be growing as a result, soon advancing to more skilled labor who will be in competition with the workforces in developed countries. Productivity is also growing, but is concentrated within a group of highly skilled few. These skilled few will have the means to perform work that required several workers in the past. Now they can do more with less, through technology. According to Avent, all this will lead to an abundance of labor because the labor markets will (unsuccessfully) struggle to digest all these displaced and would-be workers (Avent 2016: 5):

> There is no iron law that says that new, more profitable firms will create exactly enough of the right kinds of work to absorb those kicked out of shrinking occupations. On the contrary, displaced workers are quite often in an unusually bad position to be re-hired. They have

> spent years, or decades, accumulating know-how of declining value (...). They often live in the wrong places too. (Avent 2016: 47)

Whereas the highly skilled group of workers will become more and more productive through new technologies, displaced workers are unlikely to profit from this development as the "productivity is built on a level of education and training that can't easily be attained by displaced factory workers, or indeed by most workers" (Avent 2016: 47).

Avent admits that in the past, to say that humanity has too many workers was to defy a basic tenet of economics, buying into the "lump to labour fallacy: the view that there is only so much work to go around—a lump" (Avent 2016: 6). He claims

> Economists don't believe in the lump problem—the idea that there are only a finite number of jobs in any economy. But they do acknowledge the severe disruption that comes to the individual workers when displaced by new technology. That person has two options: to learn to live on lower wages, or find a way to acquire more valuable skills. (Avent 2016: 7)

However, the success of this depends on the number of people who are trying to do either of the two at once, which could become exponentially larger with the fast pace of automation in unchartered territory such as simple factory work, warehouses, retail, education, or health care and the growth of the workforce on a worldwide scale (Avent 2016: 8). According to Avent, society will need to adjust to this situation, which means stagnating wages for many workers and rising inequality.

Also commenting on the "lump of labor fallacy," Daniel Susskind claims that in today's world of advanced technological progress, this fallacy idea could turn out to be a fallacy of its own. He agrees that some work is complemented by technology and thus the demand for work generally might grow. Yet, he argues, there is no economic law stating that "human beings will necessarily be better placed to perform the tasks that are involved in meeting that demand" (Susskind 2020: 126). Susskind argues that with recent advances in technology like AI that has developed independently and unmodeled on human intelligence, the "lump of work" might as well grow, yet humans might not be best equipped anymore to fulfill those tasks because machines will be able to perform better.

Through these developments, there might be groups of people in society who face a "fading connection to the world of work" (Avent 2016: 8) because their human capital in the labor market has become outdated through technological progress. This does not mean that people will "not have any human capital. They almost certainly will, having spent large parts of their lives acquiring education or training (...). The problem is that, in a world with less work, this human capital might turn out to be worthless. (...) the human capital may be of the wrong type (...) [or] there may not be enough demand for human capital at all" (Susskind 2020: 135). Additionally, Susskind argues that in a more technologically advanced world, the "flow of income many people receive from their work may dry up to a trickle, but the flow of income going to those who own the latest systems and machines (...) is likely to be quite considerable" (Susskind 2020: 135).

The USA is already a society where a large portion of income is flowing to the owners of capital and technological progress could accelerate this trend even further.

In order not to stifle technological progress, but address the distribution of wealth in the future, Ryan Avent argues, unpleasant tasks could be automated, and working hours could be shared. Yet, more distribution is only possible if the wealth is shared without the need to keep everyone in society working.

> [The] promise of the digital revolution is an end to work. The logical endpoint is an economy in which clever software and dexterous machines and abundant energy mean that human work is unnecessary. We are generations away from this promise, just as societies in the early nineteenth century were generations away from achieving the mass industrial prosperity of the post-war decades. But the battle to create the institutions that will eventually support mass digital prosperity has begun. (Avent 2016: 23)

Avent subscribes to the notion that the total replacement of jobs by machines is the desired endpoint to automation. Avent is thus among the experts who see a massive overhaul of society and work through technology on the horizon. He can also be found on the more pessimistic side of experts who demand drastic measures when it comes to technology and labor.

Although Avent's argumentation is more extreme than others, he is not the only one who sees problematic phases for workers in the future. In their study, authors Benedikt Frey and Michael Osborne find that about 47% of US employment are in the "risk category" of automation (Frey and Osborne 2017: 265). In their model, it is predicted that most workers in the categories of transportation and logistics, as well as office and administrative support, are going to be replaced by automation. Moreover, production workers are going to have a harder time finding a job in the future.

> These findings are consistent with recent technological developments documented in the literature. More surprisingly, we find that a substantial share of employment in service occupations, where most US job growth has occurred over the past decades (. . .), are highly susceptible to computerisation. Additional support for this finding is provided by the recent growth in the market for service robots (. . .) and the gradually diminishment of the comparative advantage of human labour in tasks involving mobility and dexterity (. . .). (Frey and Osborne 2017: 268)

Additionally, machine learning advances are going to put enormous pressure on a wide range of occupations in the near future. Yet, the more current wave of automation will be followed by a slow-down due to an "engineering bottleneck" (Frey and Osborne 2017: 266) and a "technological plateau" (Frey and Osborne 2017: 266). This will further lead to labor substitution when technological improvements are successively implemented, mostly in the medium risk category. Human skills are still at a comparative advantage in areas that require complex perception and manipulation. Yet, the advantage of humans could diminish over time, especially with advancements in machine learning in new arears such as perception or the handling of irregular objects by robots, for instance (Frey and Osborne 2017: 266).

Frey and Osborne also measure that, rather than "reducing the demand for middle-income occupations, which has been the pattern over the past decades, our model predicts that computerisation will mainly substitute for low-skill and low-wage jobs in the near future. By contrast, high-skill and high-wage occupations are the least susceptible to computer capital" (Frey and Osborne 2017: 267). This means that especially low-skill workers will need to find new "tasks that are non-susceptible to computerisation—i.e., tasks requiring creative and social intelligence. For workers to win the race, however, they will have to acquire creative and social skills" (Frey and Osborne 2017: 269). Frey and Osborne's predictions for the near future point to the replacement of lower-skill occupations, rather than many median income jobs, which goes against assumptions of other experts. Yet, they also see further technological progress as the main impact in other areas of work, further replacing more advanced occupations in the long run. Thus, it remains contested among researchers which category of work is going to witness the strongest replacement tendencies in the future. But it is clear that automation will displace many jobs and change the nature of almost all remaining jobs as well.

In their report *Jobs Lost, Jobs Gained* from 2017, McKinsey Global Institute (MGI) offers yet another perspective on automation's impact on jobs. While there is the potential to automate about half of all work activities globally in a few decades, it is not likely that this will actually happen. Technical, economic, and social factors play into these projections. Their projections estimate that "between almost zero and one-third of work activities could be displaced by 2030, with a midpoint of 15 percent. The proportion varies widely across countries, with advanced economies more affected by automation than developing ones, reflecting higher wage rates and thus economic incentives to automate" (Manyika 2017: vi). But even if your job will not be replaced by 2030, MGI still argues that the transitions that lie ahead could exceed historical patterns witnessed during the transition from an agrarian to a manufacturing society. They suggest that by 2030, 75–375 million workers worldwide will need to switch occupations or adapt to new job requirements by increasing their skill levels. "Income polarization could continue in the United States and other advanced economies, where demand for high-wage occupations may grow the most while middle-wage occupations decline—assuming the current wage structures persist" (Manyika 2017: vi). The gains from automation-induced productivity growth can only be enjoyed by people if they will be able to find new work in a short period of time after displacement. Therefore, MGI argues in favor of lifelong learning and training, enhancing worker reemployment, and strengthening transition phases for workers (Manyika 2017: vi).

Tech-savvy workers have the skills that seem to be most desirable in today's economy. They are in high demand, and therefore their compensations have grown in comparison to other workers outside of the tech industry. The most digitized industries also display the fastest wage growth. Yet, these industries do not employ the majority of workers or even a very large group of workers in the USA (Manyika et al. 2015: 12). Additionally, as Chris Benner et al. show in their report on the Silicon Valley region, it is only a very small elite of innovators and managers inside the tech firms that really reap the benefits of growth in the sector (Benner et al. 2018). Inside the knowledge worker group, those that work directly in information technology (IT) make up about 4.6 million people, based on census data from 2014 (Fig. 2.4), which amounts to about 2.9% of the overall workforce. Yet, looking back in time, the group of IT workers has been growing tremendously. In 1970, only about 450,000 people worked in IT.

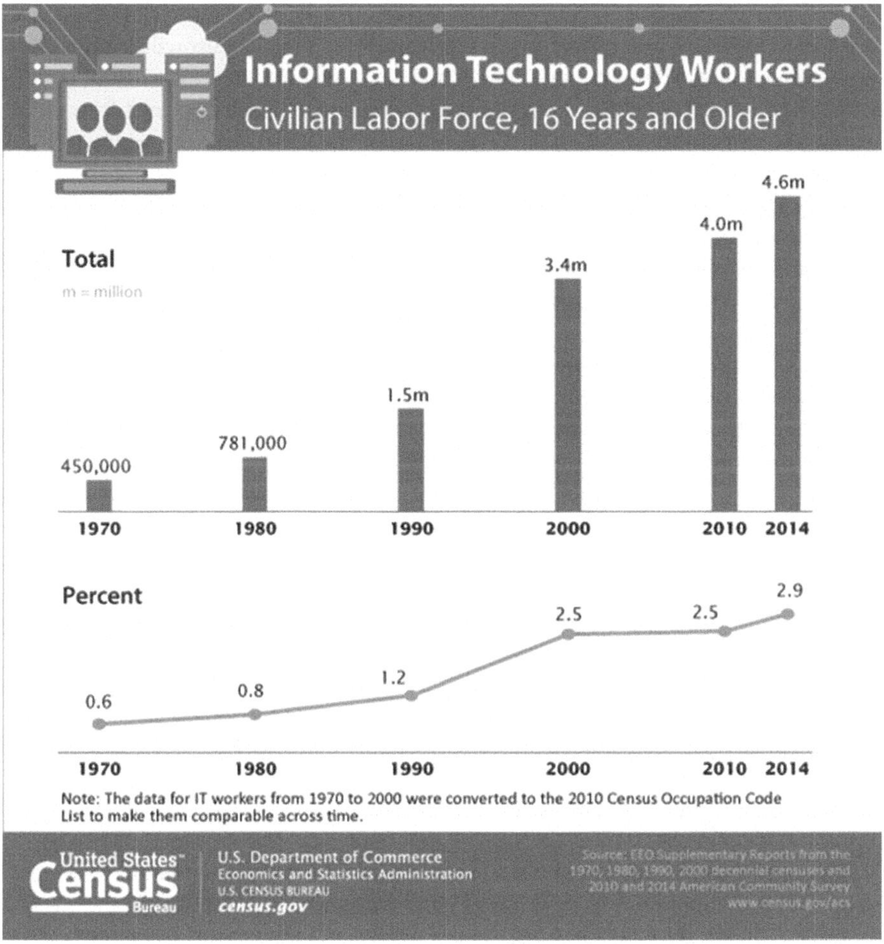

Fig. 2.4 Information technology workers in the USA, 1970–2014 (Census-Bureau 2016)

Many of the knowledge workers are employed in boom areas such as Silicon Valley, but only a very small number of workers in this area benefit significantly from their skills and innovation in the new industry today.

> For nearly all but the highest paid workers (those at the 80th percentile), earnings continued to decline from 2007/9 to 2015/17. For workers at the middle of the wage distribution (median), wages declined 5.6% in the current economic recovery; by 2015/17, the median wage was a full 14% less than in 1995/97 (in inflation adjusted terms). Wages at the bottom (10th percentile) also fell, but less sharply than did the median wage, as rising minimum wages both at the state level and in many cities helped to soften the impact of declining real wages for the lowest paying jobs. (Benner et al. 2018: 4)

In the most recent years of study, 2010–2017, Silicon Valley's regional economy grew faster in GDP than any other metropolitan area in the country. Yet, only the top

10% of households saw income growth higher than in other regions in the USA, whereas the 90 remaining percent saw a lower average income growth than in other metropolitan areas (Benner et al. 2018: 5). Thus, the very large majority of people have not benefitted from the boom of the area. Especially since the Great Recession, "economic growth resumed—yet across most of the labor market, wages did not recover the ground lost during the Great Recession. On the contrary, the economic recovery following the Great Recession, despite marking one of the longest continuous periods of economic growth, not only failed to lift wages, but for nearly 90 percent of jobs, the recovery pushed real wages further down" (Benner et al. 2018: 4). This is true for most of the workers in the USA who are not located in the IT sector.

Thus, for most of the other workers who are not the creative "superstars" of a firm, wages have been stagnating and good jobs are hard to come by. A lot of this can be attributed to institutions like higher education, who have not kept pace with the technological progress. The lack of adequate education is one of the key issues concerning stagnating wages and fewer jobs (Brynjolfsson and McAfee 2012: 7).

The relationship of education and technological progress continues to be discussed when it comes to inequality in the USA with some experts arguing that the rise in inequality is based on the lack of adequate education and skill sets. Thus, the most important issue for the future would not be the replacement of workers through technology, but the lack of adequate education and re-training of workers.

In 1975, Jan Tinbergen already talked about the idea of "returns to skill" and that those returns were dependent on supply factors of skilled workers. He described a "race between education and technology," meaning that "Technological change was argued to be skills-biased—i.e. it increases the demand for more skilled workers and therefore their wage premium in the labor market. To keep inequality in check, the supply of skills needs to increase to meet that demand" (Broecke et al. 2016: 9).

Higher education and certain skills are thus vital when talking about the American labor market. Wages have been stagnant and labor participation rates are low. Many Americans do not see a viable chance in the American economy for themselves. This has been apparent for some time. During his last term in office, President Obama emphasized that the USA had to do more to increase education levels further in order to be competitive in a changing market of the future. This starts with access to education for the youngest children to lifelong learning and training opportunities for older workers. During his last days in office, the Obama White House even published a Paper called *Artificial Intelligence, Automation, and the Economy* (EOP 2016), which shows that the administration considered this topic extremely important for the future. In this paper, the Obama administration advocated, for instance, in favor of policies to smoothen transition periods and to assist job seekers after losing their jobs (EOP 2016). In his last State of the Union Address, President Obama supported the idea of free community college education and talked about the potential of the new economy. Focusing on the future rather than his past time in office, President Obama talked about how all Americans should get a fair shot in the new economy and make technology work for everyone. Education plays a crucial part in this (McDonough 2016). Yet, access to education and educational attainment in the USA are increasingly becoming an issue for families, largely due to the high costs of higher education and, as a consequence, the high debt burden.

David Autor emphasizes too that the so-called college premium or rather the return to cognitive skill plays a role in the rise of unequal earnings and accounts for differences in income among the "other 99%"—so those who have not benefitted from wealth and income growth at the very top. In fact, the difference in income between high-school trained and 4-year-college-trained workers accounted for about $17,400 in yearly income in 1979. In 2012, this gap had risen to almost $35,000 (for male workers). Thus, the college payoff rose steadily over the years. For postsecondary education, the trend is even more pronounced (Autor 2014: 844). A study by PIAAC (Program for the International Assessment of Adult Competencies) found that among OECD countries, the USA "stands out as having the highest measured return to skill, with a premium of 28% per unit increment to cognitive ability. Concretely, comparing two U.S. workers who are one standard deviation above and one standard deviation below the population average of cognitive ability, we would expect their full-time weekly earnings to differ by 50 to 60%" (Autor 2014: 845). For certain areas of expertise, the workers' economic value thus increases when this expertise is scarce (Autor 2014: 845).

Even though costs for education continue to rise, college education generally remains a good investment. Wages of college graduates have continued to grow over the last 30 years and have even risen more starkly for specialized (post-graduate) education so that the "real lifetime earnings premium to college education has likely never been higher" (Autor 2014: 847). Additionally, a Pew research study found that "from 1971 to 2015, only one educational attainment group did not lose income status: college graduates" (Pew-Research-Center 2015: 25). However, whether your college education really pays off is a more complex story. Many families and students who want to make such an investment for their future are burdened with rising debts, which also increases pressure to find good jobs after college, something that is often dependent on the present state of the economy. This fear of indebtedness for the rest of your life seems to put off more and more Americans from gaining secondary or postsecondary education, as they do not see a guaranteed return to that investment. And those Americans who have a 4-year-college degree are finding it hard to access the labor market, or are often "underemployed," which means they do not have jobs that fit their education levels or career prospects (Stern and Kravitz 2016: Ch 2 Position 657–660). Additionally, whether the investment of a college education really pays off largely depends on which college students attend and what major subject students choose. There are many colleges, where graduates never really have any return on the costs of their education (Cassidy 2015). Post-bachelor degree levels of education, or a renowned university, seem to pay off more than just a regular college degree (Cassidy 2015).

With underemployment rising, there are many college graduates who can simply not find an adequate job.

> [T]echnological progress generates an ever-increasing need for highly educated, highly skilled workers. But, beginning in about 2000, for reasons that are still not fully understood, the pace of job creation in high-paying, highly skilled fields slowed significantly. (. . .) Since

> 2000 (. . .) the demand for highly educated workers declined, while job growth in low-paying occupations increased strongly. 'High-skilled workers have moved down the occupational ladder and have begun to perform jobs traditionally performed by lower-skilled workers,' (. . .), thus 'pushing low-skilled workers even further down the occupational ladder.' (Cassidy 2015)

Even though college education remains a good investment overall, it largely depends on the respective university, field of study, and the state of the economy, whether that investment will pay off. Thus, competition for jobs in lower-skilled areas increases with more and more educated people trying to find an occupation in these sectors.

There is also more and more talk about vocational training methods that could be implemented in the USA and more political stakeholders are advocating in favor of it. Germany is often hailed as the prime example where vocational training is a great career path. Yet, the German system looks back on a long tradition and could certainly not be implemented in the same way in the USA. Yet, the USA's community college system could be a place where some of the merits of vocational training could be implemented on a larger scale. As said before, the Obama administration, as well as other liberal political actors, has already pushed for more affordable community college education and there are some states like Tennessee where tuition-free community college education is already available (Chen 2017; Wermund 2019). Online learning initiatives could also improve the situation for some students (Cassidy 2015). Yet, community colleges in many states often remain underfunded to really make a difference for a large number of students.

Unlike many other experts, Ryan Avent sees education as only a limited response to the digital advancement of our time. Looking at the historical development of the Industrial Revolution and beyond, education has indeed played a major role in the spread of wealth. Many occupations were wiped out through automation, while other occupations appeared as a result of technological advancements, many of them low-skilled. But also the demand for higher-skilled personnel rose, such as technicians, engineers, or managing clerks (Avent 2016: 53). Due to this, countries increased their efforts to skill the population. Today, 90% of Americans have some secondary education and about 41% hold a bachelor-level degree. This push for educational attainment has led to economic growth, as well as to the more widespread distribution of the gains of this growth (Avent 2016: 54).

Today, however, Avent claims that "the skill-upgrading approach to more and better employment, which worked so well for most of the industrial era, has run out of steam. Cracks in the façade were apparent by the early 1980s in America, when growth in the share of people obtaining a university degree levelled off; in Europe, which long lagged behind America in educational attainment, this plateau occurred later" (Avent 2016: 55). Avent further argues that there is a limit to how far a population can be upskilled, claiming that many

> of those who don't currently make it through a college programme lack the cognitive ability to do so. Others could be helped through with better preparation and more attention. But the human and financial resources needed to improve the performance of less-prepared students

> mean that it is much harder and more costly to raise college completion rates from 40 per cent to 45 per cent than it was to lift them from 20 per cent to 25 per cent. (Avent 2016: 55)

As there is a limit to the cognitive abilities of the population, some countries might have reached a plateau of education that is no longer increasing. Completing college is still a ticket to higher pay. Yet, it is not the road to rapidly growing pay as in the past. Avent says that the "low-hanging educational fruit has been picked" and "growth in opportunities in moderately skilled positions is struggling to keep up with the effective labour that can be applied in those industries. Therefore, less of the burden of adjustment to technology can be borne by education this time around" (Avent 2016: 57). This means that there will be even more pressure on wages in the future. Avent argues that skilled workers today are facing the same "disruptive forces that battered less-skilled workers over the last generation: automation, globalization and rising productivity" (Avent 2016: 57).

In the past, sectors like education, health care, or government services have absorbed much of the excess workers when productivity grew. These sectors are considered "low-productivity sponges" (Avent 2016: 70) because so far, they were not able to considerably increase their productivity. Yet, Avent highlights that even in these areas, technological advancement moves ahead, making them more productive in the long run. One example is higher education where electronic and digital services are changing the way education has worked for decades (Avent 2016: 73). Schlogl and Sumner argue that there are several "automation prone" and "automation resistant sectors" where labor might still be in demand. Automation resistant sectors today can be found in tech, finance, or services, but also in those manufacturing and agricultural jobs that have survived past waves of automation (Schlogl and Sumner 2018: 14). There will always be jobs that are resistant to automation, but the question remains whether they will generate an income that allows for a decent standard of living.

Generally, the question is whether there is actually going to be mass *employment* in the age of technology as we have seen it during the twentieth century. The Internet could offer the possibility to increase niche markets for consumers where everyone will find exactly what he or she is looking for. In some cases, this seems to be possible, for instance, for YouTube stars or sellers on Etsy. They offer a highly specialized product for a specific group of consumers worldwide (Avent 2016: 74).

> Some analyses suggest that these sorts of niche work could become part of a 'gig economy' that provided supplemental income and work for lots of people. That is, as 'regular' work, in well-defined jobs for large employers, provides workers with less wage growth and fewer hours, they will increasingly turn to a few hours driving an Uber, or a side business selling craft goods, to top up their income. (Avent 2016: 75)

But how big is the gig economy's potential? For some, it might offer enough opportunity to live from it, but in total numbers it has, so far, not contributed significantly to the global labor force in any way. Yet, it points to the fact that part-time work also becomes more common among workers, especially in times of crisis (Avent 2016: 75). In general, the gig economy, which will be detailed in Chap. 3, might disrupt markets more than it has potential for job growth. It could reduce costs of critical goods and services for consumers, yet this can only happen if the wage level of gig workers remains low. Therefore, the gig economy only offers limited potential for adequate pay (Avent 2016: 76).

There are researchers, who are skeptical of the so-called skill premium altogether, at least when it comes to the role it plays in rising inequality in the USA. Other factors including the significant fall of the real worth of the minimum wage and the continuous decline of unionization also contributed to lower wages for non-college educated workers (Mishel and Bernstein 2003: 208). David Autor also admits that there are other reasons than the skill premium that led to a rise in inequality among the "other 99%." This includes the drop in real earnings of non-college-educated workers and high school dropouts that has fallen significantly over the years. Additionally, the rise in inequality was fueled through de-unionization, globalization, and the reduction of the federal marginal tax rates. Autor also mentions the influence of special interest in policy-making and slack regulation and oversight in public policy when accounting for the rise in inequality among workers (Autor 2014: 489f.).

2.2.4.3 New Work Arrangements

Apart from a change in the availability of high-quality jobs and changing skill levels that demand higher educational attainment, there is also another development that is changing the labor market: New work arrangements. The gig economy as a recent addition to a more independent labor market was already mentioned. Yet, the independent workforce in the USA is more complex than that and has been growing for decades.

The example of Silicon Valley illustrates this development. Here, the high-tech firms usually pay a good wage. However, over the last few decades, the share of those steady employees that serve or support the tech companies, but are not involved in the creative processes, has been sharply reduced. All big companies are "outsourcing domestically" to contracting firms to drive down labor costs, and high-tech firms are no exception (Benner et al. 2018: 6).

This trend across many sectors leads to a separation between service workers and those driving the industry "creatively." It also reduces the wages and benefits of these service workers because subcontractors usually take a cut of the revenue for profit (Benner et al. 2018: 7). Contracted workers are often also experiencing more income volatility than steady workers. "Research by the Pew Trusts found that between 2014 and 2015, just over a third of all American households experienced income volatility (defined as a household income swing of more than 25%). Those who experience income volatility in a given year 'report lower financial well-being and less savings than those with stable income'" (Benner et al. 2018: 9). Generally, income volatility is an issue for many American households and their financial security. The growing demand for a flexible labor force and the growth of on-demand services seems to increase volatility. Especially for lower-skilled workers, "more flexibility equals unpredictability and income volatility. Low-wage jobs with steady recurring income are surprisingly rare" (Aspen 2016: 5). Workers experience volatility in earnings because of precarious and changing schedules in working hours, or because of independent contracting, gig work, or self-employment.

In general, there are several new forms of work that shape the American labor force today: "Although industrial production shaped employment patterns during the early to mid-1900s, the current period is characterized by an increase of a multitude of jobs in biotechnology, finance, research, and other advanced occupations, which signifies the rise of a newly emergent knowledge society" (Kwon 2015: 174). Additionally, there are a growing number of self-employed workers or small entrepreneurs that (partly) work from home full-time or part-time:

> What is certainly significant, and on the rise, is the development of self-employment, and of 'supplementers,' either full-time or part-time, as part of the broader trend toward the disaggregation of labor and the formation of virtual business networks (...). This does not imply the end of the office, but the diversification of working sites for a large fraction of the population, and particularly for its most dynamic, professional segment. Increasingly mobile tele-computing equipment will enhance this trend toward the office-on-the-run, in the most literal sense. (Castells 2010: 426)

This on-the-go work has been increasing and diversifying in recent years, even more within the gig or sharing economy.

As indicated before, even in Silicon Valley, it has increasingly become the norm for tech firms to hire more contractors. Sometimes they even have more contractors than stable employees.

> [In] Silicon Valley, we have estimated that there are somewhere between 20–40,000 people in low and medium wage occupations who contract directly with high-tech firms in the valley, and up to 78,000 in the 'potentially contracted' workforce—which includes those whose wages and working conditions are affected by the contracting. This potentially contracted workforce are disproportionately people of color; their average wages are 30% less than those of comparable direct-hire employees of high-tech firms. (Benner et al. 2018: 24)

At Google's Alphabet, for example, contractors outnumbered stable employees for the first time in 2018. According to a 2018 article on this "shadow workforce," "Investors watch employee headcount closely at these tech powerhouses, expecting that they keep posting impressive gains by maintaining skinnier workforces than older corporate titans. Hiring contractors keeps the official headcount low, and frees up millions of dollars to retain superstars in fields like artificial intelligence" (Bergen and Eidelson 2018). These contractors usually do not enjoy the benefits associated with working at a big tech giant. Many of them do not even have health insurance. And there is more and more discontent about this situation. In 2018, Google workers wrote a letter to their CEO demanding equal treatment of contractors (De Vynck 2018).

But there is not only the problem of contracting in general. A continuing problem for contractors is worker misclassification:

> Worker misclassification is not new—it occurs in many industries, most of which are not considered high-tech—but it has emerged as a new, supposedly 'innovative' business model

> for a number of emerging platform economy companies with major venture capital backing. While ride-hailing companies like Lyft or Uber and delivery services like Postmates, Doordash, and Amazon Flex claim to act as 'digital marketplaces' for workers, the level of control they exert on how these workers deliver service and are compensated for that service more closely resembles the traditional employee-employer relationship than a truly independent contractor. (Benner et al. 2018: 25)

For some of the new digital platforms, potential worker misclassification seems to have become part of their business model and conflicts over the status of these workers remains contested.

In general, contracting as a main or secondary source of income has become much easier through the proliferation of mobile Internet and smart devices. Recent data show that "that 8.4% of US workers participate in independent contractor work as their primary job, a 22% increase over the last decade. A much larger fraction, 30% (. . .) participate in independent work as a primary or secondary activity" (Chen et al. 2017: 2). Of this independent work, the fastest growing part are digital platforms "that instantaneously match buyers and sellers" (Chen et al. 2017: 2). These arrangements pose risks and opportunities. Independent workers often value the flexibility the platforms can offer, different from traditional employment situation.

> [There] is evidence that many US workers would prefer to work fewer hours per week than required by the schedule set by their employer, if they could do so at their current hourly wages. Consistent with this, the Council of Economic Advisors reports data from the National Study of Employers that suggests that 36% of firms with over 50 employees would allow 'some employees' to transition from full-time to part-time work and back again while remaining in the same position or level, but that only 6% would allow it for 'most or all' workers. (Chen et al. 2017: 3)

The platform economy becomes especially interesting for the group of workers which has less flexibility and influence in steady work arrangements than higher wage employees. Often they cannot set their own hours, but are dependent on what the employer decides (Chen et al. 2017: 4). This shows that there are viable flexible work arrangement options available in the platform economy, but most of all because available stable jobs often do not offer good options for workers in that regard. For some workers more flexibility also means more income volatility, which many cannot bear given their low-wage level. Thus, problematic issues such as income volatility, lack of benefits, or job security remain. Some of the workers in the platform economy are high-skilled and highly educated individuals, and most of them supplement their income from a stable occupation, due to, for instance, underemployment or low wages. To some extent, they are thus crowding out lower-skilled Americans from their traditional employment in the lower-skilled service sector.

Generally, the success of the new platform working arrangements must be seen as part of a larger trend among Americans to engage in independent work. In the *State of Independence in America Report* from 2018, MBO partners found that there are about 41.1 million Americans working independently (at least 15 hours a week) who were responsible for $1.28 trillion in revenue for the US economy, which accounts for 6.2% of the US GDP (MBOpartners 2019: 2). This number is likely to further increase and MBO partners estimate that by 2021, 46–48% of all Americans will have worked independently at some point in their lives, or will work independently full-time or alongside other employment (MBOpartners 2016: 4). Until 2014, the Census Bureau found that the full-time self-employed[9] Americans had made up a steady 10.9% of the total employment in the USA (Beckhusen 2014: 3).

Among the independent workers, the majority, 37%, describe themselves as "self-employed," 14% describe themselves as independent contractors or offering professional services, 13% are business owners, 6% are consultants, and 6% free-lancers.[10] Among the different generations, millennials now make up the biggest share of independent workers (about 40%, 21–36 years old), followed by the Baby Boomers (about 31%, 52–70 years old), Generation X (27%, 37–51 years old), and the Matures (2%, 71 and older). In general, most people seem satisfied to be independent with about 80% of respondents claiming they are independent by choice (MBOpartners 2019: 5). On the other end of the spectrum, one in 10 said that it was beyond their control to move to independent work. Flexibility and more control over their careers were among the most important reasons to move into independence (MBOpartners 2016: 6). Interestingly, the younger the independent worker, the more educated they are (6 out of 10 millennials have a college degree) and 83% of independents are service providers. 47% of independents report that they earn more than if they were employed[11] (MBOpartners 2016: 7). Overall, some structural changes have led to the growth of the independent workforce over time, which include the emergence of highly skilled independents, companies demanding flexible labor, the expansion of platforms and marketplaces, and demographic changes like the aging Baby Boomers and the growth of working-age millennials (MBOpartners 2019: 5).

In 2019, the latest report by MBO pointed to another trend among independents in the American workforce, the "occasional independent and the side hustle" (MBOpartners 2019: 6). MBO presents persistent weak wage growth as one reason why there are more occasional independents. This group needs the extra income to pay for rising costs of living, education, and health care, or to cover unforeseen expenses. In 2019, the group of occasional independents made up about 14–15 million people in the USA. They are looking for occasional work and the "side gig" on online platforms and marketplaces (MBOpartners 2019: 6f).

McKinsey Global Institute (MGI) also looked at the status of independent work in a 2016 report called *Independent Work: Choice, Necessity, and the Gig Economy.*

[9]The Census Bureau's definition of self-employed is much narrower than other estimates and usually only takes into account the full-time self-employed.

[10]"Self-employed" usually means that you are working on your own for an employer who only has a say in the results you are delivering. Freelancers are usually even more independent, not affiliated with any institution or partner, often working for several clients at the same time (Ewer 2020).

[11]17.9% of full-time independents earned more than $100,000; 28% earned more than $75,000; average gross income generated from independent work was $64,450 while median family income is $53,657.

The sole concentration on full-time jobs does not do justice to the way many workers are making a living today. Independent work has become more common but often does not neatly fit into the official labor statistics. That is why MGI tried to fill in the gaps surrounding the status of independent work in the USA. The report focused on labor services, as well as people who rent and sell goods independently, with a high degree of autonomy, payment by assignment or sale, and a short-term relationship between the worker and client (Manyika et al. 2016: iv). Thus, they also included millions of "self-employed, freelancers, and temporary workers—as well as individuals renting out rooms on Airbnb, driving for Uber, or selling goods on eBay (...)" (Manyika et al. 2016: 1). This MGI research suggests that the independent workforce in the USA (and globally) could be much larger than previously thought. Traditionally, most of the workers who supplement their income are not counted in the official statistics and therefore the official numbers are often smaller (Manyika et al. 2016: 1f). The MGI estimates that between 20 and 30% of the working population in the USA engages in independent work. That accounts for about 54–68 million workers in the USA. Unlike the study by MBO, McKinsey does not find the majority of independents to be millennials. MGI estimates that less than 25% of independents are under the age of 25 (MBO sees millennials between 21 and 36 years of age). In general, the independent workforce is very diverse, but it is not dominated by low-wage workers. Low-wage workers are much more dependent on stable income and cannot easily cope with the volatility of independent work arrangements. Construction, transportation, and personal services but also professionals such as therapists, lawyers, or doctors are among the independent group in the workforce (Manyika et al. 2016: 5). Digital platforms are transforming independent work as they enhance the ability to match, gain information, and be available at most times. Yet, for the very well-known platforms such as Uber, Lyft, TaskRabbit, or Upwork, only about 4% of the working-age population reports using them to make an income. Yet, as these platforms continue to grow, the potential for making an income through them will increase. This can also be seen with e-commerce platforms such as eBay or Etsy, or with renting platforms such as Airbnb (Manyika et al. 2016: 12). Additionally, as indicated before, the number of occasional earners on these platforms seems to be growing.

Another report from 2017 that focuses on California also looks at independent work, and what is often referred to as "gig work" in more detail. Anette Bernhardt et al. define gig work as independent contracting. For this side of the independent workforce, there is much more data available. Full-time gig workers are rare and they share essential interests and issues with independent contractors. Often, they are even the same workers, working on and off platforms. For California, estimates see 8.5% of the labor force working independently as a main job, and 7.2% of the national workforce. There is an additional 6.1% of workers who have both wage income and earnings from self-employment (Bernhardt and Thomason 2017: 1). Bernhardt et al. do not necessarily see a rise in gig work on platforms confirmed in the data that is available so far, although the public debate is often focused on this development. In a first look at the available data, they argue that it might be a stable number of independents as a main job over the years, while the group of supplementers might grow (Bernhardt and Thomason 2017: 1). This is consistent with what MBO partners found.

According to MGI, there are four key groups among independents, including "free agents" who voluntarily choose to work independently (30%); then there are "casual earners" (40%), "reluctants" (14%), and the "financially strapped" (16%). Thus, most of the independent workers, about 70%, are either independent by choice or are earning a supplemental income while retaining a steady job (Manyika et al. 2016: iv). Although the more reluctant independents are not the majority among the group, the "magnitude of the problem is still striking" (Manyika et al. 2016: 7), according to MGI.

> Scaling up the results of our survey suggests that 50 million Americans and Europeans are independent out of necessity, and more than 20 million of them rely on independent work as their primary source of income. For them, independent work is simply better than the alternative of unemployment or an undesirable traditional job. Temporary workers are clearly a part of this story. (Manyika et al. 2016: 7)

Not surprisingly, those who choose independency voluntarily rather than out of necessity report higher levels of satisfaction with the job than others (Manyika et al. 2016: 10).

Apart from the fast "digital transformation" (Manyika et al. 2016: iv) there are other trends that fuel the growth of the independent sector, including "aspirations of traditional workers who wish to become independent, the large unemployed and inactive populations who want to work, and increased demand for independent services from both consumers and organizations" (Manyika et al. 2016: iv). Independent work can have benefits for the economy as a whole, for example, by "cushioning unemployment" (Manyika et al. 2016: iv), improving labor force participation, and increasing demand and productivity. At the same time, consumers benefit greatly from new services. Workers might also enjoy more of an autonomous and flexible way of working (Manyika et al. 2016: iv). Companies can also benefit from hiring independents but should consider the trade-offs of a faster churn and less control over workers. Contractors need to be treated "fairly and ethically" (Manyika et al. 2016: 16) as MGI says, which is not always the reality. Additionally, the fact that wages have been largely stagnant and costs of living have risen seems to have motivated more Americans to seek additional income through "side gigs" or second jobs, of which many are independent and facilitated through online platforms (MBOpartners 2019: 18). There might also be a flow of workers shifting back and forth between independent work and traditional employment in the future. "Instead of viewing independent work or traditional employment as separate and distinct paths, careers will become more gig-based, both within and across organizations" (MBOpartners 2019: 19).

Downsides to this trend are the continued issues around the provision of social benefits for independent workers that are usually associated with steady employment structures. Moreover, income volatility and access to credit or training are an issue for independents. MGI suggest either policy changes or innovations by private intermediaries to make the situation easier for independents (Manyika et al. 2016:

iv). MGI mentions the discussions around the portability of social benefits for workers so that they can transition easier from job to job without losing health care or other social provisions. Additionally, creating a category between employed and independent to give workers more labor market protections is also mentioned (Manyika et al. 2016: 15). Private companies also tailor to independents by offering working spaces, training, or financial solutions to smoothen income volatility (Manyika et al. 2016: 16). All this could be become more important if the group of independents continues to grow in the future. "In addition to drawing people out of traditional jobs, independent work may reengage some portion of the inactive and unemployed population. (...) Flexible opportunities are especially well suited to students, retirees, the disabled, and caregivers who stay at home—groups that already make up roughly 40 percent of casual earners in the MGI survey" (Manyika et al. 2016: 13f). Overall, however, much of the public debate around independent work is polarized and happens against the backdrop of a general concern about the quality of jobs and digital technologies transforming the world of work for everyone (Manyika et al. 2016: 15).

References

Arntz M, Gregory T, Zierahn U (2017) Revisiting the risk of automation. Econ Lett 159:157–160

Aspen (2016) Income volatility: a primer. Aspen Institute, Financial Security Program (FSP)

Autor DH (2014) Skills, education, and the rise of earnings inequality among the 'other 99 percent'. Science 344(6186):843–851

Autor DH (2016) Why are there still so many jobs? The history and future of workplace automation and anxiety. MIT IDE Research Brief. MIT Initiative on the Digital Economy

Avent R (2016) The wealth of humans: work and its absence in the twenty-first century. Allen Lane/ Penguin, New York/London

Bartels LM (2006) Is the water rising? Reflections on inequality and American democracy. PS Polit Sci Polit 39(01):39–42

Beckhusen J (2014) Employment transitions among the self-employed during the great recession. Paper presented at the AAEA annual meeting, Minneapolis, MN

Benner C, Giusta G, Auerhahn L, Brownstein B, Buchanan J (2018) Still Walking the lifelong tightrope: technology, insecurity and the future of work. Everett Program, Working Partnerships, USA

Bergen M, Eidelson J (2018) Inside Google's shadow workforce. Bloomberg. https://www.bloomberg.com/amp/news/articles/2018-07-25/inside-google-s-shadow-workforce?__twitter_impression=true. Accessed 11 Dec 2018

Bernhardt A, Thomason S (2017) What do we know about gig work in California? An analysis of independent contracting (trans: Center UBL). UC Berkeley Center for Labor and Education, Berkeley, CA

BLS (2020) Occupational outlook handbook: most new jobs. U.S. Bureau of Labor Statistics. https://www.bls.gov/ooh/most-new-jobs.htm. Accessed 3 Mar 2020

Broecke S, Quintini G, Vandeweyer M (2016) Wage inequality and cognitive skills: re-opening the debate. NBER working paper series, vol 21965. National Bureau of Economic Research, Cambridge, MA

Brynjolfsson E, McAfee A (2012) Race against the machine: how the digital revolution is accelerating innovation, driving productivity, and irreversibly transforming employment and the economy research brief. MIT Center for Digital Business

Brynjolfsson E, McAfee A (2014) The second machine age: work, progress, and prosperity in a time of brilliant technologies. W.W. Norton, New York

Cassidy J (2015) College calculus: what's the real value of higher education? The New Yorker, 7 Sept 2015

Castells M (2010) The rise of the network society, vol I. The information age: economy, society, and culture, 2 edn. Wiley-Blackwell, Chichester, UK

Census-Bureau (2016) Number of IT workers has increased tenfold since 1970, Census Bureau Reports. United States Census Bureau. https://www.census.gov/newsroom/press-releases/2016/cb16-139.html. Accessed 3 Mar 2020

Chen DW (2017) Free tuition? Tennessee could tutor New York. The New York Times. https://www.nytimes.com/2017/05/14/nyregion/for-cuomos-free-tuition-plan-lessons-from-tennessee.html. Accessed 5 Mar 2019

Chen MK, Chevalier JA, Rossi PE, Oehlsen E (2017) The value of flexible work: evidence from Uber drivers. NBER working paper series, vol 23296. National Bureau of Economic Research, Cambridge, MA

Chetty R, Grusky D, Hell M, Hendren N, Manduca R, Narang J (2016) The fading American dream: trends in absolute income mobility since 1940. NBER working paper series, vol 22910. National Bureau of Economic Research, Cambridge, MA

Cooper D, McCausland WD, Theodossiou I (2013) Income inequality and wellbeing: the plight of the poor and the curse of permanent inequality. J Econ Issues 47(4):939–958. https://doi.org/10.2753/jei0021-3624470407

Davidson P (2013) Income inequality and hollowing out the middle class. J Post Keynesian Econ 36 (2):381–384. https://doi.org/10.2753/pke0160-3477360209

De Vynck G (2018) Googlers write to CEO demanding equal treatment for contractors. Bloomberg. https://www.bloomberg.com/news/articles/2018-12-05/googlers-write-to-ceo-demanding-equal-treatment-for-contractors?te=1&nl=dealbook&emc=edit_dk_20181206. Accessed 11 Dec 2018

DiMaggio P, Hargittai E (2001) From the 'digital divide'to 'digital inequality': studying Internet use as penetration increases, vol 4, issue 1. Center for Arts and Cultural Policy Studies, Woodrow Wilson School, Princeton University, Princeton, NJ, pp 1–25

EOP (2016) Artificial intelligence, automation, and the economy. Executive Office of the President, Washington, DC

Ewer T (2020) The difference between freelancers, solopreneurs, and the self-employed. Bidsketch. https://www.bidsketch.com/blog/everything-else/freelancer-solopreneur-self-employed/. Accessed 18 July 2020

Fitts AS (2017) Tech as we know it would not exist without immigrants. Wired. https://www.wired.com/story/tech-as-we-know-it-would-not-exist-without-immigrants/. Accessed 2 Mar 2020

Fligstein N (2010) Politics, the reorganization of the economy, and income inequality, 1980–2009. Polit Soc 38(2):233–242. https://doi.org/10.1177/0032329210365047

Frenken K, Schor J (2017) Putting the sharing economy into perspective. Environ Innovat Soc Transit 23:3–10

Frey CB, Osborne MA (2017) The future of employment: how susceptible are jobs to computerisation. Technol Forecast Soc Change 114:254–280

Goldin C, Margo RA (1992) The great compression: the wage structure in the United States at mid-century. Q J Econ 107(1):1–34

Goode L (2018) AI-powered apps could make us more creative—or less human. Wired. https://www.wired.com/story/ai-powered-apps-more-creative-or-less-human/. Accessed 2 Mar 2020

GSMA (2017) Number of mobile subscribers worldwide hits 5 billion. GSMA. https://www.gsma.com/newsroom/press-release/number-mobile-subscribers-worldwide-hits-5-billion/. Accessed 15 June 2017

GSMA (2019) The mobile economy 2019. GSMA Association
Henderson AW (2018) Elizabeth Warren proposes breaking up tech giants like Amazon and Facebook. The New York Times. https://www.nytimes.com/2019/03/08/us/politics/elizabeth-warren-amazon.html. Accessed 13 March 2019
Hooten C (2017) Refreshing our understanding of the Internet Economy Internet Association. https://internetassociation.org/publications/refreshing-understanding-internet-economy-ia-report/. Accessed 10 May 2021
Katz L, Krueger AB (2017) Documenting decline in U.S. economic mobility. Science 356 (6336):382–383
Kearney MS, Hershbein B, Boddy D (2015) The future of work in the age of the machine. Hamilton Project Framing Paper. The Hamilton Project, Brookings
Kenney M, Zysman J (2016) The rise of the platform economy. Issues Sci Technol XXXII(3)
Komlos J, Schubert H (2020) Reagonomics—Wegbereiter des Trumpismus. ZBW (Leibniz-Informationszentrum Wirtschaft). Wirtschaftsdienst 2020:64–71
Kwon R (2015) A new kuznetsian dynamic: the knowledge economy and income inequality in the United States, 1917-2008. Sociol Q 57(1):174–204. https://doi.org/10.1111/tsq.12106
Lapowsky I (2019) Visa rejections for tech workers spike under Trump. WIRED. https://www.wired.com/story/h-1b-visa-rejections-spike-undertrump. Accessed 29 April 2019
Loveless M (2013) The deterioration of democratic political culture: consequences of the perception of inequality. Soc Justice Res 26(4):471–491. https://doi.org/10.1007/s11211-013-0198-7
Luhby T (2018) Almost half of US families can't afford basics like rent and food. CNN Business. https://money.cnn.com/2018/05/17/news/economy/us-middle-class-basics-study/index.html. Accessed 26 Nov 2018
Manyika J (2017) Jobs lost, jobs gained: workforce transitions in a time of automation. McKinsey Global Institute, San Francisco, CA
Manyika J, Chui M, Bughin J, Dobbs R, Bisson P, Marrs A (2013) Disruptive technologies: advances that will transform life, business and the global economy. McKinsey Global Institute, San Francisco, CA
Manyika J, Ramaswamy S, Khanna S, Sarrazin H, Pinkus G, Sethupathy G, Yaffe A (2015) Digital America: a tale of the haves and have-mores. McKinsey, San Francisco, CA
Manyika J, Lund S, Bughin J, Robinson K, Mischke J, Mahajan D (2016) Independent work: choice, necessity, and the gig economy. McKinsey Global Institute, San Francisco, CA
Manyika J, Chui M, Miremadi M, Bughin J, George K, Willmott P, Dewhurst M (2017) A future that works: automation, employment, and productivity. McKinsey Global Institute, San Francisco, CA
Mayer D (2016) Why Google was smart to drop its "don't be evil" motto. Fast Company. https://www.fastcompany.com/3056389/why-google-was-smart-to-drop-its-dont-be-evil-motto.
MBOpartners (2016) America's independents: a rising economic force. State of independence in America report, vol 6. MBO Partners
MBOpartners (2019) The state of independence in America: the changing nature of the American workforce. Herndon, VA
McAfee A, Brynjolfsson E (2017) Machine, platform, crowd: harnessing our digital future (Kindle version). Norton, New York
McDonough D (2016) Back to work: what comes after the president's final state of the Union address. The White House. https://obamawhitehouse.archives.gov/blog/2016/01/12/back-work-what-comes-after-presidents-final-state-union-address. Accessed 14 Mar 2019
Mishel L, Bernstein J (2003) Wage inequality and the new economy in the US: does IT-led grwoth generate wage inequality. Can Pub Pol Analyse De Politiques 24 (suppl):203–221
Neckerman KM, Torche F (2007) Inequality: causes and consequences. Annu Rev Sociol 33 (1):335–357. https://doi.org/10.1146/annurev.soc.33.040406.131755
Pew-Research-Center (2015) The middle-class is losing ground: no longer the majority and falling behind financially. Pew Research Center. https://www.pewresearch.org/social-trends/2015/12/09/the-american-middle-class-is-losing-ground/. Accessed 10 May 2021

Pew-Research-Center (2020) Trends in income and wealth inequality. Pew Research Center. https://www.pewsocialtrends.org/2020/01/09/trends-in-income-and-wealth-inequality/. Accessed 16 June 2020

Piketty T, Saez E (2014) Inequality in the long run. Science 344(6186):838–843. https://doi.org/10.1126/science.1251936

Prause J (2016) Digitization vs. digitalization—wordplay or world view? SAP. https://news.sap.com/digitization-vs-digitalization-wordplay-or-world-view/. Accessed 13 Jan 2017

Rose SJ (2018) Manufacturing employment: fact and fiction. Urban Institute, Washington, DC

Rubin A, Segal D (2015) The effects of economic growth on income inequality in the US. J Macroecon 45:258–273. https://doi.org/10.1016/j.jmacro.2015.05.007

Schlogl L, Sumner A (2018) The rise of the robot reserve army: automation and the future of economic development, work, and wages in developing countries. Center for Global Development Working Paper (July 2018)

Schor J (2016) What can we do about economic inequality? Anglican Theol Rev 98(1):23–31

Schwab K, Samans R (2016) The future of jobs: employment, skills and workforce strategy for the fourth industrial revolution. Global Challenge Insight Report. World Economic Forum, Geneva

Singer N (2018) Tech's ethical 'dark side': Harvard, Stanford and others want to address it. The New York Times. https://www.nytimes.com/2018/02/12/business/computer-science-ethics-courses.html. Accessed 26 Nov 2018

Staab P (2016) Falsche Versprechen: Wachstum im digitalen Kapitalismus. Kleine Reihe. Hamburger Edition HIS Verlag, Hamburg

Stern A, Kravitz L (2016) Raising the floor. Public Affairs, New York

Sundararajan A (2016) The sharing economy: the end of employment and the rise of crowd-based capitalism (Kindle edition). MIT Press, Cambridge, MA

Supply-Side Economics (2019) Britannica Academic

Susskind D (2020) A world without work: technology, automation, and how we should respond. Metropolitan Books, New York

Thompson C (2018) How to teach artificial intelligence some common sense. WIRED. https://www.wired.com/story/how-to-teach-artificial-intelligencecommon-sense. Accessed 26 Nov 2018

Valdez A (2019) This big Facebook critic fears tech's business model. WIRED. https://www.wired.com/story/this-big-facebook-critic-fears-techs-businessmodel/. Accessed 13 March 2019

Wermund B (2019) The red state that loves free college. Politico. https://www.politico.com/agenda/story/2019/01/16/tennessee-free-college-000867. Accessed 29 Nov 2019

World Bank (2021) World Bank, GINI Index for the United States [SIPOVGINIUSA]. Retrieved from FRED, Federal Reserve Bank of St. Louis. https://fred.stlouisfed.org/series/SIPOVGINIUSA#0. Accessed 10 May 2021

Chapter 3
A New World of Work: The Sharing Economy Platforms

Technology has always played a major role in the transformation of work and society. Today, discussions about the consequences of ongoing automation also include the rise of the platform economy, which has contributed to a more diverse workforce in the USA. In the following, the so-called sharing economy platforms will be presented as an example of how technology continues to restructure the economy and the workforce in the USA today.

3.1 Sharing, Gig, On-Demand: Crucial Definitions

There are many examples of platforms that could be considered part of the sharing economy. Some of the most well-known platforms are Uber and Lyft that let you hail a ride through their smartphone apps, Airbnb for renting out or booking accommodation around the world, Postmates, UberEats, or Instacart that deliver food and groceries to your doorstep, TaskRabbit that lets you hire people to do repairs or odd jobs around the house, Turo that organizes peer-to-peer car sharing, BlaBlaCar a ride-sharing platform, Upwork or Amazon's Mechanical Turk that offers a platform to connect (micro) tasks with freelancers, and Etsy a platform where hand-made and artisanal products are sold. All of these platforms connect consumers with those offering a product or service, acting mainly as the intermediary, and infrastructure where the exchange can take place safely and conveniently. There are many different platforms offering a wide range of products that include selling, renting, or booking services. That is why defining the so-called sharing economy is not an entirely easy task. Many different experts have attempted to define what the sharing economy is essentially about:

> [Digital platforms] are diverse in function and structure. Google and Facebook are digital platforms that offer search and social media, but they also provide an infrastructure on which other platforms are built. Amazon is a marketplace, as are Etsy and eBay. Amazon Web Services provides infrastructure and tools with which others can build yet more platforms.

N. Rauscher, *The Future of Work in the United States*, Contributions to Economics,
https://doi.org/10.1007/978-3-030-82307-8_3

> Airbnb and Uber use these newly available cloud tools to force deep changes in a variety of incumbent businesses. Together they are provoking reorganization of a wide variety of markets, work arrangements, and ultimately value creation and capture. (Kenney and Zysman 2016)

The Internet Association, a lobbying group of several Internet firms, labels the sharing economy as an "on-demand" or "peer-to-peer" economy, "changing the way we shop, travel, do our laundry, rent cars, and improve our homes" (Internet Association 2015).

The term "sharing" is controversial in general, as it suggests an altruistic behavior or an alternative behavior to capitalism that, in many instances, is not the case in the sharing economy. A different label for the sharing economy might therefore be more suitable, especially because it has sparked a debate about how the new services impact the nature of jobs, and our day-to-day lives (Pew-Research-Center 2016b). JP Morgan defines the sharing platforms as the "Online Platform Economy" (Farrell and Greig 2016: 8). The Department of Commerce calls them "digital matching firms" (Telles 2016). Others argue that perhaps "these new services providers are not that different from traditional 'brick-and-mortar' companies that share profits with shareholders but not necessarily with their employees. The term 'platform capitalism' has been used to characterize the principle of the sharing economy" (van Welsum 2016: 2). For former Labor Secretary Robert Reich, it is even a "share-the-scraps" economy; others call it the peer, mesh, on-demand, platform, or gig economy.

With so many terms used by both mainstream media and academia, some clarification is needed. In the following, the most widely used terms are presented and assessed.

Collaborative Consumption

As a leading expert in the field of collaborative consumption, Rachel Botsman attempts to give an overview of the terms most often used when talking about the new economy. She mentions "collaborative economy" as an "economy built on distributed networks of connected individuals and communities versus centralized institutions, transforming how we can produce, consume, finance, and learn" (Botsman 2013). Airbnb might be an example here, as well as Zopa, a peer-to-peer financing platform. Botsman also talks about the label "collaborative consumption" (CC) as "an economic model based on sharing, swapping, trading, or renting products and services, enabling access over ownership" (Botsman 2013). This new form of consumption "reinvents" (Botsman 2013) how we consume, but not necessarily what we consume. Collaborative consumption is based on "redistribution markets" that make use of underutilized assets, including "non-product assets such as space, skills and money" that are exchanged in new ways, as well as "product service systems that grant access but not ownership" (Botsman 2013).

Juho Hamari et al. define collaborative consumption as "the peer-to-peer-based activity of obtaining, giving, or sharing the access to goods and services, coordinated through community-based online services. CC has been expected to alleviate societal problems such as hyper-consumption, pollution, and poverty by lowering the cost of economic coordination with communities" (Hamari et al. 2016: 1). For Russel Belk, there is only a slight difference in his definition of collaborative consumption. He sees CC as

> people coordinating the acquisition and distribution of a resource for a fee or other compensation. By including other compensation, the definition also encompasses bartering, trading, and swapping, which involve giving and receiving non-monetary compensation. But this definition of collaborative consumption excludes sharing activities like those of Couchsurfing because there is no compensation involved. (Belk 2013: 1597)

Thus, CC is defined as the middle ground between sharing activity and marketplace exchange. This definition puts an emphasis on the alternative nature of the sharing economy, valuing access rather than ownership and the collaborative idea behind sharing in general that can also take place without immediate monetary compensation.

Sharing Economy

Botsman also comments on the "sharing economy," which she labels as an "economic model based on sharing underutilized assets from spaces to skills to stuff for monetary or non-monetary benefits" (Botsman 2013). It includes many peer-to-peer (P2P) activities but also business-to-consumer (B2C) activities (Botsman 2013). Botsman is clearly a supporter of the term "collaborative economy" that she uses in her book *What's Mine Is Yours: How Collaborative Consumption is Changing the Way We Live*. She sees the development toward collaborative consumption as truly disruptive and not just as a startup trend. With the spread of technology, it is now possible to match supply and demand in new ways, especially in areas that are "ripe for disruption" (Botsman 2014), as she puts it. Those areas are usually marked by limited access, redundant intermediaries, broken trust, and complex experiences. New collaborative economy models are then able to address real problems in these systems in a new and often more efficient way that gets consumers on board (Botsman 2014).

Arun Sundararajan, author of the book *The Sharing Economy: The End of Employment and the Rise of Crowed-Based Capitalism*, favors the label "sharing economy" although he includes a wide range of activities and platforms like Couchsurfing, Airbnb, Lyft, Postmates, TaskRabbit, Etsy, and many more that others would not consider "sharing platforms." He consciously includes almost all platforms associated with the platform economy. He has different explanations for this: Although he finds "'crowd-based capitalism' most precisely descriptive of the subject matter (...), [he] continue[s] to use 'sharing economy' (...) because it maximizes the number of people who seem to get what [he is] (...) talking about" (Sundararajan 2016: Pos 669 Ch 1). Additionally, it maximizes the impact of his book because the term sharing economy has defined the discourse around this subject for a long time (Sundararajan 2016: Pos 730 Ch 1). He defines the sharing economy or crowd-based capitalism, as largely market-based, with high-impact capital, based on crowd-based networks rather than centralized institutions, blurring the lines between the personal and professional and fully and casually employed, as well as independent and dependent workers (Sundararajan 2016: Pos 654 Ch 1).

Sundararajan also comments on the other labels associated with the sharing economy. For example, he also lays out Rachel Botsman's book, where she controversially claims that hyper-consumption has been an issue of the twentieth century that society will leave behind. The twenty-first century will now be marked by collaborative consumption, which is driven by reputation systems and the community, not through advertising and ownership (Sundararajan 2016: Pos 684 Ch 1). Sundararajan also mentions another author Lisa Gansky and her idea of *the Mesh*, which applies to "'a type of network that allows any node to link in any direction with any other node in the system.' In other words, it is rhizomatic rather than linear" (Sundararajan 2016: Pos 704). Gansky published her idea in 2011 and claimed that it "will trump the ownership society" (Gansky 2011: 1). Mobile Internet on smartphones offers unique opportunities for businesses to offer better choices and access to consumers. Gansky emphasizes how resources can be used much more sustainably and efficiently through Mesh businesses. She also argues that the products and services are of better quality and more trustworthy through the existence of rating systems. Mesh businesses cannot afford to launch unsatisfactory products anymore. Lastly, she alludes to the Great Recession and claims that there is "more to life than money" (Gansky 2011: 2f), meaning that people are looking for a sense of "connection and community" (Gansky 2011: 2f) that is offered by Mesh businesses rather than by established businesses. Sundararajan might not be as overly positive as Gansky about the potential of the sharing economy, yet he also frequently alludes to the gift economy and other community-based exchanges that are part of the sharing economy. Such activities have existed for centuries and now have the potential to move to a digital form (Sundararajan 2016: Pos 226 Intro.). Although it now seems clear that the sharing economy platforms have not led to a large-scale ascent of the gift economy or have trumped the ownership society in a grand fashion, the platforms have often led to a new way of consumption of established products. One example is the ride-hailing company Uber. Taxi companies have existed before, yet Uber has democratized and innovated ride-hailing services.

Juliet Schor and Koen Frenken also comment on the use of the term "sharing economy." They argue that it is a misleading term because it is not novel behavior. *Sharing* has been part of human behavior for centuries. They say that "the claim that sharing is new ignores the higher levels of sharing that the working class, poor and communities of color have historically practiced and have partially maintained in the face of the growth of markets" (Frenken and Schor 2017: 2). So, what is actually new about the sharing economy is the "stranger sharing" (Frenken and Schor 2017: 2) that is supported by the rise of technology. Stranger sharing means that you are now able to share with whomever you match with on a platform, without the personal connections sharing included before. Russel Belk also comments on this phenomenon, saying that when

> sharing is an inclusive act that is likely to make the recipient a part of a pseudo-family and our aggregate extended self, it can be described as 'sharing in'. On the other hand, when sharing involves dividing something between relative strangers or when it is intended as a

> one-time act such as providing someone with spare change, directions, or the time of day, it is described as 'sharing out.' (Belk 2013: 1596)

The availability of mobile Internet ensures accessibility and the platforms' reputation systems enhance trust. However, Schor and Frenken limit the scope of the sharing economy in their understanding:

> We talk about sharing in many contexts, such as sharing on social media, or sharing secrets, sharing experiences, or sharing friends. As such, there's plausibility to using the term to denote a person renting out an asset such as a room, a car or a durable good. But it is certainly stretching the term beyond reasonable usage to say that paying a person $8 to make a pizza delivery (as on Postmates) or a bit more to clean one's house or put together Ikea furniture (as on TaskRabbit) has anything to do with sharing. (Frenken and Schor 2017: 2)

In their understanding, many platforms want to remain under the "big tent" label of the sharing economy as it is often used as "a socially progressive feel-good rhetoric" (Frenken and Schor 2017: 1). So for them, the term sharing economy can be used for "consumers granting each other temporary access to under-utilized physical assets ('idle capacity'), possibly for money" (Frenken and Schor 2017: 2).

For other services, Frenken and Schor suggest the wider term "on-demand economy." To illustrate the distinction, they give the example of ride-sharing- vs. ride-hailing, as well as Airbnb: Sharing a ride on car-pooling platforms such as BlaBlaCar would be part of the sharing economy. However, hailing a ride via Uber or Lyft would be an "on-demand" service, as you are creating new capacity and are not using underutilized assets. For Airbnb, renting out a room would be part of the sharing economy but buying an apartment to rent it out year-round would not count as "sharing." In this definition, platforms that enable selling of second-hand or hand-made goods would also not count as part of the sharing economy as they are selling, not granting access. In fact, there are many activities that are associated with the sharing economy that rather appear like short-term rental services, which can be called "pseudo-sharing" (Belk 2013: 1597). Yet, for most platforms the distinction between "sharing" and "pseudo-sharing" is irrelevant. They present themselves as part of the sharing economy world, if they fit in or not.

Gig Economy

The term "gig economy" has also become quite common, often appearing in mainstream media, for example in articles such as *Is the Gig Economy Working?* (Heller 2017) or *The Gig Economy Celebrates Working Yourself To Death* (Tolentino 2017) in *The New Yorker*. These articles comment on the changing nature of the American workforce and the "gigging trend." But scholars use this term as well, for example Timothy Aeppel from the *MIT Initiative on the Digital Economy*. Gigging alludes to the activity of working as a freelancer or contractor through platforms, hunting for the next short-term opportunity to work. Often, gig work is highly flexible in time and pay. This definition puts the worker in the center of attention and not so much the platform or the activity itself. However, full-time gig work on digital platforms is still very rare. Estimates (reliable numbers are still broadly missing) see only a fraction of the overall workforce gigging full-time. Yet, occasional gigs are much more common. People might have a stable job and "gig" on the side. (Aeppel 2016: 1) In a recent study by the UC Berkeley Center for Labor Research and Education from 2017 that looks at gig work in California, the researchers included gig workers in the category of independent contractors. They argue that very few workers only work on on-demand platforms. Many use diverse ways to garner clients. Additionally, they often share the same issues when it comes to their working lives. JP Morgan goes in the same direction, defining the online platform economy as a subset of the gig economy, claiming that the gig economy could be defined as the "overall contingent worker landscape, which is also sometimes called the gig economy" (Farrell et al. 2018: 7). In California, home of many sharing economy platforms, the number of independent contractors is around 8.5%, slightly higher than the national average. However, there seems to be a much larger share of workers supplementing their income with gig work or contracting (Bernhardt and Thomason 2017: 1). Additionally, it remains complicated to empirically measure who is really a gig worker because, in many cases, workers do not see their gigs as "real work" but as something else, which makes it even harder to gain information. Gig work is seen more and more as part of a broader trend, the rise of alternative work arrangements such as contracting or independent work. This often turns out to be a challenge to labor standards. (Aeppel 2016: 2).

Platform Economy

The term "platform economy" alludes to all digital platforms including business giants like Amazon, Facebook, Google, and newer participants such as Uber or Etsy. The "digital platforms are multisided digital frameworks that shape the terms on which participants interact with one another" (Kenney and Zysman 2016). They are based on

> the application of an array of computable algorithms to myriad activities, from consumption and leisure to services and manufacturing. The movement of these algorithms to the cloud, where they can be easily accessed, created the infrastructure on which, and out of which, entire platform-based markets and ecosystems operate. (Kenney and Zysman 2016)

The platform economy is thus a large concept that includes marketplaces, social media, or search engines. Yet, the distinction between the terms sharing and platform economy remains difficult. Sharing economy companies are also platforms and the label is in constant transformation. The "boosters [of the platform economy] have called it the creative economy or the sharing economy, whereas those less convinced of its beneficence have dubbed it the gig economy, the precariat, or the 1099 economy, focusing on its impact on workers and how they are compensated. And there are wide variations within these labels" (Kenney and Zysman 2016). The term "(digital) platform economy" encompasses a growing number of digital activities.

Defining the "sharing economy" remains a difficult task. Many use the different terms interchangeably, not thinking about the distinctions the terms entail. Sharing economy still seems to be the most widely used term, followed by gig economy. The usage of terms in public and political discourse will further be investigated in the corpus analysis following in Chaps. 4–6, looking at the terms *sharing economy, gig economy,* and *platform economy* specifically.

For the purpose of this book, however, the term "sharing economy platforms" is going to be used. As Arun Sundararajan has argued the term "sharing economy" might not be the best suited term, but it remains the most widely used one. The term is very proliferated in the political and public debate on the issue. "Platform economy" might be the more suitable term, yet "platform economy" is just not as widely used as "sharing economy." For the purpose of this work, the term "sharing economy platforms" seems to be most suitable. It combines the larger phenomenon of the platform economy, which has a profound effect on the American economy as a whole, with the term "sharing economy." The term "sharing economy" cannot be easily abandoned because it so widely used and recognized. Additionally, it is helpful in grasping the self-understanding of many of the platform businesses. Many of the companies try to frame their activities in extremely positive and "feel-good" (Frenken and Schor 2017: 1) ways. They are very concerned about appearing as innovative, consumer-friendly, and eco-friendly in their offerings, as well as an empowering "tool" for their workers who can (and must) work independently and flexibly.

The term "sharing economy platforms" is not limited to communal sharing activities. Especially when sharing economy platforms first began to become more widely known, the collaborative and communal aspect and the aspects of "idling capacity" and sustainability were strong components of the self-understanding and success of the platforms. They were also seen in line with traditional ways of sharing and the gift economy that have always existed in human society. Technology added the layer of "stranger sharing." Yet, over time the views on sharing economy platforms became more nuanced, as was indicated by the use of different terms such as on-demand, gig, or platform economy.

What is of interest in this book is how people are using platforms as a means to work and make an income and how platforms are an example for the push toward alternative and independent work arrangements. This includes people working as a freelancer or being active on several platforms at the same time, driving for Uber and Lyft, renting out rooms on Airbnb, renting out equipment (ShareGrid), their car on Turo, or a parking space on JustPark, delivering things via Instacart or Postmates, coworking in shared spaces, carrying out tasks over crowd-working platforms such as Mechanical Turk, setting up their own shops on Etsy, or looking for gigs on TaskRabbit. Gig workers on platforms are a very small group within all independent contractors or self-employed workers in the USA today (Bernhardt and Thomason 2017: 2). Yet, as one group of the independent workforce they shed light on the opportunities and issues surrounding the rise of alternative work arrangements in the USA.

Although the implications are not yet clear, it is likely that the sharing economy platforms in a broad sense could have an enormous impact on the future of work for many Americans as the workforce becomes more diverse and independent. Technology, and especially platforms, could play a major role in this development.

3.2 The Sharing Economy Platforms

In many instances, the sharing economy platforms are widely used, but not widely recognized. In 2016, 72% of Americans had used at least one of the 11 different on-demand services that a Pew research survey tested. Yet, at the same time, 73% of Americans were not familiar with the term "sharing economy." Terms like "crowdfunding" or "gig economy" are also not well known. Exposure to sharing economy platforms varies extremely between demographic groups: People under the age of 45, urban residents, college graduates, and households with a high annual income are more likely to have used (some) on-demand services. Older people, people with lower education levels and lower incomes, and people living in rural areas are less likely to have used the services extensively (Pew-Research-Center 2016b).

When it comes to opportunities of earning money through platforms, the picture remains mixed as well. Another Pew research survey from late 2016 found that about 8% of Americans have earned money using a digital platform to take a job or task, and that 18% of Americans have earned money selling something online. Only about 1% of Americans have rented out something over a platform. Adding all these up, about 24% of Americans have earned money through the platform economy in the year 2016 (Pew-Research-Center 2016a: 2). The overall independent workforce in the USA with both independents and online platform workers (which is a small group), as well as anyone who is self-employed, is freelancing, or temporarily working, is estimated to make up about 20–30% of the working-age population in the USA (Manyika et al. 2016: 1).

Of those who have earned money via the platforms, there are "casual users" (Pew-Research-Center 2016a: 15) who like the extra money or enjoy doing it but are not dependent on it. About 42% say that they do it for fun or to have something to do in their spare time (Pew-Research-Center 2016a: 15). On the other end, there are "dedicated users" (Pew-Research-Center 2016a: 3) who rely to a greater extent on the income earned through the platforms. About 37% of the survey respondents say that working on a gig platform helps fill gaps or fluctuations in income (Pew-Research-Center 2016a: 15). Among those who sell things online, 80% say that the extra income is not essential but nice to have (Pew-Research-Center 2016a: 16).

Dedicated users are more likely to come from low-income households, to be non-white, and to not have attended college. These users are motivated by the flexibility of the self-set schedule, and also by the fact that not many other jobs are available to them (Pew-Research-Center 2016a: 5). In general, however, users of online platforms tend to be better-educated and younger. The public continues to have mixed feelings about working in the gig economy. On the one hand, people have a positive view about the flexibility it offers (68%). On the other hand, people feel that workers are burdened financially (21%) and that companies take advantage of workers (23%). Only 16% think that these kinds of jobs offer possibilities for career building (Pew-Research-Center 2016a: 6). Intensive users of on-demand services are generally more positive about working in the gig economy (Pew-Research-Center 2016a: 24).

With these numbers on sharing economy use and a first look at the definitions around sharing economy platforms, it is necessary to take a closer look at what the sharing economy platforms really are, who uses them, and what overall impact they might have on the future of work in the USA.

According to the Internet economy's own lobbying group the *Internet Association*, the sharing economy platforms generated $15 billion in global revenues in 2013 with 3.2 million people earning an income through peer-to-peer networks, most of them part-time. They estimate that by 2020 about 7.6 million people will provide services and earn money through sharing economy platforms. Service providers usually work as so-called micro-entrepreneurs, independently from an employer, which provides them with flexibility and new opportunities. For consumers the sharing economy platforms often deliver alternatives to existing services, e.g., in the area of ridesharing (Internet Association 2015: 1f). As a lobbying group, the Internet Association is naturally rather positive about the potential of sharing economy platforms. But the question remains, what is so novel about the sharing economy platforms?

As said before, sharing is a basic human behavior. Structurally speaking, platforms such as eBay or Craigslist existed before the advent of what we now call the sharing economy platforms. The digital platforms of today "are complicated mixtures of software, hardware, operations, and networks. The key aspect is that they provide a set of shared techniques, technologies, and interfaces to a broad set of users who can build what they want on a stable substrate. Android and IOS are platforms. (...) Indeed, platforms can grow on platforms" (Kenney and Zysman 2016). So, the Internet, especially Web 2.0, and a change in consumer behavior that puts trust in online payment services favor access to ownership, and collaborative consumption practices were important factors in the development of the sharing economy platforms (Belk 2013: 1595). Collaborative consumption through online platforms such as websites or mobile apps relies on social dynamics for the actual sharing and collaboration. The platforms themselves usually do not control the content on the platform, only acting as a coordinator or intermediary, and the development of platforms depend on social dynamics such as enjoyment or self-marketing of a community (Hamari et al. 2016: 4). Many customers today are using the web to research their purchases first with users of the platforms turning to social media, for instance, in order to retrieve information about products, which leads to commercial sources losing more and more influence in the purchasing process (Hamari et al. 2016: 5).

Today, one can say that the early platforms such as eBay paved the way for the newcomers. In this way,

> sharing platforms facilitate sharing among people who do not know each other and who do not have friends or connections in common. (...) The platforms reduce risk by posting information on users via feedback and ratings. This points to another novel dimension—the use of digital technology to reduce transaction costs, create opportunities in real time, and crowdsource information. The uniqueness of these new sharing economy platforms is that it

mobilizes technology, markets, and the 'wisdom of crowds' to bring strangers together. (Schor 2014: 8)

To put it differently, the introduction of apps and online platforms has created a convenient and safe place for producers and costumers to meet, connect, and transact in one "seamless process" available anywhere and anytime on mobile devices, which have also allowed for more and more customization and specialization opportunities for the users (van Welsum 2016: 3). "Digital enablers" such as smartphones, wireless broadband, and trust systems made it easier for the new platforms to succeed (Sundararajan 2016: Pos 1173 Ch 2).

The peer-to-peer (P2P) aspect of the platforms, as well as the seamless structure on mobile devices that takes ratings and safety into account, is part of the "newness" of the sharing economy platforms. Although platforms such as Craigslist have facilitated P2P exchange before, it was more risky to do so because Craigslist does not provide any background checks or insurance in case of noncompliance. The new platforms have introduced well-working mobile apps that can be used anytime and anywhere, and are built on a rating and trust system (Sundararajan 2016: Pos 1236 Ch 2). Juliet Schor calls this the "stranger sharing" aspect of the sharing economy platforms.

For Sundararajan, there are four aspects that were critical to the emergence of the sharing economy platforms: "(1) the consumerization of the digital; (2) the digitization of the physical; (3) the emergence of decentralized peer-to-peer, and (4) the digitization of trust" (Sundararajan 2016: Pos 1294 Ch 2). The proliferation of the Internet has made consumption easy and flawless through digital applications. The growth of e-commerce is one example for that. In another step, the physical world has also become digitized. For many services or products, there is now an easy digital alternative to use. Just think of Google Maps. Additionally, there is more access to decentralized peers through the Internet, with the help of platforms. Their transactions are based on the trust systems built into the platform structures. There are also new business-to-consumer (B2C) or business-to-business (B2B) applications that have grown in efficiency due to digital platforms (Eichhorst and Spermann 2015: 4). Another key element or idea of the sharing economy platforms is that people can share their "underutilized assets" or skillsets (Olson and Kemp 2015: 1). Rachel Botsman calls this "idling capacity" in her book *What's Mine is Yours*. It stands for the idea that in this common space, you can put to use skill sets that others might need and things you only occasionally use yourself. This behavior was also associated with more sustainable consumption and behavior, especially in the beginning of the sharing economy platforms. However, this notion has come under question in recent years when it became clear that the sharing economy platforms are not necessarily about collaborative consumption or making available underutilized assets, but are a commercial alternative in the market rather than a truly sustainable alternative of any kind. Yet, some more collaborative and sustainable platforms such as Couchsurfing or second-hand platforms still remain part of the platform economy.

In contrast to the initial "alternative" outlook of the sharing economy platforms in early years, the success of platforms is in fact largely built on the backing of venture capital (Sundararajan 2016: Pos 628f. Ch 1). Yet, some experts like Arun Sundararajan also believe that the sharing economy platforms are an "in-between" of commercial and community aspects. In fact, he thinks that "some of the shifts we will see in capitalist exchange over the coming years will reflect a reintegration of gift economies into a system that has become inefficiently impersonal and commercial" (Sundararajan 2016: Pos 847 Ch 1). For example, he sees the rating aspect of the sharing economy platforms also as a *gift* of some sort because the users do the rating out of their own accord without necessarily getting something in return, just because they know that a good rating will also benefit the host/seller/provider in the years to come (Sundararajan 2016: Pos 952 Ch 1), and that it will be helpful for other customers. Additionally, there are several crowdfunding platforms that allow people to fund a wide variety of projects without a return, just because they think that the world could need a certain object or service (Sundararajan 2016: Pos 962f Ch 1). Despite the examples mentioned here, it remains questionable if sharing economy platforms such as Uber or Airbnb can be seen as anything other than commercial entities. They might have been born out of a desire for alternative consumption, but early on they have attracted huge venture capital to scale up their businesses. In this sense, many platforms have quickly moved on from any alternative notion to emphasizing growth at all costs.

Among the most well-known examples of the sharing economy platforms are ride-hailing apps like Uber or Lyft, home-sharing platforms like Airbnb or HomeAway, crowdfunding sites like KickStarter or GoFundMe, or other service platforms like TaskRabbit, Fiverr, Instacart, Favor, and Postmates. Then there are crowd-working sites like Amazon's Mechanical Turk, Clickworker, Upwork, CloudCrowd, WorkHub, etc. Additionally, there are online marketplaces like Amazon Marketplace or Etsy that can be used to sell products, second-hand, artisanal, and hand-crafted goods from producers directly to the customers. Approximately 22% of Americans have bought hand-crafted or artisanal products online, especially younger people (Pew-Research-Center 2016b). In general, there is a lot of turnover of these platforms. Some only have a very limited life span and only exist in certain regions, while others never really take off at all. Then there are the big players that reach a global impact, such as Uber, Airbnb, or Upwork. There is a wide variety of sharing economy platforms, some closer to the "gift economy" idea, some closer to the market economy ideal. An example for the former would be Couchsurfing, which is practically a gift economy platform because there is no exchange of money, only a rating activity. On the other end of the spectrum, there is Airbnb, a commercial rental site. But even this platform shows aspects of "gift economy" exchanges, such as staying in someone's private home, getting to know the host, or even just the rating of the room afterward (Sundararajan 2016: Pos 1031 Ch 1).

In general, the wide variety of sharing economy platforms makes it difficult to assess them systematically. Yet, taking a study by JP Morgan into account, one could group the sharing economy platforms into two categories, labor and capital platforms. On labor platforms people perform a given task; on capital platforms people rent or sell goods (Farrell and Greig 2016: 1). Both are used by people to "make a career" or rather to make an income in some way. A more detailed view of the different platform types is offered by Michael Olson and Samuel Kemp. Based on the skillset-sharing and asset sharing opportunities they divide the sharing economy into different types. The first are "sharing platforms" comprised of companies that connect business needs with individuals flexibly. Only few people work on these platforms as their main employment. Secondly, there are "specialist outsourcing" platforms where projects or consultations can be uploaded and specialists offer their services. Creative projects or technical problems are often posted there (e.g., HourlyNerd,[1] oDesk, Freelancer, eYeka, UpCounsel). Thirdly, there are "crowdsourcing" platforms where tasks are uploaded with instructions and worked on by a worker or panels (e.g., CrowdSource Solutions, CloudCrowd, CrowdFlower). Moreover, there are space sharing platforms where excess office space can be rented out (e.g., LiquidSpace, PivotDesk, ShareDesk, StoreFront, Breather). Lastly, there are also business-to-business employee sharing or equipment/asset sharing platforms, which are still largely unexplored business models (Olson and Kemp 2015: 36f). Moreover, there are service platforms that offer meal sharing, task sharing, and financial services. Among those there are P2P (peer-to-peer)-lending sites, crowdsource investment platforms, and even shared insurance platforms (Olson and Kemp 2015: 40ff). Parallel to the platforms themselves, there is also growing activity of advocacy groups around sharing. There are "sharing economy advocacy organisations (e.g., Collaborative Consumption and Ouishare); innovation intermediaries and funders promoting the development of the sharing economy (e.g., Nesta and the Nominet Trust); and national associations of sharing economy organisations seeking to develop best practice (e.g., ShareCo in the UK)" (Martin et al. 2015).

The sharing economy platforms become economically interesting for users and renters when the assets or services offered on the platform are less expensive than other commercial offerings, or if there is no commercial substitute for what is offered. Often both of these apply (Olson and Kemp 2015: 5). What makes the sharing economy platforms so easy to use and successful are different factors: The Internet is the largest component of its success. Additionally, the readiness to use P2P networks and online communities has grown and the willingness to engage with strangers over the net has become normal. The holistic rating systems, the easy-to-use payment systems, and mobile Internet access have also helped to make the sharing economy platforms successful. The Great Recession with many people losing their jobs might have also helped to spread the sharing economy idea more widely as people looked for alternative employment methods and inexpensive alternatives to other commercial products. Sharing platforms were readily at hand and easy to access in that situation (Olson and Kemp 2015: 8f).

---

[1]Now Catalant.

The rating systems are a decisive part of the sharing economy platforms. Although eBay or Amazon sellers also have ratings, the sharing economy platforms have integrated different forms of rating systems:

> [The] design choice is now the norm on many platforms—indeed, it represents a broader trend of platforms' providing more information to market participants—not only about products and services, but about the people buying and selling them. This also demonstrates the large degree of flexibility that online marketplaces have in their market-design choices (much more than is typically found in traditional markets). (Luca 2016: 4)

Many platforms have decided that sellers and users are both participating in the rating systems and that more information about both of them is available (on some platforms, sellers/hosts/taskers and users are the same). These new rating systems make the decisions on platforms easier and often safer for users, yet they can be problematic as well:

> The design choice of allowing hosts to reject guests on the basis of profile elements such as name, picture, and number of Facebook friends is a double-edged sword. On the one hand, it has the potential to make market participants feel more comfortable with each other, in part by reducing social distance. However, this design choice also facilitates discrimination—for example, African-American guests (and hosts) are discriminated against on Airbnb. This is part of a broader trend of discrimination that has been documented in online marketplaces including eBay, Craigslist, and Prosper. In labor market contexts, there is extensive evidence of discrimination against minority job applicants. Online labor markets such as Upwork are designed in a way that makes it easy for discrimination to manifest in online contexts as well. (Luca 2016: 5)

Trust-infusing mechanisms such as rating systems remain a critical part of the sharing economy platforms, despite their shortcomings. Trust needs to be built up in the sharing economy, as face-to-face interaction is lacking. Trust is introduced through the technology behind the sharing platforms, and it is unlikely that the platforms would be so successful without the infusion of trust into the transactions: "Trust remains important but is built through the technology. In the vocabulary of Airbnb, 'trust is what makes it work'" (Richardson 2015: 125). Through the development of technology and different systems of safety and verification on the platforms, users feel at ease using them.

3.2.1 Users and Providers of the Sharing Economy Platforms

Users of sharing economy services tend to be young, urban, and well-educated, with higher household incomes. In a Pew survey, men and women were equally likely to use most sharing and on-demand platforms.

> As is true of social media platforms, these shared, collaborative and on-demand services have a significant amount of user overlap. And in much the same way that the vast majority of Twitter and Instagram users also use Facebook, certain shared and on-demand services are widely popular among users of various other services. In particular, a substantial majority of shared and on-demand service users indicate that they have purchased used or second-hand goods online. (Pew-Research-Center 2016b)

Crowd-working sites remain a niche with only about 4% of Americans reporting to have hired someone online for a task, just like shared office spaces, where also only 4% of Americans have worked so far. Yet, Americans under the age of 50 are far more likely to have done so (Pew-Research-Center 2016b).

All in all, several studies suggest that a big driver for consumers to use sharing economy sites are monetary benefits or cost-saving. Additionally, there are convenience and social aspects (interacting with new people) that users value on the sharing economy platforms (Tussyadiah 2016: 73f; Hamari et al. 2016: 6). Environmental considerations, at least for renting accommodation on sharing economy platforms, do not seem to play a large role (Tussyadiah 2016: 78). Yet, the environment could possibly be a bigger factor in other areas, such as car sharing or second-hand goods. In general, however, there is a tendency that "although consumers may be ideologically and ethically minded, their aspirations may not translate into sustainable behavior" (Hamari et al. 2016: 7). Although users might claim that ecological considerations are important to them, sustainable behavior can be "costly both in terms of coordination and direct cost (. . .) [Moreover,] people lack the means of deriving benefits from signaling such behavior (and thus not be able to gain recognition from the behavior). (. . .) There is not enough information for the consumers about sustainable consumption" (Hamari et al. 2016: 7). This is called the "attitude-behavior gap" (Hamari et al. 2016: 7). Thus, the initial claims that the sharing economy and its users are motivated by the will to lead a more environmentally sustainable life were likely overblown.

On the contrary, enjoyment both as users and providers rather than sustainability is a major factor when participating on sharing economy platforms. Firstly, some people derive joy "from the activity itself and value derived from acting appropriately—that is, conforming to norms" (Hamari et al. 2016: 5). Secondly, people enjoy participating in online projects such as open source activities (e.g., Wikipedia) because they feel competent and are interested in the activity. Additionally, participants gain a reputation online, also through customer and user reviews, and enjoy this part about the activity (Hamari et al. 2016: 6). Eventually, "results suggest that enjoyment plays an essential role in attitude formation and use intentions. Some people might take part in CC [Collaborative Consumption] simply because it is fun and provides a meaningful way to interact with other members of the community" (Hamari et al. 2016: 9).

The enjoyment aspect is further emphasized through the structure of the platforms themselves. Often, the platforms put great emphasis on "gamification" of their structures, meaning that the platforms build structures that resemble online games where accomplishments are rewarded and where providers are encouraged to keep going (Mason 2018). Moreover, many of the people working on sharing economy platforms such as Etsy or Turo (formerly known as RelayRides) have a "day job" and start selling or offering something on a platform because they enjoy it. Without the structure of platforms like Etsy, almost none of the providers would be able to sell or offer anything to a worldwide audience. The infrastructure of the platform is key in this economic activity. Especially Etsy offers a possibility for people who enjoy arts and crafts to offer their products to a worldwide audience instantly. Many of these people thus run a "microbusiness" in addition to their day job. Yet, only because these businesses are small, it does not mean that microbusinesses have no impact on the economy. Studies from the UK and the USA show that these areas are among the fastest-growing in recent years (Sundararajan 2016: Pos 2388f Ch 5).

Of course, there are "big players" operating inside of the sharing economy, for example in ride-hailing, car sharing, or on rental sites like Airbnb. Yet, there are many private individuals who are sharing their personal assets on the platforms as well. What is their motivation to do so? Accessing a sample group on Mechanical Turk, as well as participants on sharing platforms, a survey among "sharers" found that the strongest motivations to "share" seem to be "social-hedonic" motives, meaning the excitement to meet new people. Additionally, "moral" motives (sharing is the right thing to do and points to generosity) were a motivating factor. Least significant are monetary aspects (saving money by sharing fixed costs or maximizing on investment). Sociability is the strongest driver for sharing goods on online platforms, which might not be surprising, as it involves meeting or trusting strangers in some way. Monetary considerations might be considered as necessary, also to infuse trust into the sharing activity. However, monetary compensation *alone* is not sufficient to motivate sharing. Even for groups who prefer commercial platforms rather than noncommercial sharing platforms, monetary aspects were only one of several motivations. Corroborating this, research shows that altruistic motivation and monetary motives can coexist (Bucher et al. 2016: 322f).

This coexistence of monetary and altruistic motivations in sharing via Internet platforms is also in line with how the platforms conduct themselves. They are keen to paint a positive, valuable, and useful picture of themselves, offering a possibility for committed individuals to do good, and earn some money with it at the same time. They often evoke the picture of empowerment for small businesses to succeed in a global market. As Michael Olson and Samuel Kemp put it: "The community aspects add a layer to the sharing economy that is both difficult to quantify and easily romanticized, which creates an attractive marketplace for both users and sharers, it is a communal marketplace" (Olson and Kemp 2015: 10). This notion strongly alludes to the "trusting and sharing mentality of the Internet" (Olson and Kemp 2015: 10) that has its origins in the Internet's beginnings and in counterculture. Initially, the Internet was seen in idealistic terms, promising freedom and opportunity for everyone. Even though the initial hopes of what the Internet would accomplish have faded, the sharing economy platforms can still be seen as an extension to this early notion. Many of the sharing economy platforms emphasize their positive and empowering outlook and claim that their economic activity actually changes the world for the better. In line with this, many of the largest sharing economy platforms were able to build strong brands. Airbnb is a prime example for this. Initially, Airbnb was a platform matching a room or couch with travelers who did not have the funds to afford a hotel but wanted to see the world and meet locals. In fact, the name stems from an anecdote of one of the founders saying he started the company by offering an "airbed" and breakfast for travelers. Nowadays, Airbnb has moved on from these beginnings to become a commercial actor with many professionals being active on the site. Often, whole apartments or houses in desirable holiday destinations can be rented, igniting criticism in many cities as locals are crowded out of these areas. Yet, private, nonprofessional hosts are also still active on Airbnb and many use the platform to make some extra money living in expensive urban areas. Thus, Airbnb is an example of a sharing economy platform that retains some of its early sharing aspects, but that has moved on to become commercially successful as well. Airbnb built its brand around the customer experience; second only came the technological platform, which was also well designed (Olson and Kemp 2015: 20).

Many platforms like Airbnb manage to build their brand around an "outsider" idea to the traditional economy, borrowing from the early ideas of the Internet as a communal place:

> The sharing economy busts a lot of the assumptions of our finance-obsessed, over-leveraged culture. It seems the perfect locally rooted, small-is-beautiful antidote to an economic crisis precipitated by reckless financial giants too big to fail. But it's not just tangible things like beds, bikes, and breastmilk that are being shared. Equally important is the community *ethos* of sharing. The message of collective empowerment through human contact is its own viral product, touted by Harvard Business School professors and time-banking activists alike. Is the industry's egalitarian impulse real or a kind of window dressing? (Lee in Nadeem et al. 2016: 17)

For Juliet Schor, most of these platforms are indeed merely engaging in window dressing and "feel-good" rhetoric of sociability and sustainability nowadays. Many platforms are now practically managing a labor force but accumulate profits mostly for some providers and owners of the platforms (Schor in Nadeem et al. 2016: 14). Arun Sundararajan also emphasizes the "hierarchical" experience of crowd-based marketplaces that have invested heavily in branding (Sundararajan 2016: Pos 2196 Ch 4).

Yet, there is no denying that sharing economy platforms have become so successful because of changing attitudes toward consumption. People value the perceived community aspect of the platforms that indicates an "alternative" to mass consumption in some way. They are also more prone to value the access rather than ownership idea where it fits their lifestyle and where it makes them feel good about their behavior. Buying second-hand or from an artisanal designer also fits this new attitude toward (local) consumption that highlights niche markets and the individualized product or service. Additionally, consumers value the romanticized notion of an alternative to the traditional capitalist offerings. The platform founders themselves often truly believe(d) that their platform would really make a difference for consumption as a whole, for consumers, the environment, and the empowerment of the individual. Many sharing economy platforms continue to present their activity in this way.

At the same time, many platforms have in fact left behind their idealistic starting phase and moved on to become major global players. As mentioned before, sharing economy platforms are a magnet for venture capital and many platforms we know today would not exist without it. After initial investment, when the service infrastructure, platform, and app are created, the transaction costs for services over the platforms are close to zero. These near-zero marginal costs are one aspect of the success of digital products. This is why the sharing economy platforms are so attractive to investors. They expect high returns on their investment due to fast exponential growth. Network effects enhance this growth even further. The business model can usually be rolled out internationally as well (Eichhorst and Spermann 2015: 5). Initial investment for sharing giants like Uber or Airbnb is high. Airbnb attracted $2.3 billion, Uber even $6 billion in early investment, and many platforms go public later on. Yet, their success on Wall Street remains questionable so far. On the other end of the spectrum, many new startups that attract investors never really make it off the ground, burning through the investment money at great pace. This shows how much investors are expecting from the sharing economy platforms, but that Silicon Valley also remains a risky investment target with many platforms never really becoming profitable (Eichhorst and Spermann 2015: 6).

As of now, the sharing economy platforms remain a relatively small part of the overall US economy, even a "sharing economy niche" (Martin 2016: 151). In this niche, the sharing economy is framed in different ways. There is positive framing of the platforms claiming they stand for economic opportunity, more sustainable forms of consumption, and a pathway to decentralized and a sustainable economy overall. On the other end, critics see the sharing economy creating unregulated marketplaces, reinforcing neoliberalism and an incoherent field of innovation (Martin 2016: 153). Initially the sharing economy was framed by Botsman and others as a unique alternative to hyper-consumption, but has since been taken over by "regime actors" who have framed the sharing economy in mostly economic opportunity aspects, emphasizing giant success stories like those of Uber and Airbnb (Martin 2016: 158). Looking at the future of some of the sharing economy platforms, it remains to be seen whether those platforms will ever live up to a more sustainable promise. More on the specific discourse around the sharing economy will follow in Sect. 6.3.

3.2.2 Sharing Economy Platforms: An Ambiguous Trend

> The meteoric rise of the sharing economy has raised a compelling set of questions. Is it really about sharing? Is there anything new here? Does it represent a better model for organizing work and consumption? After more than three years of studying these initiatives, I can definitively say that the answers to these questions are: maybe, maybe, and maybe. (Schor in: Nadeem et al. 2016: 14)

Whether you are a sharing economy advocate or a critic, it is certain that the sharing economy platforms are leaving their mark on the American economy and the labor market. There are researchers like Arun Sundararajan who advocate in favor of the sharing economy platforms and do not see them as a threat to the future of work:

> Increased Variety = Increased Consumption. The sharing economy creates new consumption experiences of higher quality and greater variety. It is thus very likely that, rather than merely substituting old forms of commerce with new digitally enabled ones, new economic activity will be enabled. Put differently, we grow the pie, rather than simply carving it up differently. (Sundararajan 2016: Pos 2644 Ch 5)

In this view, sharing economy activities are growing the market, rather than supplanting it, because platforms provide new experiences and demand. Sharing economy platforms hold "great potential to address some of the economic disparities in today's economy, democratizing access to a higher standard of living, and to do so by growing rather than suppressing markets" (Sundararajan 2016: Pos 2829 Ch 5).

There is a wide range of sharing economy platforms, "from financially successful companies like Airbnb, a peer-to-peer lodging service, to smaller initiatives such as repair collectives and tool libraries" (Schor 2014: 2). But the question is whether the "the popular claim that the sharing economy is fairer, lower-carbon, and more transparent, participatory, and socially-connected is anything more than rhetoric" (Schor 2014: 2). In general, there are sharing economy platforms that offer a "true" alternative to capitalism in the way of small-scale, sustainable efforts like local food swaps, maker-spaces, coworking spaces, neighborhood platforms, or, for example, driver-organized taxi initiatives that challenge the might of Uber or Lyft.[2] These platforms are often nonprofit community-based platforms that are peer-to-peer rather than business-to-consumer (Schor 2014: 6). These initiatives are driven by the premise that users want to create "a fairer, more sustainable, and more socially connected" society (Schor 2014: 3). Whether users really translate that idealistic view in a change of consumer behavior is questionable however. Research has shown that "many respondents emphasize the value of sharing and collaboration, and some are highly critical of capitalism, the operation of the market, and the business-as-usual economy. Ideological motivation, however, varies by site, with less exhibited by earners on platforms such as Airbnb and RelayRides and more by participants in time banks and food swaps" (Schor 2014: 7).

There are "direct economic benefits" (Frenken and Schor 2017: 6) of the use of the sharing economy platforms because "Millions of transactions now take place that did not happen in the past, because the transaction costs involved in stranger sharing were simply too high" (Frenken and Schor 2017: 4). Yet, the big platforms are in the hand of venture capital and are not owned by a collective or the workers on the platform. Therefore, profits are not "shared" in any extensive way:

> the distribution of increased income and welfare are likely to be uneven. Sharing economy websites are two-sided platforms characterized by strong network externalities, creating the tendency towards natural monopoly and allowing for high margins to be charged by the platform. Note here that ratings account for a significant part of the value of the platform. Even though the ratings are the products of platform users, the value generated is appropriated by the platform itself. (...) The second group of people profiting most are owners of valuable assets. (Frenken and Schor 2017: 5)

The platforms benefit from their network power and can usually charge large margins. Workers usually do not have a say in any platform-wide decisions and often do not benefit from them. It is likely that the more economic considerations become

---

[2]Schor gives the example of a taxi cooperative in Portland, Oregon, where drivers formed their own platform and so became driver-owned (Schor 2014: 12).

central when participating in online sharing activities, the more social interactions will decline (Frenken and Schor 2017: 5).

Thus, the sharing economy platforms remain quite paradoxical, caught in between the air of alternativeness and the rules of the digital market that produce winner-take-all situations. Some local efforts of true sharing remain. Yet, the big players scale up their business worldwide and move away from any initial sharing ideal. This paradox exists because the sharing economy "has been framed both as part of the capitalist economy and as an alternative: simultaneously 'neoliberalism on steroids' and a remedy for a hyper-consumerist culture" (Richardson 2015: 121). This development points to the fact that our economic activity is far from homogenous and that "entanglements of culture and economy" (Richardson 2015: 121) are displayed in our consumer behavior. Rather than to look at the economy as a whole, we need to look at "economic niches" that occur on all ends of the spectrum. In this way, the sharing economy platforms can be understood as part of a generally heterogeneous economy. However, the paradox remains in the name, as it suggests a "promise (. . .) as an antidote" and "performs a narrative of collaboration and community" (Richardson 2015: 122) while failing to live up to this promise. Sharing economy platforms seem to act as an alternative *within* capitalism, not *from* it. The origins of the sharing economy platforms lie within hacker cyber culture; they have now been extended to the mainstream (Richardson 2015: 123).

When it comes to societal hierarchies, the sharing economy platforms offer positive and negative aspects as well. Platforms can be an easy access to labor or income, regardless of class, gender, or racial background. Yet, in some instances, inequalities that plague society are reproduced, despite the buffer of the digital platforms:

> [In] research at a food swap (. . .) a type of class privilege, limited the trades members were willing to make. (. . .) In our time bank research, we found that some people screen potential trading partners by grammar and education, and that many highly educated people were unwilling to offer their most valuable skills (. . .). A recent study also reported evidence of racial discrimination among Airbnb users, finding that non-black hosts were able to charge 12% more than blacks for comparable properties. (Schor et al. 2016: 80)

Other claims about racial discrimination pertain at Lyft and Uber, with drivers canceling rides for black customers more often than others (White 2016). Inequality and discrimination is hard to overcome, in gender, race, or class, and there might be a trade-off between inequality and market volume (Schor et al. 2016: 80). There are hopes that in the future machine-learning practices and more responsibility of the platforms could tackle discriminatory behavior. Programs could possibly identify such behavior by hosts and platforms could make anti-discriminatory policies more up-front in their activities (Sundararajan 2016).

All in all, "sharing" remains a paradoxical entity: "The truth of the matter is that the sharing economy is a floating signifier for a diverse range of activities. Some are genuinely collaborative and communal, while others are hotly competitive and profit-driven. A good many others are suspended somewhere in between" (Nadeem et al. 2016: 13). Whether truly communal, or just feel-good rhetoric, the sharing economy platforms are most controversial when it comes to the "gig" aspect, meaning its relationship to the labor force.

3.3 The Platform Economy and Labor

> I think that there's this sort of cultural notion that nobody is quite a worker anymore. Everyone is an entrepreneur (Stern and Kravitz 2016: Ch 5 Position 2045).

As we have seen in the chapter on automation, there are significant indications that millions of jobs could change profoundly or could disappear in the near future through the further development and introduction of technology. If jobs are not replaced, the demand for skills will certainly change. Additionally, jobs will be created that we cannot even imagine today. However, the future of work for Americans is not only characterized by these unforeseeable developments but also by the push toward alternative work arrangements such as independent work. The growth of the sharing economy platforms shows how much digital platforms have evolved and how they are becoming part of our everyday lives. More and more platform services offer flexible work or other income options. This can be seen as part of the general growth of the independent workforce in the USA.

> [If] the industrial revolution was organized around the factory, today's changes are organized around these digital platforms, loosely defined. Indeed, we are in the midst of a reorganization of our economy in which the platform owners are seemingly developing power that may be even more formidable than was that of the factory owners in the early industrial revolution. The proliferation of labels is simply a reflection of the recognition that platforms are already having powerful consequences for society, markets, and firms, and that we are unclear about their dynamics and directions. Whatever we call the transformation, the consequences are dramatic. (Kenney and Zysman 2016)

The consequences of these new digital platforms are not yet known and estimates vary significantly. Labor markets could become more efficient due to matching platforms. Yet, the labor market could also fragment with the growth of part-time work that lacks social benefits usually granted through employment. "For now, it is not clear whether these digital platforms are simply introducing digital intermediaries or actually increasing the extent of gig or contract work" (Kenney and Zysman 2016).

Moreover, there are issues associated with so-called micro entrepreneurs (self-employed entrepreneurs on a very small scale) who are part of the sharing economy platforms. Many of the new platforms spread the notion of "being your own boss" and succeeding on your own, which is supposed to be much better than being employed because you are independent and not bound to any restrictions from above.

> America's 'religion of entrepreneurship' has a powerful pull (. . .). 'People think that they can begin their own business and succeed. (. . .) But, by embracing this fantasy of being an entrepreneur, too many workers are surrendering their potential power to the big corporations.' (. . .). 'It's an appealing bait and switch for a company to go to a worker and say,

> 'Culturally, you're not a worker anymore. Congratulations! You're now an entrepreneur.' When the fact is that you're doing exactly what you were doing yesterday and your set of choices is just as constrained.' (Stern and Kravitz 2016: Ch 5 Position 2046)

Many platforms in fact only hire independents and do not consider them employees under any circumstances. This has led to many problems with potential misclassification of workers in the new economy. There are industries where misclassification is more common than in others such as home care, janitorial services, trucking, or hospitality (Bernhardt and Thomason 2017: 1). Although this problem has existed before, for example in the construction sector, some platforms seem to have integrated misclassification into their business model. With platforms like Uber, for example, there is an ongoing discussion whether their drivers should be considered employed or not. Lawsuits by drivers reach American courts again and again because of claims that Uber is exerting a level of control over drivers that is not compatible with independent contracting. A recent law introduced in California tightened the rules on hiring contractors and would have made many platform workers employees (Conger and Scheiber 2019). Yet, through a ballot initiative that was heavily pushed by platforms like Uber, this initiative toward classifying platform workers as employees was stopped. For now, drivers for Uber or comparable gig workers remain independent contractors in California (Dickey 2020). As of now, the issue remains contested.

3.3.1 The Example of Uber

Uber is one of the most widely known and influential sharing economy platforms. Often, Uber acts as a stand-in for the overall debate around sharing economy platforms, especially when it comes to the situation of platform workers. Uber is seen as a prime example for platform businesses and a more independent future of work (Hall and Krueger 2016: 2). As such, Uber is both hailed as the most successful and as the worst example for the on-demand economy, depending on the perspective.

Founded by Travis Kalanick, Uber set out to change the transportation industry for good, tapping into the "the power of the two-sided network effects that the company had created" (McAfee and Brynjolfsson 2017: Ch VIII Position 2970). Kalanick argued that the taxi industry was overregulated, and in many instances, corrupt, which resulted in inferior service for costumers. Through Uber, new competition would improve market choice. Since its founding, UberX (quasi taxi service) and UberPool (car-pooling), as well as other services that vary from region to region, have been added to the transportation platform.[3] Uber did not offer a

---

[3]UberPop means that people can use their private cars to do the ride-hailing service, without much regulation for car and driver, etc. UberPop is not available in all locations. UberBlack offers luxury cars with drivers. There is also UberSelect that offers better cars but charges higher prices than the

unique new product but an upgrade to the traditional taxi service. Everyone who has used Uber will probably admit that the Uber smartphone app works extremely well. It is user-friendly and integrates tracking and a cash-less payment method in one seamless process. The matching is instant and in the Bay Area, as well as in LA and San Diego where the app was tested, Uber drivers pulled up almost immediately after booking a ride on the app. The cars are usually well-kept and of better quality than traditional taxis have been. The app shows how many cars and which options are available. After the ride is over, all transactions such as payment, tipping, rating, or leaving a message for the driver can be completed through the app. You can also see a photo of the driver, how many rides the driver has already completed, the reviews, and the type of car. For big cities like San Francisco it seems that Uber taps into an area that is not adequately covered by convenient public transportation and offers a relatively inexpensive and flexible alternative. With the different options from sharing a car on UberPool to UberSelect where a more high-end car is available, Uber offers options for many groups of consumers, even for the less affluent who could have never afforded regular taxi rides. Some employers now even seem to cover ride-hailing expenses for their employees to get to work. For the consumer side, Uber offers a seamless service that is working perfectly and is relatively inexpensive, safe, and convenient, especially compared to the former taxi service. However, in San Francisco and other big cities, the roads are already very congested and adding even more cars through Uber and other platforms is certainly adding to this congestion problem. Additionally, traditional taxi drivers come under a lot of pressure with so much competition (not only Uber but other services such as Lyft also operate in many cities). In fact, in San Francisco barely any regular taxis seem to operate anymore. It is likely that a lot of full-time taxi drivers in the USA are losing their jobs because of ride-sharing platforms.

For investors, Uber was certainly a great investment target, and the company grew fast. From near-zero in mid-2012 to more than 460,000 drivers in the end of 2015, the number of active Uber drivers doubled almost every 6 months (Hall and Krueger 2016: 2). By 2016, the platform had reportedly generated $20 billion in annual gross bookings, and was valued at $68 billion, raising $15 billion from investors (McAfee and Brynjolfsson 2017: Ch VIII 2975). However, Uber has still not made a profit. In 2019, Uber went public with an IPO of about $82 billion, somewhat of a disappointment for many investors, as Uber had claimed much higher stakes before (de la Merced and Conger 2019). The first months of trading have remained somewhat questionable because Uber still struggles to prove it is able to make a profit. In 2020, Uber and other ride-hailing services have experienced the next deep crisis with most of their business disappearing almost overnight due to restrictions and stay-at-home orders caused by reactions to the global COVID-19

regular service. UberAssist is available in certain areas and offers the rider additional help, for example for getting in and out of the car. Uber has also entered the food delivery business with UberEats.

pandemic. For the foreseeable future, any estimates as to when Uber will become profitable have thus been abandoned (Conger et al. 2020).

But even before the difficult public offering and the new problems due to a global health crisis, Uber was rocked by several scandals, especially in 2017 when reports surfaced about sexual harassment and a toxic business culture at Uber's workplaces. After more and more reports about Uber's internal struggles became public, Travis Kalanick stepped down as CEO. For labor advocates, Uber's struggles did not come as a surprise. For many, Uber seems to embody everything that is wrong with the sharing or on-demand economy: Uncertain working hours and low pay, actual misclassification of workers, no benefits due to the status of micro-entrepreneur, and the possibility to be removed from the platform without your consent. Additionally, Uber and its competitors are using their influence to try and shape labor law on the state and local level. In states like Texas, proposals surfaced that would exempt companies that use digital networks from having to qualify their workers as employees (Scheiber 2019).

As indicated before, platforms like Uber have also been heavily lobbying to pass Proposition 22 in California as a ballot initiative in the 2020 elections, thus ensuring that gig workers retain their independent contractor status (Dickey 2020). Uber and other platforms used their direct access to customers and drivers over their apps to reach out and push their view about the classification of gig workers, namely that they want to and should remain independent contractors. This is one of the most important issue for companies like Uber. If they cannot maintain the contracting basis for drivers, the business model of the platforms would have to change profoundly, and services could no longer be offered at low rates. Often, companies can save between 20 and 30% of labor costs by using contractors instead of employees. Thus, in many states, platforms like Uber or Lyft work toward exempting most (digital platform) gig workers from the employment status (Scheiber 2019). The motivation behind these moves is ambiguous. On the one hand, for labor advocates, it is clear that the platforms want to ensure the continuation of the contracting basis for workers and thus save costs. Additionally, critics see the proposals as a motivation for other companies to reclassify their workers as contractors simply by using a digital interface for communication. On the other hand, companies claim that they are pushing this agenda in order to be able to provide more benefits and services for workers on platforms without immediately being classified as a regular employer (Scheiber 2019). Additionally, they usually claim that most gig workers want to remain independent. All in all, labor laws in relation to platform companies like Uber remain a contested issue for law-makers and courts.

Despite these controversies, numbers show that the Uber platform is not unpopular among many workers in the USA. As of 2016, about 800,000 drivers were active on Uber in the USA (Buchak 2018: 2). They seem to be attracted by the flexible schedules that depend on the drivers' desires. Uber cannot, under normal circumstances, force drivers to take rides or prevent them from taking rides. That is one of the most crucial arguments for Uber to classify their drivers as contractors. Additionally,

> most driver-partners do not appear to turn to Uber out of desperation or because they face an absence of other opportunities in the job market—only eight percent were unemployed just before they started working on the Uber platform—but rather because the nature of the work, the flexibility, and the compensation appeals to them compared with other available options. Even as the national unemployment rate fell to 5 percent, the number of active Uber drivers continued to rise. (Hall and Krueger 2016: 3)

During a research trip to California, a small number of drivers shared their experience driving for Uber with me.[4] Most of them seemed to like the job, or at least they did not say otherwise in front of a customer. Although the drivers were aware of some drawbacks like covering your own car expenses and insurance, they still liked the option to drive for Uber. One full-time driver said he had formerly driven a taxi and preferred Uber to that. However, another full-time driver said he only did it to get by (flexibly) and did not like the Uber platform. He had purchased the vehicle specifically to be able to work as a driver and wanted to finance another job training by driving for Uber. A study on the ride-hailing market in New York City actually revealed that purchasing a vehicle specifically for driving it on platforms like Uber has become a common practice for Uber drivers in some cities. The majority of them work full-time as a driver. However, as earnings have gone down in cities like New York with more drivers on the road, it becomes increasingly difficult to cover the expenses associated with purchasing a new car (Bellafante 2018).

Yet, most of the drivers I talked to were content with the service and liked the flexibility alongside their other stable jobs. From what the drivers had to say, it can be assumed that it is a mixture of necessity and easy access that leads people to drive for Uber. Especially for the supplemental drivers, it seems unlikely that they would want to get another stable job if Uber was not available with its easy and flexible access. This is in line with larger surveys of Uber drivers as well (Hall and Krueger 2016). Yet, the drivers seemed to be in need of extra income in some way; otherwise drivers would most likely not spend their free time driving around the city. With California having become very expensive when it comes to cost of living, it is likely that many people are looking for ways to earn extra income. For the full-time drivers, Uber basically seemed to be close to a taxi driver job only with their own car and more flexibility. Moreover, many drivers are not only active on Uber but also on other ride-hailing platforms like Lyft at the same time. Most of the drivers had a better-than-average car and looked out for the convenience and cleanliness for riders. As said before, for customers Uber certainly is a very good service because of the seamless process of getting a ride and the apparent upgrade of service and cleanliness compared to many traditional taxi providers.

So, interestingly, many workers do not see Uber as the nightmare it is sometimes portrayed as. Many seem to choose this kind of work option because of flexibility reasons or to supplement their income, alongside their other job. Others might turn to it because all other available job options are even worse in quality or do not fit their

[4]Only a small and unrepresentative number of drivers could be interviewed personally. Therefore, their opinions are only a glimpse into what Uber drivers think and are in no way representative of all Uber drivers in the USA.

needs. Bad (and good) jobs exist in all categories, in employed arrangements, as well as in independent arrangements (Bernhardt and Thomason 2017: 6). Yet, as stated before, it is mostly the middle-income workers with another job who might start driving with their own car for ride-sharing apps like Uber. The group of lower income individuals who could benefit from driving for Uber often do not own their own car or their car is not eligible because of a lack of standards and quality. Therefore, many individuals actually decide to borrow the necessary capital to get a better car in order to be able to drive for Uber (Buchak 2018: 2). In this way, the capital investment of buying a car adds dual welfare benefits as a productive capital asset (driving for Uber), and as a consumer durable good (Buchak 2018: 3). On the other hand, as said before, shrinking and volatile income for Uber drivers in places like New York City might make it problematic for these drivers to cover expenses. New York has since introduced driver restrictions. Some argue that this could reduce welfare effects which could fall back on riders (who might have to pay higher rates) (Buchak 2018: 3). Others see the cap on the number of drivers and cars on ride-hailing platforms also as a means to stabilize income for the existing drivers (Bellafante 2018).

Drawing once again from personal research in California in 2018, Uber is now also active in bringing drivers together with car rental firms like Hertz, who have started a partnership with Uber in different US cities. Through Hertz, drivers who want to work on the Uber platform could get an eligible car for a fixed rate a week with insurance and mileage covered. This is another way to attract drivers and give people access to eligible vehicles who might otherwise be unable to work on the platform. But, again, buying a car or renting one to drive for Uber puts pressure on drivers to complete a certain amount of rides in order to refinance their fixed expenses, while earnings for ride-hailing platform drivers have actually steeply decreased over the years (Farrell et al. 2018: 4).

The flexibility aspect that many Uber drivers value has always been an important factor for all independent contractors. This seems to continue in the sharing economy as well. Studies confirm that many workers highly value work flexibility that the platforms can offer. They would prefer more flexible work arrangements in stable jobs, parental-leave options, or other arrangements that are not in line with the standard nine-to-five job. Especially families with children are struggling to combine family and career. More changes to the healthcare system might reduce job lock and more people might take advantage of the possibilities of the on-demand economy (Hall and Krueger 2016: 3). So far, many drivers are covering healthcare through another job or through a spouse, which is convenient for platforms like Uber. But these numbers only accounted for 38% of the drivers in 2015. Other drivers need to make their own arrangements for health care or are not covered (Hall and Krueger 2016: 12). Additionally, drivers are not reimbursed for expenses such as gasoline, maintenance, or insurance, and can only deduct some expenses from their taxes (Hall and Krueger 2016: 26).

Additional factors such as general social benefits, flexible schedules, access to training and promotions, health and safety on the job, bargaining rights, and violations of labor laws (e.g., wage theft) are also decisive when judging the quality of a job, may it be traditional or self-employed, and this remains true for the sharing economy as well (Bernhardt and Thomason 2017: 6). However, an advantage that Uber continues to argue for is that drivers on the platform make more money than minimum wage in other similar jobs. These claims might be overrated, as Mason points out:

> Retention is a problem in large part because the economics of driving are so bad. Researchers have struggled to establish exactly how much money drivers make, but (. . .) a consensus on driver pay seems to be emerging: drivers make, on average, between $9.21 (£7.17) and $10.87 (£8.46) per hour. What these findings confirm is what many of us in the game already know: in most major US cities, drivers are pulling in wages that fall below local minimum-wage requirements. (Mason 2018)

Other studies come to the same conclusions about low pay from driving on ride-hailing platforms (Farrell et al. 2018), also because Uber's service depends on large numbers of drivers idling in order to cover customer requests on a short-notice basis (Parrott and Reich 2018: 5).

Through issues like low pay or lack of an eligible car, Uber struggles to keep drivers on the platform and conduct more rides. Especially in dense areas like the Bay Area this becomes more and more problematic. As said before, from research in the area, I could see that Uber was very popular but that it seemed to have problems finding enough drivers. This could be seen, for instance, through radio ads that specifically offered bonuses for new drivers who registered on Uber and delivered a certain number of rides. And the Bay Area offered a Hertz partnership for people interested in driving for Uber but do not have their own car.

Generally, gig workers, such as drivers for Uber, do not seem to represent the extremely desperate. People working for Uber reflect the general workforce much more evenly than the cohort driving taxis or working as a chauffeur. Yet, more young people drive for Uber (Hall and Krueger 2016: 6). Also, Uber drivers are more likely to identify as white than taxi drivers or chauffeurs, and they usually have a higher educational degree than taxi drivers or the general workforce. Forty-eight percent of Uber drivers report that they have a college degree, only 41% of the general workforce, and only 18% among taxi drivers have a college degree (Hall and Krueger 2016: 8). Although Uber drivers might not be among the extremely desperate, they also do not seem to belong to the group of workers whose income covers expenses comfortably enough to not look for supplemental earnings. As said before, most drivers seem to be in a situation where a higher or an extra income is needed in some way.

Despite the issues surrounding expenses and pay, Uber displays certain features that are not comparable to former services. For instance, the rating system. Using this makes it possible to build a good reputation on the site so that earnings might go up for good drivers, which is an incentive taxi drivers did not have in the past (Hall and Krueger 2016: 32). At the same time, the rating systems and structures of Uber or its competitors like Lyft put the workers on these platforms in a stressful position. The platforms use incentives based on gamification that are designed to motivate drivers to log on to the platform and work. On the one hand, they are designed in a way that completing certain tasks comes close to moving up levels, comparable to a game. On the other hand, the algorithms used to calculate tasks or evaluate the drivers are often opaque and might feel unfair to drivers.

> [Gamification] is the use of game elements—point-scoring, levels, competition with others, measurable evidence of accomplishment, ratings and rules of play—in non-game contexts. Games deliver an instantaneous, visceral experience of success and reward, and they are increasingly used in the workplace to promote emotional engagement with the work process, to increase workers' psychological investment in completing otherwise uninspiring tasks, and to influence, or 'nudge', workers' behaviour. (Mason 2018)

Another reason to use gamification elements is worker retention, which is a problem for ride-hailing sites like Uber or Lyft. "According to Uber, 50% of drivers stop using the application within their first two months, and a recent report from the Institute of Transportation Studies at the University of California in Davis suggests that just 4% of ride-hail drivers make it past their first year" (Mason 2018). This means that these platforms need to find ways to keep drivers engaged on the site, and they try to do that through the use of rating systems and gamification aspects based on algorithms. All this is done to promote drivers to perform better and to keep them engaged: "And this is the thing that is so brilliant and awful about the gamification of Lyft and Uber: it preys on our desire to be of service, to be liked, to be good" (Mason 2018). Uber cannot force any driver to take up jobs or decline them, nor can the platform decide when and for how long a driver is working. Yet, Uber can remove drivers from the site and usually settles all disputes with riders. Uber algorithms also decide the rates the driver charges, as well as the margin taken off. Uber also demands certain minimum standards from drivers and decides if these are met or not. Thus, the Uber platform infrastructure does exert a certain amount of control over drivers, which is also desirable, at least for customers, when it comes to safety and quality. The question remains whether this is enough to qualify Uber as an employer.

Uber remains one of the most well-known examples of the sharing economy platforms. It also remains one of the most controversial ones. On the one hand, it offers a great product to consumers and has changed the transportation industry in the USA profoundly, especially in the areas on the West Coast where public transportation service is much more absent from people's lives than in European countries. Yet, many of these areas are already plagued by congestion and pollution through heavy traffic. Uber and its competitors have not alleviated the problem but most likely worsened it. Again, this shows that the sustainable promise of the sharing economy platforms has been overblown. But Uber is maybe most controversial when it comes to the impact on labor, in this case, its drivers. Are they truly independent contractors or are they employees? Many lawsuits have been fought over these issues and this will most probably continue in the future. It is unlikely that the issues around the use of independent contracting are going to be settled any time soon.

3.3.2 The Future of Work: Platform Work

Uber is only one example of the large array of sharing economy platforms that were founded in the last decade. But the larger implications of working conditions on these platforms are still hard to fully assess. There are those who see a lot of opportunity in the platform economy, and there are people like former Labor Secretary Robert Reich who see it as a race to the bottom of labor standards. He frequently called the sharing economy "share-the-scraps" economy (Sundararajan 2016: Pos 3640 Ch 7). "In this dystopian view of the future, work will be defined by low wages, the elimination of benefits, and high levels of job insecurity. People will work longer hours for less money, income will be fragmented, the safety net will be a distant memory, and work environments will have less ideal and less carefully monitored conditions" (Sundararajan 2016: Pos 3645f Ch 7). But there are also the sharing economy "enthusiasts" who do not share these dystopian ideas. In their view, the future of work will rather be

> one defined by increased flexibility, fluidity, innovation, and creativity. In this utopian future, individuals will be empowered entrepreneurs who take control of their own destinies on an unprecedented scale. Innovative new products and services will flow from platforms that are gateways to innovation (...). Average workers will work fewer hours on a more flexible schedule from wherever they want and make more money doing work that they choose. (Sundararajan 2016: Pos 3645f Ch 7)

Both of these visions seem to be overblown, but it shows that there seem to be at least two opposing sides to sharing economy platforms and their impact on labor in the future. One side considers them the way toward a "precariat" of workers, the other insists on great opportunities. But predictions are still hard to make as data is not widely available. One study conducted by JP Morgan in 2016 was able to shed some light onto a part of the sharing economy platforms. The study distinguishes between labor and capital platforms and offers a dataset of 260,000 customers who offered goods or services on one of 30 platforms (Farrell and Greig 2016: 1). The initial interest of JP Morgan was to find out whether working on the sharing economy platforms would help people with income volatility.

In one part of the study, JP Morgan looked at the online platform economy specifically, as many people see "the Online Platform Economy as the 'future of work.' The next question is whether the platform economy will become the 'future of income'" (Farrell and Greig 2016: 20) as well. For some people, it could be a chance to earn some money on the side as the most active participants on the platform are also those who experience the most income volatility. The study found that over the period of 2012–2015 labor platforms grew more rapidly than capital platforms,[5] but capital platforms remained larger overall. Across the 4 years of the study, 21% of customers in the dataset participated in labor platforms, 78% in capital platforms, and only 2% in both of them (Farrell and Greig 2016: 21). In an

[5]Labor platforms included TaskRabbit or Uber; capital platforms include Airbnb, eBay, Amazon Marketplace, or Etsy.

updated version of their study from 2018, JP Morgan found that among the labor platforms, transportation (drivers transporting people or goods) and "non-transport work" defined as "workers offering services such as dog walking, home repair, or telemedicine" (Farrell et al. 2018: 2) dominated. Capital Platforms could be divided into selling (independents using online marketplaces) and leasing (renting out of homes or parking spaces). Their 2018 dataset included 39 million JP Morgan Chase accounts and 128 platforms. They found that 2.3 million families participated in the online platform economy between October 2012 and March 2018 (Farrell et al. 2018: 2).

Summarizing their results, the JP Morgan study suggests that over the 4 years, earnings from those participating in platform work were substantial, but remained a secondary source of income overall. People often only participated sporadically once they had joined a platform. This remained true for the 2018 data as well. The largest fraction of participants reported earnings for 1–3 months a year. Overall, it remained a minor income source (Farrell et al. 2018: 3). In general, the platform economy grew tremendously over the past few years, driven by new participants, not by a deepening engagement of older participants. Yet, the overall size is still small compared to traditional employment. Labor platforms were used as a source to compensate for dips in earnings; capital platforms were used to generate additional income on top of the regular earnings. The activity on labor platforms shows that people were less likely to have a non-platform job at the time of usage of these platforms and that their non-platform income was also lower (Farrell and Greig 2016: 27). In general, JP Morgan suggests that the platform economy can bridge times of crises or supplement the income for families for a limited amount of time per year. In the 2018 update, most of the findings from 2016 were corroborated. However, the online platform economy had already grown tremendously from 0.3% of families earning from platform work (of the JP Morgan sample) to 1.6% in 2018. Transportation platforms have grown to dominate in terms of numbers and transaction volume. Yet, the supply of drivers increased which led to a steep decline in earnings for these drivers (Farrell et al. 2018: 2f).

Another report trying to illuminate the impact of the sharing economy platforms on workers was conducted by Airbnb itself (Sperling 2015). The report tries to show how Airbnb hosts can create an additional income over the platform, which, as Airbnb claims, helps middle-class families. Written by former White House National Economic Advisor and Director of the National Economic Council under Clinton and Obama, Gene Sperling, the report argues that income stagnation is one of the central problems for many middle-class families today. The report admits that solutions to the problem of falling family budgets are "no doubt complex and involve a multiplicity of efforts in a wide range of areas, from education and skills-training policies, to the minimum wage, to innovation and research policies, to efforts to increase demand for workers" (Sperling 2015). Yet, "innovation in the private sector can also play an important role" (Sperling 2015), and this is where Airbnb sees the potential of home sharing to tackle this problem. Many studies show that the real value of middle-class family budgets has fallen. US Census data shows that in 2001 the middle-class income was at $56,451 and had fallen to $52,770 in

2013. Comparable to what JP Morgan claims in the study mentioned before, Airbnb sees their home-sharing platform as a valid option for families to provide extra income in order to close income gaps. To further corroborate their argument, Airbnb claims that the majority of their hosts rent out only parts of their primary residences for only about 66 days/year.[6] According to internal Airbnb data, the typical single-property host thus makes up to an extra $7530 from renting out part of their residence on these 66 days/year, increasing yearly family income to about $60,000. This can also help families to cover financial squeezes in ways that are not tied to their jobs or savings. A similar claim was made by the study JP Morgan conducted among their customers. The report also suggests that many of the host families are part of the middle class, but have a significantly lower income level than the average for their cities. This raises the question whether these families' only solution is to rent out parts of their residences in an effort to maintain their livelihood in dense and costly urban areas (Sperling 2015). For boom areas such as the Bay Area where Airbnb was founded, this seems to be the case.

Although the two studies were conducted by market actors and their conclusions need to be weighed carefully, their results still indicate that some platform activities can be considered a tool for families to supplement their income and to bridge financial squeezes. Rising costs of living in many areas around the USA can seemingly only be countered with extra income sources. Everyday expenses are growing while wages are often stagnant. Middle-class households can therefore benefit from some of the platform arrangements. First, because they often have assets such as a spare room to rent out. Secondly, they have a (stable) main job that they can rely on for their general income, as well as for benefits such as health insurance. The two studies thus also show that many income opportunities such as renting out or working as a platform driver are middle-class options. Lower income families usually lack the assets that are necessary to engage in this kind of activity.

It also varies significantly where families live with places like Nevada and San Francisco displaying the highest numbers of participants on online platforms. Younger people are also more likely to participate (Farrell et al. 2018: 7). Generally, the online platform economy is growing and there are more and more people taking advantage of this source of income, at least for a limited time. Renting out is one method to earn money, but the "engine of growth" are the transportation platforms with independent drivers. Yet, with the growth of this sector, earnings have steeply declined. JP Morgan finds that there is no "evidence that the Online Platform Economy is replacing traditional sources of income for most families. (...) our findings indicate that regardless of whether or not platform work could in principle represent the 'future of work,' most participants are not putting it to the type of use that would usher in that future" (Farrell et al. 2018: 5).

[6]This data is based on Airbnb booking data from the year 2014. However, in-depth data is only available for five major cities in the USA, Portland, Oregon, Los Angeles, New York City, San Francisco, Boston.

As these studies show, the digital platform economy is growing, despite not being the model for the "future of work" more generally quite yet. With its growth and the growth of the independent workforce in the USA, however, there will be more consequences that need to be addressed. "The questions are really: what balance will there be among jobs created as the digital wave flows through our economy and society, and which workers will be displaced?" (Kenney and Zysman 2016). Within the new economy, there are many new kinds of jobs emerging.

> [The] new kinds of work that are now being created and the existing jobs that will be redefined and reorganized in the future are more difficult to forecast, so we can only speculate. Algorithms and databases are automating some kinds of work, but even as this occurs other value-creating opportunities are appearing. There will be new products and services as well as new production and service processes, which are likely to be design and creativity intensive, as well as algorithm-enabled. Some of the early indicators of the new or transformed work can be enumerated, but certainly not exhaustively counted. (Kenney and Zysman 2016)

Additionally, the present jobs are undergoing tremendous transformation. They will most likely "be reframed but not eliminated by digital technology. Uber, Airbnb, TaskRabbit, Handy, and other platform firms are transforming industries by connecting 'producers' with customers in new ways. In some cases, this is displacing or threatening existing, often regulated, service providers, such as taxis and hotels" (Kenney and Zysman 2016). Most often, platforms do not offer new services, but a more effective and inexpensive option that was previously unavailable, too expensive, or a nuisance. Therefore, people often talk about the disruption of industries through platforms. Disruption is not a negative concept per se, but part of what Joseph Schumpeter very famously coined "creative destruction" (Reinert and Reinert 2006). In order for an economy and society to move forward, old industries will go down and new ones will be created. In the platform economy, disruptions have brought about positive effects, especially for consumers, who have benefitted from better and cheaper products and services. As said before, Rachel Botsman indicates that there are certain industries that are "ripe for disruption," because their services might be outdated or not user-friendly. For example, Uber is often considered an "upgrade" of the taxi industry which many people consider monopoly-driven or even corrupt, overregulated, and not particular customer-friendly.

But the digital economy also creates entirely new forms of value creation. Platforms like Instagram or YouTube that have initially been created as forms of communication or entertainment networks "are creating entirely new value-creating activities that are formalizing into what can be seen as precarious careers, such as a YouTube producer or smartphone app developer. Finally, existing organizations are creating new digital and social media marketing departments and jobs" (Kenney and Zysman 2016). Social media advisors or social media content producers are in demand around the globe, for all kinds of businesses. Additionally, as said before, the micro-entrepreneur is growing as a job description, also called

> 'consignment workers,' who provide goods—usually but not necessarily 'virtually'—for platforms such as app stores, YouTube, or Amazon Self-Publishing. Although the vast majority of them are unsuccessful or marginally profitable, some can be enormously

> successful, and despite the fact that this phenomenon is as yet unmeasured, it is clearly creating many new opportunities for entrepreneurship. (Kenney and Zysman 2016)

The changes through the new digital economy are most probably not going to lead to a "workerless society" (Kenney and Zysman 2016). However, the "preponderance of work and value creation" (Kenney and Zysman 2016) is going to be more dispersed than in the past.

All these points just mentioned allude to a general issue of the digital platform economy, the dissolution of the traditional employer–employee relationship. In general, those we refer to as gig workers or (digital) freelancers do not enjoy the benefits that an employer–employee relationship offers such as minimum wage, social security, health insurance, retirement plans, paid vacation, liability insurance, or unemployment insurance. As said before, the move toward nontraditional work arrangements is a larger trend that is changing the US labor force. Most of the gig workers enjoy a great amount of flexibility, which they highly value, but many other benefits can only be obtained as a full-time employee. "For many Americans, the new landscape of work offers freedom, flexibility, and the ability to achieve their entrepreneurial dreams. For many more, however, it represents a harsh, uncertain place with lower wages and less bargaining power" (Stern and Kravitz 2016: Ch 5 Position 2068). Actually, there is more and more criticism about contracted workers in Silicon Valley itself, where drivers or security guards are contracted out and do not enjoy the benefits of the big companies they work for (Sheng 2018).

> Are these contractors mini-entrepreneurs, employees in all but name, or yet something else? Further, what is the proper employment category for individuals who hope to be one of the winners by producing apps, YouTube videos, or self-published books on Amazon? In these activities, there is a power law of returns by which a few big winners are remunerated by advertising, product placement payments, personal appearance fees, and even crowd-funding campaigns, while a very long tail of producers are creating the vast bulk of consigned content without monetary return. (Kenney and Zysman 2016)

Moreover, the number of those enjoying the great rewards of the likes of Google or Facebook, the business giants, is relatively small: "Take Google, the platform economy giant, which, despite its 2014 revenues of $66 billion, has only 50,000 employees. Uber has only about 1500 employees and is already a global business" (Kenney and Zysman 2016). This brings up the question what "policy and political issues arise when the orchestrators of economic activity are relatively small firms, rather than organizations as large as Ford Motor Company, General Electric, or General Motors—all of whom also require sophisticated supplier and distribution networks?" (Kenney and Zysman 2016).

In an even more pessimistic outlook, an article in *The New Yorker* from 2017 called *The Gig Economy celebrates working yourself to death* (Tolentino 2017) paints a bleak picture of those working in the gig economy: "It does require a fairly dystopian strain of doublethink for a company to celebrate how hard and how constantly its employees must work to make a living, given that these companies are themselves setting the terms" (Tolentino 2017). The article comments on the controversial advertisement of the platform *Fiverr*, which included posters of rather distressed looking young people.

> [On Fiverr a service] can be purchased for as low as five dollars— [and] recently attracted ire for an ad campaign called 'In Doers We Trust.' One ad, prominently displayed on some New York City subway cars, features a woman staring at the camera with a look of blank determination. 'You eat a coffee for lunch,' the ad proclaims. 'You follow through on your follow through. Sleep deprivation is your drug of choice. You might be a doer.' (Tolentino 2017)

This celebration of gig work arrangements is attributed to a flawed economic system that is so obsessed with self-reliance that it can celebrate "working yourself to death": "The contrast between the gig economy's rhetoric (everyone is always connecting, having fun, and killing it!) and the conditions that allow it to exist (a lack of dependable employment that pays a living wage) makes this kink in our thinking especially clear" (Tolentino 2017).

So are freelancing, independent contracting, or "gigging" under precarious circumstances becoming the "new normal?" (Hill 2015: 4). This remains to be seen. Yet, when talking about the platform economy and its relationship to labor, it is an ambiguous trend. Some people see it as a possibility for easy and flexible access to the labor market for some individuals who want to earn money (or gain additional income to supplement their earnings). The other side sees the sharing economy platforms as "architects of a growing 'precariat,' a class on the precarious edge of economic security, and argue that the impetus for sharing is not trust, but desperation" (Schor 2014: 10). In this view, the platforms, in a push toward a more independent workforce overall, are leading the way toward insecure livelihoods where an isolated workforce tries to make ends meet in an ever more (globally) competitive labor market. Additionally, the growing number of "supplementers" points to the lack of adequate stable jobs that allow for a middle-class lifestyle. Ultimately, both sides have their point. The sharing economy concept is an opportunity for growth and income in some sectors, and the independent workforce is growing in all parts of the American economy. This independent workforce is very diverse and many are not driven into independence because of economic hardship. Many people choose to work independently, while others are more reluctant or would prefer a stable employment if only better jobs were available. Yet, old business models and their employees are at risk of being replaced by new models, and with it today's stable jobs. Despite potential for easily accessible work, the question remains, what kind of jobs are created and whether labor standards can be maintained (Eichhorst and Spermann 2015: 3). The concern is that more and more businesses might switch to an on-demand workforce in areas where no special expertise is needed or where no internal sectors of a business are concerned. If the local or global labor market offers cheaper alternatives via platforms, businesses might be tempted to hire on-demand instead of a stable workforce (Eichhorst and Spermann 2015: 8). This "national outsourcing" is already practiced by many businesses, including big tech giants like Google that display a growing "shadow workforce" of contracted workers (Bergen and Eidelson 2018; Sheng 2018).

3.3.3 Platforms: Labor Reform and Regulation

> Hope is not a strategy. Neither is nostalgia. We need a strategy for the new world of work. Otherwise, the notion of a good job will vanish, as will income, dignity, and creativity. (Stern and Kravitz 2016: Ch 5 Position 2084)

With growing concern and criticism about the influence of the platform economy on the US workforce, more and more people demand reforms in order to provide benefits and a stable income (Stern and Kravitz 2016: Ch 5 Position 2079). Unlike in the past, labor unions have often lost their position as a political actor and labor broker since the level of unionization in the USA has decreased and remains on low levels in many areas. Additionally, the employer–employee relationship has broken down in many industries. Without some reform of the social security net and worker classification, businesses could be incentivized to replace their workforce with contractors, or so-called 1099 workers (named after the 1099 information filing form) wherever possible. Without being responsible for benefits such as health insurance, social security, unemployment, breaks, paid sick leave, injured workers compensation, and many other things, businesses could save up to 30% in labor costs. Businesses have already shown their willingness to cut back their American workforce by outsourcing many jobs to overseas territory. Under "the current system, employers actually have an incentive to fire their entire workforce if they can get away with it, and go 100 percent with 1099 workers, or as high a percentage of them as possible. A business owner would be foolish not to, watching as your competitors go this route and dramatically slash their labor costs by 30 percent or more" (Hill 2015: 5). Although 1099 workers have existed before the rise of the sharing economy platforms, the digital platforms make it much easier to adopt such business practices (Hill 2015: 5), and there are whole business models such as ride-hailing platforms that are based on using solely contractors. As said before, other companies such as Google are also hiring more and more contractors for anything that is not considered the core of their business.

One idea to close this 1099 loophole and to improve the situation for contractors could be to make social benefits more independent from the employment status: "Former Treasury Secretary Larry Summers, as well as many others, have proposed the idea of the 'portability' of the safety net. The United States (...) is 'unique in providing significant aspects of basic economic security through the employment contract'" (Hill 2015: 5). In fact, the introduction of Obamacare, officially called the Affordable Care Act, can be considered a first step in this direction as self-employed workers can also enroll. "One of the major selling points for passing the Affordable Care Act was that it would liberate workers to move more easily from job to job. No longer are their employment prospects hurt by 'job lock,' in which they do not dare leave a job for fear of losing their affordable health care" (Hill 2015: 6). A multi-employer plan would work in a similar manner, being independent from the employment status with workers and employers paying into it to ensure a certain level of security. Only because businesses hire temporary workers, they would not be exempt from contributing to the benefits workers need (Hill 2015: 6). Thus, in addition to what contractors or freelancers are paid, businesses would pay a few dollars into the individual security accounts of the workers. The model for such a system is the way construction workers fund their insurance and benefits system.

A portable system such as Steven Hill and others have proposed could mean a better option for on-demand workers. Businesses are still free to hire flexible workers, and those workers are able to enjoy the flexibility that they may value without the lack of benefits and the threat of insecurity:

> when asked, on-demand workers usually say they like their jobs, savoring the flexibility and the ability to be their own boss, as well as the money. Workers tend to be optimistic and trust the new labor platforms (...) but they can't decide if flexibility or security matters more. What's needed (...) is new benefit structures that limit the risk for workers, (...). (Aeppel 2016: 3)

The JP Morgan study previously mentioned also argues in favor of portable benefits when working on sharing economy platforms, especially because it could help families with income volatility. In all cases, trying to find work over the platforms seems to be a better option to overcome volatility in income than to cut household spending or take out additional loans. The study highlights issues for policymakers: A new labor force is created through the work on platforms which is not entitled to the same benefits as the stable workforce. Policies should therefore adapt benefits to be portable and to make independents eligible to social safety net programs such as unemployment insurance (Farrell and Greig 2016: 28f). It is important to state that reforms around the portability of social benefits do not want to get rid of flexible workers, but that through changes on the business and the labor side, the situation for both could be improved. As of now, companies and politics still seem to be hesitant to experiment with such a system, although the Affordable Care Act can be considered a step in this direction.

The difficulty to provide basic social benefits to freelance and gig workers is one of the key areas for calls of labor market reform. Others argue that the classification of employed vs. self-employed is not adequate anymore in the era of digital transformation. Therefore, some argue in favor of a third category of workers who are something in between employed and independent. The different statuses of employee and freelancer or self-employed contractor seem to be some of the most problematic parts of the sharing economy. If the stark separation between the categories was eased, some problems could be solved. The self-employed could be able to access social security and insurances; wages could be settled more efficiently by setting, for example, minimum pay or suggested fees. Platforms could also offer some services and benefits for those contractors that need it, without immediately qualifying as an employer. For social security, it could be valuable to make freelancers join social security networks with a possibility to opt out if you have private coverage. The question is whether platforms themselves or the person posting gigs should pay a certain amount into the social benefits system of the gig workers. This would lead to different price calculations but would also level the playing field for businesses still employing a regular workforce (Eichhorst and Spermann 2015: 23ff). As of now, platforms as well as labor leaders seem to be hesitant to embrace such a policy, fearing either higher costs or the weakening of labor standards for the general workforce.

On the business side, interest groups such as the Internet Association advocate for policymakers to only focus on consumer protection by "rooting out protectionist policies designed to stifle competition for incumbent industries" (Internet Association 2015: 2). These actors argue that a free market will regulate itself and that tech companies should have a maximum of freedom to decide their business practices. In this view, the sharing economy platforms are best left alone to impose their own self-regulatory regimes: "Sharing economy platforms already self-regulate through various mechanisms that are hardwired into the technology, including putting valuable information and data in the hands of consumers" (Internet Association 2015: 2). These include rating systems, in-platform payment systems, or GPS tracking. Apart from consumer empowerment, there are also some self-imposed efforts by platforms to improve the situation of their workers. For example, TaskRabbit introduced a site-wide minimum wage. The platform Favor allows workers to schedule shifts a week ahead of time and guarantees a $9/hour minimum wage. There are also some market-based solutions springing up in order to help with income volatility or saving for freelancers. There are even some startups like *Hello Alfred* that fully employ their workers, although these examples remain rare.

In the discussion around regulations, there are also smaller platforms and micro-entrepreneurs to consider.

> [Some] Etsy makers enter the platform with well-established businesses. But similar to most Airbnb hosts, the majority of Etsy sellers open their storefronts on the site as a hobby, investing only a bit of extra time and energy with the desire to make some spare cash. Naturally, these microentrepreneurs are not equipped to deal with different federal and state industry regulations and may not even be aware that these regulations exist. (...) Regulations, therefore, might create standards that sometimes make sense on a large scale but prove insurmountable to on a small scale. (Sundararajan 2016: Pos 3040–3044 Ch 6)

In this view, existing regulations were established with big business in mind but could stifle opportunities for small business that is encouraged by platforms like Etsy or Airbnb. Experts arguing in this way usually do not try get rid of all regulations, but they favor "peer regulation," which most often alludes to a market solution. In this sense, "peer regulation can represent an equitable way to regulate from within, one that is cost-efficient for society and leverages learning-by-doing in a way that is well suited to the scale of peer-to-peer" (Sundararajan 2016: Pos 3471 Ch 6). By delegating more responsibility toward the platforms, user data remains protected, which would not necessarily be the case if platforms had to hand over all their user data (Sundararajan 2016: Pos 3471 Ch 6).

In any case, platforms might not even wait for regulations to change but aim to be "first movers": "Platform entrepreneurs increasingly believe that if they possess a first-mover advantage, they can, in fact, remake existing law by creating new practices on their platforms that essentially establish new norms of behavior. It is often said in Silicon Valley, 'Don't ask permission; ask forgiveness'" (Kenney and Zysman 2016). As the platforms develop their own digital code, they also influence how one can use the platform. Apps like Uber have already influenced behavior and even if government wanted to change this behavior through the introduction of new regulations, they might be "constrained by the 'facts' in the software" (Kenney and Zysman 2016), namely how the app was coded. Therefore, platform businesses might influence how they can be regulated by proactively establishing new (digital) behavior and the infrastructure of their platforms. Governments often lack consistent ways to bring together these innovations with existing or new regulation.

Most platforms seem to reject regulation, especially labor regulation because of their "winner-take-all" structures that they share with many tech companies:

> [As] the power is centralized, the platform owner can become a virtual monopolist. In that case, the platform owner can squeeze the platform community—the drivers or customers on Lyft or Uber, the content providers, the consigners, the customers, essentially any of the participants in the ecosystem who are instrumental in creating the value in the first place. (. . .) In any case, a monopoly position or even a strong oligopoly might inhibit, or sharply constrain, further entrepreneurial efforts. (Kenney and Zysman 2016)

This tendency is increased through network effects. When network effects are particularly strong, as with digital platforms, monopolies are more likely because bigger networks are at an advantage and continue to grow (McAfee and Brynjolfsson 2017: Ch 6 Position 2189). Additionally, consumers only seem to value a few players in the market and are less likely to use several platforms at the same time. (McAfee and Brynjolfsson 2017: Ch 7 Position 2491). Therefore, many Internet companies are likely to become monopolists, such as Google or Amazon, and it seems to be especially hard to impose anti-trust and intellectual property rules on these globally operating Internet businesses:

> Policy and political interests among the players, even among the winners, are far from uniform. Consider such domains as antitrust policy, where the European Commission has done battle with U.S. tech companies; intellectual property, where the interests among information and communications technology firms and platform firms are less consistent than it might seem at first glance; network policy, where carriers such as AT&T have radically different interests from Netflix or Google; and labor market policies. (Kenney and Zysman 2016)

One of the areas of diverging interests is the issue of network neutrality which was considerably weakened under the Trump administration. Big broadband providers like AT&T advocate against neutrality, but businesses like Google fear that their services could be disadvantaged if neutrality is abandoned (McCabe 2019).

3.3.4 A Future Without Work? The Universal Basic Income

Apart from the discussion around changing worker classification or portability of benefits, there is a growing group of advocates who argue in favor of a more extreme solution, the universal basic income (UBI), for a future in which many people might not find good jobs nor earn enough to finance their lifestyle due to technological progress.

With the labor market changing so much, many look to the Nordic model of a more activating welfare state to improve the situation for workers, and indeed, it offers many opportunities and benefits such as training, job placement, and a basic income (Kenney and Zysman 2016). In contrast, the US welfare system is a very downsized version of the modern welfare state. After the last big welfare reform in the 1990s under Bill Clinton, the number of people receiving welfare decreased sharply, which is largely based on the temporal limitation of welfare provisions. This has led to a considerable amount of people being stuck in deep poverty. The reform also lacked a coherent strategy to effectively implement more active labor market policies (Economist 2016). Although the discussion around welfare reform has been rather mute for some time, recently there have been more and more discussions around the provision of a universal basic income (UBI) which grow louder with the rising concern over a jobless future. The discussion around the UBI in the USA is very much a tech-driven discussion that is heavily influenced by several Silicon Valley leaders.

In a 2017 article in WIRED, Issie Lapowsky describes the effects of the provision of free money on a community, which are often positive. The discussions about the UBI still largely lack any reliable data. Therefore, the example of an Eastern Band of Cherokee Indians in North Carolina is especially interesting. The tribe opened a casino on their territory, pledging to share the profits equally among their 15,000 members, basically providing a small basic income. The profits have grown over the years and have lifted many members of the community out of poverty. Additionally, the casino revenue was used to improve infrastructure, health care, and college funding for tribal members. "Now the body of research (. . .) has become a favorite point of reference for universal basic income advocates, providing some of the most compelling evidence yet of the positive effects of bestowing unconditional sums of cash on the poor" (Lapowsky 2017). And there are more examples: In the state of Alaska, the Alaska Permanent Fund hands out $1000–$2000 a year to Alaskan citizens based on oil extraction profits. Moreover, there are more and more cities and states experimenting with the UBI. For example, in the city of Utrecht and other Dutch cities, there are year-long basic income experiments in planning. In Finland, there are also pilot projects taking place. In 2016, Switzerland voted on a UBI proposition. In the end, the Swiss people rejected the proposal, but the referendum was met with a lot of interest and publicity worldwide (Stern and Kravitz 2016: Ch 8 Position 3285–3299).

The UBI idea is not new. In fact, Thomas Paine already proposed a basic income in 1795. Paine argued that each owner of cultivated land owed the community a rent for the land he held. Revenues of this ground rent could be used to fund a basic income for everyone (Stern and Kravitz 2016: Ch 8 Position 3123–3127). Since then, other thinkers were inspired by the idea of a basic income. Especially in Europe after WWI, people began to think about new ways to tackle poverty. Bertrand Russel, for example, said that "'a certain small income, sufficient for necessaries, should be secured to all, whether they work or not'" (Stern and Kravitz 2016: Ch 8 Position 3137). He also proposed that those people working for the good of the community should get bonuses, but in general, people should be free in choosing what to do with the money (Stern and Kravitz 2016: Ch 8 Position 3143f). Later in the 1960s and 1970s, the USA even came very close to introducing something like a UBI with Milton Friedman's proposal of the "negative income tax." This form of a UBI is delivered through the federal tax system providing subsidies to people whose income falls below a certain level. This was a plan to eventually replace the New Deal welfare provisions and to get rid of its expensive and ineffective bureaucracy, according to Friedman (Stern and Kravitz 2016: Ch 8 Position 3158). Another economist Friedrich August von Hayek also advocated for a basic floor of income, beneath which nobody should descend in society (Stern and Kravitz 2016: Ch 8 Position 3163). In 1967, Martin Luther King supported the idea of a basic income in order to end poverty, hunger, and the education deficit among all Americans. Supported through a presidential commission in 1969, a version of Friedman's negative income tax was recommended to Congress, with the House adopting the plan. Yet, the Senate rejected it in 1970 and again in 1972 (Stern and Kravitz 2016: Ch 8 Position 3192).

Since then, apart from the Alaska Permanent Fund which was established in the 1970s, the idea of the UBI moved more or less to the realms of academia. But since the advent of smart digital technology, many see the UBI as the solution for a "jobless" future. Lately, tech leaders like Mark Zuckerberg, Chris Hughes (Facebook), Elon Musk, or Sam Altman (Y Combinator) have been discussing the issue as a potential solution to the effects of automation and globalization and the anxiety created by it. Even politicians like Hillary Clinton have picked up the issue (for example in her book *What Happened*), as does Congress with, for example Ro Khanna, a Silicon Valley representative. He proposed a bill for a $1.4 trillion expansion of the Earned Income Tax Credit, which would effectively create a small basic income for low-income working families in the form of tax credits. In fact, the Earned Income Tax Credits have been expanded several times through bipartisan support. In Stockton, CA plans for a UBI experiment were announced, handing out $500 a month to 300,000 people. This is financed by the Economic Security Project, funded by Chris Hughes (Lapowsky 2017). There are other entrepreneurs who are interested in the issue of the UBI, such as Peter Barnes who published *With Liberty and Dividends for All* in 2014. In his book, he introduced a Paine-inspired version of the UBI. He is mainly interested in tackling pollution, arguing that companies that use our shared resources (and pollute them) should consequently pay fees to the government. The funds would be distributed among citizens and boost their income (Stern and Kravitz 2016: Ch 8 Position 3232f). As said before, the Earned Income Tax Credit already exists in the USA today and is actually a means to subsidize low to moderate income households, especially with children. It is not a *universal* basic income, but provides many low-wage workers with some extra yearly earnings. But the Earned Income Tax Credit only applies to families that are working and are filing their taxes. The absence of a safe long-term basic income through the welfare system might also be part of why the discussion around the UBI has become so widespread in the USA.

Opponents of a UBI claim that once people will be handed out free cash, they will stop working and just live on the handouts. Yet, other researchers looking at the data from the Cherokee tribe cannot confirm such claims. They have not found any impact on the overall labor participation among the members of the tribe. In fact, what they did find was mainly positive: Improved education due to longer school participation, as well as reduced crime rates with increases in household income (Lapowsky 2017). Additionally, advocates of the UBI claim that it would finally level the playing field on the job market, giving workers much more room to bargain for better conditions. Moreover, a UBI would not exceed a certain amount of money, raising the floor for many people, and making it possible to afford their basic needs, but it would not support any luxurious lifestyle (Stern and Kravitz 2016: Ch 8 Position 3606).

The UBI is seen as a possible solution for a future without enough work for everyone. Others claim that the UBI encourages entrepreneurship. Even though people claim that entrepreneurs are unusually prone to risk-taking, other studies show that a deciding factor is that entrepreneurs come from families with financial assets (Stern and Kravitz 2016: Ch 8 Position 3453). If people had a financial buffer to fall back on, they could be more willing to try their own business ideas. However, it is questionable if anything like the UBI is going to go forward with the USA's "sacred nature of hard work" (Stern and Kravitz 2016: Ch 8 Position 3632) engraved in its culture.

The popularity of the UBI idea can also be seen against the backdrop of rising inequality where the average income of the top 0.01% of Americans has tripled since 1980 and the bottom 90% has seen virtually no increases. A UBI can be seen as a way to offer people some security, regardless of whether they have a stable job and social benefits. Chis Hughes, one of the Facebook founders, claims that "'I'm proud of the work we did at Facebook, but I've also been very clear that the financial rewards I got were disproportionate to the work we put in. (. . .) In human history, you have not had self-made wealth among twentysomethings on the order of magnitude we have today'" (Lapowsky 2017). In order to tackle this problem of extreme inequality among Americans, Hughes founded the Economic Security Project in order to look into the potential of the UBI.

But even proponents of the UBI do not agree on the concept, including the amount of money or whether the "universal" part is desirable, basically bestowing already wealthy people with the same amount of cash as the poor. Moreover, it is questionable if the other social provisions such as Medicare, Medicaid, food stamps, and other provisions should be abandoned in favor of the UBI. Naturally, the UBI cannot be the solution to all problems of today and tomorrow. Drug addiction will not be eradicated by the introduction of UBI, nor will the disappearance of many unionized jobs be balanced out by cash provisions. Yet, some see the UBI as a measure to lessen the consequences of extreme poverty, especially also for future generations. The children of those receiving the cash from the Cherokee tribe, for example, have a lot more opportunities today than their parents ever had. The impact of these unconditional payments can often be best evaluated in future generations. Therefore, it is certainly not a fast-track solution to today's inequality issues:

> if anything is to be learned from the Cherokee experiment, it's this: To imagine that a basic income, or something like it, would suddenly satisfy the disillusioned, out-of-work Rust Belt worker is as wrongheaded as imagining it would do no good at all, or drive people to stop working. There is a third possibility: that an infusion of cash into struggling households would lift up the youth in those households (. . .), until finally, when they come of age, they are better prepared for the brave new world of work, whether the robots are coming or not. (Lapowsky 2017)

The UBI is usually debated in the context of a future where there might not be enough work for everyone. In an article from The Atlantic called *A World without Work*, author Derek Thompson entertains this idea and its consequences. Total unemployment is unlikely, in his view, especially with technology only gradually changing the job market:

> What does the 'end of work' mean, exactly? It does not mean the imminence of total unemployment, nor is the United States remotely likely to face, say, 30 or 50 percent unemployment within the next decade. Rather, technology could exert a slow but continual downward pressure on the value and availability of work—that is, on wages and on the share of prime-age workers with full-time jobs. Eventually, by degrees, that could create a new normal, where the expectation that work will be a central feature of adult life dissipates for a significant portion of society. (Thompson 2015)

Experts already see slower job growth, even after the recessions, whereas automation is moving on fast. With these developments, is "*any job truly safe?*" (Thompson 2015). More computer power and automation means that our everyday products become much cheaper, even former luxury products. And this will most likely grow wealth, but only "aggregated up to the level of the national economy" (Thompson 2015), not necessarily for the individual person who might lose his or her job. If this happens, then one of the main pillars of identification in the USA, hard work, will lose its significance: "The sanctity and preeminence of work lie at the heart of the country's politics, economics, and social interactions. What might happen if work goes away?" (Thompson 2015)

Technology has diminished human labor as a driver for economic growth. Economic growth and job growth are not necessarily linked anymore. This can also be seen in the most valuable firms today, as they employ rather low numbers of people. The labor force participation rate also remains lower in the USA than in many other countries (OECD 2020). Underemployment of recent graduates is also growing, even years after the Great Recession. People with college degrees are now more likely to take a job that was usually filled by a person with lower education. Opponents of the technology argument say that so far, no machines have fully replaced humans and human solutions and machines exist side by side. Often, companies take many years to fully implement technology that replaces humans. While this seems to be the case, in the meantime, the need for human labor in many occupations is likely to gradually decrease. "The most-common occupations in the United States are retail salesperson, cashier, food and beverage server, and office clerk. Together, these four jobs employ 15.4 million people—nearly 10 percent of the labor force, or more workers than there are in Texas and Massachusetts combined. Each is highly susceptible to automation" (Thompson 2015).

Other experts would say that the human mind cannot be replaced, especially when it comes to creative tasks. Yet, as argued before, experts like Andrew McAfee and Erik Brynjolfsson have shown that machines get better and better at coming up with their own ideas. Additionally, the creative part of the job market is easily overstated, according to Derek Thompson. Nine out of ten jobs today have existed 100 years ago and just about 5% of the jobs generated between 1993 and 2013 came from the high-tech sector. The high-tech sector does not require a large amount of workers and will most likely not be the source of many people's income in the future (Thompson 2015). In their occupational projections, the US Bureau of Labor Statistics sees most future jobs in low-skill occupations, and considerably fewer in the high-tech sector (BLS 2020). Moreover, many people will not be able to reach the educational attainment necessary to pursue a career in high tech, and it will most certainly not be those who have been replaced through machines that go on to receive the highest academic merits (Avent 2016). So will we really run out of jobs?

> Is that certain—or certainly imminent? No. The signs so far are murky and suggestive. The most fundamental and wrenching job restructurings and contractions tend to happen during recessions: we'll know more after the next couple of downturns. But the possibility seems significant enough—and the consequences disruptive enough—that we owe it to ourselves to start thinking about what society could look like without universal work. (Thompson 2015)

Technology's largest impact on jobs and wages is most likely not imminent or even fatal. The next few decades, as well as the pace and severity of the business cycle, will show how much pressure technology will truly put on work and income in the future. Yet, there are many people who try to advance worker interests today by raising the minimum wage, build union power, or try to tackle existing income inequality. These are important measures to make existing jobs more valuable and to facilitate a pathway to a middle-class lifestyle. There are also others who want to "mediate" between present problems on the job market and possible issues of the future. They advocate for better education, better infrastructure, fostering innovation, more stimulus for the economy, raising the minimum wage, simplifying the tax system, or proposing a shorter work week (Stern and Kravitz 2016: Ch 7 Position 2805). Work-sharing is mentioned as one possible solution to tackle a future where employment might disappear or growth remains weak. Unions have argued in favor of work hour sharing between the employed and unemployed for a long time, in order to achieve higher employment and more sustainable growth. During the Great Recession, the topic has also received greater attention as shortened working hours were introduced in Germany to prevent lay-offs (Zwickl et al. 2015: 246f.). Thus, work sharing might be an option for sustaining employment in times of crises, as well as a means to reconcile family and a career. Yet, if the future of employment as a whole is unknown and even today wages are not high enough to get by, work sharing cannot be the sole solution to improve the overall situation of today's and tomorrow's workers.

It remains questionable if the USA, a country that champions hard work and was built on the foundations of a Protestant work ethic, can come to terms with a situation where there might not be enough work for everyone to live on. As of now, there are already many people who work full-time, but are not earning a living wage or are unable to maintain a middle-class lifestyle. Future predictions are murky. As Derek Thompson has said, it is likely that technology will gradually be adopted throughout all economic sectors and that the next few economic downturns will show how many jobs will be replaced by technology after all. It seems clear, however, that there is a growing concern throughout the Western world that the consistent historical pattern of technological progress with the replacement and subsequent creation of new jobs might be fading in the digital society we are growing into.

3.3.5 *Present and Future of the Platform Economy in the World of Work*

As seen in the discussion above, many digital platforms offer a flexible and independent way to work with easy and fast access to all kinds of opportunities that many people might value more than a steady nine-to-five job. For consumers, the sharing economy platforms are certainly a great deal as they have "democratized luxury services by making amateur chauffeurs, chefs and personal assistants available to perform occasional work once largely dominated by full-time professionals. Venture capital firms seem convinced" (Singer 2014). Many platforms were able to accumulate massive backing by big investors, catapulting some of their founders to extreme wealth in a short amount of time. But for the labor force, the situation remains uncertain. There seems to be a general push toward independent work in the American economy and these independents are very diverse. Yet, the growing group of independent "supplementers" points to an overall need for extra income among many workers today and those occasional independents might crowd out full-time workers in certain areas such as transportation.

The question remains if workers will be able to improve their situation in the future and whether the platforms themselves will be helpful in doing so. As long as other sources for stable employment exist, independent (platform) work can be a supplementary option. And there are some signs that platforms are willing to make some improvements. TaskRabbit has started to offer discounts on health insurance and accounting services; Lyft is teaming up with the Freelancers Union so that their drivers can be eligible for a health plan and other benefit programs (Singer 2014). These are first steps in the direction of offering the workforce better working conditions in the platform economy.

There are also more and more initiatives that want to address general issues freelancers face today. Examples of union-like organizations that were created include Coworker.org or the Freelancers Union (Stern and Kravitz 2016: Ch 5 Position 2104). There are also more and more tech and platform workers themselves who push for unionization on the local level, such as Kickstarter or Instacart workers (Gurley 2020). Established unions have been slow or noncooperative in response to the growth of the gig economy and the independent workforce. Most union leaders seem to be stuck in the "single-minded devotion to the collective bargaining model as the only way to represent workers" (Stern and Kravitz 2016: Ch 7 Position 2694). The question remains how politicians on all levels (federal, state, local) will respond to this development, whether they will strengthen the position of workers or whether they will leave the workers' situation as it is, hoping the platforms themselves or the market might find solutions. On the local level, such as in Seattle or California, there are more and more efforts by government to give gig workers more bargaining power or to reclassify them (Wingfield and Isaac 2015; Conger and Scheiber 2019).

The American people are often not aware of the issues surrounding independent work or the platform economy. A Pew survey from 2016 found that users' views on how best to regulate ride-hailing or home-sharing services (as two of the most well-known sharing services) stand in contrast to their overall political leanings. Even politically liberal users tended to support the idea that both services should be legal and tax-free and should exist outside of regulatory structures (Pew-Research-Center 2016a). Additionally, when it comes to regulation there is a lot of variation from state to state, city to city, as many labor regulations are set locally.

The question is whether critics are right that "for-profit platforms have coopted what began as a progressive, socially transformative idea" (Schor 2014: 10) and are squeezing it out for as much profit as they can, or whether they are going to accept some form of regulation. It seems that in certain areas such as taxation or insurance, platforms support regulation (Schor 2014: 10). Yet, the situation of the independent labor force remains an unsolved issue. As said before, there are signs that platforms like Uber are working on the local and state level to push lawmakers for exemption laws for their digital contracting businesses.

In general, the situation of workers, in and out of the sharing economy, is dependent on how the labor market as a whole will develop. That is why there is

> difficulty assessing the impact of these new earning opportunities [because] they [were] being introduced during a period of high unemployment and rapid labor market restructuring. Working conditions and protections are already being eroded, real wages are declining, and labor's share of national income in the US has declined to historic lows. If the labor market continues to worsen for workers, their conditions will continue to erode, and it will not be because of sharing opportunities. Alternatively, if labor markets improve, sharers can demand more of the platforms because they have better alternatives. (Schor 2014: 10)

In the past 10 years, the US economy has seen a historic economic boom period: Growth rates were up and unemployment rates down. Nevertheless, labor participation has not picked up to the same extent. Some people have opted out of the workforce altogether because of a lack of good jobs. Some of them opt for independent work but not all do. The growth of the independent workforce and alternative work arrangements is a long-term trend that seems to continue despite higher growth rates and lower unemployment. Yet, the problems that many platforms have with worker retainment could also point to the fact that people value other options than gig work if they are available.

Thus, politicians are faced with numerous issues concerning independent work in the future. Some market regulations might have to be adapted to the new digital competition in order to protect consumers and workers. This also includes more and more calls for competition enforcement in the digital market.

The issues of social security for the new digital workforce also have to be addressed, as well as taxation of the new services (Eichhorst and Spermann 2015: 3). Businesses and investors expect the platforms to grow tremendously over the next decades. This could also lead to new markets being accessed and new competition replacing old business models (Eichhorst and Spermann 2015: 6ff). Although many platforms reject regulation at first, they usually fare well with it once some regulation is introduced, also because users have more security, which can ultimately lead to more consumption. There are already some examples of platforms trying to improve the situation of their providers, as well as carrying out regulation such as tax collection. However, the status and situation of providers, or workers on the platforms, remains an unsolved issue and the source of much of the controversy surrounding the image and value of digital (labor) platforms.

Especially with the unknown future of employment, there still is hope that the sharing economy platforms could make a difference and transform the economy into a more sustainable and empowering way of consumption. With the growth of the independent workforce, platforms are seen as a way toward easy and fast access to additional work. Consumers can personalize their consumption in creative ways "as technology returns the tools of the assembly line to individuals, democratizing the means of mass production. Something like this future is already present in the small but growing number of industrial shops called 'makerspaces' that have popped up in the United States and around the world" (Thompson 2015). Even the most commercial providers of the sharing economy platforms try to establish a brand around personal consumption, awareness for the environment, individuality, and "doing the right thing." They also champion their providers as entrepreneurs (if they want or not) who are no longer "wage slaves" but their own boss. This positive framing of the sharing economy platforms, although less pronounced than in the beginning, seems to prevail to some extent. More on the different views of the sharing economy platforms will follow later in this book (Chaps. 4–6).

Apart from the influence of sharing economy platforms on the future workforce, there is a general anxiety that future employment will be undermined more and more through further automation. This includes the dislocation of workers, as well as the push toward more alternative work arrangements. There are experts like Steven Hill who argue in favor of a multi-employer, portable benefits' system in order to close the 1099 loophole that incentivizes employers to switch to contractors wherever they can. Additionally, there are more and more calls to alter the categories of employed and self-employed in order to adapt to the new circumstances of more and more independents in the US economy. The local attempts to shape labor legislation to exempt workers contracted over digital platforms from employment status show the determination of platforms to maintain their business model of contracting. This could make the situation of digital independents more certain in their (online) activities but would exclude them from any employment benefits. However, even in the current situation platforms could provide their workers with more services without having to employ them right away and, in fact, some platforms do. Moreover, the universal basic income (UBI) is discussed as an option to tackle a future without enough work and income for everyone, albeit remaining a niche topic.

The future of employment in the era of digital automation is unknown. It remains to be seen how labor markets will fare after the next economic downturns and whether job growth will remain slow and mostly located in low-wage sectors. All in all, the future impact of the platform economy is going to be immense and most likely impact our lives even more than it already does. Especially with the further development of AI and the Internet of Things, more and more technology and related platforms are going to enter our lives. The question remains if the platform economy is going to be largely a target for big investment or also a way to establish more "everyone-to-everyone" transactions and a desirable access to easy and flexible work. The issues surrounding the platform economy, such as legal rules, taxation, or labor issues, will remain contested areas well into the future.

References

Aeppel T (2016) How the on-demand/gig economy is redefining work. MIT IDE Research Brief. MIT Initiative on the Digital Economy

Avent R (2016) The wealth of humans: work and its absence in the twenty-first century. Allen Lane/ Penguin, New York/London

Belk R (2013) You are what you can access: sharing and collaborative consumption online. J Bus Res 67(8):1595–1600. https://doi.org/10.1016/j.jbusres.2013.10.001

Bellafante G (2018) Uber and the false hopes of the sharing economy. The New York Times. https://www.nytimes.com/2018/08/09/nyregion/uber-nyc-vote-drivers-ride-sharing.html. Accessed 19 July 2020

Bergen M, Eidelson J (2018) Inside Google's shadow workforce. Bloomberg. https://www.bloomberg.com/amp/news/articles/2018-07-25/inside-google-s-shadow-workforce?__twitter_impression=true. Accessed 11 Dec 2018

Bernhardt A, Thomason S (2017) What do we know about gig work in California? An analysis of independent contracting (trans: Center UBL). UC Berkeley Center for Labor and Education, Berkeley, CA

BLS (2020) Occupational outlook handbook: most new jobs. U.S. Bureau of Labor Statistics. https://www.bls.gov/ooh/most-new-jobs.htm. Accessed 3 Mar 2020

Botsman R (2013) The sharing economy lacks a shared definition. FastCompany. https://www.fastcompany.com/3022028/the-sharing-economy-lacks-a-shared-definition#4. Accessed 1 June 2017

Botsman R (2014) Collaborative economy: a transformative lens, not a start-up trend. http://www.collaborativeconsumption.com/2014/11/27/collaborative-economy-a-transformative-lens-not-a-start-up-trend/. Accessed 1 June 2017

Buchak G (2018) Financing the gig economy. University of Chicago, Chicago

Bucher E, Fieseler C, Lutz C (2016) What's mine is yours (for a nominal fee)—exploring the spectrum of utilitarian to altruistic motives for Internet-mediated sharing. Comput Hum Behav 62:316–326. https://doi.org/10.1016/j.chb.2016.04.002

Conger K, Scheiber N (2019) California bill makes app-based companies treat workers as employees. The New York Times. https://www.nytimes.com/2019/09/11/technology/california-gig-economy-bill.html. Accessed 5 Mar 2020

Conger K, Satariano A, Isaac M (2020) Pandemic erodes gig economy work. The New York Times. https://www.nytimes.com/2020/03/18/technology/gig-economy-pandemic.html. Accessed 17 June 2020

de la Merced MJ, Conger K (2019) Uber I.P.O. values ride-hailing giant at $82.4 billion. The New York Times. https://www.nytimes.com/2019/05/09/technology/uber-ipo-stock-price.html. Accessed 10 May 2019

Dickey MR (2020) CA ballot measure that keeps gig workers as independent contractors passes. TechCrunch. https://techcrunch.com/2020/11/03/prop-22-results/. Accessed 13 Mar 2021

Economist (2016) Welfare reform—a patchy record at 20. The Economist. https://www.economist.com/leaders/2016/08/20/a-patchy-record-at-20. Accessed 8 Apr 2019

Eichhorst W, Spermann A (2015) Sharing economy—Chancen, Risiken und Gestaltungsmöglichkeiten für den Arbeitsmarkt. IZA Research Report, vol 69. IZA, Bonn

Farrell D, Greig F (2016) Paychecks, paydays, and the online platform economy: big data on income volatility. JPMorgan Chase Institute

Farrell D, Greig F, Hamoudi A (2018) The online platform economy in 2018: drivers, workers, sellers, and lessors. JPMorgan Chase & Co Institute. https://www.jpmorganchase.com/institute/research/labor-markets/report-ope-2018.htm. Accessed 10 May 2021

Frenken K, Schor J (2017) Putting the sharing economy into perspective. Environ Innovat Soc Transit 23:3–10

Gansky L (2011) The Mesh: six reasons why the Sharing Society (aka The Mesh) will Trump the ownership society. ChangeThis. https://mktgsensei.com/AMAE/Consumer%20Behavior/The%20Mesh%20Manifesto.pdf. Accessed 10 May 2021

Gurley LK (2020) Instacart workers win historic union election. Vice. https://www.vice.com/en_us/article/qjdvgm/instacart-workers-win-historic-union-election. Accessed 5 Mar 2020

Hall JV, Krueger AB (2016) An analysis of the labor market for Uber's driver-partners in the United States. NBER working paper series, vol 22843. National Bureau of Economic Research, Cambridge, MA

Hamari J, Sjöklint M, Ukkonen A (2016) The sharing economy: why people participate in collaborative consumption. J Assoc Inform Sci Technol 67(9):2047–2059. https://doi.org/10.1002/asi.23552

Heller N (2017) Is the gig economy working? The New Yorker. http://www.newyorker.com/magazine/2017/05/15/is-the-gig-economy-working?mbid=nl_170508_Daily&CNDID=49221241&spMailingID=10976418&spUserID=MTg0OTkxNzg0Nzg3S0&spJobID=1160695595&spReportId=MTE2MDY5NTU5NQS2. Accessed 10 May 2017

Hill S (2015) New economy, new social contract: a plan for a safety net in a mulitemployer world. Economic Growth Program. New America. New York

Internet Association (2015) The sharing economy sharing economy. Internet Association

Kenney M, Zysman J (2016) The rise of the platform economy. Issues Sci Technol XXXII(3)

Lapowsky I (2017) Free money: the surprising effects of a basic income supplied by government. WIRED. https://www.wired.com/story/free-money-the-surprising-effects-of-a-basic-income-supplied-by-government/?mbid=nl_111317_daily_list1_p2. Accessed 16 Nov 2017

Luca M (2016) Designing online marketplaces: trust and reputation mechanisms. NBER Working Paper Series, vol 22616. National Bureau of Economic Research, Cambridge, MA

Manyika J, Lund S, Bughin J, Robinson K, Mischke J, Mahajan D (2016) Independent work: choice, necessity, and the gig economy. McKinsey Global Institute, San Francisco, CA

Martin CJ (2016) The sharing economy: a pathway to sustainability or a nightmarish form of neoliberal capitalism? Ecol Econ 121:149–159. https://doi.org/10.1016/j.ecolecon.2015.11.027

Martin CJ, Upham P, Budd L (2015) Commercial orientation in grassroots social innovation: insights from the sharing economy. Ecol Econ 118:240–251. https://doi.org/10.1016/j.ecolecon.2015.08.001

Mason S (2018) Level up—high score, low pay: why the gig economy loves gamification. The Guardian. https://www.theguardian.com/business/2018/nov/20/high-score-low-pay-gamification-lyft-uber-drivers-ride-hailing-gig-economy. Accessed 17 Dec 2018

McAfee A, Brynjolfsson E (2017) Machine, platform, crowd: harnessing our digital future (Kindle version). Norton, New York

McCabe D (2019) Court upholds net neutrality repeal, with some caveats. The New York Times. https://www.nytimes.com/2019/10/01/technology/net-neutrality-repeal-broadband.html. Accessed 5 Mar 2020

Nadeem S, Schor J, Walker ET, Lee CW, Parigi P, Cook K (2016) Viewpoints on the sharing economy. Contexts 14(1):12–19

OECD (2020) OECD economic surveys: United States 2020. OECD, Paris

Olson MJ, Kemp SJ (2015) Sharing economy: an in-depth look at its evolution and trajectory across industries. Piper Jaffray Investment Research

Parrott JA, Reich M (2018) An earnings standard for New York City's app-based drivers: economic analysis and policy assessment. The New School Center for New York City Affairs, Center on Wage and Employment Dynamics, University of California, Berkeley, New York City

Pew-Research-Center (2016a) Gig work, online selling and home sharing. Pew Research Center. https://www.pewresearch.org/internet/2016/11/17/gig-work-online-selling-and-home-sharing/. Accessed 10 May 2021

Pew-Research-Center (2016b) Shared, collaborative and on demand: the new digital economy. Pew Research Center. http://www.pewinternet.org/2016/05/19/the-new-digital-economy/. Accessed 10 May 2021

Reinert H, Reinert ES (2006) Creative destruction in economics: Nietzsche, Sombart, Schumpeter. In: Friedrich Nietzsche (1844-1900). Springer, Boston, MA, pp 55–85

Richardson L (2015) Performing the sharing economy. Geoforum 67:121–129. https://doi.org/10.1016/j.geoforum.2015.11.004

Scheiber N (2019) Is gig work a job? Uber and others are maneuvering to shape the answer. The New York Times. https://www.nytimes.com/2019/03/26/business/economy/gig-economy-lobbying.html. Accessed 8 Apr 2019

Schor J (2014) Debating the sharing economy. Great Transition Initiative

Schor JB, Fitzmaurice C, Carfagna LB, Attwood-Charles W, Poteat ED (2016) Paradoxes of openness and distinction in the sharing economy. Poetics 54:66–81. https://doi.org/10.1016/j.poetic.2015.11.001

Sheng E (2018) Silicon Valley's dirty secret: using a shadow workforce of contract employees to drive profits. CNBC. https://www.cnbc.com/2018/10/22/silicon-valley-using-contract-employees-to-drive-profits.html. Accessed 5 Nov 2018

Singer N (2014) In the sharing economy, workers find both freedom and uncertainty. New York Times. https://www.nytimes.com/2014/08/17/technology/in-the-sharing-economy-workers-find-both-freedom-and-uncertainty.html?_r=0. Accessed 9 Dec 2016

Sperling G (2015) How Airbnb combats middle class income stagnation. Airbnb

Stern A, Kravitz L (2016) Raising the floor. Public Affairs, New York

Sundararajan A (2016) The sharing economy: the end of employment and the rise of crowd-based capitalism (Kindle edition). MIT Press, Cambridge, MA

Telles RJ (2016) Digital matching firms: a new definiton in the "sharing economy" space. ESA Issue Brief, vol #01-16. US Department of Commerce Economics and Statistics Administration, Office of the Chief Economist, Washington, DC

Thompson D (2015) A world without work. The Atlantic, July/August 2015 Issue

Tolentino J (2017) The gig economy celebrates working yourself to death. The New Yorker. http://www.newyorker.com/culture/jia-tolentino/the-gig-economy-celebrates-working-yourself-to-death. Accessed 10 May 2017

Tussyadiah IP (2016) Factors of satisfaction and intention to use peer-to-peer accommodation. Int J Hospit Manag 55:70–80. https://doi.org/10.1016/j.ijhm.2016.03.005

van Welsum D (2016) Sharing is caring? Not quite. Some observations about "the sharing economy". World Development Report 2016 Digital Dividends. World Bank

White GB (2016) Uber and Lyft Are failing black riders. The Atlantic. https://www.theatlantic.com/business/archive/2016/10/uber-lyft-and-the-false-promise-of-fair-rides/506000/. Accessed 6 Mar 2020

Wingfield N, Isaac M (2015) Seattle will allow Uber and Lyft drivers to form unions. The New York Times. https://www.nytimes.com/2015/12/15/technology/seattle-clears-the-way-for-uber-drivers-to-form-a-union.html. Accessed 5 Mar 2020

Zwickl K, Disslbacher F, Stagl S (2015) Work-sharing for a sustainable economy. Ecol Econ 121:246–253. https://doi.org/10.1016/j.ecolecon.2015.06.009

Chapter 4
Corpus Analysis: Automation, the Future of Work, and the Platform Economy Reflected in Political and Public Discourse

The previous chapters of this book have analyzed several different concepts and developments crucial to technological progress in recent years such as the Network Society, automation, digitization, and the platform economy. A special focus was put on sharing economy platforms and their impact on the future of work in the USA. In recent years, the term *future of work* seems to encompass a lot of the questions around and consequences of the impact of technology on the world of work, both negative and positive. The future of work has emerged as a crucial topic in academia and as well as in the public and can be found in many articles and publications around the topic of technological progress. In the following, this book moves on from tracing the developments of technological progress including more recent trends in the digital realm and the impact of technology on income inequality and the labor market in the USA to the discourse around the future of work that is prevalent in the USA today.

4.1 Political and Public Discourse[1] as Source Material

> It is difficult to conceive of any political action which does not involve using language: political speeches, newspaper editorials, press conferences, Acts of Parliament, declarations of war and peace negotiations, to name but a few. Language is vital to the process of

[1]Discourse as a term is not easy to define. Linguistically, it is all units of language above the level of the sentence. However, there are further definitions, seeing discourse as not only a group of sentences but also as a practice, a way of talking and thinking about a subject by a certain community (McEnery and Hardie 2012: 133f). In a poststructuralist definition, "discourse is not studied to find out about 'the real world', but rather to find out how 'the real world' is talked about" (McEnery and Hardie 2012: 135). Discourse in this book mainly refers to the amount of all expression or manifestations around a certain topic by a group of actors. In this case, the subject matter is technological progress that is discussed by political stakeholders and the public.

N. Rauscher, *The Future of Work in the United States*, Contributions to Economics,
https://doi.org/10.1007/978-3-030-82307-8_4

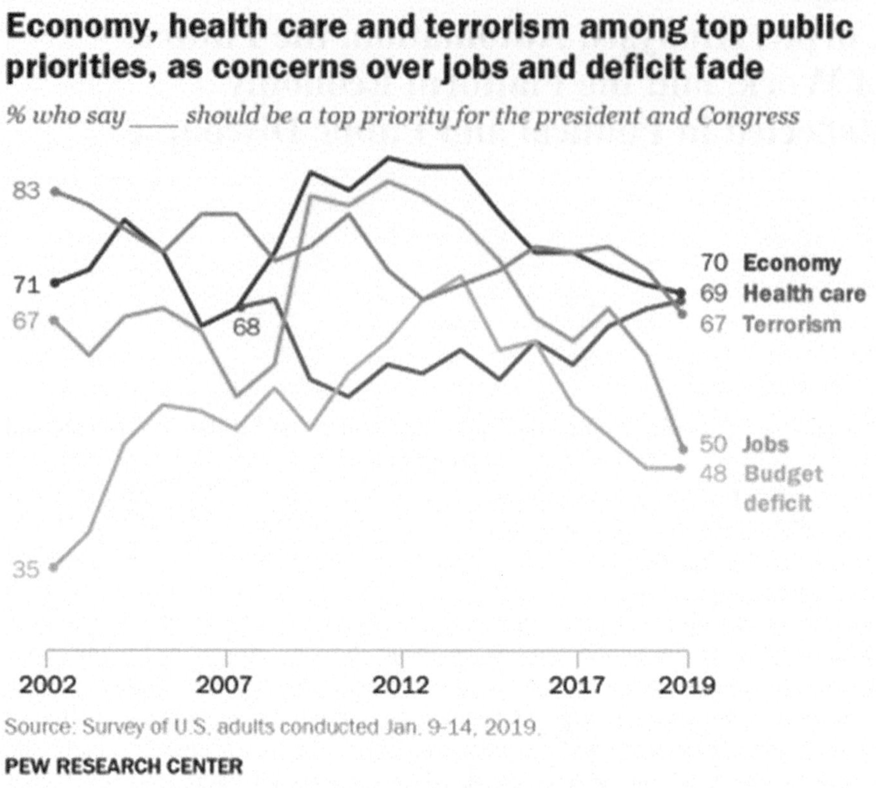

Fig. 4.1 Public priorities according to Pew Research Center (Pew-Research-Center 2019)

> transforming political will and power into social governance and all political actions are prepared, accompanied, and controlled by language. (Partington 2013: 1)

If and how societal issues are discussed in the public eye and in the political sphere can shape the way we think about these issues and can affect our policy preferences. This communication can have different channels, for example media outlets. But some issues are more important to the public than others, especially in times of elections. The economy is of great concern to most voters and is discussed in the public to a large extent. In surveys, concerns over the economy usually rank among the highest priorities for Americans (Fig. 4.1).

Political careers can be sustained or come under pressure depending on the economic outlook, something that is not totally under the control of politics or economic actors alone. Perceptions of the economy might be even more important than the actual state of the economy. Economic perceptions are reflected by the media and possibly shape our policy preferences. In the age of social media, such perceptions and preferences seem to be even more decisive and are reinforced through the platforms' own algorithms (Ellis 2019).

But certain perceptions have not only been relevant since social media platforms have become ubiquitous. For example, past studies have looked at economic conditions and attitudes toward the government and how they are linked, alluding to President Bush Sr's and Bill Clinton's presidential campaign in the 1990s. Clinton succeeded to discredit President Bush by suggesting the economy was in downturn due to the administration's ineptitude. This was one significant factor in Clinton's electoral success as support for the government and favorable economic conditions usually coincide. The Clinton campaign famously coined the slogan *It's the economy, stupid.* By the reflection and perpetuation of this particular perception of the economic conditions of the country, media outlets contributed to this effect: "Public *perceptions* of the economy matter as well. In fact, past work suggests that economic perceptions influence vote intentions and government evaluations above and beyond the impact of the actual economy (. . .)" (Soroka et al. 2015: 457). The media and the public at large are receptive to

> where the economy is going in the future, in addition to—and at least sometimes more than—where it has been or currently is. (. . .) this has consequences for public assessments of the economy, which themselves also affect media coverage. All of this matters, we believe, for the way in which the economy matters for political behavior. (Soroka et al. 2015: 458)

Therefore, political communication and economic trends mutually affect each other constantly: "if media matter, and if media capture—mostly, at least—the tone of changes in the future economy, then we should expect to see public opinion react not so much to what currently is going on in the economy, but what is likely to be going on soon" (Soroka et al. 2015: 471).

The examples the authors present here are illustrative to show that strategic political communication and political and public discourse around certain themes can stir and mark people's perception. If and in which way a topic is picked up by political actors and the media can shape the public perception around certain areas. This book looks at how the discourse around the topics of automation, the future of work, and the platform economy is shaped in political and public settings. As said before, the economy is an important reference point for people's decisions and their attitudes toward the future. How the economy will develop under the influence of more and more technological progress is of great interest to a lot of people. It can be seen as a driver for economic opportunity, which has been the case for the last two centuries. At the same time, technological progress has always ignited fears of job loss and economic marginalization. Therefore, this work aims to study the discourse around the themes of technological progress in the USA (automation, the platform economy, the future of work) using textual data. By drawing from existing tools and methods of corpus linguistics such as computational analysis of textual data, frequency analysis, or collocation analysis, as well as by combining this quantitative approach with a qualitative analysis of the textual material, this book will provide insights into the discourse around technological progress in the USA. The political discourse around these issues will be investigated using exemplary material from committee hearings from the US Congress. The public discourse will be investigated through the examination of journalistic articles from different outlets, namely the *New York Times*, the *Washington Post*, and the *Wall Street Journal*.

Using textual data as the basis for this research may raise the question why it is worthwhile to study language and discourse at all. Language and discourse can deliver significant points of reference for the treatment of a subject. Discourse "signals the particular view of language in use (...) as an element of social life which is closely interconnected with other elements" (Fairclough 2007: 3). And indeed, the study of language as pioneered by corpus linguists on whose research this work draws is becoming more and more integrated into other disciplines in the humanities and social sciences. Many scholars outside of the field of linguistics have realized how much our "social and cultural world that we as human beings inhabit exists, and is expressed and recorded, to a very large degree by means of language" (McEnery and Hardie 2012: 230). Language and texts can have social effects; in fact, texts are elements of social events that can "have causal effects—i.e., they bring about changes" (Fairclough 2007: 8). Fairclough argues that texts bring about changes in our knowledge, in our beliefs, attitudes, or values, which is the most immediate effect texts can have. Discourse goes beyond the mere text as it is also a practice, "a characteristic type of language use found in a group of texts, or at large in the language community. Further, discourse are not only ways of talking about something, they are also ways of thinking about it" (McEnery and Hardie 2012: 133). In this way, studying discourse aims "to uncover how groups of people conceptualise themselves, their social setting, other groups of people and the issues that matter to them" (McEnery and Hardie 2012: 133). In the long run, language and texts can shape people's identities, contribute to change in a larger setting like international affairs, industrial relations, education, etc. (Fairclough 2007: 8). "In sum, texts have causal effects upon, and contribute to changes in, people (beliefs, attitudes, etc.), actions, social relations, and the material world" (Fairclough 2007: 8).

Although Fairclough believes that texts can have the ability to change, the causality aspect of them is complex.

> We need, however, to be clear what sort of causality this is. It is not a simple mechanical causality—we cannot for instance claim that particular features of texts automatically bring about particular changes in people's knowledge or behavior or particular social or political effects. Nor is causality the same as regularity: there may be no regular cause-effect pattern associated with a particular type of text or particular features of texts, but that does not mean that there are no causal effects. (Fairclough 2007: 8)

Causal effects cannot easily be traced back to certain parts or features of texts. Nevertheless, this does not mean that texts have no causal effects at all. Therefore, analysis of discourse, language, and texts is complex, remains partial, and might not be as complete as we might wish for (Fairclough 2007: 14). Additionally, a textual analysis is always, in a way, subjective. "There is no such thing as an 'objective' analysis of text, if by that we mean an analysis which simply describes what is 'there' in the text without being 'biased' by the 'subjectivity' of the analyst" (Fairclough 2007: 14). Like all other analyses, the researcher brings his or her background to the table and looks at her subject in a certain way. This is not different with textual data. Nevertheless, there is much to be gained from studying discourse as it is the expression of actors' attitudes toward certain subjects and lets us make assumptions about conceptualizations and changes in these attitudes. The use of textual corpora helps in this regard because of the "incremental effect of discourse" (Baker 2006: 13). Discourses are part of society and "are circulated and strengthened (...) via language use," which makes it the task of a discourse researcher to illuminate these underlying discourses with the help of (large) corpora that allow us to discover and analyze language data and language use without being solely reliant on our intuition (or biases) (Baker 2006: 13).

It is vital to study discourse as it can be seen as a social organization that can illuminate certain actors and social practices that shape this discourse. In this setting, language has a key function. Language has "become more salient, more important than it used to be, and in fact a crucial aspect of the social transformations which are going on—one cannot make sense of them without thinking about language"(Fairclough 2007: 203). One does not need to be a linguist to think this way. Other social researchers are looking at language and its importance. Fairclough mentions the French sociologist Pierre Bourdieu who wrote about the neoliberal turn in the world. He stressed the importance of neoliberal discourse and the performative power of language in order to remove obstacles on the way toward "New Capitalism" (Fairclough 2007: 203). Fairclough also mentions that language is an element with ever greater importance in today's 'knowledge society' where information is key: "The greater salience of 'knowledge' or 'information' in economic and social processes and changes amounts in practical terms to the greater salience of language and discourse—this is the form in which 'knowledge' is produced, distributed, and consumed" (Fairclough 2007: 204).

There are many more scholars who have looked into the meaning of the study of discourse, and they all look at discourse in a different way (McEnery and Hardie 2012: 135). However, it can be useful to look at discourse not in order to "find out about 'the real world', but rather to find out how 'the real world' is talked about" (McEnery and Hardie 2012: 135). All this shows that it is a viable and necessary endeavor in our time of the 'information age' to look at language and texts, at discourse generally, in order to discern how certain topics and issues are treated.

> The universalist view states that we understand our world in terms of conceptual primes, and language simply reflects these possibilities. Language is the vehicle for expressing our system of thought, with this system being independent of the language itself. The relativist argues language and thought are inextricably intertwined, in that available linguistic resources affect our understanding of the world. Our world is not given to us directly but is continually mediated by language. (Wilson 2015: 777)

Therefore, this book takes a look at the discourse around technological progress and how this topic is reflected in the public and political realm in the USA. The aim of this work is to compare "technological change discourse" in the public and political sphere in order to illuminate how these themes are mediated by language and how this gives meaning to our understanding of said topics.

There are several studies in and outside of linguistics that look at political discourse specifically, which is in itself a term that cannot be easily defined. Political discourse can be seen as a piece of talk or text produced by or for political actors; it could also refer to the study of political language "where the focus is on aspects of language structure as it constitutes and displays specific political functions" (Wilson 2015: 775f). Yet, "while linguistic analysis is central to political discourse, it must be seen as a tool in explaining the operation of such discourse and not an end in itself; political discourse should be seen as intersecting a range of communicative modalities and theories" (Wilson 2015: 776). In the same way, this work considers linguistic analysis of political and public discourse as a tool to illuminate discourse and not as an end in itself. The linguistic tools can be used in political discourse studies to answer questions about "how the world is presented to the public through particular forms of linguistic representation. For example, how (...) are actions and events perceived and described? Which modes of reference are used to signify places, objects and institutions within particular positive or negative frames?" (Wilson 2015: 776). The concern of political discourse study is to look at how language is used to serve a specific goal. To this end, all levels of language can be involved and can be part of discourse studies, such as lexis, grammar, or pragmatics (Wilson 2015: 787).

Apart from political discourse there are several studies that focus on media discourse. Some of the main approaches to media discourse include discourse analysis, sociolinguistic studies, and more broadly "non-linguistic" (Cotter 2015: 798) studies of media material. Analytical discourse studies of media material might look at all kinds of "discourse-level matters related to larger stretches of talk and text beyond the word or sentence level" (Cotter 2015: 798) such as participants, topic, and genre. There are several approaches to the media discourse, for instance framing, priming, or metaphor studies. Colleen Cotter refers to studies in political science, media studies, cultural studies, or history as "non-linguistic" research, whereas this work does not make such a stark distinction and argues that even in projects from political science, economics, and other disciplines the use of linguistic tools and methods is useful to gain insights into discourses.

Yet, indeed, corpus-based approaches to the study of language and discourse are still one of the more uncommon methodologies in the social sciences. But due to the ever-growing availability of big amounts of data, many researchers become interested and able to use textual corpora. As the field of corpus linguistics has shown for a long time, it is a viable method to examine language and the context of language use on a grand scale. With more and more data available in digital form, researchers must find ways to make use of this vast amount of data in a comprehensive manner. Today, we have the ability to combine quantitative and qualitative analysis as techniques to investigate big amounts of digital text. Close reading techniques still play a very crucial role. They are combined with the quantitative analysis to produce more rounded picture of the discourse in question. In the field of digital humanities, researchers from different areas of the humanities and social sciences are developing approaches to investigate their field of interest, working together with computational linguists or data scientists. With progress in such fields as machine learning, analysis techniques are only going to improve and will be more widely available to researchers. Especially in the field of political communication, where language is one of the most important tools, these corpus study approaches will become more widely used.

4.2 Corpus Linguistics as Method

> Corpora allow us to observe language, but they are not language itself. (McEnery and Hardie 2012: 26)

In this work, the tools derived and explored by corpus linguists are used in order to examine different corpora of text. Corpus linguistics can deliver a number of ways to look into language and language use itself, over time, in different areas, or among different groups in society, for example. There are usually corpus-based or corpus-driven studies in corpus linguistics. The corpus-driven analyses see the corpus as central. The corpora usually drive the research question. A corpus-based approach usually formulates a question or hypothesis that the researcher wants to examine in the data in "order to validate it, refute it or refine it" (McEnery and Hardie 2012: 6). In another form of distinction, these approaches fall under the headline of "corpus-as-theory" or "corpus-as-method" with the latter referring to the approach used in this work. These concepts were detailed by Elena Tognini-Bonelli in her 2001 book *Corpus Linguistics at Work* (Tognini-Bonelli 2001).

Corpus-as-theory would reject any explanation of language "not directly derived from the analyst's interaction with the data" (McEnery and Hardie 2012: 148), whereas the corpus-as-method approach looks at corpora and corpus techniques as sources of empirical data "that may be deployed in support or refutation of any explanatory theory about language—even a theory devised in whole or in part without reference to corpus data" (McEnery and Hardie 2012: 148). Using the approach of corpus linguistics as a method, it can "be used in interaction with an established analytical framework which may, in and of itself, have nothing to do with corpus linguistics (. . .)" (McEnery and Hardie 2012: 149). This work can even be labeled a corpus-informed research study as the corpora compiled and used here can be seen as a "bank of examples to illustrate a theory" (McEnery and Hardie 2012: 17) and does not aim to make general statements about language use or can aim for "total accountability" (McEnery and Hardie 2012: 18).

The focus of this work is not a purely linguistic one. In this book, the tools and digital applications developed by corpus linguists are used to explore different texts. The focus is not language analysis in a narrow sense, but how keywords in a non-linguistic sense appear and are used across a certain amount of time and in different contexts, such as political and public debates. In this way, this works aims to identify different themes[2] in the discourse around technological progress and its impact on the economy. The themes around the topics of automation, the future of work, and the platform economy that are identified in the discourse material point to different attitudes toward technological progress and the future of work in the USA. These differing attitudes are embodied in the extent of the topics in the material (frequency) as well as in the way the topics are treated (collocations of keywords and content). In order to analyze these differing attitudes, this book includes a frequency analysis of certain terms alluding to the different topics as well as a collocation analysis of certain key terms. Additionally, there is a close qualitative reading of specific terms in context that follows the frequency analysis to identify how the themes are reflected in a similar or different manner across the material and different sources.

Looking at political and public discourses around technological progress in this way is significant as discourses influence the progress of technology itself. Political actors debate and influence factors like support of research areas, funding of projects, and policies that will support or hinder technological development such as infrastructure spending, immigration, or education reforms. Some of these specific policies will be discussed in the analysis of the material later on. The attitudes of policy-makers, as well as the treatment of technological development in the public sphere (media discourses), influence people's attitudes toward technology, their enthusiasm and acceptance, as well as possible concerns or fears, which in turn influence the adoption of technology. Discourses can reflect differing and even contradictory narratives and attitudes toward technological change and the future of work, but all these are important to illuminate how the public and political actors are making sense of the future, which in turn can impact their behavior.

Through the research in this book the contexts of specific themes in political and public discourse are identified in order to see whether there is a difference between the political and public discussions and between different sources. Therefore, different exploratory corpora, or "snapshot corpora" (McEnery and Hardie 2012: 9), were compiled that are not representative of general language use. Yet, this work aims to "seek balance and representativeness within a given sampling frame" (McEnery and Hardie 2012: 9) as much as possible. The results can therefore not be used to make claims about the use of certain terms in general language but only in the specific contexts examined here. This specific context can be labeled "current technological progress discourse in the USA." The corpora are built around the terms *automation*, *digitization*, and the *sharing economy* and are explored through quantitative methods and through a thorough qualitative reading of many of the specific sources. Quantitative and qualitative readings are equally important to corpus linguistics (McEnery and Hardie 2012: 2) and to this study as well. Corpora, "while a helpful guide or source of examples, cannot give sufficient access to

---

[2]The OED (Oxford English Dictionary) defines theme as the subject of discourse, discussion, conversation, etc., or as a topic. In linguistics it is that "part of a sentence which indicates what is being talked about" (OED 2020).

language to the extent that so-called 'qualitative' approaches to the date should be abandoned" (McEnery and Hardie 2012: 17). Therefore, quantitative measures and close reading are combined in this book in order to approach discourses as effectively as possible and to identify themes and trends in these discourses. This includes familiarization with the sources to a great extent. Inferences from the texts can only be made if the researcher is familiar with the context such as author, institution, or specific outlet, which is always a crucial part of corpus linguistic studies. Therefore, an intensive engagement with the texts is necessary.

4.3 Methodology: The Corpora on Congressional Hearings and Media Sources

For the purpose of this book, a two-tier approach of a quantitative corpus-based method and a qualitative reading of a smaller set of texts was chosen. In this way, we will arrive at a broader understanding of the discourse related to technological change in the economy.

Different sources and genres of text data were chosen in order to be able to look at political and public debates. In order to approach the political discourse, a corpus of congressional hearings was compiled. A number of 5 years of hearings strikes a balance between a manageable size and a meaningful comprehensiveness in terms of the discussion of the themes of interest. The hearings were held between 2013 and 2017 in congressional committees either in the House of Representatives, the US Senate, or in a Joint Committee of the two chambers.

For the public discourse, text data from different media sources was selected, as two of the most widely read news outlets in the USA, *The New York Times* (NYT) and *The Washington Post*, along with their online content, are serving as a source for discourse material. Both *The New York Times* and *The Washington Post*, although widely acclaimed journalistic outlets, can be associated with a more liberal—in the American context—approach to politics, the economy, and society. In the following chapters, this part of the data will therefore be referred to as the "liberal media data."

On a more conservative and business-oriented side, *The Wall Street Journal* together with its online content is the largest newspaper that is comparable to outlets such as *The New York Times* and *The Washington Post* when it comes to circulation and impact on a national or even international scale. Therefore, *The Wall Street Journal* (*WSJ*) and its online content will be compared to the more liberal media outlets and to the congressional material respectively in order to arrive at a more balanced picture of the discourse around the topic of technological progress and its impact on the economy.

Naturally, these outlets are in no way the only significant outlets shaping public opinion today. There are several other sources, especially digitally based ones such as blogs that are important in the opinion-making process of today's political landscape in the USA. Additionally, TV-based outlets are very important for most

Americans when it comes to news and information seeking, on all sides of the political spectrum. Conservative minded Americans often seek out *Fox News* as their main and most-trusted source of information (Pew-Research-Center 2020). The *WSJ*, in this work taken as a more "conservative" source compared to the *NYT* and *Washington Post*, reflects only a certain group within the conservative spectrum, which is referred to here as "business-friendly." This notion is not representative of all conservatives in the USA but is reflected more intensely in the *WSJ*. For many progressives in the USA today, the *NYT* and *Washington Post* are also not the only trusted sources anymore, yet they are still widely read. Thus, despite some shortcomings, the three outlets *NYT*, *Washington Post*, and *WSJ* were chosen for this research as a representation of public discourse on the topic of technological progress in the USA. All three are outlets that have a national presence and are still highly relevant as agenda-setters and the "fourth estate" in the country, which cannot be easily ignored by political actors in Washington. Additionally, they are engaged in a wide array of topics of which the economy and technological progress shaping this economy is one part. They are also relevant in the sense that they report in great detail about significant stakeholders and the goings-on in government institutions in Washington whereby certain aspects of political and public discourses reinforce each other.

4.3.1 Compiling the Data

As the US Congress is a working parliament and not a debating parliament, it does most of its important work and debate inside its committees in the House of Representatives and the Senate. There, witnesses and experts are invited to dig deeper into issues that are of concern to the committee and therefore society. Who is invited and what is discussed also points to the attitudes of the members of Congress and to the salience of an issue. There are political decisions behind the invitation of some experts, but they are not only political. Oftentimes, highly specialized issues call for expert knowledge and thus pundits are invited to testify.

In order to compile the Congress material to investigate the topics around the "technological progress discourse," the GPO,[3] the US Government Publishing Office was consulted and more specifically its Federal Digital System (FDsys).[4] The website offers a wide collection of different government publications, including collections of records of congressional hearings of both the House and the Senate throughout the years. The hearings in Congress are defined as "meetings or sessions of a Senate, House, or joint committee of Congress, usually open to the public, to obtain information and opinions on proposed legislation, conduct an investigation,

[3]Congressional hearings can be searched under: https://www.govinfo.gov/app/collection/chrg

[4]The FDsys has been discontinued as it was used in this work. The same collections of hearings can now be found under: https://www.govinfo.gov/app/collection/chrg

or evaluate/oversee the activities or a government department or the implementation of a Federal law. In addition, hearings may also be purely exploratory in nature, providing testimony and data about topics of current interest" (Office USGP 2018). Most of the hearings' records are published between 2 months and 2 years after the hearings. Although the GPO's website includes a disclaimer that not all hearing records (and other material) are made available through its website, it constitutes the largest and most comprehensive digital collection of congressional hearings attainable. Additionally, the material was especially well suited for a corpus-based investigation as the material is available in a range of formats.

The hearings offer a more comprehensive look and reflection of political discourse at a certain time. As said before, hearings are often sources to obtain information about current topics from experts in their field. It is therefore a valuable source to examine whether certain issues are reflected in the political discussion and are recognized by the members of Congress. When a hearing is called on a certain topic, it is clear that it ranks high on the political agenda of the committee. There is rarely a hot debate in front of the whole House or Senate. Often, Congress members speak in front of their chamber only for the record. The committee work, however, is the more "hands-on" job and includes more in-depth discussion and information concerning various topics.

One would think that there are only certain committees that deal with the issue of technological progress and its impact on the economy, and especially with the impact of automation (digitization), the platform economy, and the future of work. However, the topics span a wider range of committees in Congress than initially anticipated. Technological progress and innovations in the digital sphere are making inroads into all kinds of fields, e.g., in health care, small business, transportation, governance, trade, data storage, and security, only to name a few. Thus, the search for this project was broadened to all hearings, irrespective of the committee that dealt with the issues of interest. Instead of focusing on specific committees, three main terms were used to compile the corpora. The terms are three broad issues investigated in this book: *automation*, *digitization*, and *sharing economy*. For the collection of the hearings, the somewhat nonspecific terms were broad enough, and at the same time suitable to obtain specific records of hearings on the subjects of concern, namely technological progress and its impact on the economy, and more specifically on automation itself, the platform economy, and the future of work.

Automation as a term is much more salient than the term *digitization* in the English language, which will be shown in more detail later in the book. The term *automation* is most often used in the English language when referring to technological progress, even though we are moving away from mere mechanization into the digital sphere. Nevertheless, *digitization* as a term is interesting to contrast with *automation*. Additionally, it delivers results from other areas than *automation* as it is used in different contexts. The term *sharing economy* is a term that was derived from the literature on the platform economy that was reviewed for this book. Objectively, the term *platform economy* is much more suitable of what is of interest in this study. However, the term *platform economy* is not used to any great extent outside of specific (academic or technical) literature. It was therefore not suited as a term for compiling the corpus data. Instead, the somewhat misleading term *sharing economy* is used here. As detailed before, many of the platforms that started under a sharing idea have mostly moved on to commercial usage or were never in any way "collaborative" or "shared" to begin with. Nevertheless, the term *sharing economy* remains widely used in the public and political discourse, which will be shown later, and delivered the most promising search results. With these three main terms, two highly specialized corpora of hearing records from the House and Senate were built, excluding hearings that do not concern these main subject areas and thus preventing the data to be flawed.[5]

This eventually brought the corpus to a total number of 241 hearing records. One hundred and fifty-one hearings were conducted in the House of Representatives; 90 hearings were conducted in the Senate. After dividing them by year, there are the following collections of hearing records (see Table 4.1): From the House there are 30 hearings in the year 2013, 19 hearings in 2014, 28 hearings in 2015, 33 hearings in 2016, and 41 hearings in 2017. In the Senate, there are 10 hearings for the year 2013, 20 for 2014, 21 for 2015, 16 for 2016, and 23 for the year 2017. The total size of the corpus based on the House hearings is 151 files, 5,069,940 tokens. The size of the corpus based on the Senate hearings is 90 files, 3,884,016 tokens. Although the size of the Senate corpus is smaller, using the analysis software LancsBox[6] (Brezina et al. 2018), it is possible to compare results of both corpora as the frequency analysis output of results is *per 10,000 tokens*. Tokens, in the corpus linguistic sense, roughly refer to "word.[7]"

As said before, sources from Congress will be compared with sources from the public sphere, namely media sources. *The New York Times* and *The Washington Post* were the main sources on the "liberal" side, including their online publications. *The Wall Street Journal* as well as the *Wall Street Journal Online*, Eastern Edition, were used to refer to the more conservative, "business-friendly" side of the public discourse. The corpora from the media sources were compiled in a similar manner as the congressional corpora.

The corpora based on *The New York Times* and *Washington Post* were put together with the help of the LexisNexis[8] platform. The platform can be used to

[5]Hearings that were excluded were concerned with health, immigration, agriculture, appropriations of the fiscal year of departments, food, energy, pending legislation, border protections, veterans, international relations, tourism, and defense. Hearings on nominations (Senate) were also excluded. Records from hearings that were included are mostly concerned with the economy, labor, transportation, innovation, finance, trade, education, infrastructure, regulations, robotics, artificial intelligence, entrepreneurship, cybersecurity, jobs, small business, and inequality.

[6]For the analysis of the congressional material, LancsBox version 3.0.2 was used. The material from the *NYT*, *Washington Post*, and *WSJ* was analyzed with LancsBox version 4.5. Minor changes in the results can occur from the updated version of the software.

[7]Token is any instance of a particular word form in a text (e.g., singular and plural of a word) (McEnery and Hardie 2012: 50).

[8]Now called NexisUni. At the time of publishing, the *Washington Post* was no longer available on the NexisUni platform.

Table 4.1 Corpora based on congressional material

	Total number of hearings	2013	2014	2015	2016	2017	Size of corpus (tokens)
House	151	30 (1,233,806)	19 (485,639)	28 (837,229)	33 (1,012,743)	41 (1,500,523)	5,069,940
Senate	90	10 (405,511)	20 (719,335)	21 (965340)	16 (662,181)	23 (1,131,629)	3,884,016
Total	241	40	39	49	49	65	8,953,956

Number of hearings per year; token size per year
Source: Author

search for specific media sources—in this case, data from *The New York Times* and *The Washington Post*. LexisNexis includes data from written content of the newspapers as well as the online publications (washingtonpost.com) and blogs (Washington Post Blogs, New York Times Blogs). The database was searched using the three main terms in mind, *automation*, *digitization*, and *sharing economy* that were already used when compiling the congressional material. In total, the media corpus originally consisted of 4805 different articles.[9] After cleaning the data, the corpus based on the sources from *The New York Times* and *The Washington Post* contains 4701 articles (104 article duplicates were removed) and amounts to 5,297,270 tokens, and spans the years 2013 through 2017 (Table 4.2). Comparing it to the congressional hearings corpus: the congressional hearings corpus consists of 8,953,956 tokens (the congressional Hearings Corpus only features 241 separate files, but this is due to the fact that congressional hearings are much longer than journalistic articles).[10]

The material from the *Wall Street Journal* (*WSJ*) (see Table 4.2) was compiled in the same manner as the other media sources through a database which was searched using again the three main search terms (*automation, digitization, sharing economy*). In this case, the database ABI/INFORM Collection by ProQuest was used.[11] After cleaning this corpus of duplicate articles, the total amount of *WSJ* and online edition data amounted to a number of 1965 articles (originally 1991), and 1,744,157 tokens. In comparison to the other media sources (*NYT* + online, *Washington Post* + online), this seems a comparable size. The material amounts to roughly a third of the corpus size of the *NYT* and *Washington Post* outlets.

[9]After a first analysis of the corpora, duplicates of articles had to be removed. They naturally occurred in the data because the search terms delivered some identical results. Some duplicate articles remain in the corpus data as some articles appeared in different outlets (e.g., print and online) or reappeared on different dates. These duplicates are significant because they point to the relevance of the articles and subject matters in those articles.

[10]The three corpora are different in size with the congressional corpus being the largest with 8,953,956 tokens, the media corpus based on the *NYT* and the *Washington Post* the second largest with 5,297,270 tokens, and the corpus based on the *WSJ* the third largest with a size of 1,744,157 tokens. Ideally, the corpora have similar sizes, yet these corpora vary in size because of the different source material (congressional hearings are very long and include a lot of material that is not relevant for content analysis), as well as a diverging number of actual sources (*NYT* and *Washington Post* with online content and blogs vs. *WSJ* with online content). However, as these are exploratory corpora and they are not compared directly to infer any overall use of language, the size differences are neglected in this study. Additionally, all of the corpora are very large in size, which avoids the risk of "cherry-picking" material. All of the results are put out in *per 10,000 tokens* and are therefore relative to compare.

[11]In the database, the *WSJ* is available in print from 1984 to today, and the online edition is available from 2010 onward. The database allowed us to download specific sections: for the keyword *automation*, the "automation section" was downloaded, for the keyword *digitization*, all sections were downloaded (there were very few), and for the keyword *sharing economy*, specific sections were excluded as they did not concern the subjects of interest. For example, sections on banking, air travel, international trade, or international relations were excluded. This way, a more cohesive and manageable corpus of articles could be built.

Table 4.2 Corpora based on media material

	2013	2014	2015	2016	2017	Total size of corpus (tokens)	Total number of articles
Liberal Media Corpus (*NYT*, *WaPost* incl. online content)	428 (451,728)	797 (811,077)	835 (896,776)	1051 (1,202,959)	1590 (1,934,730)	5,297,270	4701
WSJ (incl. online content)	241 (224,578)	278 (245,729)	409 (357,806)	594 (504,068)	443 (411,976)	1,744,157	1965

Source: Author

Table 4.3 House and Senate hearings as basis for keywords

Year	House	Senate
2014	The Power of Connection: Peer-to-Peer Businesses (Committee on Small Business)	
2015	The Disrupter Series: How the Sharing Economy Creates Jobs, Benefits Consumers, and Raises Policy Questions (Subcommittee on Commerce, Manufacturing and Trade) The Opportunities and Risks of the Sharing Economy (Subcommittee on Commerce, Manufacturing and Trade)	
2016	The Sharing Economy: A Taxing Experience for New Entrepreneurs, Part I (Committee on Small Business) The Disrupter Series: Advanced Robotics (Subcommittee on Commerce, Manufacturing and Trade) The 21st Century Workforce: How Current Rules and Regulations Affect Innovation and Flexibility in Michigan's Workplaces (Subcommittee on Workforce Protections)	The Economic Report of the President (Joint Economic Committee) The Transformative Impact of Robots and Automation (Joint Economic Committee) The Dawn of Artificial Intelligence (Subcommittee on Space, Science, and Competitiveness)
2017	Helping Americans get back to work: Implementation of the Workforce Innovation and Opportunity Act (Subcommittee on Higher Education and Workforce Development) Closing the Skills Gap and Boosting US Competitiveness (Transportation Committee)	The Decline of Economic Opportunity in the United States: Causes and Consequences (Joint Economic Committee)

Source: Author

4.3.2 *Identifying Keywords*[12]

Before starting the analysis of the corpora, a pattern was devised with which to examine them. At first, twelve hearings from the congressional data were closely examined in order to get a first impression of the subject matters and the discussions concerning technological progress in the political realm. The hearings were chosen because of their clear relation to the subject matter of automation, the platform economy (sharing economy), and the future of work. These hearings (Table 4.3) include two files from the Committee on Small Business *The Power of Connection: Peer-to-Peer Businesses* from 2014 and *The Sharing Economy: A Taxing Experience for New Entrepreneurs, Part I* (2016); three files from the Joint Economic

[12]Keywords were not derived from use of corpus linguistic software LancsBox in a quantitative manner as a statistical measure, but from a qualitative reading of texts to identify key issues and terms. Keywords in this sense thus refer to the key issues and terms around certain themes in the texts.

Committee including *The Economic Report of the President* (2016), *The Transformative Impact of Robots and Automation* (2016), and *The Decline of Economic Opportunity in the United States: Causes and Consequences* (2017); three files from the Subcommittee on Commerce, Manufacturing and Trade including *The Disrupter Series: How the Sharing Economy Creates Jobs, Benefits Consumers, and Raises Policy Questions* (2015), *The Disrupter Series: Advanced Robotics* (2016), and *The Opportunities and Risks of the Sharing Economy* (2015); one file from the Subcommittee on Space, Science, and Competitiveness *The Dawn of Artificial Intelligence* (2016); one file from the Subcommittee on Workforce Protections *The 21st Century Workforce: How Current Rules and Regulations Affect Innovation and Flexibility in Michigan's Workplaces* (2016); one file from the Subcommittee on Higher Education and Workforce Development *Helping Americans get back to work: Implementation of the Workforce Innovation and Opportunity Act* (2017); and one file from the Transportation Committee *Closing the Skills Gap and Boosting US Competitiveness* (2017).

After reading through the hearings, specific topics and issues that were discussed in relation to a more automated and digital future could be identified by reference to certain keywords. The topics were divided into five broader categories. These categories are *Future Trends, Inequality, Technology, Policies,* and *Platform Economy* (see Table 4.4). The categories consist of the keywords identified through the close reading of the Congress hearings. For example, under *Future Trends*, we find keywords such as *future of work, automation, disruption, digital revolution*, etc. Under the headline of *Policies* we find keywords like *education, higher education, infrastructure, portable benefits, skills gap, or universal basic income*. Under the headline of *Platform Economy*, there are keywords like *gig economy, sharing economy, platform economy, peer-to-peer, gig worker*, etc. (For a full list see Table 4.4). This extensive keyword list was used to conduct the quantitative analysis of all corpora.[13] In the frequency analysis following in Chap. 5, a sample of the keywords displayed in this list will be examined in more depth.

4.4 A First Glance at the Congressional Material

In the following chapter, some of the initially examined hearings will be discussed in more detail, before going into the quantitative corpus analysis using the keyword list. This way, we will gain a first impression of the political discourse around the topics of technological progress.

[13]For several of the keywords, the meaning can be ambiguous. Yet, as the keyword list is rather extensive the analysis still aims for a well-rounded picture of the discourse around these issues. Additionally, the frequency analysis of the keywords is followed by a close contextual reading of the actual hearing or media article. This way, the ambiguous meaning of some of the keywords in the list can be neglected.

Table 4.4 Keyword list

Future trends	Inequality	Technology	Policies	Platform economy
Future, future of work	Replacement, displacement, relocation	New technology, digital technology	Education, secondary education, higher education, workforce training, apprenticeship, vocational training, vocational education, community college, affordability	Gig economy, sharing economy, on-demand economy, sharing economy platform* Platform economy, digital platform*, Uber economy, collaborative economy, collaborative consumption
Automation, digitization	Polarization	robotics, self-driving cars, autonomously-driving cars	Social security, social safety net, portable benefits, portability	Small business owner*, small business, micro-entrepreneur*, micro-entrepreneur, peer-to-peer, peer-to-peer business, peer-to-peer platform*, on-demand, online platform*
Robots, robotics	Flexibility	Internet of Things, cloud computing, artificial intelligence, AI, deep learning, machine learning	job classification, worker classification, classification of workers	Supplementing, nontraditional work arrangement*
Transformation	Unemployment, underemployment		Labor participation	Self-employ*, millennial*
Disruption, disruptive	Creativ*, creative jobs, communication, social skills, analytical skills, technical skills		Minimum wage, skill gap, skills gap, skills, upskilling, lifelong learning	gig worker*, independent contractor*, independent worker*, piecework, freelance*
Technological development, Technological revolution	Prosperity, winner-take-all economy		Universal basic income, UBI, earned income tax credit, wage insurance program	Uber, Airbnb, InstaCart, TaskRabbit, Postmate*

(continued)

Table 4.4 (continued)

Future trends	Inequality	Technology	Policies	Platform economy
Digital revolution	Income Inequality, inequality		Infrastructure	
American Dream, Millennials			Consumer protection, data privacy, cybersecurity	
			Minimum wage	

Source: Author

The * is used in corpus analysis software as a wildcard, i.e., to search for different forms of the word such as plural form, adjective, etc., e.g., freelance* would search for freelance, freelancer, freelancing, etc

Most of the hearings from Table 4.3 were conducted in committees in the House of Representatives. The House seems to conduct more hearings that are concerned with current developments than the Senate. As the House members are elected every 2 years, they are confronted very imminently with current issues and events that their voters care about. Between the two chambers, the House is the one representing the "popular" vote that reacts to changes more immediately. Additionally, the fact that there are 435 members in the House compared to 100 Senators makes it easier for Representatives to focus on specific issues and certain (sub)committees. The number of committees and subcommittees in the House and Senate is comparable, yet a Senator has to cover much more ground in the committees than a Representative in the House. Although the Senate also has expert staff, it seems to be more feasible for a member of the House to specialize in a specific issue. This could be among the reasons why the House sets more hearings on very current events. The Senate is also the more traditional and deliberative chamber of the two. Together with the limits of time of a US Senator, it is therefore understandable that the Senate holds hearings on long-term trends rather than what seem to be current and short-term trends. Yet, there is also the Joint Economic Committee, which consists of House and Senate members. This committee was designed to "review economic conditions and to recommend improvements in economic policy" (Congress 2019) additional to the Council of Economic Advisors. This committee holds hearings that deal with long-term trends such as technological and structural change of the US economy and involves both House and Senate members.

Indeed, some of the hearings in the Joint Economic Committee stand out in their reflection of the technological trends that are of concern for this book. One such hearing in the Joint Economic Committee from 2016 is called *The Transformative Impact of Robots and Automation* (Congress 2016e). This topic was picked up for a Joint Committee hearing, which points to the relevance of the topic to lawmakers from all sides. The hearing centers around the question of how advances in robotics and automation are changing the US economy as a whole and what impact this has on the workforce (replacement), on education, on the social safety net, or on government policies (Congress 2016e: 2). As witnesses, Andrew McAfee, researcher at the MIT, Adam Keiper from the Ethics and Public Policy Center, D.C., and Dr. Harry Holzer, professor at Georgetown University, Washington D.C., were invited. The hearing is held in order to improve the understanding of Congress in assessment of some studies that point in a fatalistic direction when it comes to the future of jobs. Other studies again do not seem to paint such a bleak picture. As automation boosts productivity, it advances innovation. But workers might be affected in a negative way and need support. Prosperity cannot be shared widely if a significant number of well-paying jobs in the USA will disappear (Congress 2016e: 3f). Therefore, lawmakers invited experts to talk about these issues and arrive at a more balanced picture.

As hearings are designed to gather information and expert knowledge on any given field, inviting MIT's Andrew McAfee who has published widely on the topic of automation was a crucial step. In his statement before the Joint Economic Committee, McAfee points out what he and his colleagues call the "great decoupling" of output and productivity growth on the one hand and the meagre growth of jobs and median income on the other hand:

> more recently we noticed what my coauthor and I call 'the great de-coupling.' The two lines related to output have continued to go on a pretty healthy upward trajectory, while the two lines related to the workforce have in a sense stalled out. And, by some measures, the median American household or family is worse off in income terms than they were at the turn of the century. (Congress 2016e: 6)

He argues that at the base of this development is technological progress, which has automated many routine jobs, both physical and knowledge work. He also shows that in the area of manufacturing, the USA has seen rising output while manufacturing employment steadily declined. Moreover, he is sure that through further technological progress in the areas of 3D printing, artificial intelligence (AI), deep learning, or machine learning systems, more and more human work will be replaced:

> And the main thing that I think is going to happen is that these phenomena that we have already seen in the workforce, this hollowing out of the middle class, the pressures that we see on the average American family, who that middle class was built on the back of routine physical and knowledge work, I expect these phenomena to continue, and for some of these challenges to accentuate because technological development is not slowing down. I believe it is speeding up. And it is eating into areas where it has not been present before. (Congress 2016e: 6)

As mentioned in the previous chapters of this book, McAfee and his colleagues do not believe that mass unemployment is around the corner; in fact, the USA has been producing more jobs at the time of writing than in the years before. Yet, many of these jobs require different skill sets than in the past and that is why McAfee calls Congress to adopt policies that encourage entrepreneurship, build up modern infrastructure, reform immigration, and foster education and training. He also emphasizes that the USA should focus on original research in areas such as machine learning and AI (Congress 2016e: 7).

Adam Keiper continues the discussion with emphasizing that through the technological advances of the last few years, our lives as consumers and citizens have significantly improved. Technology has made goods cheaper and better and thus added to prosperity. Yet, he also thinks that the current phase of automation is quite different from previous ones because machines get better at cognitive work and start manipulating the physical world on their own. He thinks that, generally, policy ideas like advancing lifelong learning, upskilling, and making the workforce more flexible could help workers to adapt. Yet, he especially sees flexibility as a two-edged sword because workers also want to have the time and means to build up a family or to pursue other things in their leisure time instead of constantly being available for work. He also mentions thoughts about the universal basic income (UBI) that might become more relevant as technological change progresses and the nature of work does as well (Congress 2016e: 8).

Harry Holzer argues that past estimates of how many workers will be replaced by automation have always been overblown. He therefore thinks that today's fears could also be overblown and argues in favor of a more nuanced understanding of the impact of automation and other factors on jobs and income:

> Even if technology hasn't eliminated large numbers of jobs in the aggregate, it can and has reduced earnings among large groups of workers. In the past 35 years, the digital revolution, globalization, and weakening institutions like labor unions together have reduced employment and good-paying job categories, especially for those workers with only a high school education or less. The jobs most affected were goods-producing jobs for men, clerical jobs for women. But at the same time, wages and jobs have increased for workers who either have the technical skills to deal with the new technology like machinists, technicians, and engineers, or who have other skills that complement the machinery. Those skills could be analytical, or communication skills, or even creative skills. There is a strong skill bias in the technology that actually helps some workers and hurts others. (Congress 2016e: 9)

Holzer describes a further polarization of the job market that Andrew McAfee also talks about. He thinks that the top tier of income is growing, while the middle and the bottom is shrinking because of technological change, globalization, and weak institutions in the USA. Only through better education, in his eyes, can the hollowing out of the middle class be prevented. He also thinks that if "the labor market becomes more unstable, we do need to make sure that universal benefits are available and portable. Health care, paid family leave, etc. And then finally, we actually might need to invest in more job creation if the pace of displacement picks up and overwhelms the labor market" (Congress 2016e: 10).

In the hearing, further questions are asked about labor participation in the USA, which is at a record low. Prof. Holzer thinks that this is not due to machines replacing humans, but it is about declining wages of many workers:

> All the forces that have reduced the wages of less-educated workers— technology, globalization, weakening institutions—as those wages have stagnated and declined, a lot of workers simply don't believe it is in their interest or worth their while to stay in the labor force. And I think that is why they leave, and that is why dealing with stagnant wages through, or separately from the technology, I think is our prime concern right now. (Congress 2016e: 13)

Holzer thinks that the main problem is not that machines displace humans altogether, but that they put more and more pressure on the income of today's workers, especially if they are less educated.

But how can people benefit from technological advancement? Andrew McAfee sees both potential and problems in the education system, which might still be stuck in the past. Instead of learning about how to use new technologies or develop it, students learn things that machines can already do better, like memorizing large amounts of facts or basic math. But today, workers need different skills to succeed like performing non-routine tasks, creative thinking, or social skills (Congress 2016e: 13f).

McAfee is very much in favor of Silicon Valley's view of the "permissionless innovation" (Congress 2016e: 18), where the government does not intervene if it is not absolutely necessary. Yet, the witnesses are not there to advocate for no regulation at all. Many regulations are there to prevent market failure and inequities produced by the market (Congress 2016e: 19). Moreover, the ideas of apprenticeship programs and stronger community college education are discussed to overcome educational difficulties (Congress 2016e: 22). The question remains whether the investment in higher education will really pay off. Also, the issue of "subsidizing non-work" (Congress 2016e: 23), so something along the lines of a UBI, is discussed briefly. There are discussions about how it could be implemented in a more distant future when a higher number of people might not find enough work anymore because of high productivity and advanced technology. Yet, dis-incentivizing work is a challenge, because it would replace work as a structuring and dignifying act in everyone's lives (Congress 2016e: 23).

During the hearing, unionization in the new economy also plays a role. When asked about the potential of unionization and the labor movement in the new economy, Dr. Holzer responds that the new economy is not a very fruitful ground for labor organization:

> the model of unionism that we have in America was developed mid-20th century. It was very well suited to that kind of economy, and it is less well suited to an economy with a lot of dynamics, and a lot of fluidity in and out of jobs, and dramatic new competition. (...) I think we're struggling for a new institutional model that fits the new reality of the 21st century labor market. (Congress 2016e: 29)

But apart from unionization, there are other issues that are discussed. McAfee argues that

> Education and reskilling is obviously crucial. The only thing I would add is, I am a huge fan of an expansion of the Earned Income Tax Credit. Whereas, if we have people who are trying to do the right thing and get out there in the workforce and work at a relatively low wage job like child care, like elder care, let's top their wage up with a subsidy. I actually prefer that to a substantial increase in the minimum wage because that might have a disincentive effect on the employers from employing that person. I would like to see our system work so that we directly incentivize both the employer to employ that person, and that person to get out there and do that job via topping up their wages. (Congress 2016e: 31)

As mentioned before, the UBI is also discussed on a few occasions during the hearing. Adam Keiper comments on the UBI and the idea of a negative income tax.

Both solutions would guarantee an income and could potentially incentivize good behavior in society. Yet, the question remains how work as a concept can be replaced by something as meaningful to people in their lives (Congress 2016e: 57f). He also speaks about the UBI in relation to questions about the affordability of social security in the future.

Another hearing that touches upon the challenges of a more technologically advanced future in the Joint Economic Committee, *The Economic Report of the President* from 2016, discusses the overall state of the economy, but also mentions more specific issues the economy is facing in the future. It was the last economic report by the Obama Administration and its Council of Economic Advisors and so it can also serve as a summary of what has been achieved since the beginning of the Obama presidency and the Great Recession.

The chairman of the committee Daniel Coats (Rep) comments on the report highlighting the issue of inequality in the USA, which is still on the rise: "The CEA's report we will discuss today devotes significant attention to inequality as a defining challenge of the 21st Century. (. . .) For the American Dream to remain attainable for future generations, we must accept the reality of our fiscal situation and act responsibly by addressing it immediately" (Congress 2016c: 2). Carolyn B. Maloney (Dem) highlights the achievements of the Obama Administration regarding the recovery from the Great Recession that can be seen in low unemployment numbers and the overall recovery from the most severe downturn of the economy since the Great Depression: "Let's remember, when George Bush left the Oval Office, the economy was in a death spiral" (Congress 2016c: 3). Regarding the more immediate things that need to be done to make the economy grow and help American workers, Maloney says that the

> Report notes that the economy faces long-term structural challenges. (. . .) We also face the devastating effects of off-shoring of American jobs and job losses due to automation and technical changes. These challenges are not a surprise. They have been on economists' radar for years. So what should we do? I agree with your assessment that we need to rebuild the Nation's crumbling infrastructure, invest in early childhood education, implement paid leave, achieve equal pay for equal work, and make college more affordable. I want to close by looking at economic inequality, one of the central issues of our time (. . .) We need to recommit ourselves to policies that expand opportunities and narrow inequality. (Congress 2016c: 3f)

As the Chairman of the Council of Economic Advisers, Jason Furman presents the report of the president and was invited to the Joint Committee to comment on it. Naturally, as part of the administration, he sees the state of the economy rather positively, stressing continued growth and declining unemployment, which was at its lowest rate since 2008 at 4.9%. Yet, he also sees inequality as a continuing challenge to American society. Furman argues:

> Despite progress since the Great Recession, the unequal distribution of income, wealth, and opportunity remains one of the greatest challenges facing our economy. (. . .) Some of the increase we have seen is a natural consequence of competitive markets, a result of differences in productivity as technology evolves, but some of the increase may reflect the rising influence of what economists call economic rents: the income captured by companies and workers beyond what their productivity justifies. (Congress 2016c: 5)

Like many economists, Furman argues that some degree of inequality is natural in market economies and develops over time. Yet, he does admit that there are developments in inequality that are undesirable, especially when they put strain on the whole of society and the economy. He argues that inequality of income leads to inequality of opportunity eventually. When asked about why the top 1% of US earners capture most of the income in the USA, a phenomenon that is much more pronounced in the USA than elsewhere, Furman responds that the USA has invested less in education and upskilling of workers that complements the technological advancement of recent years. He also mentions the low minimum wage, which he sees as a contributing factor in rising inequality. In order to expand economic opportunity, he wants to support higher labor participation suggesting more child care and parental leave or reducing tax penalties for second earners (Congress 2016c: 8).

About future automation, Furman says:

> In theory, automation should not present any problem at all. We have had automation for thousands of years, and we always find more jobs for people. [Yet,] in practice that can come at a cost, either in terms of inequality if you do not have the skills to benefit from it, or some people who get displaced do not find another job and you might call it transitional or temporary, but that could last for decades. (Congress 2016c: 16)

Thus, Furman does not see a different quality in the automation that is occurring in the USA today. But he emphasizes that the skills gap leads to undesired consequences of automation processes. In general, however, automation has always happened and solutions were always found.

Furman clearly draws from the traditional toolbox when trying to tackle worker replacement and the rise in inequality. For example, he sees the low minimum wage as a problem. Being asked whether raising the minimum wage could not even accelerate automation for the lower-skilled, Furman responds that

> the evidence that I have seen for moderate increases in the minimum wage phased in over time, similar to the types of proposals that have been put forward in Congress, has found that they don't have adverse effects on employment. But certainly if you were to raise the minimum wage to $30 an hour, you know, I would expect you would have a tradeoff. (…). I think it is important as part of an overall strategy to make sure our workers have more skills and more productivity. (…). I think it certainly has implications for how we design our social safety net, and I think that is an important conversation to have. (…) I think Earned Income Tax Credit has worked. But I think we should be thinking hard about these questions going forward, as well. (Congress 2016c: 17)

Thus, Furman argues phasing in a moderate minimum wage, as well as combining it with policies like the earned income tax credit that can help future low-wage workers. About the future of work, Furman says:

> For thousands of years we have invented new machines. They have replaced things people used to do. (…). The problem is when that happens really abruptly, and when you are not prepared for it the consequence of that can be one of two things. One is inequality. (…) And if you see a lot of lower wage jobs replaced, that is reducing the demand for those types of workers. That lowers their wages. That raises inequality. So one bad side effect is inequality. The second is I certainly believe that over time if you lose a job you will be able to find another job, and hopefully a better job. But (…) that process can be long and painful. (…).

> What we should be doing in this regard is making sure people have more skills to take advantage of so that they are complementing the innovations and benefitting more from them. Making sure we have a labor market that is better at moving people from job to job. The President had proposed a wage insurance program that would help get people back on their feet by insuring them against some of the wage losses associated with a job, as they move into a new job. And there is probably a lot more than that that we need to do (. . .). (Congress 2016c: 28f)

Furman argues that issues due to structural change have always happened, but the problem is the speed of this change that workers cannot keep up with. Inequality could therefore rise. Political actors should react with labor market reform to make it easier to move into new jobs and to support those who face wage losses.

In another hearing in the Joint Economic Committee from 2017 called *The Decline of Economic Opportunity in the United States: Causes and Consequences,* consequences of technological progress were further discussed, as well as the state of the economy 1 year later under the new Trump Administration. The hearing focuses on the alleged decline of economic opportunity and the overall state of the economy that could, for example, be witnessed by the decline in startups or the number of entrepreneurs. Although the previously discussed Economic Report of the President pointed out that there had been significant improvements and recovery since the Great Recession, the Trump Administration paints a bleaker picture. Although the economy was supposedly on the rise, many people feel otherwise. Incomes have not increased and costs of living keep rising. The hearing also sees a problem in the stagnating numbers of entrepreneurial activity that reflects uncertainties in the economy as a whole.

The statement by John Lettieri, Senior Director for Policy and Strategy Econ Innovation Group who testifies in the hearing, reflects on this issue:

> Well, in this supposed age of the gig economy, automation, and artificial intelligence, conventional wisdom would certainly have us believe people are suffering from too much and too rapid change across the economic landscape. But I disagree. In fact, I believe our economy features far too little change and churn in critical areas. In short, economic dynamism is fading rapidly, and the cycle of creative destruction seems broken. (Congress 2017: 8)

John Lettieri argues that the lack of dynamism in the economy can have severe consequences:

> For workers, it means fewer labor market opportunities and fewer pathways to achieving the American Dream. For markets, it has corresponded with an era of declining competition and increased concentration among elite firms. And for regions, it means shrinking industrial bases and more profound geographic disparities. (Congress 2017: 9)

He also stresses that GDP growth alone is not the only goal to be achieved when opportunities for the American workforce need to be improved:

> Faster GDP growth, while obviously a critically important goal, should not be expected to solve opportunity deficits in America today. The reason is inequality. It is already the case that not enough GDP growth is reaching those who have been left behind. Why should we believe that more growth is the full answer, especially absent policies that more directly help connect left-behind people and places to that growth? (Congress 2017: 10)

Mr. Lettieri also comments on the new economy, saying:

> So we have obviously always had technological transformation in the economy. We have always had these great leaps that really redefine the economy overnight and open up new types of industries and opportunities. The problem today is that, while we have those types of transformations occurring, they are not, A, spreading to the benefit of as wide an array of people as they once did, and B, we have policies and trends in place that actually mute those benefits in a really perverse way. So it is not that there isn't change occurring; it is that there is not enough coming in to replace that which is dying out. So this is what I mention in terms of creative disruption. When you don't have the creative part of that equation in place, it feels to people like too much destruction, but it is really just the rate of creation has dramatically changed. (Congress 2017: 12)

In this testimony, the well-known "creative destruction" quality of innovation is mentioned. Yet, the expert witness argues that despite innovative business ventures like the gig economy, the "creative" part of the innovation delivering new and better jobs is still missing in large parts of the economy. That is why the American workforce is frustrated and pessimistic about their economic outlook.

Another hearing that was initially examined is titled *The 21st Century Workforce: How Current Rules and Regulations Affect Innovation and Flexibility in Michigan's Workplaces* and took place in front of the Subcommittee on Workforce Protections in the House (Congress 2016a). Current regulations of the labor market were discussed and whether they are still up-to-date.

In a flexible economy in which more and more millennial workers are taking part, the question arises if rules and regulations need an update. Representative Walberg (Rep) is sure an update is needed for the twenty-first century workforce:

> Today, the regulations guiding the law's implementation are rigid, outdated, and simply are not working for the twenty-first century workforce. Millennials are now the majority of the workforce, and they, like most in the workforce, do not want a flawed regulatory structure that constrains flexibility and innovation by creating confusion and uncertainty in today's workplaces. Unfortunately, the current law raises more questions than it provides answers. (Congress 2016a: 2)

As usual, experts were invited to the hearing, commenting on the issue. Jared Meyer from the Manhattan Institute for Policy Research and author of *Uber Positive: Why Americans Love the Sharing Economy* talks about how the American workforce has changed: "The American economy is changing, and millennials' attitudes about work and their careers are changing with it. The rapid rise of the so-called sharing economy embodies many young Americans' new economic ideal, one driven by technology, convenience, and flexibility" (Congress 2016a: 19). Another expert present was Dale Belman, Professor at the School of Human Resources and Labor Relations, Michigan State University. He is not as enthusiastic as Meyer about the new prospects of the economy represented by the platform economy. He comments on the issue of inequality arguing that the idea of "shared prosperity" has recently been abandoned in favor of a so-called winner-take-all economy. Mr. Belman testifies:

> We can see this in stagnant real wages over the last 35 years, only slow improvement in family incomes, and that only because families are working more hours largely by moving

> women into the labor force. Likewise, levels of income and wealth and equality have risen to levels that rival the 1920s and the Gilded Age. Abandoning the path to shared prosperity appears not only in outsourcing, offshoring, tax inversions, and other headline-grabbing changes, but also in the details of protective labor law. (Congress 2016a: 31)

The new Internet giants have a tendency to develop into winner-take-all entities as the Internet nurtures network effects and often leads to monopolies. Consumers like a certain amount of choice, but only a few services and platforms are able to survive alongside each other. This leads to heavy concentration and power of the platform businesses in the market, which eventually also affects people working on and for the platforms.

Touching on the even bigger trend of artificial intelligence and its influence on the future of American society and jobs, yet another hearing took place in 2016 called *The Dawn of Artificial Intelligence*. The hearing was held in the Subcommittee on Space, Science, and Competitiveness in the Committee on Commerce, Science, and Transportation in the Senate (Congress 2016b). In his opening statement, Senator Ted Cruz (Rep) stresses the importance of AI for the development of transformative applications like the autonomously driving car, healthcare applications, and consumer products like Alexa or Google Home and how all of these developments will contribute to economic growth (Congress 2016b: 1f). Senator Gary Peters (Dem) comments on the application of AI that is already in place. Through the advances in computer processing and cloud computing, this field will witness exponential growth in the next few years and decades. Although there are many benefits to the introduction of AI, the Senator also emphasizes that the American workforce is under pressure and that Congress must act so that workers are not left behind (Congress 2016b: 3f). Bill Nelson (Dem) also highlights the issue of replacement of workers through introduction of robots and other intelligent machines. He mentions that in the event of more automation in the trucking industry, for example, one of the most common occupations in the USA could come under pressure (Congress 2016b: 4f).

In his statement, the invited expert Eric Horvitz, Technical Fellow and Director, Microsoft Research, brings forward the fast advancement of AI and its implications. With the likely benefits of increased productivity and value creation, there is growing concern about the effect on jobs and income disparities that might grow through AI. His suggestions are to increase training and retraining of workers so that "skills are aligned with needs" (Congress 2016b: 8) and more investment in STEM education. He stresses that one important issue to solve is the skills gap, leading to a widening income gap between those who have the skills desirable and those who do not. He thinks that women, young people, and workers in rural areas and underserved communities are most affected by this gap (Congress 2016b: 15). In another statement in this hearing, Dr. Andrew W. Moore from the Carnegie Mellon University's School of Computer Science argues along the lines of Andrew McAfee and his colleagues who anticipate a different relationship of humans and machines in the future. The nature of humans' work will evolve and will demand different skills (Congress 2016b: 22f).

The issues of the *sharing economy* were discussed on several occasions in the hearings initially investigated. Sometimes the sharing economy was mentioned in specific hearings on the subject; sometimes it came up during other discussions, for instance when talking about the trends of automation and digitization in general. One of the earliest hearings on the sharing economy was held before the Committee on Small Business in the House of Representatives in 2014: *The Power of Connection: Peer-to-Peer Businesses.* The hearing engages with the new phenomenon that draws more and more attention. In the hearing, it becomes clear that the understanding of these new platforms is still very limited, but they it is seen as an important issue for Congress to discuss. Chairman Graves (Rep) begins by saying that the "newness of these platforms limits our ability to know the true economic impact, these new businesses appear to be creating significant shifts in the economy and demonstrate potential for significant economic growth and job creation" (Congress 2014: 1). Representative Velazquez (Dem) sees the success of the sharing economy platforms a little differently:

> One reason for this sector's rapid growth may be rooted in broader economic struggles. With job growth still sluggish, enterprising Americans and dislocated workers are seeking new ways to replace revenue. Renting out rooms, providing lifts in their car, and selling homemade goods, food goods, have all become ways for ordinary Americans to experiment with entrepreneurship and stay afloat during tougher economic times. (. . .) It is important this Committee fully understands what is happening in the new sharing economy and has a grasp on how we can minimize risk for consumers while maximizing growth and productivity from peer-to-peer business models. (Congress 2014: 2)

One of the experts invited to the meeting is Arun Sundararajan. As he elaborates in his book *The Sharing Economy*, Sundararajan believes in the sharing economy's ability to

> stimulate consumption, raise productivity, catalyze innovation, and facilitate entrepreneurship. (. . .) These platforms enable entrepreneurs, people who want to supply goods and services, to fulfill demand from consumers, people who want to buy, rent, or consume. Thus, they create millions of new, very small businesses or what are being called micro-entrepreneurs. (Congress 2014: 3)

Sundararajan believes that the peer-to-peer businesses will have a positive effect on economic growth in general and will be a means to provide work and an income in a more nontraditional sense. He also argues that new and better goods and services will come out of the peer-to-peer sector, which offers new ways of consumption. It also holds the potential to experiment with entrepreneurship and use underutilized assets, making these more efficient (Congress 2014: 4).

Yet, from the other experts invited to the panel one can see that the sharing economy was still a very new field and that many of the platforms failed after a short time. Beth Stevens from Sidecar was invited to testify in 2014. Sidecar closed down in 2015 and was acquired by GM. Alan Mond, Co-Founder of 1000 Tools, was also invited. His tool-sharing platform is no longer in operation. This shows that there are a lot of ups and downs in the sharing economy and that many of the startups never really take off.

As a fourth expert in the hearing, Philip Auerswald from George Mason University comments on the "newness" of the sharing economy platforms as well:

> So is there any fundamentally new about the sorts of peer-to-peer businesses that have been proliferating in the past five years? Yes. The difference between the past and the present is in the platforms over which people find one another, conclude transactions, and establish reputations. The triple revolutions in computation, communications, and algorithmic power (…). (Congress 2014: 9)

Philip Auerswald is optimistic that the sharing economy will pose a solution for the meager job growth that many of the new digital businesses display. Auerswald testifies:

> While some scale-ups creates large numbers of new jobs, many do not. Companies like Apple, Google, Facebook, Instagram, and Twitter have all achieved valuations in the tens and even hundreds of billions of dollars but they directly employ far fewer people per dollar of revenue than their Fortune 500 counterparts did a generation ago. This is where peer-to-peer platforms come into play. By their very structure, peer-to-peer platforms scale out success to reach tens of thousands, even hundreds of thousands of people with opportunities to create viable livelihoods for themselves. (…) The issue is not whether new livelihoods based on peer-to-peer business models are better or worse than the industrial-aged jobs that are disappearing from large corporations. The real point is when jobs are eliminated in the process of digital disruption, they will not be coming back in their old form. As that happens, we humans have no choice but to fall back on our fundamental social skillset, creating and sharing with one another. There is, however, one big difference. Unlike our isolated ancestors of millennia past, Americans in this century are empowered by architectures of collaboration that allow for the creation of new and diverse livelihood at unprecedented rates. Therein lies the power of today's peer-to-peer economy. (Congress 2014: 14)

Auerswald is thus very hopeful that platforms will actually provide a new way toward careers and a stable livelihood, a view that will consequently be challenged in the following years.

Apart from this early hearing on technological innovations like the sharing economy, the House of Representatives in fact held a whole series on new industries called *The Disrupter Series*. One hearing in this series was specifically dedicated to the sharing economy. In 2015, the hearing *The Disrupter Series: How the Sharing Economy Creates Jobs, Benefits Consumers, and Raises Policy Questions* took place in the Subcommittee on Commerce, Manufacturing, and Trade in the House of Representatives.

One of the witnesses is the Co-Director of the Center for Economic and Policy Research (CEPR), Dean Baker. He emphasizes the ideals of the sharing economy, which is to use idling objects to their full potential, for example renting out a spare room, or to give people the option to work in their spare time for extra income. Yet, Baker also talks about the possible risks of a growing sharing economy and details different aspects of possible reform: labor regulations including the classification of workers, consumer protection, regulations of property rights, and rules prohibiting discrimination in the provision of the services, as well as taxation of users activity and platform owners (Congress 2015b: 2f). Congress should also strengthen gig workers' rights to bargain collectively and settle who is eligible for employee-like protections like the minimum wage, hours regulations, or social benefits like unemployment insurance. As for consumer protection, many non-sharing economy companies have to meet safety and nondiscriminatory standards, which should be applied to sharing economy businesses as well (e.g., background checks on employees, fire protection standards, or disability access standards). Moreover, some sharing economy businesses blur the line between commercial and residential use of property (e.g., Airbnb or Uber) and Baker asks for a discussion on how best to reform or regulate this phenomenon (Congress 2015b: 3ff). In general, Baker concludes by saying: "We want companies to compete to provide better and cheaper services, not to determine who can more effectively game the regulatory structure and the tax code" (Congress 2015b: 12).

Apart from the witnesses, several of the committee members comment on the concept of the sharing economy themselves. Michael C. Burgess (Rep), for instance, states that what

> sharing platforms provide are often in addition to, not necessarily instead of, the streams of income available through traditional employment sources. The sharing economy has captured the entrepreneurial spirit of many Americans already. Those who engage in freelance jobs are expected to skyrocket to 40 percent of the workforce in the next 5 years, and almost 8 million will be participating in a sharing economy. (Congress 2015a: 2)

Burgess wants to discuss the possibilities of accountability and consumer protections inside the platform economy and whether Congress has to respond in any way to the new companies: "generally speaking, the sharing economy companies do face regulations, like most other firms, under the typical patchwork of Federal and State laws, and I, for one, am more concerned about existing regulations hurting new jobs than I am about the need for new regulations" (Congress 2015a: 2).

Janice D. Schakowsky (Dem) emphasizes the gig aspect of the sharing economy and how job preferences might change over time:

> For many millennials the gig economy model of employment may be appealing for a time, providing scheduling flexibility that many young people desire. But for many older workers, who used to have full time employment, or younger workers, seeking steady full time work, this transformational change is not always positive. The model of this economy (...) often eliminates benefits, like health care and pensions, and it means more questions about whether they can make ends meet (...). The gig economy companies argue that the individuals who generate earnings through the use of their technology are independent contractors. (...) Making that claim may enable gig economy companies to avoid legal liability (...) [and] enables them to avoid Social Security contributions, and requirements to provide overtime pay, Workers' Compensation, and Unemployment benefits. The workers are atomized, and unable to collectively bargain in their own interest. (...) these entities are very often directly involved in almost every aspect of the transactions that occur by way of their technology. (Congress 2015a: 3f)

She continues by saying that gig platforms might have an unfair advantage if they do not ensure licensing, tax, or zoning requirements, something that other players in the market have to do. In her view, platforms should meet all existing requirements in order to ensure fair competition (Congress 2015a: 4).

Apart from Dean Baker, the *Disrupter Series* hearing on the sharing economy also features other witnesses. One of them is a "driving partner" (Uber calls its drivers "partners") for Uber, Luceele Smith who gives some insights in her work in the sharing economy environment. Smith highlights the flexibility that the ride-sharing platform offers, as well as the autonomy that lets her decide her own schedule and the amount of time she wants to work. She uses Uber to generate supplementary income, as many drivers do. She also highlights the contact with people that she enjoys during her drives. Yet, the most important thing that she emphasizes is the nontraditional work arrangements that she prefers, setting your own goals and schedule, which is virtually impossible in many other jobs (Congress 2015a: 8).

Another statement during the hearing is given by Michael Beckerman, President and CEO of the Internet Association. The Internet Association is "the unified voice of the Internet economy and its global community of users. We are dedicated to advancing public policy solutions to strengthen and protect Internet freedom, to foster innovation and growth, and to empower the global community of Internet users" (Congress 2015a: 10). As a lobby group for business actors in the Internet economy, Beckerman naturally advocates for little regulation and emphasizes how innovative the new companies are:

> These companies have an extraordinary story to tell, a story about job creation, about economic growth, opportunity, and life changing flexibility. Ride sharing and home sharing do get most of the attention, but these business models are really just the tip of the iceberg. Companies like Instacart, Washio, TaskRabbit, GetAround, Handy, and Thumbtack, who is here with us today, are changing the way we shop, do our laundry, rent cars, improve our homes, and so much more. The incredible consumer benefits of these platforms pales in comparison to the benefits of flexible earning opportunities for those that opt-in to meet consumer demand. (Congress 2015a: 10)

Beckerman also talks about local differences, which he as a lobbyist for Internet businesses rebukes by saying that what

> we are seeing across the country is a tale of two cities. In some communities, regulators embrace new technology and competition. In these communities, consumers in the local economy have seen job creation and growth. Unfortunately, there are other communities where policymakers and regulators have put up roadblocks that block consumer choice and competition. In these areas, the community is worse off when arbitrary barriers are placed on new entrants to the market. Competition is stamped out, growth is stifled, and opportunities are lost. (Congress 2015a: 10)

Beckerman is rather vocal about the benefits of digital platforms, painting a widely positive picture of consumer surplus and opportunities with virtually no downsides. He slams regulators who want to stifle the platforms wholeheartedly. He suggests that political action is only necessary if there are consumer protection concerns. He also emphasizes that there are many self-regulatory measures that the platforms take to provide a better consumer experience (Congress 2015a: 11).

Alex Chriss, Vice President of QuickBooks Self-Employed Business, also testifies and talks about the self-employment aspects of the sharing economy:

> In the past few years we have noticed an acceleration of a trend that began decades ago. We believe this trend to be a massive shift in employment towards a more independent, or self-employed workforce. Intuit recently conducted a study forecasting that self-employed will grow to represent 43 percent of the workforce by 2020. A very fast growing segment of this

new workforce is the sharing economy. According to our data, 3.2 million Americans are earning income from the sharing economy. Within 5 years, our survey suggests the total population of sharing economy workers will more than double, to 7.6 million. (Congress 2015a: 43)

Chriss emphasizes that the tax structure in the USA is a burden on many of the workers in the sharing economy because it treats them as small business owners, when many are not (Congress 2015a: 43). Many sharing economy platforms would like to help their workers but shy away from doing so because they do not want to trigger issues around the employer status or worker classification (Congress 2015a: 44).

Jonathan Lieber from Thumbtack also testifies in the hearing, going deeper into the issue of self-employment. He worked for the Thumbtack network, connecting professionals with customers. He emphasizes that worker classification issues are not new, especially for small businesses. He decries that government has built a two-tier system for individuals who work in larger companies full-time, and everyone else. This way, self-employment is not supported because becoming self-employed often means leaving behind all state-supported benefits associated with employment. Lieber argues:

And although Congress has attempted to extend some of these benefits outside the workplace through the Affordable Care Act and tax-free savings vehicles, like IRAs, there is more that could be done. To the extent possible, benefits should be tied to the worker, and not their place of work, or their form of compensation. (Congress 2015a: 64)

But how do these platforms differ in their way of treating independent contractors? Dean Baker argues that in traditional circumstances, contractors have control over their time, their wage rate, and what they do. Yet, this differs on digital platforms:

I sometimes write a paper, sometimes I will be paid on commission. Well, if someone contacts me, they say, 'We need this in two weeks,' I am going to decide what it looks like, I will decide the content. That is really not the case with Uber. They specify the rules. In a lot of ways, that is a good thing. We want to make sure that, when you drive an Uber, the car's safe, other conditions are met, but that is not the situation of an independent contractor. (Congress 2015a: 75)

Going into even more detail on the issues of the sharing economy, 2016 saw two more hearings in Congress, this time on taxation in the sharing economy. The Committee on Small Business in the House of Representatives held these hearings titled *The Sharing Economy: A Taxing Experience for New Entrepreneurs (Part I, II)*. These two hearings are mainly concerned with taxation but also comment on the larger structure of these new platforms. The fact that two hearings are called on the subject of the sharing economy and taxation shows how prevalent the topic has become. Chairman Chabot (Rep) stressed that the committee members were

here to examine an exciting new phenomenon in our society, the sharing economy. This new economy goes by many names—app, gig, on-demand, peer-to-peer, online platform, and collaborative. We have even heard it called the 'Uber economy.' (...) No matter what you call it, the sharing economy is changing the face of American entrepreneurship and small businesses before our very eyes. The dizzying pace of this change has presented many new

> opportunities and new challenges for the millions of Americans who participate in it. These new platforms have dramatically changed the ways companies provide goods and services, giving their workers unprecedented freedom and independence. This new generation of workers wants to set their own hours and decide which jobs to take. They may work with one on-demand platform or multiple platforms. (. . .) This is the essence of economic liberty and a testament to the power of the free market. (Congress 2016d: 1)

Representative Velazquez (Dem) stresses economic opportunity but also economic struggles as the reason behind the success of the platforms. She argues that one

> reason for this sector's rapid growth may be rooted in broader economic struggles. With job growth still sluggish, enterprising Americans and dislocated workers are seeking new ways to replace revenue. Others seek more flexibility and work-life balance. Renting out rooms and providing lifts in their car have all become ways for ordinary Americans to experiment with entrepreneurship. While the explosive growth of these networks has created new opportunities, the rapid rise raises questions. While many of the workers in the shared economy enjoy flexibility, they must be protected from unscrupulous business practices. (Congress 2016d: 2)

Worker classification is again raised as an issue, which many businesses and courts are trying to solve. It remains an issue to support innovation and to protect the workers at the same time. "Control is a critical factor to this question. If the employer controls the worker, how can the worker be truly independent? With the rise of the sharing economy, this question has become harder to answer as workers are connected to consumers through online intermediaries" (Congress 2016d: 2).

In the statement by the expert witness Caroline Bruckner, Executive-in-Residence at Kogod Tax Policy Center, she explains that under the current tax code, everyone who is active on on-demand platforms is a small business owner. The earnings gathered through platforms are not easily identifiable by existing government research or publicly available taxpayer filing data. She therefore suggests an update to the tax code in order to treat these workers more fairly and not burden them unnecessarily (Congress 2016d: 4). She further says:

> This reflects the explosive growth of the on-demand platform economy but is just the latest example of a 66.5 percent increase in alternative work arrangements for U.S. workers from 2005 to 2015. Second, although people do cycle in and out of the on-demand platform economy, during months in which people are actively using platforms to earn income, average monthly income ranges from $533 to $314 per month. (Congress 2016d: 5)

Bruckner argues that work on the sharing economy platform is growing, alongside the overall growth of alternative work arrangements, but that earnings from platform work often remain a secondary source of income overall. She goes on to say that after investigating providers and sellers on the platforms, her team found that many of them lack the understanding of self-employed tax filing obligations.

The Vice President of TaskRabbit was also called as a witness in the hearing, stating TaskRabbit's commitment to the new economy and the opportunities it offered to the "taskers." Most taskers supplement their steady income with work on the platform, enjoying the low barriers to entry and flexibility of the platform.

Yet, in his view, the growing debate on the classification of these taskers is a potential threat to the growth of the platform economy (Congress 2016d: 6f).

The issue of worker classification in the sharing economy comes up in other hearings as well. For example, in *The 21st Century Workforce: How Current Rules and Regulations Affect Innovation and Flexibility of Michigan's Workplaces*, Jared Meyer, author and fellow at Manhattan Institute for Policy Research, argues that

> Companies such as Uber and Airbnb offer the technical platform and support to allow transactions between buyers and sellers to easily take place. For this reason, these types of companies are often referred to as 'intermediaries.' Those who partner with intermediaries are classified as independent contractors, not employees. The flexibility that independent contractor status offers workers is vital to the success of the sharing economy. While some workers use these platforms full-time, the vast majority use them for part-time work and supplemental income. (…) Furthermore, half of Lyft drivers work another job while partnering with the company, and two-thirds of Uber drivers work another job as well. (Congress 2016a: 19)

Thus, Meyer would not argue in favor of an employee classification for platform workers as it could destroy the business model of the sharing economy platforms and thus easy and flexible ways of income for many. He thinks it makes little sense to extend benefits like the minimum wage, overtime pay, unemployment insurance, etc., to independent contractors, as platform intermediaries do not control working hours. These business models are also hard to combine with minimum wage and overtime pay rules. But most of all, Meyer advocates for government action when it comes to the issue of worker classification. Government should not hand this responsibility over to the court system (Congress 2016a: 20). When asked about how the platforms could offer provisions for their workers, and still keep them as independent contractors, Meyer argues in favor of portable benefits, an idea that sharing economy businesses support (Congress 2016a: 63).

Dale Belman, professor at the School of Human Resources and Labor Relations, Michigan State University who testifies at the same hearing, thinks differently of the so-called gig economy. He argues that albeit all the talk of how innovative and new the gig economy is, many of the issues discussed have been debated for a long time, for example in the construction industry. Working in construction shares many characteristics with the gig economy as employment is temporary, employers change often, and misclassification is frequent. Construction workers also often struggle to gain benefits such as health care or pensions. Therefore, Belman suggests a better enforcement of minimum labor standards, in construction and gig work, instead of creating new laws or categories (Congress 2016a: 36).

4.4.1 Impressions from the Congressional Hearings

After the initial examination of some the congressional hearings, there are some things that stand out. In general, the most important subjects discussed were issues around if and how the developments of automation and technological advancement change the American economy and the workforce, and how politics needs to react in order to strengthen growth, but also to protect and support the American labor force.

Productivity and job growth were key issues that were discussed at length in the hearings. But with new technological development, it is questionable if they will still go hand in hand. Some experts already see a decoupling of productivity growth on the one hand, and job and income growth on the other. This ultimately leads to a hollowing out of the middle class, especially because many middle-income jobs have been replaced more and more by automation processes. This can be seen in manufacturing for instance. Manufacturing output has been growing, yet manufacturing employment is in decline. Therefore, experts demand that the government should focus on ensuring that the prosperity produced in the new economy will be shared more widely.

The discussion around whether the concerns about the future are valid has not subsided. So far, technological advancement has always made some jobs obsolete, but created new and better jobs in other places. Concerns about the future were often overblown. Moreover, many see the advance of robotics and artificial intelligence (AI) as rather positive as it will eventually support and improve human work. This discussion is also reflected in the hearings. Some members and experts do not see automation processes as a concerning issue for the future. Only the transition phase poses a problem, especially when this phase is making many jobs obsolete at the same time, without enough time for the workforce to adapt. They see globalization, offshoring of jobs, and weak labor unions as equally important as automation when talking about the threat to income and good jobs. Yet, others see a new quality to the technological progress of today because machines are increasingly getting better at human tasks such as cognitive and creative work. Especially AI is a key technology for the future that is in fact already part of many of our appliances today, such as smartphones or home appliances such as Amazon's Alexa or Google Home. There is concern that AI is going to replace many common jobs such as truck driving in the future when automated cars will have become the norm. More high-skilled occupations will be in demand, but the question remains how many routine workers can really be upskilled to do other jobs. Jobs that pay under $20 per hour could prove likely to be automated, meaning that a vast group of workers could lose their occupation due to technology.

Consumer benefits of the new economy are mentioned over and over in the hearings, both by lawmakers and by business advocates. The sharing economy platforms and other technologies have brought many advantages to consumers, which are notoriously hard to measure. Congress members were therefore also very interested in the consumer safety side of the new economy. They frequently ask about consumer data and privacy concerning digital services and platforms. Additionally, concerns were voiced especially about the platforms adhering to anti-discrimination or worker classification rules. Yet, Congress was also concerned about maintaining the innovative edge of the new economy. They want to make sure that the rules governing the economy do not stifle innovation and economic growth. There usually is a debate about the right set of rules and regulations on the one hand and "permissionless innovation" on the other hand.

The skills gap was another issue that was discussed extensively and throughout many hearings. The skills gap is most often mentioned as the reason for rising inequality and stagnating incomes. Many experts argue that many American workers do not have the skills that are in high demand in the economy and therefore they cannot benefit from economic growth. They are stuck in occupations that have increasingly come under threat. Experts therefore argue for upskilling in fields where skills will be adaptable and not easily automated. These include creative fields and social skill sets, as well as entrepreneurial skills. Yet, some do admit that many of the occupations that are not easily automated, for example in the field of care work, usually do not pay well. Therefore, some argue in favor of government support for workers in poorly paying sectors.

Another issue related to the skills gap is access to education in the USA. Higher education is much more expensive in the USA than in other countries. But many jobs of the future demand some graduate education or specific training beyond a 4-year college degree. Therefore, the USA must invest more in its education system. Moreover, many experts have argued in favor of research and development based in the USA. It is questionable considering the competition from Asia, if the USA can keep up its position in the production of technological goods. Therefore, Congress wants to strengthen the US competitiveness in this field. Many experts raised concerns that the US economy is less dynamic than in the past despite the progress in automation and the gig economy.

Inequality as a broad issue was also mentioned in some of the hearings. For example, it was discussed with the Economic Adviser of the President in the Joint Economic Committee. Many economists see a certain amount of inequality as natural to a market economy. Yet, the rise in inequality that has occurred in the USA in recent years is a problem for the whole of the American economy and workforce. There are several factors mentioned that led to the rise in inequality, including an aging society that puts the social security net under pressure, offshoring of jobs due to globalization, as well as job and income losses due to automation and technological change. Moreover, a rise in inequality is blamed on the rise in "rents," meaning that certain companies and workers have captured much larger gains and incomes than their productivity would justify. This leads to a hollowing out of middle income. However, some experts did not see automation and technological advancement as a problem per se. Innovation is generally good for the economy. Yet, the actual problem with inequality, as argued in some of the testimony, is that inequality in wealth and income eventually leads to inequality of opportunity. This inequality of opportunity is also mentioned when talking about dynamism of the American workforce and economy. Inequality is a barrier to dynamism as people lack the means to upskill and look for better opportunities for themselves because they are already struggling to make ends meet. Employers lack the skilled workforce they need. Additionally, the prosperity that is created through the advances in technology is not shared widely. Consumers have benefitted from technological progress as services and goods have become cheaper. Yet, there is no economic law that says that the prosperity created through growth is shared equally or fairly among all. Therefore, Congress discusses the fact that there are many groups in society that have been left behind despite technological advancement.

In the congressional hearings, GDP and other economic measurements are often mentioned as inadequate to really reflect the changes in the economy. Certain economic indicators also do not reflect the actual situation of households very well. Although the economy has been growing since the end of Great Recession, many families still feel the economic pinch. In the last recession, many people lost their jobs and most of their household wealth, and have still not fully recovered.

In this context, some Representatives and Senators see the success of the gig economy in terms of wider economic struggles where many families look for further income to maintain their standard of living. Others see the sharing or gig economy as a positive way to experiment with entrepreneurship, which should be supported. Especially in the early hearings on the sharing economy, things like opportunity, entrepreneurship, and "idling capacity" were stressed. The sharing economy was presented as a new way of consumption and making an income at the same time. Hearings on small business also painted a picture of the sharing economy as a hub for small entrepreneurs who are unduly burdened with taxes. With more hearings on the matter, the understanding of the type of work on sharing economy platforms grew and economic struggles became more present as an argument for the success of the platforms. The entrepreneurial opportunities of the sharing economy continued to be voiced by Congress members, however.

There was also a lot of debate about how the attitudes toward work have been changing. Especially working time has changed tremendously because of technological advances. Both employers and employees see the new possibilities they have using technology in the workplace. Many of the smart technologies make it possible to work from home or on the road, blurring leisure and working time. This demands more flexibility but is often also a chance for employees to organize their lives in a more independent way. Innovative ways to work become more prominent, including freelance or independent work. Yet, these ways of working are often in conflict with existing labor laws, which has been the basis for much debate in Congress. Are the new technologies only a vehicle for employers to extract more productivity from workers without giving them protections under the law? Or are the technologies a way to actually work in a flexible and autonomous fashion that lets workers decide about family, leisure, and working time? The rise of the platform economy and sharing economy platforms seems to point in the direction of more nontraditional work arrangements, a trend that has been going on for years. While some see it as a sign of slow recovery and status loss of the middle class, others see in the rise of the sharing economy a growing demand from workers to have flexible options to work that are in line with their private lives. More free market inclined politicians thus clearly stress the flexibility and opportunity aspect and see the platform economy as the essence of the free market and economic liberty. On the other end of the spectrum there are those experts that do not see any difference between the sharing economy and ordinary piecemeal work. The construction industry is one example that is close to the platform economy when it comes to the situation of labor. Construction workers have faced similar problems as gig workers for years, as many employers do not comply with existing standards. Therefore, some experts suggest focusing on compliance with existing labor regulation instead of creating new regulation.

Many platforms claim to be intermediaries who only connect supply and demand. Yet, most platforms do exert more control over the workers of the platform than they want to admit. This includes fees, payment methods and rates, standards of behavior, or removal from the platform. Therefore, some experts see platforms as ordinary employers who do not want to adhere to labor standards. Others agree with this saying that only because many people do gig work on the side with another main job, it does not mean that labor regulations should be ignored. However, many acknowledge the growth of nontraditional work arrangements overall, which means that some regulation might need updating. Usually, it is crucial how much control an employer exerts over the worker, which then determines if the worker is classified as independent or employed. Some experts argue that if you do not control working hours, there is no control in the traditional sense and therefore a digital platform is not an employer. Platforms are therefore not bound by rules like minimum wage and overtime pay. But if the behavior of platforms really exempts them from employer status is a question that remains unresolved. This issue has increasingly led to litigation in different cities and states. As the on-demand attitude is spreading, some experts ask for better support of the self-employed workforce by the government. All in all, there is often a call for protection of workers on the one hand and a support of the flexible arrangements on the other hand. Also, there are several unresolved issues that sharing platforms have raised, including residential vs. commercial use of property, stable provisions of income, legal liability, and taxation issues.

4.4.2 Suggested Policies in Context of the Future of Work

Certain policies were suggested by experts and lawmakers in order to ease issues connected to the future of work and to support further growth through automation and the platform economy.

One common suggestion from politicians of both parties was an update and improvement of the ailing US infrastructure. Internet availability, access, and speed need to be improved. Additionally, the education system and the area of original research at universities and in fields like machine learning and AI call for updates. Especially the education system is in focus throughout the selection of hearings first examined. Due to technological progress and automation, many jobs disappear or demand advanced skills. Therefore, experts and Congress members argue in favor of lifelong learning and upskilling of the workforce. Otherwise, the chances of finding a well-paying job in the future are rather bleak. Inside the education system, technical skills are important. Yet, also creative and social skills are mentioned several times. These are skills that are considered less prone to automation and could therefore last into the future. There are also calls to make the education system more accessible and affordable in order to bring more people into higher education. Additionally, there were many debates focusing on the support for community colleges and apprenticeship programs that are more common in places like Germany.

Some experts argued in favor of new and less restrictive immigration reform in order to attract the best talent to the USA and improve competitiveness. Entrepreneurship should also be supported by government. Other legislation that was suggested included portable social benefits and a new classification of workers. Moreover, policies were suggested to support workers in low-wage jobs such as wage insurance programs. The universal basic income (UBI) was only discussed in a limited manner. The UBI is mostly mentioned in connection with technological progress and the replacement of many workers in the more distant future. Occasionally, the UBI is mentioned in connection with the social security system that could run out of money in due time. Although the UBI itself is not a frequent topic, there are other measures mentioned that resemble the UBI such as the negative income tax, calls for "subsidizing non-work" for people who lose their jobs, a wage insurance program, as well as the earned income tax credit (EITC). The former would insure people against wage loss when they have to move into new jobs that might pay less than previous jobs. Earned income tax credits would subsidize job creation and worker retainment from the government side, in comparison to the minimum wage. Instead of raising the wage floor, the EITC system subsidizes low-income households with tax credits. In the future, this could ensure that people working in low-income jobs like elderly or health care will still be able to make a living. The EITC as a policy was mentioned by several politicians from both parties and different experts.

Apart from policies focusing on the workforce, there were frequent calls to improve consumer safety and handle data privacy issues for platforms. Cyberattacks on consumer data need to be prevented and better security systems should be in place. Additionally, there are demands to regulate property rights when commercial and private usages are blurred. Moreover, anti-discrimination rules and better information on taxation of many activities in the platform economy should be upheld and provided. In general, there is often the call to regulate platforms or digital businesses if consumer safety is concerned but not for competitive reasons. The self-regulatory function of the market is emphasized in this context. These calls mostly come from the business side but are supported by many legislators.

In order to tackle inequality, there are several policies mentioned. Infrastructure building and education reform are among them. There are calls for better (early childhood) education, paid parental or sick leave for workers, better child care for workers, equal pay for equal work, improving affordability of education, and reducing the tax penalties for second earners in a household. Education and skill-building are seen as the main factors in this equation. These policies should be designed to enhance economic opportunity and the labor participation rate. There are also frequent calls to raise the minimum wage moderately, despite fears of automation in the fields where the minimum wage is crucial.

In relation to the platform economy, there were frequent calls to make the available social benefits portable when someone has multiple employers throughout their career and lifetime. In general, there were also demands for better support of the group of self-employed and independents that is a growing part of the US labor market. Some see measures like the Affordable Care Act as a first step to give the small-scale self-employed means to ensure their social status and benefits. Tax-free savings for retirement and social benefits that are tied to the worker, not the job, are frequently mentioned. Also, there is a need to collect more data about the group of self-employed in order to find out what they really need and demand. In relation to the benefits, an update of the tax code is argued for because in the eyes of the tax system every gig worker is a small business owner. This is often a heavy burden on the small-scale activities that make some extra income.

An update of the classification of workers is also frequently discussed. As mentioned before, some see the platforms as just another regular employer who wants to get around the existing rules and regulations. Yet, some aspects of digital platforms could be classified as a new form of the employer–employee relationship, something in between independent and employed, in fact. Platforms usually do not control the times and hours worked, yet they often impose some rules like pricing or standards, which they can also change unilaterally. Therefore, many see the gig workers as caught in between the independent contractor status and employee. Some legislators therefore call for an update of these classifications of workers as they do not reflect the current reality anymore. Many legislators want to strengthen gig workers' right to bargain collectively (independents are usually prohibited from bargaining collectively), as well as give them protections that are quite the same as those for regular employees such as minimum wage, hours regulations, and unemployment benefits. Others do not want to enforce these measures because it might ruin the business model of platforms and because it does not reflect the interests of the platform workers correctly who mostly just want to earn something on the side.

In general, one can say that debates and policies that are suggested to ease the difficulties of the transition to a more digitized economy are mostly not innovative. Policies that focus mostly on better infrastructure and especially education do not differ greatly from measures that were used in the past to alleviate issues of inequality or technological transition. And of course, they are necessary. The USA lags behind other developed nations when it comes to educating their citizens. So, much of the situation could be improved if the so-called skills gap was reduced and Americans had access to better and (higher) education. Moreover, infrastructure reform is something that has been discussed for a long time but has not come to fruition. Yet, there still seem to be few ideas about what to do when automation progresses and good jobs will be even harder to come by for most Americans. There might be more and more middle-skill jobs that disappear due to the advances in technology such as AI. Apart from the universal basic income (and measures that resemble it like the negative income tax) that was only briefly mentioned, there seems to be no sense of urgency among many of the legislators to really look into that issue further.

In the end, most of them seem convinced that jobs will disappear, but will eventually come back in other places and better form. The American citizens only have to be trained in a better way to be able to get these jobs and participate in the economic growth of the new economy. One of the biggest obstacles to this development, however, still remains: Rising inequality among Americans. As former Economic Adviser Furman said, inequality of income eventually leads to inequality of opportunity, which poses a problem for the entire American society. Additionally, the American education system is neither affordable nor fit enough in its current form to train or upskill a big part of the American workforce. An improved community college system, as well as more on-the-job training, could help in the situation but can hardly be enough. The USA also needs to train more people in higher education. Still, it remains questionable which kinds of skills are best suited to adapt to an ever-more digitized economy and which skills can secure a well-paying job. Moreover, there is some acknowledgment that this transition phase of replacement, technological unemployment, and reskilling could take years and could end up being problematic and painful for many workers.

As for the platform economy, it is clear that the success of it points to several issues: First, it appears that more and more people are looking for further income through different sources and the platform economy offers an easy and fast access to it. The income from a stable middle-income job is apparently not enough anymore to sustain a middle-class lifestyle. Second, it points to a bigger trend, the rise of nontraditional forms of work. This segment of the labor market has been growing for years and is further advanced through the success of smart technologies. Attitudes and behavior of both employers and workers have changed and we have moved toward an on-demand economy in many ways. More and more workers are not interested in a nine-to-five job for the rest of their lives. They want to make sure they can strike a work–life balance, sometimes by working on your own independently. They also might want to have the chance to earn extra income when they deem it necessary with something they might enjoy. Platforms are often an easy way to do so. Employers have an interest in hiring independents as they are a way to save labor costs. But they also want to hire independents because they are flexible and can work on a project basis in an on-demand manner. Independents are also often a way to hire creative talent. This should not obscure, however, that not all platform work is a great opportunity and makes everyone an entrepreneur or small business owner. Much of the platform or overall independent work done by gig workers or contractors is something they need and not the fulfillment of their dreams. Many workers who are independent would prefer a more stable form of employment and engage in these "side hustles" because they need to make ends meet.

The debates in the Congress hearings investigated here are a good indicator to show that digitization and automation are processes that are ongoing, and the height of their impact is not yet here. These trends will continue to trigger discussions in many different policy fields. The platform economy is also hotly debated on many occasions. It seems that platforms are already here to stay, and their business model is spreading throughout the world and in all kinds of sectors. Debates around platforms include the allusion to the opportunities platforms offer to workers who enjoy the flexible and easy access to work. Yet, platforms remain contested when it comes to labor and consumer safety standards. In order to sustain the platform business models and give workers a fair share, there is much talk about portable social benefits. This is not only interesting for gig workers, but for the whole group of the small-scale self-employed. If benefits are accessible and affordable, many of the issues around gigging could be eased. As many legislators have said, the success of the platform economy could point to larger economic struggles among Americans who look for cheaper products and easy ways to gain extra income. Therefore, policies discussed in Congress often try to find a compromise between, on the one hand, sustaining the platforms, and, on the other hand, supporting the livelihoods of workers who sustain these businesses and make them successful. From what could be seen in the hearings in Congress, there are mostly two sides. One that wants as little regulation as possible and wants sharing economy platforms to grow and strife as they are. They emphasize the great consumer experience, the improved services, as well as the flexible ways to work. The other side sees platforms as predatory business models taking advantage of vulnerable and desperate workers. They say that platforms are just like other employers who do not want to adhere to existing labor standards such as minimum wage and overtime pay. In order to make the sharing economy platforms work for everyone, Congress will continuously be asked to strike a balance between the two.

References

Baker P (2006) Using corpora in discourse analysis. Continuum, London

Brezina V, Timperley M, McEnery T (2018) #LancsBox v. 3-4.x [software]. http://corpora.lancs.ac.uk/lancsbox

Congress (2014) The power of connection: peer-to-peer businesses. U.S. Government Publishing Office, Washington, DC

Congress (2015a) The disrupter series: how the sharing economy creates jobs, benefits consumers, and raises policy questions. U.S. Government Publishing Office, Washington, DC

Congress (2015b) The opportunities and risks of the sharing economy. U.S. Government Publishing Office, Washington, DC

Congress (2016a) The 21st century workforce: how current rules and regulations affect innovation and flexibility in Michigan's workplaces. U.S. Government Publishing Office, Washington, DC

Congress (2016b) The dawn of artificial intelligence. U.S. Government Publishing Office, Washington, DC

Congress (2016c) The economic report of the president. U.S. Government Publishing Office, Washington, DC

Congress (2016d) The sharing economy: a taxing experience for new entrepreneurs, Part I. U.S. Government Publishing Office, Washington, DC

Congress (2016e) The transformative impact of robots and automation. U.S. Government Publishing Office, Washington, DC

Congress (2017) The decline of economic opportunity in the United States: causes and consequences. U.S. Government Publishing Office, Washington, DC

Congress (2019) Joint Economic Committee. https://www.jec.senate.gov/public/index.cfm/about. Accessed 23 Jan 2020

Cotter C (2015) Discourse and media. In: Tannen D, Hamilton HE, Schiffrin D (eds) The handbook of discourse analysis, 2nd edn. Wiley, New York, pp 795–821

Ellis EG (2019) Why social media companies frown on 'gaming the algorithm'. Wired. https://www.wired.com/story/platforms-gaming-algorithm/. Accessed 20 July 2020

Fairclough N (2007) Analysing discourse: textual analysis for social research. Routledge, New York

McEnery T, Hardie A (2012) Corpus linguistics: method, theory and practice. Cambridge textbooks in linguistics (Kindle edition). Cambridge University Press, Cambridge, UK

OED (2020) Oxford English Dictionary. https://www-oed-com.ubproxy.ub.uni-heidelberg.de/view/Entry/200321?rskey=XAWSzq&result=1#eid. Accessed 21 July 2020

Office USGP (2018) Congressional hearings. https://www.gpo.gov/fdsys/browse/collection.action?collectionCode=CHRG&browsePath=110&isCollapsed=true&leafLevelBrowse=false&ycord=5.555555820465088. Accessed 19 Feb 2018

Partington A (2013) Corpus analysis of political language. The encyclopedia of applied linguistics. Blackwell, Oxford. https://doi.org/10.1002/9781405198431.wbeal0250

Pew-Research-Center (2019) Public's 2019 priorities: economy, health care, education and security all near top of list. Pew Research Center. https://www.people-press.org/2019/01/24/publics-2019-priorities-economy-health-care-education-and-security-all-near-top-of-list/. Accessed 10 May 2021

Pew-Research-Center (2020) U.S. media polarization and the 2020 election: a nation divided. Pew Research Center. https://www.journalism.org/2020/01/24/u-s-media-polarization-and-the-2020-election-a-nation-divided/. Accessed 21 July 2020

Soroka SN, Stecula DA, Wlezien C (2015) It's (change in) the (future) economy, stupid: economic indicators, the media, and public opinion. Am J Polit Sci 59(2):457–474. https://doi.org/10.1111/ajps.12145

Tognini-Bonelli E (2001) Corpus linguistics at work. John Benjamins, Amsterdam

Wilson J (2015) Political discourse. In: Tannen D, Hamilton HE, Schiffrin D (eds) The handbook of discourse analysis, 2nd edn. Wiley, New York, pp 775–793. https://doi.org/10.1002/9781118584194

Chapter 5
Quantitative Analysis: Frequency Analysis

After initially examining some congressional hearings detailed in the previous chapter, we now turn to a more in-depth analysis of the textual material used in this book. The keyword list (Table 4.4) is used as a basis for a detailed frequency analysis of the corpus data. Using a quantitative approach to the corpora, based on both the congressional and media sources, allows for an overview of how the topics and issues of concern appear in the textual data, especially over time, and how intensively they are discussed in the sources other than through a qualitative close reading analysis.

In this chapter, the results for a selection of keywords from the five keyword categories *future trends*, *platform economy*, *technology*, *policies*, and *inequality* are presented and discussed. Thereafter, the qualitative analysis of the material will look at collocations of the terms *automation* and *digitization*, the *future of work*, and the *sharing economy* (*gig economy* and *platform economy*) in more detail as well as identify and compare the central themes around these issues in the source material.

For the first part of this chapter, a frequency analysis was conducted through the use of the corpus-linguistic software LancsBox (Brezina et al. 2018). With the help of this software different text corpora can be uploaded and examined. As said before, there are two corpora based on the congressional material: The House Corpus and the Senate Corpus (each of them is also divided into the years 2013–2017). Additionally, there are two corpora based on the media material: The liberal media corpus (containing the sources of the *NYT* and *Washington Post*) and the *Wall Street Journal* (*WSJ*) Corpus (both of the media corpora were also divided into years,

In this study, frequency data of the snapshot corpora are used without significance testing, which is more common in some strands of corpus linguistics like neo-Firthian studies (McEnery and Hardie 2012: 126). Although neo-Firthian approaches are usually not associated with corpus-as-method approaches but corpus-as-theory approaches, there are strands of methodologist approaches to be found in neo-Firthian corpus linguistics as well (McEnery and Hardie 2012: 167). The quantitative analysis here is solely based on relative frequencies. This means, keywords here are displayed only relative to one another in the respective corpus.

N. Rauscher, *The Future of Work in the United States*, Contributions to Economics,
https://doi.org/10.1007/978-3-030-82307-8_5

Table 5.1 Example of collocation parameters notation (CPN)

Statistic ID	Statistic name	Statistic cutoff value	L(eft) and R(ight) span	Minimum collocate frequency (C)	Minimum collocation frequency (NC)	Filter
4b	MI2	3	L5–R5	5	1	Function words removed

Based on Brezina (2018: 75)

respectively). In order to conduct the frequency analysis, the corpora were queried for all the keywords of the different categories shown in Table 4.4. A selection of the results is displayed in this chapter. Their occurrences were documented and are displayed below as normalized frequencies in "per 10,000 tokens," meaning how often the keyword appears in the amount of 10,000 tokens (or words) in the corpus.

In a subsequent step of the analysis that will follow in Chap. 6, the collocations of certain key terms are examined in the corpus data. Collocations are "combinations of words that habitually co-occur in texts and corpora" (Brezina 2018) and are significant as meaning-making elements of other words they occur with. Instead of mere frequency, collocations are based on a so-called association or collocation measure, which is a statistical measurement to calculate the strength of the association between different words. With this specific statistical measure certain themes and attitudes can be traced in the examined discourse. Collocations can indicate the views and assessments of terms and themes in different sources of text depending on the outlet or author.[1] In the collocation analysis of this book, MI score[2] was used. The collocations are then reported using different parameters. An example of such parameters are displayed in Table 5.1.[3]

[1]Mere frequency analysis of collocations usually delivers a generic set of mostly function words like *my, the, is,* etc., which are frequent with every word in the English language. Therefore, better results can be achieved by the use of an association measure such as MI score (Mutual Information Score), MI2, log Dice, Delta P, or others (Brezina 2018). The MI score seemed most appropriate for the data and research question of this work, as it highlights "rare exclusivity of the collocational relationship, favouring collocates which occur almost exclusively in the company of the node, even though this may be only once or twice in the entire corpus" (Brezina 2018). The MI score highlights not only frequency but so-called *exclusivity*, meaning the "collocation relationship where words occur only or predominantly in each other's company" (Brezina 2018).

[2]Although MI scores might be higher for low-frequency words than for high-frequency words and this can be misleading, it is actually very suitable for this analysis as the keywords and phrases of interest are often low frequency even in the highly specialized corpus and are rather specific in their usage. Proper names or technical terms are highlighted to a greater extent by MI (SketchEngine 2020; HarperCollins 2008).

[3]In the analysis of this work, MI($\geq$7), collocation frequency 5 was the default setting, which differed from the LancsBox default setting (MI($\geq$3), collocation frequency 5) because it led to overpopulated graphs. Therefore, a higher MI was set. In some instances throughout the collocation analysis, the settings had to be changed, which is indicated in the tables. Changes to the MI and collocation frequency settings were necessary in some instances to produce fewer collocations (overpopulated graph) or more collocations than with the original setting.

Table 5.2 Liberal media: future trends, per 10,000 tokens (all the following charts displaying data on frequency were produced by the author)

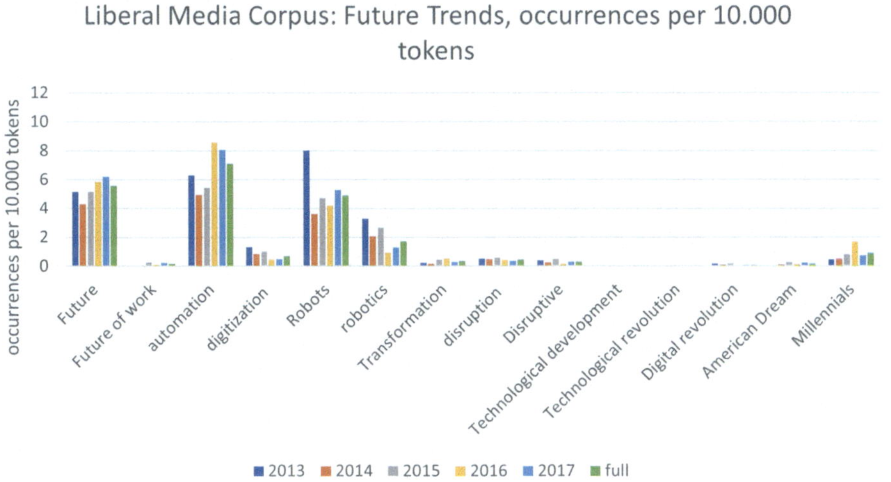

Source: Author

To visualize the results of the collocation analysis, tables of the most important collocations are displayed, as well as graphs that are computed by LancsBox. The collocation graphs can be useful as they are "a visual representation of the collocational relationship between a node and its collocates" (Brezina 2018) and will therefore be included below.

In the following, the frequency analysis of the keywords will first be presented, before moving on to the qualitative analysis of certain terms in the source material.

5.1 Future Trends[4]

As said before, the keyword list (Table 4.4) was used to examine the corpus data. Taking into account the first category, *future trends*, the corpora were examined for specific keywords such as *future, future of work, automation, digitization, robots, robotics, transformation, disruption, disruptive, technological development, technological revolution, digital revolution, American Dream, and millennials.*

Looking across the NYT and Washington Post Corpus (Table 5.2), the WSJ Corpus (Table 5.3), and the data from the House (Table 5.4) and the Senate

[4]The tables that show the diffusion of these terms are based on occurrences per 10,000 tokens, which means the occurrences of a specific term in the range of 10,000 words in the corpus, which makes it comparable with other corpus data independent of their respective sizes.

Table 5.3 *WSJ*: future trends, per 10,000 tokens

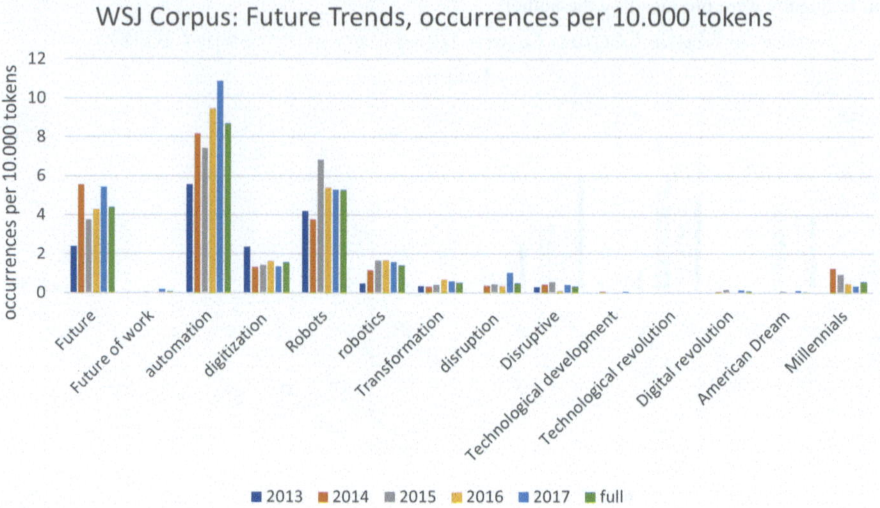

Source: Author

Table 5.4 House: future trends, per 10,000 tokens

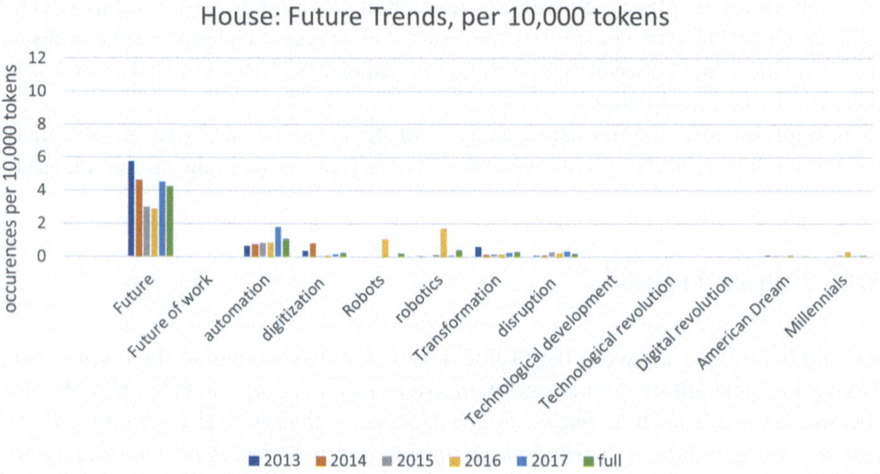

Source: Author

(Table 5.5), one can make different observations. First of all, we see many similarities. The term *future* features most prominently in the Senate and House data sets, as well as second most prominently in the liberal media data. It is only the third most prominent term in the WSJ data, after *automation* and *robots*. The most prominent

Table 5.5 Senate: future trends, per 10,000 tokens

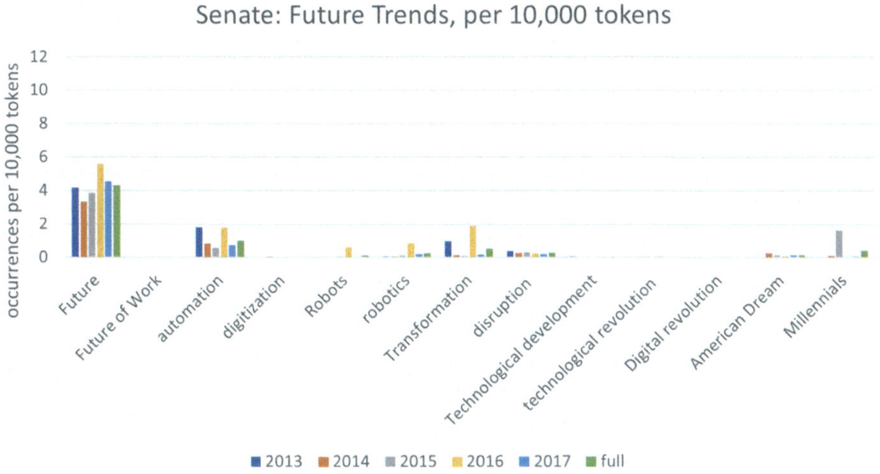

Source: Author

keyword in the liberal media data as well as in the WSJ data is *automation*. Yet, the term *future* is very broad; therefore, it is not surprising that it occurs quite frequently in sets that are based on technological trends. It seems only natural for it to be the most frequent term in the sources from Congress as politicians often discuss the future outlook of the country. As said before, the economic outlook of a country is very important to the public at large and so it seems reasonable that *future* occurs very frequently in the corpora concerned with future impact on the economy.

Looking at more specific keywords, we can see more similarities. The terms *disruption/disruptive* are not featured very prominently among either of the sets and seem to remain on a steady low level through the years. Although the trends of automation, digitization, and the sharing economy are often presented as disrupters, this is not necessarily intensively reflected in this data set, at least not by using the term *disruption*. Although there is a whole *Disrupter Series* in the hearings in Congress that deals with innovative technology, the term itself is not widely used in neither the congressional nor the media data. *Disruption* in the economy points to innovation but can also threaten the status quo. Using the term sparsely might therefore be wise for politicians. This is further confirmed by the very rare occurrences of the terms *transformation, technological development, technological revolution*, and *digital revolution*. *Transformation* remains the only term that is steadily occurring throughout the years but also on a very low level compared to the terms *future*, *automation,* or the more specific term *robots*. One can still estimate that *transformation* and *disruption* occur at roughly the same rather low rate throughout all the data sets.

It is also interesting to look at the phrase *future of work*. This phrase is virtually not featured in the four data sets at all. It occurs a little more frequently in the media outlets based on the *NYT* and the *Washington Post*, but is still at a very low rate. The *WSJ* material only features the term at a very low rate as well, although this might be less surprising than in the liberal sources. The *WSJ* is more business-oriented and deals to a lesser extent with the plight of the (future) labor force. The focus of the *WSJ* is, for example, mergers and acquisitions and to a lesser extent news related to the workforce. Whereas *future* occurs frequently in all sources, *future of work* does not. This could indicate that the phrase is not yet a fixed expression for the future developments concerning the labor force and the nature of work. It could be possible that the term is a rather recent one and therefore does not occur frequently. Another possibility would be that it is a term only used by experts or insiders.

The results for *automation* are very different. It is not surprising that the term features heavily in the corpora as it was one of the three main search terms to compile the data. Yet, one can see that it features much more prominently in the media outlets than in the congressional hearings data. In the *WSJ* material it appears even more frequently (8.7 per 10,000 tokens) than in the liberal media sources (7.13). The term *automation* roughly appears seven times as much in the liberal media outlets than in the congressional data (1.09 in the House and 1.01 in the Senate) and eight times as much in the *WSJ* material than in the congressional material. Looking at the data, *automation* is thus the most frequent keyword that occurs in the media data. Comparing *automation* to *digitization,* the latter is much less prominent than the term *automation*, in all four data sets. Yet, as *digitization* could be seen as a part of *automation*, this could explain some of the results. However, the WSJ material features *digitization* in more than double the instances (1.59) than the liberal media material (0.69). In all sources used for this book, even in academic and scientific sources, *automation* remains much more frequent than *digitization* and is a term that encompasses different levels of technological progress. *Digitization* is used in rather specific circumstances such as the preservation of certain material. More on how these two terms differ in the source material will be discussed in Sect. 6.1.

Another interesting case is *robots* and *robotics*. Both these terms do not occur frequently in the congressional data but occur quite frequently in the media outlets. *Robots* occurs even more than *robotics*, whereas in the congressional data, it is the reverse (Robots—House: 0.24 per 10,000 tokens, Senate: 0.13, Robotics—House: 0.42, Senate: 0.25). In the *WSJ* material, *robots* is the second most frequent term (5.29) after *automation* (8.7), and is even more frequent than in the liberal media data (4.93). *Robotics* occurs at a rate of 1.43 in the *WSJ* material, and at a rate of 1.72 in the liberal media material. This is a much lower rate than *robots*. This could indicate that the discussion around *automation* in the media outlets focuses specifically on the introduction of robots into the workplace or the production cycles. The *WSJ* material, for example, discusses specific production types and companies in much more detail than the liberal media sources, which could explain the salience of the term *robots*. The frequent occurrence of *robots* could also be due to the fact that journalistic articles appeal to a non-specific audience and *robots* is just an easier

Table 5.6 Liberal media: automation, digitization, future of work, per 10,000 tokens

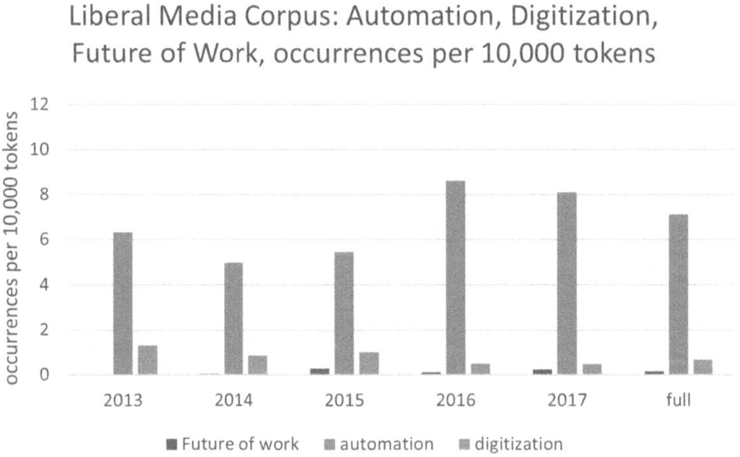

Source: Author

and broader term to use when referring to intelligent machines. Everyone thinks they know what a *robot* is, and it often invokes certain associations in the readers, both positive (taking over dangerous and heavy tasks) and negative (taking away jobs from humans, turning against humans). *Robotics* refers to the actual development and application of robots and is therefore less salient than *robots* itself. Using the term *robot*, the author or speaker often refers to intelligent machines or even artificial intelligence, which is in fact not the same.

Millennials as a term also occurs quite differently in the media outlets and in the congressional hearings. Although it is not a highly frequent term in either of the media outlets, it does occur much more often than in the House or the Senate material. In the liberal media data, the term *millennials* appears about twice as much (0.91) as in the Senate data (0.45), and about nine times as much as in the House hearings (0.1). In the *WSJ* material it features a lot less than in the liberal media data (0.59). This might also be influenced by the readership of the news outlets with the more liberal millennial generation favoring the *NYT* and the *Washington Post*. The very low frequency in the congressional data could suggest that the focus in the discussion around *automation* and its implications for the younger generation does not play a major role in the discussions in Congress and takes up a bigger share of coverage in the media outlets.

Let us look at the term *automation* and *digitization* a little more closely. The following charts (Tables 5.6, 5.7, 5.8, and 5.9) illustrate again more clearly that *automation* is the most used one out of the terms *automation*, *digitization*, and *future of work*. Compared to *digitization*, it is used much more frequently over the years.

Before going into detail in the qualitative analysis that follows in Sect. 6.1, one can already say that *digitization* often occurs as a "method," meaning it refers to

Table 5.7 WSJ: automation, digitization, future of work, per 10,000 tokens

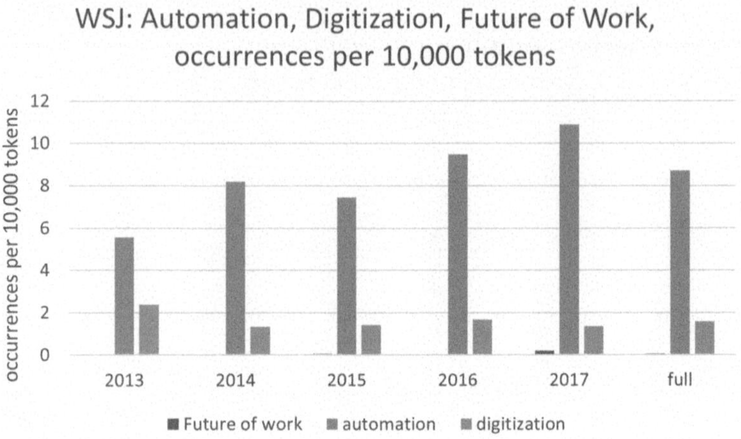

Source: Author

Table 5.8 House: automation, digitization, future of work, per 10,000 tokens

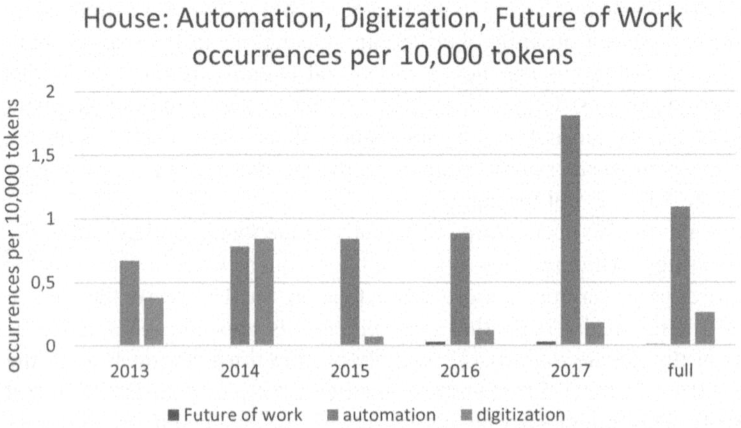

Source: Author

strategies to preserve or examine data with digital methods. It is not used as frequently in the context of work or the economy. *Automation* as a term is used much more often in the context of work, introduction of robots in the workplace, and also in the context of processes that would fall under the theme of *digitization*. *Digitization* progress is often seen as part of the overall development of *automation*. As mentioned before, the term *future of work* does not occur frequently in any of the data sets. The context of the term will be detailed later in Sect. 6.2.

Table 5.9 Senate: automation, digitization, future of work, per 10,000 tokens

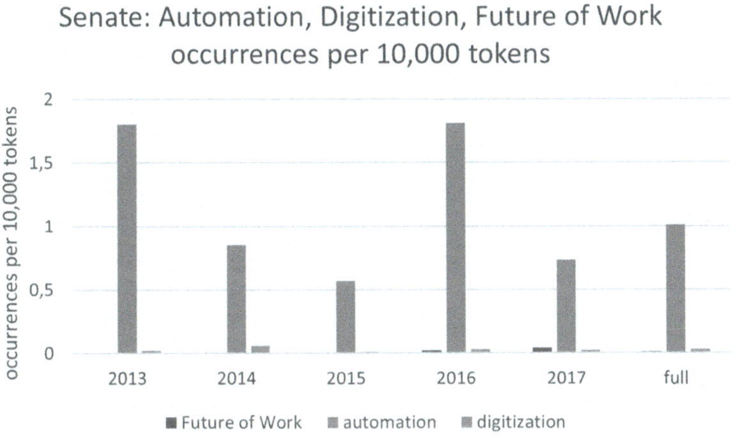

Source: Author

Table 5.10 Liberal media: platform economy, per 10,000 tokens

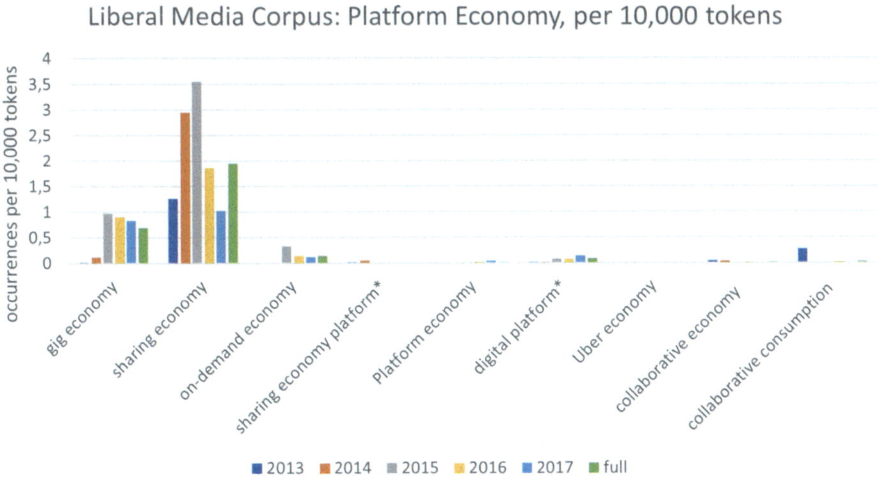

Source: Author

5.2 Platform Economy

Looking at the corpus material for the keyword category *platform economy* (Tables 5.10, 5.11, 5.12, and 5.13), first, the most widely known terms are analyzed. In the following tables, we can see the terms *gig economy, sharing economy,*

Table 5.11 *WSJ*: platform economy, per 10,000 tokens

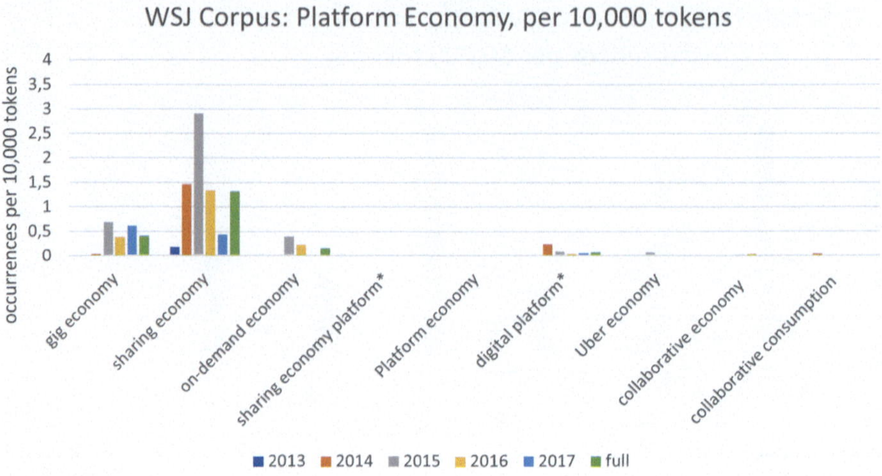

Source: Author

Table 5.12 House: platform economy, per 10,000 tokens

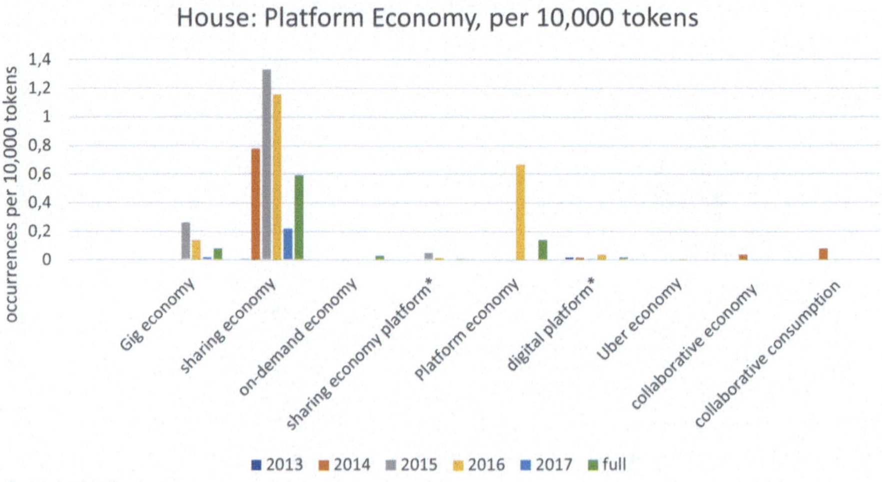

Source: Author

on-demand economy, sharing economy platform, platform economy, digital platform*, Uber economy, collaborative economy*, and *collaborative consumption*.

The term *sharing economy* is the most prominent term in all four data sets. This is unsurprising as it was one of the main search terms to compile the data. However, one can clearly see that among the other terms, *gig economy* is the other most

Table 5.13 Senate: platform economy, per 10,000 tokens

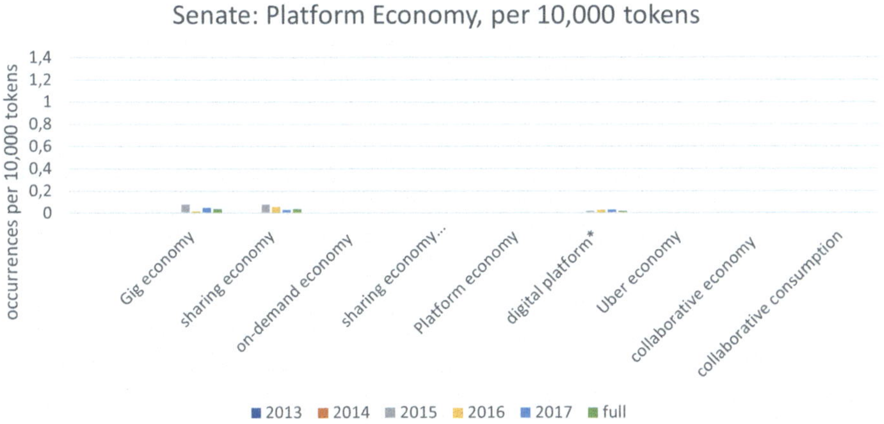

Source: Author

prevalent. One can also see that *sharing economy* as a term, as well as *gig economy*, appears to a much greater extent in the data from the media outlets (Tables 5.10 and 5.11) than in the Congress data (Tables 5.12 and 5.13). In the liberal media corpus, *sharing economy* appears 1.96 times per 10,000 tokens (Table 5.10); in the *WSJ* material, it appears at a lower rate with 1.32 (Table 5.11). In the House it appears 0.59 times per 10,000 tokens (Table 5.12), and in the Senate 0.04 times, so at a very low rate (Table 5.13).

Thus, *sharing economy* appears about three times more often in the liberal media and more than twice as much in the *WSJ* data than in the House data. It appears about 50 times more often in the liberal media data and about 30 times as much in the *WSJ* data as in the Senate data. Thus, one can say that in the media outlets the term is much more salient than in the congressional data where the House displays the higher salience of the term as it holds specific hearings on the topic, which corroborates the findings from the first cycle of qualitative reading of the sources.

As said before, the somewhat misleading term *sharing economy* is still widely used in the sources examined here. Often these articles refer to new platforms such as Uber or Airbnb. As said above, this book uses the term *sharing economy platforms* to allude more strongly to the platform nature of the businesses. One cannot, however, ignore the prevalent use of *sharing economy* altogether. Inside the Congress debates, the House hearings discuss the topic of the *sharing economy* to a greater extent than the Senate hearings. The term *sharing economy* appears over ten times as much in the House hearings than in the Senate hearings. The House Committee on Small Business, for example, discusses the implications that arise from the new digital applications quite intensively. The *Disrupter Series*, which deals with a wide range of technological innovations, also takes place in the House. This could point to the fact that the House is more responsive to current trends such as the rise of the digital sharing economy platforms than the Senate where the discussion around this topic seems to be much more limited.

The term *gig economy* is clearly the second most prevalent among the platform terms. It appears at a rate of 0.69 per 10,000 in the liberal media data, and 0.41 in the *WSJ* material. By contrast, it occurs only 0.08 times per 10,000 in the House data, and 0.04 times in the Senate data. The term *gig economy* is therefore very limited in its appearance in the congressional data. The term appears much more prominently in the media data, more than 8 times more often in the liberal media data, and 5 times as much in the *WSJ* material than in the House, and more than 17 times and 10 times more often than in the Senate data, respectively. Even more than the term *sharing economy*, the term *gig economy* is a rather recent one and does not appear to a larger extent in the data examined here. Interestingly, in the media data, the term *gig economy* only begins to appear in 2015 and is virtually absent in the years before that. 2015 is the year it appears most often in the liberal media sources, as well as in the *WSJ* material, and gradually recedes in the following years. A reason for this could be a widely cited report on the *sharing economy* that was published in 2015 by PricewaterhouseCoopers (*The Sharing Economy* (PricewaterhouseCoopers 2015)). Generally, the *sharing economy* began to draw more attention in 2015 and afterward with several reports about it being published (e.g., by JP Morgan in *Paychecks, Paydays, and the Online Platform Economy* (Farrell 2016) or in Germany by IZA Institute for the Randstad Foundation called *Sharing Economy—Chancen, Risiken und Gestaltungsoptionen für den Arbeitsmarkt* (Eichhorst and Spermann 2015)). Also, several of the big players like Uber and Airbnb became more widely known as they had expanded their reach in the market.

For all the other terms examined here, it is clear that they do not feature prominently in either of the data sets. It becomes especially clear that the terms focusing on the *collaborative economy* do not feature prominently in the data sets at all. The collaborative aspect of this new economy that was propagated in the beginning by pundits like Rachel Botsman has not prevailed in any major sense. In the media data, in both the liberal and the *WSJ* material, you can also see the occurrence of the term *on-demand economy* to some extent, yet it is not frequent compared to the *gig economy* or *sharing economy*. The maybe most appropriate term *platform economy*, or this work's term *sharing economy platforms*, is almost entirely absent from either of the data sets. In fact, the term *platform economy* does not appear at all in the data set from the *WSJ* nor in the Senate data. This term seems to remain a rather technical term that has not made it to mainstream use. In the qualitative analysis following in the next chapters, these terms will be discussed in the detailed context they occur in.

It is also interesting to see in how many hearings in Congress the term *sharing economy* actually occurs. In the whole corpus of 151 hearings in the House, there are 15 hearings where the term *sharing economy* actually appears (Table 5.14). Out of the 90 hearings from the Senate, there are 9 hearings that feature the term (Table 5.15). This shows that one-tenth of the hearings in both chambers of Congress that were examined here deal with the topic of the *sharing economy* in some way. It is noticeable, however, that these hearings occur to a larger extent starting in 2015. In

Table 5.14 House: number of hearings featuring "sharing economy"

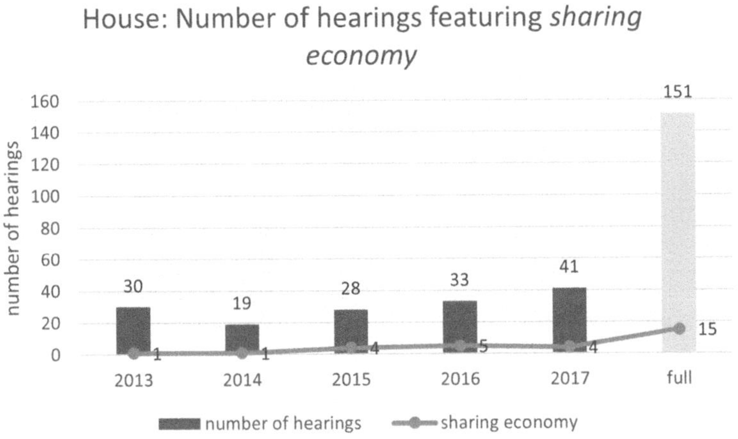

Source: Author

Table 5.15 Senate: number of hearings featuring "sharing economy"

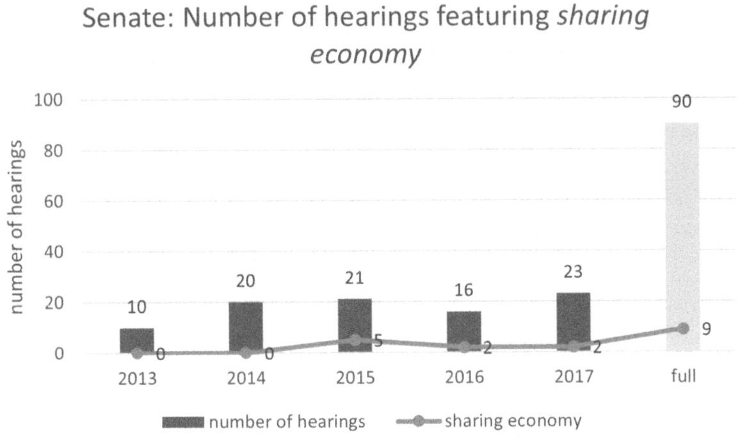

Source: Author

2013 and 2014 combined, there are no hearings featuring the term in the Senate, and only two in the House. Starting in 2015, there are several hearings per year that include the term *sharing economy*. As said before, it could also be observed that the year 2015 saw greater attention for the *sharing economy* in the media outlets. This was probably due to the greater reach of several big platform players but could also be due to several economic studies that looked at the phenomenon of the *sharing economy* more closely. This apparently led to a greater interest in the *sharing economy* after 2015 in Congress as well as in the media.

Table 5.16 Liberal media: platform economy—workers, per 10,000 tokens

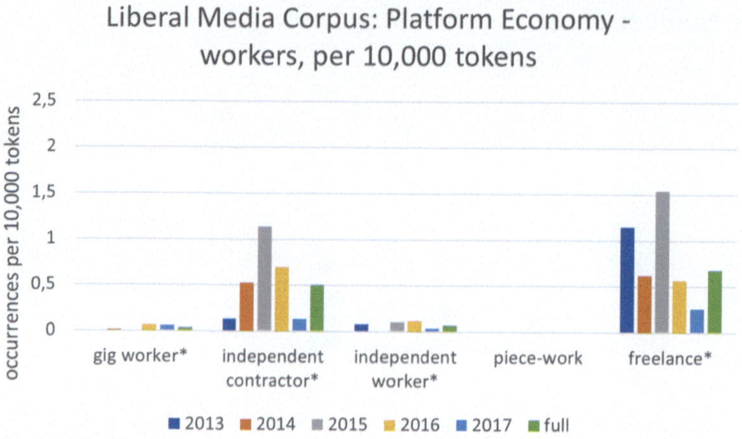

Source: Author

Table 5.17 WSJ: platform economy—workers, per 10,000 tokens

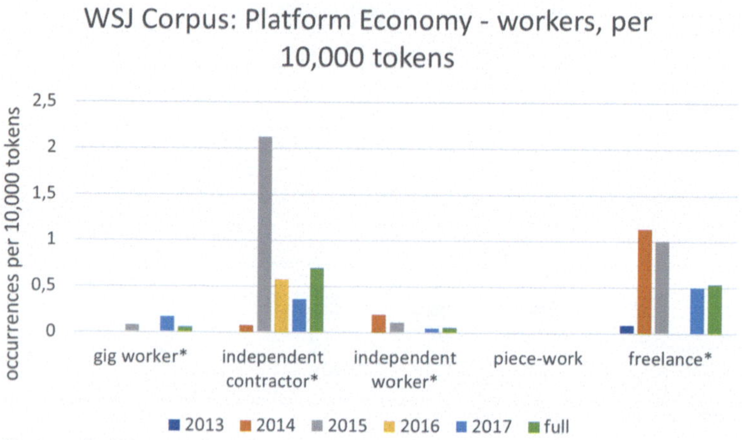

Source: Author

Another interesting point to examine are the workers of the platform economy. In all four data sets, the term *independent contractor** features most prominently out of the examined terms that included *gig worker**, *independent contractor**, *independent worker**, *freelance**, and *piece-work*. It is also the most neutral and all-encompassing term, which makes it likely to appear more often. In the liberal media corpus, it appears 0.5 per 10,000 tokens (Table 5.16); in the *WSJ* material it appears slightly more often at a rate of 0.7 (Table 5.17). In the House it appears at a rate of 0.07 (Table 5.18), and in the Senate, it appears 0.03 per 10,000 tokens

Table 5.18 House: platform economy—workers, per 10,000 tokens

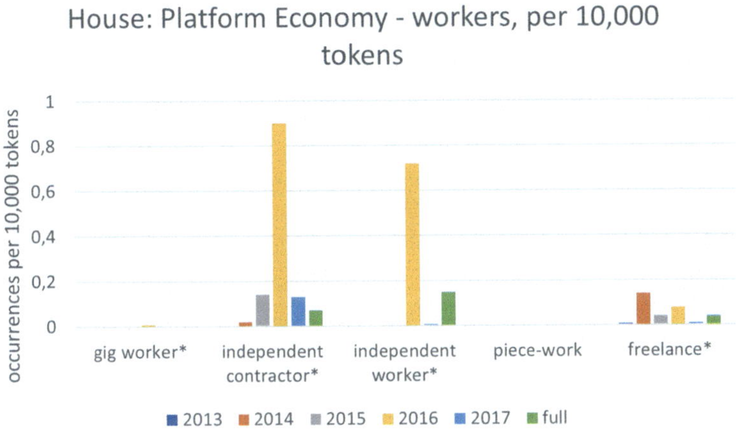

Source: Author

Table 5.19 Senate: platform economy—workers, per 10,000 tokens

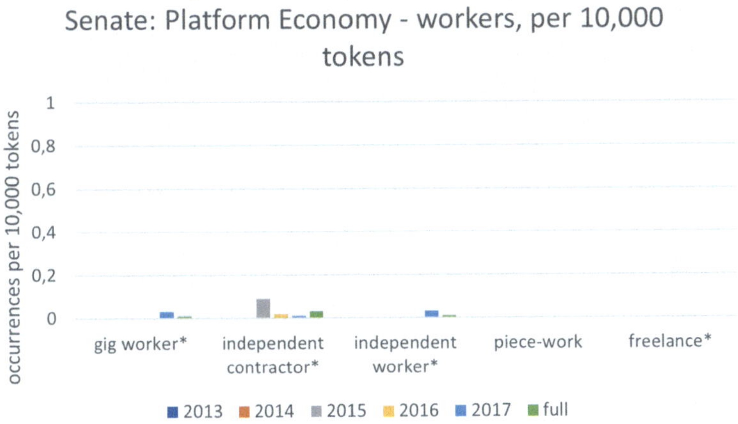

Source: Author

(Table 5.19). In the liberal media data, the term *freelance** is actually the most prominent term with 0.68 occurrences per 10,000 tokens. The *WSJ* material features it slightly less often with 0.54. *Independent contractor** is the most frequent term in the *WSJ* material. In the House data, *independent worker** is the most prominent with 0.15 per 10,000 tokens. And in the Senate data, *independent contractor** features most prominently among the workers' terms. Yet, all terms that refer to workers of the *platform economy* are rare in all data sets.

The term *gig worker** appears a lot less prominently than *independent contractor**. But in the media data, it appears more often than in the Congress data. You can

Table 5.20 Liberal media: platform economy—platforms, per 10,000 tokens

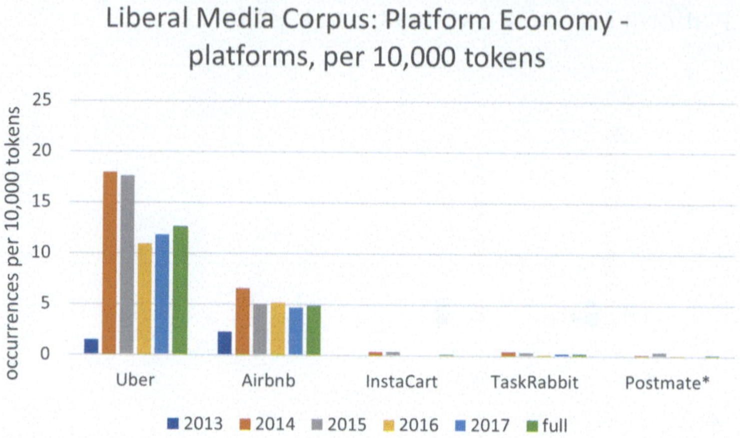

Source: Author

also see that *gig worker** only began to appear in 2015 or later, so alongside higher frequency of the term *sharing* and *gig economy*. Before 2015, it is virtually absent from the media data, just like the term *gig economy*. In the Senate data, *gig worker** only appears in 2017, and in the House data it only appears in data from 2016. The 2016 occurrences of *independent contractor* and *independent worker* in the House data can mainly be associated with hearings on the *sharing economy* and taxation for small business. In general, the term *gig worker* is a rather recent term, and it is not widely used. Compared to *independent contractor*, *gig worker* is a much more specific term and normally only refers to people working solely on digital platforms, which is a very small number of workers. *Independent contractor*, however, refers to a much larger group of workers that has existed well before the rise of the platform economy. Handymen, cleaners, builders, or other professionals are all independent contractors. In general, this group is highly heterogeneous and encompasses a wide range of occupations.

The term *freelance** is also interesting to examine. It is a lot more prominent as a term in the media data than in the Congress data, where it rarely appears at all. *Freelancing* is a term that precedes *gig work* and is also more encompassing than *gig work*. Instead of *gig economy*, the *freelance economy* is also thrown around in the public discourse, for example by the Freelancers Union. The more independent types of work of today are often associated with *freelancers*. In general, *freelancers* seem to be associated more with creative, non-physical work, whereas *gig workers* are often Uber drivers, deliverymen, or shoppers on platforms like Instacart, so engaged in what could be considered more "blue-collar" occupations.

When looking at the *platform economy*, it is also interesting to look at some of the business giants that are associated with the rise of the *sharing economy* (Tables 5.20, 5.21, 5.22, and 5.23).

Table 5.21 *WSJ*: platform economy—platforms, per 10,000 tokens

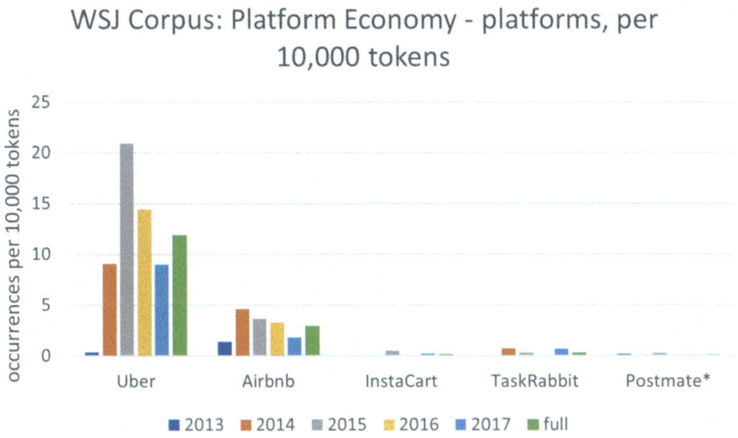

Source: Author

Table 5.22 House: platform economy—platforms, per 10,000 tokens

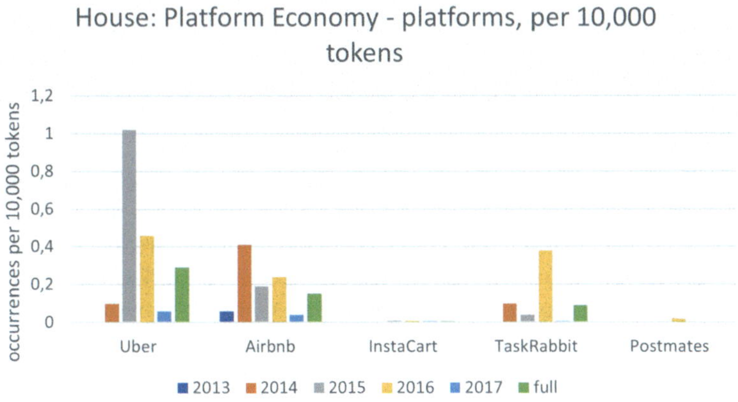

Source: Author

We can see that in all data sets, *Uber* appears most often by far, compared to all other featured companies. *Airbnb* is the second most frequent term but lags far behind *Uber*. *Instacart*, *Postmates,* or *TaskRabbit* do not occur very frequently in any of the data sets. *Uber* clearly is one of the most well-known companies in this comparison and is very prominent. This is reflected in the media attention, as well as in the attention that it gets in politics.

In general, *Uber* starts to feature more prominently in the conversation starting in 2014 in the media data, both from the liberal sources and the *WSJ*. There is a big jump from virtual nonexistence in the 2013 data to the following years. Overall, the

Table 5.23 Senate: platform economy—platforms, per 10,000 tokens

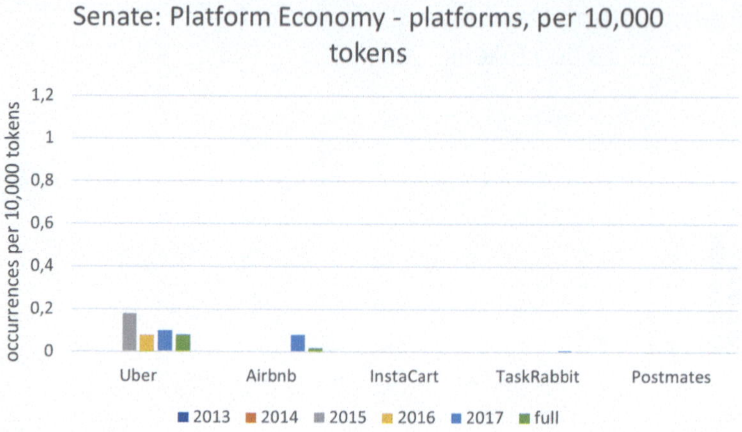

Source: Author

term *Uber* appears at a similar rate in both media corpora (12.69/10,000 tokens for the liberal media, Table 5.20; 11.92/10,000 for the *WSJ*, Table 5.21). Only in 2015 does it start to appear more often in the Congress data, but at a very low rate. It only appears at a rate of 0.29 per 10,000 tokens in the House data (Table 5.22), and 0.08 in the Senate data (Table 5.23).

The differences here are extreme. *Uber* seems to be a very popular topic in the media in general. This could have to do with *Uber's* aggressive strategy to conquer the ride-sharing market and "fight" the taxi industry. All media outlets also report from urban areas (NYC and Washington, D.C.) where the platforms are much more popular than in more rural areas of the country. Especially in New York City, where both the taxi industry and the housing market are highly regulated, both *Uber* and *Airbnb* have faced extensive criticism. They were challenged for their behavior toward workers, for further congesting streets, or for worsening the overall critical situation of the housing market. The extensive occurrence of *Uber* could also reflect its aggressive and notorious business culture of the early years that frequently made headlines. In any way, Uber is often used as the prototype and example of the new platform economy businesses and might be the most well-known of them. Other than *Airbnb*, for example, *Uber* is also more often attacked for its treatment of workers and for possible violation of worker classification rules. *Airbnb* is not associated with gig or platform work as it focuses on renting. Because of these various reasons, *Uber* is the platform that is most often referred to when talking about the *sharing* or *platform economy* and what effect it has on incumbent businesses and workers. Of all the companies mentioned, it is the most prominent in the public and in the political discourse.

In the academic discourse around the platform economy, *TaskRabbit* is also mentioned quite frequently. Yet, it does not feature very prominently in the data

Table 5.24 Liberal media: technology, per 10,000 tokens

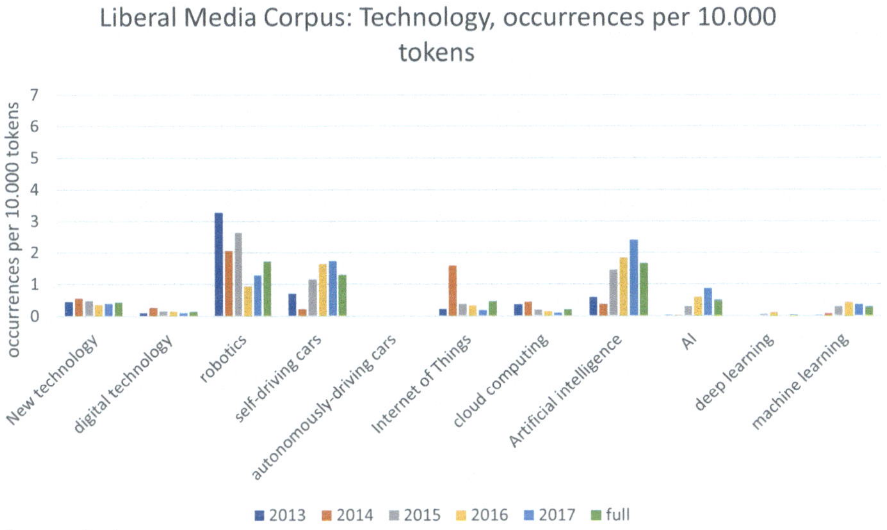

Source: Author

examined here. As a company it is not as well known as *Airbnb* or *Uber*, but it is often discussed as an example for the business model of independent contracting or gig work. The platform matches handymen, cleaners, or other professionals with customers but does not employ them. Since its beginnings, *TaskRabbit* has seen several changes to its policies, for example the introduction of a site-wide minimum wage. As will be discussed later, *TaskRabbit* appears several times in the media data to report that the company was acquired by IKEA in 2017. *Instacart* and *Postmates*, both delivery services, are also not very well known and not as ubiquitous as *Uber*. They are also more recent additions to the platform economy market and might therefore not appear very frequently in either data set. As they are delivery services, they operate locally and often one or the other service is more prominent in a given city. However, they often rely on contracted work, like *TaskRabbit* or *Uber*, and are therefore interesting to look at when discussing the development of independent work in the *platform economy*.

5.3 Technology

Looking at the keyword category of *technology* (Tables 5.24, 5.25, 5.26, and 5.27), there are different trends that can be observed. For once, *artificial intelligence/AI* seems to be among the most prominent terms in this category in all four data sets with only the House data displaying very low frequencies of the terms. In the liberal

Table 5.25 *WSJ*: technology, per 10,000 tokens

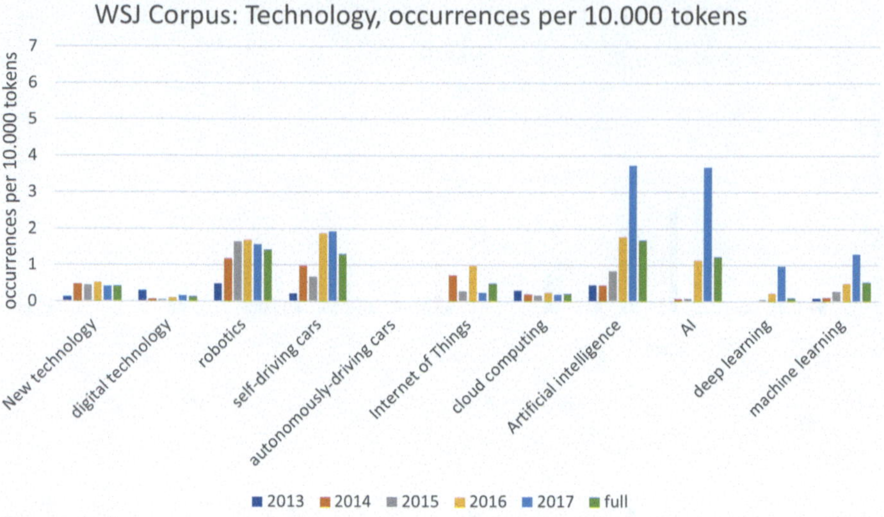

Source: Author

Table 5.26 House: technology, per 10,000 tokens

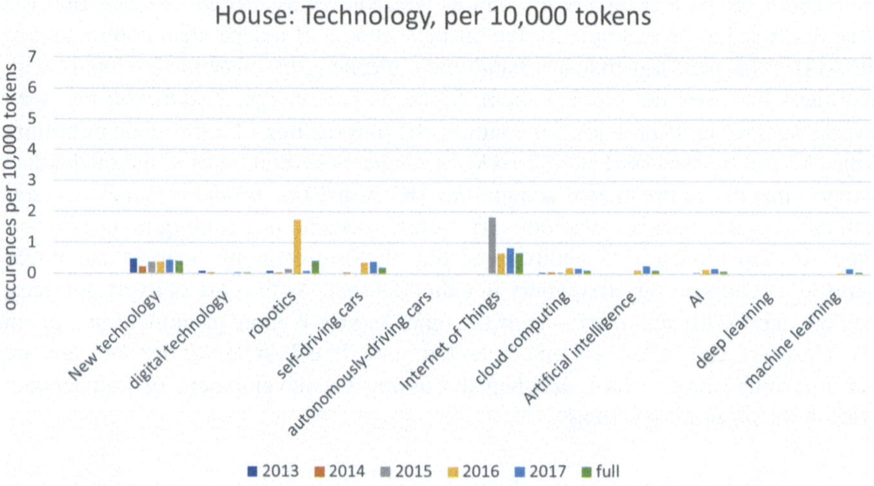

Source: Author

media corpus *artificial intelligence* appears 1.66 per 10,000 tokens; in the *WSJ* material it appears at a similar rate with 1.7. In the House data, it only appears 0.11 per 10,000 tokens and in the Senate data 0.4 (the abbreviation *AI* appears 1.4 per 10,000 tokens, however). In the congressional data, it is obvious that the term

Table 5.27 Senate: technology, per 10,000 tokens

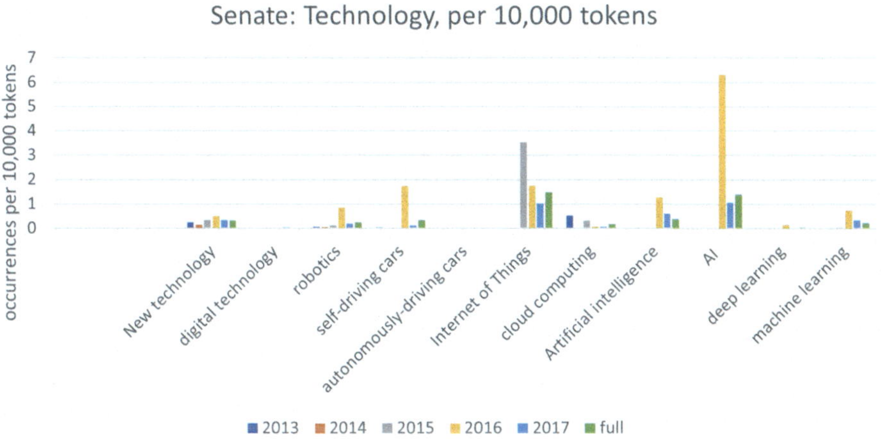

Source: Author

and abbreviation appears much more often in the Senate than in the House, which is due to a specific hearing on the topic of *AI* in the Senate in 2016. It is also noteworthy that the more specific terms of *machine learning* or *deep learning* do not appear to a similar degree as *AI* in the corpus data overall. There are some outlier years, but all in all, these two technological developments are not featured frequently in the corpus data.

What is also apparent is that the term *Internet of Things* is much more prominent in the Congress data than in the media data. In the House data, it appears with 0.68 per 10,000 tokens in the Senate data with 1.48, in the liberal media data at a rate of 0.48, and in the *WSJ* material 0.5 per 10,000 tokens. Especially in the Senate data, it appears much more often than in the other sources. The *Internet of Things* is concerned with former “analogue” utilities that become more and more advanced so that many appliances become “smart” in a way that they are able to communicate with the user and access the Internet so that they can be controlled by the user from anywhere, anytime. The impact and possible regulation of these utilities seems to be of concern to Congress.

What is also noteworthy is that *self-driving cars* are a much more prominent topic in the media data than in the congressional hearings. In the liberal media data as well as in the *WSJ*, the term features 1.3 times per 10,000 tokens. In the House data, it features 0.2 per 10,000 tokens, and in the Senate data, it features 0.34 times per 10,000 tokens.

Although it would seem that both the *Internet of Things* and *self-driving cars* would demand new specific regulation and therefore exploratory hearings in Congress, the years 2013–2017 show that the *Internet of Things* is a more prominent topic with lawmakers than *self-driving cars*. The topic of *self-driving cars* features more than four times as much in the media data than in the Congressional data,

Table 5.28 House: number of hearings featuring "AI" and "Internet of Things"

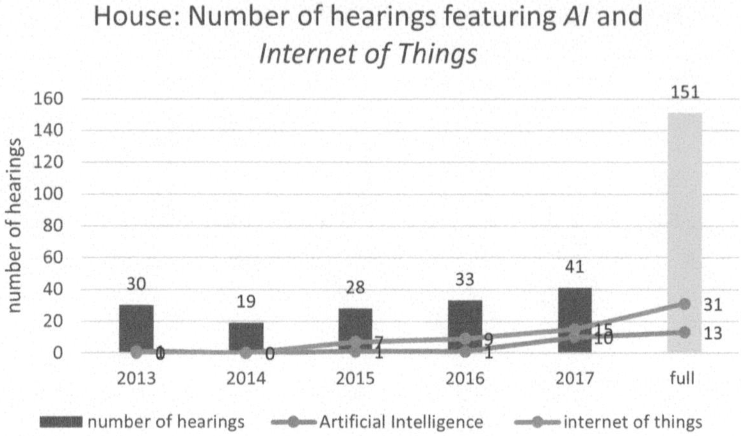

Source: Author

Table 5.29 Senate: number of hearings featuring "AI" and "Internet of Things"

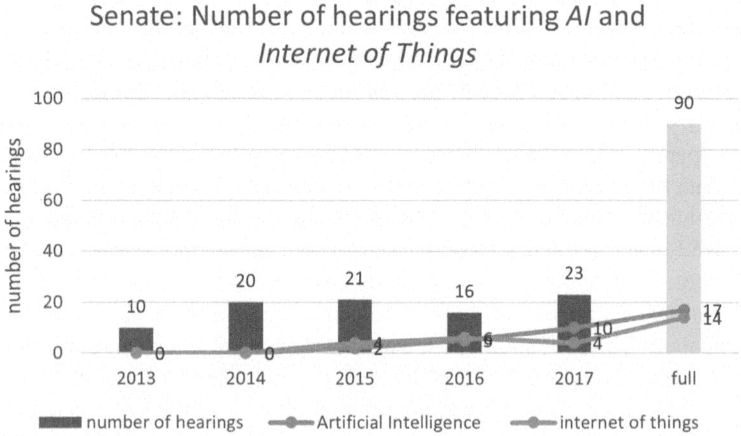

Source: Author

which points to a larger interest of readers in the topic of technologically advanced cars specifically. The higher frequency of *Internet of Things* in Congress compared to *self-driving cars* could also point to the fact that the *self-driving car* is seen as part of the *Internet of Things*, a "smart" utility for the future.

In Tables 5.28 and 5.29, one can also see a comparison between the number of hearings that feature the term *artificial intelligence* and *Internet of Things*. In the House, there are noticeably more hearings that feature the term *Internet of Things*.

There are 31 hearings held in the House that feature the term *Internet of Things*, whereas there are only 13 hearings in which *artificial intelligence* occurs. In the Senate, the number of hearings featuring the two terms is more comparable with 17 hearings that feature the term *artificial intelligence* and 14 featuring the term *Internet of Things*. As said before, *AI* is more frequent in the Senate data overall, and it is also more frequent in the total number of hearings. *artificial intelligence* could rather be described as general-purpose technology that might come to fruition in many different fields. It might therefore be more of a general discussion around the impact of *AI* in the Senate. The *Internet of Things* appears to be a more practical development of concrete applications such as smartphones, smart watches, or smart home appliances.

The term *robotics*, which was already briefly mentioned above, is one of the more frequent terms in the media data. The term is not occurring to a comparable extent in the congressional data. The terms *new technology*, *digital technology*, or *cloud computing* are also not as common in the source material as other terms.

5.4 Policies

If we look at the keyword category of *policies* (Tables 5.30, 5.31, 5.32, and 5.33), there are very stark contrasts in frequency between the congressional data and the media data. This might not be surprising as Congress is naturally much more concerned with actual policy proposals to address certain developments or issues

Table 5.30 House: policies, per 10,000 tokens

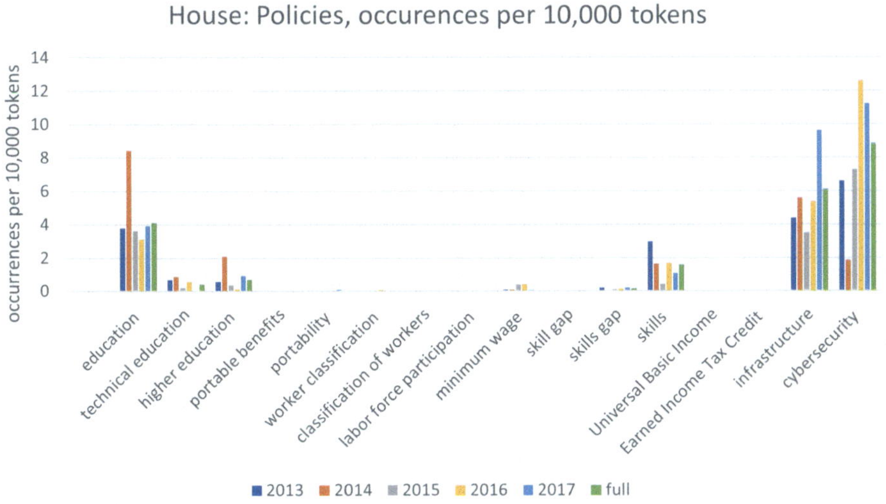

Source: Author

Table 5.31 Senate: policies, per 10,000 tokens

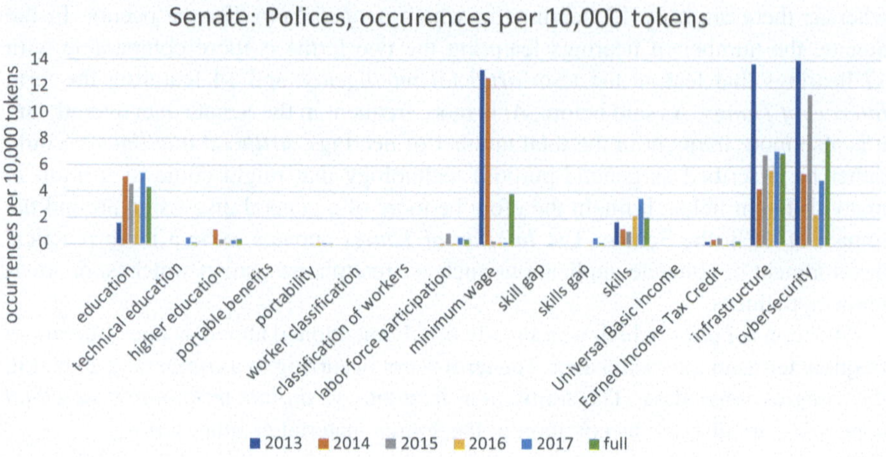

Source: Author

Table 5.32 Liberal media: policies, per 10,000 tokens

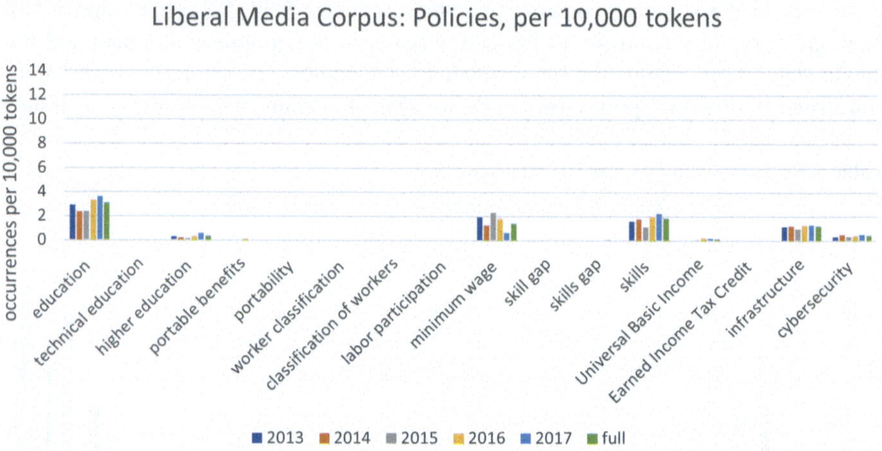

Source: Author

than the media. Media outlets are not asked to provide specific proposals as much as politicians in Congress are.

The most frequent term in the data from both chambers in Congress is *cybersecurity*. It occurs at a rate of 8.85 per 10,000 tokens in the House data and at a rate of 7.95 in the Senate data. *Cybersecurity* is an issue that is discussed across a rather large field of Congress committees. There are even more hearings concerned with

Table 5.33 *WSJ*: policies, per 10,000 tokens

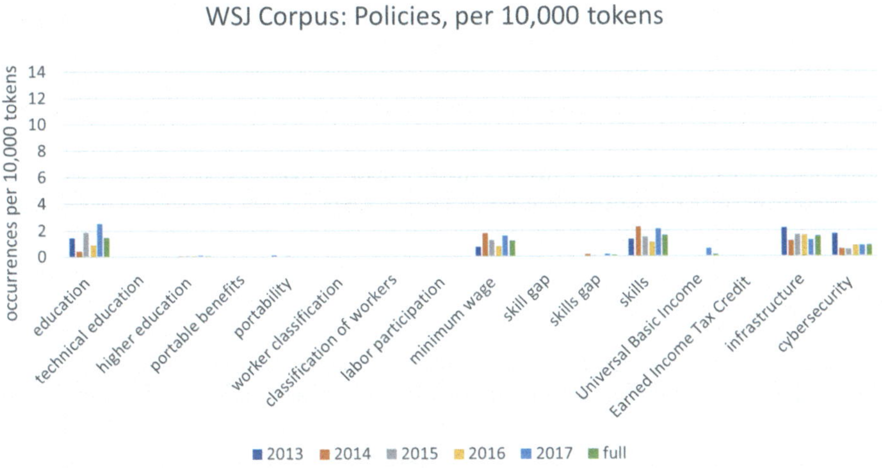

Source: Author

cybersecurity if one included hearings on defense or homeland security. Yet, *cybersecurity* is also of concern for businesses and consumers, especially with the new tech companies (and platforms) collecting more and more data. Online payment systems or rating systems are also part of the success story for platform businesses, and *cybersecurity* is of great concern to these systems as well. Additionally, the use of social media and possibility of manipulation was also a topic of concern for Congress over the years. Congress is expected to find ways of securing data and privacy in the digital age, and this topic is likely to prevail as an issue in the coming years.

The second most prominent term in both chambers from the category of *policies* is *infrastructure* (6.13/10,000 tokens in the House, 6.98 in the Senate). This is followed by the third most frequent term in this category, *education* (4.12/10,000 tokens in the House data, 4.33 in the Senate data). In the Senate, the fourth most frequent term is *minimum wage* (3.89/10,000 tokens), which is not frequent in the House data. Yet, as the Senate data also features the Joint Economic Committee hearings where members from both chambers meet, it does not mean that the topic of the *minimum wage* is not discussed by House members. In the House, the fourth most frequent term is *skills* (1.62/10,000 tokens), which is even more frequent in the Senate (2.09/10,000 tokens). All of the aforementioned terms (*infrastructure, education, minimum wage, skills*) are policy fields that are constantly discussed in Congress. Especially infrastructure reform has been a hotly debated issue for a long time, but a reform has not yet been passed. Educational reform and how to better train American workers in order to give them the skills necessary for the demands of the new economy is also an issue that is discussed on both sides of the aisle. There are several topics that are discussed in the context of education, which include new skills, training programs, student tuition fees, and apprenticeship programs, but also better primary or secondary education. The *minimum wage* is also often discussed in the context of the quality of jobs. The federal minimum wage has not increased in years, but several states have raised their state-wide minimum wage to react to higher costs of living in some of the urban economic centers. The low *minimum wage* in many parts of the country is often taken as an example of the low-quality jobs many Americans face in the labor market today.

Apart from these most frequent terms in the congressional data, one can see that terms such as *portable benefits/portability*, *worker classification*, *labor participation*, or *universal basic income* do not occur in the data to any great extent compared to the other terms.

The *earned income tax credit* also does not occur very frequently in the Congress data, although it is a program that has bipartisan support and has frequently been extended. It is one of the most expensive programs for the federal government and is directed at working American households (with children) who have a low income. It can also be claimed by a self-employed worker and can amount to a few thousand dollars a year.

Looking at the category of *policies* in the media data, there are some similarities and differences to the congressional data. First, all the terms in this category occur at a much lower rate. The term *cybersecurity,* in particular, appears a lot less frequently in the media data than in the congressional data (0.47/10,000 tokens in the liberal media corpus, 0.88 in *WSJ* sources). Thus, *cybersecurity* is 10–20 times more frequent in the congressional data than in the media data.

Education (3.1/10,000 tokens in the liberal media, 1.5 in the *WSJ*) and *Infrastructure* (1.22/10,000 in the liberal media, 1.57 in the WSJ) are also two terms that are much more frequent in the congressional data. *Infrastructure* is around four times more frequent in the congressional data than in the media data. *Skills* (1.86/10,000 tokens in the liberal media data, 1.62 in the WSJ) appears at a similar rate in the congressional data and in the media data but is in itself a more infrequent term across the sets. *Minimum Wage* (1.4/10,000 tokens in the liberal media, 1.22 in the WSJ) as a term is much more frequent in the Senate data; in fact, it occurs more than twice as often in the Senate data than in the media data.

As said before, political actors are of course discussing policy proposals much more intensively than media outlets. It is therefore not surprising that the keywords in the category *policies* are much more frequent in the congressional data than in the media data. The fields of *education* and *infrastructure*, for example, are extensively discussed in Congress. In Tables 5.34, 5.35, 5.36, and 5.37, one can see the number of hearings in Congress featuring the terms. In the House, 123 of 151 hearing records feature the term *education*, so the majority of hearings. The same is true for the Senate data, where the term *education* appears in 80 out of 90 hearings.

In order to contrast the two fields, in Tables 5.36 and 5.37 one can see the hearings featuring the term *infrastructure* and *skills gap*. *Skills gap* is something that is often discussed around the topic of the new economy as Americans often lack the adequate skills to make the most of the new opportunities. The *skills gap* also has to do with a lack in *infrastructure* (lack of internet access, lack of affordable housing,

Table 5.34 House: number of hearings featuring 'education'

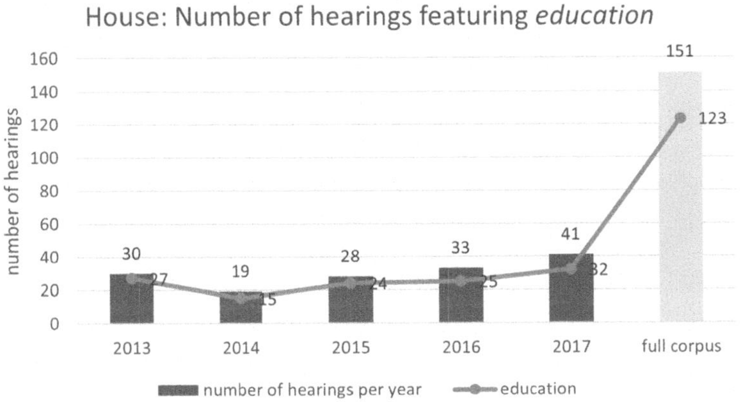

Source: Author

Table 5.35 Senate: number of hearings featuring 'education'

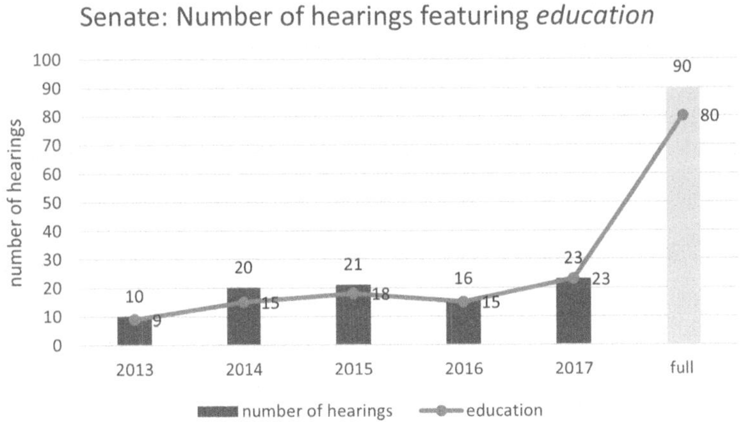

Source: Author

mediocre school buildings, and lack of affordable child care, schools, and colleges, etc.), but the more specific term occurs at a much lower rate than *infrastructure* itself. This might indicate that the debates are focused on the basic idea of *infrastructure* reform but are not emphasizing specific ways to address the *skills gap* among Americans. There are only 14 out of 151 hearings in the House that feature the specific term *skills gap*, and 12 out of 90 hearings in Senate.

Table 5.36 Senate: number of hearings featuring "skills gap" and "infrastructure"

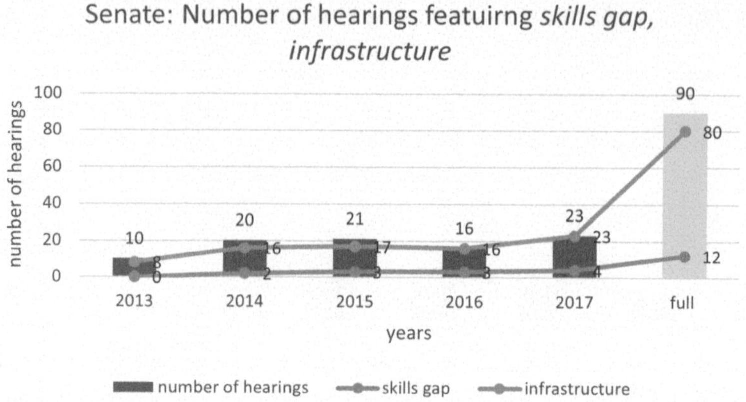

Source: Author

Table 5.37 House: number of hearings featuring "skills gap" and "infrastructure"

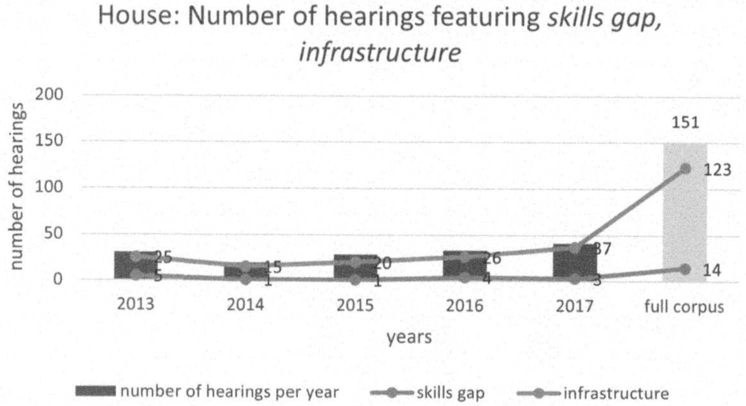

Source: Author

5.5 Inequality

The keyword category *inequality* (Tables 5.38, 5.39, 5.40, and 5.41) does not display very high frequencies in the corpora overall. In this category, the term *inequality* itself is not among the most frequent. It occurs at a rate of 1.06 per 10,000 tokens in the liberal media data, 0.42 in the WSJ data, 0.06 in the House data, and 1.26 in the Senate data. The high frequency of *income inequality* and *inequality* in 2014 in the Senate data is due to one specific hearing in the Senate called *Income Inequality in the United States* held in the Joint Economic Committee on January 16, 2014, which

Table 5.38 Liberal media: inequality, per 10,000 tokens

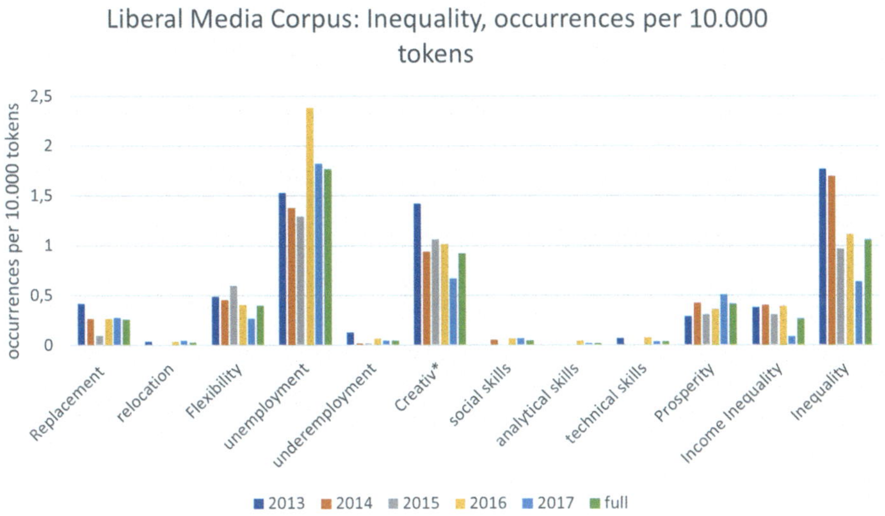

Source: Author

Table 5.39 *WSJ*: inequality, per 10,000 tokens

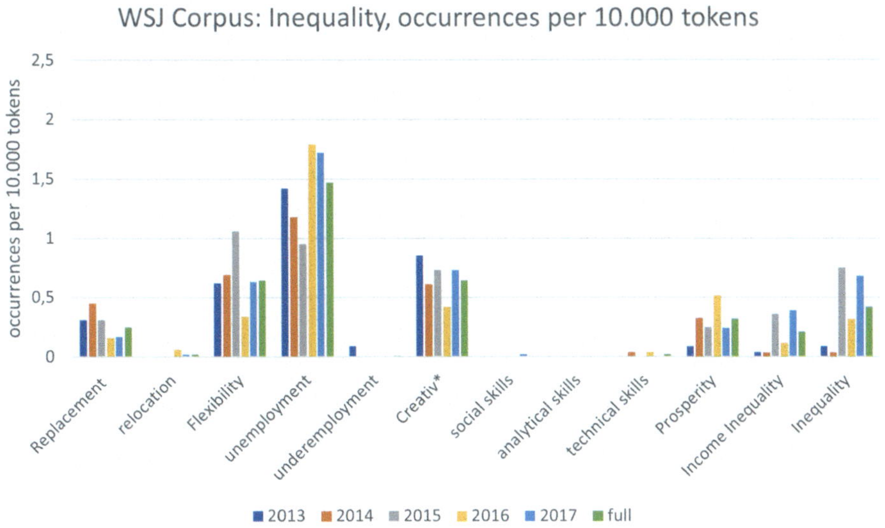

Source: Author

Table 5.40 House: inequality, per 10,000 tokens

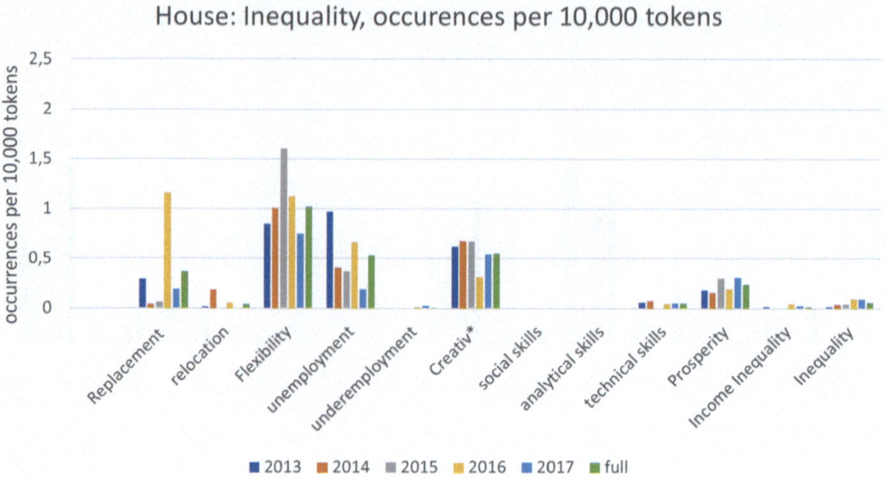

Source: Author

Table 5.41 Senate: inequality, per 10,000 tokens

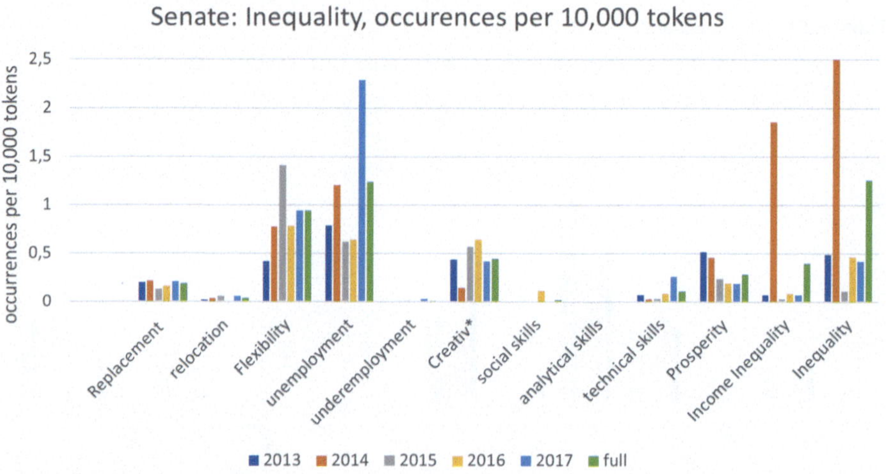

Source: Author

provides for the higher frequency of the terms in the Senate data. The low overall frequency of *inequality* in the data sets points to the fact that the issue is not discussed to a great extent in the discourse around technological development that is examined in this work. Other terms are much more frequent in the data sets, which means that *inequality* as a term is not prevalent in the discussions or that it might be discussed in other ways.

Apart from *inequality* itself, several other terms were analyzed in this category. Terms like *unemployment*, *creativ**, or *flexibility* are often discussed referring to the economy as a whole, but also to the structural changes (such as technological progress) the economy is undergoing. Additionally, the structural changes in the economy are often accompanied by fears of *replacement* or *relocation*. Different skill sets could be in demand in the future such as *social*, *analytical*, or *technical skills*.

Job loss is also often associated with the restructuring of the economy, but the term did not deliver any large differences in results compared to the term *unemployment*. *Unemployment* occurs at a rate of 1.77 per 10,000 tokens in the liberal media data, 1.47 in the WSJ, 0.53 in the House, and 1.24 in the Senate and is therefore the overall most frequent term in this category across the data sets. *Unemployment* is always a topic of interest to the public, so it is not so surprising that it is discussed extensively. However, the frequency is not as high as for other terms, which could also point to the fact that *unemployment* is not a crucial discussion point when dealing with technological progress. Additionally, the years 2013–2017 were years where the USA witnessed an economic recovery after the Great Recession, with *unemployment* numbers steadily falling. This might also be a reason why *unemployment* is not of greater concern in this period.

*Creativ** (e.g., creative, creatives, creatively, creativity) as a term in this category was used to see whether creativity or occupations demanding creative skills were discussed, which is often pointed to when talking about job loss due to technology. Some experts argue that machines cannot easily replace creative tasks (of course *creative* is a word that is also used in completely different contexts). Overall, this is not a very frequent term in any of the data sets. *Creativ** occurs with a rate of 0.92 per 10,000 tokens in the liberal media, 0.64 in the WSJ, 0.55 in the House, and 0.45 in the Senate.

Flexibility is a topic that is often associated with the discussion of structural changes in the economy. Especially for the platform economy where many people work as independents, *flexibility* is a given. It can also be seen as an opportunity to have more control over one's own schedule. *Flexibility* occurs 0.4 times per 10,000 tokens in the liberal media data, 0.64 in the *WSJ*, 1.02 in the House, and 0.94 in the Senate. Thus, overall, this term is also not very frequent in the data but occurs a little more frequently in the congressional data.

Replacement and *relocation* are terms that are not frequent in any of the data sets. Neither are the more specific terms *social skills*, *analytical skills*, and *technical skills*.

After having looked at the keyword categories and the frequency data of the different keywords, we will turn to a more specific qualitative analysis. For the purpose of this book, there are certain keywords that are especially interesting to examine in their contexts. First, the terms *digitization* and *automation* will be investigated and contrasted across the different source material. After that first close investigation of two keywords, the term *future of work* will be further examined. Eventually, the analysis will turn to the use of the term *sharing economy* and how it compares to the alternatives *gig economy* and *platform economy*. As said before, through the use of collocations and contextual reading of some of the most important terms, this analysis aims to identify underlying themes and attitudes toward these issues in the different sources in order to arrive at a more rounded picture of the treatment of these issues in public and political discourse.

References

Brezina V (2018) Statistics in corpus linguistics. a practical guide. Cambridge University Press, Cambridge, UK. https://doi.org/10.1017/9781316410899

Brezina V, Timperley M, McEnery T (2018) #LancsBox v. 3-4.x [software]. http://corpora.lancs.ac.uk/lancsbox

Eichhorst W, Spermann A (2015) Sharing economy—Chancen, Risiken und Gestaltungsmöglichkeiten für den Arbeitsmarkt. IZA Research Report, vol 69. IZA, Bonn

HarperCollins (2008) A guide to statistics: t-score and mutual information. https://wordbanks.harpercollins.co.uk/other_doc/statistics.html. Accessed 8 Jan 2019

McEnery T, Hardie A (2012) Corpus linguistics: method, theory and practice. Cambridge textbooks in linguistics (Kindle edition). Cambridge University Press, Cambridge, UK

PricewaterhouseCoopers (2015) The sharing economy. PricewaterhouseCoopers LLP. https://www.pwc.fr/fr/assets/files/pdf/2015/05/pwc_etude_sharing_economy.pdf

SketchEngine (2020) MI score. https://www.sketchengine.eu/my_keywords/mi-score/. Accessed 9 Jan 2020

Chapter 6
Qualitative Analysis: Collocations and Contextual Reading

After having examined the relative frequency of specific keyword categories and a first look at some of the keywords in the congressional material, the analysis of political and public discourse around technological progress and its impact on the economy in the USA will now turn to a more in-depth examination of certain terms and themes. The following analysis will look at collocations of the different terms before turning to a close contextual reading of the congressional hearings and media articles. In the contextual analysis of the terms, certain specific hearings and articles will be presented in more depth than others in order to give examples of the use of the terms in context and to identify overarching themes in which the terms occur. The hearings and articles were chosen because the identified terms (*automation, digitization, future of work, platform economy*) occurred in the text (either once or several times) and were then grouped around certain thematic topics the hearings or articles were concerned with. The material from the Senate, the House of Representatives, the media sources containing *The New York Times* (NYT), and *Washington Post* material, as well as the material from the *Wall Street Journal* (*WSJ*), will be discussed separately.

6.1 Digitization and Automation

Digitization and *automation* are two of the key concepts when talking about technological progress. In some countries, like Germany, the term *digitization* is mostly used to refer to the more recent technological developments that go beyond mere mechanization. Smart robotics, algorithms, and artificial intelligence are often associated with *digitization*. Yet, in the English-speaking world, the term is not as widely used in this way. *Automation* remains the more commonly used term and includes new technological development in the digital sphere as well. But what exactly do these two terms entail? What exactly does the political and public discourse around technological progress reflect when *digitization* and *automation*

N. Rauscher, *The Future of Work in the United States*, Contributions to Economics,
https://doi.org/10.1007/978-3-030-82307-8_6

are discussed? In the following, *digitization* will first be examined in the context of congressional hearings from the Senate and the House of Representatives, followed by an investigation of the public discourse through the media material. The term *automation* will subsequently also be investigated in this way.

6.1.1 Digitization in the Congressional Material

As detailed above, the terms *automation* and *digitization* occur to a very different extent in the congressional material when looking at frequency. In Tables 6.1 and 6.2, one can see which hearings in the Congress material actually feature the two terms alongside the term *future of work*, which is even more infrequent than *digitization* but will be investigated in the next chapter. Once again, it becomes clear that *digitization* occurs much more infrequently than *automation*. In the House, there are 119 hearings that feature the term *automation*, but only 20 that feature *digitization* (Table 6.1). In the Senate, there are 75 hearings across the time frame of 2013–2017 that feature the term *automation*, but only 9 that include the term *digitization* (Table 6.2).

On the one hand, this shows that the term *automation* is much more commonly used than *digitization*. On the other hand, it could indicate that *digitization* is seen as part of the *automation* process and is often not mentioned specifically but included in the concept of *automation* toward more digital products and services. But moving beyond a mere frequency analysis, the question arises how the terms *automation* and *digitization* are actually used in context.

Table 6.1 House: number of hearings featuring "automation," "digitization," "future of work"

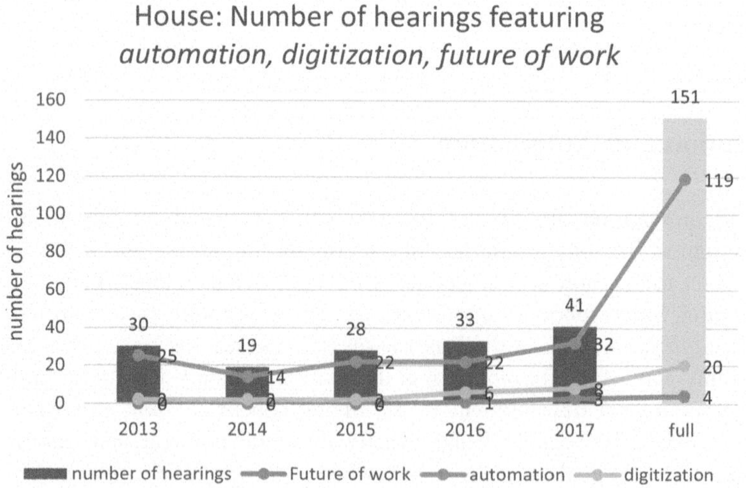

Source: Author

Table 6.2 Senate: number of hearings featuring "automation," "digitization," "future of work"

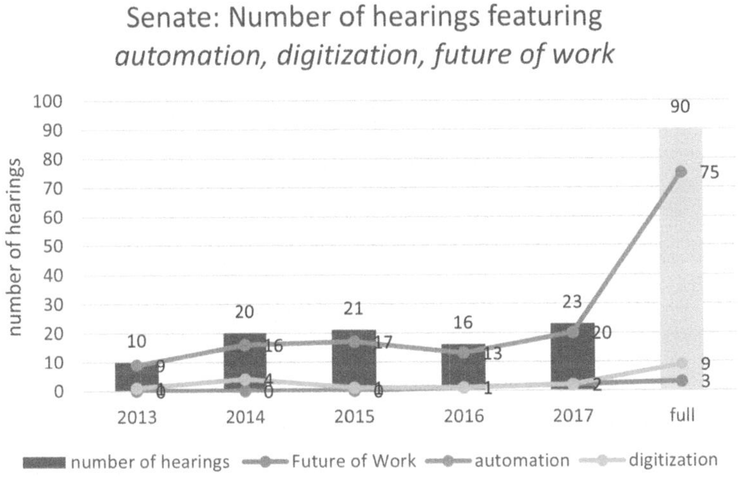

Source: Author

As indicated above, collocations[1] are "the company words keep." These are words that commonly co-occur with the word of interest (node) and give an indication of how this word is used in the context examined. In the following, collocation graphs and collocation lists of the different terms are discussed. The collocation graphs can display different dimensions of the relationship between words, including strength of the association (the closer to the node, the stronger the relationship), frequency of the collocate (the more intense the color the more frequent the collocate), and position of the collocate in the text (left, right, middle) (Brezina 2018). This representation in graphs can be used to visualize networks of nodes (words) with each other. In general, collocation "graphs and networks are useful summaries of complex meanings of words in texts and corpora. These networks can provide useful information about key topics in texts and discourses as well as their connection" (Brezina 2018).

As indicated above, the Senate data does not feature the term *digitization* to a large extent. There are only 9 out of 90 hearings where the term occurs (Table 6.2), and in total the term appears only 9 times. This amounts to a relative frequency of

---

[1]These collocation graphs and tables were produced with LancsBox 4.5 version using MI score. The default setting used in this work was MI ≥ 7.0, minimum collocation frequency 5, word span 5 <> 5. This minimum collocation frequency means that the collocate appears at least 5 times or more in the data together with the search term (node). Word span 5<>5 means that 5 words to the left and right of the node are considered in the collocation search. In some instances, these settings had to be adjusted to populate or depopulate the graphs and tables. A lower MI score and minimum collocation frequencies lower than 5 were used in some instances where the search term was very rare. The word span was not altered throughout the searches.

Table 6.3 Senate: collocation graph of digitization MI $\geq$ 5, minimum collocate frequency 1

Source: Author, using #LancsBox

0.03 per 10,000 tokens, which is very low compared to some other terms, especially compared to *automation*, which will be discussed later.

In Tables 6.3 and 6.4, the collocations of *digitization* in the Senate data are displayed. As there are so few instances of *digitization* in the Senate material, a lower than usual MI score (MI $\geq$ 5[2]) and the lowest minimum collocate frequency (1) were chosen to compute the collocation list and graph. The graph therefore displays a rather large set of collocations. But one has to bear in mind that most of these only occur once in the Senate material (6.4). Yet, they still indicate the contexts in which *digitization* occurs in the Senate data. The collocates can be grouped around different themes. For example, there are several collocates that refer to new technology such as *blockchain, grid, technology, numerically-controlled, communications, net, advances, machine,* and *data. Digitization* has led to the advance of data-driven technology such as communication technology or other smart machines.

[2]MI $\geq$ 5 still points to statistical significance.

Table 6.4 Senate: collocates of digitization MI ≥ 5, minimum collocate frequency 1

digitization

Freq: 10 Collocates: 66

Index	Status	Stat (03 - MI)	Collocate	▼ Stat	Freq (coll.)	Freq (corpus)
1	O	L	need—the	18.56699613702832	1	1
2	O	L	numerically-controlled	18.56699613702832	1	1
3	O	L	seeding	16.982220405035616	1	3
4	O	R	modularity	16.245180100476553	1	5
5	O	R	toric	15.397195645385073	1	9
6	O	L	scanning	14.86672881993196	1	13
7	O	R	eroded	14.567136211307847	1	16
8	O	L	rewarded	13.437873206084504	1	35
9	O	L	widespread	12.68450978183086	2	118
10	O	L	preservation	12.338334330639466	1	75
11	O	R	legacy	12.227298314246342	1	81
12	O	R	blockchain	12.043592526811734	1	92
13	O	R	1990s	11.709169707399237	1	116
14	O	L	immediately	11.377328922801318	1	146
15	O	R	massive	11.183446178654881	1	167
16	O	L	machine	10.916100549396223	1	201
17	O	R	shift	10.818959650307985	1	215
18	O	L	advances	10.727948939415327	1	229
19	O	R	tremendous	10.715402330261462	1	231
20	O	R	offers	10.666284056234163	1	239
21	O	L	via	10.636414948712511	1	244
22	O	R	grid	10.249739845283214	1	319
23	O	R	survey	10.187772567548338	1	333
24	O	L	limit	10.027992462760134	1	372
25	O	R	mccaskill	9.856344822194325	1	419
26	O	L	although	9.648288024145176	1	484
27	O	R	increases	9.633461311982249	1	489
28	O	R	lives	9.633461311982249	1	489
29	O	L	net	9.164139706399848	1	677
30	O	L	communications	9.136699494981613	1	690
31	O	L	capabilities	9.10158506293431	1	707
32	O	L	become	9.043589481535584	1	736
33	O	L	tools	9.01064559726247	1	753
34	O	R	wages	8.985951356587199	1	766
35	O	L	available	8.656509126342442	2	1925
36	O	R	his	8.574213409241546	1	1019
37	O	L	needed	8.522757479726017	1	1056
38	O	R	second	8.509159994792988	1	1066
39	O	L	protect	8.4508076464515	1	1110
40	O	R	further	8.346773265606974	1	1193
41	O	L	another	8.30858561500734	1	1225
42	O	L	funding	8.269089331865006	1	1259
43	O	L	markets	8.235115203444574	1	1289
44	O	L	doing	8.030904371604914	1	1485
45	O	L	potential	7.995399214264404	1	1522
46	O	L	come	7.977500609240755	1	1541
47	O	L	he	7.865845145730549	1	1665
48	O	L	benefits	7.598485075962896	1	2004
49	O	R	jobs	7.444323669473551	1	2230
50	O	L	working	7.261659971546631	1	2531
51	O	L	things	7.206304573413671	1	2630
52	O	L	important	6.864978997165129	1	3332
53	O	L	us	6.725980561253761	1	3669
54	O	R	technology	6.693707630253464	1	3752
55	O	L	were	6.620976519454246	1	3946
56	O	L	who	6.456668423901361	1	4422
57	O	R	data	6.103116579688431	1	5650
58	O	R	think	5.763625973729063	1	7149
59	O	R	all	5.554178052261413	1	8266
60	O	R	there	5.5427046220256395	1	8332
61	O	R	but	5.265369758415925	1	10098
62	O	R	so	5.1862848530528725	1	10667
63	O	R	they	5.159618375529232	1	10866
64	O	R	senator	5.0338219806357625	1	11856
65	O	M	have	5.020377812520873	2	23934
66	O	R	will	5.011963496162214	1	12037

Source: Author, using #LancsBox

There are other collocates that point to advances and progress, such as *further, will, increases, offers, widespread, potential, immediately, tremendous,* and *become*. The collocates *preservation, scanning, tools, machine, data,* and *legacy* point to *digitization* as a method of preserving "analogue" data, which is often associated with the term *digitization*. *Jobs, wages, working,* and *markets* point to the influence of *digitization* on the world of work and the economy as a whole.

Looking in more detail at the Senate hearings where *digitization* occurs, the hearing *Income Inequality in the United States* (Joint Economic Committee, 2014) was investigated. Automation is generally portrayed here as developments in computers, software, machine tools, and *digitization*, which puts further pressure on jobs and wages. *Digitization* is thus seen as being part of the current wave of automation. The hearing also mentions the income growth added by technological advancement and *digitization* for well-educated and well-connected workers. Technological progress has led to a further polarization of the labor market in which highly specialized workers can profit from *digitization* more directly than lower-skilled workers. *Digitization* is further mentioned in the context of corporate innovation and the possibilities of offshoring in a globalized market, especially for the manufacturing industry (*Rebuilding American Manufacturing*, Committee on Banking, Housing, and Urban Affairs, Subcommittee on Economic Policy, 2013). It is also mentioned in the context of preserving historical data (*Resources as Revenue,* Committee on Energy and Natural Resources, 2014), or when talking about big data sets (*The Connected World: Examining the Internet of Things*, Committee on Commerce, Science, and Transportation, 2015; *The Dawn of Artificial Intelligence*, Committee on Commerce, Science, and Transportation, Subcommittee on Space, Science, and Competitiveness, 2016). Additionally, *digitization* as a term occurs when talking about advances in technology, computing power, or new technology such as the blockchain (*The Dynamic Gains from Free Digital Trade*, Joint Economic Committee, 2017). The advances in "prowess of algorithms" or machine learning practices are also mentioned in the Senate material (*The Dawn of Artificial Intelligence*, Committee on Commerce, Science, and Transportation, Subcommittee on Space, Science, and Competitiveness, 2016). In total, the term *digitization* only occurs once or twice in the respective hearings mentioned above and only nine times overall, so the treatment of the term in the Senate material is very limited.

In the hearings in the House of Representatives, the term *digitization* is mentioned much more often than in the Senate. Overall, there are 20 out of 151 hearings where the term *digitization* occurs (Table 6.1) and 133 actual instances of the term in the House data. That amounts to a relative frequency of 0.26 per 10,000 tokens. Compared to the Senate data, this is a significant difference in the number of occurrences of this term. In Tables 6.5 and 6.6, the collocations of *digitization* in the House data are displayed. In order to depopulate the graph, a higher collocation frequency was chosen in comparison to the Senate data (which only displays collocates that occur one time in the data). A MI ≥ 5 threshold and a minimum collocation frequency of 4 was chosen.

The strongest collocates are *mass*, followed by *orphan* and *metadata*. *Orphan* relates to an issue in the realm of intellectual property that is discussed in the

Table 6.5 House: collocation graph of digitization MI ≥ 5, minimum collocate frequency 4

Source: Author, using #LancsBox

material, namely "orphan works" which are copyright protected works of which the rights holder is not determined or not detectable. *Orphan* works and *mass digitization* actually occur in the same context. In this case, their occurrences are mainly based on a specific hearing in the Committee on the Judiciary, Subcommittee on Courts, Intellectual Property, and the Internet from 2013 called *A Case Study for Consensus Building: The Copyright Principles Project* as well as another hearing in the Committee on the Judiciary on copyright issues, *U.S. Copyright Office: Its Functions and Resources*, held in 2015. Together with other collocates in the graph such as *music, preservation, efforts, libraries, works, print,* and *access* this points to the main use of *digitization* as a term in the House material overall, namely *digitization* as a method of preserving and digitizing existing data, may it be print or music, in order to make it accessible for audiences and preserve it for the next generation. In these discussions, the issue of copyright and intellectual property is often crucial.

Examining the hearings from the House more closely, the prevalence of the copyright topic in the debate around *digitization* efforts becomes even more

Table 6.6 House: collocates of digitization MI ≥ 5, minimum collocate frequency 4

digitization

Freq: 133 Collocates: 20

Index	Status	Stat (03 - MI)	Collocate	▼ Stat	Freq (coll.)	Freq (corpus)
1	O	L	mass	12.70919834346679	39	222
2	O	L	orphan	12.633252549570146	14	84
3	O	M	metadata	11.970280662638805	4	38
4	O	R	music	10.791949688099647	4	86
5	O	R	preservation	10.422353050380243	9	250
6	O	R	guidelines	9.245521897139655	5	314
7	O	L	works	9.20450338998821	18	1163
8	O	L	print	8.956119098775744	4	307
9	O	R	libraries	8.47337981230926	4	429
10	O	R	projects	8.109689205385168	9	1242
11	O	R	energy	6.845037780682084	7	2321
12	O	L	benefits	6.716774405854509	5	1812
13	O	R	efforts	6.238788185943246	4	2019
14	O	L	issues	6.173819466515386	5	2640
15	O	R	does	5.797200613090799	4	2742
16	O	L	things	5.661324403944803	5	3766
17	O	R	access	5.533026675110225	4	3293
18	O	R	federal	5.321448668891564	7	6673
19	O	M	way	5.296000804625904	4	3881
20	O	R	should	5.183689740336861	5	5244

Source: Author, using #LancsBox

apparent. The hearings in the House material that feature the term *digitization* most often are *Preservation and Reuse of Copyrighted Works* (Committee on the Judiciary, Subcommittee on Courts, Intellectual Property, and the Internet, 2014), *GPO in 2023: Keeping America Informed in a Post-Print World* (Committee on House Administration, 2013), and *A Case Study for Consensus Building: The Copyright Principles Project* (Committee on the Judiciary, Subcommittee on Courts, Intellectual Property, and the Internet, 2013). Two other hearings are concerned with *U.S. Copyright Office: Its Functions and Resources* (Committee on the Judiciary, 2015) and *Copyright Issues in Education and for the Visually Impaired* (Committee on the Judiciary, Subcommittee on Courts, Intellectual Property, and the Internet, 2014). There are a few other hearings where the term *digitization* appears more infrequently than in the hearings mentioned above, but these are the most significant. As could be seen in the collocation list and graph, most of the contexts where the term *digitization* occurs are concerned with copyright issues. Many of the large-scale projects in recent years that make use of mass *digitization* of data such as Google Books have raised questions about who can retain intellectual property rights in a global digital world. Intellectual property and copyright issues are therefore crucial issues in the House when *digitization* is discussed.

Two other themes that are touched upon in the House material when it comes to *digitization* are consumer protection (*Powering America: Technology's Role in Empowering Consumers*, Committee on Energy and Commerce, Subcommittee on Energy, 2017) and cybersecurity (*Examining Cybersecurity Responsibilities at HHS*, Committee on Energy and Commerce, Subcommittee on Health, 2016). Looking at the frequency of *cybersecurity* as a term in the congressional material overall described previously, this is hardly surprising. Cybersecurity is a topic that has been of great concern to Congress throughout the years and across many fields of policy-making, also in the foreign policy realm, for example. Consumer rights and protections in a more digital economy are also crucial topics. In the 2017 hearing on "powering America," technology is mainly portrayed as an empowering tool for consumers, which is a notion that can be seen in many instances across the source material. Technological advancement has had great beneficial effects for consumers, making many products better, more affordable, and easier to access at all times. Consumers have also gained tremendous information access through technology.

One can see from the House hearings that the term *digitization* mostly occurs in instances where copyright issues are discussed. Intellectual property and its retainment remain critical issues in a global digital world. *Digitization* is also examined in the context of protections in the form of consumer protection and cybersecurity. Especially cybersecurity is a topic that is discussed in a wide array of contexts and different committees in Congress. Unlike in the hearings in the Senate, the term *digitization* in the House material is less connected with technological development and advances such as the blockchain or artificial intelligence. The Senate hearings featuring the term *digitization* touch upon the influence of technology on specific industries such as manufacturing, as well as on the economy as a whole. Some of the Senate hearings mentioned above were more directly concerned with the influence of (digital) technology on the workplace, on wages, and inequality in the future. All of these instances are very rare, however. Yet, the term *digitization* is reliantly used across the congressional material in reference to the method of digitizing large amounts of data of different kinds in order to preserve them and make them more easily accessible. The term *digitization* is also used in reference to issues connected to these efforts, e.g., copyright.

6.1.2 Digitization in the Liberal Media Material

In the liberal media material based on the *NYT* and *Washington Post*, the term *digitization* occurs 368 times in absolute terms with a relative frequency of 0.69 per 10,000 tokens. 2013 is the year that displays the highest frequency of the term *digitization* with 1.31 occurrences per 10,000 tokens, followed by 2015 (1.00), 2014 (0.85), 2016 (0.49), and 2017 (0.47). Compared to the congressional material, the relative frequencies of the term over the years are much higher. However, the *Wall Street Journal* material displays an even higher frequency of the term overall, which

Table 6.7 Liberal media: collocation graph of digitization MI ≥ 7, minimum collocate frequency 5

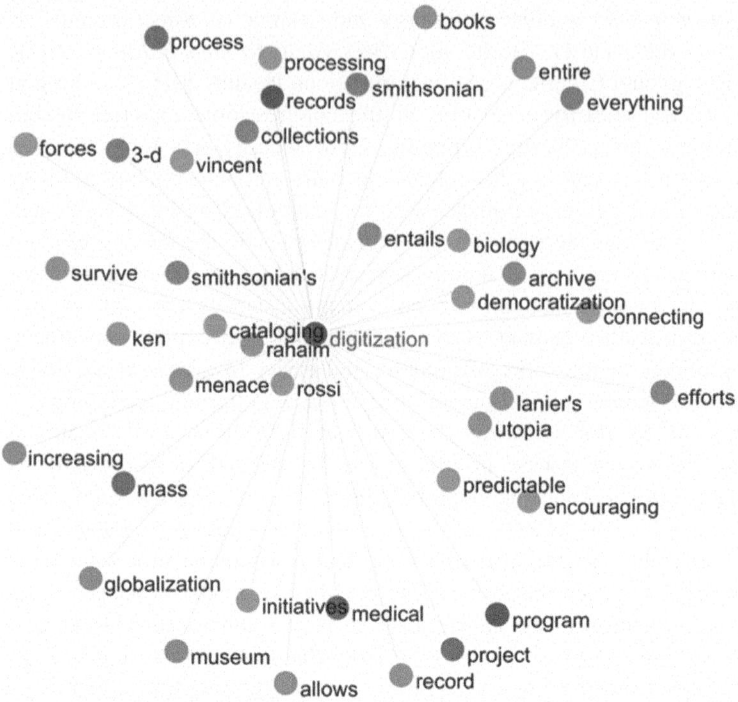

Source: Author, using #LancsBox

will be detailed in Sect. 6.1.3. Compared to the term *automation*, the frequency of *digitization* in the liberal media material is still much lower.

Looking at Tables 6.7 and 6.8 (MI ≥ 7 default setting, minimum collocation frequency 5), one can see the collocates of *digitization* in the liberal media material. Most of the collocates displayed in the tables refer to *digitization* as a method used to preserve and store analogue data digitally. These collocates include *process, processing, records, books, collections, archive, record, mass, cataloging,* and *3-d.* Then there are a few collocates referring to the institutions engaging in digitization processes to store and preserve data such as the Smithsonian institutions, museums, or libraries: *smithsonian's, smithsonian, archive*, and *museum. Democratizing* and *survive* refer to the underlying reasons institutions engage in digitization efforts: to preserve data, for example *medical* or data in *biology*, and to make it accessible to more people around the globe (*globalization*).

In the material from the liberal media sources, there are two general themes in which *digitization* occurs. One refers to further **innovation** in the field of automation and technology. The other theme is **digitization as method**, for example used to digitize documents or artifacts.

Table 6.8 Liberal media: collocates of digitization MI $\geq$ 7, minimum collocate frequency 5

digitization

Freq: 368 Collocates: 39

Index	Status	Stat (03 - MI)	Collocate	▼ Stat	Freq (coll.)	Freq (corpus)
1	○	L	rossi	13.327758283175047	5	7
2	○	L	rahaim	13.228198349601245	6	9
3	○	L	cataloging	12.434623101346395	5	13
4	○	R	entails	12.169311453312968	8	25
5	○	L	menace	11.54013650010952	6	29
6	○	L	smithsonian's	11.339221171078343	9	50
7	○	R	democratization	11.327730990677994	5	28
8	○	R	biology	10.925633284734891	5	37
9	○	R	utopia	10.565228867971712	6	57
10	○	R	predictable	10.353727687879294	5	55
11	○	L	ken	10.35372537217363	6	66
12	○	R	lanier's	10.35372537217363	6	66
13	○	R	archive	10.128654185138693	7	90
14	○	L	collections	10.005799863322764	9	126
15	○	L	vincent	9.88715696285915	5	76
16	○	R	records	9.412932661641765	26	549
17	○	L	mass	9.362493746183679	15	328
18	○	R	smithsonian	9.157802956767759	10	252
19	○	L	survive	8.86673546496802	6	185
20	○	L	3-d	8.78635558182436	10	326
21	○	R	encouraging	8.751377534602675	5	167
22	○	R	connecting	8.700455318721762	5	173
23	○	R	medical	8.692139593554629	20	696
24	○	R	initiatives	8.68387152583822	5	175
25	○	R	processing	8.58818722036775	5	187
26	●		digitization	7.874555395967876	6	368
27	○	L	increasing	7.617694798233103	7	513
28	○	L	globalization	7.448082818949896	7	577
29	○	R	program	7.401644625618986	24	2043
30	○	R	books	7.384097789459934	6	517
31	○	L	process	7.350214739460008	14	1235
32	○	R	entire	7.314448851578259	7	633
33	○	R	project	7.197313842270911	13	1275
34	○	L	forces	7.140730014225526	5	510
35	○	L	museum	7.138710521762392	7	715
36	○	R	everything	7.096164225354132	10	1052
37	○	R	allows	7.056043842303	6	649
38	○	R	record	7.023078421057895	6	664
39	○	R	efforts	7.009024415465116	8	894

Source: Author, using #LancsBox

The theme referred to as **digitization as technological innovation** is concerned with innovation that spurs economic growth. For example, in a 2015 article on the Washington Post Blogs called *Take note Republicans and Democrats, this is what a pro-innovation platform looks like*, Larry Downes writes about the 2016 elections and what candidates should do to embrace a (political) platform that is truly committed to "economic growth, innovation, and competitive advantage in the global market." Recent development in Silicon Valley has brought about so-called disruptive innovations. As an example, the sharing economy is mentioned. *Digitization* is used here in the context of the transformation of industries. These innovations encompass both values from Republicans who champion limited government and limitless innovation, and Democrats who support consumer empowerment. *Digitization* again appears when talking about the replacement of jobs that have become obsolete due to digital services or products, such as the video store clerk or bank teller. The theme of innovation is mentioned several times, for example in another article from 2015 in the *Washington Post* called *Cisco exec: Tech policy missing in 2016 race*, by Andrea Peterson, which argues that the next era of *digitization* is on the horizon. This should be encouraged, but it also calls for adequate training. Otherwise, innovation cannot be advanced and the growth of the economy is in question. *Technology That Transforms Life (and Funds' Returns)* Tim Gray from 2014 in the *NYT* argues that the growth of the economy will be based on continued *digitization*, mass consumerism, modern medicine, and emerging markets. He also mentions a possible renaissance of American manufacturing and the North American energy revival as sources of growth.

In several articles in the liberal media material, "*digitization of everything*" on a global scale is also discussed. *Digitization* and "globalization" are frequently used together. It is argued that there is little that Silicon Valley will not try to digitize and that digital products are moving into realms that were unknown before (*Today in Small Business: Same-Day Delivery*, 2014 by Gene Marks on the NYT Blogs). Connecting it to the theories of the so-called Second Machine Age, *digitization* is mentioned in the context of computer processing, AI, and network communication, for example in *How smart machines will drive the global economy* in the *Washington Pos*t by Steven Pearlstein in 2014. The pervasiveness of *digitization* is mentioned again in the context of AI: Farhad Manjoo writes about the "digitization of everything and everyone around you" in *What the Tax Bill Fails to Address: Technology's Tsunami, State of the Art,* 2017 in the *NYT*. Another factor pushing *digitization* forward is the smartphone, which is described as one of the most rapidly adopted technologies in history. The smartphone has now become the hub of further *digitization* (*The Doctor Is On*, by Sandeep Jauhar, 2015, NYT).

On a global scale, *digitization* and social networking technology make it possible to analyze massive amounts of data. However, this brings about privacy issues as well (*NSA snooping is legal. It isn't constitutional*, Washington Post, 2013, Laura K. Donohue). However, *digitization* is not only a global phenomenon, but has an impact on the rural-urban development and polarization as well. *Digitization* of the economy leads to an accelerating trend of clustering of workers and firms in larger cities. The skill demand is profoundly changing certain areas and what they have been valued for in the past. This new urbanization is discussed, for example, in *Reaching Out to the Voters the Left Left Behind* by Thomas B. Edsall, 2017 in the NYT. The article details how the gap between rural and urban areas is widening. If Democrats want to win back rural voters, they need to address this issue. Locations in urban centers are in demand by big corporations because of the concentration of highly skilled workers, universities, supply chains, STEM workers, and industry clusters. Especially the high-tech sector depends on that. Apart from the more specific articles mentioned here, there are also several articles where *digitization* occurs that are concerned with e-government, online learning, or self-driving cars.

As said before, there is a second theme that can be identified in the discourse on *digitization* in the liberal media sources, which will be referred to as **digitization as method.** In the articles concerned with this theme, the processing and accessing of documents is discussed, e.g., in the legal community, in health care, in archival work, or in libraries and museums. *Digitization* as a method is used for cataloguing and preserving objects or texts. With the rise of Big Data, there are many more opportunities to make use of data in many different fields. E-books or digital film are also mentioned in this context. For governments and citizens, *digitization* might be beneficial in providing digital services and accessing public documents.

Some of the articles discussing *digitization* as method include *Smithsonian's Clough: There's much unfinished* (2014) by Peggy McGlone on washingtonpost.com, in which the Smithsonian secretary G. Wayne Clough talks about the efforts to digitize the 138 million items in the Smithsonian collection. He argues that "Digitization is democratization" as it gives more people access to the collections. *Digitization* in museum work is a large topic and discussed in several other articles such as *A Museum at the Forefront of Digitization* (2015), *NYT*, by Stephen Heyman. Apart from museums, archives and libraries are also concerned with *digitization* as a method as can be seen in articles like *Applying new technology to digitize huge archives* by Steven Overly, 2015, in the *Washington Post* or *Hayden tapped for Library of Congress* (2016) by Peggy McGlone in the *Washington Post*. Again, *digitization* is mentioned in the context of making special collections available online. Big Data efforts and their implications are also discussed, for example in the 2015 *NYT* article *Roberto Calasso, Italy's Publishing Maestro*, by Stephen Heyman that talks about *digitization* in the context of Google Books, a project which "blurs the distinction between information and knowledge." In the mind of some people, information equals knowledge, and through *digitization* of more and more material, we automatically gain more knowledge. But Roberto Calasso argues, information and knowledge are decidedly not the same. Another article from 2017 in the *Washington Post* also talks about the possibilities of Big Data: *Sorry Sherlock* by Michael Ravnitzky. Through the *digitization* of big amounts of data, for example historical texts, our understanding of events or language can change. Big Data is also relevant in the healthcare sector (*Along with Obamacare, start-ups now in limbo*, 2017, by Elizabeth Dwoskin, *Washington Post*) where a lot of investment in digital health is made to digitize medical records and services. These are only some examples of the many more articles in the *NYT* and *Washington Post* referring to all of these issues.

In the material from the liberal media sources, the second theme identified here, "*digitization as method*," is very prevalent compared to the other theme, "*digitization as technological innovation*." This can already be seen in the collocations of *digitization* in this material that mostly concern the processes and institutions that are engaging in digitizing data such as archives, museums, or the Smithsonian institutions. This is comparable to the use of the term in the congressional material. Especially in the House, the term *digitization* mostly occurs when copyright issues or intellectual property are discussed, both of which play a big role in digitizing efforts. In the liberal media material, the focus is not so much on the copyright issue, but rather the actual processes and the data that is targeted in *digitization* efforts. Many museums and archives push for *digitization* as it means "democratizing" their collections by making them accessible to more people. On the other hand, *digitization* is also used in reference to advanced technology that disrupts markets on a worldwide scale. The "Second Machine Age" brings digital products into areas that had not seen a lot of innovation before, for example health care. Now things like AI change whole branches entirely. Indeed, one could think that there is a "digitization of everything" under way changing not only the economy but also impacting geographical locations with many rural areas being left out of the opportunities of the new economy.

6.1.3 Digitization in the WSJ *Material*

In the corpus based on the *Wall Street Journal* (*WSJ*), *digitization* appears 277 times in absolute terms and with a frequency of 1.59 per 10,000 tokens. Compared to the liberal media material, the frequency of the term *digitization* is more than double in the *WSJ*. 2013 marks the highest frequency (2.36 per 10,000 tokens), followed by 2016 (1.66), 2015 (1.43), 2017 (1.36), and 2014 (1.34). Comparing it to the term *automation*, *automation* appears with a frequency of 8.7 per 10,000 tokens and a total of 1518 mentions in the texts. *Automation* as a term thus appears more than five times as often as *digitization*. Overall, however, the *WSJ* material displays the highest frequency of the term *digitization* across the different sources investigated here.

In Tables 6.9 and 6.10, the collocations (MI $\geq$ 7, minimum collocation frequency 5) of *digitization* in the *WSJ* are displayed. *Searchable* is one of the strongest collocates; all others are fairly consistent in their strength. Of course, digitized collections and data are much more *searchable* than analogue data, for example for researchers. The quality and speed of *digitization* is indicated with the collocates *rapid, advanced, wave, increasing*, and *trend*. *Documents* and *records* are objects that are digitized more and more. Again, the idea of "digitization of everything" is also pointed at with the collocate *everything*. Other fields where *digitization* plays a role are mentioned with *mobility, regulation,* and *workplace*. Innovations in transportation and driving, for instance the self-driving car, are changing people's *mobility* profoundly. In some instances, there is a lot of discussion around whether these innovations demand new *regulation*. *Digitization* also has an impact on the *workplace* where the nature of work is changing. *Globalization* and *digitization* also co-occur here which was the case in the liberal media material as well. *Globalization* and technological progress go hand in hand and reinforce one another.

In the *WSJ* material, there are also some overarching themes in which the term *digitization* occurs. Interestingly, these themes are very similar to the treatment of

Table 6.9 *WSJ*: collocation graph of digitization MI ≥ 7, minimum collocate frequency 5

Source: Author, using #LancsBox

digitization in the liberal media material. Once again, they can be referred to as **digitization as method** and **digitization as technological innovation**.

The **digitization as method** theme includes articles that talk about ways to digitize existing material such as books, art, archives, or other big data sets, but also new ways of distribution and formats such as e-books, digital film and TV, or music. For example, in *As Trash Goes, Authors' Clutter In the Right Hands Is Very Bankable—Ken Lopez Gets Top Dollar From Libraries* and *Uncashed Checks, Salt Shakers*, by Barry Newman from 2013, *digitization* is used in the context of digitizing paper documents, which makes them more searchable in a database of libraries. In *Years of Magical Thinking Conjured Up the Works in this Library—From Prestidigitation to Escapology, Manhattan Repository Holds Tricks of Trade*, by Demetria Gallegos, 2013, the author alludes to libraries' online databases offering the digitized data of well-known personalities. There are several more articles on *digitization* efforts of archives and digital applications in libraries such as *World News: Vatican to Digitize Historic Archives*, by Liam Moloney, 2014; *City News: Library Expands Free Wi-Fi*, by Mike Vilensky, 2014; and *City News; Pushing History Into the Digital Age*, by Melanie Grayce Wes, 2015.

Table 6.10 *WSJ*: collocates of digitization MI ≥ 7, minimum collocate frequency 5

digitization

Freq: 277 Collocates: 16

Index	Status	Stat (03 - MI)	Collocate	▼ Stat	Freq (coll.)	Freq (corpus)
1	O	R	searchable	11.772131821600045	5	9
2	O	L	globalization	9.274351141709541	6	61
3	O	R	mobility	8.62012807297552	8	128
4	O	R	workplace	8.269629014514381	5	102
5	O	L	rapid	7.942056167863103	5	128
6	O	R	documents	7.8335305431568445	5	138
7	O	L	wave	7.812771410013835	5	140
8	O	R	everything	7.698881178916984	10	303
9	O	L	generation	7.41849395543103	5	184
10	O	R	projects	7.328572497993582	6	235
11	O	R	gas	7.3054300953903235	5	199
12	O	L	trend	7.3054300953903235	5	199
13	O	L	regulation	7.248568650137948	5	207
14	O	R	records	7.193862413212362	5	215
15	O	L	advanced	7.053312512587239	5	237
16	O	L	increasing	7.053312512587239	5	237

Source: Author, using #LancsBox

Digitization also opens up the possibility to consume products such as film or books in different formats. This is discussed in *Review—Don't Burn Your Books—Print Is Here to Stay—The e-book had its moment, but sales are slowing; Readers still want to turn those crisp, bound pages*, by Nicholas Carr from 2013. Carr talks about *digitization* of music, photos, and maps and their (possible) disappearance in other formats. This is also happening to books to some extent, but it is still unlikely that printed books will disappear entirely. The article *Google Books Challenge Is Rejected*, by Jacob Gershman and Jeffrey A. Trachtenberg, 2013, talks about the *digitization* of books by Google and whether it is a fair use or exploitation of author rights. Big Data such as the Google Books project is discussed on a number of occasions, for example in *Review: Books: When More Trumps Better*, by Evgeny Morozov, 2013. The term *digitization* here appears together with "datafication." Art, music, film, and TV all face tremendous challenges through digital applications and technology, and there are several articles talking about this. For instance, there is the article on the New York City Philharmonic orchestra *Philharmonic Unveils Trove Online*, by Jennifer Maloney, 2013, which talks about the *digitization* project of the New York Philharmonic's archives that gives insights into art, business, and personalities of the institution. Again, all the articles mentioned above (only a sample of all the articles that appeared on the subject) mainly deal with *digitization* as a method for preserving existing material and the different formats of products today.

The next broader theme that can be observed in the *WSJ* material is **digitization as technological innovation**. In this area, the *WSJ* material talks about different branches in the economy that are fueled through *digitization*. One of these branches is health care. Health care used to be a sector in which *digitization* and automation and thus productivity growth were very limited, but in recent years technology has become more and more important. There are several articles alluding to more *digitization* in the healthcare sector and also possible issues such as privacy concerns: *Boss Talk: Updating Doctors' Offices Via Cloud Services*, Jon Kamp, 2013; *U.S. News: Poor Prognosis for Privacy—Rules That Give Patients More Control of Their Records Face Technical Problems*, by Melinda Beck, 2013; *The Wireless Revolution Hits Medicine: Eric Topol talks about the upheaval that's coming as the digitization of health care meets the smartphone*, by Ron Winslow, 2013; *Weekend Investor: The New Basic: Securing Your Medical Data*, by Constance Gustke, 2014; *Three Ways to Find More Disease Cures*, by Michael Milken, 2016; and *Health Care Risk Underlined By Insider Threat Finding*, by Jeff Stone, 2017.

Apart from health care, there are articles that talk about *digitization's* impact on manufacturing and the economy as a whole. There are several articles on new digital technology in the production process of manufacturing industries, for example, *Manufacturing: Unleashing Innovation (A Special Report)—A Revolution In the Making: Digital Technology is transforming manufacturing, making it leaner and smarter, and raising the prospect of an American industrial renaissance*, by John Koten, 2013. *Digitization* is mentioned together with the rise of 3D printing, which offers a whole new range of possibilities for manufacturing. Another article on manufacturing is called *Will the U.S. See a Major Manufacturing Revival?*, 2014. Several experts comment on this question, among them Dominic Barton, global managing director of McKinsey & Co, who sees technological innovation as the most important driver for such a revival. Here he mentions *digitization* as the first such driver, followed by data analytics, advanced automation, the Internet of Things, and additive manufacturing, which are all transforming the manufacturing landscape. The Internet of Things is again in focus in *CIO Networks (A Special Report)—Why Most Firms Better Get Moving: Cisco's John Chambers on digital disruptions ahead*, by Scott Thurm, 2015. Here, *digitization* is mentioned together with the "Internet of Everything," which is ushering in transitions in the market and demands adaption from companies.

A year before (2013), in *The Experts: What Is the No. 1 Technology Issue Facing Companies Today?*, experts were asked about their take on the title's question. *Digitization* is seen as one such issue. *Digitization* is going to fuel growth and output and will create many new jobs. All companies want to be a part of this growth, but they need to focus on their strategy not on the technology alone. In another expert round *The Experts: How to Knock Down the Wall Around IT*, 2013, the "wall" between IT and everyone else in a company is discussed. This does not reflect a modern take on business-making when *digitization* is moving ahead quickly and requires every industry to integrate IT into their processes. Another article looks at the transformation processes of the future in a special report: *WSJ 125 (A Special Report)—125 Years of Change; And More Change; How has the business world been transformed? Let us count the many ways*, by John Steele Gordon, 2014. *Digitization* here is mentioned together with "mechanization," which have both changed the workplace. *Digitization* is displayed as one trend among many, like the rise and fall of great industries over the past 125 years in the American economic ecosystem.

There are also some large (manufacturing) companies like Siemens that are mentioned when talking about *digitization*: for example, *Siemens Provides Details on Strategic Revamp; German Conglomerate Outlines Plans After Reporting Rise in Second-Quarter Profit*, by Friedrich Geiger, 2014. Siemens focuses on further automation and *digitization*, which are mentioned together here. The article alludes to a profound structural change in the company. Siemens is mentioned several times over the years. Another German business, BMW, is mentioned in *Business News; New BMW Amps Up Car Electronics—coming 7 series reflects shift from horse-power to smart cars that park and drive themselves*, by William Boston, 2015. BMW is working on the *digitization* of mobility. Generally, electronic mobility as well as the *digitization* of the automobile industry more generally features consistently throughout the *WSJ* material, e.g., in *Business News—The Week Ahead: Car Makers Face Text of Tech Prowess*, by William Boston, 2015. *Digitization* and startups, venture capital, and global supply chains are also part of the *WSJ* material over the years. As seen above, Germany's take on *digitization* is mentioned in several articles such as *Cisco Steps Up Investments in Germany, Slack Competitor*, by Don Clark, 2016, or in *EU Offers Plan to Harmonize Members' Digital Initiatives. New governance framework would seek to coordinate 30 national and regional efforts*, by Natalia Drozdiak, 2016. *Digitization* is mentioned in the context of Germany's Industry 4.0 efforts or Netherlands Smart Industry, as well as in the context of the overall *digitization* of goods and services in the EU. The German robotic company Kuka is also mentioned several times, especially in 2016. Kuka focuses on *digitization* in the manufacturing processes through advanced robotics and was acquired by Chinese investors.

Jobs are the focus in the article *What Jobs Will Robots Have in the Future?* (2014). This is another article in which several experts are asked about their opinion on automation and *digitization*, and how they are transforming the workplace. "Dark sides" of both trends are mentioned such as job loss. With technology encroaching more and more into areas where human jobs seemed to be safe for a long time, there might be a large-scale change in the availability of jobs in all kinds of areas. With AI, for example, there is also the danger of malfunctioning machines that could pose dangers to humans. On the other hand, robots can increase the quality of life and save costs, which increases growth rates and consumer welfare. As the title suggests, the focus of this article is not workers losing their jobs through *digitization*, but robots and their capacities in the future. There are several other articles in the *WSJ* where robots and their impact on jobs are discussed.

The 2015 article *Go Big or Go Home*, by Philip Delves Broughton, looks at the book *Bold* by Peter H. Diamandis who talks about the innovators of Silicon Valley. *Digitization* is mentioned here in connection with failed businesses like Kodak who missed the trend and crashed in the era of digital photography. The financial industry and *digitization* are mentioned in *Goldman: Not Just for the Rich*, by Justin Baer, 2015. New innovations in the financial market are also mentioned in *Bitcoin Catches On with Gold Bugs*, by Stephanie Yang, 2016. In the article *CIO Network (A Special*

Report)—The Wall Street Journal CIO Network: At the Helm of the Digital Transformation, by Steven Rosenbush, 2016, the accelerating *digitization* of the market as a whole is described. Two other industries that are mentioned in the context of *digitization* are the supermarket industry that has introduced more and more digital services, as well as the construction industry, e.g., in *Trends: (A Special Report) Building a Better Building: The construction industry has lagged behind others in going digital; That's changing quickly—with impressive results*, by Robb M. Stewart, 2016.

Globalization and *digitization* are the focus of *C-Suite Strategies (A Special Report)—Venture Capital, for Everywhere Else: Steve Case says people outside Silicon Valley feel left out and left behind; he has a plan*, by Deborah Gage, 2017. In this article, *digitization* and globalization are discussed as trends that have a large impact on many developments, for example on elections. Blue states and red states in the USA are unequally affected by the two trends with red states missing out on almost all of the venture capital and thus missing out on innovation. This picks up on the idea of the urban–rural divide that was mentioned in the liberal media material but looks at Republican and Democratic states more specifically. Red states, often more rural, do not seem to be the champions of innovation in a digitized world which leads to the population being left out of opportunities and participation in the economy. Blue Democratic states, often more urban, attract more venture capital and therefore innovation. This idea is an interesting take on the political landscape of the USA, but it is an isolated article in the *WSJ* material investigated here.

In several instances, *digitization* and mobility, as well as disruptive technology companies or "game changers," are mentioned together in the *WSJ* material, especially in the year 2017. Additionally, the relationship between *digitization* and the security of data is an important topic in 2017. Robots also remain an important issue of 2017, e.g., in *Robots Will Save the Economy* by Bret Swanson and Michael Mandel, 2017. *Digitization* and e-commerce in retail are the focus here. E-commerce has added thousands of jobs, more than physical shops would have. This focus on *digitization* in retail intensifies in 2017. Also in 2017, the book by Andrew McAfee and Erik Brynjolfsson called *Machine, Platform, Crowd*, which was mentioned in this book, was published and was discussed in *The Future on Fast Forward*, by Randall Stross, 2017. The book deals with the possible "digitization of everything" that the authors see coming. Education for this not-so-distant future is the focus of the article *CEO Council (A Special Report)—Preparing Youth for Future Jobs: Betsy DeVos says the education system has tended to look backward rather than forward*, by Matt Murray, 2017, in which the then Secretary of Education is interviewed and is asked about the impact of *digitization*. *Digitization* is mentioned together with artificial intelligence and the increasing transformation of the workplace. Are US workers prepared for it? In the article, Betsy DeVos argues that a 4-year college degree alone cannot be the solution and that parents and children need to be offered different options. Vocational training and school choice programs in the different states are advocated by her. International affairs, security risks (cybersecurity and cyberwar), and net neutrality are three other topics that show up in the *WSJ* material on *digitization*.

The broader themes around *digitization* in the *WSJ* material can be divided into two main areas. On the one hand, the term often alludes to the method of preserving existing material such as books, archives, or other forms of art. It also alludes to new digital formats such as (e-)books, digital music, film, or art. On the other hand, there are several articles that mention *digitization* as a driver for innovation in the economy such as in the fields of health care, manufacturing, e-commerce, retail, the construction industry, and others. This focus is much stronger in the *WSJ* material than in the other material investigated. The focus here lies on the innovative capacity of *digitization* through the introduction of robots, for instance, and on specific businesses who implement these innovations. In the *WSJ* material, the opportunities for innovation and the economy as a whole are clearly emphasized over any possible "dark sides." Generally, the *WSJ* material is much more detailed in its use of *digitization* as a term compared to the congressional and liberal media material investigated in this work. The *WSJ* also displays the highest relative frequency of the term in the material. There is a special focus on specific companies and business branches engaging in *digitization* efforts and their impact on economic growth and productivity. In the other material, the "digitization as a method" theme is significantly stronger than in the *WSJ* material. Tending to the business-oriented reader, the *WSJ* gives more specific details on the digitization strategies of specific countries and companies and how *digitization* is implemented in the production cycle or in new areas altogether. In this sense, *digitization* is seen as a step in the ongoing restructuring process of the American economy fueled through automation.

6.1.4 Automation in the Congressional Material

As indicated before, the term *automation* is much more frequent than the term *digitization* overall. In the congressional data, this is also the case. First, the Senate material will be investigated. In the hearings from the Senate, the term *automation* occurs 392 times in absolute terms with a relative frequency of 1.01 per 10,000 tokens. The term also appears in 75 out of 90 Senate hearings investigated here. *Digitization*, in comparison, only appeared in 9 out of 90 hearings.

In Tables 6.11 and 6.12, the collocations of *automation* in the Senate material are displayed. There are several collocates that refer to driving or cars; these include *self-driving, route, vehicle, sensors, driving*, and *cruise*. *Cruise* refers to Cruise Automation which is a company that belongs to General Motors and works on self-driving cars. Although it could not be immediately observed in the frequency data, the issue of self-driving cars is treated rather frequently when *automation* is discussed in Congress, as it is an area where new regulation and safety issues are of concern. In fact, *vehicle* is the most frequent collocate here (Table 6.12). Additionally, the collocate *eram* also refers to the field of transportation and *automation*. ERAM is an abbreviation for "En Route Automation Modernization Program" which is a federal program for the modernization of infrastructure capabilities. It is mainly talked about in hearings on the future of aviation.

Table 6.11 Senate: collocation graph of automation MI ≥ 7, minimum collocate frequency 5

Source: Author, using #LancsBox

Artificial, robots, industrial, robotics, and *cognitive* point to the progress of technology in the field of smart machines and their industrial application. Artificial intelligence and smart robotics are entering more and more fields. They are discussed in a specific hearing on the matter in front of the Joint Economic Committee called *The Transformative Impact of Robots and Automation.* The collocates *levels, degree, increasing, increasingly,* and *continuum* point to the extent and fast pace of *automation*.

The two Senate hearings that feature the term *automation* the most are directly concerned with the influence of technology on the economy as a whole. They look at robotics and artificial intelligence specifically. The first hearing is called *The Transformative Impact of Robots and Automation* (2016) in front of the Joint Economic Committee. This hearing is mainly concerned with how robots, *automation,* and new technology are transforming the economy. In the hearing, members and witnesses discuss the influence of technology on jobs, but also how to best use technology for innovation and productivity. The second hearing called *The Dawn of Artificial*

Table 6.12 Senate: collocates of automation MI ≥ 7, minimum collocate frequency 5

automation

Freq: 392 Collocates: 23

Index	Status	Stat (03 - MI)	Collocate	▼ Stat	Freq (coll.)	Freq (corpus)
1	○	R	continuum	11.13673633108979	5	22
2	○	R	eram	11.005736123043855	11	53
3	○	R	robotics	10.244478478531745	12	98
4	○	L	cruise	10.041565551696069	5	47
5	○	L	robots	9.923728126442919	5	51
6	○	R	routine	9.771730525892501	6	68
7	○	L	route	9.583066941898345	12	155
8	○	R	cognitive	9.508696120058575	5	68
9	○	R	modernization	9.080454890792689	10	183
10	○	L	terminal	9.059214426193254	7	130
11	○	R	involves	8.827973578266159	5	109
12	○	R	artificial	8.512676064858717	8	217
13	●		automation	8.244481337077142	12	392
14	○	L	vehicle	8.10795087468528	33	1185
15	○	L	sensors	7.895716232636799	5	208
16	○	L	self-driving	7.793102332053806	6	268
17	○	L	levels	7.737009560486711	16	743
18	○	L	full	7.452226130659913	14	792
19	○	L	increasing	7.427773128547769	13	748
20	○	L	degree	7.412698091503444	7	407
21	○	L	industrial	7.191014241321413	5	339
22	○	M	increasingly	7.179710454200781	6	410
23	○	L	driving	7.1222253011714	9	640

Source: Author, using #LancsBox

Intelligence (Committee on Commerce, Science, and Transportation, Subcommittee on Space, Science, and Competitiveness, 2016) discusses the influence of technology on the economy further. For example, it is mentioned how *automation* and manufacturing have made the USA an industrial and military powerhouse. In order to maintain this status, new technology like AI needs to be harnessed in the right way. Both these hearings were already discussed in more detail in Sect. 4.4.

The focus on the subjects of *automation*, robotics, and artificial intelligence in the Senate hearings points to their large impact on the economy as a whole and their role in the debate around technological progress in the USA. Especially the hearing *The Transformative Impact of Robots and Automation* (2016) discusses potential action of Congress in the fields of the workforce, education, social security, and other government policy in order to steer the impact of *automation* in a desirable direction. Here, expert witnesses like Andrew McAfee talk in great detail about *automation* and its impact. On the one hand, it boosts productivity, but on the other hand, there is a decoupling of this productivity from job and income growth. Many Americans have not seen their wages increase in the last few decades and job growth has been slow as well. Technological progress is one reason behind this trend as many fields have invested in *automation* technology to produce "more with less." This is especially apparent in the manufacturing sector. Through new innovations like AI and machine learning this effect will increase and affect different fields than before. This could lead to even more polarization in the job market with few people on top and many more in low-wage jobs. Therefore, education and infrastructure, entrepreneurship, and immigration reform are discussed in Congress. Many other witnesses argue along the same lines, supporting the fact that technology has brought about enormous benefits for consumers and the average citizen by producing superior and cheaper goods and services. None of the political actors or witnesses really see a future without work on the horizon, but the skills necessary to be successful in the future will change fundamentally. Therefore, technological progress does put enormous pressure on the workforce already.

There are several other hearings where the term *automation* occurs. However, most of the other hearings are not as specific in the treatment of technological progress and its impact on the American economy as the two hearings just mentioned. They are mainly concerned with other topics that include **transportation, infrastructure, cybersecurity, and monetary policy**.

There are several hearings on the topic of future **transportation and infrastructure,** for example, *The Road Ahead: Advanced Vehicle Technology and its Implications* (2013) in the Committee on Commerce, Science, and Transportation or *Nextgen: A Review of Progress, Challenges, and Opportunities for Improving Aviation Safety and Efficiency* (2014) in the Committee on Commerce, Science, and Transportation, Subcommittee on Aviation Operations, Safety, and Security that discuss technological development in aviation and car-making. There are several more hearings that touch upon the issue of transportation such as *Continuing to Improve Truck Safety on our Nation's Highways* (2017) in the Committee on Commerce, Science, and Transportation, Subcommittee on Surface Transportation and Merchant Marine Infrastructure, Safety and Security. Trucking is one of the most common occupations in the USA so more *automation* in this field could have large consequences. *Technologies Transforming Transportation: Is the Government Keeping Up?* (2015) in the Committee on Commerce, Science, and Transportation, Subcommittee on Surface Transportation and Merchant Marine Infrastructure, Safety and Security and *Hands-off: The Future of Self-Driving Cars* (2016) in the Committee on Commerce, Science, and Transportation also talk about transportation and especially about self-driving cars. Self-driving cars raise all kinds of issues and questions such as liability in case of accidents. Then there is also *Keeping Goods Moving: Continuing to Enhance Multimodal Freight Policy and Infrastructure* (2017) in the Committee on Commerce, Science, and Transportation, Subcommittee on Surface Transportation and Merchant Marine Infrastructure, Safety and Security and *Surface Transportation Reauthorization: Examining the Safety and Effectiveness of our Transportation Systems* (2014), both of which look into infrastructure in more depth. All the hearings mentioned here feature the term *automation* more prominently than the rest of the material and are mainly concerned with the impact of further *automation* in transportation and infrastructure.

As could be seen in the frequency analysis, **cybersecurity** is an important and intensely discussed issue in many different committees throughout Congress. More powerful automated processes and algorithms have attracted the interest of lawmakers in different fields. In the Senate, one such hearing on the issue is *The*

Promises and Perils of Emerging Technologies for Cybersecurity (2017) in the Committee on Commerce, Science, and Transportation.

Interestingly, there are several hearings in the Senate concerned with **monetary policy** that feature the term *automation* more prominently, for example the *Federal Reserve's Second Monetary Policy Report for 2016* (2016), Committee on Banking, Housing, and Urban Affairs; *The Semiannual Monetary Policy Report to the Congress* (2017), Committee on Banking, Housing, and Urban Affairs; and *The Economic Outlook with Federal Reserve Chair Janet Yellen* (2017). In the latter, for instance, Senators talk to Janet Yellen about the influence of advanced technology like AI, the Internet of Things, or quantum computing on almost every trait of life. As these technologies disrupt the economy and the labor market, Yellen is asked about the Fed's use of new data to assess the impact of technology in monetary policy and whether this has influenced the Fed's decisions. The Fed is using technology to collect data from surveys of household and economic decision-making in order to track the long-ranging effects of rising inequality that has occurred in the USA. Yet, Yellen testifies that the Fed does not have the tools to target specific groups who have been left behind in recent decades or who might be more vulnerable to shocks such as technological disruptions in the economy.

In the hearing *Federal Reserve's Second Monetary Policy Report for 2016*, *automation* is also mentioned in the context of its wider impact on the economy. For example, *automation* and routine work are mentioned in the same context. Routine tasks can increasingly be replaced by *automation*. If routine work is replaced by automated processes, what effect does this have on the economy in the long run? Here, productivity growth is mentioned as an outcome of *automation*. Yet, the replacement of workers on the one hand, and their employment in a new occupation on the other, can take much longer than in the past. Some experts are contemplating whether the historical pattern of *automation* (old jobs are replaced, but new ones emerge) might be upended with the current wave of *automation*.

Additionally, *automation* is used in the context of distribution of wealth and income, which could have an influence on the whole of the economy. In the hearing *The Semiannual Monetary Policy Report to the Congress*, *automation's* impact on employment is further discussed, for example in the context of saving for your retirement. In this context, the displacement of jobs through globalization was the focus of recent years, less so *automation*. Yet, *automation* has been a big disrupter of employment. Fed Chair Janet Yellen discusses *automation* as a driver of growth, but also mentions that those with less education have had a disadvantage in recent years. This was especially apparent in manufacturing which has been affected by globalization as well. Yellen argues for more attention on the downward pressure on income of these groups.

In general, one can say that in the Senate most hearings where *automation* occurs talk about transportation and infrastructure. There are also several hearings on monetary policy where experts and the then Fed Chair were testifying. In these hearings, the impact of *automation* on the economy as a whole is discussed, always with regard to monetary policy by the Fed. But these hearings are not specifically dedicated to *automation* and its impact. There are only a few specific instances, where the impact of *automation* is discussed regarding new technology and the transformation of the economy as a whole. Augmented reality, artificial intelligence, and advanced robotics are the focus of these hearings that take a closer look at the disruptive impact of further *automation* on today's economy, especially with respect to intelligent machines and programs such as robots and software. In these hearings, expert witnesses argue in favor of technological progress because it has boosted growth and has brought enormous benefits for consumers. However, they also see more and more pressure for the workforce who might not be well equipped for the automated future. Skills necessary for success in the new economy will change and many different economic sectors will be affected at the same time. It could be a painful process for many workers to lose their jobs and look for an adequate new occupation. The threat of a further polarized labor market with very few "superstars" at the top and many more who are stuck in low-wage service jobs is not a desirable future scenario. In this regard, education and infrastructure reforms are discussed. Immigration reform and policies to support entrepreneurship and original research are also debated. Although there are not many hearings dedicated to *automation* specifically, there are several instances where its impact is discussed in the Senate. The hearing *The Transformative Impact of Robots and Automation* (2016) before the Joint Economic Committee stands out in this regard. Held in front of the Joint Committee, it already indicates the far-reaching importance of the topic. Members from both the House and the Senate are there to hear the testimony of expert witnesses and researchers on the topic and to discuss policy recommendations for the future. It is clear that the discussion around *automation* is not part of the day-to-day issues of Congress, but this specific hearing discusses developments that will change the face of the American economy in the decades to come. Even if some of these developments are hard to predict, it is clear that the impact of technology in the future ranks high on the agenda of Congress.

In the hearings in the House, the term *automation* occurs 551 times in absolute numbers in 119 out of 151 files. This amounts to a relative frequency of 1.09 per 10,000 tokens. The relative frequency of *automation* in the Senate (1.01) and the House is thus rather similar despite more occurrences in the House overall. In Tables 6.13 and 6.14, the collocations of *automation* in the House material are displayed. Just like in the Senate data, there are many collocates that refer to (innovation in) the car industry, such as *self-driving, route, cars, driving, driver, vehicle, vehicles,* and *crashes.* The *self-driving* car is one of the most debated innovations in recent years, despite the fact that autonomous vehicles have not arrived in a grand fashion yet. As indicated before, *self-driving cars* as a term is not an especially frequent term in the corpus data, yet it appears as a collocate in both the Senate and the House data. Therefore, despite low frequency, the collocate analysis reveals that it is a topic discussed when the wider topic of *automation* is debated in Congress.

The collocates *levels, full, faster*, and *increasing* point to the fast pace of *automation* that reaches different sectors than in the past and drives the economy ahead. *Automation* is often painted as a "driver for innovation." These innovations are found in areas like *robotics* or *communication*, for example. Moreover, there are

Table 6.13 House: collocation graph of automation MI ≥ 7, minimum collocate frequency 5

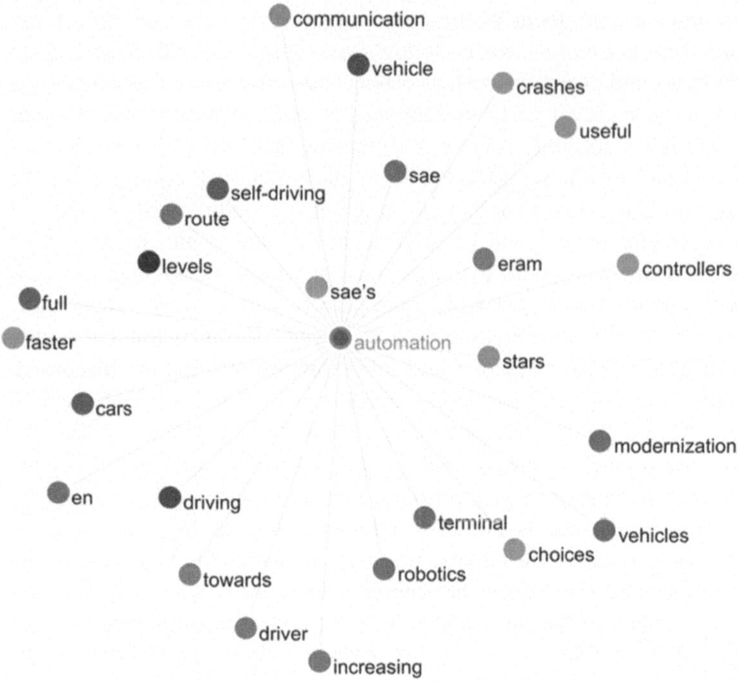

Source: Author, using #LancsBox

a few other collocates that are actually abbreviations, such as *eram* (ERAM, En Route Automation Modernization Program), which refers to the federal program for the modernization of infrastructure previously mentioned. Then there are *sae* and *sae's* which refer to SAE, the Society of Automotive Engineers. This association issues a classification system for *automation* in driving (SAE J3016) which talks about different levels of *automation* from driving with an assistance system to fully automated vehicles. The collocate *stars* also refers to an abbreviation, the Standard Terminal Replacement System (STARS), which is an *automation* system in the area of aviation and air travel. Many of these abbreviations are used in the hearings on *automation* in aviation. The collocate *controllers* also points to aviation (air controller). *Automation* is an important topic in the field of aviation safety and is advancing fast in this field, both in ground control and in the planes themselves.

In the material from the House, there are several foci surrounding *automation*. For instance, the **self-driving car** is discussed on a number of occasions. Additionally, the **Disrupter Series** talks about a number of specific innovations. Then there are

Table 6.14 House: collocates of automation MI ≥ 7, minimum collocate frequency 5

automation

Freq: 551 Collocates: 26

Index	Status	Stat (03 - MI)	Collocate	▼ Stat	Freq (coll.)	Freq (corpus)
1	O	L	sae's	13.167489716822589	5	5
2	O	R	stars	11.052001247642684	6	26
3	O	R	eram	10.734508639568446	10	54
4	O	L	sae	10.475589374804768	13	84
5	O	L	self-driving	10.071542201201023	20	171
6	O	M	terminal	9.952454322419468	14	130
7	O	L	levels	9.787223879096912	80	833
8	O	L	route	9.70803704382714	12	132
9	O	L	driving	9.167468088136044	41	656
10	O	L	robotics	9.126439892552694	13	214
11	O	L	cars	8.427928798718058	21	561
12	O	L	vehicle	8.24790425297389	34	1029
13	O	R	choices	8.24146720264332	5	152
14	O	R	modernization	8.113737286203085	14	465
15	O	L	towards	8.10377463140091	9	301
16	O	R	controllers	7.7278470313330905	5	217
17	●		automation	7.646521940673817	12	551
18	O	R	crashes	7.612879079901988	5	235
19	O	L	driver	7.538112411756993	10	495
20	O	R	useful	7.471659341948641	6	311
21	O	L	full	7.371002056549234	19	1056
22	O	L	en	7.183159309127996	13	823
23	O	L	increasing	7.110018140705237	10	666
24	O	L	faster	7.054767600948064	5	346
25	O	R	vehicles	7.045072089426893	15	1045
26	O	L	communication	7.017720818336572	7	497

Source: Author, using #LancsBox

hearings concerned with **transportation and infrastructure**, **national security**, and **entrepreneurship and small business**.

There is one hearing that displays most of the occurrences of the term *automation* in the House material: *Self-Driving Cars: Levels of Automation* (2017) in the Committee on Energy and Commerce, Subcommittee on Digital Commerce and Consumer Protection. **Self-driving cars** have become a hotly debated issue. The field of self-driving vehicles potentially needs new regulation as it poses new security threats or liability issues. The innovation of the self-driving car is also discussed in a whole series dedicated to potentially disruptive innovations, **the *Disrupter Series*,**[3] which is held in the Committee on Energy and Commerce, Subcommittee on Commerce, Manufacturing, and Trade. Among them are *The Disrupter Series: Mobile Payments* (2015), *The Disrupter Series: How the Sharing Economy Creates Jobs, Benefits Consumers, and Raises Policy Questions* (2015),

[3]The *Disrupter Series* hearings feature the term *automation* to a different extent; *Mobile Payments* and the *Sharing Economy* hearing do not feature the term *automation* in large numbers but talk about innovations in the respective field.

The Disrupter Series: Advanced Robotics (2016), *Disrupter Series: Self-Driving Cars* (2016), *Disrupter Series: Update on IOT Opportunities and Challenges* (2017), *Disrupter Series: Smart Communities* (2017), and *Disrupter Series: Improving Consumers' Financial Options with Fintech* (2017). The series even continues after 2017. Through this series of hearings, the House members try to get an overview of cutting-edge innovations which have the potential to leave a mark on the American economy as a whole.

As the title of the series suggests, most of these technologies have the potential to disrupt traditional businesses and are all tied to technological progress. Smart technologies using Big Data as a basis are the most important innovations of recent years. These developments are reflected here in debates around the self-driving car, the sharing economy, the Internet of Things, Smart Communities, or Fintech. It seems that the House of Representatives puts a lot of effort in gaining a perspective on recent technological developments from many different fields. In *The Disrupter Series: Mobile Payments*, Representative Michael C. Burgess (Rep) characterizes the series as "covering a variety of technologies that are redefining our lives and improving our or [sic] economic condition." In this hearing (*The Disrupter Series: Mobile Payments*, 2015), the enormous consumer benefits of new applications on our smartphones are discussed that let you pay for goods and services online and via apps. The lawmakers stress that they need to understand the new innovation in order to address security and consumer protection vulnerabilities.

Another hearing from the series, *Disrupter Series: Advanced Robotics* (2016), looks at the large field of applications of advanced robotics such as manufacturing robots, smart prosthetics, or drones. However, the "future workforce trends" are also of interest, stressing that more jobs will include some "automation component" which raises the question which skills will be necessary to adapt to this new environment. Technology has the capability to augment and improve human work, not just replace it. Consumer protection and privacy, but also ethical questions of robotics in a more technically advanced society, is of concern to lawmakers. Moreover, research facilities advancing research and development need to be supported. The *Disrupter Series* hearing on the sharing economy stresses the innovative character of the sharing economy which gives people new opportunities. But the sharing economy is critically assessed as well, especially in relation to the "gig character" of the work through platforms. More details on the sharing economy will follow in Sect. 6.3.

Similar to the Senate material, there are several hearings in the House that deal **with transportation and infrastructure** under the influence of more and more *automation*. There is also a special emphasis on "next generation" air travel and aviation, which are fundamentally altered through more *automation*. Hearings on this issue include *Causes of Delays to the FAA's Nextgen Program* (2013) in the Committee on Transportation and Infrastructure, Subcommittee on Aviation, *Building a 21st Century Infrastructure for America: Enabling Innovation in the National Airspace* (2017) in the Committee on Transportation and Infrastructure, Subcommittee on Aviation, *Federal Aviation Administration Reauthorization: Enabling a 21st Century Aviation System* (2015) in the Committee on Transportation and Infrastructure, Subcommittee on Aviation, *The Need to Reform the Federal Aviation*

Administration and Air Traffic Control to Build a 21st Century Aviation System for America (2017) in the Committee on Transportation and Infrastructure, or *Unmanned Aircraft Systems Research and Development* (2015) in the Committee on Science, Space, and Technology.

Apart from air travel, reforms of the American infrastructure system are also discussed. The improvement of roads, the future of "surface transportation," autonomous vehicles, and their communication with each other, as well as drones, are some of the topics that are debated in these hearings. They include *Fast Act Implementation: Improving the Safety of the Nation's Roads* (2017) in the Committee on Transportation and Infrastructure, Subcommittee on Highways and Transit; *Building the Foundation for Surface Transportation Reauthorization* (2014), Committee on Transportation and Infrastructure; *How Autonomous Vehicles will shape the Future of Surface Transportation* (2013) in the Committee on Transportation and Infrastructure, Subcommittee on Highways and Transit; *US Surface Transportation: Technology Driving the Future* (2015) in the Committee on Science, Space, and Technology, Subcommittee on Research and Technology; *Vehicle-to-Vehicle Communications and Connected Roadways of the Future* (2015), Committee on Energy and Commerce, Subcommittee on Commerce, Manufacturing, and Trade; *The Future of Surface Transportation* (2014), Committee on Science, Space, and Technology, Subcommittee on Research and Technology; and *Drones: The Next Generation of Commerce?* (2015), Committee on Oversight and Government Reform.

All of the hearings on air travel and infrastructure are held under the assumption that further *automation* will fundamentally shape and change transportation and infrastructure needs in the future. They will potentially make transport more convenient and faster, but these developments also point to broader discussions around *automation* such as safety of travelers, drivers and civilians, liability in case of accidents with autonomous vehicles, and the impact on jobs when more autonomous vehicles are entering the market.

There are also a number of hearings that discuss *automation* in relation to **national security**. For example, there are *Checkpoint of the Future: Evaluating TSA's Innovation Task Force Initiative* (2017) in the Committee on Homeland Security, Subcommittee on Transportation and Protective Security, *The Future of the Transportation Security Administration* (2017) in the Committee on Homeland Security, Subcommittee on Transportation and Protective Security, and *Security Clearance Investigation Challenges and Reforms* (2017) in the Committee on Oversight and Government Reform, Subcommittee on Government Operations. These hearings are from the year 2017. Lawmakers have become increasingly aware that further *automation* and technological progress also pose new security risks, which is why cybersecurity is a topic that is also of keen interest to lawmakers from many different committees. Cybersecurity and *automation* are therefore specifically discussed in several hearings. These include *Oversight of the Cybersecurity Act of 2015* (2016) in the Committee on Homeland Security, Subcommittee on Cybersecurity, Infrastructure Protection, and Security Technologies, *Federal Cybersecurity Detection, Response and Mitigation* (2016) in the Committee on Oversight and Government Reform, Subcommittee on Information Technology, *Protecting*

Maritime Facilities in the 21st Century: Are our Nation's Ports at Risk for a Cyber Attack? (2015) in the Committee on Homeland Security, Subcommittee on Border and Maritime Security, *Examining the President's Cybersecurity Information-Sharing Proposal* (2015), Committee on Homeland Security, *Challenges of Recruiting and Retaining a Cybersecurity Work Force* (2017) in the Committee on Homeland Security, Subcommittee on Cybersecurity and Infrastructure Protection, *Cyber Side-Effects: How Secure is the Personal Information Entered into the Flawed HealthCare.gov?* (2013), Committee on Homeland Security, *Cyber Preparedness and Response at the Local Level* (2016) in the Committee on Homeland Security, Subcommittee on Cybersecurity, Infrastructure, Protection, and Security, *Cyber Threats and Security Solutions* (2013) in the Committee on Energy and Commerce, and *Promoting Security in Wireless Technology* (2017), Committee on Energy and Commerce, Subcommittee on Communications and Technology.

Apart from infrastructure, transportation, or cybersecurity, *automation* is discussed in hearings that look at **entrepreneurship and small business**. For example, the hearing *Reversing the Entrepreneurship Decline* (2017) in the Committee on Small Business discusses the status of entrepreneurship in the USA and different approaches to how entrepreneurship can be enhanced, such as improved availability of broadband Internet or access to capital.

Many entrepreneurs in the USA are in fact small business owners. Therefore, there are several hearings that discuss different aspects of small business that mention the term *automation*: *Struggling to Grow: Assessing the Challenges for Small Business in Rural America* (2016) in the Committee on Small Business, Subcommittee on Economic Growth, Tax and Capital Access, *Small Business: The Key to Economic Growth* (2017), Committee on Small Business, Subcommittee on Economic Growth, Tax and Capital Access, *Modern Tool in a Modern World: How App Technology is Benefitting Small Business* (2015) in the Committee on Small Business, Subcommittee on Health and Technology, *The New Faces of American Manufacturing* (2016), Committee on Small Business, *How the Administration's Regulatory Onslaught is Affecting Workers and Job Creators* (2015), Committee on Education and the Workforce, Subcommittee on Workforce Protections, and *Small Businesses: Promoting Greater Information Sharing for Stronger Cybersecurity* (2017), Committee on Small Business. Most of these hearings look at how to support small businesses in the USA and how technological progress is affecting them. *Automation* is seen as both a challenge and an opportunity. Small businesses are an engine of growth in all of the USA, also the more rural parts. But often, these small businesses in rural areas face difficult challenges such as the lack of high-speed Internet and a lack of cybersecurity protection. Overall, however, small businesses can benefit immensely from advanced technology as it opens up new opportunities and markets.

There are several other hearings that mention the term *automation*, yet it only appears very rarely in those instances. In general, one can see that the main focus of the House hearings that feature the term *automation* more prominently is technology. With the *Disrupter Series,* there is a strong and ongoing emphasis on technological progress that lawmakers are interested in. They want to stay informed when it comes to new technology, and therefore, they are inviting experts from diverse fields to talk about innovations such as self-driving cars, the sharing economy, robotics, the Internet of Things, Smart Communities, or FinTech. Self-driving cars feature most prominently among these issues when *automation* is concerned. Understanding new technology is the main focus of the *Disrupter Series,* but larger debates about *automation* also feature in these hearings, for example when it comes to workers who have to acquire new skills for an automated future. Apart from that, infrastructure and transportation are the main areas where the term *automation* occurs in the House hearings. Additionally, aspects of national security and cybersecurity are prominent topics in the hearings that deal with *automation.* Entrepreneurship is also mentioned: *automation* is seen as both a challenge and an opportunity for entrepreneurs and small business owners.

Overall, specific technological innovations and their impact on the USA as a whole are the strongest issues discussed when it comes to *automation* in the House of Representatives. This is a strong contrast to the hearings in the Senate where such a far-reaching emphasis on very recent innovation cannot be found. There is one specific hearing in the Senate that stands out in this regard, which talks about *The Transformative Impact of Robots and Automation* (2016), which takes place in front of the Joint Economic Committee where lawmakers from the House and Senate are present. This is a very far-reaching hearing that covers crucial aspects of the discussion around *automation* and features prominent experts like Andrew McAfee. Yet, the *Disrupter Series* in the House that includes several hearings is much more detailed in its approach to new technology and wants to gain a wide perspective into many different fields. The *Disrupter Series* continues after 2017 as well. Once again, the House seems to be more inclined to discuss very current trends that impact the American economy, whereas the Senate seems to look at the bigger picture and long-term trends. This can also be seen in the hearings in the Senate where *automation* and monetary policy are discussed with the Fed. These hearings look at long-term trends in the American economy and how government agencies and institutions can assess and steer these developments in a beneficial way. In both chambers, however, infrastructure and transportation are very significant issues when discussing *automation.* Especially the field of autonomous vehicles is debated on many occasions, both for aviation and for surface transportation. Infrastructure and transportation are going to be transformed through *automation* technology, and although these developments have not been introduced in a grand fashion yet, they pose regulatory challenges for Congress.

6.1.5 Automation in the Liberal Media Material

In the media corpus based on the *New York Times* (NYT) and *Washington Post*, the terms *automation* and *digitization* occur at a very different rate. Similar to all other material investigated in this book, *automation* is much more frequent than *digitization.* The term *automation* occurs about 3778 times in absolute terms, with a relative

Table 6.15 Liberal media: collocation graph of automation MI ≥ 7, minimum collocate frequency 7

Source: Author, using #LancsBox

frequency of 7.13 per 10,000 tokens. *Digitization* only occurs 0.69 per 10,000 tokens so there is a very stark contrast between the two terms. The year displaying the highest relative frequencies of the term *automation* is 2016 (8.59 occurrences per 10,000 tokens), followed by 2017 (8.09), 2013 (6.31), 2015 (5.45), and 2014 (4.98). Thus, the two most recent years investigated here display the highest frequency of *automation* as a term, which could point to an increased interest in the topic in the media. The term is common throughout the years, however, especially compared to other terms like *digitization*.

In Tables 6.15 and 6.16, the collocations of *automation* in the liberal media material are displayed.[4] Many of the collocates can be grouped around certain themes. For once, *cruise, rockwell,* and *eram* refer to two companies (Cruise Automation and Rockwell Automation) and a program (ERAM) used in *automation* development. Cruise Automation is working on self-driving vehicles and is owned by GM. The collocate *cruise* is the second most frequent collocate of *automation* (Table 6.16), pointing to the extensive coverage of Cruise Automation in the liberal media material. Rockwell Automation specializes in industrial production *automation*. ERAM is the aforementioned abbreviation for a federal program "En Route

[4]The minimum collocation frequency was increased to 7 from the default setting 5 to depopulate the graph as there are so many instances of *automation* in the liberal media corpus. The MI score remained at the default setting.

Table 6.16 Liberal media: collocates of automation MI $\geq$ 7, minimum collocate frequency 7

automation

Freq: 3,778 Collocates: 46

Index	Status	Stat (03 - MI)	Collocate	▼ Stat	Freq (coll.)	Freq (corpus)
1	O	R	eram	9.388237024533401	11	23
2	O	R	destroys	9.172269208548801	7	17
3	O	L	cruise	9.062433367844468	87	228
4	O	R	elimination	8.867431740561448	7	21
5	O	R	computerization	8.867426145727563	13	39
6	O	L	rockwell	8.867419618448821	30	90
7	O	L	assisted	8.830902227891976	13	40
8	O	L	overreliance	8.800320850751143	7	22
9	O	L	darker	8.764331977526519	9	29
10	O	R	modernization	8.645034124021445	14	49
11	O	R	outsourcing	8.645027197112425	54	189
12	O	R	replaces	8.562565036920347	17	63
13	O	L	globalization	8.546739974728908	154	577
14	O	R	offshoring	8.369919958978278	17	72
15	O	L	labor-saving	8.336911429029058	9	39
16	O	R	hart	8.282457117727667	22	99
17	O	R	good-paying	8.26795075969395	11	50
18	O	L	relentless	8.259738367078539	14	64
19	O	R	displace	8.148599222781186	16	79
20	O	R	subsidiary	8.1304490328541	17	85
21	O	R	fireplaces	8.101879880657629	10	51
22	O	R	eliminated	8.021746396220996	23	124
23	O	R	displacing	7.9605290228404195	8	45
24	O	L	killer	7.957616058801027	22	124
25	O	L	en	7.916326292917964	15	87
26	O	L	susceptible	7.837679201964019	8	49
27	O	R	eliminating	7.817667302357058	19	118
28	O	L	abb	7.800303494081603	7	44
29	O	R	sake	7.7894215724774485	9	57
30	O	L	farewell	7.715415464324122	12	80
31	O	L	pearl	7.703440376960914	18	121
32	O	L	partial	7.691567000939978	9	61
33	O	L	cockpit	7.622308446463561	9	64
34	O	M	accelerating	7.545494917742554	10	75
35	O	L	outsourced	7.5454872808461815	8	60
36	O	L	vogt	7.5318149856383885	7	53
37	O	L	haas	7.5263771180962245	10	76
38	O	L	efficiencies	7.521641999497143	8	61
39	O	L	blaming	7.478378870511295	7	55
40	O	R	reduces	7.352842202904226	7	60
41	O	R	kits	7.302633804532636	8	71
42	O	L	wave	7.202507360385188	39	371
43	O	R	threatens	7.1512088951314725	7	69
44	O	L	relying	7.143630191511381	11	109
45	O	L	bankers	7.083151046746722	9	93
46	O	R	pressures	7.0118039452663545	7	76

Source: Author, using #LancsBox

Automation Modernization Program." The collocates *partial* and *assisted* point to the different levels of *automation* which range from total *automation* to *partial* and *assisted automation* in certain products (e.g., in cars).

Cockpit and *bankers* point to two sectors in which *automation* is becoming crucial, in aviation and the banking industry. Both in the cockpit of a plane and in airport ground control, *automation* is becoming more and more common and advanced. The banking sector also faces profound challenges through *automation.* With innovations in the Fintech industry many human roles in banks might be replaced in the coming years, for example in loans or trading.

The collocates *efficiencies, computerization, modernization*, and *globalization* point to larger developments of which *automation* is one part. *Modernization* is unthinkable without *computerization* and *automation*, which have gone hand in hand and have advanced *efficiency*. Technological progress and *globalization* are the two major developments of the late twentieth and early twenty-first century that continue to have a profound impact on the economy and the workforce. In fact, *globalization* is the most frequent collocate of *automation* in this corpus data (Table 6.6). In many instances, *globalization* and *automation* are mentioned in unison.

But moving away from these rather neutral terms, some other collocates already point to a certain attitude toward technological development in the liberal media material. Collocates like *overreliance, relying*, *susceptible, accelerating,* and *relentless* might point to the notion that *automation* can have undesirable effects when we rely too heavily on machines (*overreliance*). Additionally, *susceptible*, *accelerating,* and *relentless* point to the fact that many fields are *susceptible* to *automation* and that it is a fast-paced process which does not leave a lot of room and time for adaption (*relentless*). Then there are other collocates that clearly point to the negative effects of *automation*, especially on the workforce. These include *elimination*, *eliminating, eliminated*, *labor-saving*, *outsourcing*, *outsourced*, *displace, displacing*, *replaces*, *reduces*, and *pressures*. All these collocates clearly refer to the effect *automation* has on jobs, namely that it will *eliminate*, *displace*, and *reduce* workers, which puts *pressure* on them. Additionally, through advanced technology, *outsourcing* becomes much more worthwhile for businesses. Instant communication and control become possible around the clock and around the globe. Apart from these collocates that refer to *automation* as a "job reducer," *automation* is related to even more negative associations in the liberal media material. Collocates like *darker, killer*, *destroys*, and *threatens* are clearly negative in association with *automation*, and they paint this development as a significant threat.

The term *automation* is so frequent in the liberal media material that only a few examples can be presented in more depth. Most of these examples are articles that display the term several times or could be associated with one of the themes stated here. The broader themes in which the term *automation* occurs most frequently in the liberal media data include **artificial intelligence and robots, the sharing economy, automation-past and present,** and **automation and the future of jobs.**

In the first theme, **artificial Intelligence and robots**, *automation* is used, for example, in the context of the displacement of workers through intelligent machines. One example is the article *Radical proposition: Get paid for using company Web sites* by Evgeny Morozov (2013) on washingtonpost.com that uses *automation* in the context of the self-driving car displacing the cab driver in the future. The same topic is dealt with in *The 5 most important turning points for technology in 2015* on the Washington Post Blogs by Brian Fung where Fung claims that the year 2015 is a major driver for *automation* and self-driving cars. There are many other articles that speak about the potential of driverless vehicles in the future. Just like in the congressional material, self-driving vehicles are a hotly debated issue throughout the years, despite the fact that they have not arrived to the extent anticipated a few years ago.

The article *Why investors can be optimistic*, by Robert F. Bruner on washingtonpost.com from 2014, uses *automation* in the context of AI to allude to disruptions in the economy that lead to winners and losers. Workers on the middle level of corporate organizations could turn out to be the losers of this development as their jobs are rather susceptible to *automation*. In a *NYT* article from 2017 called *How Efficiency is Wiping Out the Middle Class* by David Siegel, the term *automation* is used again in connection with AI and details the author's belief that it can bring good to the world. However, there are also worrisome effects of AI. Despite being a driver of efficiency, middle-class workers, e.g., in the industrial Midwest, might be negatively affected by it. The article argues that the negative effects computers and AI have had on employment have been underestimated, even in these early stages. Although recent political campaigns have tried to blame job loss in manufacturing on trade and immigration, industrial *automation* can be seen as the real reason behind the hollowing out of the middle class and the displacement of middle-skill jobs.

Automation and the introduction of robots are often seen as the same, especially in manufacturing. In articles from 2013 and 2014, robots seem to take up more space. Looking again at the frequency analysis (Table 5.2), especially the year 2013 stands out when it comes to the topic of *robots* and *robotics,* displaying the highest frequencies of these terms in the liberal media material. For example, in *Raging (Again) Against the Robots*, by Catherine Rampell in the *NYT*, 2013, old-time anxieties about robots and machines taking over the world are invoked. The tyranny of machines is juxtaposed with *automation* leading to better living standards and safer workspaces. Historically, displaced workers themselves had to bear the consequences of further *automation*, but overall, labor has benefitted through mechanization over time. The question remains, whether today's transformation will be more difficult than in the past with the accelerating speed of the new technology entering so many sectors. In another article around the same topic from 2013 called *In 1949, He Imagined an Age of Robots*, by John Markoff in the NYT, science fiction is again invoked for visions of a future when robots will be taking over. These visions have always been fed by fears of the dehumanizing effects of machines on society and work. In another article, *Job creators—or terminators?* by Cecilia Kang 2013 on washingtonpost.com, she also alludes to this effect—and science fiction. Robots will be able to take over more advanced human tasks. This means more productivity for industries without hiring more (human) personnel. All in all, the articles dealing with *automation* and robotics are torn between two themes. On the one hand, there are fears that robots will make human jobs obsolete on a large scale. These fears have always accompanied *automation* and have also been fed by (dystopian) science fiction visions in countless books and movies. On the other hand, the theme that robots will create better jobs in the long run and will create safer work environments has also always prevailed in the debate around *automation*. Both themes exist alongside each other in the reporting around *automation* in the liberal media material.

Another topic that is tied to the reporting on *automation* in the material from the *NYT* and *Washington Post* is the Internet of Things (IoT) and smart home appliances. In the liberal media outlets, there are several articles alluding to possible new fields of application for intelligent devices to automate your home, to make it safer, or to save energy. Another part of the debate around *automation* and robotics is the question of smart machines in warfare that is also part of the conversation to some extent.

Apart from AI and robotics, the **sharing economy** is another broader theme in the liberal media material when *automation* is discussed. For example, in the article *Sleepless in a Sharing Economy* in the *NYT* from 2014, the term *automation* is used to talk about shifts in the economy that are a threat to the "traditional economic model that sustained industrial and postindustrial society." Trends like robots and advanced *automation* are presented here as job killers of traditional employment that lead to a greater "sharing economy character" of the whole economy. On the Washington Post Blogs, there is another article from 2014 called *Why 2015 will be the year of India's next technology revolution. This is the year to teach the world how to promote the public good through new digital infrastructure* by Vivek Wadhwa. Here, *automation* again appears in the context of the sharing economy and companies like Uber. *Automation* moves into all kinds of settings, for example by making it possible to hire short-term formal and informal workers like technicians, maids, or painters through new applications. The author calls this "app-based automation." The article *The political economy of a world without work* by Daniel W. Drezner from 2015 on Washington Post Blogs goes in the same direction. *Automation* here is again used in the context of the sharing economy and how the two effects combined are a threat to traditional employment.

A Washington Post Blog article called *What vocational education students need today—but aren't likely to get under Trump* from 2017 by Valerie Strauss uses *automation* in the context of computerization and the fast-changing nature of work. Apart from *automation*, the nature of work is further changing through globalization and the rise of the gig economy. The article then goes on to explore vocational training as a possible way to educate young people in a different way.

There are also several articles dealing with *automation* and the sharing economy that comment on the 2016 presidential race. The 2015 *Washington Post* article *Clinton to reveal strategy to lift the middle class* by Philip Rucker and Jim Tankersley talks about candidate Hillary Clinton's agenda to support the middle class economically. *Automation*, new technology, and sharing economy businesses like Uber are presented here as trends that are threatening middle-class jobs on a worldwide scale. Like *automation* more generally, the sharing economy is presented as another threat to middle-class jobs as the short-term work over platforms does not offer protections nor benefits for workers. There are several other articles talking about Clinton's agenda concerning technology and the issues arising through *automation*, the sharing economy, and the future of work in general.

Apart from the allusions to AI and the sharing economy, there is another bigger theme concerning *automation* in the liberal media material that is referred to here as "**Automation–past and present**." In the articles grouped around this theme, *automation* is discussed in historical context as well as in comparison to more present debates around the topic. In fact, *automation* has been of concern since the times of Adam Smith and is alluded to in historical terms quite often throughout the liberal media material. The article *We're heading into a jobless future, no matter what the government does; Robots will drive our cars, manufacture our goods, and do our chores* by Vivek Wadhwa from 2014 talks about past *automation* processes. *Automation* is presented here as a process that has eliminated jobs over the centuries and already in *automation's* infancy there were protests against it. The Luddites in nineteenth-century England are one example of such early protests. They saw their jobs threatened and replaced through advanced machinery and tried to eliminate the competition by storming factories and crashing the machines. Eventually, they were unsuccessful and *automation* created new jobs, new industries, and greater prosperity in the long run. Yet, this development took time and the Luddites never profited from it. They rightly did not foresee a better future for themselves. In order to benefit from *automation* in the long run, there has to be greater educational attainment. But uncertainty remains about what kind of skills will be beneficial in this future. In the article mentioned here, the author claims that there will be an increase in employment in the coming years, before the number of available jobs will dip eventually due to technological progress. In order to set up a more automated future in countries like the USA, there will first be a lot of new jobs to fill as engineers and programmers, for example, before this stream of new jobs could dry up. The author claims that the "future is very bright for some countries in the short term, and in the long term is uncertain for all."

Another article called *Will robots steal our jobs? The humble loom suggests not.*[5] in the *Washington Post* from 2014 by James Bessen comments on what Karl Marx observed about *automation*. Marx claimed it could eventually lead to mass unemployment, but because overall demand increased, that did not happen. Yet, there were certain sectors where this was actually the case. Taking the textile industry as an example, the author claims that at some point in the twentieth century, demand did not increase anymore, and when technology was fully implemented and integrated, it slowly displaced jobs. This happened in places like Lowell, Massachusetts, which used to be famous for its textile mills. Publishing is another example of an industry that witnessed this development. Today, we see technology moving into the area of white-collar jobs as well, which could influence job security in many different fields. Yet, there is no established pattern when it comes to the adoption of technology. Some innovations might be adapted rather quickly in some industries, but it might take decades for their benefits to spread to all parts of society. Therefore,

[5]Published January 25, 2014, under washingtonpost.com under this headline; the print edition used a different title.

the article suggests ongoing learning possibilities and occupational changes over time in order for workers to stay afloat.

In *The robots are coming*, by Robert J. Samuelson in the *Washington Post*, 2015, *automation* fears are mentioned again in historical context. In 1964, President Lyndon B. Johnson created a commission to look into the effects of *automation*. In the 1960s, fears among Americans ran high about the possible negative impact of *automation* on many occupations. The commission's report tried to alleviate fears by arguing that the economy has always adapted to technological shocks. Technology has led to lower prices and superior value of products, in turn creating more demand and growth in the economy overall. Therefore, the federal government in the 1960s did not see any reason to fear *automation*.

In articles like *What Hollywood Can Teach Us about the Future of Work*, by Adam Davidson in the *NYT* from 2015, *automation* is mentioned in a more up-to-date context and not so much in historical terms. *Automation* is discussed as being part of the so-called Hollywood model. New technologies have always been embraced by Hollywood productions, but the author claims that the impact of *automation* was less severe because of the project-based nature of Hollywood work. The era of "traditional" robots and *automation*, marked by expensive machines and giant robots, is ending and we are entering an era of a new human–robot partnership, according to the article. Another article that touches upon the impact of *automation* today is the called *Global innovation may have a 1 percent problem* (2016) by Dominic Basulto on the Washington Post Blogs, which talks about inequality in today's world and how innovation in *automation* and robotics might even worsen this problem. *Automation* technology has the potential to eliminate jobs on the one hand. On the other hand, it boosts returns for the owners of capital and the means of production. Therefore, especially the so-called 1% could benefit from further *automation*, while workers might be hit more painfully. In *A Plan in Case Robots Take the Jobs: Give Everyone a Basic Income* by Farhad Manjoo for the *NYT* from 2016, *automation* is mentioned in the context of (future) employment. Economists have different attitudes and ideas when talking about *automation's* impact on future employment. For instance, the article talks about how further *automation* pushes the idea of the universal basic income (UBI) among tech leaders. Tech workers are not afraid of further *automation*. They rather see more *automation* as a form of social progress. Thus, among the tech community, the UBI is seen as the most optimistic vision for this socially progressive future.

There are also (former) politicians who comment on *automation's* impact and what can be done to improve the situation for the workforce today. For instance, an article by Senator Mark Warner (Dem) in the *Washington Post* from 2016 called *How to weave a 21st century safety net* talks about how *automation* and global competitive pressure are "seismic shifts" in today's economy, which many politicians have failed to acknowledge. These shifts need the attention of politics to find ways to protect the American workforce in the future. He talks about giving the idea of portable social benefits more credit, especially in the field of the gig economy, as well as strengthening lifelong learning and the educational infrastructure. He also argues in favor of more long-term investment and less short-sightedness by investors. In another article by former Treasury Secretary Lawrence H. Summers called *Why we need unions* from 2017 in the *Washington Post*, *automation* appears in the context of replacing workers with technology, which has given employers more bargaining power compared to workers. When workers are faced with the threat of displacement through domestic (contractors, gig workers) or international outsourcing, they are unlikely to demand higher wages. Summers claims that through these developments, the employers' power to hold down wages has increased and has been one reason for wage stagnation in recent years.

Apart from specific technological innovations such as AI or the sharing economy, as well as past and present takes on *automation's* advancement, another big theme in which *automation* appears very frequently in the material from the *NYT* and *Washington Post* is its specific impact on jobs ("**automation and the future of jobs**"). As said before, most fears associated with *automation* are in regard to whether machines will eventually take over most or all human jobs, leaving workers struggling to make ends meet. One article talking about the impact on jobs specifically is *Ignoring the Tech Tsunami*, by Farhad Manjoo in the *NYT* from 2017. This article discusses *automation* and its potential to replace jobs for good, bringing about a future without enough jobs for everyone. Here, again, the idea of the universal basic income is mentioned, an idea pushed by the tech community. In addition, there is interest in new unemployment insurance measures, skills training, and other policies to address short-term job displacement caused by technology. The article reviews Republican and Democratic plans for the future economy, for example mentioning the earned income tax credit which is a policy that is generally supported by both partisan sides. In another article called *Stocks & Bots*, by Nathaniel Popper from 2016 in the *NYT*, a study by the Department of Labor is mentioned that is concerned with the impact of *automation* on jobs. The study shows that *automation* is not only about robots on the factory floors anymore, but that software is increasingly doing work educated people used to do. Reasons for this development are dropping prices in computers and the rise of machine learning. Furthermore, not all jobs are affected by *automation* to the same extent. Jobs in health care, for example, are less affected; whereas jobs as a truck or cab driver could be much more affected by *automation*. Investment and law firms also have great potential for automating tasks, which is seen both as an opportunity and as a threat. The article assumes that technology seems to be more about labor-saving than job-creating. Although *automation* does create jobs, they are not created as quickly as others are replaced. The theme of *automation* and job loss is pursued in several other articles throughout the years in the liberal media material, tracing similar arguments mentioned here. Staff cuts, general fear of job loss and workers becoming obsolete, or even the lack of availability of jobs altogether in the future are themes that prevail throughout the material. For example in an article called *After Jobs Dry Up, What Then?* (2015) by Katrin Bennhold in the International *NYT* a prominent and widely cited Oxford study is mentioned that argues that 74% of jobs in the USA are susceptible to *automation* in the next two decades. The study argues that some new jobs are created for human workers, but many more might be replaced. The concern expressed in the study is that *automation* is moving extremely fast, too fast to counteract effectively. Again, the idea of a basic income or a negative income tax are mentioned in order to remove some pressure from workers who will struggle to find well-paying jobs in the future.

Despite several studies pointing to job loss in the future, the material also mentions sectors that have always been less affected by *automation*. These include (to a certain extent) health care or education. Additionally, there are new jobs emerging that we might not even know about today. The question will remain however, what kind of jobs these will be and whether they will be low-skill and low-pay or well-paying, secure jobs. An article concerned with this double-edged development is *This Robot Wants to Be Your Co-Worker* by John Markoff in the *NYT* from 2013. In this article, Andrew McAfee and Erik Brynjolfsson and their concept of the "Race against the Machine" is presented. They argue that *automation* is pushing into new areas that were previously thought to be un-automatable. This could mean job loss and a change in the nature of work for many different sectors. However, the two experts argue that *automation* can create good and well-paying jobs at the same time.

In *The Economics of a Higher Wage Floor* by Jared Bernstein on the NYT Blogs from 2013, the author challenges an argument that is often presented in order to argue against a higher minimum wage, namely that a higher minimum wage might spark layoffs and push businesses to automate even faster. Bernstein does not support this idea, but instead argues that in order to help low-wage workers a certain wage floor is necessary. Measures like the earned income tax credit are not enough. He calls for an increase of the minimum wage so that low-wage workers can earn a living. Low-wage work has always existed, even before advanced *automation* remains a problem. He argues that the earned income tax credit adds to the income of low-wage workers, which is a positive development. Yet, a tax credit should not be a rationale for not increasing wages. The earned income tax credit is a form of income redistribution through the tax code, but it can also be seen as a subsidy for low-wage work. Tax credits would have to be increased every few years to really help those who receive them, but this is not the case. He argues for both a higher minimum wage and tax credits in order to increase income and help workers. Jared Bernstein also presented his arguments in Congress where he testified as a senior fellow at the Center on Budget and Policy Priorities in Washington.

Despite advocates like Bernstein, the image of the minimum wage as a job killer and *automation* pusher remains a frequent argument used against it, especially by Republicans. In another post called *Farhad and Mike's Week in Tech: Robots vs. Jobs*, in the *NYT* on the Web from 2015, the topic of an increased minimum wage as a threat to employment is picked up again. They ask whether a higher minimum wage really leads to higher incentives to automate. However, the authors do not see the introduction of more automated processes or robots in the workplace as the most pressing issue. Rather, they talk about the rise of "1099 work." This means the replacement of stable labor with contracted, short-term "1099 workers." Additionally, they mention studies from McKinsey Global Institute, for example, that argue that AI is moving much faster and is more transformative than previously anticipated.

In another article, the impact of *automation* and international trade on jobs is discussed. Both are seen as a threat to middle-class jobs (*The Quality of Jobs: The New Normal and the Old Normal* on the NYT Blogs, 2013 by Laura D'Andrea Tyson). Labor force participation in the USA continues to be rather low despite the recovery after the 2008 recession. One reason behind a low labor force participation rate could be the low quality of jobs. In general, the composition of jobs in the USA is portrayed as unhealthy. In comparison to well-paying jobs, too many low-wage jobs are created. Different reasons for this development are presented, including little unionization, a low minimum wage, technological change, and globalization. The labor market seems to become even more polarized, splitting into demand for highly skilled and low-skilled workers, with the middle losing out. The labor force participation rate is further discussed in *The economy's big mystery. Why workers are disappearing from the job market* by Zachary A. Goldfarb from 2014 on washingtonpost.com. In this article, the author argues that labor force participation is low because even before the Great Recession, labor markets were weaker than previously thought. For men, it was especially challenging to retain a job because of further advances in workplace *automation* and expanding trade. But all demographic groups have seen dips in participation since the Great Recession. In this article, infrastructure spending is seen as the most vital project to fight this development.

In the material from the liberal media sources, *automation* is discussed to a large extent. There are over 3700 individual instances of the term in the material and only a few specific articles could be discussed here. However, the occurrences of *automation* in the liberal media material can largely be grouped around certain themes. For once, there are several articles on advances of AI and smart robotics. In this discussion, the potential of the self-driving vehicle is discussed extensively. This is corroborated by the collocations of *automation* in the liberal media material, which point to the salience of the self-driving car as a topic through collocates referring to the company Cruise Automation, for example. As truck-driving is one of the most common occupations in the USA, the impact of self-driving vehicles could be severe in this sector. Generally, there are going to be winners and losers from further *automation*, with some of the losers most likely being middle-class workers.

However, AI and robots will also lead to more efficiency and growth in the USA. In many instances, when the articles talk about *automation*, they actually mean the introduction of robots, for example on the factory floor. Yet, technological progress has always been accompanied by fears about the implications and possibly negative consequences of this progress: a notion that can be traced throughout the media coverage in the *NYT* and *Washington Post* over the years. On the one hand, there are fears that robots will have negative effects on the number of available jobs. On the other hand, they also promise safer and better workplaces by taking over undesirable tasks. These dual narratives run throughout history when it comes to *automation*. Even when industrialization first began in earnest in the nineteenth century, fears were running high. Several of the articles in the liberal media material allude to Luddite thinking, evoking fears of advanced machines taking over most of the jobs and leaving humans behind. The allusions to the Luddites also imply that the conflict and opposition to machines are eventually fruitless and unnecessary. Technology has always advanced and has brought about more prosperity for all. However, the history of the Luddites also shows that there often is considerable time between the painful disruption from technology and its eventual beneficial effects. In the meantime, whole industries might disappear as could be seen in the downfall of the textile industry in the Northeast of the USA in the twentieth century. Today, new fears of *automation* are emerging as not only blue-collar but also white-collar jobs could be affected more severely through the adoption of new technology. Additionally, the nature and arrangement of work are also changing through *automation*, as the growth of the sharing economy points out. New applications make it easy to hire short-term temporary workers, which raises questions of job security and benefits. In this context, the universal basic income is discussed in some instances.

Generally speaking, *automation* is discussed at great length when it comes to the future of jobs. There are new forms of work such as in the sharing economy. Project-based, short-term work will become more and more common. But there might also be a more large-scale disruption of the job market in the long run when automated technology moves into more and more spheres. Estimates of such disruptions are far-reaching and vary significantly. Moreover, there will always be certain sectors that will be less affected by *automation* than others, for example health care. The question of a decent wage in these areas remains, however. Infrastructure and education reform, the support of unionization, a raise of the minimum wage, the earned income tax credit, and the UBI are discussed as possible solutions to the disruptions through *automation* in the liberal media material.

6.1.6 Automation in the WSJ *Material*

As one of the major search keywords to put together the corpora, it is expected that the term *automation* appears very frequently all across the corpus data. Yet, the *Wall Street Journal* (*WSJ*) actually displays the highest relative frequency of the term compared to all the other corpora. *Automation* occurs with a relative frequency of 8.7 per 10,000 tokens in the *WSJ* material, and there are a total of 1518 occurrences of the term in absolute terms. The year 2017 shows the highest frequency with 10.9 occurrences per 10,000 tokens, followed by 2016 (9.5), 2014 (8.2), 2015 (7.4), and 2013 (5.6). We can see that there is a rise in relative frequency of the term over the years, with the exception of 2015. This shows that the coverage of *automation* becomes more intense over the years, indicating that the subject of *automation* becomes more and more important to authors and readers of the *WSJ*.

In Tables 6.17 and 6.18, the collocations of *automation* in the *WSJ* material are displayed. The collocates can again be grouped around certain themes. For instance, there are several collocates that refer to companies and services such as *cruise, honeywell's, sales-force, emerson, rockwell,* and *grohmann. Cruise* refers to Cruise Automation, which now belongs to General Motors and is concerned with self-driving vehicle research and development. As such, it is a topic of interest to the *WSJ* and its readers who are looking for updates from the business world. In fact, *cruise* is

Table 6.17 *WSJ*: collocation graph for automation MI ≥ 7, minimum collocate frequency 5

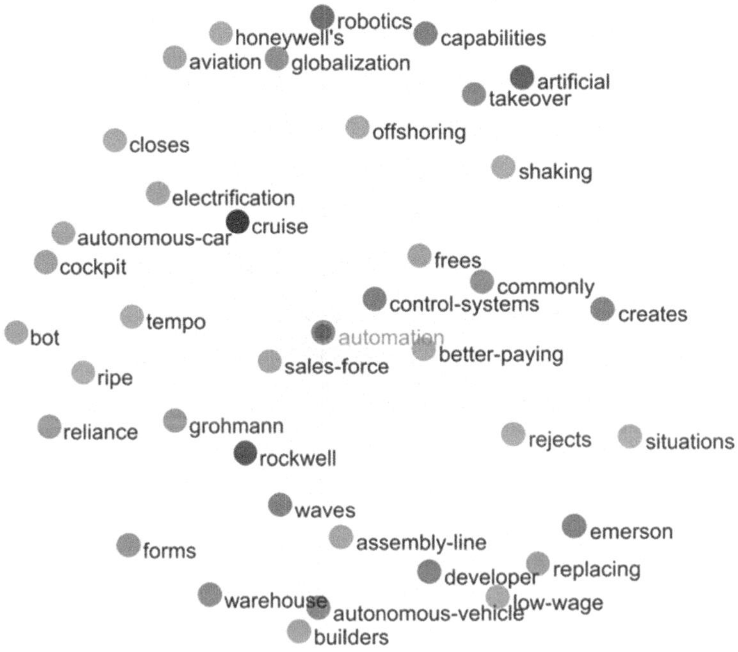

Source: Author, using #LancsBox

the most frequent collocate here (Table 6.18). *Rockwell* is the second most frequent collocate which also refers to a company, Rockwell Automation, which is concerned with industrial robotics. Emerson Electric Company (*emerson*) is also a company offering *automation* solutions for production. Honeywell is a large American conglomerate that offers *automation* and control solutions. Sales-Force Automation Software (*sales-force*) is an application to automate sales in a company. Grohmann Automation, which now belongs to Tesla, is a German firm that is concerned with automated production. All in all, the collocates referring directly to specific companies are rather frequent among the collocates in the *WSJ* material.

Apart from the frequent direct allusion to companies, there are collocates that refer to different branches where *automation* has an impact such as *aviation*, *warehouse*, *cockpit*, and *assembly line*. As mentioned before, *aviation* is a sector where many automated processes have already been implemented and are becoming even more crucial. Warehouses and assembly lines are heavily affected by *automation* as well. New machines and robots take over many tasks from human workers in warehouses and on the factory floor. *Electrification*, *globalization*, and *offshoring* are processes that are associated with further *automation*. Historically, *electrification* in the nineteenth and twentieth century was crucial for economic growth.

Table 6.18 *WSJ*: collocates of automation MI $\geq$ 7, minimum collocate frequency 5

automation

Freq: 1,518 Collocates: 38

Index	Status	Stat (03 - MI)	Collocate	▼ Stat	Freq (coll.)	Freq (corpus)
1	O	R	control-systems	10.164882625043033	16	16
2	O	L	sales-force	10.164866912063832	6	6
3	O	R	better-paying	9.67945804259817	5	7
4	O	R	frees	9.427926458746478	6	10
5	O	L	cruise	9.212051388431394	171	331
6	O	L	rockwell	9.164887024707863	75	150
7	O	R	commonly	8.901853456906972	10	24
8	O	L	grohmann	8.811246353605307	9	23
9	O	L	waves	8.7604962109404	17	45
10	O	L	tempo	8.579929552191402	5	15
11	O	L	assembly-line	8.427926458746688	6	20
12	O	L	offshoring	8.399354348780298	5	17
13	O	R	rejects	8.316883972593056	5	18
14	O	L	electrification	8.290420649446649	6	22
15	O	L	ripe	7.963249447050292	5	23
16	O	R	shaking	7.963249447050292	5	23
17	O	R	developer	7.755495201241965	16	85
18	O	L	autonomous-vehicle	7.579923750418329	13	78
19	O	L	globalization	7.556076215873884	10	61
20	O	R	creates	7.5459775428680285	14	86
21	O	L	autonomous-car	7.540393034168331	6	37
22	O	R	takeover	7.5019217473433555	12	76
23	O	L	closes	7.486810719930721	5	32
24	O	L	warehouse	7.4543944799361626	11	72
25	O	L	cockpit	7.448681739647165	7	46
26	O	L	forms	7.4207264544719305	10	67
27	O	L	reliance	7.4040731224284935	9	61
28	O	L	builders	7.290414935587697	6	44
29	O	L	bot	7.195259282974533	6	47
30	O	L	aviation	7.135137526374007	6	49
31	O	R	replacing	7.114258177463079	7	58
32	O	L	robotics	7.105992330015987	30	250
33	O	M	capabilities	7.0987964833918955	16	134
34	O	R	emerson	7.0987964833918955	16	134
35	O	L	honeywell's	7.094495541877189	5	42
36	O	R	low-wage	7.094495541877189	5	42
37	O	R	situations	7.027380529754272	5	44
38	O	R	artificial	7.011934328301006	38	338

Source: Author, using #LancsBox

Globalization as a phenomenon has been significant over the last 200 years. With further *automation*, *globalization* and *offshoring* have become possible to an even greater extent.

The collocates *autonomous-car*, *autonomous-vehicle*, and *control-systems* allude to another crucial topic in the *automation* debate, the self-driving vehicle. Across all of the material, the push toward autonomous driving is reported and discussed extensively. Another area that is discussed when it comes to *automation* is *robotics*. *Bot* and *artificial* also point in the direction of smart robotics. Artificial intelligence and robotics are often discussed in the same context, and there are more and more sectors in which the two are implemented.

The collocates *low-wage* and *replacing* are pointing at the implications for workers when it comes to *automation*, namely machines replacing human jobs and the rise of low-wage work. Compared to other collocates, however, the two are rather rare in frequency. On the other hand, there are several collocates that present *automation* in a more positive light; these include *frees, capabilities, creates, ripe*, and *better-paying*. There are many allusions to some sectors being *ripe* for disruption, and *automation* actually *frees* up *capabilities* and *creates* new opportunities for businesses and workers by also delivering *better-paying* jobs in the long run. These collocates are in rather stark contrast to the collocates in the liberal media material that referred to the "job killer" aspect of *automation*. In the *WSJ*, the opportunity aspect as well as the business side of *automation* seems to be emphasized more strongly. This cannot only be inferred from the positive collocates just mentioned, but also from the use of the collocates directly referring to companies engaging in *automation*, as well as to the processes and sectors where *automation* is strongest.

For the material from the *WSJ*, different contexts can again be identified in which the term *automation* occurs most often. In the following, only a selection of articles can be examined in more depth as there is a large set of specific instances. The themes in which the term *automation* most often occurs include **artificial intelligence and the Internet of Things, automation and (the future of) jobs, robots and robotics, the UBI and the minimum wage,** and **technological progress and tech businesses in the US economy**. Some of the categories are comparable to those used in the examination of the liberal media material, but the *WSJ* material also features other contexts in which *automation* occurs.

In the *WSJ* material **artificial Intelligence and the Internet of Things** are discussed on several occasions in the context of *automation*. Driverless cars and transport are among the most important issues, for example, *Off Duty—Gear&Gadgets: The Driverless Road Ahead—Computer guided cars are no longer a Jetsonian fantasy* and *Dan Neil finds out just how close we're getting* by Dan Neil from 2013 which reports on the newest innovations in self-driving vehicles. Almost all large automakers have heavily invested in driverless research and development. One company that is mentioned heavily is GM who acquired Cruise Automation (e.g., *GM, Lyft to Test Self-Driving Electric Taxis, GM's Cruise Automation Wades Into HD Mapping to Aid Autonomous-Car Effort, New Federal Guidelines Coming for Self-Driving Cars,* by Mike Colias, 2017). 2017 also sees more articles on the possibility of "robo-taxis" coming to the USA, meaning self-driving taxis. Additionally, there are several articles on air travel where more *automation* is a big topic, e.g., *U.S. News: Air-Safety Panel Hits Pilot Reliance on Automation* by Andy Pasztor, 2013. This article talks about pilots' heavy reliance on *automation* which can lead to poor manual flying skills. Apart from air travel, the *automation* of harbors and ports is another topic, for example in *Cross Country: How to Free U.S. Ports From Chronic Union Problems* by Douglas Holtz-Eakin, 2014. The use of *automation* in warehouses is another issue discussed in the *WSJ*, mentioned especially in 2016 and 2017.

Apart from self-driving cars and transportation, *automation* is also discussed in the context of the Internet of Things. Especially automated home appliances and gadgets are discussed in many articles over the years, for example in *Phone Home: How Close is an Automated Household?* by Geoffrey A Fowler, 2014. There are several companies which are trying to get into the smart home business as it is a huge market for the future. Examples are Google Home or Amazon's Alexa. This topic is not only discussed positively, as one can see in *Do smart homes really bring an advantage? In Keywords: Smart Home? I'll Keep My Dumb One for Now* by Christopher Mims, 2014. Apart from the Internet of Things, there are several articles on the military and cybersecurity, which are both important and large topics (e.g., in *Killer Robots and the Laws of War*, Kenneth Anderson and Matthew Waxman, 2013, or *Keywords: We're Fighting Killer Robots the wrong way*, 2015). The issues of cybersecurity and surveillance data is the focus of many articles when talking about *automation* in general. Throughout all the corpus material, not only the *WSJ* material, cybersecurity and data privacy are mentioned quite frequently.

Another larger theme in which the term *automation* appears in the *WSJ* material is **automation and (the future of) jobs**. In the articles discussed in this context, the introduction of machines and replacement of human workers are in focus. But robots will not only take over human tasks, but will also change the nature of work in many instances. For example, in *Corporate News: Honeywell Takes Lessons From Japan* by Bob Tita from 2013 *automation* is mentioned in the context of the reassignment of workers in a company in order to become more productive and efficient. Training but also job cuts are mentioned for those who cannot be reassigned. The issue of robots taking over human jobs is discussed in several more articles. For example in *Review: A Strategy for Keeping the Robots at Bay—Automation is making inroads in every industry—but if you're nimble, you can avoid being replaced by a machine* by Matthew Lynn in 2013, the author talks about a future vision when robots will be working for us and humans will be freed from hard work. Strangely, according to the author, this future never seems to materialize. Rather, people are working harder, being "bound to our smartphones and email." But with recent advances in AI, some version of this future scenario might finally be arriving. Mentioning recent reports by McKinsey and a book by Carnegie Mellon professor Reza Nourbakhsh called *Robot Futures,* the article talks about work taken over by robots. In this wave of *automation*, not only labor-intensive work is taken over; knowledge work also becomes more and more susceptible to *automation*. Although it remains unknown how fast *automation* is really proceeding, it is clear that all developed nations will continue to lose many manufacturing jobs due to technology. Service jobs could also be automated to a certain extent. To quote the article, "intelligent machines could rip through dozens of what today look like relatively secure, well-paid occupations." The article goes on to talk about "future-proof" careers and skill sets that include robot development, marketing your "human" skills, and taking over creative or complex jobs. The author assumes that entering a new industry is also a way to remain relevant as a worker. The article also speaks about the growth of industries "selling things to robots" although it remains unclear what exactly that means.

In another article on robots and work, called *Managing in the Middle: Robots Need Supervisors Too* by Lauren Weber from 2013, the changing nature of work is discussed. Through *automation*, the workforce is shrinking, and workers are expected to improve performance and productivity. Automated processes enter all kinds of fields, not only production, and supervisors are now asked to oversee these processes rather than overseeing employees. Therefore, they will have to amass more technical knowledge themselves. Andrew McAfee is quoted here saying that middle management seems to be exceptional in this sense, as it will not be affected as much by *automation* as some other (management) fields. An example of a more susceptible field is the back office, as mentioned in *Business Technology: CIO Journal*, 2013. Here *automation* is used in the context of job loss in back-office occupations. About 3.7 million jobs could be lost, according to the article, most likely in the area of "transactional positions" such as data operations or accounting. Prospects are better for specialized skills that help shift the company to a global stage like IT, finance, human resources, and procurement.

As could already be seen, *automation*, the further introduction of machines, and the impact on jobs are discussed on several occasions in the *WSJ* material. There are in fact even more articles directly concerned with ***robots and robotics***. *Automation* and robotics are strongly connected in the material from the *WSJ* and robots are presented as the main source of disruption for workers as they will replace them in many instances of blue- and white-collar jobs. In fact, in many instances, *automation* and robots are equated. Middle-skilled workers are expected to be hit quite severely by the introduction of robots in the future. The *WSJ* material also mentions Luddite thinking in this context. With this historical allusion, it is emphasized that a reversal or a fight against *automation* and machines is eventually unreasonable and unnecessary.

There is, for example, *Robots Take on More Elaborate Tasks Amid Worker Shortage; Automation gains could reduce need for human workers in many fields*, by James R. Hagerty from 2015, which talks about the fact that robots are now able to take on more complicated tasks, which might reduce the number of workers needed in the long run. Another article reports on the conference *South by Southwest* from 2014, in *WSJ.D Technology: Digits*. Many experts argue that *automation* will eliminate a lot of jobs, especially in manufacturing and that it will lead to major shifts in the labor market. *Automation* and robots will disrupt entire industries, for example in the trucking industry. However, the jobs that will be eliminated are not the ones that you "would want for your children." The jobs eliminated by robots are often undesirable for many workers. At the conference, several ideas are discussed that address the problem of job loss through *automation* by taking up ideas like taxing economic output rather than income and a negative income tax (a form of UBI) which would guarantee a basic income. The *WSJ* article calls these ideas "outlandish."

In the article *Big time automation making us dumb and unemployed: In Review: Books: Learning to Roomba* by Daniel J. Levitin, the author talks about the book *The Glass Cage* by Nicholas Carr from 2014. In this book, Carr warns that too much reliance on technology is not only making us dumb but also unemployed, especially in the middle-skilled section of the labor market. There is demand for high-skilled and low-skilled labor but not so much for the middle. Carr argues that people actually become less skilled when they rely too heavily on computers to do their work. The author of the review sees positive sides in Carr's book as it quotes many relevant facts, but there should be more of a middle ground. Machines now do many things for us, but if we make an effort, we can become the "masters of machines" and not the other way around, according to the author. We should still be capable of acting when machines fail. The author argues that *automation* is "what you make of it." *Automation* can be used to advance humanity, or to bring it down. The priorities must shift in the direction of advancing humanity, focusing on the strength and weaknesses humans have.

In yet another article called *What Jobs Will Robots Have in the Future?* (2014), experts were asked about how *automation* and digitization will possibly transform the workplace and what role robots play specifically. Again, the replacement of blue- and white-collar jobs by robots is discussed, especially the development of robots taking over nonroutine tasks more and more. This is an issue for workers but creates economic value as well. The issue of overreliance on machines as well as the fast pace of *automation* eliminating jobs is also discussed. Especially with a wave of smart devices that work autonomously, robots will be a threat to many occupations. The service industry could also be "ripe" for *automation* and new technology could be implemented in lots of ways. The argument in favor of *automation* has always been that it frees us from mundane forms of work to do more innovative things. So far, this has not come to pass on a large scale. Yet, there are many experts that see robots mainly taking over jobs that are dirty and dangerous, and not the ones that require human understanding and creativity. On the business side, most companies need to re-imagine themselves and implement a digital strategy that will be rewarded in the market. In this article, the *WSJ* tries to give a holistic view of opinions about *automation* by including experts from business, academia, and think tanks.

Jobs and the Clever Robot: Experts rethink belief that tech lifts employment as machines take on skills once thought uniquely human by Timothy Aeppel from 2015 also takes up the issue of robots in the workplace. The article quotes Erik Brynjolfsson and his colleagues saying that MIT experts have so far dismissed the notion that most human jobs will be eliminated by robots. However, even their opinion has changed. This change comes in the wake of the most recent innovations leading technology to the tipping point of mastering truly human tasks. Brynjolfsson sees a future in which more wealth is created through less (human) labor, but also a future where people want to work but cannot find an adequate job. The MIT experts also see middle-skilled jobs disappearing, while demand for the lower and upper ends of the skill level will grow. This has led to the polarization of the labor market, wage stagnation, and a rise in inequality in recent years. The article also alludes to past eras of vast *automation* and mechanization, for example in the nineteenth-century textile industry. So far, *automation* has always replaced labor, but the lump of labor fallacy is still relevant.

There is no finite amount of labor, at least so far. Is this going to change? This topic is picked up in the book review on *Rise of Robots* by Martin Ford from 2015 (*WSJ* article: *Soon They'll Be Driving It, Too* by Sumit Paul-Choudhury). The review says that, at best, there is circumstantial evidence that this wave of *automation* is different from the ones before. One-fifth of US jobs are highly creative, like in the entertainment industry or architecture. Those jobs are not likely to be automated. Yet, everyone else does face the threat of *automation* to some extent. The book's author Martin Ford does not see large numbers of low-skilled workers acquiring higher skills to move up the employment ladder. The *WSJ* article questions this, however, saying that smart machines have the ability to give workers new opportunities. The article argues in favor of technological solutions for a technological problem instead of a political solution. The book argues for a guaranteed basic income to address consequences of technological advancement. The *WSJ* reviewing the book sees this as a "drastic prescription" and is clearly not in favor of such a policy.

In general, many *WSJ* articles support the notion that there is no need to worry about the machines (*The Robots are Coming, but Don't Worry Yet*, by James R. Hagerty from 2015). There is still no progress in instilling machines with common sense, which is the fundamental advantage of humans so far. Additionally, *automation* will create machines that work alongside us and will also deliver lots of new jobs (*From WSJ.D: Before Taking Your Job, a Robot May Work Next to You*, by Elizabeth Dwoskin from 2015). New jobs will be in demand in areas such as software, engineering, designing, maintenance, support, or training. However, there are areas that could see a lot of losses for middle-skilled workers, like the healthcare sector (*Midlevel Health Jobs Shrink; Cost Cuts, Technology Hurt Semi-skilled Hospital Fields; 'B.A. Is Now Entry-Level'* by Ben Casselman from 2013). Especially through new technology, but also through cost-awareness of hospitals, there is more demand for high-skilled and low-skilled workers, but the middle is eroding. While many have seen secure jobs disappearing in manufacturing, health care had always been a sector where middle-skilled people could thrive. But a speedy advancement in technology is changing that.

2016 also sees several articles with a focus on robots in the workplace, especially in service sector jobs, for example, in *Service industry automation: Why Restaurant Automation Is On the Menu* by Andy Puzder, 2016. This article describes *automation* processes in sectors like hospitality. This sector has profited from changing consumer preferences, as well as from reduced costs of technology. This has advanced *automation* in this field. Additionally, government policies like minimum wage increases are portrayed as drivers for a more automated service industry. Digital *automation* and good customer service are becoming more and more important for firms. Therefore, they are building up their automated processes such as automated call centers. A year later, the 2017 article *Robot Baristas Serve Up the Future of Coffee at Café X; Automation is eliminating jobs for factory workers and Uber drivers—will your morning fix soon come from a precision caffeine machine?* by Geoffrey A Fowler alludes to even more change in the service industry with more automated machines being created to fulfill tasks formerly done by human workers. Here the example is a barista being replaced by a robot in coffee shops.

Apart from the service industry, robots in manufacturing are an important topic, as seen in *Latest Robots Lend an Arm: Manufacturers are reshaping factory floors with 'collaborative automatons'* by Andrew Tangel from 2016 or in *Manufacturing revival? In Will the U.S. See a Major Manufacturing Revival?* (2014). In the latter, different experts talk about the possibility of a manufacturing revival in the USA, citing technology, digitization, *automation*, data analytics, the Internet of Things, and additive manufacturing as the most crucial factors. The USA has traditionally adapted technology quite willingly and should benefit from the disruption from technology, provided it can retain a large talent base and maintain an innovative edge in the future.

But robots continue to move into new areas. This development is due to even smarter machines, as highlighted in *Some tips on Job Security in the Robot Age; Co-author Tom Davenport of the new book "Only Humans Need Apply" speaks on knowledge workers*, by Lauren Weber, 2016. This article discusses a new wave of *automation* that threatens professional workers. As in several other articles, there are allusions to the nineteenth-century Luddites who tried to stop *automation* and replacement of their jobs, which ultimately failed. Yet, there are ways to succeed in the *automation* age, for example working in or with tech, or the complete opposite, doing empathic work. The idea of the UBI is mentioned (in the book reviewed in this article), but there is more emphasis on the idea of giving people jobs rather than money. People should focus on jobs that computers *cannot* do better than humans, and these could very well lie outside the STEM fields. As was the case in the liberal media material, there are several more articles in the *WSJ* that allude to the Luddites who feared impoverishment due to a lack of well-paying work that they used to fulfill. They tried to prevent further *automation* by trashing the machines that threatened to replace them. The allusions to the Luddites in the material reviewed in this book are mainly made to show that fighting against machines is unnecessary and eventually unsuccessful. Technology is going to progress, no matter what. In the end, everyone is going to benefit and in the long run there will be better conditions and higher living standards for all, so the story goes.

Another example that goes in the same direction by citing the Luddites is *Keywords: Technology's Long-Term Toll on the Middle Class,* by Christopher Mims from 2017, where the author discusses dystopian future visions, especially concerning growing inequality. Allusions to the Luddites are made because they attacked the machines that threatened them but were ultimately doomed to fail. The article assumes that today, millions of truck drivers are not very different from the Luddites of the nineteenth century as many of them could be displaced with the large-scale arrival of automated driving. *Automation* is seen as being in its fourth revolution, rapidly advancing in AI, Biotech, nanotech, and other areas. Yet, the *WSJ* author, not an advocate of Luddite thinking, argues in favor of *automation* as it creates more jobs than it destroys, a development that has always accompanied *automation*. However, it is indeed admitted that today's jobs are often not comparable to the lost ones. Jobs used to pay more and were more secure and rewarding. Especially grave is the effect on the middle class where manufacturing and clerical jobs are lost, and people are pushed into the service sector more and more. Wages, benefits, and job security are different in this sector, and thus, the job market becomes more and more polarized. One solution to address polarization in the job market is to solve the skills gap for the labor force through specific training. Education is too blunt of a tool, according to the author, to really address the skills gap as workers need to acquire very specific skills to remain employable. The article *Management: Increasingly, Automation Reshapes Workplace Tasks*, by Lauren Weber from 2017, goes in the same direction saying that at the 2017 Davos meeting of the World Economic Forum, experts talked about changing work patterns in many jobs. Only a small number of jobs are likely to be automated entirely. Yet, all jobs will profoundly change through technology and will demand different skill sets.

Luddite thinking is again mentioned in *Bill Gates vs. the Robots*, by Andy Kessler in 2017. In many instances in the *WSJ* material, Luddite thinking is portrayed as workers' vain stubbornness to hold on to a past that will not come back. Bill Gates is mentioned here because he expressed his sympathy for people smashing the robots. Gates suggests that job-killing robots could be taxed in the future. The *WSJ* author does not hide the fact that he disapproves of this idea calling it "the dumbest idea since Messrs. Smoot and Hawley rampaged through the U.S. capitol in 1930." The author emphasizes all the good that technological advances have brought to the economy. And he adds that Gates' inventions have actually replaced many jobs as well. *Automation* is mentioned in the context of the American Dream saying that better jobs are the fulfillment of the American Dream, not mundane ones. The author argues in favor of technology as it delivers dramatically lowered costs and prices that benefit everyone. The author dismisses calls for less growth (rejecting the so-called de-growth movement) or less consumption and argues in favor of innovation in all its forms.

The next article called *U.S. News—Capital Account: Robots Aren't Killing Our Jobs Fast Enough*, by Grep Ip from 2017, goes in the same direction, calling the idea of a robot apocalypse "baffling and misguided." Ip claims that many sectors are actually too resistant to *automation* for their own good and are holding back a rising standard of living. Evidence shows that there are many jobs available and that they are not disappearing as suspected. Productivity per worker is not advancing fast enough to claim that the machines are displacing workers any time soon, according to the article. The article *Don't Fear the Robots; Smart machines will replace some jobs, but they will create many more by generating new wealth and higher demand for products and services* by Jerry Kaplan from 2017 argues the same, saying that the upsides clearly trump the downsides when it comes to *automation.* The historical pattern of replacement and creation of new jobs will remain the same. There are several other articles alluding to the same argument, for example *Automation's Surprise Benefits: More Jobs—E-commerce more than compensates for layoffs by traditional retailers*, by Grep Ip from 2017 where retail workers are the focus, or *Management: A Future Without Jobs? Think Again—Artificial Intelligence and automation will create new roles for humans, studies say,* by Vanessa Fuhrmans from 2017. The latter article mentions tech leaders like Elon Musk who say that there is the need for a new social safety net. Moreover, there is the 2015 article *At Startups, People Are 'New Infrastructure', Uber, Instacart and other are building not on the elimination of humans, but on their wholesale recruitment*, by Christopher Mims, which presents Silicon Valley's platform companies as beneficial to the "human factor" in new work arrangements.

According to the *WSJ* articles, in many cases, it is not robots but misplaced public policy that eliminates jobs. This can be seen in articles like *Management: Forget Robots: Bad Public Policies Can Kill More Jobs*, by Lauren Weber, 2017. The UBI and career coaching are mentioned as being practiced in places like Finland or Ontario, but not in the USA. Policy-makers and businesses in the USA should support displaced workers, invest in education and training, fund job-creating projects in downtrodden areas, and fund infrastructure in order to get people into good jobs. Higher wages can be an incentive to automate more quickly, so governments and businesses need to choose wisely which *automation* tools to adopt, how to regulate, and how to adjust wages. This is also discussed in *Three New Predictions for Automation and Jobs; Jobs will change, forcing workers to adapt and global productivity will rise*, by Lauren Weber from 2017.

As could already be seen, there are several articles in the *WSJ* that mention **the UBI.** Additionally, there are several articles mentioning the **minimum wage** or other reforms of the social policy reforms. By and large, these ideas are dismissed by the *WSJ* and openly opposed. The articles mentioned above talk about ideas by Elon Musk or Bill Gates about possible reforms such as the UBI, new social safety net measures, or a robot tax. Other articles on the matter include *Zuckerberg's Opiate for the Masses*, by Andy Kessler from 2017, which reports on Facebook founder Mark Zuckerberg's call to Harvard graduates to explore a new social contract for their generation. Zuckerberg argues that progress is more important in the economy than just growth. In this context, Zuckerberg also mentions the idea of the UBI. The *WSJ* author is not hiding his disdain for these ideas, as can be assumed from the title of the article ("opiate for the masses") and calls this idea the most "bankrupt idea since socialism." Silicon Valley is advocating the idea of the UBI with well-known figures like Elon Musk and Robert Reich who is quoted here. These ideas are openly dismissed in the article. The *WSJ* seems to generally favor the notion that *automation* has always created more jobs than were destroyed. There had been critical views and fears of replacement before, but they never came to pass. Yet, paying people for doing nothing will never get them back into the workforce. Instead, in order to advance everyone in society, the education system needs reform. The author claims the USA is turning into Europe (which he decidedly opposes) with Obama's push toward universal health care and now new ideas such as the UBI, which would come close to a downfall of capitalism altogether. He claims that some people need help and should not be "dying in the streets," but it does not help to create freeloaders for no reason. The author claims that the new ideas from Silicon Valley are nothing more than giving away other people's money.

Apart from the UBI, the minimum wage is also discussed in the *WSJ* on a number of occasions. For example, in the article *Workers with Technology; Burger-Flipping Robot May Be on Horizon* by Sarah Needlman and Angus Loten from 2013. When minimum wages increase, some small businesses fear that they will not be able to afford their workers anymore so they might push for automated services instead. With now so many inexpensive smart technologies available such as tablets or smartphones, small businesses can afford to implement more automated processes. But studies that are supposed to show the impact of an increased minimum wage on jobs are often politicized and do not make a clear statement one way or the other. One issue that is crucial for many small companies, which has not been solved by the invention of machines, is that humans tend to do multiple tasks spontaneously, which a machine cannot. This might prevent firms from over-relying on technology.

There are several more articles that deal with the issue of the minimum wage, *automation*, and the possible reduction of the number of workers, for example, *The Employee of the Month Has a Battery*, by Michael Saltsman from 2014. In this article, *automation* is directly connected to the minimum wage, with CEOs of large companies claiming that a high minimum wage is a driver for more *automation*. This claim is often made despite studies failing to really prove this trend. The article argues that government makes entry-level labor more expensive through all kinds of labor standards and that is why companies turn to technology to cut costs. However, the article also says that labor-saving devices are not a new phenomenon in these industries but have existed long before advanced technology. A reason for this has always been the low profit margins in areas such as retail, hospitality, and grocery stores. Efficiency is thus increased with new technology, but at the same time the cut in labor in the service industry can be dramatic for workers. The author claims that technology is often moving ahead with or without expensive labor costs, but that through the enormous spikes in minimum wage requirements in some states, faster implementation of technology is encouraged.

This article is followed by several letters to the editor in *Raising the Minimum Wage Will Cost Many Their Jobs*, 2014. The readers, some of them from the field of automated industries themselves, point to the huge potential for automated processes and that they are entering all branches of the economy. In their opinion, a $15 minimum wage would serve as an incentive to implement technology and would lead to the layoff of many low-skilled workers. Similar sentiments are expressed in the following articles: *A post-Labor Day, Minimum-Wage Hangover; The evidence is already coming in: Mandatory increases in Los Angeles, San Francisco and Seattle have cost thousands of jobs*, by Andy Puzder from 2015; *The Minimum Wage Should Be Called the Robots Employment Act*, by Andy Puzder from 2017; and *Cross Country: San Francisco's Problem Isn't Robots; It's the $15 Wage Floor*, by Michael Saltsman, also from 2017. In all these articles, the increase of the minimum wage, especially a rather stark one to $15 per hour in places like California and Seattle, is seen mainly through the lens of increased incentive to automate. It is emphasized that a high minimum wage does not benefit the worker, but that it leads to layoffs and faster *automation* in the long run. In the article, *Obamacare as Job Killer: Face It, ObamaCare May Help Some but it's a Job Killer* from 2014, the introduction of the Affordable Care Act is also presented as a job killer. In the same sentiment as mentioned before, the Affordable Care Act and the minimum wage help some groups of workers, but generally threaten jobs because they dis-incentivize employment, according to the articles. There are also several letters to the editor supporting the idea of Obamacare incentivizing the replacement of workers through *automation*.

In general, the *WSJ* material on *automation* and the introduction of robots in the workplace argues that middle-skilled jobs could be replaced to a larger degree than high- and low-skilled work. Yet, there is no need to fear this development. With allusions to the Luddites of the nineteenth century who were ultimately unsuccessful in preventing technological progress, the threats and fears of a more automated future are dismissed. The *WSJ* material emphasizes that in the long run the introduction of robots in all kinds of branches is a good development overall and only marginal groups might be negatively affected by it. The *WSJ* clearly furthers the narrative of technological change bringing about more jobs than it destroys. That is why they find most reform calls such as the UBI ludicrous and misplaced. The material from the *WSJ* also dismisses the introduction of a significantly higher minimum wage as this would drive *automation* ahead even faster.

Another theme around *automation* in the *WSJ* is **technological progress and tech businesses**. In this context, the trajectory of the **US economy** as a whole is in focus, in addition to specific technological developments and companies. *Automation* also plays a role in reports and articles talking about job gains and unemployment statistics in the *WSJ*. This is one of the most important themes in the investigation around the term *automation* in the *WSJ* material. The *WSJ* is a business-oriented news outlet, and therefore, the readers are interested in the outlook of the economy, the stock market, and the health and strategies of specific companies. For example, there are many reports on overall market success or weakness of certain companies over the years. Additionally, the *WSJ* reports on takeovers, mergers and acquisitions, sales, and costs in certain industries. Many of the industries apply or develop automated processes, and one key point of interest is how their stocks perform. China is also a large topic with many articles discussing production and the technological progress of this production in China, for example in *China's Hunger for Robots Marks Significant Shift*, by Timothy Aeppel and Mark Magnier, 2015. Some overall topics when *automation* and the state of the economy are discussed include artificial intelligence, machine learning, cloud computing, data analytics, global supply chains, or offshoring. Robotics are again discussed in this context. This can be seen, for example, in *Robots Will Save the Economy; The problem today is too little technology. Physical industries haven't kept up,* by Bret Swanson and Michael Mandel, 2017. As an ongoing trend that has pushed the economy forward for decades, *automation* is discussed in this context as a driver of growth and something that is naturally occurring when the economy is advancing. *Automation* is seen as a strong factor for growth.

As said before, there is a set of articles that deals with specific companies and the technical advances they are developing or implementing. For example, in *Business Technology: How many Turns in a Screw? Big Data Knows* by James R. Hagerty from 2013, *automation* is mentioned in "Rockwell Automation Inc." This company is frequently mentioned throughout the years in the *WSJ* material. *Bring in the Robots* by Holman W. Jenkins Jr. from 2013 deals with technological advances in aircrafts, trains, and other transportation devices. Human intervention in many of these devices is reduced but not replaced entirely. The article talks about the fact that when there is a mixture of automated and un-automated (human) processes involved, the whole structure is worse off. The article also claims that there will be a lack of workers to fill jobs, for example due to an aging society. *Automation* is a way out of that scenario. The article *Keeping Plants Running from Afar—Factory-Automation Gear Helps Manufacturers Deal With Problems Amid Skilled-Worker Shortages* by James R. Hagerty from 2013 also talks about advances in *automation*. Through technology, factories can be monitored from afar, which allows them to run all day without interruption. The article sees this as a way to address skilled worker shortages, especially in remote areas.

America's Toilet Turnaround—After Years of Moving Work Overseas, Remaining Factories Ramp up U.S. Output by James R. Hagerty from 2013 mentions the introduction of new techniques that can maintain production in the USA. Another new possibility for companies in the USA is mentioned in *Data and cloud: Leadership—Data and the cloud break down barriers between business units, helping to streamline production*, by Angus Loten and John Simons, 2017, which talks about cloud computing as a way to improve business practices. In a similar article called *Driving U.S. Factories: Foreign Robotics—Manufacturing rebound means buying modern machinery from overseas*, by Daniel Michaels from 2017, modern robotics are portrayed as driving US companies, especially in manufacturing.

But robots are not only used in manufacturing, they are increasingly used for routine tasks in the service industry such as retail, detailed in the article *Business News: Retailers Are Checking Out Automation—As online competition squeezes profits, chains recruit machines for routine tasks*, by Sarah Nassauer, 2017. This article talks about routine tasks that are more easily automated, even in retail, where the competition from online sellers is stark. In other service sector branches, such as banking, *automation* is another hot topic, which is changing the industry profoundly. In *Fintech automation helps to save money for the future: Savings Strategies for Young People* by Lindsay Gellman, innovation in the banking sector is already discussed in 2014. In *Automation Stalks Financial Advisers—Algorithms generate investment advice, undercut traditional 1% fees* by Jason Zweig, Anne Tergesen, and Andrea Fuller from 2017, algorithms rather than people are seen as the future of banking and investment. All the articles mentioned here show again that artificial intelligence is a significant topic when talking about *automation*. AI will make it possible for machines or algorithms to learn and deliver results without human intervention. Additionally, cloud computing and platform software, for example to monitor production in manufacturing, become bigger topics. All these technologies are driving the American economy but are also a way to replace "the human factor" or at least reduce it drastically so that you can actually produce more with less (labor). This development is portrayed as positive and a stimulus to the American economy overall.

As indicated before, the *WSJ* reports on several specific companies that are either front-runners in the *automation* business or investing heavily in it. Some firms that are mentioned are Honeywell, Siemens, Groupon, Cadence Design Systems Inc., GE, Bayer, Google, Nest Labs Inc, Rockwell Automation, PepsiCo, several different auto makers across the globe, Cruise Automation, Tesla, Uber, Instacart, Airbnb, Apple, Kuka, Waymo, or Ford. Platform industries are mentioned occasionally, like Uber or Airbnb, but they do not appear very intensively in this context. Foxconn is another company that is mentioned over and over in the context of *automation*, for example in *Foxconn is Subject of Bribery Probe by Aries Poon*, 2013. Foxconn is a Chinese firm producing Apple products in China. Foxconn has been in the news over riots that had broken out at some facilities in China. After these uprisings, Chinese officials allegedly considered moving the production to other regions and introducing more automated processes. In this context, *automation* indeed serves as a way to eliminate the "human factor" and stripping Chinese workers of their ability to demand better working conditions. The *WSJ* material does not discuss this aspect, however.

The auto industry features quite intensively throughout the material, especially when GM acquired Cruise Automation, which produced a lot of headlines, especially in the years 2016 and 2017. *Automation* in the car industry is generally a big topic with many new players moving into the market, which can be seen in *Apple Drops Hints About Working on Self-Driving Cars, In letter to U.S. transportation regulators, Apple said it is investing heavily in machine learning and automation*, by Tim Higgins and Tripp Mickle, 2016. Even companies that have not produced any cars before are now considering investing in autonomous driving technology. Apart from the auto industry, more recent articles in the *WSJ* also feature innovation in the mining industry and how *automation* is used to improve and update the production.

Apart from the auto industry there are other industries mentioned in the *WSJ* material such as telecommunication providers Verizon and AT&T who are looking into ways to use remote *automation* and online platforms as detailed in *Wireless Carriers Move Beyond Smartphones* by Thomas Gryta, 2013. In *India's Drug Firms Push Automation* by Sean McLain from 2014, *automation* is seen as a way toward better quality of drug production for the American market. Despite an abundance of cheap labor, India's drug-making facilities move toward more *automation* to produce the quality demanded by FDA regulations. However, a push toward more *automation* is not always easy and there are many challenges that companies face in a more automated economy (e.g., *'Digital' Clients Pose Big Challenges* by Thomas Coyle, 2013). Offering digital services is a great stretch for some firms and pleasing customers in a digital setting is not easy.

Again, the articles in the *WSJ* mentioned here focus on specific players in the market. All of them are investing heavily in *automation* processes that will eliminate the human factor in many situations. This can be a way toward superior quality and safety of products while being more efficient in the long run as well. This pushes productivity and economic growth and delivers inexpensive consumer goods benefitting all Americans. Many sectors are implementing automated processes where this seemed impossible in the past like the retail sector or self-driving vehicle production. The advantages of this development are clearly in focus for the *WSJ*: better quality, fewer accidents, reliable production, and lower costs in the long run. Even developing countries are therefore pushing *automation* even though they still have an abundance of cheap labor. In the context of specific development and companies, the implications for labor are rarely discussed.

It is clear that *automation* is an important topic in the material from the *WSJ* as it is one of the main developments driving businesses and the economy forward.

Progress in *automation* is also seen as a natural development in economic growth. Even though it is not the focus of the *WSJ* reporting on *automation*, there are nevertheless several articles that include questions about the future of work. Yet, the stance of the *WSJ* comes across rather clearly. By alluding to the Luddites several times and how their fight against the machines was clearly futile, the *WSJ* expresses the view that *automation* has always brought job loss, but worrying about it is misplaced. There will be more and better jobs eventually. Workers will benefit if they can adapt to this new environment through higher education. This is a narrative that is shared by many economists and experts when they focus on the overall economic gains from technological progress. In this context, the effects of technological development on certain groups in society are less intensively discussed.

The material from the *WSJ* specifically emphasizes the impact of robots on the nature of work and the economy as a whole. Possible job loss is not the focus. It seems that robots and *automation* often mean the same thing in the material from the *WSJ*. Robots are moving into different areas than before, also into white-collar jobs. This could lead to less demand for middle-skilled workers and higher demand of high- and low-skilled workers. The polarization of the labor market could therefore be painful for certain groups. Yet, many *WSJ* articles put an emphasis on *automation's* impact on businesses and the economy as a whole, which they see as positive overall. The focus is clearly not the repercussions for workers in the future. What they call for is education and training possibilities and also more action by businesses themselves who should invest in upskilling their workforce, on which they depend to succeed.

In line with the more business-friendly outlook of the *WSJ*, there are fewer calls for action by the government and more emphasis on action taken by the economic actors themselves. It is also clear that the *WSJ* dismisses calls for a broader social safety net or reforms such as a significantly higher minimum wage. The minimum wage is repeatedly portrayed as a driver for *automation*, instead of a support for low-wage workers. More radically new ideas such as the UBI are portrayed as rather outlandish and the *WSJ* clearly rejects those who advocate in favor of such new policies such as Silicon Valley heavyweights Bill Gates, Elon Musk, or Mark Zuckerberg whose stances on liberal social policy are clearly opposed. Apart from the contexts and themes mentioned above, the *WSJ* material on *automation* included several letters to the editor where readers expressed their concerns about further *automation* in the future. In some instances, the readers seemed more concerned about future *automation* than the authors writing for the *WSJ*.

6.1.7 Digitization and Automation in Political and Public Discourse

Generally, one can say that the contexts in which *digitization* and *automation* are used across the public and political discourse investigated here differ greatly.

Although *digitization* is used to refer to technological progress and its impact on the economy in places like Germany, the US discourse does not display the use of *digitization* in this way in many instances. The development of AI, smart robotics, and the development of algorithms are associated with *digitization*. Yet, in the discourse investigated here, *automation* remains the term that is most often used when talking about technological progress of any kind. *Digitization* is used in reference to new technology in some instances, but in the majority of cases, it refers to things like Big Data initiatives or as a method to digitize "analogue" material of all kinds. When frequencies of the two terms are compared, it is also obvious that *automation* is used in the majority of cases, whereas *digitization* as a term is rather rare overall.

Especially in the Senate material, there were only very few cases where the term *digitization* could be found. Yet, if it appears, it is in the context of the impact of technology on specific industries such as manufacturing, the workplace, income, and inequality rather than in reference to *digitization* as a method. In the *WSJ*, there is also a much more intense discussion of *digitization* as technological innovation than in the other sources examined here. First of all, the *WSJ* displays the highest frequency of the term *digitization* overall. Additionally, it features more detailed discussions on digital innovation in different fields such as health care, manufacturing, or construction. It also features in the assessments of the success of specific companies and how they are faring with their digitizing strategy. The introduction of advanced robotics, for example, boosts productivity and economic growth.

Apart from the reference to *digitization* as technological innovation, the *WSJ* also talks about *digitization* as a method for preserving material and making it accessible. This has an influence on fields such as the book market, music, film, and art. This theme is also rather strong in the liberal media material which mentions several institutions that are engaged in digitizing their archives, for example. The House material also mostly uses *digitization* as a term in this sense, talking about copyright issues and intellectual property more intensively.

Both the liberal media material and the *WSJ* material interestingly touch upon the issue of rural areas being left out of innovation processes and the opportunities of *digitization*. The *WSJ* mentions the fact that red (Republican-led) states are receiving almost none of the venture capital that is so crucial in the new economy. Blue states led by Democrats see much more investment in that regard. The *NYT* talks about this issue in regard to the urban–rural divide arguing that rural voters are turning away from Democrats as they feel left behind. This might explain some of the polarization that is happening between rural and urban areas in the USA. These discussions remain isolated instances, however. Generally, *digitization* is most often used in connection with digitizing and storing data and Big Data initiatives and processes. The business-oriented outlet *WSJ* is most engaged in the discussion around *digitization* as technological innovation, while the other material features *digitization* in a more limited fashion.

The term *automation* in the political discourse is used in a more complex manner than the term *digitization*, and it is also much more frequent overall. Transportation and infrastructure innovation are points that are discussed rather frequently in

Congress. Especially aviation but also the self-driving vehicle are two fields in which *automation* is crucial. Additionally, cybersecurity and *automation* in the fields of national security were also discussed in both chambers.

In the Senate, there are only a few instances where *automation* is discussed in the context of specific technology (AI, robotics), but there is a larger focus on the disruption of the workforce and the economy as a whole through these innovations. Some of these hearings take place in front of the Joint Economic Committee and include testimony by high-profile experts such as Andrew McAfee from the MIT. *Automation* is seen as a booster of economic growth and productivity, which has benefitted consumers greatly. At the same time, there are several problematic issues that accompany further *automation* in recent years, such as decoupling of productivity and wage growth, which also has to do with a lack of adequate skills and access to higher education that have not kept pace with the fast-moving *automation* environment. This could lead to a further polarization of the labor market. In this regard, education and infrastructure reforms are discussed in Congress. Additionally, there are several hearings in the Senate on monetary policy that also touch upon *automation's* impact. The hearings focus on long-term trends in the American economy and how institutions like the Fed can respond to these developments.

In the House, there were several allusions to the impact of *automation* on entrepreneurship and small business. Ongoing *automation* is seen as both a challenge and an opportunity in this regard. Yet, the focus of the hearings in the House that feature the term *automation* more prominently is technology. Especially the *Disrupter Series* shows that the Representatives in the House try to get a grip on very recent innovations in various fields and the implications they have for regulation, the workforce, and the economy as a whole. The *Disrupter Series* includes specific hearings on the self-driving car, the sharing economy, the Internet of Things, FinTech, and many more. As indicated before, the House seems to hold more specific hearings in this regard than the Senate. There could be several reasons for this. For once, the average age in the House is slightly below that of the Senate, which means that some younger Representative might be more aware of and interested in recent technological developments. Moreover, the House is elected every 2 years, which makes it necessary for House members to respond actively to current events. Some of the technological innovations touch on the everyday lives of many people, and thus, Congress should be aware of them. Lastly, it seems much more feasible for members of the House to specify in certain areas than for Senators. There are 435 members of the House and only 100 Senators, but the number of committees and subcommittees is roughly the same. Therefore, members of the House have a greater possibility to dig deeper into specific issues, while Senate hearings seem to focus on long-term trends rather than very recent ones. Yet, some of the hearings investigated here were held in front of the Joint Economic Committee, which points to the significance of some of the developments, such as *automation*. There was, for instance, one specific hearing on the impact of *automation* in front of the Joint Economic Committee where high-profile experts testified (*The Transformative Impact of Robots and Automation*, 2016). Here, developments that profoundly change the trajectory and nature of the US economy in the future are discussed.

In the media sources, there was an extremely high number of instances where *automation* occurred. In fact, the *WSJ* displayed the highest relative frequency of the term *automation* overall. There are certain themes in which *automation* occurs in the media material. These include references to AI and smart robotics, with a special focus on the self-driving car. The self-driving car is discussed in reference to specific companies such as Cruise Automation (GM) that are heavily investing in the development of autonomous driving. Especially in the *WSJ*, there are numerous references to all kinds of companies that are engaged in automation R&D and implementation (Cruise, Rockwell Automation, Honeywell, etc.). There are several areas where *automation* has become crucial such as in aviation, transportation, warehouses, factory floors, or banking. Especially for business-interested readers, reports on the businesses and sectors where *automation* plays a big role are crucial to see where the economy is headed. Apart from the self-driving car, robots and robotics are discussed on several occasions in the media material. In many instances, robots are equated with *automation*, especially in fields like manufacturing. Yet, there were also many allusions to formerly low-automated sectors being "ripe" for *automation* such as the retail or healthcare sector.

Interestingly, all media outlets use historical references to assess the impact of *automation*. By invoking the struggle of the Luddites on several occasions, the fight against technological progress is mainly portrayed as pointless. *Automation* has always happened over the course of human history, and it has eventually led to more prosperity and better jobs for all. In the liberal media outlets, however, the painful process of job loss for many workers is emphasized to a greater extent than in the *WSJ*. Especially through new waves of *automation* that touch sectors known as white-collar or knowledge work, there are concerns that this wave of *automation* might be different from the past and more difficult to handle. Many middle-skill jobs are likely to disappear due to *automation*, while high- and low-skill jobs will be in higher demand. In order to address these challenges, there are more allusions to new ideas like the universal basic income in the liberal media outlets.

For the *WSJ*, however, these new ideas do not make sense and they are openly dismissed. Additionally, the *WSJ* sees a high minimum wage as an unfavorable further driver of *automation*. The *WSJ* mostly maintains the "traditional" narrative of the benefits and opportunities of *automation* through better products, safer work environments, and eventually more prosperity for all, as well as the creation of more and better jobs eventually. In this sense, the *WSJ* does not call for major government intervention to address the impact of technology in the future. Specific skills training is seen as crucial, however, and there are in fact calls for businesses to step up their efforts in training their own workforce. Other government policies such as the earned income tax credit are not discussed, neither are calls for a higher minimum wage or better healthcare provisions supported, which is a bigger concern for the liberal media outlets. Making entry-level jobs more expensive is often generally portrayed as a further driver for *automation* in the *WSJ*.

Interestingly, the liberal media outlets talk more extensively about new work arrangements such as in the sharing economy in the context of *automation*. Although independent (contract) work has existed before the advent of digital technology, the liberal media outlets directly associate the sharing economy with ongoing technological progress and *automation* processes. New applications make it much easier to hire short-term contractors to fulfill tasks, which could point to a future development that is even more complicated for workers. Not only are they facing possible job loss, wage stagnation, and a lack of access to skills training, they are also facing jobs that are less secure and offer fewer benefits than in the past (independent work). As mentioned before, more radical ideas like the UBI are discussed in the liberal media material in order to address some of the harsher impacts of technology on the future workforce. Yet, more traditional approaches such as the minimum wage, earned income tax credits, and infrastructure and education reform are also discussed.

6.2 Future of Work

After looking at the treatment of *digitization* and *automation* in political and public discourse, the analysis turns to some more specific terms that are part of the conversation around technological progress and its impact on the American economy. In the following analysis, the term *future of work* will be examined. Naturally, the discourse around the *future of work* is more elaborate than just using the phrase as such. What can be inferred from the analysis in this book is that all the specific terms around technological progress in the USA are in some way concerned with the *future of work* as well. The impact of technology on the number of available jobs, the workplace, and the nature of work are key concerns when ongoing automation is discussed. Technological progress has always ignited fears of job loss. Yet, the debate around the *future of work* is larger. Apart from whether the number of jobs will change in the future or not, the nature of work and work arrangements are also changing profoundly. All these aspects are part of the debate around the *future of work*. Yet, the phrase itself seems to have entered the discourse around technological progress only recently. It seems that it has now become more of a fixed expression to refer to the impact of technology on labor and the workplace in general. In the following, there will be a more in-depth analysis of the term and if and how it is used across the different sources.

6.2.1 Future of Work in the Congressional Material

As can be seen in Tables 6.19 and 6.20, *future of work* is rare in the congressional material overall, especially compared to other terms like *automation* or *digitization* (of course it is also a phrase and not a single term). In the House, there are only 7 instances in 4 out of the 151 hearings in the 5 years examined where the term *future*

Table 6.19 House: number of hearings featuring "automation," "digitization," "future of work"

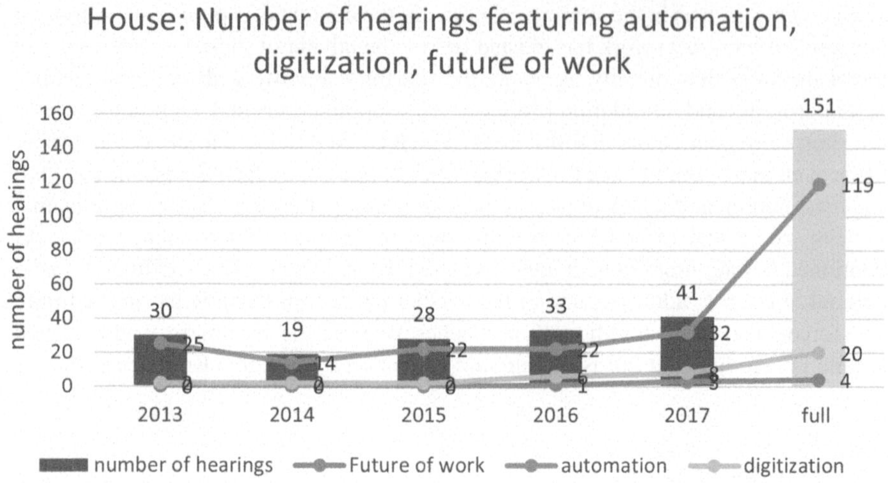

Source: Author

Table 6.20 Senate: number of hearings featuring "automation," "digitization," "future of work"

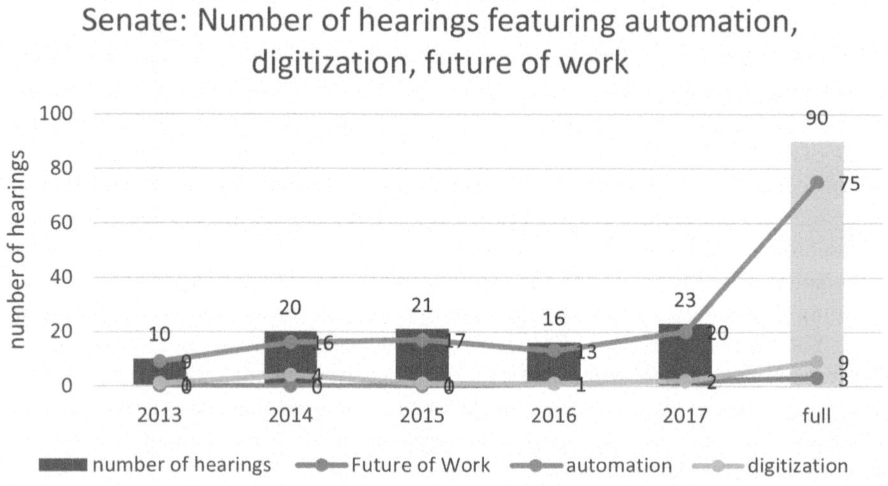

Source: Author

of work occurs. Looking at relative frequency, this only amounts to 0.01 per 10,000 tokens. The hearings in the House where the term *future of work* occurs include: *The Sharing Economy: A Taxing Experience for new Entrepreneurs, Part I* (2016, Committee on Small Business), *Federal Wage and Hour Policies in the Twenty-First Century Economy* (2017, Subcommittee on Workforce Protections, Committee on Education and the Workforce), *Disrupter Series: Smart Communities* (2017, Subcommittee on Digital Commerce and Consumer Protection, Committee on Energy and Commerce), and *Reversing the Entrepreneurship Decline* (2017, Committee on Small Business).

In the Senate (Table 6.20), there are only 5 instances in 3 out of 90 hearings where the phrase *future of work* actually occurs (relative frequency: 0.01 per 10,000 tokens). The hearings in the Senate that feature the term are *Exploring Augmented Reality* (2016, Committee on Commerce, Science, and Transportation), *The Current State of Retirement Security in the United States* (2017, Subcommittee on Economic Policy, Committee on Banking, Housing, and Urban Affairs), and *The Economic Outlook with Federal Reserve Chair Janet Yellen* (2017, Joint Economic Committee). Overall, it is interesting to see that *future of work* appears in hearings across an array of different committees, not only concerned with the workforce specifically. They include committees on small business, economic policy, transportation, or consumer protection. It is apparent that the topic of the *future of work* is of concern in many different fields.

All hearings in Congress that include the phrase *future of work* are found in 2016 or later. This indicates that the term and discussion around the *future of work* is rather new and was picked up more recently by lawmakers. It could also indicate that the term *future of work* has only recently entered the discussion as a fixed expression for future developments of labor in the digital age. In fact, the liberal media material examined in this work also features *future of work* more intensively in 2015 and later (in the *WSJ* material the relative frequency level remains low throughout the years). In general, the phrase appears rarely in all of the corpora compared to some other terms investigated in this book, and also in both the House and the Senate. The corpora are based on the themes of *automation*, *digitization*, and the *sharing economy*, but it seems that the term of *future of work* does not appear in this context to a great extent.

Looking at the Senate material in more detail, the rarity of the term *future of work* continues to be apparent. Tables 6.21 and 6.22 display the collocations of *future of work* in the Senate material.[6] Some of the more interesting collocates that are not function words include *change*, *automation*, *uncertain*, *prepare*, and *future*. *Inno* as a collocate most likely refers to *innovation* or *innovative*. These collocates point at the uncertainty of technological progress (*automation*) in the future but also the dynamic power (*innovation*) for which Americans need to prepare.

When the term *future of work* occurs in the Senate hearings, the hearings revolve around specific technology, for example augmented reality, as well as around concerns for the future in general, for example, the US social security system (retirement) and its sustainability that is in question in an aging society. Moreover, the *future of work* is part of the conversation in a hearing in front of the Joint

[6]The frequency of the collocates is very low. A lower MI ≥ 5 than usual and the lowest minimum collocate frequency score (1) were used to produce the collocate list and graph. Indeed, most of the collocates only appear once in the material (Table 6.22).

Table 6.21 Senate: collocation graph for future of work MI ≥ 5, minimum collocate frequency 1

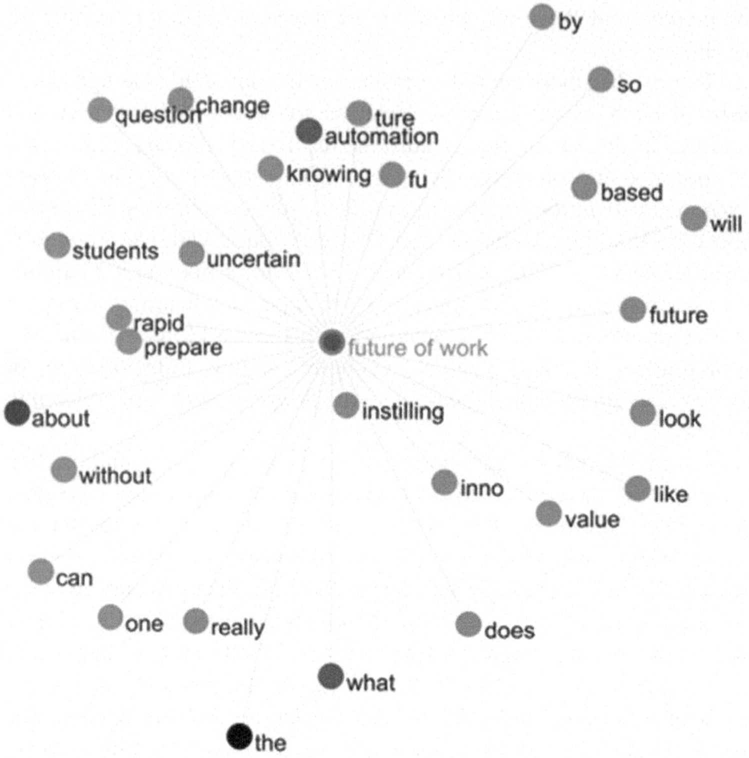

Source: Author, using #LancsBox

Economic Committee, where Janet Yellen, Fed Chair at the time, talked about the economic outlook of the USA before leaving office shortly after in 2017.

When talking about augmented reality in one of the hearings (*Exploring Augmented Reality,* 2016) the terms *future of work* and "lifelong learning" appear together, stressing how students must be prepared for the future and must find a way to improve their skill set throughout their lives. In the hearing *The Current State of Retirement Security in the United States* (2017), *future of work* appears three times, and is mentioned in connection with automation. In general, there is uncertainty about how the future will really look like for working Americans. "What does the future of labor look like?", Senators ask. Without buying into the dramatic forecasts of losing about half of today's jobs, it is still of concern how to improve the economic outlook for Americans and how to come up with a sustainable plan for future retirement, in a time when the *future of work* for the labor force is still unknown. In the hearing with Fed Chair Janet Yellen, *The Economic Outlook with Federal Reserve Chair Janet Yellen* (2017), *future of work* appears again together

Table 6.22 Senate: collocates of future of work MI ≥ 5, minimum collocate frequency 1

future of work

Freq: 5 Collocates: 28

Index	Status	Stat (03 - MI)	Collocate	▼ Stat	Freq (coll.)	Freq (corpus)
1	O	R	instilling	17.245180100476546	1	5
2	O	L	uncertain	13.636414948712533	1	61
3	O	R	fu	13.192111969555569	1	83
4	O	R	inno	13.15775681130519	1	85
5	O	L	knowing	12.982185384057237	1	96
6	O	L	prepare	12.319223443316442	1	152
7	O	M	automation	11.95244066125118	2	392
8	O	L	rapid	11.901814785341633	1	203
9	O	R	ture	11.300364224564802	1	308
10	O	R	value	9.73901313427609	1	909
11	O	L	change	9.341942232509236	1	1197
12	O	L	students	9.16840600872193	1	1350
13	O	R	based	9.05935542534836	1	1456
14	O	L	without	8.963523550399584	1	1556
15	O	R	future	8.859790819302509	1	1672
16	O	L	really	8.437222967178185	1	2241
17	O	R	does	8.341339898678344	1	2395
18	O	R	look	8.278283910167687	1	2502
19	O	L	about	8.054738625144472	3	8764
20	O	L	question	7.82610426188167	1	3423
21	O	M	what	7.576514026765822	2	8139
22	O	R	like	7.53751751953971	1	4181
23	O	L	one	6.919691408762792	1	6416
24	O	L	can	6.313745524902287	1	9765
25	O	R	so	6.186283014527189	1	10667
26	O	R	will	6.0119616341381334	1	12037
27	O	R	by	5.7263719598124965	1	14672
28	O	L	the	5.048320018872082	8	187799

Source: Author, using #LancsBox

with "automation" and "innovation" in the same sentence. There is the allusion to jobs being disrupted by these trends. Additionally, it is mentioned that government programs might come under stress because of it. The question is then posed whether and how monetary policy has to change and take the new data about these trends into account. In general, although the term *future of work* is mentioned rarely, if it appears it is mostly in the context of uncertainty, disruption, and the unknown future for labor and jobs. At the same time, it is seen in the context of innovation.

In the House, the occurrences of the term *future of work* are also rather rare. When looking at the collocates of this term in the House (Tables 6.23 and 6.24), this is also apparent.[7] However, there are some interesting collocates in the House material that seem to be more specific than in the Senate material. These include *innovative, service, pathways, startup, research, on-demand, changing, industry, workforce,* and *bipartisan*. There seem to be more specific topics that are discussed around the *future of work* in the House material. *Innovation, service, startup, research,* and *industry* point to the discussion around the dynamism in the American economy in

[7] Again, the frequency of the collocates was set to 1 and MI ≥ 5 was used, which decidedly reduces the significance of the collocates produced by the software.

Table 6.23 House: collocation graph of future of work MI ≥ 5, minimum collocate frequency 1

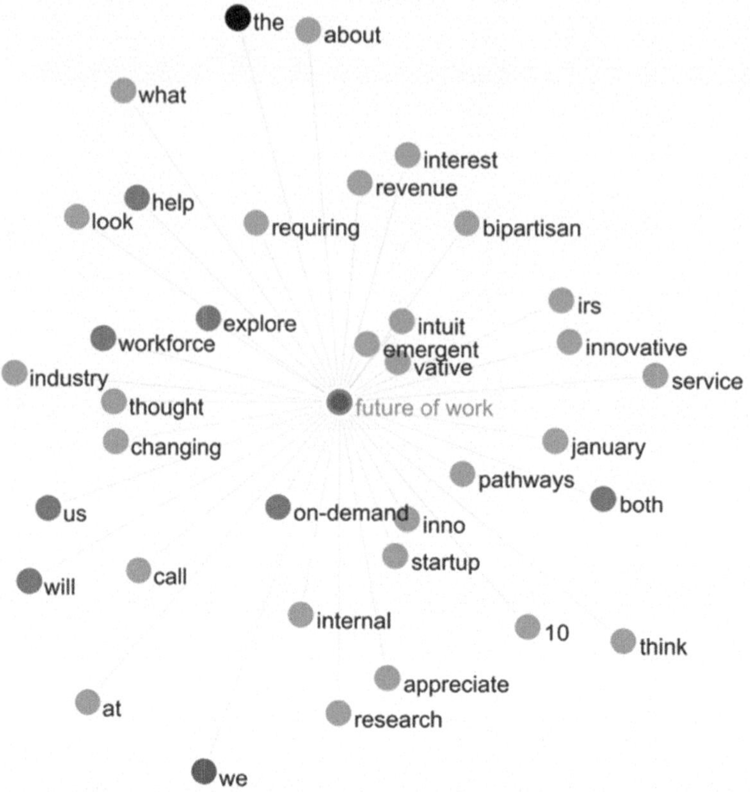

Source: Author, using #LancsBox

the future. *On-demand* points to the rise of new forms of business-making and consumption that leave their mark on the American economy. *Workforce* as a collocate points to the implications of technological innovation on the American labor force.

The House hearings that mention the *future of work* concern the state of the economy, challenges for the twenty-first century workforce, and the economy's potential for innovation and dynamism. Additionally, topics like "smart communities," the sharing economy, and (the decline of) entrepreneurism are discussed in the hearings. In *The Sharing Economy: A Taxing Experience for new Entrepreneurs, Part I* (2016), the *future of work* is mentioned in the context of a publication title. The publication is mentioned when talking about online platforms in general. Platforms are mentioned here as something that offers great value to both consumers and workers. They give workers a way to work flexibly and "on-demand," which workers generally seem to enjoy. A survey is mentioned arguing that many workers

Table 6.24 House: collocates of future of work MI ≥ 5, minimum collocate frequency 1

future of work

Freq: 7 Collocates: 36

Index	Status	Stat (03 - MI)	Collocate	▼ Stat	Freq (coll.)	Freq (corpus)
1	O	R	emergent	15.559298988593746	1	15
2	O	R	vative	15.378718137784507	1	17
3	O	R	intuit	14.421777733039763	1	33
4	O	L	on-demand	13.80795927238848	2	101
5	O	R	inno	13.378707381397417	1	68
6	O	R	pathways	13.162395873830521	1	79
7	O	L	explore	12.731463480883834	2	213
8	O	R	startup	12.488894567545813	1	126
9	O	L	requiring	11.41632447390914	1	265
10	O	R	internal	10.873716250663126	1	386
11	O	R	january	10.797288066219949	1	407
12	O	R	bipartisan	10.755366741170764	1	419
13	O	R	revenue	10.71797972444766	1	430
14	O	L	thought	10.538394800567433	1	487
15	O	L	changing	10.491757835435825	1	503
16	O	R	innovative	10.227768617625868	1	604
17	O	R	irs	10.023229694070237	1	696
18	O	L	workforce	9.943591345748773	2	1471
19	O	R	interest	9.609747327995253	1	927
20	O	L	call	9.416324473909194	1	1060
21	O	R	appreciate	8.887800436699392	1	1529
22	O	R	both	8.8840309984897	2	3066
23	O	L	help	8.615204721444446	2	3694
24	O	R	10	8.487462524588684	1	2018
25	O	R	research	7.927014158458746	1	2976
26	O	L	us	7.926771719608983	2	5953
27	O	R	service	7.774865621390257	1	3307
28	O	L	look	7.561538288666462	1	3834
29	O	L	industry	7.413944622863696	1	4247
30	O	L	will	6.4339549750660545	2	16754
31	O	R	think	6.092628016366306	1	10613
32	O	R	about	5.97019303743445	1	11553
33	O	L	what	5.775956658575069	1	13218
34	O	L	at	5.396387532392138	1	17196
35	O	L	we	5.362502641315138	3	52814
36	O	L	the	5.212263905820461	12	234442

Source: Author, using #LancsBox

would not go back to rely solely on a traditional job for income. In the hearing *Federal Wage and Hour Policies in the Twenty-First Century Economy* (2017), *future of work* again appears with "innovative" in the same sentence. In the hearing the *Disrupter Series: Smart Communities* (2017), *future of work* appears in the context of "pathways to the advanced manufacturing, cybersecurity, and data science jobs of the future." Future occupation and therefore the *future of work* will lie in these fields. In this context, the potential for disruption is also mentioned, saying that America needs to prepare for disruption in order to "harness the promise of new technology to benefit our residents." Even though disruption might be painful, it is argued, in the end it will benefit all Americans because it will improve safety, reliability, efficiency, and resilience. In *Reversing the Entrepreneurship Decline*

(2017), *future of work* is mentioned in the context of the "startup ecosystem." The hearing discusses the changing attitude of the workforce toward the workplace, especially among millennials who will soon make up the majority of the overall workforce. According to the hearing, millennials do not value traditional long-term working relationships as much as previous generations. However, this changing attitude also raises questions about the provision of social benefits, for example in the context of the so-called gig economy. In the future, the issue will be to provide social benefits normally associated with traditional work arrangements to a more diverse workforce. At the same time, these nontraditional work arrangements such as the gig economy should not be stifled. During this debate portable social benefits are also discussed.

In the hearings in the House, the phrase *future of work* is mentioned in a more "hands-on" fashion than in the Senate, touching on actual issues people face who work in the digital sphere such as the sharing or gig economy. The sharing economy platforms are seen as one part of the *future of work*, offering desirable options for both consumers and workers. Especially millennials, it is argued, are looking for other options than just the 9–5 traditional job. Yet, this also raises problems in the area of social benefit provision or taxation. *Future of work* appears in a context that is seen as innovative, yet disruptive with the potential to benefit workers, consumers, and communities. The actual *future of work* will mean the growth of the independent workforce, as well as growth in the number of high-skilled professions.

All in all, the *future of work* appears very rarely in both congressional corpora. It seems that the term has only become a fixed expression more recently. When it is mentioned in the hearings, the conversation is often centered around new forms of work such as the gig or sharing economy. It is also mentioned in the context of innovation in the economy, which is positive for consumers and communities, but potentially more difficult for workers. Uncertainty remains about the effect on labor, but also uncertainty about how to maintain social security measures such as retirement plans in a changing economy and with new ways of working. Disruption of work and further automation are also mentioned in this context. Thus, the *future of work* holds the potential for both innovation and disruption, which is more difficult to navigate. The discussion of possible solutions to these disruptions is ongoing, and their effects remain largely unknown. The hearings examined here were not conducted on the topic of the *future of work* specifically, yet they seem to be some of the first exploratory hearings on the subject with few pre-formed ideas about possible solutions and a lot of uncertainty remaining.

6.2.2 *Future of Work in the Liberal Media Material*

Compared to the congressional material, the liberal media sources display a significantly larger set of occurrences of the term *future of work*, even though it is still rare overall compared to other terms. In the liberal media corpus the term *future of work* appears 85 times in total and 0.16 times per 10,000 tokens. 2015 shows the highest

Table 6.25 Liberal media: collocation graph of future of work MI ≥ 7, minimum collocate frequency 5

Source: Author, using #LancsBox

frequency of the term with 0.27 per 10,000 tokens, followed by 2017 (0.23). The years 2016, 2014, and 2013 show much lower relative frequency levels. Compared to the congressional material the relative frequency levels of *future of work* in the liberal media material are significantly higher, especially in certain years but also overall. In the congressional material, there were only about 12 instances where the *future of work* is mentioned as such. In the liberal media material there are about seven times as many instances. The *WSJ* material displays a low frequency of the term overall, which will be detailed in the next chapter.

The collocations of *future of work* in the liberal media material are displayed in Tables 6.25 and 6.26.[8] One of the strongest collocates is *aspen*. Together with

[8] With a minimum collocate frequency of 5 and MI ≥ 7, the bar was set back to the default setting and higher than for the congressional material as the liberal media material produced more collocates. This way fewer but stronger and more frequent collocates are part of the list.

Table 6.26 Liberal media: collocates of future of work MI ≥ 7, minimum collocate frequency 5

future of work

Freq: 85 Collocates: 13

Index	Status	Stat (03 - MI)	Collocate	▼ Stat	Freq (coll.)	Freq (corpus)
1	O	L	aspen	12.856966802373195	5	42
2	O	L	co-workers	12.78051650275932	7	62
3	O	R	initiative	10.140761350563366	5	276
4	O	L	love	9.557293211292839	7	579
5	O	R	february	9.009487729780979	12	1451
6	O	L	debate	8.759103399828627	6	863
7	O	R	issue	8.502491284279932	6	1031
8	O	L	institute	8.395975377884968	5	925
9	O	L	robot	8.12923272547216	7	1558
10	O	R	nearly	7.773383226911179	6	1709
11	O	L	working	7.302170297361436	7	2764
12	O	L	future	7.203818177965313	7	2959
13	O	L	about	7.10329350678702	32	14503

Source: Author, using #LancsBox

institute and *initiative*, these collocates refer to the Future of Work Initiative that is conducted by the Aspen Institute. There are other collocates such as *issue*, *debate,* and *about* that indicate that there are intense discussions going on around the topic of the *future of work*. *Co-workers*, *working*, and *robot* point to the technological impact on the working world and labor. *Future* is naturally a frequent collocate when the *future of work* is of concern and when many consequences of further structural and technological change for the economy are discussed.

Looking at the occurrences of *future of work* more closely in the articles from the *NYT* and the *Washington Post*, there are different themes that can be identified. For once, the **sharing economy** is a specific theme that comes up in the context of how work is changing. In fact, the sharing economy and the broader implications for the *future of work* are factors in the run-up to the presidential elections in 2016. Things like the gig character, independent work, and flexibility but also worker protections and the safety net are points that are discussed. The *future of work* is portrayed as a more flexible but also insecure future for workers. Additionally, the themes of **labor protections and the changing attitudes toward work**, the **UBI**, and the introduction of **robots** in the workplace are discussed.

In the context of the **sharing economy and the *future of work***, there is for example Juliet Schor, an expert on the sharing economy, who wrote an article in *The International New York Times* in 2013 titled *After the Jobs Disappear* in which she describes new forms of work like makerspaces and crowd working. The appeal of such a vision of work in the future is described, one that looks out for sustainability and has fewer boundaries between white- and blue-collar work. The article also states that the jobs that were lost in the Great Recession due to technological change, globalization, and financialization of the economy are unlikely to come back. Therefore, people are looking for different and nontraditional paths to work. Here, she mentions again so-called makerspaces, the sharing economy, and other "Web-based services like Couchsurfing, or Airbnb, sharing office space and working in community gardens and food co-ops." The sharing economy is mentioned as having the potential to give more meaning, autonomy, and social impact to your job, something that people yearn for. Technology is portrayed as the means to make this happen. In the end, she paints the role of the sharing economy as the "future of jobs" and as an answer to soaring inequality, a shortage of jobs, and a "fraying welfare state." The *future of work* is described as more community-based and self-providing.

This early article by Schor paints a rather positive picture of the sharing economy as a source for future jobs and meaningful work. A few years later in 2015, the picture of the sharing economy seems to have become more nuanced (more details on the treatment of the sharing economy in political and public discourse will follow in Sect. 6.3). There are several articles that mention the *future of work* and the sharing economy in the 2016 run-up to the presidential elections where the platforms are discussed more critically. For example, in *Shifting gear in the Uber wars* (2015) on washingtonpost.com by Brian Fung and Jacob Bogage, *future of work* and the sharing economy are mentioned in direct context. The article argues that instead of debating the sharing economy, Democratic and liberal debates should focus on a broader discussion around the *future of work* in the twenty-first century. Here, the *future of work* is used in the context of platform companies such as Uber. They are presented as a new but unreliable sources of income. The term "sharing" is used in quotation marks to indicate that the authors do not see it as a real sharing effort or alternative behavior. Moreover, the article mentions the ambiguous response Democrats seem to have toward Silicon Valley and the rise of the sharing economy and on-demand businesses. Organized labor is even more critical when it comes to these platform businesses. The sharing economy is seen as one factor of the *future of work* with less stability and little security. Democrats are hoping to integrate the gig economy into existing structures by proposing new protections for part-time workers and targeting companies using contractors. This way, the authors argue, Democrats try to avoid a direct fight over the drawbacks and opportunities of the digital economy. The article also mentions Republicans who reject new regulation, and support companies like Uber, their philosophy, and business practices. In general, however, Republicans are not seen as the natural ally of Silicon Valley. As said before, the authors suggest to shift the debate entirely by not focusing on individual on-demand businesses but rather on the issue of the *future of work* in the twenty-first century. This can also be crucial as the issues surrounding on-demand workers are not unique to these kinds of jobs. There are many other fields and companies that use contractors and on-demand workers. There have already been some efforts to establish policies that support small-scale on-demand businesses and workers, among them the Affordable Care Act. Democratic politicians like Mark Warner (Senator from Virginia) want to regulate the on-demand economy more directly, for example by establishing ways to access social benefits for independent workers. Bernie Sanders and Hillary Clinton are also mentioned in this context. Whereas Sanders is a strong supporter of traditional labor unions and their ideals, Clinton is described as "walking the tightrope." In general, the article raises the question for

Democrats of how to protect the middle class in a time when many of them rely on unconventional jobs that fall out of the traditional labor law system. Democrats struggle to find a way to encompass Silicon Valley's innovations that could change the world for the better, but at the same time establish a safety net for the digital economy and its workers. In the end, however, the article concludes by saying that technology is not the reason for poverty growth and inequality, but that failed social policies lead to this outcome. The article argues very strongly in favor of putting the debate around the *future of work* on a different level and to look at structures and reforms rather than individual businesses. The failure of past social policies also points to the possibility of reform and remedies for the situation. Structural change can be accompanied by smart political reform. Democrats seem to be the most likely supporters of such reforms.

Another article published in the *New York Times* in 2015 called *Uber's Much More Than Just a Ride Service in This Presidential Race* by Michael Barbaro and Ashley Parker mentions the term *future of work* again in the context of online platform companies like Uber and its political implications in the presidential race. Uber is presented as the stand-in for all platform businesses and the debates around the *future of work* at the time. Several candidates in the presidential race and their attitudes toward Uber are mentioned: Jeb Bush supports Uber's idea of self-reliance, Hillary Clinton sees some "hard questions" about job security when talking about Uber, Rand Paul sees no necessity of government regulation of the new companies, and Martin O'Malley argues for new labor laws. The term *future of work* is then related to issues around responsibilities of employers, virtues of technology, and workplace regulations. Uber is seen as a symbol of economic aspiration. At the same time, it invokes anxiety about rising inequality and the lack of good jobs. Steven Hill is quoted here as an expert in the field of sharing economy companies. The article argues that both supporters and critics of Uber seem to blur the usual demographic and ideological lines. Emphasizing their free market paradigm, Republicans, the article argues, are making attempts to win over Democratic strongholds and supporters. Democrats, on the other hand, are somewhat reluctant to criticize the digital giants over their treatment of workers too harshly because they do not want to alienate young liberal voters who like the new companies. Other companies like TaskRabbit or Airbnb are also mentioned in this regard. The Freelancers Union argues that the issues of on-demand workers will become decisive in the 2016 elections. Millennials are portrayed here as a vital electoral group that identifies heavily with new companies like Uber. As in other articles before, Democrats are portrayed as the political actors asked to find solutions for the *future of work* in the twenty-first century to ensure workers' protections while not stifling innovation and job opportunities.

Another article from the *Washington Post* from 2015 called *Bush tries to woo Silicon Valley* by Ed O'Keefe alludes again to the debate around the *future of work* and the sharing economy as a subject for the presidential candidates during the 2016 elections. Jeb Bush and Hillary Clinton both visited Silicon Valley during their campaigns. As said before, Clinton is quoted here saying that she has no problem with the likes of Uber, but that they nevertheless raise questions about the *future of work* and workplace protections. Again, the term *future of work* is heavily associated with the sharing economy and its most popular actors such as Uber or Airbnb. The article also stresses the rather close ties of Democrats and Silicon Valley, with some former Democratic politicians having moved on to work for Silicon Valley companies. Clinton's campaign stance toward Silicon Valley is again mentioned on the Washington Post Blogs in the article *Hillary Clinton's tech agenda is really a huge economic plan in disguise; The Democratic candidate wants to put high-speed Internet in every U.S. household* by Brian Fung from 2016. In that article, Fung describes Clinton's economic strategy which also takes into account disruptions through technological innovation. Ideas include flexible and portable benefits for contractors. The author claims that this is a nod to the ongoing national debate around the "future of work and increasing automation and the rise of the sharing economy." The author claims that Clinton's tech plan is detailed and ambitious with policy plans for many controversial issues, in contrast to Donald Trump who had not published a tech plan.

Another article detailing the *future of work* in the context of the sharing economy emphasizes once more that politicians are increasingly interested in and aware of the "gig economy." The *NYT* article *Politicians Turn to Start-Ups for Grasp of 'Gig Economy'* from 2015 by Katie Benner uses the term *future of work* in the context of the political debate around the concept, especially in the context of on-demand platforms and startups. The discussion includes questions about rising inequality and the security of jobs in times of a growing gig economy. Again, platforms are seen as a way to make money as a freelancer, but at the same time they lack a social benefits structure for workers. The article shows that platform companies are not only offering work in the field of ride-sharing but are moving into all sorts of spheres. This also grabs the attention of policy-makers. With some of the gig platforms becoming more well known, politicians are pushed to be more active in the debate around the *future of work* and platforms. In the article, "future of labor" is also used as a term, alluding more directly to the shifts in the nature of work, but also to uneven protections for workers based on the federalist system in the USA that lets states set most labor regulations individually. The term *future of work* is again used when talking about "the larger debate" around it, an expression that is repeatedly used in many articles.

Apart from frequent allusions to the sharing economy, there are several articles throughout the liberal media material that put the *future of work* in the context of **labor protections and the (changing) attitudes toward work**. Misclassification of workers as independent contractors and the lack of the safety net are two of the issues debated here. Additionally, a growing independent workforce points to changing attitudes toward work altogether.

The NYT article *Job Growth in Past Decades Was in Temp and Contract* by Neil Irwin from 2016 talks about job growth and the *future of work*. Again, the sharing economy is mentioned. But the author soon turns to a broader trend, namely the shift from traditional jobs to independent contracting and temporary work. The article details that most of the growth in jobs in recent years has been in nontraditional employment and that this had profound implications for social insurance because it is usually tied to the employer in the USA. The article claims that slow job recovery as well as the rise of technology has led many people to seek alternative employment. The article ends with the question whether the twentieth-century employer-based social insurance of workers will be carried over to the twenty-first century.

In the next article from the *Washington Post* from 2016 by Jenna Portnoy, *Workers' benefits compel Warner,* the social safety net issue is again picked up. Virginia Senator Mark Warner is portrayed in this article as someone who is concerned with twenty-first century worker benefits that ensure a health and retirement plan for all American workers. When workers change jobs frequently, seek alternative work on platforms, freelance, or do part-time work, receiving benefits can become a problem. Workers are thus less prepared for injuries, health issues, unexpected expenses, or retirement. Warner therefore thinks about a safety net for freelance workers. An Aspen Institute initiative for the *future of work* that studies portable benefits is also mentioned in this context. The same is discussed in a blog post on Washington Post Blogs in 2016 also by Jenna Portnoy called *Saving capitalism: A restless senator's new obsession; Mark R. Warner, the 'other senator' from Virginia, can't stop talking about the future of work* also talks about many of the points just mentioned.

The next article called *A whole new part of the sharing economy is being sued for mistreating workers* published in a Washington Post Blog article in 2015 by Brian Fung mentions the *future of work* again in the context of the sharing economy. Workers of platform services have brought a lawsuit claiming they are in fact employed and not independent. Fung paints this lawsuit as only one part of an ongoing battle between sharing economy platforms and workers. Other disputes around misclassification of workers include the company Uber for example. The term *future of work* is used in this article in the context of making the safety net work for all, also in an uncertain job market that includes freelancing and part-time jobs. Additionally, popular companies like Uber or GrubHub (a delivery service) are mentioned here in the direct context of the term *future of work.*

The article *A safety-net movement for on-demand workers* by Lydia DePillis from 2015 in the *Washington Post* mentions the term *future of work* once more in the context of the Aspen Institute's *Future of Work Initiative*. The Aspen Institute tries to present ways to combine the on-demand or gig economy that consumers love with worker protections. The Labor Department also focuses on the *future of work* with a special *Future of Work* symposium held in Washington. The article states that although the number of people working exclusively on platforms is small, it could grow exponentially over time. The Aspen Institute tries to bring together two separate camps: those who think most platform workers are misclassified and should be employees, and the other camp who want to protect platform businesses from having to employ workers. Yet, there is a discussion about a middle road. The Hamilton Project is also mentioned here. They introduce the idea of a new category in labor law, the "independent worker," encompassing some employee protections but not all. However, there is also criticism of this approach for example by the National Employment Law Project. They argue that inventing a whole new worker category for a relatively small number of people in the labor market could be overreaching.

In *Future tense: Concern about the quantity and quality of future jobs* by Jared Bernstein on the Washington Post Blogs from 2015, the term *future of work* is again used in the context of future policy-making in the area of labor law. The author sees no need to worry about the rise of robots, but rather about the right policy when addressing the *future of work*. He argues that there is the potential to steer the *future of work* in a certain direction when quantity and quality of jobs are supported by public policy. This policy should be directed at fighting growing inequality and should support bargaining power, the article argues. Robust consumer demand can be a source of growth, but only if people have enough income to spend. If growth remains robust, new jobs are created but their quality is often decided outside of the market through policy. For freelancers, it is essential to determine how they are classified, if they can get health coverage, and if they can organize collectively. These possibilities are often out of reach for independent workers, as seen in Uber's business model (*Uber's Business Model Could Change Your Work* by Farhad Manjoo from 2015 in the *New York Times*).

The "Uberization" is mentioned several times in the context of the *future of work*. Platforms like Uber have the potential to upend traditional job descriptions and ways of working by using and implementing dynamic measures of supply and demand, performance tracking, or customer satisfaction data. Uber is the prime example of a company using these tracking measures on workers. Now, it is copied by other firms in different settings. Again, the article alludes to the fact that new streams of income and flexible work arrangements are upsides of this economy. Arun Sundararajan is quoted as a supporter of sharing economy platforms. On the downsides are less security, less regulation, and no further career prospects. Robert Reich is quoted saying he considers the new way of business-making nonsense and advocates instead for well-paying, regular jobs, which most of the on-demand workers would prefer. The article further states that the larger concern relevant for the *future of work* is not necessarily a lack of benefits but a lack of agency. In a future when computers or algorithms decide for you what to do, when to do it, and how much you earn, the concern for efficiency trumps workers' concerns. The author goes on to say that being tracked by algorithms and monetizing one's downtime on Uber or other platforms, as some experts would suggest, is a hellish scenario.

Another article in the *NYT* from 2015 takes a totally different approach and talks about another model that could point into a more positive *future of work* using the "Hollywood model" as an example, which was already mentioned in the previous chapter (*What Hollywood Can Teach Us about the Future of Work* by Adam Davidson). The article presents a form of work that is common in Hollywood but that could be a model for other branches as well in order to achieve more quality for independent work. The so-called Hollywood model is a form of work that is project-based, where a team is assembled for exact tasks, works precisely together, and is disbanded at the end of the project. This model is contrasted with the corporate model that looks for long-term workers with open-ended jobs, or the gig economy model that takes care of very short-term tasks without any further engagement. The

Hollywood model is used, according to the article, in construction, restaurant startups, or cosmetic companies, where temporary teams of specialists are needed. The article claims that our working lives are moving into the direction of the Hollywood model because we are exiting the era of mass production when physical capital was key. The Hollywood model is far more adaptable to specific products. Management and owners of capital could benefit from such a more flexible model. But the author claims that from his observations on (actual) Hollywood sets, workers can also benefit from this arrangement. Workers on the sets, from make-up to construction, are highly organized in unions and are in high demand, both of which guarantees good wages. The article also claims that automation, although essential to Hollywood production, has had a less disruptive impact because of the project-based model. Technology is adapted by the individual craftsman or -woman to use on the project and does not require large capital investment. The author goes on to say that we are entering the era of the human–robot partnership, in which humans figure out what needs to be done and then letting the robot do the task.

Apart from new forms of project-based work in the sharing economy or in other models, the term *future of work* also occurs in the context of the **universal basic income (UBI)**. An article in the *NYT* from 2016 called *A Plan in Case Robots Take the Jobs: Give Everyone a Basic Income* by Farhad Manjoo elaborates on the idea of automation and its effect on employment in the future. Taking a rather hypothetical stance, the article imagines a future when robots take over most tasks, making humans redundant. In such a future scenario, another form of income is needed. Thus, the idea of the UBI is brought up. The UBI is supported by many tech entrepreneurs, but also by some libertarians, conservatives, and progressives. In an idealistic future, machines take over manual labor and humans are able to become artists, scholars, or entrepreneurs, the article suggests. But reality is different: The *future of work,* again related to developments like gig work, makes people feel uncertain about their future. Although technology has created jobs, the rise of the gig economy and companies like Uber points to a more insecure future. People now seem to realize that the *future of work* is a much more immediate concern for them and they begin to think about possible solutions to this uncertainty in the form of the UBI, for instance.

The 2017 article in the NYT called *Capitalism Has a Problem. Is Free Money the Answer?* by Peter S. Goodman also talks about the UBI. In this article, the term *future of work* is mentioned in the context of automation and a loss of well-paying jobs. This explains some of the interest in the UBI idea. The article states that capitalism is facing the problem that there are not enough well-paying jobs in the world anymore and that workers are increasingly worried about maintaining their lifestyle. In order to tame populist backlash, many advocate in favor of a universal basic income to "soften the edges of capitalism." The idea of the UBI is gaining momentum around the world, with many trials being initiated in different cities and regions around the globe. However, affordability of the UBI remains an issue. In the USA, for example, handing everyone \$10,000 every year, which would still be well under the poverty line, would mean eight times the spending of social services today. Labor leaders are also critical of such a provision, as it devalues work. They also fear that poor people would be worse off with other provisions being abandoned in favor of the UBI. The article also mentions Silicon Valley leaders pushing the UBI idea in order to tame the consequences of their own making, namely more automated technology. Advocates of the UBI paint it as freeing people from the bureaucracies of the welfare system and letting them decide what best to do with their money. The article claims the UBI is also witnessing such momentum because of the ever widening gap between the rich and the poor. Another article from the same year shows again that the UBI is a favorite topic of the Silicon Valley tech elite who tries to find answers to the consequences of technological progress (NYT, 2017, *The Future of Not Working, The Future of Work* by Annie Lowrey).

In other articles that deal with the *future of work*, the potential of **robots** is discussed. Are they going to lead us into a future without enough jobs for humans? How will education have to change to give workers the right skills to succeed in such a future scenario?

In 2014 on washingtonpost.com, the article *Will robots destroy jobs, or create them?* details some expert views on potential job loss in the future. The experts are rather divided with about 52% of them not seeing robots displacing most jobs, while 48% have a more dystopian view. The article mentions a PEW research study that implies that the new waves of technological change could hit people differently than anticipated. Change may happen quickly, making it hard to adjust. This could create a larger gap between winners and losers of this change. The basis of the report were open-ended questions about the impact of robotics and artificial intelligence on the *future of work* that were put to 12,000 tech experts, Internet analysts, and members of the public concerned with technological trends. The answers ranged from "not concerned" to "very alarmed."

As mentioned before, there are several conferences and workshops on the *future of work* that also look at the potential of machines and robots. One of them is mentioned in the *NYT* article from 2015 called *After Jobs Dry Up, What Then?* by Katrin Bennhold. The article details that economic growth is no longer a good indicator of economic well-being as growth has created fewer jobs of lower quality than in the past. The article states that "the main metrics for economic success now appear to be decoupling from labor markets, the main source of income and meaning for citizens." The term *future of work* is used here to refer to what some call a new industrial revolution or the Second Machine Age. These processes point to the growing influence of machines and computers on the world of work, which could lead to human work becoming scarcer. The article mentions a famous study conducted by Oxford economists claiming that 74% of employment in the USA is susceptible to automation over the next 20 years. In order to address the issue of fewer jobs and lower pay, the aforementioned basic income or the negative income tax is discussed, an idea spread by the likes of Milton Friedman. Other experts are quoted arguing in favor of the Nordic model of flexible labor markets and a strong social safety net. However, both the Nordic model and a basic income would require fundamental rethinking in countries such as the USA.

How *Thriving in the Robot Workplace* will be possible is the topic of another article by Alexandra Levit in the *NYT* from 2016. In this article, the term *future of work* appears together with automation and people's fears of job loss through robots. However, according to the article, there will always be certain jobs that require a lot of human interaction such as teaching or caregiving which are not easily automatable. Yet, with the advances of machines in areas of "emotional intelligence" through deep learning mechanisms and new "social robotics," even these areas could face the introduction of robots. But even though there are many advances in the area of social services it might take decades before these machines are really adopted. Through lifelong learning, the author claims, humans will find the roles best suited to their qualities.

In *Learning to Love Our Robot Co-Worker; The Future of Work*, by Kim Tingley from 2017, the author describes some of these new qualities such as humans adjusting to work with and alongside robots. In this article, the author alludes to the fact that many people feel threatened by the future we might face. That is why many manufacturing workers have voted for Donald Trump who promised to bring back the jobs that were lost in recent years. However, these jobs cannot and will not come back because many of them were automated. The manufacturing industry has become much more productive in recent years, but employment is decreasing. Robots are not only coming to the factory floor, but to all branches of life. There are even more collaborative robots who are designed to take up more flexible roles and are easier to integrate with human employees. The article presents different views of how robots might impact the future, from a bleak outlook of robots taking over, to the idea that we will work alongside them, to everything in between. Which scenario will be fulfilled depends on the adoption processes, and future laws and regulations.

When talking about the *future of work* and robots, education is also a major topic. The *NYT* article *How to Prepare for an Automated Future; Robot Revolution*, from 2017 by Claire Cain Miller, highlights the need for adequate education when it comes to the *future of work* and claims that it is questionable if the right institutions will emerge in time to train workers. The author claims that although we do not know how fast and how many jobs machines will displace, we know that this impact will happen eventually, and it will happen to many branches in the economy. The logical consequence would be to educate people differently so they will be able to compete in the labor market and work alongside robots or other machines. Experts are confident that new skills can be identified, and people can be trained. However, the political will and the funding for a shift in educational reform is often missing, according to the article. College will remain a vital source for education and skill training, as automation will require higher education. However, just any degree will not do. Education from other sources seems to be needed as well. Lifelong learning will be required for workers in order to maintain a career. Experts remain optimistic about the amount of jobs available if people pick up the skills necessary. Here the term "future of jobs" is used in the context of future optimism. However, the article also features more pessimistic expert views saying that in the future we will need to think about ways to share wealth when many people might be forced out of the workforce and their occupations become redundant.

Education is again the main topic in the *Washington Post* article *Preparing college students for the automated future* by Jeffrey J. Selingo from 2017. In this article, automation is identified as the bigger job killer than outsourcing or immigration. Former President Barack Obama's farewell speech is quoted, saying that the next wave of economic dislocation will come from automation in the workplace. Fears of job loss have always accompanied technological advances. So far, education has been a way out. However, the article claims that it is unclear if the same is true today. Therefore, the *future of work* will require new ways of thinking in higher education. Very few institutions of higher education are actually preparing for the changes of the *future of work*, which is already problematic for students today. It would be especially important to teach technical and social skills together so that people will be able to switch between jobs and tasks. These skills include coding and data analytics, but also creativity, entrepreneurship, ethics, and culture. The article states that if higher education institutions manage to train students differently, the *future of work* might not be as bleak as some people fear.

A year later, newly elected President Donald Trump takes a different stance, blaming Mexico and China for the job loss in the USA (Washington Post Blog, 2017, *Coming technology will likely destroy millions of jobs. Is Trump ready? We need to develop an American Dream 2.0 for how society can function in the Smart Machine Age).* The article details that President Trump has not addressed the impact of technology on the US job market to any great extent. Here, the term *future of work* is used in allusion to upholding the American Dream, despite deep societal changes through technology.

In the liberal media material, we can find several instances in which the term *future of work* occurs and is discussed. Compared to both the congressional and the *WSJ* material that will follow in the next chapter, there are many more occurrences and specific themes that are associated with the *future of work*. What is quite apparent is that the sharing economy is seen as one significant aspect of the *future of work* that also points to larger developments. The sharing or gig economy provides flexible ways to work on an independent (contractor) basis. The group of independents in the workforce is growing overall, not only the group of platform workers. This points to, on the one hand, the demand for flexible work and income; on the other hand, it raises questions about social provisions and security for these workers. If the future will bring a more independent workforce, the liberal media outlets see it as the task of political actors, especially Democrats, to find answers to these new challenges.

Some of the articles argue for a large-scale shift in the debates among liberals to address the *future of work* more broadly instead of concentrating on individual market actors like Uber. Republicans seem to be more willing to accept the status quo and often reject new regulation in the labor market, at least so far. During the 2015–2016 election cycle, the implications of companies like Uber on the *future of work* and the "future of income" were already discussed to some extent. Uber is often used as a stand-in for all the gig and sharing economy platforms which have a big influence on the labor market already. The growth of these platforms points to the fact that it has become more common to rely on a flexible workforce. The

"Hollywood model" of project-based work is presented as a more desirable alternative to the gig environment, championing independent specialists who are unionized and well-paid.

Apart from the sharing economy and a more flexible workforce in the future, the liberal media outlets also discuss other topics when it comes to the *future of work*. For instance, the consequences of ongoing automation and in this regard the large-scale entry of robots in the workplace are debated. In this context, many articles talk about a new relationship of humans and robots. Workers need to prepare for a more automated workplace where they will work alongside or with robots as they will enter all kinds of branches. This will also require different and more specific training. Judging from views expressed in the material investigated in this chapter, many remain doubtful that the current American education system can deliver the training opportunities needed to succeed in a more automated future. It also remains somewhat opaque which skills will be safe from automation in the future and which skills will provide a good income and switching between jobs and tasks.

With the entry of algorithms and more machines into the workplace, fears of replacement will prevail. The extent of the replacement or the changing nature of work is yet unknown. No matter if these concerns are actually valid or not, there are debates about future scenarios when jobs become scarce and machines have replaced many human workers who will not be able to find another comparable occupation. In this context, the idea of the universal basic income gains traction, especially among the tech elite in Silicon Valley. It is an unlikely coalition of entrepreneurs, progressives, libertarians, and conservative economists who have advocated for something like a basic income over the years. It seems like the tech leaders are becoming uneasy about the impact of some of their own innovations, while libertarians and conservatives have always aimed to replace the established welfare system with something resembling a basic income. However, not all progressives support the idea of the UBI. Especially labor leaders generally reject the idea of an unconditional basic income. They are concerned about the devaluing effect on work and that a UBI would wipe out all other welfare provisions for the poor, while being much more expensive than the current social security system.

The material in the liberal media corpus also included allusions to the fact that blaming immigration and trade for the loss of jobs, for instance, in the manufacturing sector as Donald Trump has done, will not help workers in the future. Automation has wiped out many more jobs than trade or migration, but so far there seems to be no consensus among lawmakers about how to address this future coherently.

6.2.3 *Future of Work in the* WSJ *Material*

In the *Wall Street Journal* (*WSJ*) material that was investigated for this book, the term *future of work* appears very rarely with a total of 12 times and a relative frequency of 0.07 per 10,000 tokens overall. There is very little variation of this very low frequency over the years with the highest relative frequency score in the

Table 6.27 *WSJ*: collocation graph of future of work MI ≥ 5, minimum collocate frequency 2

Source: Author, using #LancsBox

year 2017 (0.19 per 10,000 tokens). Thus, one can see that in comparison to the liberal media material, the *WSJ* talks in a much more limited fashion about the *future of work* as a term.

In Tables 6.27 and 6.28, the collocations of *future of work* in the *WSJ* are displayed.[9] Apart from several function words like *which, if, we, do, for,* etc., there are some more interesting collocates as well. For example, *flexible*, *prepare*, and *workers* indicate that the *future of work* is becoming more *flexible* for *workers* who need to *prepare* for this new situation. Additionally, there are *vanguard*, *san francisco*, *american*, and *automation* that point to dynamism and innovation (*vanguard*) in the economy and the American center of avant-garde technology (*San Francisco*), where a lot of the new applications (*automation*) are developed. *Cognizant* as a collocate is a proper name. It is mentioned in the article *Management: A Future Without Jobs? Think Again—Artificial Intelligence and automation will create new roles for humans, studies say* by Vanessa Fuhrmans from 2017 that

[9]The minimum collocate frequency was set to 2 and the MI ≥ 5. Most of the collocates displayed here only appear twice in the *WSJ* material.

Table 6.28 *WSJ*: collocates of future of work MI ≥ 5, minimum collocate frequency 2

future of work

Freq: 12 Collocates: 31

Index	Status	Stat (03 - MI)	Collocate	▼ Stat	Freq (coll.)	Freq (corpus)
1	O	L	cognizant's	17.149118066197037	2	2
2	O	R	jane	15.827164808974981	2	5
3	O	R	supervisor	14.242219083094856	2	15
4	O	R	n't,	14.14910233968642	2	16
5	O	L	prepare	12.959281443129177	4	73
6	O	L	vanguard	12.171828157591152	2	63
7	O	L	flexible	12.126736704164605	2	65
8	O	R	kim	11.999358542669684	2	71
9	O	R	cognizant	11.979182580395278	2	72
10	O	R	released	10.872981485544786	2	155
11	O	L	light	10.143481278458692	2	257
12	O	L	americans	9.689674295240973	2	352
13	O	R	francisco	9.390882938531915	2	433
14	O	L	center	9.364471523808122	2	441
15	O	R	san	8.908314880649202	2	605
16	O	L	american	8.67134797728315	2	713
17	O	R	being	8.324147535104425	2	907
18	O	R	do	8.274124793846639	4	1878
19	O	R	only	7.815950817363493	2	1290
20	O	L	automation	7.5811500560224205	2	1518
21	O	R	two	7.521572252623046	2	1582
22	O	L	workers	7.2787415181112305	2	1872
23	O	R	all	6.887598918856631	2	2455
24	O	R	if	6.772438128117447	2	2659
25	O	R	people	6.615289838106889	2	2965
26	O	R	other	6.552916444039385	2	3096
27	O	R	who	6.371850850815745	2	3510
28	O	R	we	6.221698598795134	2	3895
29	O	R	which	6.067289917911588	2	4335
30	O	L	for	5.65117122024107	6	17353
31	O	L	new	5.534856459584229	2	6270

Source: Author, using #LancsBox

mentions the *Cognizant's Center for the Future of Work*. In general, the collocates of *future of work* in the *WSJ* material seem to be less specific than in the liberal media material, which is hardly surprising given that there are only about 12 instances where the term actually occurs in the material.

Looking a little more closely at the *WSJ* material, one can see that in the year 2017 the term *future of work* occurs the most (0.19 per 10,000 tokens), for example, in the article *Management: Increasingly, Automation Reshapes Workplace Tasks* (2017) by Lauren Weber. Here, the author describes the World Economic Forum in Davos and how automation and the *future of work* are increasingly discussed at such events, even introducing special reports on the matter. The article mentions a study by McKinsey Global Institute which projects a maximum of 5% of jobs being totally taken over by machines. The report argues that most jobs will not be replaced but rather change dramatically, "forcing workers to adapt." Through this development, productivity will increase on a global scale. The article further looks at who benefits from this development through a report by Accenture. The report concludes that it is up to corporate leaders to help workers make use of their "human" skills such as social and emotional intelligence in the future. Strategic retraining could reduce the vulnerability to job loss. When asking workers, most feel optimistic about automation. However, many of the featured respondents, about half of them, were highly skilled, and the rest was split into low- and middle-skilled workers. Highly skilled workers might be more optimistic about their future given the benefit of higher education on the job market. The article also mentions that one in four workers does not know which skills are necessary in the future. It makes sense, the article claims, that highly skilled workers are much more confident about the future when it comes to replacement of their jobs as they are engaged in more complex tasks or have an easier time switching between jobs. For lower-skilled workers, this might be more complicated.

In several letters to the editor of the *WSJ* from 2017, the theme of the *future of work* is also addressed. In *The Decline of Human Labor is Dangerous*, several letters by readers are published who see the *future of work* as rather threatening. One of the readers speaks from personal experience as a robotic-equipment manufacturer who has seen the development in the field firsthand. The reader argues that today's technological power has exceeded many dreams and visions of what was thought to be achievable. The reader does not think that robots will take away all jobs; there are going to be new and interesting ones as well. But he sees a threshold "in a race to the bottom cycle" that drives the value of labor down dramatically. Even the threat of such a situation is the reason we should not just wait and see what happens, according to the reader. In the next letter, the prevalence of service jobs is discussed. Most people in these jobs do not earn a sustainable living wage. This reader is worried about the development of inequality with the outlook that only those people will thrive who happen to own stocks in automation industries or who have the educational skills of a high-profile worker. The service sector workforce will likely not benefit from a more automated future. The last letter mentions the term *future of work* literally, saying that the USA owes it to the American workers to prepare them for this *future of work*. The reader is worried about the potentially devastating effect of accelerated automation in the USA in the near future, which must be addressed. The reader is unsure if a surge in service industry jobs will benefit masses of American workers. Retraining could be an opportunity. But the reader certainly does not appreciate a wait-and-see attitude toward the problem.

In another article detailing letters to the editor (*San Francisco is Right about $15 Minimum* from 2017), a different reader expresses her concern about the *future of work* and further automation in the context of the minimum wage. She thinks that opposing the minimum wage sends the wrong signal and does nothing to prepare the workforce for the future. The opposition to a higher minimum wage which argues that it is not affordable basically presents people with the (impossible) choice between a low wage or no job at all. The challenge is to provide all levels of workers with the training and skills needed to earn a decent wage. The reader sees the minimum wage rather as a safety net, a bare minimum for people to get by, than a path toward the middle class. She is of the opinion that a "robot tax" is a way to pay for an expansion of skills training and lifelong learning opportunities in order to prepare the American worker for the *future of work.*

In opposition to what some concerned readers express, a different article in the *WSJ* paints a picture of the *future of work* where automation will create more jobs than it will replace. *Management: A Future Without Jobs? Think Again—Artificial Intelligence and automation will create new roles for humans, studies say* by Vanessa Fuhrmans from 2017 uses the term *future of work* in the context of the Cognizant's Center for the Future of Work. The center looks at, for instance, which types of jobs will disappear due to automation. The article mentions several opinions about the *future of work,* for instance citing Elon Musk who thinks that little human work will survive further automation surges and therefore argues in favor of a universal social safety net to "maintain economic order" (in other instances, this would be called a UBI). However, the article does not agree with this notion and goes on to say that there will be more jobs emerging than disappearing. Especially in building and around AI, humans are still needed in crucial roles. The article argues that jobs that were lost in retail have been replaced in "fulfillment centers" (Amazon warehouses) and that the number of jobs being created largely depends on business investment in their own workforce, on the demand for certain products and services, and on decisions made by workers themselves. Michael Reich, an economist from Berkeley, is cited here saying that business has a limited desire to replace all workers with robots as the economic cycle only works if there are people able to buy the products of the business. Future jobs will likely help to manage AI and automation. These would be high-skilled workers. On the low-skill level, the article sees a rising demand for gig workers and people tending to older people on-demand. The article includes estimates of about 19 million jobs disappearing and 21 million jobs being created over the next 15 years. Although more jobs are being created in the future, the situation is unlikely to go by without painful upheavals in the job market, according to the article.

The article *Artificial Intelligence Company B12 Raises $12.4 M* from 2016 by Cat Zakrewski also presents a rather positive outlook when it comes to the *future of work* overall. Many innovations will be created, especially in the field of AI and workers will profit from this. The company B12 is mentioned here as an example of using AI to augment human work rather than replacing it, a development that is attracting a lot of capital. The startup does not use machine learning in the classical sense and is not getting rid of the human factor, but rather tries to make the human input more efficient. Those types of companies are located in customer support, marketing, or security. The startup claims that human-assisted intelligence is the actual *future of work,* not total automation and replacement.

Apart from the articles focusing on machine-assisted work or entirely new jobs in the future, there are two articles in the *WSJ* material that mention the sharing or "on-demand economy" in the context of the *future of work.* The first is *On-Demand Workers: We are Not Robots—Is Technology Liberating or Squeezing The New Class of Freelance Labor?* by Lauren Weber and Rachel Emma Silverman from 2015. The article talks about the *future of work* in the context of micro-entrepreneurs and flexibility. Mentioning Uber and TaskRabbit by name, the authors describe the new forms of work as flexible and autonomous. Workers are only engaged at times and in jobs they desire. However, the article mentions a load of lawsuits and protests around these new companies and forms of work. From some workers' point of view, the companies issue too much control over them and give them no choice but to comply with business practices while also having to cover all financial and personal risk. The article alludes to the ambivalence of these jobs, stating that many gig workers like the extra flexible income, while some might be concerned about the isolation and confusion triggered by these platforms. The ongoing (legal) conflicts around the classification of workers are mentioned in the article as well. The often-cited argument that "app-enabled workers" on digital platforms do not seem to fit into the existing regulatory categories, namely employed or independent, is repeated in this article. Yet, the author does not see any broad new labor laws on the horizon. Thus, courts will continue to face cases on the matter and will be asked to resolve the issues. The article also mentions the growing number of freelance and independent workers in the USA overall (at least working independently to some extent) and the ongoing fight between some of the workers, their representatives (mostly in web-based communities), and the companies. Companies emphasize how people like the flexibility of the work arrangements, while many critics say that the pay and structure is not fair.

Another article on the *future of work* and sharing economy platforms called *Boss Talk: TaskRabbit Chief Aims to Recast Freelance Work; CEO Says Startups Need to Do More to Protect Workers* by Elizabeth Dwoskin from 2014 features Leah Busque, founder of TaskRabbit. She talks about the power of algorithms in the future which are going to take over a lot of decision-making processes. Apart from that, she talks about how to reform the freelance economy. For example, freelance workers on TaskRabbit can now access discounts on health insurance over TaskRabbit and the platform introduced a base wage on the site. Here, the term *future of work* appears again in the context of more flexibility and its upsides and downsides for workers. Apparently, Leah Busque does not think that automation will replace human work, but it might change the way people engage in work. She sees micro-entrepreneurs working through platforms like TaskRabbit as the future for workers. The platforms and the technology will enable a flexible workforce. In the interview, she argues, however, that access to social benefits in this new economy needs to be improved.

As said before, the term *future of work* is rather rare in the *WSJ* material. Most of the time, the term only appears later in the corpus, especially in the material from 2017. Only recently, the term *future of work* seems to have become a fixed expression in the debate around a more automated future and its implications on the labor force. In general, the *WSJ* as a more conservative and business-oriented newspaper seems to be less concerned with the plight of the future workforce than the more liberal outlets. It seems natural for the *WSJ* to emphasize the business side rather than the labor side when talking about the future. The articles mentioned above look at some of the well-known problems of gig workers, like classification issues and lawsuits, but generally see independent workers as a big part of the *future of work* overall. Flexibility is the overarching theme, which is generally seen as more positive than negative. Workers seem to demand more flexibility, and therefore, they engage in things like platform work. This is likely to increase in the future.

Apart from a growing flexible workforce, the term *future of work* is associated with automation more generally. The *WSJ* mentions several reports and studies that do not see large-scale replacement of jobs in the future, but rather a changing nature of jobs and work. In the *WSJ* material a more automated future is seen as positive with a more high-skilled workforce benefitting from this development. Ideas like a basic income are not discussed at any length. In fact, it is only mentioned when alluding to ideas of Silicon Valley leaders like Elon Musk, but is painted as a rather outlandish idea because automation will most likely produce more jobs than it will replace. However, skill sets need to change. In order to get a more skilled workforce, the articles also allude to businesses' obligation to invest in their workforce if they want to stay on top in the future. This could benefit the business and the labor side in the long run. Therefore, for the *WSJ*, there not only needs to be a state-funded educational infrastructure, but there is also a need to act on the business side. Interestingly, the readers who sent letters to the editor and were published in the *WSJ* seem to be more concerned about the future of the American worker, seeing automation as a fast-moving threat that could entail unintended consequences. Especially the growth of the low-skilled, low-pay service sector in the USA is of concern to these readers because these jobs cannot serve as a source for an adequate income or career path in the long run.

6.2.4 Future of Work in Political and Public Discourse

Overall, there are important differences in the treatment of the term *future of work* in the sources investigated in this book. First of all, the extent of the treatment of the subject differs across the sources. The congressional material investigated here does not feature many occurrences of the term *future of work* overall. The Senate hearings mention the term in general allusions to the future in the economy under more technological change like augmented reality, as well as the sustainability of the American security systems and dynamism of the American economy. The hearings in the House seem to be a little more specific than the hearings in the Senate. The sharing economy is a specific topic in this case, pointing to a more flexible workforce in the future. In general, the *future of work* is both innovative and disruptive with uncertain effects on the labor force. Disruption, it seems, is seen through the lens of "creative destruction" delivering new and better jobs and products, rather than fatalistic destruction. Lawmakers see the possibility of benefits for consumers, workers, and communities in the future, as well as a more independent and high-skilled workforce. Issues surrounding this development are mentioned but remain minor next to the benefits for the future.

The *WSJ* material is also quite limited in the discussion around the *future of work*. Just like in the congressional material, there are very few actual occurrences of the term in the articles examined. When the term *future of work* appears, the debate revolves around the topics of flexibility in the labor market embodied in the growth of the gig economy and the independent workforce. In general, the *WSJ* does not support the notion that there is going to be large-scale replacement of jobs through automation in the future. Rather, more jobs will be created than lost. Yet, the *WSJ* does see the need for better and different education, also arguing in favor of businesses investing more into a skilled workforce that is needed to succeed in the future. Some of the occurrences of *future of work* in the *WSJ* material are actually part of letters to the editor with readers expressing more concern about the *future of work* than the *WSJ* as an outlet itself. In any case, the *WSJ* seems to be less concerned with the outlook of the workforce in the future than the liberal media outlets. The *WSJ* would most likely argue that this wave of innovation and automation is not different when compared to the past, which makes fears of a more automated future redundant and new policy approaches such as the UBI unnecessary.

The liberal media outlets seem to be more concerned about the *future of work*. First of all, there are many more instances where the term occurs. The extent of usage and the discussion around the term is larger and more specific. The debate is concerned with different issues. One of them clearly is the sharing economy and its impact on the workforce and economy overall. The growing independent workforce that can be seen in the rise of the sharing economy points to changing attitudes toward work. On the one hand, people value flexibility and easy access to additional income. On the other hand, a more independent workforce also raises questions about labor law, classification, and the provision of social benefits. According to the liberal media material, many independents would actually prefer a stable job and income if they had access to better quality jobs. Democrats and liberals are portrayed as being more concerned with these issues than Republicans and Democrats will be asked to find a more coherent answer to Silicon Valley innovations. Some articles in the liberal media material argue, however, that Democrats should not focus on the impact of individual businesses like Uber but should rather shift the discussion in order to take into account broader issues. What will the *future of work* and income actually look like and how can it be steered in a beneficial direction for consumers, workers, and businesses? More flexible forms of work can be positive for all sides if access to training, good pay, and career paths are actually possible. So far, Democrats have shown an ambiguous approach to Silicon Valley as many of the tech leaders and young consumers who value the new products and digital services are important electoral supporters. Many Democrats are therefore hesitant to treat big tech and their impact too harshly.

Apart from the sharing economy, the political response to Silicon Valley, and a more flexible workforce, the *future of work* is also discussed in the context of ongoing automation and the introduction of robots in the workplace in the liberal media material. Workers will most likely face a different relationship with robots in the future, increasingly working with and alongside them. Specific training and higher education will be necessary in order to give workers access to the skills for this future. At the moment, it is questionable if the American education system is capable of doing that.

Even if it remains unclear whether the future will actually see large-scale replacement of jobs, policies addressing such a scenario are also discussed in the liberal media material. Apart from reforms of social security provisions (portable benefits), the UBI is a topic that is picked up in more recent articles. As a topic, it is driven by the tech elite in Silicon Valley who seem to become aware of the impact their own technologies might have on the *future of work* and jobs. Yet, it is not only tech leaders but also political progressives and libertarians who are interested in the idea of an unconditional basic income. Libertarians and business-friendly actors see the UBI as a chance to replace the social security system as it is. Labor leaders are decidedly less excited about such an idea, pointing to the value of work and the necessity to support people through the existing welfare state programs. In some instances, the UBI is portrayed as an innovative idea to "free" people from mundane work and to give them the liberty to pursue the lifestyle they desire. Yet, this notion seems to neglect the importance of work as a purpose in life, which is a very strong component of American culture.

Although the UBI is not directly discussed in this way in the sources investigated here, it also seems possible that certain actors in the USA argue in favor of the UBI in order to build a stronger social safety net. Because welfare provisions were slashed in the last welfare reform in the 1990s, it has become increasingly apparent that a social safety net which provides a more long-term minimum basic income to the American people is missing. Additionally, the reform was rather unsuccessful in regard to active labor market policies. If in the not-so-distant future many people are displaced by machines in a short amount of time without the means of an activating welfare state to transition them into new employment, the lack of a safety net could become even more painful for many Americans. Large parts of the population already feel frustrated with their economic outlook and lack economic security, which turns out to be a large factor in their electoral choice as well. Yet, both the UBI and a more activating welfare state would mean a fundamental rethinking in the USA, which is not apparent.

Although the *future of work* as a term and topic seems to become more pronounced in both the political and public discourse over time, which is supported by more occurrences of the term in the corpus data after 2015, there seems to be a lack of a coherent answer to it. Apart from the UBI, which seems to be mainly supported by a small group of tech entrepreneurs and Silicon Valley thinkers today and repeated calls for improved education in the future, specific solutions are hardly discussed and the lack of bipartisan efforts makes it unlikely that this will change any time soon. The "traditional" narrative around automation, namely that more jobs will eventually be created than lost, seems to lead to the "wait-and-see" attitude that many *WSJ* readers were concerned about.

6.3 Platform Economy

After having looked at the overall trends of *digitization* and *automation*, as well as the more specific term *future of work* in political and public discourse, this part of the book will investigate the category of the *platform economy* in more depth. The *platform economy* has entered the debate around technological progress and its impact on the economy in recent years. The term implies all kinds of developments which will be detailed in the following chapters. One such aspect is that work arrangements are changing and are becoming more diverse, which could already be seen in allusions to the *future of work* in the previous chapter. The group of independents is growing among the US workforce and one aspect of this is platform work. Additionally, many platforms have entered our daily lives and have become ubiquitous in all kinds of spheres from communication to banking, payment systems, traveling, or shopping. As the frequency analysis has already shown, the terms around the *platform economy* are used to a very different extent. In the following, the terms *sharing economy, gig economy,* and *platform economy* will be discussed separately and in the contexts they occur in. First, corpus data, more precisely collocate data from the different corpora, will be discussed, followed by a more in-depth reading of the context of the terms and how their use might differ from term to term and from source to source.

6.3.1 Platform Economy in the Congressional Material

When looking at the results of the frequency analysis concerning the terms *sharing economy*, *gig economy*, and *platform economy* in the congressional material, the term *sharing economy* is the most common among them in the hearings from the House. In total, *sharing economy* occurs 300 times in 15 out of 151 files (0.59 per 10,000 tokens), *gig economy* appears 39 times in 6 out of 151 files (0.08 per 10,000 tokens), and *platform economy* appears 69 times in 2 out of 151 files (0.14 per 10,000 tokens). *Platform economy* appears to be more common than *gig economy*, yet it only appears in two hearings overall. In the Senate hearings included in the corpus, *gig economy* and *sharing economy* occur at the same rate, whereas *platform economy* does not appear at all. *Gig economy* appears 15 times in 7 out of 90 files from the Senate (0.04 per 10,000 tokens), and *sharing economy* appears 15 times as well, in 9 out of 90 different hearings from the Senate (0.04 per 10,000 tokens). Taking the corpora of congressional hearings as the basis, one is safe to say that the term *sharing economy* is the most frequently used term among the three. *Gig economy* follows, whereas *platform economy* is virtually not used at all (other terms are used even less). As mentioned before, the appearances of the terms were very limited before 2015, which indicates that the sharing economy platforms are still a rather recent trend.

First, the Senate data will be examined more closely before moving on to the data from the House.

6.3.1.1 Sharing Economy in the Senate Data

The most strongly associated collocate[10] of *sharing economy* in the Senate data is *gig*. "Strong collocate" means that the combination of words does not necessarily appear frequently, but if the terms appear they do so most likely in the company of one another. Thus, when *sharing economy* appears in the Senate data, *gig* is likely to appear as well. This points to the fact that the *gig* work nature is strongly associated with the *sharing economy* and it might also point to the fact that *sharing* and *gig economy* are often used interchangeably. In fact, the "*gig* or *sharing economy* platforms" are often mentioned together in this way in the congressional and media material. *Workshop* as a collocate appears because different workshops on the *sharing economy* were held in Washington D.C. by different actors over the years, for example by the Federal Trade Commission (FTC). *Platforms* itself also appears as a collocate, which together with *internet*, *economy*, *companies*, and *job* alludes to the economic side of the *sharing economy*. It is noteworthy that words alluding to collaboration or sustainability are not found in the list. The collocates *rise*, *new*, *will*, and *issues* seem to refer to the very recent nature of the *sharing economy* and to future implications it could have (Tables 6.29 and 6.30).

Moving on to the contextual analysis of the term *sharing economy* in the Senate data, it is rather clear that the hearings featuring the term are not specifically concerned with the *sharing economy* as such. Rather, the term appears in the discussion of other topics and trends such as **disruptive technology, millennials, labor participation**, or regulation and (digital) **trade** more broadly.

The term *sharing economy* appears, for example, in *Oversight of the Federal Trade Commission* (2016) in front of the Committee on Commerce, Science and Transportation. This hearing is conducted to hear testimony by the FTC. The agency reports on its activities which included organizing workshops about the "so-called sharing economy." These activities are designed to grasp the impact of these platforms and bring together different stakeholders. The term is also associated with disruption of the economy more broadly, which can be seen in the hearing *The Connected World: Examining the Internet of Things* (2015) in the Committee on Commerce, Science, and Transportation. Here, the term *sharing economy* appears in a publication title, but also in the context of other disruptive technologies like 3D printing, the Internet of Things, wearable technology, virtual and augmented reality,

[10] As the term *sharing economy* is rather infrequent in the Congress data overall, a lower MI and minimum collocate frequency score than the default (MI $\geq$ 5 and minimum collocate frequency score 2) were chosen to be able to illuminate some of the collocates that appear with the term. This means that Tables 6.29 and 6.30 include all collocates that might have appeared as rarely as two times in the overall data set and indeed only the collocate *the*, a function word, appears significantly more often than the others. Most of the collocates have a frequency of 2 or 3 (Table 6.30).

Table 6.29 Senate: collocation graph of sharing economy MI $\geq$ 5, minimum collocate frequency 2

Source: Author, using #LancsBox

commercial drones, autonomous vehicles, or robotics. It is therefore seen as one technological disrupter among many other innovations.

The hearing *Millennial Voices on Advancing the American Dream* (2015) in front of the Joint Economic Committee features some more detailed discussions of the *sharing economy*. The hearing looks at reasons why millennials have such a hard time getting off the ground financially and when it comes to employment, buying a house, or starting a family. Issues such as education, debts, unemployment, underemployment, or stagnant career paths are among the crucial points mentioned here. When the term *sharing economy* occurs, it is in the context of part-time work of the 18–34-year-olds.[11] The *sharing economy* is presented as a way to work flexibly and as some kind of entrepreneur. It also seems to have accelerated the trend toward part-time work overall. The hearing discusses that it is because of this push toward part-

[11] Millennials are usually defined as being born between 1981 and 1996 (Pew-Research-Center 2019).

Table 6.30 Senate: collocates of sharing economy MI ≥ 5, minimum collocate frequency 2

sharing economy

Freq: 15 Collocates: 16

Index	Status	Stat (03 - MI)	Collocate	▼ Stat	Freq (coll.)	Freq (corpus)
1	O	M	gig	13.937792325928063	2	33
2	O	M	workshop	12.660252619770327	2	80
3	O	R	platforms	11.124199961050431	2	232
4	O	L	rise	10.49032839656024	2	360
5	O	R	economy	8.298017705469709	3	2468
6	O	R	internet	8.206571660512939	2	1753
7	O	L	job	8.204104558356068	2	1756
8	O	M	issues	7.898037765463979	2	2171
9	O	L	including	7.654629242466892	2	2570
10	O	M	companies	7.570141369596619	2	2725
11	O	L	new	6.952204470098614	3	6273
12	O	R	at	5.799166803301125	3	13950
13	O	R	will	5.426993547352671	2	12037
14	O	M	or	5.229174038483277	2	13806
15	O	L	the	5.1637916628147	26	187799
16	O	L	with	5.093501957020252	3	22751

Source: Author, using #LancsBox

time work with the help of the *sharing economy*, that young people now often lack basic benefits such as good wages, workplace protections, or consistent workplace scheduling. Additionally, the high burden of debt in the USA that is caused by costly education is mentioned here. Although most jobs will soon require some postsecondary education beyond high school, access remains a problem because of high costs of education.

The *sharing economy* is also mentioned in this hearing when talking about the question of worker classification. Are people hired to do a job over a *sharing economy platform* employees or independent contractors? Are independent contractors only hired to save labor costs? What really defines the status of these workers? Flexibility and "individualized work model" jobs are also in demand by workers, not only by employers, and should be supported if it is what workers want. Some members of Congress caution that the battles over worker classification issues in the *sharing economy* could bring down the business model of these platforms altogether, which would not be beneficial to either side.

In another hearing from 2015 called *The Consumer Financial Protection Bureau's Semiannual Report to Congress* before the Committee on Banking, Housing, and Urban Affairs, the *sharing economy* is mentioned only once, but again in the context of millennials. It is reported that this sector is growing, especially among the group of millennials. Different terms are used here, for example *gig economy, sharing economy,* or *on-demand economy.* Similarly to the hearing mentioned before, the growth of the *sharing economy* is portrayed as having positive and negative sides. On the one hand, there are new work environments and some people are successful in putting together different sources of revenue. On the other hand, it is questionable how the lack of social benefit provision affects these groups and how this can be tackled. Estimates are mentioned saying that about one-third of the American workforce falls into the category of contingent workers at some point in their working lives. Here, one particular issue, qualifying for a mortgage, is mentioned as an issue. As a "1099 worker," you often cannot get an affordable mortgage offer due to fluctuating income. The 2015 hearing in front of the Joint Economic Committee discussed before already mentioned that this could be a reason why people working independently (like many millennials) are postponing investments like buying their own home.

Regulation remains one of the most controversial topics in the *sharing economy*. Labor law or consumer protection are among the topics discussed in this regard. The term *sharing economy* is specifically mentioned in this context in *A Growth Agenda: Reducing Unnecessary Regulatory Burdens* (2017) in front of the Commerce, Science and Transportation Committee. Gary Shapiro representing the Consumer Technology Association (CTA) testifies as an expert witness. According to Shapiro, his association works to support public policy to advance innovation and competitiveness and promote jobs and business creation. The members of the association come from different areas, including *sharing economy* and Internet companies. As many of these companies are also smaller businesses and startups, one of their primary concern is overregulation, which is the main topic of the hearing. Regulation in the context of the *sharing economy* revolves around the question whether incumbent businesses are trying to protect their business models or if new rules for areas such as consumer safety in the digital world are necessary. It is clear from the title of the hearing that the Republican side (who represents the majority of the Senate at the time) is generally in favor of "reducing the unnecessary regulatory burden" and favors deregulation where possible. Therefore, it is unlikely that they would support new regulation in the *sharing economy*. The argument is that ride-sharing and home-sharing companies have already been the regulatory target of local policy-makers who have been put under pressure by existing businesses to protect them against the newcomers. Market actors therefore question the necessity of even more regulation by the federal government. Additionally, one key component of *sharing economy* platforms is mentioned, the rating systems, which could make more consumer protection regulation obsolete. In general, technology is presented as one of the major driving forces of the US economy and the job market and therefore should not be stifled or harmed by new regulation. The business-friendly arguments see the "innovation marketplace" in less need of regulation as one of the key competitive strategies of the new tech firms is instilling trust in their activities through their platform infrastructure. If firms fail to meet the expectations, consumer reaction is swift and leads to self-regulation and better products and services, according to expert witnesses like Shapiro. Self-regulation is something that *sharing economy* platforms are striving for, represented in this hearing through Shapiro, and they clearly lobby against more regulation through lawmakers.

The term *sharing economy* also appears in *What Lower Labor Force Participation Rates Tell Us about Work Opportunities and Incentives* (2015) in front of the Joint Economic Committee. This hearing focuses on the declining labor participation rate since the early 2000s (in June 2015 the labor participation rate stood at 62.6%) and how this trend can be reversed. The *sharing economy* is mentioned in this hearing, albeit only once, in the general context of barriers to entry to the labor market. For example, occupational licensing is mentioned as such a barrier. Yet, more business-friendly actors might see the *sharing economy* as a means to overcome these barriers and to experiment with entrepreneurship. Quoting from the hearing, a statement by expert witness Dr. Mathur (scholar at the American Enterprise Institute) argues that "we are seeing that with the new sharing economy, with the new gig economy, and how people are just using the assets and skills that they have already to generate income for themselves. And I think the more we try to regulate that, I think these avenues are going to be closed to us." This quote shows that more conservative and market-friendly voices argue in defense of the current model of the *sharing economy* and are generally against regulation of the new platforms. Opportunity for additional income and work are emphasized, rather than any threatening aspect. It also becomes clear that the idea of "idling capacity" is still something that is associated with the *sharing economy* at that point in time, meaning that people already have assets that are idle (a car, a room, or their own skills) and can use them to garner further income. In the meantime (this hearing was from 2015), many of these ideas about the *sharing economy* using idling capacity have been proven improbable.

The hearing *The Dynamic Gains from Free Digital Trade for the U.S. Economy* (2017) in front of the Joint Economic Committee focuses on digital trade. The *sharing economy* is mentioned in the context of trust-building and making digital trade work for all, abroad and at home. Due to the fear that the labor force could be disrupted by new technologies like the *sharing economy*, AI, or robotics, innovation could face harmful restrictions all over the world, according to opinions in this hearing. Therefore, the USA, as a global role model, needs to find ways to "transition the displaced due to technology at home."

In general, *sharing economy platforms* also come up in the wider discussion around infrastructure improvement, especially when it comes to transportation and Internet access. The platforms deliver new ways of transportation in the twenty-first century that become more and more popular, yet many regions still face poor Internet connectivity. Congress discusses some of the questions around the future implications of some transportation products and what undesirable effects there might be.

When looking at the Senate hearings and the occurrences of *sharing economy*, one has to remember that the discussions are very limited. The term *sharing economy* is very rare in the Senate data overall, and in many hearings mentioned above, the term only appears once. Yet, one can see that the *sharing economy* is a phenomenon that is strongly associated with millennials. Why do they have such a hard time getting off the ground? Part of it is associated with the growth of nontraditional work arrangements that leads to more and more part-time and contingent work. On the one hand, those jobs often lack the benefits that are usually acquired through steady work and leads to more insecure livelihoods for many millennials. On the other hand, the *sharing economy* is seen as a way to work flexibly, something that is in demand from both employers and workers. *Sharing economy* work is also presented as a way to experiment with entrepreneurship.

In general, *sharing economy* businesses are often seen as part of a wave of disruptive technologies that leave its mark on the American economy. In this context, regulation remains controversial. Some calls for new regulation are interpreted as a way for incumbents to curb new market competition and many platforms already face local rules and regulations. Market-oriented actors therefore argue for little new regulation as long as consumers are not negatively affected. These advocates of the *sharing economy* argue that the innovative style of doing business by these platforms is actually a way around new regulation. Many businesses have built-in rating systems and are responsive to consumer concerns, thus making it unnecessary for lawmakers to act further.

6.3.1.2 Sharing Economy in the House Data

In the material from the House the term *sharing economy* appears much more often than in the Senate hearings, in total, 300 times. There are three hearings that even feature the term in their title, namely *The Disrupter Series: How the Sharing Economy Creates Jobs, Benefits Consumers, and Raises Policy Questions; The Sharing Economy: A Taxing Experience for new Entrepreneurs, Part I;* and *The Sharing Economy: A Taxing Experience for New Entrepreneurs, Part II.*

Tables 6.31 and 6.32 display the collocates of *sharing economy* in the House data.[12] The strongest collocate is *taxing*. This can be attributed to the two specific hearings on taxation issues in the *sharing economy* mentioned before. In general, taxation can be an issue for small-scale self-employed workers. Being active on *sharing economy* platforms makes it even more complicated with people only making a small income from several different clients or employers. *Entrepreneurs* is another strong collocate, also included in the hearings' titles mentioned before (*A Taxing Experience for new Entrepreneurs*). The *sharing economy* workers are often portrayed as small-scale *entrepreneurs*, also referred to as "micro-entrepreneurs."

Another relatively strong collocate group includes *economy, gig, rise*, and *growth*. Together with *companies, businesses, business*, and *billion*, these collocates allude to the business side of the *sharing economy platforms*. There are also several collocates that allude to the labor side of the *sharing economy*; these include *workers, experience, benefits*, and *challenges*. The innovative quality of the *sharing economy* is also stressed through certain collocates: *new, different, models, creates,* and *innovation*. *New* is actually the most frequent collocate in the collocate list (Table 6.32). Both issues around labor and the innovative edge are two very strong themes that are associated with the *sharing economy*. It is a rather new phenomenon

[12] Here, MI ≥ 5 was used, but the minimum collocate frequency was set to 5 as opposed to 2 in the Senate data. This means that collocates mentioned below appear at least five times in the corpus data.

Table 6.31 House: collocation graph of sharing economy MI ≥ 5, minimum collocate frequency 5

Source: Author, using #LancsBox

that needs to be assessed, and it brings significant changes to many different sectors of the economy by establishing new business models, changing behavior and demand. The *sharing economy* is also discussed in its relation to labor, often as a challenge to existing structures, for example in the field of social benefit provision, labor protections, or worker classification. The collocate *benefits* can of course also allude to benefits that the *sharing economy* brings to consumers and workers, which seems to be the case in a hearing from *The Disrupter Series* (detailed in the following).

Two terms from the *sharing economy* terminology also appear as collocates: *gig* and *peer-to-peer*. Just like in the Senate data, *gig* is also a collocate here. Together with *peer-to-peer* it alludes to the nature of the *sharing economy*, namely often made up of *gig* work, as well as taking place between *peers* who engage in "stranger sharing." The "peer-to-peer nature" was also strongly emphasized in the early years of the *sharing economy*.

Table 6.32 House: collocates of sharing economy MI ≥ 5, minimum collocate frequency 5

sharing economy

Freq: 300 Collocates: 31

Index	Status	Stat (03 - MI)	Collocate	▼ Stat	Freq (coll.)	Freq (corpus)
1	O	R	taxing	13.392476243390501	7	11
2	O	L	gig	10.32207583442389	5	66
3	O	L	so-called	9.95708227677567	7	119
4	O	M	peer-to-peer	9.593334989521455	8	175
5	O	L	rise	9.016638791796558	8	261
6	O	L	entrepreneurs	8.854720411815173	8	292
7	O	R	creates	8.16190177699336	5	295
8	O	R	platforms	7.608248607221717	5	433
9	O	R	models	7.303077005853544	5	535
10	O	R	companies	6.997630280920019	26	3438
11	O	R	workers	6.991432842111594	10	1328
12	O	R	experience	6.934713801891796	8	1105
13	O	L	economy	6.744420665528578	15	2364
14	O	R	growing	6.742591286695789	5	789
15	O	R	model	6.702152314655947	7	1136
16	O	R	income	6.57368204559095	5	887
17	O	M	tax	6.5550976096746	10	1797
18	O	R	benefits	6.2211772606865665	8	1812
19	O	L	growth	6.15754134801076	7	1657
20	O	R	new	6.129945683528318	35	8445
21	O	L	internet	6.004711563487219	6	1579
22	O	R	billion	5.851758482443969	5	1463
23	O	M	challenges	5.845689932154954	6	1763
24	O	R	innovation	5.7389387029835035	5	1582
25	O	M	whether	5.595395734098712	6	2097
26	O	R	sharing	5.522102999896089	7	2574
27	O	L	different	5.511863781631755	6	2222
28	O	R	business	5.140936371432786	11	5268
29	O	L	about	5.133526980371144	24	11553
30	O	L	including	5.116173964971562	5	2436
31	O	M	businesses	5.068696366792658	6	3021

Source: Author, using #LancsBox

So-called is another collocate of *sharing economy*. Throughout many sources, the term appears as "so-called sharing economy." This alludes to the fact that *sharing economy* is actually not the most appropriate term for the *sharing economy* platforms, but it remains one of the most widely used ones.

After having looked at the collocates for *sharing economy* in the House, the more specific contexts of the term are investigated in more depth. There are several specific hearings in the House that are dedicated to the *sharing economy*. Some of the themes discussed in these House hearings include the **nature of the sharing economy** in the early years (peer-to-peer and innovation aspects), **consumer benefits, new work arrangements and opportunities, taxation and small business, flexibility of work,** as well as **labor laws and social protections.**

The 2014 hearing *The Power of Connection: Peer-to-Peer Business* in front of the Committee on Small Business is one of the earliest hearings that specifically deals with the *sharing economy*. The new business models are discussed in more depth and different terms are thrown around to refer to this new development, including *peer-to-peer*, *on-demand*, or *sharing economy*. The focus are small businesses and entrepreneurship in this context. In this hearing, the different terms are used interchangeably, alluding to the same technological development that leaves its mark on the economy. The committee talks about how peer-to-peer "businesses create new marketplaces to access goods and services by utilizing technologies such as smartphone apps, GPS locators, and the Internet to easily and efficiently connect individuals who may be able to meet each other's needs." Here, it appears that the peer-to-peer aspect is strongly stressed. This seems to be in line with early views of the *sharing economy* that emphasized the collaborative character of the platforms. However, even though the platforms were a relatively new phenomenon in 2014, many of them were already facing issues and challenges at the local or state level. Additionally, Representative Velázquez (Dem) stresses that the success of the *sharing economy* might also point to economic struggles of Americans who try to find new income sources during harsh economic times. It might also be a way to experiment with entrepreneurship and an overall innovative way of business-making and working. Rating systems are mentioned as a key ingredient in the platform businesses, yet it remains contested if this is enough to protect consumers.

In this hearing, *sharing economy* expert Arun Sundararajan (New York University, Stern School of Business) testifies as an expert witness. Sundararajan sees the peer-to-peer businesses as a rapidly growing sector that creates work, stimulates consumption, raises productivity, catalyzes innovation, and facilitates entrepreneurship. Apart from mentioning (non-traditional) job growth, new consumer experiences, and a "gateway to entrepreneurship" that the platforms create, he also mentions the idea that underutilized assets are used, including skills and physical assets. This is in line with the early view of the *sharing economy*, not only stressing its collaborative nature, but also its sustainability by making use of underutilized assets and "idling capacity." Just like in his book *The Sharing Economy*, which was published shortly after, Sundararajan advocates in favor of self-regulation of platforms.

There are two more witnesses, Beth Stevens from Sidecar and Alan Mond from 1000Tools (tool lending platform) who also testify in this hearing. Both of the platforms just mentioned do no longer exist at the time of writing or have been bought up (Sidecar), pointing to the volatility of the platform market in the early years.

Philip Auerswald (George Mason University), another witness to the hearing, also uses "peer-to-peer economy" interchangeably with the term *sharing economy* and argues that it is not such a new phenomenon. In fact, the only new aspect is the utilization of computation, communications, and algorithmic power, which have all led to "lowered costs of finding a provider of a service, assessing their reliability, and ensuring that the transaction can be performed in an equitable manner." Auerswald thinks that for the federal government there is no need for political action as long as platforms mostly stay in the realm of local transportation, hospitality, food service, and the rental of consumer goods. If more *sharing economy* businesses are moving into other areas such as health care, energy, or education, this might be a different issue as these fields are of specific interest to society and regulations in these fields are more complex. This might mean more government intervention.

He furthermore mentions that while innovations "scale up" businesses as can be seen with platforms or other big tech firms like Apple, Google or Facebook, they have not created a lot of new jobs. Yet, Auerswald argues, the peer-to-peer aspect can play another role here: "By their very structure, peer-to-peer platforms scale out successes to reach tens of thousands, even hundreds of thousands of people with opportunities to create viable livelihoods for themselves." He expresses the hope that platforms will actually serve as a bigger factor in job growth in the future. In 2014, when the platforms were still new, this view was more commonplace. Yet, in the meantime, the early hopes of platforms serving as a career opportunity and as source for good jobs seem to be much more limited.

Looking at other House hearings on the *sharing economy*, there is one hearing from *The Disrupter Series* that stands out (*The Disrupter Series: How the Sharing Economy Creates Jobs, Benefits Consumers, and Raises Policy Questions*, 2015, Committee on Energy and Commerce, Subcommittee on Commerce, Manufacturing, and Trade). This hearing alone features the term *sharing economy* 103 times. The main focus here is the *sharing economy* itself and the hearing includes many themes around this new phenomenon that come up in other hearings as well.

In the beginning, Chairman Michael Burgess (Rep) states that the *sharing economy* is "actually putting people to work," unlike other sectors of the economy, according to the Congressman. The private sector and the *sharing economy* are presented as fostering innovation and job creation. These platforms are presented as a source of income that is supplementing wages from traditional work. Additionally, platforms are presented as capturing the "entrepreneurial spirit of many Americans." The term *sharing economy* also appears in connection with freelance work, which is expected to grow tremendously over the coming years. In order to support this development, Burgess argues, government involvement should remain small, as the platforms themselves have already built-in mechanisms to foster consumer protection and accountability. The platforms already face regulation on the federal and state level and should not have to cope with more. Only in branches like privacy, safety, or cybersecurity should the government be concerned.

However, there are also opposing and more critical voices when it comes to the *sharing economy*. In the same hearing, Congresswoman Janice Schakowsky (Dem) expresses different views about the *sharing economy*, increasingly calling it the *gig economy*. She thinks this phenomenon deserves more scrutiny as a fast-growing sector in the economy that brings about consumer benefits but also more negative consequences. For millennials especially, the work environment of the *gig economy* is only appealing for a while, as long as steadiness of employment and social benefits are not of primary concern yet. The worker classification problem is mentioned here as well, meaning that *sharing economy* workers are generally categorized as independent contractors, not as employees. Platforms consider themselves intermediaries, not traditional employers. But critical members of Congress increasingly see this as an excuse to bow out of social benefit provisions for workers. Uber and the many legal battles over worker classification are mentioned here as an example.

Another issue mentioned in the context of the *sharing economy* is the protection of data. The platforms collect a lot of data but might not store it securely enough. Schakowsky argues that "[a]ll of these issues must be addressed if we are to ensure that the sharing economy is as much about improving the lives of working Americans as it is about increasing the market caps of gig economy companies."

In the same hearing, Fred Upton (Rep) also comments on the *sharing economy*, but again in more positive terms. He sees it as a promising sign in the economic recovery as it connects self-employed or small businesses with consumers who demand specific goods and services. The *sharing economy* therefore stimulates economic activity, income, and growth in the economy overall. Upton argues that in the light of many disruptions that are part of the series of hearings (*The Disrupter Series*), it is important to understand their impact on consumers, job creation, and the economy as a whole. He advocates for little regulation in this sector in order not to stifle job growth in a time when it is still hard to find new jobs. He also argues in favor of flexibility and autonomy of the industry. Moreover, new niche markets are emerging and striving because of the *sharing economy* platforms.

This 2015 *Disrupter Series* hearing on the *sharing economy* goes on to hear testimony of several witnesses including a so-called driver-partner for Uber (Luceele Smith), the president and CEO of the Internet Association (Mr. Michael Beckerman), the Assistant Vice President of Property and Casualty Insurance Association of America (Bob Passmore), the Co-Director of the Center for Economic and Policy Research (Dean Baker), the Vice President of Quickbooks Self-Employed Segment, Intuit Inc. (Alex Chriss), and the Chief Economist at Thumbtack Inc. (Jon Lieber). The witnesses talk about different aspects of the *sharing economy*, for example how driving for Uber provides the opportunity to work flexibly and in an interesting environment with a lot of customer contact (Luceele Smith). Other witnesses also talk about how the Internet economy advances Internet freedom, innovation, and growth on a global scale (Michael Beckerman, Internet Association), and how the *sharing economy* platforms, as part of the larger group of Internet firms, are already the target of local, state, federal, and global regulations. Beckerman, as the advocate of market actors, argues that the *sharing economy* platforms are only intermediaries that match supply and demand. Thus, *sharing economy* firms, through self-regulation and a focus on costumers, deliver better consumer products at a lower price and better service.

Another witness (Dean Baker, Center for Economic and Policy Research) is more critical and advocates for more caution when it comes to the *sharing economy*. It does indeed offer innovative opportunities, but it also undermines some regulations that were put in place for good reason. These include labor regulations, consumer and quality regulations, property rights, anti-discrimination laws, and taxation. Additionally, Baker argues, issues arise for people working on platforms because they are counted as small business owners when it comes to the US tax structure. This poses problems for many people as they do not know how to handle their income correctly. Thus, certain reforms are suggested by witnesses like Baker including an update of government programs supporting the self-employed, as well as an update to the tax code, allowing *sharing economy* platforms to offer guidance to their independent contractors without qualifying as an employer. Additionally, it is emphasized that the social security system might not match the realities of working Americans anymore. Becoming self-employed should not mean giving up all social benefits, which is why the idea of a portable benefits structure is discussed.

In this hearing, the *sharing economy* is generally associated with an "on-demand" nature, in the context of consumer goods and services but also for finding work. This makes the *sharing economy* popular among consumers and some groups of workers. This seems to point to a wider change of preferences in regard to consumption and work. In this context, the *sharing economy* is also presented as a way of "testing the waters" for entrepreneurship. Moreover, the hearing features discussions around the employer–employee relationship in the *sharing economy*, for example in the context of Uber, and what criteria qualify a platform as an employer (e.g., extent of control exerted over workers). These discussions around the classification of workers are not new, however. Apart from the *sharing economy,* fields like real estate or construction have faced the same issues around classification.

Apart from the 2015 *Disrupter Series* hearing on the *sharing economy* that touched upon many different issues, there are other hearings in the House that deal with specific aspects of the *sharing economy*. Taxation is among these aspects. There are two specific hearings on the *sharing economy* and taxation in the realm of small-scale entrepreneurs: *The Sharing Economy: A Taxing Experience for new Entrepreneurs*, Part I and Part II (2016), in front of the Committee on Small Business. This shows that small business is considered to be highly affected by the *sharing economy* and that taxation seems to remain a complicated issue.

In Part I of the hearing, the timeliness of the tax code in regard to the *sharing economy* and small businesses is the main issue (Part II goes into more detail on the same issues). Right in the beginning of Part I, Chairman Steve Chabot (Rep) mentions other terms the *sharing economy* goes by, using terms like "app, gig, on-demand, peer-to-peer, online platform, and collaborative." He also refers to the *sharing economy* as "Uber economy," a term that is not used in any other context. This shows that the *sharing economy* and other terms from the field are often used interchangeably. Yet, Chabot argues, no matter what you call it, it "is changing the face of American entrepreneurship and small business before our very eyes." The *sharing economy* is presented as bringing opportunities to millions of Americans, especially providing more freedom and independence to set your own hours and ways of work. Chairman Chabot presents the *sharing economy* as the "essence of economic liberty and a testament to the power of the free market."

Another Representative, ranking member Nydia Velázquez (Dem), is more critical and doubles down on the idea that the rise of the *sharing economy* could have to do with wider economic struggles of Americans. Many people are seeking alternative ways to employment and extra income because of a slow economy. She stated the same sentiments in the hearing on the *sharing economy* from 2014 mentioned before, emphasizing the economic struggles of many Americans. There might also be those workers participating in the *sharing economy* who seek flexibility and work–life balance or want to experiment with entrepreneurship. Yet, a slow economic recovery and lack of good traditional job opportunities also have to do with the success of the *sharing economy*. In this context, Velázquez also discusses the issue of worker classification again, which remains unsolved. Innovation and new business practices are important in the American economy, Velázquez argues, but everyone needs to abide by existing laws.

In the subsequent rest of the hearing, further details and issues around the *sharing economy* are debated with witnesses. Caroline Bruckner (American University Kogod School of Business), who is invited to testify at the hearing, mentions the *sharing economy* in the wider context of alternative work arrangements, which have increased by 66.5% between 2005 and 2015, she claims. She also mentions that work in and income from the *sharing economy* remain marginal. These activities mainly serve as extra income, not as a main job. When it comes to taxation, most self-employed workers lack adequate information and understanding of complying with the tax code, which is also a problem for *sharing economy* workers.

In line with Bruckner's argument, another witness, Rob Willey, Vice President of TaskRabbit, argues that most of the people active on TaskRabbit do this as a flexible part-time job. *Sharing economy* platforms have basically no barriers to entry, which makes them easy and accessible for many. He also mentions worker classification, which was designed for another era, in his opinion. Now, there is uncertainty about what platforms can or cannot do for the worker. For example, when it comes to tax compliance TaskRabbit could offer more information to their contractors, but in fact does not in order to avoid the risk of qualifying as an employer in the eyes of the law.

Other witnesses in the hearing (Morgan Reed, Executive Director of ACT App Association and Joe Kennedy, Innovation Technology and Innovation Foundation) comment on issues such as small businesses and the tax code and high consumer and worker satisfaction in the *sharing economy*, but also on the displacement and disruption of existing businesses by *sharing economy* platforms. The issue of worker classification is again mentioned in this context. Work arrangements are constantly changing and witness Joe Kennedy argues, "Congress cannot dictate the shape of future work arrangements. It can, however, play a large role in helping workers get the kind of support they need to have good careers that fit into their increasingly complicated lives." In general, there is a lot of debate about worker classification in this hearing as it also touches more generally on taxing obligations, also of employers.

Apart from these specific hearings on the *sharing economy* as such, there are several other hearings in the House that feature the term to a greater extent. In these hearings, taxation and small business remain a concern, as can be seen in the hearing *Small Business Tax Reform: Modernizing the Code for the Nation's Job Creators* (2017) in front of Committee on Small Business. Here, the *sharing economy* appears in the context of technology changing the business model of many small companies and that the tax code is overly complicated and has not kept pace with innovation. The term *sharing economy* again appears in the context of worker classification here, saying that the definition of worker, independent contractor, and employee is critical for the platform business model. There is more talk about how the categories of workers could be updated in order to give independents in the *sharing economy* better opportunities, for example by getting access to training, so that better services and products can be provided and the business model can be maintained.

The term *sharing economy* is also mentioned together with the term "micro-entrepreneur" and "flexibility" as well as "gig." All these terms point to the nature of the *sharing economy*, creating gig work for the self-employed (micro-entrepreneurs) in a highly flexible manner. The growing independent workforce in the USA is also a topic in this context. In this regard, there are suggestions to adjust the tax threshold for income from self-employment so people do not have to pay taxes on very marginal income. Again, "testing the waters" for entrepreneurship is also mentioned in this context.

The hearing *The 21st Century Workforce: How Current Rules and Regulations Affect Innovation and Flexibility in Michigan's Workplaces* (2016) in front of the Committee on Education and the Workforce is also not specifically concerned with the *sharing economy*. But it is concerned with broader trends that the *sharing economy* is part of. The term *sharing economy* appears when witness Jared Meyer (author of the book *Uber Positive: Why Americans Love the Sharing Economy*) testifies in front of the Congress members. He talks about changing attitudes toward work and careers, especially among the millennial generation. The *sharing economy* has witnessed such a success as it embodies the new ideal of convenience and flexibility in the working world. Meyer also connects *sharing economy*, part-time work, and supplementing income, which is the most common activity on the platforms. He sees ongoing issues around the *sharing economy* especially in connection with the independent contractor status of workers. In his view, preserving this status is crucial because it offers people the means to smoothen out earnings and "to do everything from meeting rent to paying down student loans or funding a new business venture." Again, entrepreneurship is strongly associated with the *sharing economy* here. Yet, Meyer argues that overall entrepreneurship is in decline in the USA. A reason for this is federal labor regulation that aims at making most people employees, according to Meyer. Because the work on *sharing economy* platforms is done on the side, he does not see the need to employ these workers or extend labor benefits. In general, Meyer strongly connects the *sharing economy* with "working on your own," working extra hours, and "working on your smartphone."

Apart from Meyer, another witness, Mark Wilson from H.R. Policy, uses *sharing economy* and *gig economy* interchangeably and talks about how discussions around labor regulation and worker classification are not new. Yet, labor standards have not been updated to match the digital age. The hearing also discusses the issue of portability of social benefits such as health care or retirement, which have not been offered by platforms so far, also due to the unresolved employee-or-contractor issue.

There are several other hearings in the House that feature the term *sharing economy* (yet only rarely) but are not immediately concerned with it. In these hearings, issues like regulation, flexibility, independent contracting, the Sharing Economy Caucus in Congress, or social media are discussed.[13]

From the hearings conducted in the House, one can see that the *sharing economy* is definitely a more prominent subject than in the Senate. There are several hearings that specifically deal with and talk about different aspects of the *sharing economy*. In general, there is the view that on-demand attitudes have entered all branches of life, including the world of work. The *sharing economy* is seen as the result of both growing on-demand consumption and the demand for more flexible work, both by workers and by employers. This is often associated with a "millennial" lifestyle in the hearings investigated here. Looking at the earlier hearings, it also becomes clear that the peer-to-peer aspect as well as the sustainability or "idling capacity" aspect of the *sharing economy* had a strong appeal. Yet, this aspect has faded somewhat over time. Many peer-to-peer platforms did not make it off the ground, were bought up, or failed.

Generally, the small business aspect of platforms, as well as the issue of taxation, is very prominent in the hearings in the House. The notion that many of these platforms create so-called micro-entrepreneurs who might want to test the waters of entrepreneurship is mentioned throughout different hearings. In this context, a complicated tax code is seen as an obstacle for many small-scale businesses who could potentially benefit from the *sharing economy*. The platform infrastructure can either be used by existing small businesses or the platforms actually produce new small-scale business owners. But the majority of this group seem to only earn a marginal income from this activity.

Throughout the hearings, it is clear that contesting views prevail about the *sharing economy*. On the one hand, there are those who see the *sharing economy* as "putting people to work" when the rest of the economy is not able to, giving workers a taste of entrepreneurship and the flexibility and work–life balance that they seek. Platforms are an innovative way to do business and work. On the other hand, there are those who see the *sharing economy* more critically, stressing economic struggles of Americans, the lack of social benefits, as well as the problems of worker classification. It is mostly agreed upon that the consumer experience is positive and that the platforms deliver a certain level of consumer protection with their rating systems and the installment of trust in their transactions (self-regulation). However, the issue of undermining existing labor laws remains. Here, the *sharing*

[13] Some of these hearings include *Triple Threat to Workers and Households: Impacts of Federal Regulations on Jobs, Wages and Startups* (2016), Committee on the Judiciary; *Occupational Licensing: Regulation and Competition* (2017), Committee on the Judiciary; *Federal Wage and Hour Policies in the Twenty-First Century Economy* (2017), Committee on Education and the Workforce; *Disrupter Series: Update on IOT Opportunities and Challenges* (2017), Committee on Energy and Commerce, *IRS Puts Small Business Through Audit Wringer* (2016), Committee on Small Business; *The Future of Housing in America: 50 Years of HUD and Its Impact on Federal Housing Policy* (2015), Committee on Financial Services; and *Emergency MGMT 2.0: How #SocialMedia & New Tech Are Transforming Preparedness, Response, & Recovery #Disasters* (2013), Committee on Homeland Security.

economy is seen in line with the growth of nontraditional work arrangements overall (independent contractors, freelancers, self-employed). In other areas outside of platforms, classification issues have always existed and now seem to be replicated on digital platforms. What exactly defines an employer in these new arrangements remains an unresolved issue. Additionally, most workers only earn part-time on the platforms, supplementing their fluctuating steady incomes, so do they need and want the same provisions as full-time employees? This remains a contested issue. Is it worth upending the business model of these platforms, blocking the access to flexible work and income, by pushing through existing labor laws? Or, a third option, do labor laws require an update for the twenty-first century digital workplace, including taxation, classification, or portability of benefits? In these areas, the opinions of lawmakers seem to follow party lines with Republicans advocating for self-regulation and no interference of the federal government, while Democrats see the need to at least enforce existing regulation and labor standards.

6.3.1.3 Gig Economy in the Senate Data

In the Senate corpus, the terms *gig economy* and *sharing economy* occur at closely the same rate. *Gig economy* appears 15 times in 7 out of 90 files from the Senate (0.04 per 10,000 tokens). *Sharing economy* appears 15 times as well, in 9 out of 90 different hearings from the Senate (0.04 per 10,000 tokens). As indicated before, this is a very low rate overall.

When looking at the collocations for *gig economy* in the Senate data (Tables 6.33 and 6.34), all the collocates are very infrequent and might only appear about two times in the data. The terms *artificial, automation, age, intelligence,* and *sharing* are among the strongest collocates. In a lot of cases, *sharing* and *gig economy* appear together or are used interchangeably. *Benefits* and *economy* are two more collocates that are not function words.

The collocates of *gig economy* in the Senate seem to be rather unspecific, pointing to the limited engagement with this phenomenon. The collocates in the House data displayed in the next part seem to be a bit more specific. Yet, broader themes like *automation, artificial intelligence,* and *economy* come up as collocates in the Senate data. This could indicate a broader discussion of the phenomenon of the *gig economy* in connection with larger technological trends that leave their mark on the whole of the economy. The Senate data also includes the hearings of the Joint Economic Committee of House and Senate, which often allocates hearings to bigger themes of economic transition.

The Senate hearings featuring the term *gig economy* the most are taking place in the Joint Economic Committee. Most of these hearings were already mentioned during the examination of the term *sharing economy* in the Congress data.

The first hearing is called *Millennial Voices on Advancing the American Dream* (2015) in the Joint Economic Committee. According to this hearing, millennials seem to have a larger stake in the so-called *gig economy* and are used to changing jobs more often. Also, the issue of a lack of social benefits is mentioned again using

Table 6.33 Senate: collocation graph of gig economy MI ≥ 5, minimum collocate frequency 2

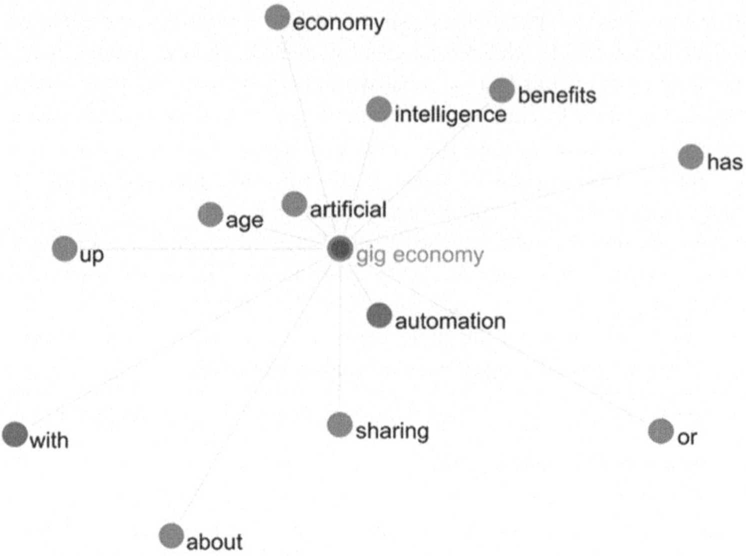

Source: Author, using #LancsBox

Table 6.34 Senate: collocates of gig economy MI ≥ 5, minimum collocate frequency 2

gig economy

Freq: 15 Collocates: 12

Index	Status	Stat (03 - MI)	Collocate	▼ Stat	Freq (coll.)	Freq (corpus)
1	O	M	artificial	11.22062957904392	2	217
2	O	R	automation	10.952434943610756	3	392
3	O	L	age	9.863240700106077	2	556
4	O	M	intelligence	9.60063853003763	2	667
5	O	M	sharing	8.97375297659857	2	1030
6	O	R	benefits	8.013515025900132	2	2004
7	O	M	economy	7.71305520474901	2	2468
8	O	L	up	7.059225835683538	2	3883
9	O	M	about	5.884808061335382	2	8764
10	O	R	has	5.389257626989959	2	12356
11	O	R	or	5.229174038483277	2	13806
12	O	L	with	5.093501957020252	3	22751

Source: Author, using #LancsBox

the term *gig economy* in this context. The term also comes up when talking about alternatives for traditional retirement plans and the overall rise of part-time and contract work, as well as temporary employment. Overall, for millennials and other American workers, employment patterns are changing and the *gig economy* is part of this. With the increase of "part-time, on-demand, 'gig' economy work," there is the discussion of how social benefits could move from job to job along with the worker. The hearing *The Current State of Retirement Security in the United States* (2017) before the Committee on Banking, Housing, and Urban Affairs, Subcommittee on Economic Policy, goes in the same direction, mentioning independent or gig work which becomes more and more common among Americans, especially with the rise of well-known companies like Uber, Lyft, Airbnb, TaskRabbit, eBay, or Etsy.

In *The Decline of Economic Opportunity in the United States: Causes and Consequences* (2017) before the Joint Economic Committee the term *gig economy* is put in the context of overall structural change and technological progress with the "leaps in automation, artificial intelligence, and a gig economy on one hand and the decline of dynamism (. . .) on the other." The hearing focuses on the decline in entrepreneurial dynamism in the USA overall. According to witness testimony in the hearing, this is indicated by sinking startup rates, and by lower numbers of people switching jobs.

In the following hearings the term *gig economy* only appears once: In *What Labor Force Participation Rates Tell Us About Work Opportunities and Incentives* (2015) in the Joint Economic Committee, *gig economy* is used when talking about the *sharing economy*. As said before, these terms are often used interchangeably. In *The Economic Report of the President* (2016) before the Joint Economic Committee the term appears when talking about millennials' struggles in a "volatile economy" and that they are often unable to accumulate savings for later in their lives. In *The Dynamic Gains from Free Digital Trade for the U.S. Economy* (2017) before the Joint Economic Committee, the term *gig economy* is used when talking about different labor market policies including the portability of social benefits, wage insurance, and training programs. In *The Consumer Financial Protection Bureau's Semiannual Report to Congress* (2015) in the Committee on Banking, Housing, and Urban Affairs, the term is used interchangeably with *sharing economy* and *on-demand economy* and how these trends are on the rise among millennials.

In general, the term *gig economy* is very rarely used in the material from the Senate and is also used interchangeably with the term *sharing economy*. Most hearings that feature the term in some way are conducted in the Joint Economic Committee where broader issues shaping the American economy are discussed. If *gig economy* occurs, it is often associated with millennial lifestyle and struggles in the labor market such as income volatility, a lack of savings, or a lack of access to specific training. The *gig economy* is seen as part of the structural change in the economy due to technology, which produces all kinds of issues for the American labor force in the future.

The *gig economy* is also seen as part of the trend toward more flexible and short-term work arrangements and the growing group of independents in the labor market overall. This raises the question of social benefits provision that is usually tied to employment. In this context, the possibility of portable benefits is discussed.

Additionally, the term *gig economy* appears in connection with large-scale trends such as automation and artificial intelligence. Lawmakers seem to be concerned about the outlook of the American economy more generally. Although technological developments change the economy and society profoundly, it is questionable whether the American economy is dynamic enough to make the most of this progress when it comes to innovation, entrepreneurship, or human capital.

The term *platform economy* does not appear in the Senate material. As said before, this term is rather rare in all of the data sets and seems to be a more technical and expert term that is not widely used by political or public actors. In the following analysis of the House data and the media sources, the term *platform economy* will be discussed in some more detail.

6.3.1.4 Gig Economy in the House Data

The House material examined here features the term *gig economy* as well as the term *platform economy*, which is absent in the data from the Senate and the *Wall Street Journal* detailed later. *Gig economy* is much more frequent in the House data than *platform economy*, however. In the network graph (Table 6.35), one can see some of the connections between all three terms. The collocates *income*, *business**, *companies*, and *tax* are connecting the three terms. These collocates already indicate some of the main issues that are discussed around the context of platforms, namely as a new source of supplementing *income*. Through the new income that is made on the side, *tax* issues have come up for platforms as well as for the so-called micro-entrepreneurs. New *business* models have developed due to technological progress and have produced some of the most valuable *companies* of the last few years.

Tables 6.36 and 6.37 show the collocates of *gig economy* in the House data.[14]

One of the strongest collocates that can be observed in Table 6.36 is *discourages*. Yet, it only appears two times in the material. *Discourages* is used in the phrase "uncertainty and litigation which discourages companies from supporting gig economy workers" in a statement by Joe Kennedy (ITIF) in *The Sharing Economy: A Taxing Experience for new Entrepreneurs, Part I,* in front of the Committee on Small Business. Kennedy alludes to the fact that platforms are discouraged to offer its independent workers any services as this makes it more likely that platforms qualify as employers. This touches upon one of the most controversial issues of the *gig economy*—do digital platforms ever qualify as employers and what determines this?

Another collocate that is strongly associated with *gig economy* in the House data is *millennials*. As indicated in the analysis of the Congress data before, *millennials* are often associated with the *sharing* or *gig economy* which are seen as part of their lifestyle.

[14]The term *gig economy* appears 39 times in 6 out of 151 files (0.08 per 10,000 tokens) in the House data. Using MI ≥ 7 and a minimum collocate frequency score of 2, a larger set of collocates was produced than for the Senate data. Yet, as one can see in Table 6.37, the collocates are very infrequent, most of them only appearing 2–3 times.

Table 6.35 House: collocation network graph of sharing economy, gig economy, platform economy MI ≥ 5, minimum collocate frequency 5

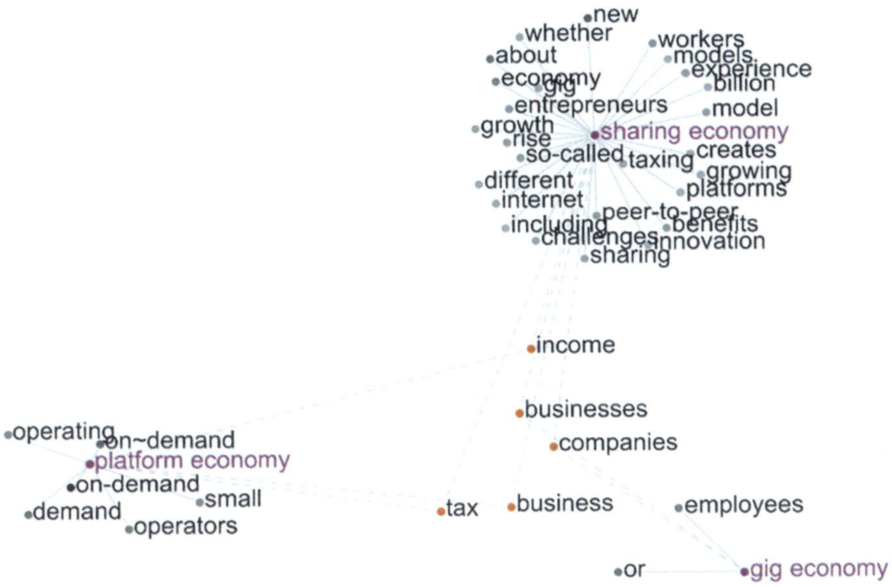

Source: Author, using #LancsBox

The most frequent collocates in the House data are *businesses*, *companies*, *employees*, *sharing*, *protection*, *additional,* and *ensure*. All of these collocates seem to point to either the business side or the labor side of the *gig economy*. Of course, new gig *businesses* and companies have developed in the *sharing* economy market. As I said before, *gig* and *sharing economy* are often used interchangeably. The question of whether gig workers should qualify as *employees* is an ongoing topic when talking about the *gig economy*, as well as whether *protections* can or should be provided for these workers. Often, these workers seek *additional* income in the *gig economy*. Collocates like *protect*, *benefits*, *workers*, *temporary*, *supporting*, *retirement*, or *enable* could also be associated with labor issues in a broader sense.

Customers, *claim*, *covered*, *liability, consumers*, and *insurance* could point to other important issues that are discussed around the *gig economy*, for example who is liable for ensuring customer safety. Customer service and consumer satisfaction are usually highly valued in the *gig economy* and platforms often claim to deliver better products and services than incumbent businesses.

As said before, the term *gig economy* is rarer than the term *sharing economy* in the House data. There are certain hearings where it appears more intensively than in others. Yet, most of these hearings are the same that are concerned with the *sharing economy*.

For example, in *The Disrupter Series: How the Sharing Economy Creates Jobs, Benefits Consumers, and Raises Policy Questions* (2015) in the Committee on

Table 6.36 House: collocation graph of gig economy MI ≥ 7, minimum collocate frequency 2

Source: Author, using #LancsBox

Energy and Commerce, the term *gig economy* is mentioned, for example by Janice Schakoswky (Dem) who replaces "sharing" with "gig" right at the beginning of her opening statement: "Thank you, Mr. Chairman, for holding this hearing on the sharing, some call gig, economy. This is a topic absolutely deserving of our attention, discussion, scrutiny." She is more critical of the *gig* or *sharing economy* than others, emphasizing the questionable business model that puts those at risk who are in need of a more stable employment. The term *gig economy* thus appears when talking about issues like independent contracting, legal liability of platforms, and minimum labor standards for platform work. Also, the *gig economy* is used in the context of using and storing consumer data. In the sentence "All of these issues must be addressed if we are to ensure that the sharing economy is as much about improving the lives of working Americans as it is about increasing the market caps of gig economy companies," the terms *sharing economy* and *gig economy* are used to refer, on the one hand, to the opportunities platforms offer for working Americans (*sharing economy*) and, on the other hand, to the large and problematic corporate nature of the platform companies (*gig economy*). It seems that the term *gig*

Table 6.37 House: collocates of gig economy, MI ≥ 7, minimum collocate frequency 2

gig economy

Freq: 39 Collocates: 40

Index	Status	Stat (03 - MI)	Collocate	▼ Stat	Freq (coll.)	Freq (corpus)
1	O	L	discourages	14.08120292985237	2	15
2	O	L	caps	13.130125981737455	2	29
3	O	L	millennials	12.287671623990216	2	52
4	O	M	insur	12.033908225689878	2	62
5	O	R	temporary	11.329897491857192	2	101
6	O	R	argue	11.193696109379495	2	111
7	O	L	claim	10.675225290587568	2	159
8	O	L	adequately	10.578716930898171	2	170
9	O	L	retirement	10.520502851726265	2	177
10	O	L	covered	10.1054663855329	2	236
11	O	M	ance	9.874367906598927	2	277
12	O	R	largely	9.828238726637132	2	286
13	O	R	nature	9.678253833733665	3	476
14	O	R	avoid	9.492253626754527	2	361
15	O	R	liability	9.418253957058775	2	380
16	O	L	supporting	9.344253183134905	2	400
17	O	R	topic	9.308630076187544	2	410
18	O	L	size	9.203474933699189	2	441
19	O	R	legal	8.810689399097203	2	579
20	O	R	businesses	8.74922708259799	10	3021
21	O	L	enable	8.744934991136148	2	606
22	O	R	employees	8.650933759892139	5	1617
23	O	M	protection	8.55139770939603	4	1386
24	O	L	whole	8.520503884811875	2	708
25	O	R	model	8.423325088933062	3	1136
26	O	R	companies	8.240755524284207	8	3438
27	O	R	additional	8.23238739059581	4	1729
28	O	R	individuals	8.219925081684185	2	872
29	O	R	workers	8.198032420253064	3	1328
30	O	L	customers	8.146807289027375	3	1376
31	O	R	ensure	7.842177346518358	4	2266
32	O	L	required	7.792122065527969	2	1173
33	O	R	space	7.726014801525625	2	1228
34	O	L	protect	7.66280388076372	2	1283
35	O	M	sharing	7.658313156877259	4	2574
36	O	M	insurance	7.6393813757328894	2	1304
37	O	R	consumers	7.469456124997528	2	1467
38	O	L	own	7.4220551514002	2	1516
39	O	L	making	7.3148001562587215	2	1633
40	O	L	benefits	7.164742270106399	2	1812

Source: Author, using #LancsBox

economy is more often used than the term *sharing economy* when addressing problematic sides of the new digital platforms.

In the hearing *The Sharing Economy: A Taxing Experience for New Entrepreneurs, Part I* (2016) in the Committee on Small Business, the term *gig economy* is used similarly to the hearing before, replacing *sharing economy* in contexts where workers are the focus. In this context, the uncertainty around the gig worker status or a lack of worker support by platforms is mentioned. Many platforms are reluctant to offer any services to workers for fear of qualifying as a full employer. *Gig economy* also occurs in the context of two of the most well-known platforms in ride-hailing, Uber and Lyft, who have introduced a business model based on "gig platform workers." These two companies continue to be involved in high-profile litigation because of their business model, which is also discussed among lawmakers.

The labor force is also in focus in *The 21st Century Workforce: How Current Rules and Regulations Affect Innovation and Flexibility in Michigan's Workplaces* (2016) in front of the Committee on Education and the Workforce, Subcommittee on Workforce Protections. In this hearing, one of the witnesses states that the *gig economy* appears to be new, exciting, and different, when it is actually none of these things. As mentioned above, sectors like the construction industry have faced similar questions and issues like the *gig economy* for years. Therefore, it is questionable if there is the need for a new category of workers (gig worker) or new labor laws. In fact, it would be important to ensure existing standards first, according to testimony in this hearing.

There are several more hearings where the term *gig economy* only appears once or twice. These include the hearing *Reversing the Entrepreneurship Decline* (2017) in the Committee on Small Business where *gig economy* is again used in the context of workers' rights, and *Federal Wage and Hour Policies in the Twenty-First Century Economy* (2017) in the Committee on Education and the Workforce, Subcommittee on Workforce Protections, where the term *gig economy* appears when talking about changing ideals when it comes to work, for example more flexibility. In the *Disrupter Series: Improving Consumers' Financial Options with Fintech* (2017) in the Committee on Energy and Commerce, Subcommittee of Digital Commerce and Consumer Protection, the term *gig economy* is mentioned together with *on-demand economy* and stresses the "new face of entrepreneurship," namely the small-scale self-employed (in other contexts called micro-entrepreneurs) who represent the future as "hard-working people [who] have the freedom and flexibility to set their own schedules and work toward their own goals" and who represent a "business of one."

All in all, the hearings that feature the term *gig economy* in the House material are the same that talk directly about the *sharing economy*. In many instances, the terms are used interchangeably. But it seems that there are different connotations when the terms *sharing* or *gig economy* are used. *Gig economy* is more often used by some stakeholders when workers' issues or more problematic aspects of digital platforms are discussed. In other instances, or when emphasizing the opportunities of the new platforms, *sharing economy* seems to be used more often.

In the hearings investigated here, the term *gig economy* usually occurs when workers' rights (contracting, liability, minimum labor standards) or new ways of working in the digital age are discussed more generally. Flexibility and "new entrepreneurship" are also two themes in this context. Unlike the *sharing economy*, the term *gig economy* seems to have never been as strongly associated with ideas such as opportunity, alternative consumption, peer-to-peer collaboration or sustainability.

6.3.1.5 Platform Economy in the House Data

Platform economy is the third term that is investigated in the congressional material. It only appears in the House data. The Senate records investigated here do not feature any instance of the term *platform economy*. At first glance, this corroborates the fact that the term is extremely rare and somewhat of an expert term. However, it could also be that the specific section of Senate data investigated in this work does not feature the term.

The strongest collocates for *platform economy* in the House data are *on-demand*, *sparked*, and *emergence* (Table 6.38).[15] These three collocates might indicate that platforms *sparked* the emergence and growth of *on-demand* services. With the new technology of platforms, *on-demand* services became feasible. *On-demand* in various forms appears as a strong collocate, meaning that when the term *platform economy* occurs, *on-demand* is also likely to occur. The term "on-demand economy" is rather rare in the corpus data overall, but on-demand service platforms are some of the major players in the *platform economy* market (e.g., TaskRabbit, Instacart, or Uber). *On-demand* is the most frequent in this collocate list with more than 40 occurrences of its various forms.

Income, *demand*, *operators*, *operating*, and *tax* are other frequent collocates. *Operators* and *tax* might refer to the operators earning extra *income* on the platforms and who are running into the aforementioned *tax* issues. The collocate *income* occurs in several instances, which indicates that platforms are strongly associated with the possibility of earning (extra) *income*.

Interestingly, *TaskRabbit* appears as a collocate here, which was not the case in the collocation analysis of the terms *gig* or *sharing economy*. *TaskRabbit* is not as widely known or successful as Uber or Airbnb. Yet, *TaskRabbit* as a platform for hiring workers for any given task is often associated with platform work (Table 6.39).

There are only two hearings from the House where the term *platform economy* actually occurs. The hearing *The Sharing Economy: A Taxing Experience for new Entrepreneurs Part I* (2016) in front of the Committee on Small Business features 68 occurrences of *platform economy*. This high number of occurrences is due to witness testimony by Caroline Bruckner in this hearing. She is a tax professor looking at taxation issues for small businesses under the influence of online platforms. She argues that the *platform economy* poses difficult compliance and tax issues for small businesses. In the eyes of the law, all self-employed are considered

[15] In order to produce a larger collocate list below, the minimum collocate frequency was decreased to 2. There are a few collocates that appear more often, but most collocates only appear 2–3 times (Table 6.39).

Table 6.38 House: collocation graph of platform economy MI ≥ 7, minimum collocate frequency 2

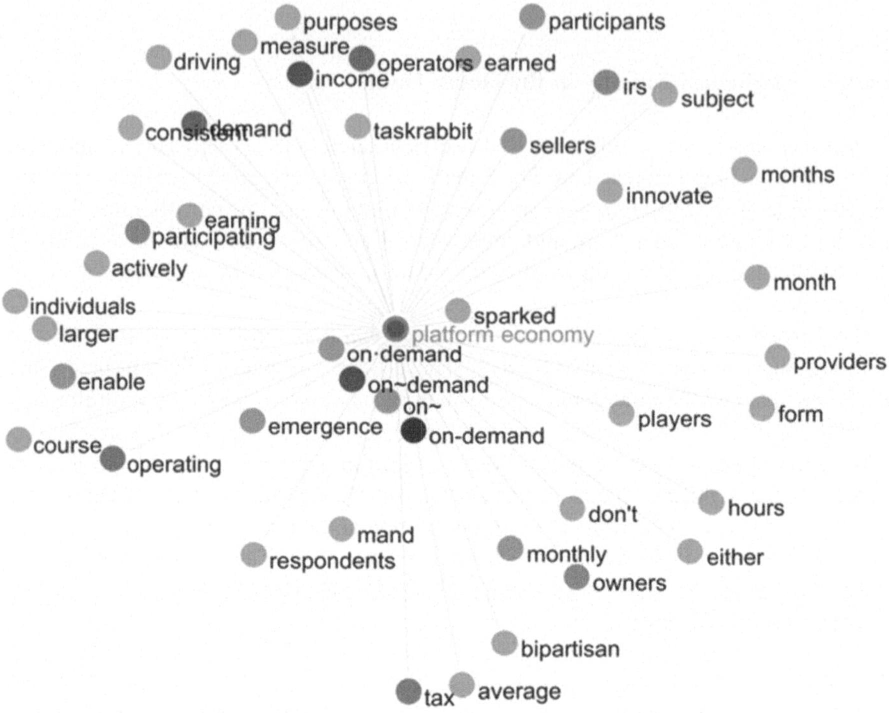

Source: Author, using #LancsBox

small business owners even if they only earn a marginal income from platforms like Airbnb, TaskRabbit, Lyft, Uber, Instacart, or others. She quotes from her report on the issue called *Shortchanged: The Tax Compliance Challenges of Small Business Operators Driving the On-Demand Platform Economy* (Kogod Tax Policy Center) which she provides to Congress. The fact that *on-demand* is the strongest collocate of *platform economy* (Table 6.38) is due to the testimony of Bruckner. She mostly uses the term "on-demand platform economy" whenever she talks about platforms. As said before, tax issues are the most important considerations in this hearing in front of the Small Business Committee, which also explains the prevalence of the collocate *tax*. The issues of a growing part-time, flexible workforce (that might earn income over platforms) are also discussed in the context of the *platform economy* in this hearing.

As said above, *TaskRabbit* is also a collocate of *platform economy* in the House material. This is mainly due to the fact that Rob Wiley, Vice President of TaskRabbit, also testifies in the hearing *The Sharing Economy: A Taxing Experience for new Entrepreneurs Part I* (2016). He emphasizes that in his view, people earning income over platforms are in fact small business owners. Wiley also argues that

Table 6.39 House: collocates of platform economy MI $\geq$ 7, minimum collocate frequency 2

platform economy

Freq: 69 Collocates: 43

Index	Status	Stat (03 - MI)	Collocate	▼ Stat	Freq (coll.)	Freq (corp...
1	O	L	on·demand	15.164946907194636	3	6
2	O	R	sparked	15.164946907194636	2	4
3	O	L	on~demand	15.110512667760466	13	27
4	O	L	on~	14.942606729970557	3	7
5	O	L	on-demand	14.207200488501176	26	101
6	O	L	emergence	12.580004723403478	3	36
7	O	L	taskrabbit	11.6103813983972	2	47
8	O	L	mand	11.580014881975776	2	48
9	O	R	sellers	11.24213486138255	3	91
10	O	L	earning	10.975147396625534	2	73
11	O	R	players	10.843046240230402	2	80
12	O	R	monthly	10.590061087541212	3	143
13	O	R	don't	10.521112659716685	2	100
14	O	R	innovate	10.492543077275565	2	102
15	O	L	respondents	10.1315490304522	2	131
16	O	L	participating	9.990045267597118	4	289
17	O	L	income	9.957142614396282	12	887
18	O	L	operators	9.930665577552894	7	527
19	O	M	earned	9.755577483109326	2	170
20	O	L	demand	9.647300968094122	8	733
21	O	L	actively	9.240156977973252	2	243
22	O	R	owners	9.134302846029804	4	523
23	O	L	operating	9.091721460643692	6	808
24	O	R	irs	8.722026530633459	4	696
25	O	L	measure	8.681153603422679	2	358
26	O	L	consistent	8.550259453181532	2	392
27	O	L	purposes	8.528346176939923	2	398
28	O	L	enable	8.506758356444003	3	606
29	O	M	bipartisan	8.454164039220878	2	419
30	O	R	participants	8.270152704722697	3	714
31	O	L	larger	8.150949779759857	2	517
32	O	R	subject	7.950651181671427	2	594
33	O	R	hours	7.900527498023292	2	615
34	O	R	month	7.83181480325515	2	645
35	O	L	driving	7.807418316624562	2	656
36	O	M	average	7.699403779231588	2	707
37	O	L	tax	7.675523305051704	5	1797
38	O	R	either	7.655195480566407	2	729
39	O	R	form	7.581887502861774	2	767
40	O	L	individuals	7.396786068068794	2	872
41	O	R	providers	7.396786068068794	2	872
42	O	R	months	7.359226325759862	2	895
43	O	L	course	7.1029236901846575	2	1069

Source: Author, using #LancsBox

many people supplement their income through platform work today. Both witnesses seem to argue in favor of simplifying and improving the situation for platform workers (small business owners in their view) when it comes to taxation.

This notion is again expressed in the 2017 hearing *Small Business Tax Reform: Modernizing the Code for the Nation's Job Creators* in the Committee on Small Business. There is only one instance where the term *platform economy* occurs. It is used as "on-demand platform economy" again by Caroline Bruckner who testifies in this hearing again. A bipartisan bill demanding common sense tax changes to make it easier for "the growing sharing economy" as well as the self-employed and small business owners is discussed in this hearing.

Although the term *platform economy* is featured in the House material, there are essentially only two hearings where the term actually occurs. Both hearings feature testimony by the same witness, Caroline Bruckner. In line with what this book argues, this shows that *platform economy* as a term is not prevalent in the public and political discourse around the *sharing* or *gig economy* and is mainly used by experts. Bruckner testifies as an expert witness, an academic, who probably strives for a neutral and suitable term for what she investigates. The term does not seem to be prevalent outside of expert circles.

Both hearings show that the *platform economy* is generally often discussed in the House in relation to taxation issues for small business owners. Platform workers are seen as part of the overall self-employed, independent workforce. Small business owners face specific challenges when it comes to taxation and many argue in favor of a simplification of the law. People working on platforms are, at least in these hearings, equated with small business owners. In the eyes of the (tax) law, this is actually true. However, it is questionable whether gig workers can really be equated with actual business owners. It is suggested to address issues such as the threshold for self-employed to report taxes or to reinstate deductibles for healthcare costs for the group of self-employed workers. This could also help the group of independent platform workers. These reform ideas point again to the fact that many self-employed (platform) workers only earn a marginal income with platform work and just want to make some extra income on top of their stable earnings.

6.3.1.6 Sharing, Gig, and Platform Economy in the Congressional Data

When looking at the use of the terms *sharing*, *gig*, and *platform economy* in the congressional data investigated here, there are several themes that can be identified. First of all, the *sharing economy* maintains some of its original positive outlook. It is presented as an opportunity for a different kind of consumption under collaborative and peer-to-peer aspects. In the earlier material, sustainability and "idling capacity" are also associated with the *sharing economy*. For consumers, the *sharing economy* has always been considered a great benefit. Many consumers have happily embraced many of the platforms because of the affordability and quality of the products and the platform infrastructure that includes rating systems to instill trust and make stranger sharing possible.

Most of all, however, the Congress material investigated here displays a strong emphasis on the *sharing economy* as a way toward entrepreneurship for the single individual. Everyone can become a micro-entrepreneur on the basis of the digital platform infrastructure. This is an opportunity to make extra income or to "test the waters" of entrepreneurism. For business-friendly actors, this epitomizes the free market spirit prevalent in the USA. This theme of the *sharing economy* as a pathway to economic opportunity is prevalent throughout the debates in Congress and is not necessarily tied to one party affiliation. Throughout the congressional material, the initial peer-to-peer or sustainability (idling capacity) assumptions seem to be abandoned more and more in favor of economic opportunity aspects of the *sharing economy*.

Apart from the overarching theme of economic opportunity, the *sharing economy* platforms are regularly discussed in the context of small business, emphasizing how the digital platform structure helps and produces new small-scale self-employed entities. Yet, these "micro-entrepreneurs" also face struggles such as correct compliance with the tax code.

Apart from taxation, Republican and Democratic lawmakers discuss more broadly whether and how the activities of platforms should be regulated and whether labor laws should be changed to accommodate these new activities. Worker (mis)-classification or compliance with minimum labor standards is discussed on several occasions throughout the congressional material. The allocation of social benefits is also discussed.

When the debate moves to the changing labor market that becomes more volatile and flexible, the term *gig economy* is often used, emphasizing that many jobs today are short-term, flexible, and insecure. The term *gig economy* is therefore more prevalent in contexts where issues or downsides of the new digital platforms are discussed such as their large corporate structure or the issues around worker classification. Additionally, the success of the *gig economy* is associated with a slow economy where other good employment is hard to find.

Moreover, the *sharing* or *gig economy* is also strongly associated with millennials and their changing lifestyle and working lives. They often embrace the new platforms as consumers and users, but are also more affected by their impact on the labor market, i.e., more insecure career paths overall. Although gig workers themselves are rare, they face issues similar to those of a generally more independent labor force. Here, labor laws such as classification or minimum pay, but also the allocation of social benefits (e.g., health care or retirement), are the most crucial issues.

In general, both the *gig* and *sharing economy* are seen in line with larger trends such as further automation, the rise of artificial intelligence, or the Internet of Things. The *platform economy* is not very prominent overall and remains an expert term. Generally, however, the three terms discussed here are very often used interchangeably, even in the same sentence or context.

6.3.2 *Platform Economy* in the Liberal Media Material

After having assessed the terms *sharing*, *gig*, and *platform economy* in the congressional material, the investigation will move on to the context of these terms in the public discourse, starting with the material from the *New York Times* (*NYT*) and *Washington Post*.

The term *sharing economy* features most prominently in this material with 1039 separate occurrences and a relative frequency of 1.96 per 10,000 tokens. This is rather unsurprising as it is one of the terms that was used to initially compile the corpora. The second most prominent term is *gig economy*, which occurs 367 times in the material with a relative frequency of 0.69 per 10,000 tokens. The least prolific term of the three is *platform economy*, with only 12 occurrences in total and a relative frequency of 0.02 per 10,000 tokens. Here, it can again be seen that the extent of the use of these terms varies to a great extent. The specific contexts of these terms are investigated in the following beginning with the least prolific term *platform economy*, followed by the term *gig economy* and *sharing economy*, respectively.

Before looking at the liberal media material in more detail, there is one specific article from the *NYT* that looks at the terminology of the platform economy in more detail. As indicated before, it is rather common that all the terms are used interchangeably. This points to the fact that there is still no overall consensus on what these terms really refer to and what they encompass. The article *The Whatchamacallit Economy* in the *NYT* from 2016 by Steven Greenhouse discusses this issue. Greenhouse argues that *sharing economy* is actually not an appropriate term because the activity it refers to has little to do with what we would generally consider "sharing"—an argument expressed by other sharing economy experts as well. The article mentions several terms that are used instead, some of which were also investigated in this book. They include *on-demand economy*, *peer-to-peer economy*, *crowd-based economy*, *gig economy*, or *collaborative economy*. Arun Sundararajan, the author of *The Sharing Economy*, is quoted saying that the term *sharing economy* has survived because it was used first in academia and in the public debate. The term referred to the usage of underutilized assets and was regarded as a sustainable way of life in the earlier 2000s. Rachel Botsman is also quoted here, saying the "Uberification of everything" is under way, blurring the idea of what "sharing" is really about. For Botsman who has coined the term *collaborative economy*, only those companies who have a clear value-driven approach count as "sharing platforms." *Gig economy* as a term is also imprecise as it suggests that gig work is something new when it has actually been around for a long time (independent contracting). Other experts in the field of platforms like Geoffrey G. Parker embrace the term *platform economy*, but he also admits that it is very broad, encompassing many different companies like Google, Facebook, or on-demand companies like Uber. For Parker, as an expert in the field of engineering, it seems more natural to embrace the term *platform economy* rather than other more unspecific terms. But as Sundararajan argues in this article, the term *sharing economy* might be inaccurate, yet we continue to rely on it as it is so widely used by different corporations, the public, Silicon Valley, and other experts. The term *sharing economy* can therefore not be ignored or easily replaced.

The same is argued throughout this book. The *sharing economy* as a term might be imprecise but is still widely in use. However, there are nuances in the meaning of the different terms *sharing economy*, *gig economy,* and *platform economy* that were already touched upon in the examination of the congressional material. This will be investigated further in the following chapters.

6.3.2.1 Platform Economy in the Liberal Media Data

All the articles mentioned in this part of the analysis are from the years 2016 or 2017. This points to the fact that the term *platform economy* is a very recent addition to the discourse around the *sharing economy*.

A first look at the collocations of *platform economy* (Tables 6.40 and 6.41) in the liberal media material shows that the strongest collocate is *connotation*. Looking at

Table 6.40 Liberal media: collocation graph of platform economy MI ≥ 7, minimum collocate frequency 2

Source: Author, using #LancsBox

Table 6.41 Liberal media: collocates of platform economy MI ≥ 7, minimum collocate frequency 2

platform economy

Freq: 12 Collocates: 23

Index	Status	Stat (03 - MI)	Collocate	▼ Stat	Freq (coll.)	Freq (corpus)
1	O	L	connotation	16.75186644627033	2	8
2	O	R	posing	15.359539925418837	2	21
3	O	R	geoffrey	14.996957715359729	2	27
4	O	L	earns	14.318885810247089	5	108
5	O	R	parker	13.7976516463195	2	62
6	O	R	g.	13.107994971766193	2	100
7	O	L	embrace	11.821110316030163	2	244
8	O	R	grand	11.675032450953942	2	270
9	O	L	earned	11.394295801759997	2	328
10	O	R	survey	11.300637502269396	3	525
11	O	R	receive	11.224372353632836	2	369
12	O	R	earnings	10.90635812012494	2	460
13	O	L	digital	10.175931060724269	5	1908
14	O	L	bad	9.764584551833421	2	1015
15	O	L	money	9.650135610357932	5	2747
16	O	R	questions	9.618706029680114	2	1123
17	O	R	general	9.216573045221566	2	1484
18	O	R	recent	9.200460696413726	3	2251
19	O	L	income	9.16594697215165	2	1537
20	O	R	according	8.755139822735863	3	3065
21	O	R	did	8.375723086815288	2	2658
22	O	L	uber	7.6225655744117	3	6720
23	O	L	from	7.072871234998975	7	22952

Source: Author, using #LancsBox

the corpus material, *connotation* is used in the context of the rather notorious *connotation* the peer-to-peer aspect of the *platform economy* used to have in the early 2000s when it was mostly associated with sharing illegal content on platforms like Napster. But nowadays, the *platform economy* has largely moved on from this gray legal area.

Geoffrey Parker is also a rather strong collocate. He was mentioned above in the article *The Whatchamacallit Economy* in the *NYT* from 2016 by Steven Greenhouse. He published a book called *Platform Revolution* in 2016, is an expert in the field of platform economics, and is therefore appearing in strong connection to the term *platform economy*.

The collocates *earns*, *digital*, *money*, *recent*, *survey*, *according*, and *from* are not very frequent (2–7 occurrences overall), but they could point to the fact that people have begun to *earn* money on (*digital*) platforms in *recent* times. The collocate *survey* could point to several surveys conducted around the *platform economy*, for example one by the PEW Research Center mentioned in the following.

Generally, collocates like *recent*, *earned*, *embrace*, *questions,* and *bad* could point to the rather novel (*recent*) nature of the platforms, which people *embrace* or *question*. It is used to *earn* extra income but has questionable (*bad*) implications.

Uber as one of the most prominent examples of the *platform economy* is also a collocate that appears in the list.

One of the rare occasions of *platform economy* appearing in the material from the *New York Times* (*NYT*) and *Washington Post* is a section in the *Washington Post* in 2016 called *On-Demand Economy: Billions of taxes may get unreported, study finds* which reports on taxation issues. Often, earnings from platforms are not reported and thus the state loses tax revenue every year. As the section title already indicates, the *platform economy* is equated with the "on-demand economy." The article uses the term *platform economy* in the context of specific on-demand platforms such as Airbnb, Etsy, or Lyft. Using these, about 2.5 million Americans have earned an income in 2014, according to the article. However, mentioning a study by the American University, the majority of people earning an income on platforms do not receive earning statements and are confused about how to report them.

In another article in the *Washington Post* from 2017 called *Side hustles are the new norm. Here's how much they really pay,* Abha Bhattarai mentions the term *platform economy*, again together with other terms like *gig economy*. The terms *platform economy* or "digital *platform economy*" are mentioned in the context of a PEW survey that claims that about one in four Americans earn money from digital platforms. The article details that there are those who supplement their regular income and those who rely on platform work to make a living. There are enormous differences between the people who engage in the *platform economy*, ranging from occasional renting or supplementing to working around a tight schedule.

An article from the *NYT* called *Platform Companies Are Becoming More Powerful—but What Exactly Do They Want?* by John Herrman from 2017 uses the term *platform economy* as a more general term to refer to all kinds of companies, including Uber. The article reports on Uber and his founder and then-CEO Travis Kalanick and the relationship of the company to the drivers, which seems to be ambiguous. On the one hand, Uber relies heavily on a large pool of drivers who deliver their service around the clock; on the other hand, drivers irrevocably remain independent from the company. This is a reason why Uber, as part of the *platform economy*, has been mired in controversies. The term *platform business* is also used here to refer to the matchmaking structure of many of the new tech companies. The article claims that successful platforms create their own marketplaces or even sometimes end up controlling whole sectors. Companies like Airbnb, eBay, TaskRabbit, or Fiverr but also Facebook or Google are part of the *platform economy*. The article defines these platforms as "asset-light," "employee-light," "low on liability," and "aspiring toward monopolies." Additionally, platforms are described as "intoxicating to investors." The article claims that criticism about the *platform economy* has been slow to emerge and tensions have often been ignored, especially when it comes to labor issues because platform work has emerged in areas that are used to precarious working conditions. However, the tensions between platforms, the customers, the workers, and the environment they operate in are growing.

Another article also focuses on struggles of the likes of Uber (*European Court Deals New Blow to Uber, Ruling It's a Cab Service* by Liz Alderman from 2017), but this time in the realm of litigation. The term *platform economy* is mentioned here in the context of legal action against Uber, for example in Europe. The article claims that court cases will illuminate what it is really like to work in the *platform economy*.

As said before the term *platform economy* is very rare in the liberal media material. Although it is a rather neutral and appropriate term for the activities described, it is just not used in a grand fashion. In the articles mentioned here, it is also used rather vaguely. It tends to refer to new (*sharing economy*) platforms like Uber, but Facebook and Google are also thrown in the mix. In the instances mentioned here, the term is used when reporting on problems and issues with these platforms, for example when it comes to taxation, labor standards, or the growing market power of some platforms.

The usage of a more neutral term such as *platform economy* instead of *sharing economy* could point to the fact that the media have recently started to strive for a more neutral way to report on digital platforms without invoking old tropes that were associated with the *sharing economy* such as sustainability, community, or empowerment. This also goes hand in hand with the fact that the articles mentioned above are only from the years 2016 and 2017.

6.3.2.2 Gig Economy in the Liberal Media Data

As mentioned before, there are more proliferate terms in the textual data than *platform economy*, for example *gig economy*. The term appears to be more directly concerned with working conditions and workers themselves. There is a wide range of articles in the *NYT* and the *Washington Post* that mention the term, and there are several more specific themes that can be traced in the liberal media data. The investigation of the material is grouped around the following themes: **gig workers, freelancers, independents**, the **ambiguous relationship of (liberal) politicians and the gig economy, Uber, flexibility,** the **universal basic income, social provisions and labor law,** and **ideology**.

Before going into detail about the different themes, collocates for the term *gig economy* are going to be examined (Tables 6.42 and 6.43). The most frequent collocate of *gig economy* in the liberal media material is *so-called*. Throughout the whole media material, but in fact in all of the material investigated in this book, the terms *sharing economy* and *gig economy* are often accompanied by the word *so-called*. As indicated before, there is a certain awareness that the terms are not completely accurate, and this is most often expressed by putting *so-called* in front of them. Another way to express this is the utilization of quotation marks, which is also often the case. Looking at Table 6.43, there are at least 30 instances where *so-called* appears as a collocate of *gig economy*.

Apart from that, many of the collocates of *gig economy* can be grouped around the theme of labor: *independent, temporary, contingent, classify, exploitation, part-time, on-demand, worker, freelancers*, or *positions* are all concerned with the situation of workers. Most of these terms point to a more flexible labor market where people work in temporary jobs or as independents. The collocate *exploitation* indicates that these developments are seen as questionable by the outlets examined

Table 6.42 Liberal media: collocation graph of gig economy MI $\geq$ 7, minimum collocate frequency 5

Source: Author, using #LancsBox

here. Classification (*classify*) of workers as an issue also shows up in the collocation graph.

Although *opportunities* also occurs as a collocate and is in fact a little more frequent, *exploitation* is a much stronger collocate (it is located closer to the node *gig economy*), which indicates that the term *gig economy* is likely to occur with the word *exploitation* in the texts. Economic opportunities as well as problematic issues around labor such as exploitation of workers are continuously discussed around the *gig economy* over the years.

In the liberal media material investigated, there is another article that picks up the problem of terminology in the context of the *gig economy*. The article *The dean of American labor reporters explains everything*, on the Washington Post Blogs from 2014 by Lydia DePillis, talks about the fact that the term *sharing economy* is not really suitable for many of the platforms. *Gig economy* is used instead. Companies like Uber, Lyft, or Airbnb are part of this economy. Some workers value the *gig economy* because of the freedom it gives them; others would prefer stable

Table 6.43 Liberal media: collocates of gig economy MI ≥ 7, minimum collocate frequency 5

gig economy

Freq: 367 Collocates: 32

Index	Status	Stat (03 - MI)	Collocate	▼ Stat	Freq (coll.)	Freq (corpus)
1	O	R	wrongly	11.969004740113629	5	18
2	O	R	fashioned	11.679463389731168	5	22
3	O	R	exploitation	11.272659298057865	6	35
4	O	R	tribunal	11.09451246664625	5	33
5	O	R	classify	11.00962489222406	5	35
6	O	L	ripple	10.781359099513766	5	41
7	O	R	safeguards	10.781359099513766	5	41
8	O	L	prevalent	10.679480756220343	5	44
9	O	L	britain's	10.424662391502938	10	105
10	O	R	contingent	10.232013674861562	5	60
11	O	L	so-called	9.903899582207783	31	467
12	O	L	wider	9.513201553321865	8	158
13	O	R	freelancers	9.504099467881593	8	159
14	O	L	seeks	9.303909753964483	6	137
15	O	R	taskrabbit	9.232017920011268	6	144
16	O	L	part-time	9.160357963446227	9	227
17	O	R	exciting	9.14455632733683	6	153
18	O	R	ruled	9.051444425794715	5	136
19	O	L	on-demand	8.86702210209249	11	340
20	O	R	blame	8.747820112352889	7	235
21	O	L	nick	8.704279429136555	5	173
22	O	L	affect	8.330481900303607	6	269
23	O	R	positions	8.30918601378414	8	364
24	O	R	independent	8.087117599307984	14	743
25	O	R	temporary	7.8957355829286024	5	303
26	O	R	opportunities	7.765319047545304	9	597
27	O	R	creating	7.5969326646472854	11	820
28	O	L	worker	7.509148019051476	9	713
29	O	L	net	7.382352806557368	6	519
30	O	L	rise	7.252658358934126	11	1041
31	O	R	helping	7.173125589407924	5	500
32	O	L	increasingly	7.102735913818036	9	945

Source: Author, using #LancsBox

employment especially due to the *gig economy's* income volatility. The article also talks about inequality and puts the *gig economy* into the context of the broader discussion around inequality in the USA. Another article from 2017 in the *NYT* called *Platform Companies Are Becoming More Powerful—but What Exactly Do They Want?* by John Herrman does not talk about the terminology specifically, but rather about the platform technology behind the "*gig*" or "*sharing economy,*" which plays a big part in their market success.

As said before, there are different themes that can be associated with the use of *gig economy* over the years. One such area of interest is referred to as **gig workers, freelancers, independents.** Despite remaining somewhat unclear on terminology, there are generally many articles in the liberal media material that use the term *gig economy* in the context of self-employed workers. The "unique" thing about the *gig* *economy* is that only independents work in it. This is a fact that is often (critically) discussed in the liberal media sources.

For example, in the article *Going It Alone, Together* in the NYT from 2013 by Steven Greenhouse, the term *gig economy* is used to talk about the life of someone working as an independent contractor. Independent contracting is much more common than one might think and is not only limited to branches like construction. The article claims that there is a growing group of workers, independent contractors, temp workers, contract employees, or freelancers, who are hired by companies on a short-term basis to cut costs. The article sees a growing "freelance economy" emerging in the USA, made up of workers such as software developers, graphic artists, accountants, consultants, nannies, writers, editors, designers, or sellers on Etsy. The term "freelance economy" might have been used here instead of the term *gig economy* because in 2013 the term was even less proliferate than it is today. In the article, more traditional independent jobs as well as online platform jobs are discussed. Some of these workers are even represented by a union, the Freelancers Union. The article claims that one of the key issues in this part of the economy is healthcare coverage. But even if people have health care, they might prefer a stable job, rather than the independent status. Others value the flexibility. Sara Horowitz from the Freelancers Union is quoted saying that the middle class is at risk of being pushed down toward working-class and working-poor status and that the freelancers are the first group witnessing this.

In a 2014 article in the *NYT* by Natasha Singer called *Check App. Accept Job. Repeat.* the term *gig economy* is used when talking about new working patterns fueled by technology, for example working through apps. Other terms referring to this activity are mentioned such as *sharing economy*, "peer economy," or "collaborative economy." Taking gigs is very flexible, but also very uncertain for platform workers who look for jobs on a day-to-day basis. Yet, people have worked in such arrangements before the advent of digital technology. In the past, this was called piecemeal work.

The term *gig economy* is again associated with the term "freelance" in the next article called *Freelancers in the 'Gig Economy' Find a Mix of Freedom and Uncertainty* (2014) by Rachel L. Swarns in the *NYT*. Freelancers are presented as the prototype working in the *gig economy*. Instead of calling them "gig workers," "freelancers" is used, which might be due to the fact that "gig worker" is not a common term (especially not in 2014), which was reflected in the frequency analysis of this book. The *gig economy* is made up of many different professions, but many freelancers in the *gig economy* do not have a high income; many make less than $25,000 a year. They also often lack basic benefits that are associated with stable employment like a fixed income, health benefits, paid vacation, or a retirement plan. Yet, taking up freelance work might be a solution for someone who cannot find stable employment. Although gig work is not ideal, it might be better than having no job at all.

The terms *gig economy* and *sharing economy* are often used interchangeably. That is also the case in Mark Warner's column in the *Washington Post* in 2015 called *Facing the gig economy*. The US Senator is mentioned in many instances throughout the sources in the *NYT* and *Washington Post* as one of the most vocal politicians on the subject of the *gig economy*. Warner served as Governor of Virginia and became a US Senator in 2008. He himself was involved in venture capital investing into telecommunications technology in the 1980s. He is more present in the media material until 2015; after that his presence seems to fade more and more when the *gig economy* is concerned. This might be due to the fact that as a Senator he is not part of committees specifically engaged with the subject. In the corpus on congressional material investigated here, Warner does not appear as often as in the liberal media material where he comments frequently on the topic of the *gig* or *sharing economy*. In this column, he comments on the changing structure of the US workforce, which is increasingly made up of freelancers, independent contractors, or the self-employed. In this article, *gig economy* and *sharing economy* are again used interchangeably, even in the same sentence, and Warner associates it with companies like Uber, TaskRabbit, or Etsy.

In a *Washington Post* Blog article from 2016 called *Uber and other companies like it make up a surprisingly small share of the gig economy*, Karen Turner also talks about big players of the gig economy, for example Uber. The article associates the rise of nontraditional work and work arrangements with technological change and a slow labor market. The article details the report by McKinsey Global Institute that talks about the growth of the independent sector, of which *gig economy* platforms are just a very small part. Yet, their hiring structure usually depends entirely on independents, which is further detailed in the 2015 article *What Amazon's Uber-like delivery service means for the sharing economy; Thanks to Amazon Flex, the gig economy of the future could look very different*, Washington Post Blogs, by Brian Fung. The positive testimony toward Uber in front of a House subcommittee by Luceele Smith, an Uber driver, which was mentioned in a previous chapter is mentioned in this article as well. In general, this article talks about how a stronger labor market might make it hard to attract enough independents because most people still seem to prefer stable employment if they have the choice.

Stable employment is very rare in the *gig economy*, but one such example is presented in the article *A Start-Up Shies Away from the Gig Economy* by Nick Wingfield, NYT, 2016. The article claims that the debate on whether to hire employees or freelancers has triggered a national debate about protections and the quality of jobs. The startup Redfin took on full-time employees instead of contractors, but faced backlash from investors over this decision because it slows down growth of the company. Redfin remains an outsider in Silicon Valley where almost all companies rely heavily on contractors or where whole business models are based on hiring contractors.

The lack of high-quality employment opportunities is again discussed in the *Washington Post* in 2017 in *Economy creating fewer job options for middle class* by Aaron Gregg. In this article, *gig economy* appears together with general technological progress as two possible reasons why there are fewer good options for middle-class workers. Two studies by Brookings and the George Mason University mentioned in this article indicate that digital technology has primarily created high-wage and low-wage jobs, while the middle class has suffered. Additionally, part-time and contract work with little to no social benefits are becoming a bigger part of the labor market. The "*gig economy*" is, however, very diverse and some independents are high-skilled experts who can demand a much higher income.

The next theme in which the *gig economy* is discussed in the liberal media material is the rather **ambiguous relationship of (liberal) politicians and the gig economy.** As the *gig* or *sharing economy* platforms become more widely known, politicians are trying to understand their impact and need to address possible issues. Democrats who are usually supported by Silicon Valley (and the users of the *sharing economy*, young urban voters) have a harder time embracing platforms wholeheartedly because they raise questions about labor protections and "good jobs." They might also worsen issues such as traffic congestion or a lack of affordable housing in cities. However, the companies also offer opportunities, are innovators, and offer better products or services in many instances.

An article in the *NYT* called *Republicans and the Politics of Uber* from 2015 by Vikas Bajaj talks about politicians and their relationship to Silicon Valley, also in the context of the presidential race of 2016 and whether Republicans or Democrats can be considered allies of *gig economy* companies. The issue of (mis)classification and independent contracting is brought up in this context. Many policy-makers are struggling with *gig economy* firms and their ways of doing business. But on the local level, issues around the *gig economy* are mostly not marked by political or ideological boundaries. Therefore, in certain cities conservative and liberal policymakers may be found on either side of the battle over the impact of actors like Uber, the article claims. However, the *gig economy's* users are more likely part of the Democratic voting block: less white, younger, and living in urban areas. Republicans might have a harder time attracting these groups regardless of their ties to the *gig economy*.

More ambiguous attitudes toward the *gig economy* trend are presented in an article in the *NYT* from 2015 called *Politicians Turn to Start-Ups for Grasp of 'Gig Economy'* by Katie Benner. Here, online platforms are used to illustrate what the "*gig economy*" is about. Politicians like the aforementioned Senator Mark Warner of Virginia or Jeb Bush but also the White House administration increasingly turn toward the topic of the *gig economy*, also in the run-up to the presidential elections of 2016. The article presents the topic of the *gig economy* and tech startups as some of the most important themes of the election cycle in which income inequality is a major topic. Platforms also play a role in the inequality debate by contributing to the rise of gig work, for example. Politicians are therefore increasingly interested in how these startups and business models work. They look at the matching structure of platforms, as well as business practices that exercise more control over workers such as managing prices or dispatching drivers (Uber). The article states that the number of platform workers is growing and thus lawmakers have to react to controversial issues such as legal battles over the definition of employment or contracting. In this context, the term "future of labor" is used to refer to these new forms of work. Apart from several politicians visiting Silicon Valley, the article mentions expert witnesses called to testify in Congress on the matter of the *gig economy* as well. As mentioned before, an Uber driver was invited to speak before Congress, and other expert witnesses like the chief economist of Thumbtack, Jon Lieber, are invited to testify in *The Disrupter Series: How the Sharing Economy Creates Jobs, Benefits Consumers and Raises Policy Questions*.

But policy-makers do not always have to travel to the West Coast to learn more about the *gig economy*. There are actors in Washington itself who conduct workshops or initiatives on the matter. If the group of independents is growing, there might be issues with the availability of social safety net provisions, which is detailed in *A safety-net movement for on-demand workers* by Lydia DePillis from 2015 in the *Washington Post*. The term *gig economy* appears when talking about an initiative by the Aspen Institute that looks at how those workers allegedly caught in between self-employed and employed can be protected while not gauging the growth of this sector. The article mentions other *Future of Work* initiatives, for example by the Department of Labor, the Hamilton Project or the Brookings Institution. The article also mentions that there is a lot of discussion around whether platform workers are misclassified or not.

Lawmakers are concerned about the future of jobs and want to know what this future will look like. This topic is treated, for example, by the Washington Post Blog article from 2015 called *Future tense: Concern about the quantity and quality of future jobs* by Jared Bernstein. Bernstein who has also testified on several occasions in Congress on matters such as taxation, stagnating wages, the middle class, or the state of economic opportunity in the USA paints different future scenarios of the world of work in his guest article.[16] One such scenario is the rise of the *gig economy*, meaning the growth of the group of freelancers, independents, and contingent workers. Although this development has been going on for decades, technology is accelerating the trend. In the text, the Bernstein exchanges the term *gig economy* with the *sharing economy* quite frequently. The article claims that the size of the *gig economy* remains mostly unknown. Additionally, the "becoming your own boss" notion of gigging is easily romanticized, according to the article. The idea of everyone suddenly becoming an entrepreneur is most often disappointed when people realize they are only engaged in small-scale gigs. In reality, this is often insecure and stressful low-wage work. The article goes on to say that while many people are concerned about the number of jobs in the future, it is more the quality of jobs that should be of concern, especially with inequality rising and bargaining power declining. If many people hold jobs in the future that do not pay well, demand is going to falter and economic growth could go down as well.

The article *The Resistance* by Joel Achenbach from 2015 in the *Washington Post* also uses the term *gig economy* in juxtaposition with the *sharing economy* to talk about some politicians' attitude toward this trend. Some think that the gig aspect of the new economy hurts workers. Companies like Uber, Airbnb, and Amazon Mechanical Turk are mentioned in this context. The article talks about political progressives' changing attitude toward the tech economy. They are not thrilled by

---

[16] Jared Bernstein testified, for example, in *The Decline of Economic Opportunity in the United States: Causes and Consequences*, Joint Economic Committee, 2017.

the huge profits tech companies make, the gender and racial disparities it portrays, and the rise of a tech elite. The article claims that the progressives' embrace of the *sharing economy* ended when they realized that it had developed toward a *gig economy*. Just like the Internet has disappointed many hopes for a more equal society, so did the *sharing economy* not live up to its expectations. There are some local and rare cases where the sharing idea is still alive (e.g., detailed in *A New Wrinkle in the Gig Economy: Workers Get Most of the Money,* NYT, 2016, by Amy Cortese about the project Stocksy.com that is based on a cooperative structure). In general, however, the promise of a fairer economy that was associated with the *sharing economy* has faded. In its stead, the *gig economy* has risen, meaning highly flexible work schedules, volatile pay, and little security for workers.

In a *NYT* article from 2017, these unfulfilled expectations of the *gig economy* are further discussed: *The Gig Economy's False Promise* by the Editorial Board. The *gig economy's* promise entailed that everyone could be their own boss and an entrepreneur through technology, the article claims. In reality, however, many people work long hours and have a stressful work schedule. Workers are often exploited by the new firms and the law does not protect them. The article claims that gig workers are often poorer and more likely from a minority background than the general population and generally lack basic work protections. Although the article states that the use of independent contracting is hardly anything new, the new *gig economy* businesses claim that being an independent is actually better than being employed. The article goes on to give a few examples of officials and workers pushing back against the *gig economy*, for example in Seattle where ride-hailing company drivers successfully lobbied for the right to unionize. Without guaranteed legal protections, the article claims, once agreed-upon norms of employment and work are going to disappear.

As could already be seen in the articles mentioned in this chapter, **Uber** plays an important role in many of the articles from the liberal media material. In the discussion around the term *gig economy*, Uber is especially prevalent because it stands for one of the biggest and most controversial actors among the platforms. Uber is seen as responsible for the surge in insecure gig arrangements in many places and is generally portrayed as the prime example of a *gig economy* business.

The articles from the *NYT* and the *Washington Post* deal with different topics associated with Uber such as the classification of workers. This remains an issue throughout the source material. Possible misclassification of workers has led to several lawsuits against Uber in different cities throughout the USA. In some of these lawsuits drivers were successful, but this has not led to a fundamental shift in the hiring strategy of Uber or other platform businesses. However, after founder and former CEO Travis Kalanick stepped down, Uber tried to rework its business culture and public perception. The article *How Uber Pushes Drivers' Buttons* by Noam Scheiber from 2017 in the *NYT* comments on this. For example, it describes how Uber and other companies use psychological tools and techniques to influence drivers and incentivize them to work, for instance through "gamification." This also has to do with low driver retention. Uber struggles to keep drivers working longer than just a few months. Additionally, with the hiring practice of Uber there is no control over workers' hours, which is the main argument used by Uber to defend their claim that they are not an employer. By hiring freelance drivers, Uber can minimize labor costs, but has difficulties compelling drivers to work at specific times, which makes it hard to establish the seamless transport of passengers Uber strives for. Other articles detail lawsuits Uber faces abroad, for example in Britain or with the EU where the issues range from minimum pay, or licensing, to breached transportation guidelines. There are also several articles detailing Uber's security issues and whether it invests enough in background checks of drivers.

Uber is one of the most well-known actors in the *gig economy* and has raised issues around platforms' hiring practices. Many argue that these practices have fueled the growth of a workforce that is highly flexible. **Flexibility** is another broader theme that is associated with the *gig economy* in the liberal media material. This flexibility often leads to people facing income volatility and seeking multiple jobs at the same time.

There are several articles in the liberal media material that deal with these issues. For example: *Side hustles are the new norm. Here's how much they really pay* in the *Washington Post* from 2017 by Abha Bhattarai. This is an article on the "*gig economy*" that discusses the reality of many gig workers who have several sources of income and do not work full-time on gig platforms. The article mentions some popular platforms like Lyft, Airbnb, or TaskRabbit, which have made the *gig economy* popular. The article comments on the fact that most people use the platforms as a side job: 85% of people make less than $500 a month on average with the services. Airbnb lets hosts earn the most with a median income of $440 a month, compared to $210 from Lyft, $40 from Etsy, $70 from Postmates, $110 on TaskRabbit, and $155 from Uber. These results are based on a study by Earnest, a loan provider in San Francisco. The data implies that many people working on platforms are making some extra money on the side. A bigger implication is, however, that many people are working several jobs to make ends meet, on platforms or elsewhere. The article offers a slow job market, growing income inequality, stagnant wages, and increasing student loan debt as possible reasons for this development. Although at the time the USA was at near full employment, the quality of jobs has been eroding and therefore people look for further income, the article claims. Arun Sundararajan is quoted saying that we need to rethink employer–employee relationships as the structures of the economy are changing and there are more ways toward an income today than just traditional employment.

The next article from the *NYT* called *Steady Paycheck, Shaky Income, Rising Angst* by Patricia Cohen from 2017 goes in the same direction. The article comments on income volatility once more, stating that even a regular job might not deliver a steady income anymore. The *gig economy* is mentioned here as being behind this trend toward more income volatility. In many jobs, working hours are unreliable, which makes it hard for families to organize. However, the *gig economy* can also be used to smoothen some of the income insecurity. In general, however, people seem to prefer stable and predictable work to gig work whenever they can get it.

The 2017 *NYT* article *Glum, Glummer, Glummest* by Jon Pareles gives a rather gloomy outlook not only for workers in general, but for the millennial generation specifically. Income inequality and student debts are putting many millennials in tough spots in their lives. They often work in dead-end retail service jobs or in highly flexible *gig economy* jobs to make ends meet. Additionally, they are worried that they will not be able to rely on the social safety net anymore.

Other articles such as the 2017 article *Why some families who save constantly are still struggling to make ends meet*, by Jonnelle Marte on the Washington Post Blogs, look at the situation of families who are often unable to save money for tougher times. The article claims that inconsistent paychecks and unpredictable expenses are to blame. That is why many people have to dip into savings for everyday expenses. The *gig economy* is not portrayed as the main reason for income volatility in this article. Rather, there are other jobs that are highly dependent on tips and commission and can lead to volatile income over the year. These kinds of jobs might also be a reason why people seek extra income on *gig economy* platforms.

The aforementioned articles show that the liberal media outlets are rather critical of some aspects of the *gig economy*, especially when it comes to the overall impact on the workforce that has to deal with more flexibility, income volatility, and insecure career paths. But what can be done to address issues like low and volatile wages, a lack of basic social security, and the overall challenge to find a good job? Different policy proposals are discussed by the liberal media sources in the context of the *gig economy*. For example, the **universal basic income** (UBI) is one option that is mentioned in the material. **Social provisions** like the Affordable Care Act or portable social benefits are also discussed. Additionally, **labor law** is discussed for example in the context of the classification of workers or bargaining power.

There are several instances where the idea of the UBI is discussed in relation to the *gig economy*. An article in the *NYT* from 2016 called *A Plan in Case Robots Take the Jobs: Give Everyone a Basic Income* by Farhad Manjoo uses the term *gig economy* to talk about uncertainty for workers in the future. Even when technology has created jobs in recent years, the author claims, these jobs were often part of the "so-called *gig economy*" and are not stable. Another article goes in the same direction (NYT, 2016 by Peter S. Goodman, *Free Money for the Jobless*) and uses the term *gig economy* in the context of the ongoing replacement of stable jobs by contract work, which is in line with other developments such as the introduction of robots in the workplace, and a push toward new ways of doing work altogether. This notion is pursued in another article in the *Washington Post* from 2017, *Before the next tech revolution* by Christine Emba. She comments on the 10-year anniversary of the iPhone. The *gig economy* is mentioned because the smartphone ushered in a new era of app-based companies such as Uber. The smartphone did not only transform ways of communication, but also many other branches of society and work. The article claims that the "*gig economy*" is making work more precarious and incentivizes us to work more at all times. Tech developments like AI or machine learning could also potentially take over more human jobs, making the situation for human workers even more insecure. The article claims that society is not ready to talk in earnest about the possibility of automation leading to a massive underclass. The only things discussed are some forms of retraining or the UBI. According to the article, society has adopted a wait-and-see attitude toward the future which could become problematic: industrialization has lasted over decades and has still spurred many clashes in politics and society. The smartphone has changed many branches of society in only 10 years, which means that society has to address these issues faster.

Apart from the UBI that could be considered a rather radical idea to address issues of a flexible and independent workforce in the future, there are other policies that are discussed in the context of the *gig economy*, for example, healthcare provisions. The 2017 article *Along with Obamacare, start-ups now in limbo* in the *Washington Post*, for example, talks about the fact that "Obamacare" has spurred the development of startups whose fate is now tied to the survival of the Affordable Care Act. Millions of dollars have been invested in digital healthcare startups. Additionally, many "*gig economy*" companies such as Uber have profited from Obamacare because since the reform their flexible workers have an easier time purchasing health care. Because of this, tech leaders have been among the greatest advocates of maintaining the Affordable Care Act.

In addition to health care, the possibility of a portable social safety net is discussed in the context of the *gig economy*. Sara Horowitz, the director of the Freelancers Union, wrote an article in 2015 about this issue called *Help for the Way We Work Now*. She equates *gig economy* with the "freelance economy," which gives flexibility and independence to workers. Although freelancers make up a big part of the workforce (about a third, according to her), they still lack basic benefits and protections, which is a central challenge for policy-makers. Horowitz advocates for a portable safety net for freelance workers. She argues that politicians have not realized the urgency of this problem and that they are using "outdated language" that has nothing to do with how people work today or will work tomorrow.

The possibility of portable social benefits is discussed in another article in the *NYT* by Noam Scheiber from 2016 called *Care.com Creates a $500 Limited Benefit for Gig-Economy Workers*. This article talks about Care.com (a nanny and babysitting service platform) which began to set aside up to $500 a year for workers to use for health care, transportation, or education expenses. This is seen as a move to address the problem of gig workers who receive income from multiple sources but have no benefit structure to pay into. Care.com's solution is seen as a first step to provide something like portable benefits to gig workers. The article claims that several people, including tech leaders, are pushing the idea of portable benefits. Yet, there has been little progress in this direction. The article in the *NYT* called *Redefining 'Labor' in the Gig Economy* by Cecilia Kang from 2015 also looks at the issue of portable benefits. The article looks at a coalition of think tanks, tech startups, and unions that think about possible reforms to improve the situation for workers. Upending the companies by classifying all independents as employees could mean the end of many gig platforms, which is something that nobody really wants, including the workers.

As can already be seen in the article mentioned above, there are several issues around labor that are discussed when it comes to the *gig economy*. One very crucial aspect is worker classification. This topic is picked up in an article from 2015 in the *NYT*, *Employees, Contractors and Those in Between* by Noam Scheiber. The term "so-called *gig economy*" is again used in this instance. Here, Alan B. Krueger, former Chief Economist under President Obama, and Seth D. Harris, former Deputy Labor Secretary, argue in favor of *gig economy* workers receiving more rights and protections. However, they also argue that forcing traditional employment structures on these workers could be an existential threat to this "online-intermediate work" that many people engage in. Yet, gig or on-demand workers do also not fit every business model, as there is a lot of turnover and less availability of workers at undesirable times or locations. Some companies like Munchery or Instacart are therefore rethinking their models based solely on gig workers. Generally, companies need to ask themselves if they want and need a certain amount of control over their workforce, which can trigger a different worker classification. Exerting more control usually means companies qualify as an employer. For some *gig economy* platforms like ride-hailing firms (Uber or Lyft), some form of control is desirable. For example, companies want to be able to react in cases of low-rated drivers and a lack in customer service. These drivers might be deactivated because they are harmful to the business and the customers. The article argues that for these cases, the labor laws should be updated in order to define the status of employees and independents for twenty-first century needs.

Worker classification and categorization are discussed in several other articles in the liberal media material. In some instances, there is a focus on labor organization and bargaining power of these new (gig) workers. For example, in *Shifting gears in the Uber wars* from 2015 in the *Washington Post* by Brian Fung and Jacob Bogage, the term *gig economy* is used when talking about the labor movement. The USA's biggest labor organization, the AFL-CIO, is quoted saying that gig work is not a new phenomenon, but has been around for years, for example in construction or the entertainment business. In their view, Uber and the other platform businesses are just another chapter in the struggle between employers and workers. Although Uber is credited for the trend toward more independent work, the trend has started well before the company was even founded and misclassification issues have also existed before Uber.

Defining 'Employee' in the Gig Economy in the *NYT* from 2015 again talks about the history of workers' protections and the new *gig economy*. Labor protections have been denied by employers in the past. Now, new companies like Uber are continuing to do so in a grand fashion. Hiring independents and thereby saving labor costs is one reason behind the fast growth rates of some of the app-based companies. Whether workers are actually misclassified is usually decided in court using a specific system. Among other things, it must be determined whether the work is an integral part of the employer's business, how much control the employer exerts over the worker, and whether the relationship is open-ended or limited. But problems about the determination of this classification remain.

Another article by Noam Scheiber in the *NYT* called *Solo Workers Unite to Tame their Gig Jobs* from 2016 is also concerned with labor and its possible organization in the online *gig economy*. The article talks about how workers often feel squeezed and dehumanized by business decisions that the gig companies make. Here, the workers are portrayed as looking for independence, but often ending up at the mercy of the powerful companies they work for. These companies make decisions without involving the workers in any way. Uber is again mentioned as an example. In some areas, the workers are beginning to connect in order to fight for better treatment from platforms. This does not only happen at Uber, but also at other companies like Postmates or Amazon's Mechanical Turk. Additionally, other worker alliances of independent workers are reaching out to *gig economy* companies and workers. Yet, not all platforms face the same labor disputes. There are platforms where struggles are rare like eBay or Etsy. These platforms focus on selling instead of gig work. Platform drivers, for example on Uber, are often more limited in their independence than so-called micro-entrepreneurs because of the rating system, pricing system, and other rules set by Uber and others.

Other actors quoted in the liberal media material also emphasize the need for more bargaining power for (gig) workers. Former Treasury Secretary and Economic Adviser under Obama, Lawrence Summers, writes *Why we need unions* in 2017 in the *Washington Post*. He mentions the *gig economy* in the context of an overall loss of bargaining power through different channels (outsourcing, automation, and the *gig economy*). This loss of bargaining power has ultimately held down wages, according to Summers.

Another article on the Washington Post Blogs from 2017 called *The increasing importance of a Labor Department that understands the threats to workers in the current economy*, by Jared Bernstein, mentions the "*gig economy*" as one factor in ongoing pressures and struggles that the labor force in the USA is facing. These factors include a decrease in unionization, a breakdown of the normative contract, an attack on immigrant workers, and pressures from technology. Additionally, a slack in the labor market makes it harder to find good jobs.

Generally, it remains hard to measure how big the *gig economy* truly is and how significant its impact on the labor force will be in the future. Many of the aforementioned articles portray the *gig economy* and the overall outlook for the labor force in the future rather gloomily, shaped by a loss of bargaining power and more and more insecurity. Yet, there are two other articles from the liberal media sources that paint a different picture of the future of the labor force, one that might be marked by labor scarcity. In the 2017 article in the *Washington Post* called *A labor problem, but also an opportunity*, by Robert J. Samuelson, the term "*gig economy*" occurs together with the terms "independent workers," "contingent workers," and "freelancers." This article has a more positive outlook toward the *gig economy*. The article sees the growth of independents as a result of a tougher labor market but also as an opportunity in the future. The author argues that in an aging society, a smaller labor force could lead employers to offer more attractive career paths in order to hold on to their workforce. The author claims that due to labor scarcity, market power might swing from employers to workers in the future and thus workers would have a better bargaining position.

The article *A new era of labor scarcity?* on the Washington Post Blogs from 2016 by the same author, Robert J. Samuelson, already detailed his position on labor scarcity. But Samuelson even tells the reader to "forget the 'gig economy'—at least for now." Here, the author argues that the *gig economy* is actually not the driving force of change in today's labor market because there are so few people working in the *gig economy*. Putting online gig work to the sidelines, the author nevertheless argues that there is a general push toward alternative work arrangements, which is the bigger driving force of change. The article argues that one in six jobs can already be considered nontraditional. These include subcontracting, temp work, independent contracting, freelancing, being self-employed, or working on call. The article mentions a study by Lawrence Katz and Alan Kruger, which raises concerns that the labor market might be divided into insiders and outsiders with very different outlooks on career possibilities. The author claims that the best hope workers in the USA have is that they are entering an era of "labor scarcity." Immigration is abating and women have already been integrated into labor market to a large extent. According to the article, this could mean that in the future there might be an advantage for workers and they will gain a better bargaining position.

There are two other articles from the liberal media sources that do not fit the other categories mentioned above but are interesting additions to the liberal discourse on the *gig economy*. These two articles deal with **ideology**, more specifically with liberalism and the rise of populism. The two articles try to draw a larger picture of the development of the American society of which the *gig economy* is one part. Firstly, there is the *Washington Post* article *Liberalism's crisis of confidence* by Sebastian Mallaby from 2017. Here the "*gig economy*" occurs in the context of advanced technological developments like the advent of smart robots. The article claims that today, in the time of another industrial revolution, liberalism is essential. Technological progress will create winners and losers in the economy and liberalism as a set of ideas can find ways to manage the outcomes of such a development as it has done in the past. But the ideals of liberalism must be asserted more confidently, according to the article.

Another article goes a step further and makes assumptions about what might happen if liberalism fails to communicate desirable solutions for the future. The Washington Post Blogs article from 2017 talks about the rise of populism (*This new poll shows that populism doesn't stem from people's economic distress; It's not about your finances. It's about how you think the rich and poor are doing* by Brian Rathbun, Evgeniia Iakhnis, Kathleen E. Powers). In this article, the ongoing support for (right-wing) populist actors is investigated. Some experts argue that the losers of globalization who are struggling financially are more likely to support populist leaders. The new economy and a polarized labor market with the *gig economy* as one part of it also come up in this debate as people feel they are left behind and are losing out in the new economy. The article claims, however, that research shows that not only the economic situation but also people's attitude about the broader societal turn determines their support or rejection of populism.

Pieces on the "*gig economy*" or the *so-called gig economy* as they occur in the liberal media sources are mostly concerned with the changing nature of work. Generally, although there might be fears of job loss in the future, it is more the quality of jobs that should worry lawmakers and workers. On the one hand, the *gig economy* points to the changing attitudes toward work but also to a different nature of work in many instances (flexible, short-term, project-based, independent). On the other hand, the *gig economy's* success might be a sign that people are already looking for extra income today because they are struggling with stagnant (volatile) incomes and growing living costs. The material investigated here is often concerned with these developments toward a more insecure labor market that has become more precarious even before the advent of digital technology. But the rise of (smart) technology is seen as a very significant factor in this development. This has triggered reform calls such as the UBI, portable social benefits, a reform of the worker classification system, or strengthening bargaining power for (gig) workers. Generally, the lack of "good jobs" that allow for a stable income and career opportunities is commented on profusely. The sources also include columns by (former) politicians who emphasize the necessity of strong labor representation and new reforms to improve the situation of independent workers.

The articles also comment on politicians' attitude toward the *gig economy* and the new businesses that are representative of this new economy such as Uber. Generally, there is some ambiguity of liberal politicians who are close to Silicon Valley leaders on many social and cultural issues, but not so much on their laissez-faire business practices. Some progressives are also increasingly critical of the ever-increasing wealth of the tech businesses and entrepreneurs. They had great hopes for the *sharing economy,* but have now been sobered up about its impact and by the rise of the *gig economy*. Republicans are portrayed as trying to get closer to Silicon Valley and their voting block, but traditionally have a tougher stance in Silicon Valley.

In general, the increase of robots and the rise of the *gig economy* are both seen as exacerbating the problem of a more precarious labor market in the future, but also as an opportunity in such a labor market. On the one hand, people are looking for ways to increase their income, for example through gig work. The *gig economy* is a welcome way to do so but remains a contested ground because of ongoing labor disputes. On the other hand, gig work is generally seen as part of a precarious labor market leading to even worse work arrangements. The liberal media outlets seem to be more critical than positive about the impact of the *gig economy* more broadly. Only a few differing opinions are mentioned, for example focusing on possible labor scarcity in the future which would improve the position of the labor force. Overall, however, opinions about gig work remain rather ambiguous with a stronger focus on the downsides of these work arrangements.

In the context of the *gig economy* in the liberal media material, there are even a few instances where the articles touch upon the wider implications of the development toward more precarious and automated future, saying that liberalism as an ideology will have to find answers for the "losers" of this development. People who are economically frustrated and feel left out of the progress generated through technology might turn toward populist leaders as an outlet for these frustrations. The liberal media outlets therefore see it as a crucial endeavor to address the issues arising through the *gig economy* and technological progress overall.

6.3.2.3 Sharing Economy in the Liberal Media Data

After having assessed the less common terms *platform* and *gig economy*, the term *sharing economy* will now be investigated in the liberal media material (Tables 6.44 and 6.45). The term *sharing economy* occurs many times in the material from the liberal media sources as it was one of the original search terms used to compile the corpus data. LancsBox produces over 1000 single occurrences of the term in the liberal media material of which only some instances will be explored in more depth. More general themes were identified around which the articles on the *sharing economy* in the *New York Times* (*NYT*) and *Washington Post* can be grouped.

But before going into detail, let us look at the collocations of *sharing economy* in the liberal media material. The collocate *so-called* is again a very frequent one. As said before, the collocates *sharing* or *gig economy* are often referred to as the *so-called sharing economy* or in quotation marks. There are over 60 instances where *so-called* appears as a collocate of *sharing economy* (Table 6.45). *Rise* is also a very frequent collocate. In many instances, the "*rise* of the *sharing economy*" or platform businesses is discussed. *Government-run* and *epitomized* are also strong collocates but appear only a few times in the corpus material overall. *Epitomized* is

Table 6.44 Liberal media: collocation graph of sharing economy MI ≥ 7, minimum collocate frequency 5

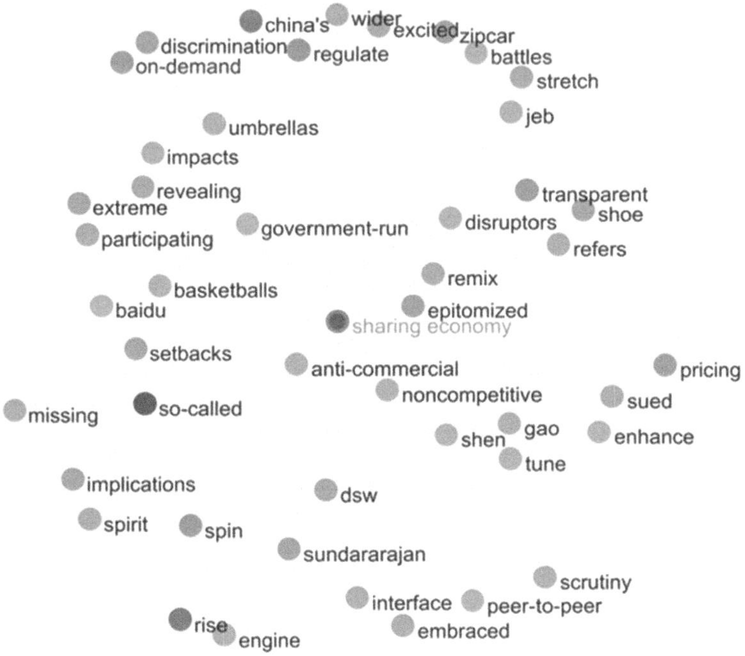

Source: Author, using #LancsBox

Table 6.45 Liberal media: collocates of sharing economy MI ≥ 7, minimum collocate frequency 5

sharing economy

Freq: 1,039 Collocates: 46

Index	Status	Stat (03 - MI)	Collocate	▼ Stat	Freq (coll.)	Freq (corpus)
1	O	L	anti-commercial	12.315275941529245	6	6
2	O	R	epitomized	11.99334784664189	8	10
3	O	R	noncompetitive	11.829794548461722	5	7
4	O	R	remix	11.440772099621494	6	11
5	O	L	government-run	10.936734936382093	5	13
6	O	R	disruptors	10.549718726605663	5	17
7	O	R	shen	10.467279034974318	5	18
8	O	L	dsw	10.215740267978363	7	30
9	O	L	basketballs	10.05224153569544	5	24
10	O	R	gao	9.682995404517712	5	31
11	O	L	setbacks	9.630769279093132	7	45
12	O	L	so-called	9.514082302684615	67	467
13	O	R	tune	9.279642715523503	5	41
14	O	R	transparent	9.11015690960189	9	83
15	O	R	refers	9.067341726899315	6	57
16	O	L	baidu	9.022486397046771	5	49
17	O	L	umbrellas	9.022486397046771	5	49
18	O	L	sundararajan	9.011490358315973	8	79
19	O	L	revealing	8.993347846641996	6	60
20	O	L	impacts	8.730313440808146	5	60
21	O	L	spin	8.683001565260641	10	124
22	O	L	participating	8.490843012372643	6	85
23	O	R	shoe	8.381160307390813	7	107
24	O	R	jeb	8.297349317879029	5	81
25	O	L	regulate	8.220114644999882	11	188
26	O	M	interface	8.158767886054365	6	107
27	O	R	sued	8.132050613179493	6	109
28	O	R	enhance	8.129405198768074	5	91
29	O	L	extreme	8.11140064717042	7	129
30	O	M	excited	7.7606843808575885	6	141
31	O	R	battles	7.6946864256456875	5	123
32	O	L	implications	7.663194904404703	7	176
33	O	R	stretch	7.642848103033899	6	153
34	O	M	wider	7.596452859036943	6	158
35	O	M	zipcar	7.560384902624786	8	216
36	O	R	peer-to-peer	7.539169165367646	5	137
37	O	M	embraced	7.5165318625416555	6	167
38	O	L	china's	7.4985782262750105	22	620
39	O	L	spirit	7.482383693632453	6	171
40	O	R	pricing	7.2904401776141	9	293
41	O	R	scrutiny	7.206745948986675	6	207
42	O	L	missing	7.179133822721894	6	211
43	O	L	engine	7.105819134746412	6	222
44	O	L	on-demand	7.075805513094068	9	340
45	O	L	rise	7.046405054228035	27	1041
46	O	L	discrimination	7.035162405163742	7	272

Source: Author, using #LancsBox

used in phrases like the *sharing economy* "epitomized in companies such as Uber." *Government-run* only occurs in one context referring to a Chinese government initiative, the "*government-run* Sharing Economy Research Center."

Apart from that, there are several other collocates that refer to what we could call the "alternative economy" aspect of the *sharing economy* in some way. These include *anti-commercial, noncompetitive, peer-to-peer, participating, on-demand, disruptors, remix*, and *transparent.* Especially in its initial phase, the *sharing economy* was strongly associated with a noncommercial and *peer-to-peer* outlook that was presented as an alternative to consumer capitalism. It was often strongly connected with *disruptors* of established markets such as Uber and the taxi industry.

There is another group of collocates that can be associated with the more problematic issues of the *sharing economy*. These collocates include *discrimination, regulate, battles, sued, scrutiny, implications, missing, extreme*, and *impacts*. These collocates seem to refer to *battles* over the right *regulation* of the platforms, but also legal battles (*sued*) that many platforms face over things like *discrimination*. *Sharing economy* platforms receive a lot of *scrutiny* as their *impact* becomes more pronounced.

The only actual platform business that comes up in the collocate list is *zipcar*, which now belongs to Avis. *Zipcar* is an international car-sharing service. New ways of transportation such as car-sharing are often discussed in connection with the *sharing economy*. Apart from *zipcar*, there are also two proper names that are part of the collocate list. One is the collocate *jeb*, which refers to Jeb Bush. There are several articles that comment on the campaign trail leading up to the 2016 presidential election. In the beginning, when Jeb Bush was still in the field, he and other politicians visited Silicon Valley to get a better grasp of the *sharing economy*. The second collocate that is a proper name is *Sundararajan*. Arun Sundararajan is the author of the book *The Sharing Economy* and is a frequently quoted expert in the field.

As mentioned before, there are certain themes in which the term *sharing economy* occurs in the liberal media material. These themes include the **sharing economy as the good economy**, **dark sides of the sharing economy**, **regulation**, **disrupters**, and **sharing economy and the future (of work)**.

The first theme, **sharing economy as the good economy**, can mainly be found in the earlier articles on the subject. The positive and hopeful framing of the *sharing economy* is strong at that time. In contrast to the *gig economy,* which seems to mainly invoke challenges such as labor disputes and insecurity, the *sharing economy* used to be associated with a positive outlook for the future. The *sharing economy* was framed as the new source of work and income where the individual was empowered and no longer a "wage slave." For example, in 2013, Juliet Schor, a well-known *sharing economy* expert, wrote an article in the *International New York Times* called *After the Jobs Disappear*. In this article, Schor comments on possible new sources of income, goods, and services in the future when employment will have become more and more insecure. The *sharing economy* is portrayed as one example of people carving out different income sources for themselves. Schor mentions all kinds of *sharing economy* efforts, some sustainable and local like makerspaces and time banks, others based on commercial online platforms like Airbnb or ride-sharing platforms. She assumes that the *sharing economy* is able to give more meaning, autonomy, and social impact to work. She says that the *sharing economy* can be seen as a return to independent production and self-provision of pre-industrialization times but with a technological touch. Yet, she sees the possibility that in the Western world the *sharing economy*, although it includes more "making," sharing, and self-organizing, can also mean fewer formal jobs.

In another 2013 article on washingtonpost.com called *The allure of sharing*, Steve Case comments further on the positive appeal of the *sharing economy*. Consumers get more choice and convenience in their lives. They put more emphasis on value access rather than possession. The article thus alludes to a shift in consumerism and consumer preference in general. The ownership ideal is somewhat abandoned in favor of the access ideal. This has the appeal of being both less consumerist and more sustainable.

The positive outlook continues in the *NYT* in 2013 with *Welcome to the 'Sharing Economy'* by Thomas L. Friedman. This article alludes to some of the most successful *sharing economy* businesses like Airbnb. The author claims that the *sharing economy* holds the potential of giving people new ways to earn a decent living when good jobs are hard to come by. The available jobs demand an ever-higher skill set that many people cannot meet. The *sharing economy* is thus an alternative. The founders of Airbnb and other platform businesses are quoted here saying that everyone can become their own boss by becoming a micro-entrepreneur. This way everyone can earn a living with the assets they already possess, like free rooms in their houses.

This idea of "idling capacity" that can be monetized in order to become a small-scale entrepreneur is further explored in another article called *How to Monetize Your Closet*, by Thomas L. Friedman from 2013 in the *NYT*. This article features details on Airbnb founders Brian Chesky and others. The *sharing economy* is equated here with the "collaborative economy" and it is portrayed as a way for the middle class to reduce their living expenses and accumulate some wealth. The assets you already own can be easily monetized through the platforms and thus extra income can be generated. The *sharing economy* is thus portrayed as the way toward new entrepreneurship and new concepts of ownership.

Another example for the positive initial framing of the *sharing economy* can be found in the article *It's Not Just Nice to Share, It's the Future* on NYT Blogs in 2013 by Tina Rosenberg. Here, "collaborative consumption" and "access instead of ownership" are used to describe the *sharing economy*. It is seen as a hip movement of light and lean consumption. *Sharing economy* activity is seen as cutting-edge, driven through technology, and hip because of its green image. It is also seen as a more community-oriented and network-based form of consumption.

There are several more articles from 2013 alluding to the peer-to-peer and anti-commercial spirit of the *sharing economy*, as well as to its sustainable image with allusions to new ways of transportation (e.g., Relay Rides), for instance. The environmentally friendly outlook is something that is picked up by several articles in the liberal media material, for example to talk about the beginning phase of car-sharing and ride-hailing platforms. At first, the idea prevailed that this was a sustainable way to use the "idling capacity" of private cars as most of them stand around unused for the majority of their life cycles. These expectations have been largely unfulfilled. But a few years ago, the *sharing economy* was still associated with a new and different spirit. The platforms seemed to point toward a more connected and meaningful way of consumption and a means to democratize commerce.

Although the very positive articles seem to be from the earlier years of this analysis, the hopes for a "better economy" in the form of the *sharing economy* have never been fully abandoned. In 2016, the *NYT* features an article called *Object Lessons: What We Collect* by William L. Hamilton that speaks of changes in ideas of ownership, especially among millennials who use the *sharing economy* intensively. The *sharing economy* here is equated with the service industry and "collaborative consumption." "Crowdsourcing" and "peer-to-peer" are also mentioned as terms to describe this behavior. Airbnb serves as the example to illustrate this change in consumer preferences.

But apart from the very positive articles mentioned above, there have always been articles that paint a more mixed picture of the *sharing economy*, weighing the upsides and downsides of the new platforms. For example, in 2014 on the Washington Post Blogs, in *Grover Norquist thinks Republicans can ride Uber to power in urban areas. That's probably a stretch; The politics of the sharing economy aren't as simple as he thinks*, Emily Badger claims that with the "*sharing economy*" it is difficult to know who the "good guys" are. Taxi drivers are pitched against amateur drivers or hotel chains against homeowners. Issues range from safety concerns, changing consumer demands, taxation, and challenges through the new economic models. There is a clash between technological change and entrenched laws that were created for good reasons. According to the article, the rise of a more nontraditional way of consumption and alternative work arrangements as embodied in the *sharing economy* brings these clashes to light. The article goes on to ask if the tensions over the *sharing economy* could help Republicans gain traction over Democrats in urban areas as Democrats seem to have a hard time embracing the new economy wholeheartedly. The author claims that there are no definitive ideological or partisan lines that can be drawn between supporters and critics of the *sharing economy*. Issues raised by the *sharing economy* are messy, says the author, for example in regard to regulations, unions, auto insurance, or taxation. Some of these issues are less partisan than others, but none of them seem to be quickly and easily resolvable.

Another early article that looks at the nature of the *sharing economy* in greater detail was written by Natasha Singer in the *NYT*, *Check App. Accept Job. Repeat.* (2014). The *sharing economy* is equated here with the "peer economy," the "collaborative economy," or the *gig economy*. Taking the life of one person as an example, the article shows that many people have started to work on platforms like TaskRabbit, Uber, or Lyft via apps. People can thus work on a flexible schedule. But the article also shows that workers often face unpredictable changes from the platforms, for example with pricing. Platforms might change their policy suddenly, taking a bigger share or reducing prices without the possibility for workers to intervene. Different reasons are presented for taking up this kind of work. Among them are long-term unemployment, rising inequality, and wage stagnation. The article claims that the reality of such a situation is that the micro-entrepreneurs championed by platforms become "micro-earners." The article thus portrays the *sharing economy* as piecemeal labor fueled by new technology. Apart from the workers' side, the article also emphasizes that consumers love the new services that make many products and services easily available and affordable. Venture capitalists and their funding of these platforms are also mentioned in the article. Overall, the article seems to caution that if people continue to seek work outside of traditional employment, a new precariat could emerge as income from these unstable jobs is low and there is no safety net for workers.

In *Unfair share*, in the *NYT* by William Alden from 2014, another mixed picture of the *sharing economy* is portrayed. The positive picture of the *sharing economy* as an opportunity remains. The *so-called sharing economy* is said to offer a new way of capitalism where normal people can turn their possessions into assets via online platforms. Airbnb and Uber are quoted as examples for a more sustainable and more virtuous future of consumption. Everyone can become an entrepreneur using their time and space. However, as the article claims, many professional operators are active on the platforms, easily outperforming amateurs. Arun Sundararajan and Juliet Schor are quoted as two well-known experts in the field. With professionals moving onto the platforms the chances and opportunities for micro-entrepreneurs are diminished as the big players get an "unfair share."

Another look at the *sharing economy* is taken in *The effect of the 'sharing economy'* on washingtonpost.com from 2014. The "*sharing economy*" is seen as a catalyst for positive change in branches of the economy that have not delivered high-quality services like the taxi industry. With competitors like Uber or Lyft, these branches are turned upside down with better technology and business models, according to the article. Highly monopolized markets are thus becoming more competitive offering better services and prices to customers. Yet, the article also mentions that it is mostly independent contractors who work in these new jobs.

The "access-rather-than-ownership" idea prevails over many of the articles on the *sharing economy* over the years, but it seems to be more pronounced in the early years. The 2014 article *Is Owning Overrated? The Rental Economy Rises* by Claire Cain Miller in the *NYT* uses all kinds of terms to refer to the "access ideal" of the *sharing economy*. For example, the *sharing economy* is called the "Rental Economy" or the "Netflix Economy." The article claims that during the recession, many of these platforms were formed in order to save money, but a gradual shift in consumption preferences and patterns also lies at the bottom of this. Juliet Schor is quoted here, saying that it is counterintuitive in an individualistic culture of America's proportions to think that renting and access as a form of consumption is successful. Nevertheless, the sharing economy shows that it is possible. Yet, a lessened emphasis on the sustainable outlook of this "access ideal" can already be seen in this article. Although some consumers might consider sustainability in their choices, the article claims that using *sharing economy* platforms is mostly a way for people to afford and maintain their past level of consumption.

In the next article in the *NYT* from 2014 called *The Technological Fix to Inequality*, by Tyler Cowen, the term *sharing economy* appears in the context of inequality, and a more mixed picture is again presented. On the one hand, technology has likely contributed to the rise of inequality. On the other hand, technology can also be part of the solution to fight inequality in the future. The *sharing economy* could make it possible to lower costs by having smaller renting spaces and to generally rent products instead of buying them, the article claims. This could be a way for low-income citizens to enjoy new services and products. New technology will become easier to handle even with fewer skills, which could also benefit millennial and future generations.

Millennials are again in focus in the *Washington Post*'s 2014 article *What causes the failure to launch* by Catherine Rampell. Millennials are described as valuing the *sharing economy* rather than the "ownership society." Yet, these ideals might not always be purely idealistic, as the article suggests. Millennials often live in tougher material circumstances than generations before them. They often delay basic steps in their lives like marriage or buying a house because it is harder for them to find a secure job and to make a living. The lack of "good jobs" is also discussed in the 2015 article in the *NYT* called *Uber Case Highlights Outdated Workers Protection Laws*, by Steven Davidoff Solomon (Professor at Berkeley). The article discusses disputes over contracting and employment. People are divided over the *sharing economy*—is it a good thing or does it lead to exploitation? Generally, a society is plagued by inequality when lower-skilled people can no longer find stable employment and a living wage. But with the new economy and the *sharing economy*, do workers actually value flexibility higher than security?

Another more mixed view of the *sharing economy* is offered by Emily Badger from the Washington Post Blogs in 2015 in *Sharing economy and outreach—will it be able to do something for the poor?* She argues that the real (questionable) promise of the "*sharing economy*" is what it can do for the poor. Will they actually benefit from the potential of the *sharing economy*? The *sharing economy* often seems like a place of well-off people, millennials, and those who are tech-savvy. But will it be something that benefits lower-income people as well? Arun Sundararajan and Samuel Fraiberger from NYU think that it will. In the article, they claim that prices for many expensive items will go down when they are available to rent and will therefore be accessible for low-income households as well. Additionally, lower-income households could rent out more valuable assets of their own if they decide to purchase them. However, there is little empirical evidence that low-income consumers are actually using these platforms, the article describes. Reasons range from a lack in infrastructure (Internet access, owning a smartphone or credit card) to trust, which is the most important ingredient in the *sharing economy*. Lower-income households are usually more skeptical about society in general and are less willing to rent out their own assets (if they have any) or trust the rating systems. Many aspects of the *sharing economy* are not really operating across socioeconomic lines and the question is whether this will ever change. The two researchers are not commenting on the nature of jobs changing through the *sharing economy* and whether this might benefit lower-income workers or put them in an even tougher position.

In the next article from 2017, the issue of working in the *sharing economy* is discussed to a greater extent. This article also features Sundararajan and is called *Side hustles are the new norm. Here's how much they really pay* in the *Washington Post* written by Abha Bhattarai. Here, the term *gig economy* is clearly preferred to the term *sharing economy* as it is about working on platforms like Lyft or

TaskRabbit. Arun Sundararajan is quoted as the author of the book *The Sharing Economy*. And in fact, the term *sharing economy* only appears in this article to refer to his book title. This article talks about gigs becoming the new norm and that families need the money to get by. Online platforms can be the point of access to supplementary income. However, it also raises questions about the burden that the workers need to carry and the overall relationship of employer and employee, which is changing.

Over time, it can be seen that the articles in the liberal media evolve from displaying a rather positive image of the *sharing economy* to a more mixed picture that also looks at downsides of this new trend. There are articles showing greater uneasiness with the initial promises of the *sharing economy* and look at the actual consequences of it in the real world. It seems that the sense of community and "purpose" are becoming selling points or are used in branding a positive image, rather than producing actual "sharing" experiences. This is an ambiguous and controversial change in the *sharing economy* that is mentioned in the liberal media material, for example on Washington Post Blogs, by Brian Fung, 2014: *Yes, Airbnb's new logo looks like a butt. That's kind of the point; Here's what the company's rebranding might do for the sharing economy.*

A more mixed picture of the *sharing economy* is painted by the liberal media outlets over time. At some point, the outlets start to spend more time discussing disputes and negative consequences of the *sharing economy* rather than the positive sides. This can be summarized under the broader theme of "**dark sides of the sharing economy**," which is a phrase actually used in some of the sources. In these instances, the articles paint a darker picture of the *sharing economy* that is somewhat departing from the hopeful outlook of the early years.

There are even two articles from the *NYT* and the *Washington Post*, published separately, which use the phrase the "dark sides of the *sharing economy*." One of these articles appeared in the *NYT* in 2014 and is titled *The Dark Side of the Sharing Economy* (by the Editorial Board). The article uses the "*sharing economy*" to talk about Airbnb and its problematic impact on housing in urban areas. The article claims that proponents of the *sharing economy* see it as a way for residents of desired areas to make ends meet in an expensive city while giving tourists a good deal at the same time. However, this ignores the fact that short-term renting offered on Airbnb is making housing less affordable in these places while also ignoring regulations such as zoning laws in many cities.

The second article alluding to the "dark sides" of the *sharing economy* quite literally appeared in the *Washington Post* in 2015 called *The dark side of a 'sharing economy'* by Catherine Rampell. This article talks about how flexible hours and "being your own boss" are valued by workers of Uber and the like. Other "peer-to-peer" companies are mentioned, for example, Airbnb, TaskRabbit, or Homejoy. The article claims, however, that the "dark side" is epitomized in a risk shift from corporations to the individual worker when it comes to liability aspects. Individual workers are faced with income volatility, their own capital investments (purchasing a new car, for example), criminal liabilities, and a general lack of protections. Risk management by a larger pool of people (corporations) and the growth of a social security net were advancements of the twentieth century that are now at risk, according to this article. Why corporations are less willing to take on the risk is debatable, says the author. It could have to do with globalization, the decline of unions, regulatory changes, new technologies, and the growing importance of financial markets. Therefore, the *sharing economy* is seen as the culmination of long-term trends that have led to more instability for workers and a declining welfare capitalism. The author discusses some remedies for this situation, especially a stronger government social safety net, for example by strengthening the Affordable Care Act.

Uber is also a frequent topic in the articles that focus on the more negative sides of the *sharing economy*. For example, this can be seen in 2015 in the *Washington Post* article *Shifting gears in the Uber wars* by Brian Fung and Jacob Bogage. In this article, Uber is practically equated with the *sharing economy*. It is seen as a means to make extra income. But at the same time, it is a nonreliable source and an insecure opportunity. The article says that Democrats are split over the treatment of the *sharing economy* as they are supported by Silicon Valley entrepreneurs politically, but also want to represent traditional working-class interests. Republicans are trying to make inroads with *sharing economy* users. However, Democratic strategists see the *sharing economy* as only one point in the larger conversation about the "future of work" on which the Democratic Party should focus. The issues of independent contracting in the *sharing economy* are mentioned, which is, however, an issue that is also not singular to the *sharing economy*. Many other businesses (such as FedEx) use it as well. Several specific Democratic politicians are mentioned in this context, among them Mark Warner, Elizabeth Warren, and presidential candidate Hillary Clinton.

There are also more and more articles that critically assess the legal conflicts that arise for *sharing economy* companies. This is detailed, for example, in *Some Setbacks for the Sharing Economy* on the NYT Blogs by David Streitfeld from 2014. Many of the businesses in the *sharing economy* are coming under more scrutiny over time. For example, Airbnb is sued over land use and zoning laws in certain cities. Uber has been the subject of legal action almost from the beginning, often because of worker classification issues.

Apart from allusions to the more positive beginnings, as well as to problematic consequences of the *sharing economy*, it is generally often portrayed as a **disrupter** of established markets in the liberal media material. One of the most prevalent ideas about the *sharing economy* is that it disrupts old and established branches like the taxi or hospitality industry. This is a theme that is addressed in several articles in the *NYT* and *Washington Post*. If certain industries are upended, new issues for policymakers arise. Political actors want to promote innovation and consumer welfare, but need to regulate risky behavior and make sure that taxation is fair and put into effect. In general, there are many articles that mention the *sharing economy* in the context of trust and credibility. Trust is one key element in the success story of the *sharing economy*. "Stranger sharing" was only made possible through elaborate rating and payment systems that were introduced to enhance trust.

Several companies move into territory that might be "ripe for disruption" or that had been resistant to change. This is for example addressed in 2014 on the NYT Blogs in *The 'Sharing Economy' Goes White-Collar* by Mike Isaac, which talks about how Uber, Airbnb, and other companies are increasingly targeting the corporate world. They are rolling out programs for corporations so that these can offer new products or services to their employees. In general, the *sharing economy* giants are diversifying their services, for example with business options (Airbnb) or by offering new services. Uber, for example, also started the UberEats delivery service or a gig worker hiring platform (Uber Works).

The disruption of old businesses is, in a way, seen as the new area of business-making (e.g., *The future of new business is disrupting old business, On Uber and the business model of disruption*, washingtonpost.com, 2015 by Barry Ritholtz). Certain companies like Uber, Airbnb, Snapgoods, RelayRides, PayPal, Instacart, Redfin, or TaskRabbit are mentioned as new and disruptive in their respective fields. They have entered markets that were monopolistic and uncompetitive with outdated products. The new competitors offer better products, often at lower prices, which explains the quick success of these companies. Incumbent businesses like the hotel industry harshly criticize the newcomers, in this case, Airbnb.

Additionally, around the new *sharing economy* giants like Airbnb or Uber, there are other smaller startups springing up tending to the big players. The *sharing economy* is also mentioned in the context of other emerging technologies like the Internet of Things or autonomous vehicles that could further disrupt other parts of the economy and workplaces.

The disruption and influence of *sharing economy* platforms on public transportation is also a frequent topic. Many of the platforms have disrupted transportation markets. Transportation platforms are often a new way to make commuting in urban areas more convenient. There is also hope that the platform technology could make it more efficient. This also goes along with calls for technological solutions to climate change. This is detailed, for example, in the 2017 *Washington Post* article *Could the rise of the sharing economy fight climate change? Up to a point.* by Sophie Yeo who quotes a study arguing that the rise of the *sharing economy* might help reduce the climate impact of dense urban areas. Individuals might be able to lower their footprint by using services like Uber or Airbnb. But there are also drawbacks to these activities, for instance that people are being lured away from public transportation. Yet, platforms offer more and more alternative transportation options such as UberPool which offers rather inexpensive rates and car-pools people inside one private car. Yet, it is still based on the use of the individual car. This worsens congestion and has a negative environmental impact. The study also suggests that if people use the extra money they have saved for carbon-intensive activities then there is no positive net effect either. This article from 2017 is increasingly rare in the liberal media material. Sustainability considerations concerning the *sharing economy* have mostly proven overrated over time. Most consumer behavior in the *sharing economy* has not led to a lower carbon footprint from more effective use of privately owned assets. The sustainability argument is not strongly discussed in the sources after some initial hopes in the beginning of the *sharing economy*.

Although *sharing economy platforms* are often portrayed as disrupters, there might also be a limit to what people actually want to share with strangers to make a small profit. In an article on the Washington Post Blogs from 2016 called *What we won't share; Our tendency to lend out our homes, cars and everything out for money has got to end somewhere* by Ana Swanson, the "*sharing economy*" is presented as a fast-expanding area but with certain limits. The article talks about a paper by John Horton (NYU, visiting economist at Uber) and Richard Zeckhauser from Harvard, which addresses the reach of the *sharing economy*. There probably will always be a market for renting out goods that are expensive, are used unpredictably, and are not extremely personal in nature, for example, lawnmowers, expensive jewelry, or tuxedos. The advent of the peer-to-peer online platform technology and matching algorithms has helped to make "stranger sharing" of these products possible and there is more potential for certain categories of these products in the future. Yet, the categories of what we really want to share are limited.

There is another bigger theme around the *sharing economy* in the articles from the *NYT* and *Washington Post*, which is **regulation**. As the *sharing economy* is a (self-declared) disrupter in many areas, there might be the need for new regulation. The introduction of new rules is not an easy endeavor, however, as political actors might be overwhelmed by the speed of disruption and by the new business practices of *sharing economy* platforms that try to circumvent existing rules and laws.

In some instances, there are articles that mention overregulation and caution against it. For example, in *Trusting the 'Sharing Economy' to Regulate Itself* in the business section of the NYT Blogs in 2014, Arun Sundararajan, author of *The Sharing Economy*, is quoted advocating in favor of "peer-to-peer" platforms like Airbnb or Uber to self-regulate. The terms "peer-to-peer" and "collaborative" are used to describe these new services; they are also associated with "individual innovation" and "entrepreneurship." The article claims that digital disruption is changing our experiences of services, and Sundararajan thinks that the platforms have the best means to regulate themselves and are doing so in many instances already. The argument in favor of deregulation highlights the consumer side of the *sharing economy* saying that the services and products it offers are superior and a great deal for users. Overregulation could take this away (e.g., *The top 7 innovations at risk from overzealous regulation* by Larry Downes, 2015 on Washington Post Blogs).

Generally, however, more articles that could be found in the liberal media material discuss the need for (new) regulation when it comes to the *sharing economy*. The article *Companies Built on Sharing Balk When It Comes to Regulators*, by David Streitfeld in the *NYT* from 2014, talks about this. The article argues that many *sharing economy* companies could only become so successful because they have dodged many regulations on their way to the top. Regulators are becoming increasingly aware that the companies are acting in ignorance of the law and are trying to address that problem. The article comments on a case against Airbnb. The company is asked to disclose host information for short-term rentals which are against the law in certain areas. Airbnb argues that the existing laws do not fit the *sharing economy* as "people" increasingly become "businesses." There are laws for people, and there are laws for businesses but nothing for the "in-between" status of small-scale *sharing economy* efforts. Moreover, the article argues that incumbent businesses often favor new regulation efforts because they see their own businesses threatened and not because new regulation might always be necessary.

An article from 2017 touches on legal issues for Uber. Uber is often portrayed as consciously trying to circumvent or ignore existing rules (Washington Post Blogs, 2017, *Uber used secret tool, extraordinary measures to sidestep government officials*, Craig Timberg, Brian Fung). This article talks about Uber as one of the most valuable firms in the *sharing economy* and how it once again faces backlash over its handling with existing restrictions and bans that it has tried to circumvent. This is not the first time that Uber faces backlash over its business practices and public conduct. In general, Uber often gets more bad press than other *sharing economy* platforms due to its controversial approach to hiring, to internal corporate culture, or its conscious attempts to circumvent existing rules. As two of the most well-known and most successful platforms of the *sharing economy*, both Uber and Airbnb are most often mentioned when certain legal troubles are discussed.

Uber is once again a subject of debate in the Washington Post Blogs 2014 article *Will the sharing economy make us all Republicans?* by Andrés Martinez. Republicans are especially keen to embrace Uber and their business model. Republicans usually favor deregulation, which is theoretically in line with Uber's interests. For liberals, it is more complicated. They usually favor regulation, but even among liberals there are actors who are questioning approaches that hinder services like Uber from operating. The article claims that there have been no breakthroughs in dealing with new economy issues like antitrust, net neutrality, or taxing in a coherent fashion across partisan lines and that this is unlikely to change.

As the *sharing economy* platforms become more well known, policy-makers and regulators are paying more attention. A 2015 NYT Blogs article called *Washington Scrutinizes the Sharing Economy*, by Rebecca R. Ruiz, reports from two conferences in Washington D.C. that examine peer-to-peer Internet companies such as Uber, the impact they might have, and the possible regulations that should be taken into consideration. The Federal Trade Commission (FTC) held a workshop where many Internet platforms such as Uber, Airbnb, and Postmates, as well as regulators and academics, were present. The other conference called Techonomy Policy was organized by the FTC and the Federal Communications Commission. Outside experts such as Arun Sundararajan were invited to talk about the sustainability of the *sharing economy*. This conference also focused on the nature of work in the *sharing economy*, somewhere in between flexibility, uncertainty, and entrepreneurship. Gary Shapiro of the Consumer Electronics Association, who also testified on the topic in Congress, is also quoted in this article.

In general, the liberal media material displays a discussion around the question of whether *sharing economy* platforms should abide by existing laws and regulations or whether there should be new ones such as new categories of workers or new tax laws for micro-entrepreneurs. In many articles, the "platform side" argues that we live in a new era where the old rules that regulated the economy do not fit anymore. That is why some of the platforms do not necessarily consider themselves bound by those rules. Additionally, many of the platforms see themselves as intermediaries only and not concerned with the laws on the ground. Platform businesses generally seem to favor no (new) regulation and emphasize "self-regulation." Yet, some critics see the need for new regulations because the old rules seem to be outdated or are often circumvented.

Apart from possible new regulation, the **sharing economy** is also discussed in the context of **the future (of work)** in the liberal media material more broadly. In which direction will the *sharing economy* develop in the next years? As said before, the very positive outlook about real "sharing" and more sustainability has faded over time. There are more and more, even obscure *sharing economy* startups that spring up offering everything from boat rentals and private storing units to Rent-A-Runway and other things.

Millennials are the generation that is continuously associated with the *sharing economy* (e.g., Washington Post Blogs, 2015, *I'm a millennial with a minivan, and I feel pretty great about it; Don't hate* by Ylan Q. Mui). The lifestyle of millennials is described as being familiar with renting, hailing rides, and owning the newest tech gadget. Millennials live in urban areas where *sharing economy* services are more common. Yet, this lifestyle can also lead to issues in the future because millennials might want and need more traditional jobs and products or services when they become older. Apart from a focus on millennials, there are several instances where the *sharing economy* is also presented as a way for elderly people to make some extra income (e.g., *Five ideas to better prepare Americans for retirement* by Dominic Basulto on the Washington Post Blogs, 2014).

When it comes to the future of work, the *sharing economy* and automation are discussed as having an impact on the traditional employment paradigm (e.g., in Washington Post Blogs, 2015, *The political economy of a world without work*, by Daniel W. Drezner). In this article, the *sharing economy* is mentioned in the context of a world without enough work for everyone. Derek Thompson's article in the Atlantic *A world without work* from 2015 that was discussed previously in this book is also mentioned in the article (Thompson 2015). Here, the *Washington Post* article questions assumptions that the *sharing economy* could be a new source of income arguing that in the end it overwhelmingly rewards the owners of capital over workers. "Post-wage arrangements" like the UBI are mentioned in this context. These possible solutions to a "world without work" remain contested, however, and often lack the political will. The author remains skeptical about the future and sees a multitude of problems that need to be addressed, of which the *sharing economy* is only one part.

More tech skepticism is discussed in other articles, for example *Techno-skeptics' objection growing louder; In the New Machine Age, they fight the tech establishment, saying human needs are getting lost in the digital revolution* on Washington Post Blogs (2015) by Joel Achenbach. In this article, the *sharing economy* is described as having been initially embraced by many but is now seen as perverted and harmful to workers. The *sharing economy*, just like the Internet itself, is a letdown for people who had hopes for a more inclusive world. Critics are uneasy about more and more labor inequality among tech workers and reject tech companies moving away from their initial ideals by becoming defense contractors, lobbyists, and advertisers, as well as the source of some of the biggest data privacy breaches of the past years.

These developments in the tech sector have been controversial and were met with backlash. That is one reason why platforms had to increase their lobbying efforts. This is discussed in the *Washington Post*'s 2016 article *Airbnb bulks up its lobbying power* by Catherine Ho. This article describes how *sharing economy* companies like Airbnb are hiking up their presence in Washington through lobbying groups because they are coming under more scrutiny from lawmakers. The article argues that Airbnb wants to sell lawmakers the narrative that Airbnb is empowering people by making it possible for middle-class families to earn extra money to pay the bills. Airbnb even commissioned a report in 2016 to prove this point which was authored by economist Gene Sperling who served in the Council of Economic Advisors (discussed previously in this book (Sperling 2015)). Airbnb also wants to defend itself against the hotel industry that pushes for Airbnb to abide by existing regulations. Elizabeth Warren, Dianne Feinstein, and Brian Schatz are quoted here who have issued a letter to the FTC asking who is running full-time businesses on Airbnb and how this is affecting local communities. The lawmakers mentioned here are concerned about growing housing prices, housing shortages, and sensitive zoning laws that could come under pressure from platforms like Airbnb.

Apart from Airbnb, Uber continues to remain highly controversial, especially over its treatment of drivers. It is questionable how this will develop in the future and how much it will have an impact on the overall (future) workforce. Although there are certain locations where drivers have gained more power, for example in New York City where the first driver association was recognized in 2016 (Washington Post Blogs, 2016, *Uber recognizes first drivers association in New York City*, by Frederick Kunkle), these instances do not point to a general shift in Uber's business practices. The association in NYC cannot engage in collective bargaining. In fact, Uber only recognized the association because drivers agreed to remain independent contractors who cannot bargain collectively. In an effort to ease some tensions, Uber said it will work with the Freelancers Union to establish portable benefits in NYC. Yet, this is only relevant for New York and does not settle cases in other states. So far, there is no sign that the employment status of drivers on Uber will be resolved any time soon.

In this context, an article by John Herrman in the *NYT* from a year later (2017) asks *Platform Companies Are Becoming More Powerful—but What Exactly Do They Want?* In this article, the term "platform" is used to refer to the *sharing economy* or *gig economy*, which are used interchangeably. The article claims that platforms are capitalism distilled to its essence. They are experimental, prone to creating externalities, but not interested in what is going on beyond their own business. They are part of the underlying change of the economy through technology, the article argues. The substructures of the *sharing economy* and claims of the "end of ownership" are part of this development. However, there are more and more tensions erupting between the big *sharing economy* businesses like Uber, the workers, and the customers. The author thinks that the tensions will become increasingly visible because they have been ignored for too long. Platforms claimed they were "perfect," without taking responsibility of how their business models affected workers and society more broadly. When platforms arrive in areas that have not been as precarious and contract-based as some of the branches platforms started in (e.g., in the taxi industry), then the tensions will boil up. In the eyes of the author of this article, conflicts will become more visible and relevant because they point to social and political changes on a larger scale.

Another article from 2017 called *How Efficiency Is Wiping Out the Middle Class* in the *NYT* by David Siegel looks at the future of the middle class. This article also uses the term *so-called sharing economy* interchangeably with *gig economy*. These trends in the new economy point to flexibility and convenience. Yet, the author "does not buy it" because he does not consider gig work a career. Platforms do not develop skills or offer wage growth, and gig work is prone to be automated when possible. Gig work is just useful to make ends meet on a short-term basis. The author points to those saying that history has taught us not to worry about jobs, they will come back despite a new Information Revolution. Yet, the article paints a different picture saying that the term "creative destruction" has become hollowed out. The term is now used to justify any (economic) destruction even if it is not creative in the Schumpeterian sense. The author suggests that policies should focus on corporations fostering career paths for the future so that the middle class will have better prospects. He thinks that not everything should be narrowed down to efficiency if it threatens the middle class so severely. Society should think about what progress really means without necessarily stopping technological advances.

Apart from creative destruction in the future, the *sharing economy* is also discussed in the context of inequality. The problem of rising inequality is addressed in the 2016 Washington Post Blogs' article *Global innovation may have a 1 percent problem* by Dominic Basulto. The *sharing economy* is presented as the result of technological progress and the emergence of successful companies like Uber and Airbnb. With this development comes the general sense that the structure of the economy might be changing overall and that the labor force might be transformed into an underpaid, part-time precariat. The article thus asks the questions if technological progress only benefits the very wealthy and does not help to address the problems of inequality rising around the world.[17]

In the liberal media material overall, the term *sharing economy* is used in the context of a wide range of topics and articles of which only a few could be detailed here. Firstly, a stream of articles could be observed, especially in the beginning of this collection (2013–2014), which portray the *sharing economy* in a very positive light, emphasizing its sustainability, peer-to-peer structure, and access rather than ownership ideal that points to the end of consumption as we know it. In this context,

[17] Outside of the US context, the *sharing economy* is often mentioned in reference to China in the liberal media material. The potential of the *sharing economy* is huge in the People's Republic and the Chinese people are open to technology and innovation. In the years 2016–2017, there are more and more articles on China and the *sharing economy* in the *NYT* and *Washington Post*.

the *sharing economy* is not only a trendy new term, but it seems to be the good and right thing to do.

Yet, there had always been those articles, and over time more of them, that were also more skeptical about the *so-called sharing economy*. Some articles express upsides and downsides of the new platforms; others are more specific about the possible "dark sides" of the *sharing economy*, mainly pointing to the questionable situation for workers on the platforms, the impact on communities (insecurity, housing prices), and the letdown of many who had hoped for a more inclusive growth and different way of consumption. In short, the *sharing economy* could not live up to the hopes of many liberal thinkers and developed more toward the "*gig economy*" which is characterized by volatility, insecurity, and flexibility rather than a true "sharing experience" emphasized in the early years. Some articles portrayed the *sharing economy* as not necessarily new and innovative, but as part of a decades-long process toward alternative work arrangements and a more independent workforce.

Apart from these more abstract considerations, the *sharing economy* platforms were displayed as disrupters of established markets (may that be good or bad) that invite scrutiny and potentially the need for new or different regulation. Uber and Airbnb were among the most debated examples here. In general, the *sharing economy* was also described as one part of a different future of work and economy under ongoing technological progress. Technology has the potential to creatively destruct the economy, but the liberal media material also cautions to not consider all destruction as creative destruction that leads us forward. In some instances, the creative part of the process seems inadequate and harmful to workers. The *sharing economy* in this sense is portrayed as a destructive force with some creative potential, delivering great consumer experiences but few true career paths toward good jobs and a middle-class lifestyle.

6.3.2.4 Sharing, Gig, and Platform Economy in the Liberal Media Data

The terms *sharing economy*, *gig economy*, and *platform economy* are used to a very different extent in the liberal media sources. As the network graph in Table 6.46 shows, the *sharing* and *gig economy* produce a much wider range of collocates than *platform economy* and are connected through some terms such as *rise, so-called, on-demand*, or *wider*. As said before, the term "*so-called sharing* or *gig economy*" is used widely across the different sources. Additionally, *on-demand* points to another term that is closely connected to the *sharing* or *gig economy*. The nature of platforms like the ride-hailing service Uber or delivery services like Postmates or Instacart are *on-demand*. Their *rise* is fueled by the instant connectedness made possible through smartphone technology and mobile Internet. This has changed many of our consumer preferences, but it also points to the "gig" nature of the platforms that fuel flexible but insecure working arrangements. From Table 6.46 one can also see that *platform economy* as a term is not connected to the other two in this analysis. As said before, *platform economy* remains a rather rare expert term that is not widely used

Table 6.46 Liberal media: network collocation graph of sharing economy, gig economy, platform economy, MI ≥ 7, minimum collocate frequency 5

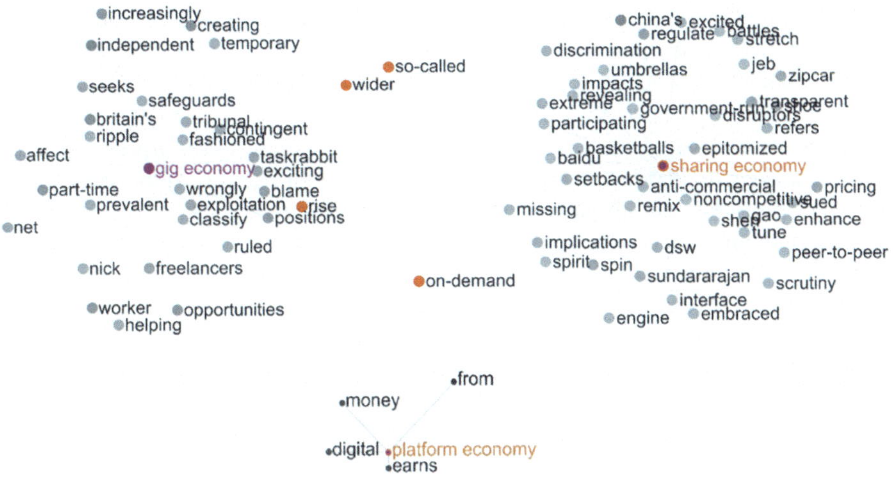

Source: Author, using #LancsBox

across the sources in the liberal media outlets, or in fact, any of the material investigated in this work.

Despite the different extent of their usage, the terms *platform economy*, *gig economy*, and *sharing economy* are often used interchangeably in the sources from the *NYT* and *Washington Post*. This is especially true for *sharing* and *gig economy*. The *sharing economy* remains the most popular term, with *gig economy* following suit. The *platform economy* is the least prevalent term, although it remains the most neutral and possibly most appropriate term of the three. It seems to remain a more all-encompassing term that includes *sharing economy* platforms but also companies like Google or Facebook.

From reading the sources more closely, it becomes apparent that at some point the term *sharing economy* was associated with a more positive outlook toward the future emphasizing new ways of (collaborative and sustainable) consumption through the newcomers in the market such as Airbnb or Uber. Yet, the term *sharing economy* was never exclusively used in this way and has become more nuanced over time. In fact, the "dark sides" of the *sharing economy* have become more apparent, also with more and more legal action the platforms were involved in.

The term *gig economy* has never had the same appeal as the term *sharing economy*. By focusing on the "gig" character of the platforms, aspects like insecurity, flexibility, and volatility of platform work were the center of attention. Although the articles also admitted that some workers may cherish the flexibility they gained, "gig work" is mostly seen more critically in the sources from the *NYT* and *Washington Post*, pointing to all kinds of implications for workers in the future. That is why the articles focusing on the *gig economy* also include several examples dealing with labor issues such as bargaining power or possible reforms to improve the situation of workers in the future. The articles around the *gig economy* seem to be less conceptual than articles on the *sharing economy*. They often focus on specific issues, practical policy proposals, and regulations.

The articles focusing on the *gig economy* and the "dark sides" of the *sharing economy* also emphasize that the success of platform work actually points to economic struggles and the absence of "good jobs" overall. Platforms are seen as a way to make extra income in an insecure and slow labor market. At the same time, however, the platforms are part of why the labor market becomes more and more insecure in the first place. The growth of alternative work arrangements in general is discussed in this context. The growing *gig economy* certainly fuels the ongoing trend toward a more diverse and independent workforce.

Over time, there are many articles dealing with technology that is profoundly changing our society and the economy as a whole; the *sharing economy* is seen as part of this. Yet, as indicated before, the *sharing economy* has lost some of its initial positive appeal and is seen less as a pathway to an "alternative economy" in any way. Although the ideas around sustainability or "idling capacity" have not disappeared in their entirety, they are much less pronounced than a few years ago. Overall, there are many articles in liberal media material that discuss platforms critically and portray them as business giants of the new economy, not much different from other Silicon Valley companies.

The liberal media sources also pick up on some of the possible policies to address the issues of the *sharing economy platforms* such as worker classification (or reform thereof), the UBI, or portable benefits such as health care or other social provisions. This is seen as part of the larger conversation around the future of work and the growth of the independent workforce in the USA.

6.3.3 Platform Economy in the WSJ *Material*

After having investigated the discourse around the platform economy in the congressional material as well as in the liberal media material, the material from the *Wall Street Journal* (*WSJ*) will now be discussed.

The term *sharing economy* appears 230 times in total in the *WSJ* corpus, at a rate of 1.32 per 10,000 tokens. *Gig economy* as a term appears 71 times in total with a relative frequency of 0.41 per 10,000 tokens. Both terms appeared at a higher relative frequency rate in the liberal media material (*sharing economy*: 1.96 times per 10,000 tokens, *gig economy*: 0.69). *Platform economy* as a term does not appear in the sample of *WSJ* material investigated here. This search term was rare in the

Table 6.47 *WSJ*: collocation graph of sharing economy MI ≥ 5, minimum collocate frequency 5

Source: Author, using #LancsBox

other material as well, but it is completely absent in the *WSJ* material investigated here and is also absent in the material from the Senate.

In the following, the terms *sharing economy* first and then *gig economy* will be investigated by identifying different themes that showcase their use and application throughout the *WSJ* material.

6.3.3.1 Sharing Economy in the *WSJ* Data

Before moving on to the specific contextual reading, the collocations of *sharing economy* in the *WSJ* are discussed (Tables 6.47 and 6.48).[18]

As could be seen in the material before, the term *so-called* is a strong collocate of *sharing economy*. There are 26 instances in the list below where *so-called* appears as a collocate of *sharing economy* (Table 6.48). This again points to the fact that the

[18] A lower MI score (MI ≥ 5) than the default was used to depopulate the graphs.

Table 6.48 *WSJ*: collocates of sharing economy MI ≥ 5, minimum collocate frequency 5

sharing economy

Freq: 230 Collocates: 24

Index	Status	Stat (03 - MI)	Collocate	▼ Stat	Freq (coll.)	Freq (corpus)
1	O	L	shackling	12.888213127026054	5	5
2	O	R	pioneered	10.888223608719464	6	24
3	O	L	vs.	10.303264601912991	6	36
4	O	L	so-called	9.611387895538318	26	252
5	O	L	democrats	8.77275042274036	12	208
6	O	R	individuals	8.254022302248114	6	149
7	O	R	apps	7.723321101177602	8	287
8	O	R	governments	7.468689517258689	5	214
9	O	R	didi	7.210155961816712	5	256
10	O	R	free	6.888228194484268	6	384
11	O	R	regulators	6.461962997963246	5	430
12	O	M	businesses	6.459867558733635	8	689
13	O	L	growing	6.146760717055814	5	535
14	O	M	that's	5.995432179765067	6	713
15	O	R	startups	5.828612979694522	5	667
16	O	R	where	5.691234689261948	11	1614
17	O	M	uber	5.673908768343067	14	2079
18	O	L	think	5.653410518176994	8	1205
19	O	L	part	5.6498231434097885	7	1057
20	O	L	working	5.582621966779855	5	791
21	O	R	workers	5.339791284225952	10	1872
22	O	L	just	5.200852241294533	8	1649
23	O	R	labor	5.1877881639061	5	1040
24	O	R	government	5.187788094796411	7	1456

Source: Author, using #LancsBox

writers contributing to the *WSJ* seem to be aware that the term *sharing economy* is not the most suitable term for what they want to describe, but that it is still largely in use. *Vs.* as a collocate indicates that the *sharing economy* is sometimes described as the *gig vs. the sharing economy.*

One of the strongest collocates is *shackling*, albeit not very frequent. This is due to an article from 2015 called *Shackling the Sharing Economy; Big Labor and the plaintiffs bar gang up on Internet start-ups*, which alludes to an alleged "attack" by unions on *sharing economy* startups described in this article. This already indicates the position many of the *WSJ* articles express, namely that the *sharing economy* should be free to develop in the market and not be "*shackled*" by things like stricter labor laws.

One group of collocates can be associated with the business side of the *sharing economy*. This includes *businesses, startups, apps*, and *uber.* As one of the most well-known platforms, *Uber* appears as a collocate, as well as the collocate *startup* that refers to the business culture of many of the platforms. Most of the platforms are *app*-based which has certainly helped their success. *Pioneered* also points to the innovative nature of the *sharing economy* platforms.

Another group of collocates can be associated with the workers' side and includes *workers, individuals, labor*, and *working*. The platforms are said to empower individuals to work whenever they want as they offer easy and flexible access. *Regulators, government*,* and *democrats* refer to political actors who are engaged with the *sharing economy*. *Democrats* appears as a collocate as there were several articles referring to Silicon Valley's relationship to Democratic politicians.

There are several larger themes that were identified when talking about the *sharing economy* in the *WSJ* material. These include **platforms and their business model**, **technological innovation**, **labor issues**, **Airbnb**, and **Uber and its larger impact**.

The first larger theme in which the term *sharing economy* appears is **platforms and their business model**. There are many articles in the *WSJ* material that inform readers about the new platform businesses. Additionally, these articles talk about the business model of the platforms and what potential they hold for the future. For example, the article *Dresses and Leftovers*, by Geoffrey Fowler and Evelyn M. Rusli from 2013, talks about the newest technology trend, apps that let you share almost everything. It mentions platforms like *Feastly*, *MamaBake.com*, *Zipcar*, *Airbnb*, *DogVacay*, and others. Rachel Botsman is quoted in this article with her book *What's Mine Is Yours*, saying that "stranger sharing" over the Internet is becoming less risky and people begin to trust each other in new ways. The term *sharing economy* is mentioned in the context of legislative concerns or whether startups violate the law. The *sharing economy* platforms' way of business-making is presented as democratizing services and turning people into micro-entrepreneurs.

Some of these new platforms have become big players, which other startups want to recreate. This is discussed in the 2014 article *Startups Want to Be the Next Airbnb, Uber; Yet at Least a Few Dozen of These 'Sharing Economy' Businesses Have Failed Since 2012*, by Sarah E. Needleman. The term *sharing economy* is used in the context of some big players like Uber and Airbnb who have gained a lot of traction. Because of this, many other entrepreneurs are introducing these business models in new startups. Sam Altman from Y Combinator is quoted saying that the *sharing economy* is reeling in a lot of investment. Yet, the article also mentions many *sharing economy* startups that have failed after only a short while. Others face difficulties by running into issues with city laws, for example. Additionally, the article mentions vivid opposition from traditional brick-and-mortar businesses toward their new digital competitors.

This shows that although many *sharing economy* startups attract so much attention and investment, there are also risks, which is the topic of *Keywords: The Risks In Today's Frothy Tech Valuations*, by Christopher Mims, 2014. The article alludes to risks of valuations, for example of *sharing economy* businesses such as Uber or Airbnb that could possibly fall short of expectations. This is again picked up in another article in 2015 called *Don't Overpay for Technology Again*, by Jason Zweig. The article alludes to the 2000s' technology euphoria around social media that led to a stock market bubble. This could happen again for *sharing economy* businesses. Some of the *sharing economy* platforms such as Pinterest, Lyft, or Uber have all estimated valuations of several billion dollars. Investors see enormous growth potential from these business models, but the *WSJ* article alludes to the fact that investors might be overpaying for technology. The article brings the *sharing economy* in connection with the early 2000s boom that resulted in growth and benefits for consumers, but that also led to the consequent bust. The article cautions investors not to cause another bubble by overpaying for technology just because of high expectations. Other articles go in a similar direction like *Voices: Weighing Opportunities in the 'Sharing Economy'—Ilina Dutt; suggestions from an advisers whose clients have been asking about investing in stocks such as Uber Technologies and Airbnb*, 2015, or *Technology Bubble? Ask Waffle House*, by Laura Stevens, 2015.

Another article touching on the business model of platforms is called *Property: Helping with home sharing—firms assist owners by delivering keys, arranging cleaning, 'type of concierge'*, by Kaya Laterman from 2014, and talks about the *sharing economy* as being "real and here to stay." Platforms even stimulate further economic activity as more and more businesses spring up around them. For example, Airbnb hosts can hire other firms to manage their rentings, for example by offering cleaning or concierge services. The platforms themselves are thus producing even more economic activity. Although these platforms seem "here to stay" there is a lot of hysteria around their business-making practices, according to the article.

This hysteria is again mentioned in a later article in the *WSJ* from 2016 called *Most Americans Don't Know about Ride-Sharing and the 'Gig Economy'*, by Josh Zumbrun. He argues that it is an illusion that the *sharing* or *gig economy* is allegedly "taking over the world." By citing a PEW research study, the article shows that the terms *sharing economy*, "on-demand economy," or *gig economy* are mostly unknown to Americans. For most of the platform activity, there is little awareness among Americans and many have never used platforms at all. They are also mostly oblivious to the issues surrounding them. The only thing that people are using more often are platforms for selling second-hand goods. Yet, the terms *sharing economy* and *gig economy* are both not established with most Americans. The article argues that gig workers on platforms are very rare and that the idea that the whole economy is becoming "Uberized" is overblown. Yet, politicians, Silicon Valley, and "thinkfluencers" are making it seem that the whole economy is turning "gig," according to the article. Most of the *WSJ* material investigated here presents the *sharing* or *gig economy* as only marginal and nothing to worry about more generally.

One issue that is discussed, however, is tax collection from these new economic activities. This topic becomes more prevalent in 2017 in the *WSJ* material. Apart from that, there are several articles that discuss the situation of *sharing economy* platforms in the EU and especially China where there is a lot of potential for future growth. In the EU, several companies have faced challenges. In China, a gradual opening to some companies and business models is discussed. China is portrayed as a country with huge potential markets in the area of platforms.

Similarly to the articles around the business models of platforms, there are many article in the *WSJ* that portray the *sharing economy* as part of **technological innovation** more broadly. For example, the article *Some Promising Trends for Startups to Propel* from 2014 mentions the term *sharing economy* together with "3D printing" or "crowdfunding," innovations that have the potential to reshape whole industries. Another article from the same year called *Mothers, Tell your*

Children to Be Software Coders, Dozens of companies are poised to follow Alibaba in going public, but there's a shortage of developers, by Andy Kessler, 2014, mentions *sharing economy* together with other innovations like cryptocurrency, nonmilitary drones, and the Internet of Things. The *sharing economy* is seen as one of the innovations of the last few years that will reshape the economy. A more niche innovation is mentioned in *Silicon Valley's Unlikely New Frontier, Startups provide legal marijuana farmers and retailers with data-driven tools*, by Elizabeth Dwoskin, 2015. In this article, marijuana is described as a new product for app-enabled *sharing economy* platforms after the drug became legal in some states in the USA. *Sharing economy* platforms provide delivery services for all kinds of products and niche markets are one target in this development.

Ride-sharing and ride-hailing as part of the *sharing economy* are other trends that are discussed in the context of technological innovation, for example in *Future of Cars: Hitching a Ride From Your Bank; French bank Société Générale will list a stake in its car-leasing business*, by Paul J. Davies, 2017. This article claims that the future of car ownership lies in the *sharing economy* and the industry needs to be aware of this. The same is argued in *The End of Car Ownership; Ride sharing and self-driving vehicles will redefine our relationship with cars. Auto makers and startups are already gearing up for the change*, by Tim Higgins, 2017. This article claims that ride-sharing will become even more popular when people become more comfortable with the *sharing economy* and use it in urban areas where they live. Owning a car can become more and more of a burden for urban residents and they will prefer to share or hail a ride when they need to instead of buying their own car. This opens up new opportunities but also poses challenges for auto makers.

The next theme associated with the term *sharing economy* in the *WSJ* material is concerned with **labor issues**. On a number of occasions, the situation of workers in the *sharing economy* and opportunities and challenges are discussed. For example, the article *BossTalk: TaskRabbit Chief Aims to Recast Freelance Work; CEO Says Startups Need to Do More to Protect Workers*, by Elizabeth Dwoskin from 2014, talks about the wider impact of platforms like TaskRabbit. The article uses terms like "freelance economy" and "micro-gig" when describing this platform. *Sharing economy* is used in the context of "venture-backed" businesses, and the future of the workforce. Automation and more flexibility for workers are presented as great concerns for workers of TaskRabbit, who are independent contractors. Automation is a concern because it might make some jobs redundant. Yet, automation is also presented as making more flexible working lives possible. In order to improve their situation, TaskRabbit is looking into possibilities of giving their contractors more options like minimum pay or healthcare discounts. In this interview, TaskRabbit expresses the hope that other platforms will do the same. There are, however, limits to what platforms can do for their workers as they are not employers, TaskRabbit argues in this article.

In 2015, there is another article looking at workers of the *sharing economy* called *On-Demand Workers: We Are Not Robots, Is Technology Liberating or Squeezing the New Class of Freelance Labor?* By Lauren Weber and Rachel Emma Silverman. The article mentions *sharing economy* businesses like Uber, Handybook, Amazon's

Mechanical Turk, or TaskRabbit, which are very popular with consumers. The article describes that these companies are relying on freelance labor or "micro-entrepreneurs," which is a highly flexible way to work. But according to the businesses themselves, this is what workers are looking for. And in general, platforms are not forcing people to work. People only do the jobs they like and when they like, a flexibility they enjoy, according to the article. Yet, the article also mentions that there are several lawsuits, protests, and online forum discussions that suggest that many workers are not as happy as companies claim. Main concerns by workers revolve around the issues of control over the terms and requirements by platforms. These are set by the companies and workers need to accept them. The platforms do not take over any of the (financial) risk that the independents carry. The article alludes to a general ambivalence between platforms and both full-time and part-time platform workers. "Peers," an independent contractor organization, is quoted saying that some workers are liberated by the options; others feel isolated and confused in the *sharing economy*. The issue of whether some of the workers should be classified as employees is also mentioned. The article also discusses the topic of whether the two established categories of workers, employees and independents, is fit for the app-enabled world. The article tries to paint a balanced picture of the matter, weighing the business and the worker side. In the end, the article draws the somewhat rare conclusion for the *WSJ* that many workers cannot afford to bring home half a paycheck (less pay and no benefits) only because they work as a freelancer.

In the next article, several letters to the editor are published under the headline: *Disruptive New Firms Challenge the Old Rule of Law; Redefining an employee as an independent contractor or paying no occupancy tax on rentals isn't revolutionary, just using technology to skirt existing laws*, 2015. All the readers' letters seem to be more critical than the *WSJ* when it comes to *sharing economy* platforms. For example, readers express a skeptical view toward *sharing economy* businesses like Uber saying that just because they use new technology, they should not be exempt from established laws. Uber often demands compliance from drivers, which is why workers are not truly independent, in the view of some readers.

The next article called *Shackling the Sharing Economy; Big Labor and the plaintiffs bar gang up on Internet start-ups*. from 2015 is quite the opposite to what the readers are concerned about. The *so-called sharing economy* is seen as a bright spot in the US "growth malaise." However, the article sees backlash building, which could lead to the failure of some of the businesses. Homejoy is presented here as an example. It was a startup platform for matching customers with house cleaners. The startup failed eventually as courts ruled that they had an employer–employee relationship with their workers. In the *WSJ* article, this is used to show that platform businesses are falling victim to the general backlash against the digital platform business model. The article accuses the political left and "Big Labor" to organize attacks against the *sharing economy* in rather drastic language ("gang up"). The article also mentions Hillary Clinton "bowing" to this movement by voicing criticism about the gig nature and the lack of workplace protections in the *sharing economy*. The article also mentions the myriad of lawsuits that all the platform businesses face because of the issue of (mis)classification of workers. This is portrayed as excessive and unnecessary. The article accuses labor groups of wanting to fight the *sharing economy* because of a lack of unionization, disruption of established service markets, and “outcompeting” unionized businesses that cannot keep up. The article sees the *sharing economy* businesses as a largely positive effect on markets. More competition is always positive for consumers and delivers higher quality. There is also a large number of workers apparently willing to do these jobs. Independent platform work is presented as a way out of under- and unemployment, often paying more than the federal minimum wage.

Although most of the articles in the *WSJ* are business-friendly, not all of them are as unambiguous as the article just discussed. For example, *Big Issues in Technology (A Special Report)—Can the Sharing Economy Provide Good Jobs?* from 2015 tries to paint a more balanced picture, quoting advocates and critics of the *sharing economy*. Platforms like Uber, TaskRabbit, or Handy are transforming the consumer access to goods and services. The article claims that about 7% of US Americans are working on *sharing economy* platforms quoting a PricewaterhouseCoopers study on *sharing economy* platforms. The article asks if there are downsides to this trend, citing worries that vulnerable people could end up in jobs without protections and benefits, but at the same time claiming that there is flexibility and autonomy to be gained. Rachel Botsman is quoted with her vision of the *sharing economy* that she paints as empowering, decentralized, and anti-hierarchical. This is changing the way we create and access goods and services. She claims that labor is profoundly impacted in a positive way, with micro-entrepreneurs appearing in all areas of the economy. Botsman argues that there are different groups in the *sharing economy*, flexers, underemployed, or formerly unemployed who cannot find a regular job, professionals who work full-time, and supplementers who hold another job. She admits that benefits such as health care are decoupled from the job on a platform, but that this is a circumstance that has always existed for the self-employed, even before the *sharing economy*. Instead of relying on the existing welfare system, she says, the market is creating an alternative social safety system, meaning income supplementing opportunities by the digital platforms. Moreover, the success of platforms can be attributed to the unattractiveness of traditional 9–5 jobs, according to Botsman. Andrew Keen (author and executive director of Futurecast) is quoted as a more critical expert in the field. He criticizes that platforms are only a good deal for their owners, but not for workers. He argues that the *sharing economy* does not provide high-quality jobs or career opportunities and creates a precariat of workers. There is an increasing inequality between owners of platforms who reap the profits and the independent workers who do not have any social benefits or security provided by their jobs. If these platforms had a traditional employer structure, they would be a lot less profitable and would not attract as much venture capital. Keen claims that this work structure reminds him of Walmart. Yet, the disrupters of Silicon Valley do not even offer the minimum federal benefits Walmart complies with. Claims of flexibility and freedom are just luring workers in, but it is a bad deal for them in the end. Keen describes the *sharing economy* as a “very selfish economy.”

Apart from looking at specific labor issues around the digital platforms themselves, the *WSJ* also features several articles on the *sharing economy* and the political agenda of the presidential candidates in 2016. Issues around the situation of workers are also discussed in these instances. For example, *A Hillary Clinton Adviser Looks Back—and Ahead; Gene Sperling is optimistic about the Democratic Party in the long run* (2016) alludes to the fact that people are not convinced that the *sharing economy* is doing much good for them. Platforms are seen as part of the overall economic situation, which is assessed as mainly negative.

Another 2016 article called *Democrats vs. Democrats on the Sharing Economy; Young Obama voters use apps like Airbnb all the time. But the party stands with unions and lawyers* by Allysia Finley talks about the Democratic agenda in the presidential campaign that includes policies to reduce inequality and to raise wages. Yet, according to the *WSJ*, this agenda brings about conflict within the block of Democratic voters who love the *sharing economy*. The attitude Democrats display toward the *sharing economy* is seen as ambivalent in this article. On the one hand, the *sharing economy* increases productivity and is making use of "underused resources" like unoccupied housing and labor. On the other hand, unions and governments are now taking aim at them. The article claims that liberal politicians want to keep people dependent on the government and therefore reject the opportunities of the *sharing economy*. But even the Democrats are split. More centrist Democrats advocate in favor of the democratizing ability of the *sharing economy*. According to the article, one should worry about politicians like Dianne Feinstein, Elizabeth Warren, and Brian Schatz who pressure the FTC to investigate the platforms like Airbnb. These efforts were also mentioned in the liberal media material, but were presented in a more positive light.

Generally, there are several articles in the *WSJ* that express concern over unionization and re-classification efforts in the *sharing economy*. The "victims" are going to be those who supplement their income, like young people and middle- or low-income families. The private sector is actually doing more for these groups than the government programs that keep them dependent, according to the *WSJ*. The next article called *An Uber Bad idea; A law to organize drivers has implications for all independent contractors*, from 2016, goes in the same direction, painting unions as a problematic economic actor. Unions are alarmed about the *sharing economy* because it empowers the individual worker, according to this article. Therefore, unions are pushing government to rewrite labor laws to make it easier for platform workers to organize. The article claims that the Sherman Antitrust Act has exempted contractors from unionizing to prevent cartels and rank up prices and that this practice should not be abandoned in the digital age.

After having looked at articles that are concerned with the platform infrastructure and labor issues, the next theme that can be identified around the term *sharing economy* in the *WSJ* material is a specific platform actor, **Airbnb**, which is frequently portrayed as one of the pioneers of the *sharing economy*. Airbnb is the center of attention in several articles in the *WSJ*. In particular, the *WSJ* quite intensively covers the lawsuit of the City of New York against Airbnb. In this lawsuit, the city demands user data from the platform in order to identify illegal listings. The issue points to two main discussion points around platforms: first, the security of user data, which platforms are most reluctant to share, and second, the possibly unlawful behavior of platform users and the rejection of responsibility for this behavior by the platforms. In this case, city officials demanded from Airbnb to disclose host information of those who rent out spaces in residential areas in NYC without a permit and without paying fees and taxes.

The first article in this area is from 2013 called *Airbnb Gets Subpoena for User Data in New York*, Brian R. Fitzgerald. The article focuses on Airbnb and their legal issues with handing over information to lawmakers on whether Airbnb hosts are offering illegal rentings. The term *so-called sharing economy* appears in the context of Airbnb but is also associated with other services like car-sharing, Uber, Lyft, and Sidecar.

In 2014, the article *Airbnb to Hand Over Anonymous User Data in New York; Agreement Ends Dispute Between Home-Rental Site and State Attorney General* by Douglas MacMillan comments on more scrutiny Airbnb faces over user data and that the company is ordered by a court ruling to hand over data. Airbnb is mentioned as one of the pioneers of the *sharing economy*, using apps to exchange goods and services. Other actors mentioned are ride-sharing services like Lyft or TaskRabbit. The article mentions one of the most controversial parts of the platforms' business model, namely whether workers are employees or independents. In most cases, platforms have portrayed themselves as only middlemen and do not consider themselves employers. The article also mentions trust as one of the most important aspects of the *sharing economy*. The lawsuits and disclosure of user data are a threat to the business model because it violates the trust the platforms are built upon, the article claims. Platform users want to be sure that their data remains private.

Apart from legal issues, Airbnb is discussed in other contexts in the *WSJ* as well. For example, the 2014 article *Hidden Income Inside Your Home: Sites like Airbnb are turning ordinary homeowners into landlords—and changing the economics of real estate* by Steven Rosenbush discusses how the concept of the *sharing economy* becomes more and more accepted, which can be seen in the success of sites like Airbnb. Airbnb is presented as a possibility to earn extra money with personal assets, like your own home. This is something that Airbnb always emphasizes, for instance in an interview with its founder in *The Weekend Interview with Brian Chesky: The 'Sharing Economy' and Its Enemies* by Andy Kessler from 2014. Airbnb Co-founder Brian Chesky talks about the company as part of the *sharing economy* universe. Chesky claims that the *sharing economy* creates a third category in the law, because people become businesses. Before, there were laws for businesses or laws for people, but "people as businesses" have not existed in the same way they do today. But on Airbnb, Chesky claims, people become (micro-) entrepreneurs and benefit from this possibility. Issues for Airbnb on the lawmakers side persist, however, for instance with questions around taxation or battles with industry incumbents.

Airbnb also tries to appeal to new customer groups over the years, which is detailed in some instances in the *WSJ*, for example in *Corporate News: Uber, Airbnb Woo Business Travelers*, by Douglas MacMillan and Karmin Craig, 2014. This article alludes to the *sharing economy* as a popular concept where consumers share car rides and apartments. Business travelers could be next. However, there are legal questions if you want to pursue business travelers and the article mentions the already complex legal issues the *sharing economy* is facing. *Sharing economy* services are presented as cheaper than other services and their users as more dedicated.

The new professionalism of the sites is further discussed in *Airbnb Moves Into Professional Vacation Rentals, Home-sharing company says offering will be limited to some markets initially*, by Drew Fitzgerald, 2015. In this article, Airbnb is pitched against competitors such as Expedia which also moves into vacation rentals. This is further explored in *Expedia to Buy Vacation Rental Site HomeAway for $3.9 Billion; Move positions Expedia to compete against home-rental businesses like Airbnb*, by Chelsey Dulaney and Drew FitzGerald, 2015. Airbnb is referred to as the "poster child of the sharing economy."

In 2017, now with more regulations for short-term rental hosts in place in New York, the *WSJ* articles argue that it has become more of a challenge to earn money with Airbnb (*A New Jersey Landlord Joins Forces with Airbnb; At a new 69-story residential tower near the Jersey City Waterfront, home-sharing services are being touted as the latest amenity to lure young renters*, by Josh Barbanel, 2017; *Airbnb Rentals Not a Bonanza for Landlords*, by Laura Kusisto, 2017). In the latter article, a study finds that only if rooms are rented out for a significant time of the year, will this create more profits than long-term rentals. This disqualifies the argument that Airbnb leads to more vacation rentals in inner cities and the crowding out of regular renters to make a bigger profit. Arun Sundararajan is quoted as one of the authors of the study who says that there is a continued blurring between commercial and personal lines in the "*so-called sharing economy*." But the fears that landlords will continue to prefer tourist rentals rather than long-term rentals are likely overblown, according to the article. Listings for entire homes by professional hosts on Airbnb have been declining, whereas private room rentals are more likely to be rented out by someone trying to make some money on the side. As new regulation is in place in New York City, Airbnb might now spread into outer boroughs and less wealthy neighborhoods. This could prove a problem for low-income areas, according to the study by Sundararajan.

Apart from the platform Airbnb, **Uber and its larger impact** is discussed again and again in the context of the *sharing economy* in the *WSJ*. For example, the article *Uber Discusses Investment at $12 Billion Valuation; Drivers-for-Hire App Firm Seeking $500 Million Investment*, by Evelyn M. Rusli from 2014, presents Uber as one of the most valuable venture-backed startups with more than $12 billion in valuation. This article describes that the unusual thing about *sharing economy* platforms like Uber is the fact that the platform only manages drivers and riders and does not own a fleet. In 2014, when the article was published this was still more unusual. Travis Kalanick, the controversial founder of Uber, and legal issues Uber faces are also discussed in the article. Despite these issues, investors seem to remain undeterred. In the article, Uber is presented as belonging to the family of the *so-called sharing economy* businesses, which put regulators in an ambiguous spot, torn between supporting new businesses and upholding policies that protect consumers.

Another *WSJ* article on Uber discusses its relationship to the taxi industry. *What the Taxi Wars Teach; On Tuesday, Uber used its $1.2 billion to hire Obama campaign manager David Plouffe*, by Holman W. Jenkins Jr, 2014. The term "taxi war" refers to Uber's disruption of the taxi industry. In cities like New York, taxi medallions used to cost a fortune and the market was considered corrupt; the new transportation apps circumvented that. The article argues that the new apps seem to have enlarged the pie rather than destroyed the taxi industry altogether, by making rides possible in outskirts and motivating new customers to take rides because they are cheaper than before. Unlike other articles in the *WSJ*, the term *sharing economy* is used here in the context of a grim picture for workers who want more than the "false promise of consumer capitalism" and contingent work. Although drivers saw themselves as entrepreneurs at first, they now fall victim to "wage slavery" enabled by technology. New York City University's Stanley Aronowitz (Professor of Sociology and Urban Education) is commenting on these problematic circumstances in the *sharing economy*. After quoting Mr. Aronowitz, the *WSJ* article goes on to say that these claims might be an overstatement, comparing it to overblown ideas of robots taking away all our jobs. The rest of the article presents the rise of the *sharing economy* platforms for workers as a sign for a slow-growth economy with fewer options for workers, but not as an altogether undesirable development.

Again and again, Uber has faced legal struggles over the status of its drivers, which is covered on many occasions in the *WSJ*. The discussion usually centers around the question of whether drivers are independents or in fact employees of the platforms. This is discussed in, for example, *Uber Driver was Employee, Not Contractor, California Commission Says; Ruling says driver was an employee, potentially paving the way for new costs to the company*, written by Lauren Weber and Douglas MacMillan in 2015. *Sharing economy* as a term is mentioned here to say that the court ruling is not applicable to other *sharing economy* platforms and is only concerned with this one case of an Uber driver. Yet, the case is seen as an indicator for how other courts might decide.

The same issue is discussed in *California's Uber Raid; A state regulator tries to blow up the 'sharing economy' business model*, 2015. Because of the court ruling mentioned above, the article argues, the whole business model of the *sharing economy* is under threat or could "blow up" as indicated in the title. The article clearly sees this as a negative development and ends with the phrase: "Let's hope California doesn't kill its own baby." The article laments that *sharing economy* companies born in Silicon Valley are now threatened in the very place they came from, California, where overzealous regulation is put in place. The article also argues that state regulators might have a different take on the employee-independent contractor issue than the courts. The article clearly rejects more regulation or policy reform in response to *sharing economy* platforms.

Another article continues the reporting on the lawsuits Uber faces: *A Lawsuit to Break the Gig Economy; Uber drivers claim they are legally employees, but that doesn't reflect reality*, by AJ Kritikos, 2015. The article reports on the lawsuit mentioned above and clearly advocates in favor of the independent contractor business model. The article expresses concern that the whole business model of platforms could go down if the case about worker re-classification prevailed in court. The article supports the platforms' argument that gig workers are not employees. Contrary opinions on this issue do not "reflect reality," according to this article.

The *WSJ* also discusses the *sharing economy* in the context of Uber in reference to another legal battle on the local level, this time in Seattle. The articles discuss a new law in the city that allows independent drivers to organize. Uber challenges this decision in court. Usually, unionization and collective bargaining is prohibited for independent contractors in order to prevent trusts and collusion. One article covering this topic is *Uber Gets a Class-Action Tutorial; Here's how the plaintiffs bar defines the 'sharing economy'* (2015). Here, the legal battles of Uber are portrayed as being connected and decisive for the whole *sharing economy*.

Another article on the case is *Seattle's Union Raid on Uber; Drivers sue to stop a law that will spread if it survives in court*, 2017. In this article, unions are presented as pressuring governments into making platforms pay extra benefits for the independent contractors they hire even though this is illegal under the current law. Seattle faces challenges to their new union law that could allow ride-sharing platform drivers to form a union. The article argues that the structure of the platforms does not allow for traditional union representation and that this should remain prohibited.

This article is followed by *Uber, Lyft Face Setback in Push to Block Seattle Union Effort; Judge dismisses a challenge to a law that enables ride-hailing drivers to unionize*, by Greg Bensinger, 2017. This article describes the dismissal of the ride-hailing platforms' challenge to the Seattle unionization law. This means that platform drivers are allowed to form a union in Seattle. This is seen as significant in the *WSJ* article, as it could point to changes for the whole business model of platforms using independent contractors. In all these articles covering the Seattle case in depth, the *WSJ* clearly argues against unionization efforts of independent contractors and sees this as a threat to the whole business model of *sharing economy* platforms. If the case prevailed and this practice spreads to other places outside of Seattle, this could mean the "downfall" of the whole platform sector, which the *WSJ* articles clearly paint as a worst-case scenario that should be prevented.

But American cities are not the only places Uber is facing struggles, which is discussed on several occasions in the *WSJ*. For example, in France where the taxi union is very strong, Uber faces strong opposition, which is detailed in *French Verdict on Uber 'Ride Sharing' in Two Weeks; Company Argues That Ban of Its 'Ride-Sharing' Service Would Be Unconstitutional*, by Sam Schechner, 2014. The article discusses Uber's legal struggles in Europe where the taxi industry is protected and where stricter rules for individual sharing (of rides, for example) are in place. Uber wants to avoid a ban arguing this might lead to a failure of the entire *sharing economy* model. There are more articles in 2015 alluding to Uber's struggle in France or in London where it was seeking new permits to operate.

Apart from legal battles Uber faces over its business model, drivers' unionization efforts, or worker classification, the *WSJ* discusses other regulations in the context of Uber critically. For example, the article *Uber Crashes the Democratic Party; The ride-share app is bringing out the inner Elizabeth Warren*, by William McGurn (2015), reports on the campaign trail of several candidates in 2016. The Democrats are painted as overbearing regulators (epitomized in Elizabeth Warren who allegedly wants to regulate everything) who will not leave the "*gig economy*" or *sharing economy* businesses like Uber alone. Republicans seem to side more intensely with companies like Uber and do not aim for more regulation. The article is clearly critical of regulation and slams Democrats as general over-regulators. Although the *WSJ* usually sides with the platforms on their demands, this article also criticizes companies like Uber for advocating in favor of Obamacare, which actually helped a lot of (gig) workers to obtain affordable health care. But even this is seen as too much interference into the market.

Generally, the *WSJ* material on the *sharing economy* shows that the *WSJ* displays a business-friendly and strong pro-market attitude. This might not be surprising for the *Wall Street Journal* as such, but this notion seems particularly strong with platform businesses. In the articles, the *sharing economy* platforms are displayed as technological innovators that have accumulated considerable valuation and market size. Their success should be enough proof that the business model is working and that there is nothing wrong with it that would demand any new or stronger regulation.

However, the issues for workers are not entirely ignored. There are in fact quite a few articles that try to paint a balanced picture of upsides and downsides of platform work. On the one hand, there is easy access and flexibility of work arrangements that some workers value. On the other hand, there is insecurity and a lack of benefits associated with platform work. Eventually, however, there seems to be a stronger emphasis on the upsides and opportunities of the *sharing economy*. This also becomes clear when the *WSJ* material directly deals with specific platforms like Airbnb and Uber, which are portrayed as "poster children" of the *sharing economy*. The *WSJ* is interested in showing the challenges that these platforms face, for instance through local laws and regulations such as zoning and renting laws (Airbnb) or classification issues of workers (Uber). In general, the *WSJ* articles are critical of all regulation inhibiting the platforms. Additionally, the articles are especially critical about the legal challenges the platforms face and paint them as existential threats to the entire business model of platforms.

The articles on Uber stand in for a larger conversation around the issues of platform workers. Are they independents or should they be employed? The *WSJ* clearly takes the side of platforms (like Uber), arguing that independents are not in an employment relationship with platforms. Therefore, platform workers should not be allowed to unionize. Due to a new law in Seattle, ride-hailing platform drivers gained the right to unionize there. This local case is taken up by the *WSJ* in several articles, painting the picture of a concerning trend of overregulating and "shackling" platforms, which inhibits their freedom in the market. Should this become the norm, the business model of platforms is under threat. Using allusions to established antitrust legislation, unionization efforts of Uber drivers in Seattle are used to condemn regulation and the influence of unions in general. (Democratic) politicians and

Table 6.49 *WSJ*: collocation graph of gig economy MI ≥ 7, minimum collocate frequency 3

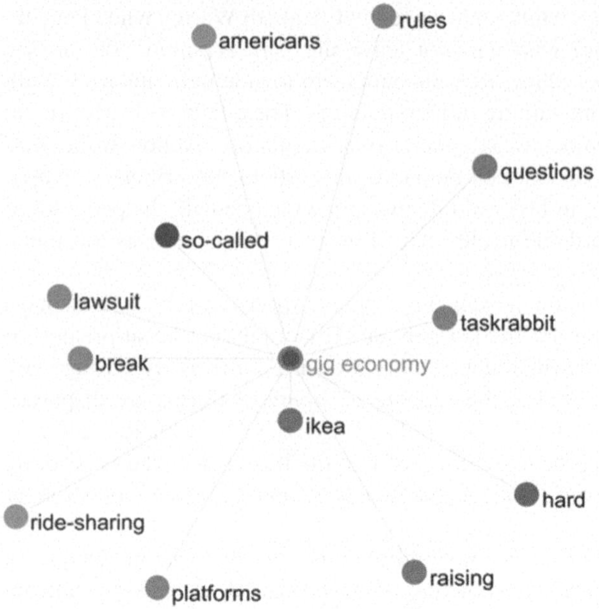

Source: Author, using #LancsBox

court rulings that strengthen rights like collective bargaining or other regulations are strongly criticized.

6.3.3.2 Gig Economy in the *WSJ* Data

The term *gig economy* in the *WSJ* material is investigated in the following by first looking at the collocates (Tables 6.49 and 6.50), before turning again to a more in-depth contextual analysis.[19]

The *gig economy* as a term was rather infrequent overall in the *WSJ* material and lower than the frequency of *gig economy* in the liberal media data. As could be seen before, *so-called* is quite a frequent collocate of *gig economy*. Similar to the other terms and the material investigated before, *so-called* is often attached to the term *gig economy* to indicate that it is a phenomenon that is not clear-cut or rather recent in nature.

[19]The minimum collocate frequency was set at a lower minimum rate to produce a few more collocates for the term, but most collocates remain rather infrequent overall (Table 6.50).

Table 6.50 *WSJ*: collocates of gig economy, MI ≥ 7, minimum collocate frequency 3

gig economy

Freq: 71 Collocates: 12

Index	Status	Stat (03 - MI)	Collocate	▼ Stat	Freq (coll.)	Freq (corpus)
1	O	L	ikea	12.311215173915379	6	29
2	O	R	taskrabbit	10.67734220509931	4	60
3	O	L	so-called	10.414308598021233	14	252
4	O	L	break	9.80287308718311	4	110
5	O	L	lawsuit	9.308109207072361	4	155
6	O	R	raising	9.185062780097859	5	211
7	O	L	platforms	8.876874992880158	4	209
8	O	R	hard	8.769536925067577	7	394
9	O	R	questions	8.751344110796131	5	285
10	O	L	ride-sharing	7.994270576606219	3	289
11	O	L	americans	7.709764969424279	3	352
12	O	M	rules	7.345829144463465	4	604

Source: Author, using #LancsBox

Apart from that, there are certain collocates that point to some problematic issues the *gig economy* is facing, including *lawsuit*, *hard*, *raising*, *questions*, and *rules*. *Ride-sharing* and *platforms* are two collocates that point to the most prevalent platform activity, *ride-sharing*, and to the *platform* nature of the *gig economy*. *TaskRabbit* and *Ikea* are two other collocates that appear with *gig economy*. *TaskRabbit* is strongly associated with digital platform work and its subsequent acquisition by *Ikea* was reported on several occasions in the *WSJ*.

From the collocates, one can clearly see that *gig economy* is associated with digital platform work such as ride-sharing or working on TaskRabbit. Additionally, collocates like *lawsuits* point to the fact that the *gig economy* faces challenges such as legal action.

Most of the articles in the *WSJ* that feature the term *gig economy* are the same that also talk about the *sharing economy*, again suggesting that the two terms are used interchangeably in many instances. The three articles mentioned here first allude to the *gig economy* and its significance more generally, for example in *What's News: Business &Finance* from 2016. The article argues that growing Silicon Valley companies like Uber have put more focus on the "*gig economy*" as such, but that new research shows that there is a broader shift away from steady employment toward more flexible work in the whole of the economy, not only among Silicon Valley companies.

In the article already mentioned above called *Most Americans Don't Know About Ride-Sharing and the 'Gig Economy'* by Josh Zumbrun from 2016, the author discusses a study by PEW Research Center arguing that most Americans are not familiar with the terms *sharing economy* and *gig economy* although mainstream public discourse seems to suggest that these businesses are "taking over the world."

Gig economy appears together with the term *on-demand* and specific technology. The *gig economy* is usually associated with renting out rooms, giving people rides, or delivering groceries. But these app-based services are not very common among Americans. According to the Pew study quoted in this article, 15% of Americans have used ride-hailing apps, 6% have had groceries delivered through a platform, and only 4% have hired someone to perform a task over a platform. The study shows, according to the article, that the *gig economy* remains in its infancy, which is consistent with other studies, for example from JP Morgan that shows that only 0.5% of Americans work in the *gig economy*.[20] The article also argues that most services of the *gig economy* did not exist only a few years ago and that it is a very recent phenomenon.

One of the platforms that is associated with an early success story of a *gig economy* platform is TaskRabbit. The company has now been acquired by IKEA, which was detailed in *IKEA to Acquire 'Gig Economy' Startup—TaskRabbit, a service for odd jobs, could help customers in assembling furniture*, by Saabira Chaudhuri and Eliot Brown, 2017. In this article, TaskRabbit is called a "trailblazer" of the *gig economy*.

Similar to the term *sharing economy*, there are different contexts in which the term *gig economy* appears in the *WSJ* material. However, they are less specific than the themes that can be associated with the *sharing economy* and there are also considerably fewer instances where *gig economy* actually occurs. These larger themes can be summarized into **labor issues** and **politics**.

In the context of **labor issues**, you can find articles mentioning gig working platforms like TaskRabbit. For example, the founder of TaskRabbit talks about the future of work for gig workers in *BossTalk: TaskRabbit Chief Aims to Recast Freelance Work; CEO Says Startups Need to Do More to Protect Workers*, by Elizabeth Dwoskin, 2014. TaskRabbit was one of the first large-scale gig working platforms and has been criticized for creating the *gig economy* that is so problematic for workers. Yet, the founder of TaskRabbit argues that this kind of work has already existed before the success of digital platforms and that TaskRabbit just offers a new option for workers to earn extra income in an easy way. This was especially attractive for workers after the 2008 crisis, the article claims.

The article *Proof of a 'Gig Economy' Revolution Is Hard to Find; Despite the hoopla over Uber, Etsy and the sharing economy, Americans are becoming less likely to be self-employed, hold multiple jobs, data show*, by Josh Zumbrun and Anna Louie Sussman from 2015, argues again that in recent years there seems to be a lot of talk about an alleged *gig economy* "revolution," as indicated in the title, especially among politicians and Silicon Valley leaders. Yet, proof of such a revolution is hard to find, according to the article. The article suggests that there are studies that show that self-employment and holding multiple jobs at the same time actually becomes less common among Americans. In this context, the article talks about the campaign

[20] In their updated version from 2018, JP Morgan estimates that this amount has tripled to 1.5% of Americans who have worked or earned money in the online platform economy (Farrell et al. 2018).

trails of Hillary Clinton and Jeb Bush who visited Silicon Valley and talked about the impact of the new informal workforce. This workforce seems to become a controversial issue in political circles, but by citing official government data, the article argues that most workers in the USA remain regularly employed. Data shows that 95% of those who have a job are on payroll from an employer and are not independent. The vast majority of workers in the USA are therefore employed. Despite the large amount of attention the *gig economy* receives, the article assumes that the trend of online gig work is marginal at best. Although the gig worker group is marginal and the issue surrounding their classification minor, according to the article, it has become a political issue and fault line between Republicans and Democrats. The *WSJ* portrays this as a sign of political confrontation between the different sides, and not as a topic that is actually of great concern economically.

One of the most common labor issues discussed around the *gig economy* is the classification of gig workers, which is illustrated in several articles in the *WSJ*, for example in an article about a California lawsuit called *A Lawsuit to Break the Gig Economy; Uber drivers claim they are legally employees, but that doesn't reflect reality*. by AJ Kritikos, 2015. As mentioned before in the investigation of the discourse around the *sharing economy*, the article alludes to a lawsuit against Uber in California pursued by drivers. According to the article, this lawsuit could "break" the rest of the *gig economy* and its "peer-to-peer structure." Although Uber faces different lawsuits, the lawsuit on whether Uber needs to employ its drivers is weighed very seriously as it would trigger all kinds of workplace protections. California has 13 factors that should guide employers and courts on whether workers are employees or not, but this determination remains somewhat subjective. Regardless of the arguments presented in this specific case, Californian courts have often upheld the rule that people count as employed if they provide an important or core service for their employer. Workers are also normally presumed employed until proven otherwise. The article argues that the labor laws dating back to the 1930s should be updated and continues to argue that the courts should accept contracts formed between *sharing economy* platforms and workers for an independent contractor relationship. Otherwise, all platforms and their business models are under threat.

The wider issues of "good jobs" in the *gig economy* are discussed in the aforementioned *Big Issues in Technology (A special Report)—Can the Sharing Economy Provide Good Jobs?* (2015). Different experts share their opinion on the matter, for example Rachel Botsman or Andrew Keen. Rachel Botsman is an advocate of the *sharing economy* and "collaborative consumption." Andrew Keen is more critical than Botsman when it comes to the *gig economy* saying that for owners of the platforms it is a great deal but not for workers. Keen argues that not everything is bad about the *sharing economy*, especially for consumers it is a great deal. The gig aspect of this is also convenient for those who just want to make some money on the side. But Keen sees a problem in the fact that these Silicon Valley businesses are not offering any good jobs, only precarious ones.

The next two articles were also already mentioned and specify disputes over unionization efforts in the *gig economy*. These articles deal with Seattle's new unionization rule for ride-hailing drivers: *Uber, Lyft Oppose Seattle's Draft Union Rules; First major city to open the door for ride-hailing and taxi drivers to unionize*, by Greg Bensinger, 2016. Seattle introduced a rule permitting ride-sharing drivers to form unions. The new rule states that if you complete a certain amount of rides in a given amount of time, you are eligible to elect and vote for a union. This excludes more infrequent drivers and favors full-time drivers. This is opposed by the ride-hailing companies, who try to challenge the new rule in court. The article is also very critical of this rule because every driver, regardless of whether they can vote, will fall under union agreements. The *so-called gig economy* could move toward more organization if Seattle's rule prevails and this practice is introduced in other cities, which is portrayed rather critically by the *WSJ* article.

Apart from the unionization issue, the employment status of the platform drivers remains a contested issue in the USA and abroad. The article *Uber Gears Up to Block Bid to Form a Union in Seattle; Ride-hailing firms ends podcasts and messages through app to persuade drivers to remain as 'partners'*, by Greg Bensinger, 2017, gives further detail on the matter. The *gig economy* is defined as making deliveries, run errands, or perform freelance tasks as a contractor over a digital platform such as Uber, Postmates, or TaskRabbit. The rest of the article refers again to the situation in Seattle where unionization is going to be opened up for ride-sharing drivers who work as freelancers (who are usually not allowed to unionize). Companies like Uber are trying to uphold the freelancer model and want to persuade drivers to support that.

In another article, a different labor issue in the *gig economy* is mentioned, this time not a legal one. It becomes more and more difficult for platforms like Uber to actually attract and retain drivers: *In a Job Market This Good, Who Needs to Work in the Gig Economy? Startups like Uber and Lyft that launched in the Great Recession strain to keep workers who don't have to take part-time work anymore*, by Kelsey Gee, 2017. The term *gig economy* is mentioned in the context of Uber, Instacart, DoorDash, or Postmates. The article reports that these companies have a hard time maintaining their workforce in a strong job market. Companies have thus started to offer benefits or bonuses to attract on-demand workers. Platforms struggle to show that platform work such as freelancing or part-time work offers some predictability and a stable income, which would attract more workers to the sites. The article sees about 4% of the American workforce earning money through platforms, which amounts to over 1 million Americans. Although investment has been strong in the *gig economy*, some investors worry that the *gig economy* comes under pressure from a stronger job market with less people looking for a job and workers not being as interested in "piecemeal jobs." In this article, the term *gig economy* is again mentioned in the context of a workforce that is changing overall. In the field of gig workers new workers constantly come in, but more than half of them exit the *gig economy* after only 1 year. This is going to be a challenge for the *gig economy* going forward, the article suggests.

One way to attract new workers can be found among an unlikely group, elderly people, which is detailed in an article called *Study Shows One Way to Extend Working Years; Research shows people who switch jobs in their 50s are more likely to be working at 65*, by Lisa Ward, 2017. The *gig economy* is presented here as a way for older workers to earn extra income, which could mean that they remain in the workforce for a longer time.

Another theme that runs through the articles of the *WSJ* around the *gig economy* is **politics.** Different political stakeholders and party actors are mentioned in these articles and their relationship with the *gig economy* is assessed. For example, the article *Uber Crashes the Democratic Party; The ride-share app is bringing out the inner Elizabeth Warren*, by William McGurn from 2015, describes several Democratic actors' take on the *gig economy*. Criticism of the *gig economy* comes from New York City Mayor de Blasio, which is setting the tone for the 2016 presidential elections, according to the article. Hillary Clinton is also mentioned commenting on the *gig economy*. In her statement, she argues that while it is unleashing innovation, there are unanswered questions about workplace protections and what a good job will look like in the future. Uber is not mentioned by name but is a big part of the conversation as it stands for some of the problematic sides of platform work. The article assumes that Clinton wants the government to regulate *gig economy* platforms, even though it makes the platforms less innovative and exciting. Republican competitors of Clinton are portrayed in contrast to this. They are described as "having fun with all this." Many Republicans side with the interests of platforms like Uber. According to the article, Republicans do not want to stifle platforms with regulation that do not fit the twenty-first century. The article cites two causes for the opposition of Democrats vis-à-vis the platforms, one being that they disrupt traditional Democratic constituencies like New York City. Secondly, innovation stirs the Democrats' "inner Elizabeth Warren," meaning that Democrats want to stifle the *gig economy* because it does not fit the established regulatory framework that they support. The article states that the Democrats' position is always to regulate, not only the *sharing* or *gig economy*, but everything in their way.

The same issues are again discussed in another article which talks about the left's alleged negative relationship with and influence on the *gig economy*. The article called *Information Age: Why Uber Drives the Left Crazy*, by Gordon L. Crovitz from 2015, reports again on NYC Mayor de Blasio who has started to crack down on Uber. In contrast to this, the article mentions other cities that display different approaches. London's Boris Johnson, for instance, is embracing Uber rather than regulating it harshly. The article also mentions the *gig economy* in the context of the 2016 presidential race again. Candidates seem divided with Hillary Clinton mentioning the *gig economy* critically in regard to workplace protections, and Marco Rubio embracing Uber and its superior service. The article argues that consumers are also not in favor of limiting the apps too much. Generally, *gig economy* platforms like Uber are worth supporting, in the eyes of this *WSJ* article, as they challenge government-enforced cartels like the taxi industry.

In the next article, politicians' attempts to regulate the *gig economy* are again presented in a very negative light: *Shackling the Sharing Economy; Big Labor and the plaintiffs bar gang up on Internet start-ups* (2015). In this article, both terms *gig* and *sharing economy* occur. As mentioned before, this article portrays the *sharing economy* as one bright spot in the economic growth malaise in the USA. Yet, the article argues that there is an increasingly organized attack on these startups. Some actors like labor activists "gang up" to fight *gig economy* platforms. This "attack" is also supported by politicians like Hillary Clinton who talks ambiguously about the *so-called gig economy*, mentioning innovation but also issues around workplace protections in the future. The article is clearly critical of any class action against the *gig economy* startups when it comes to the independent contractor status.

There are also several letters to the editor that touch upon the politicians' stance toward the platform economy. These letters are published under the headline *Innovation and the Progressive's War on Uber; Mr. de Blasio, far from being at war with Uber, has totally jettisoned his progressive values by caving in to the tech giant's pressure*, 2016. The readers are highly critical of NYC Mayor de Blasio's take on Uber but for different reasons than the *WSJ*. The readers quoted here see progressive politicians caving in to the pressure from digital platforms as they become more powerful and prevalent in urban areas such as New York. These readers argue in favor of a tougher stance vis-à-vis the platforms. Another reader mentions the *gig economy* in the context of millennials. Millennials appreciate the opportunities and consumer benefits of the *sharing* or *gig economy* but are not unaware of its downsides. They want to use the platforms, but also support improvements for workers, according to the article.

6.3.3.3 Sharing and Gig Economy in the *WSJ* Data

The terms *sharing economy* and *gig economy* are mentioned to a different extent in the material from the *WSJ*. As one can see in Table 6.51, there are a few collocates that connect the terms *sharing economy* and *gig economy* in the *WSJ* material. These include *so-called, workers,* and *Uber*. In fact, after reading the *WSJ* articles more closely, the terms *sharing* and *gig economy* appear for the most part in the same articles and are thus closely related to one another in the discourse investigated here. As said before, the two terms are often referred to as the "*so-called sharing* or *gig economy*." Additionally, *Uber* is a company that is extensively discussed in the *WSJ* material when the *sharing* and *gig economy* are concerned. One issue that is also continuously debated around the new platforms is the situation and status of *workers*.

The term *gig economy* is more often used when the situation of workers on the platforms is discussed directly, for example when unionization efforts or classification issues are presented. In many cases, the use of *sharing* and *gig economy* is interchangeable, however.

The *WSJ* material concerned with the new platforms focuses on the potential of the new startups and are generally critical of reining them in in any way, may it be by regulation, by stricter worker classification, or by unionization efforts. The articles emphasize the rise and success of platforms in recent years and quote advocates like Rachel Botsman who talk very positively about them. They also interview leaders of the *sharing economy*, like the Airbnb or TaskRabbit founders.

Table 6.51 *WSJ*: network collocation graph of sharing economy, gig economy, MI ≥ 5, minimum collocation frequency 5

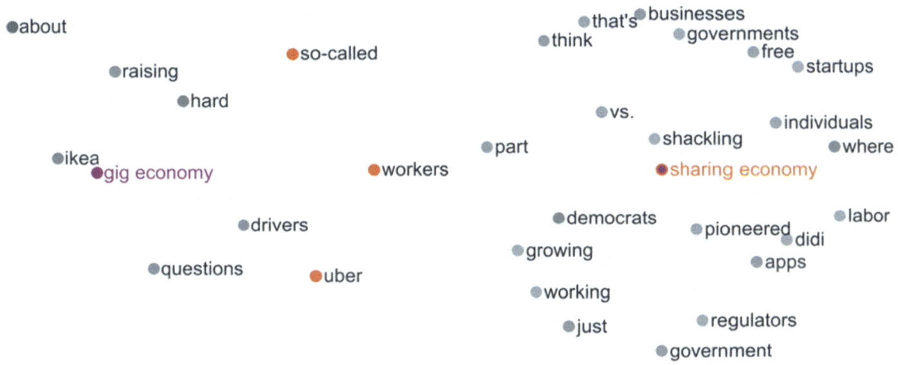

Source: Author, using #LancsBox

The continuing legal action that many platforms face is also extensively discussed throughout the *WSJ* material. These articles usually frame legal action or challenges that are brought against the *sharing* or *gig economy* platforms as negative, excessive, and generally unnecessary. Some of the cases are even portrayed as an existential threat for the whole business model of platforms. The articles are especially critical about platforms being forced to provide user data, reconsider classification of workers, or accept unionization efforts. The *WSJ* usually advocates for less regulation, rather than forcing "outdated" government regulation onto the digital market. This might not be surprising for a newspaper like the *WSJ*, but there are many articles that very specifically present unions and Democrats as launching an organized attack on the whole business model of the *sharing economy*.

When politics are discussed, Democrats are reported on mostly critically. Democrats are presented as obsessed with regulation in general, and platforms are a new target because they disrupt Democratic strongholds and contradict their view of what the economy should look like. Republicans are presented as being more positive and embracing toward the *sharing economy*. However, there is also some ambiguity as Silicon Valley companies normally side with Democrats politically. The new platform businesses seem to shake up the traditional partisan divisions quite a bit. Republicans are trying to win the support of Silicon Valley startups and their leaders, while Democrats are looking for ways to respond to platforms in light of problematic issues like workplace protections. At the same time, there are opportunities for workers in the platform economy as well.

The *WSJ* rarely criticizes the platforms, but rather presents them as a solution to a slow economy. Contested issues like precarious working conditions are mentioned as well. However, the *WSJ* usually seems to favor the entrepreneurial side of the platform businesses and emphasizes that it provides economic opportunities for many workers. They do not seem to take issues with the nature of the work on gig platforms as long as there are workers willing to take up these jobs. This seems to coincide with the fact that the term *gig economy* is mentioned less often than in other material investigated in this work, especially compared to the liberal media material. The *WSJ* emphasizes that gig workers are a marginal group among all American workers and should not be overemphasized. The more general growth of the independent workforce in the USA is not discussed in detail in the articles mentioned above.

Uber and Airbnb are the two companies that are mentioned most often in the articles by the *WSJ*. Both of them have become giants in their respective fields and are portrayed as proof of the power of the free market that produces successful global business leaders that provide superior consumer products and, at the same time, economic opportunities for many people.

6.3.4 Platform Economy in Political and Public Discourse

The platform economy in political and public discourse is most often reflected through the use of two terms, the *sharing economy* and the *gig economy*. The term *platform economy* that was also investigated is an extremely rare term that seeks neutrality but remains a technical and expert term. It can only be found in some of the sources and is most often used by an expert or researcher in the field.

The two other terms *sharing* and *gig economy* are often used interchangeably throughout all the material. They even appear as "*the so-called gig or sharing economy*" in some instances. Yet, the two terms also maintain specific connotations. Especially in the congressional and liberal media material, *sharing economy* is used in the context of a very positive outlook toward the future that emphasizes alternative, collaborative ways of consumption and more sustainability. The *sharing economy* is also painted as a great opportunity for workers to feel empowered and become their own boss. Many of these initial hopes have faded over time. Especially the argument of sustainability through the more efficient use of assets and "idling capacity" has not been fulfilled and is now largely absent from the discourse around the *sharing economy*. However, the *sharing economy* as a hub of opportunity and small-scale entrepreneurism for the individual has not disappeared in its entirety. In fact, it is still stressed by political and business-friendly actors in the debate. But even more critical voices do not reject the innovative economic opportunities of the *sharing economy* entirely.

The *gig economy* as a term has never been associated with the same positive purpose as the *sharing economy*. Nowadays, it is often used when referring to the overall structural change of the labor force that is made up of more and more independents. Generally, it seems that the use of *gig economy* as a term always reinforces the conversation about the labor side and the (problematic) issues that this form of work produces.

In the congressional material, the term *sharing economy* is rather strongly associated with the entrepreneurism and opportunity narrative. Through the online platform structure, everyone can become a (micro-)entrepreneur or a small business owner. It is seen as a means to combat a slow labor market and "put people to work." From time to time, tough economic circumstances are also presented as a reason for the success of online platforms. Platforms are also strongly associated with millennial lifestyle. This group is used to these products in their everyday lives but are also impacted by them when it comes to the overall structure of the labor market that becomes more diverse and insecure.

Generally, political actors are in agreement that consumers have benefitted from the *sharing economy* and that it often delivers cheaper and better services and products in market niches that were "ripe for disruption." However, there are different notions discussed about issues of the *sharing* and *gig economy platforms*. Regulations, for example in the areas of taxation, regional compliance, or competition, are discussed. Should these platforms have the right to forgo existing regulation because they are insisting on being digital intermediaries?

This discussion on regulation also includes the rather large debate about the classification of workers. Are gig workers independents or employees? There are different opinions on this matter, but most lawmakers do not see all gig workers as employees per se. It often depends on the platform and how much control it actually exerts over the worker. Uber as a platform exercises more control over drivers than TaskRabbit does over its workers. Capital platforms and marketplaces do not run into such issues most of the time. Thus, Uber and other gig work platforms remain the more contested and debated area of the *sharing economy* among political actors.

When the discussion moves into the area of classification or the allocation of social benefits, the term *gig economy* becomes stronger in use. "Gig" refers to the fact that many jobs today have become short-term, flexible, and more insecure than in the past. Technological progress has accelerated this trend and is part of why there is a growing group of both full-time and occasional independent workers. The *sharing economy* platforms are also often seen as part of larger technological trends such as advances in automation and the Internet of Things.

Policies that are discussed in the context of the *sharing* or *gig economy* include portable benefits (tied to the worker not the job) or a new category of workers. The Affordable Care Act is in fact presented as one step in the direction of portable benefits as it allows self-employed to get more affordable health care. In general, lawmakers are hesitant to introduce new regulation in order not to stifle innovation and consumer benefits. Platforms have introduced new and innovative economic activity and consumers love the new and advanced services. Therefore, no politician regardless of party is really interested in destroying the business model of the platform economy in its entirety.

Just like the congressional material, the material from the liberal media sources presents the *sharing economy* in a rather positive light in the beginning (2013–2014). It was seen, in a way, as "the good economy," more sustainable and collaborative, and sharing was generally considered the right thing to do. In this phase, the *sharing economy* as a term prevailed.

Although the *sharing economy* never really lost this positive connotation fully, the picture of the *sharing economy* became more nuanced over time. Especially through more and more legal action that many of the platforms faced, the "dark sides" of the platforms got more and more attention. Through reading the articles from the *NYT* and the *Washington Post* over the years, one can see that the *sharing economy* could not live up to its expectations of alternative sustainable consumption, nor to the empowerment claim of the beginning. This points to the rise of the *gig economy*. Once the gig and on-demand character of many of these platforms became clearer, the media outlets spent more time assessing the implications of a growing gig labor force. Although there is some reference to easy access and flexibility that the workers cherish, there are many articles pointing out the more problematic side of an isolated and insecure labor force "hustling on the side." In a larger context, the liberal media material spent more time pointing to the lack of good jobs overall. Therefore, it is not the quantity but rather the quality of jobs that should be of concern in the future. The articles also spent a certain amount of time discussing possible policy reforms that were also part of the discussion in Congress, namely worker classification, the UBI, the Affordable Care Act, or portable benefits.

In the material from the *WSJ*, quite a different take on the *sharing* and *gig economy* could be identified. Looking at the frequency data, you would not immediately think that there is so much difference between the liberal media material and the *WSJ* material when it comes to the *sharing* or *gig economy* in use. But after reading the articles in the *WSJ*, the portrayal of these developments is quite different. Although there are some instances where the consequences for workers in the future are discussed, such as insecurity and a lack of benefits, the emphasis of the *WSJ* lies in presenting the platforms as innovators that are best left alone in the market.

The *WSJ* material seems to be especially strong in opposing any notion to make platform workers employees or to give them the right to collectively bargain. In the eyes of the *WSJ*, this would be the end of the whole business model of the *sharing economy* platforms. In the end, this would negatively impact everyone because economic opportunities for those workers willing to work in the *sharing* or *gig economy* would be lost and a striving area of business-making and a source of growth were to be destroyed. Larger implications of the gig nature of the work are countered with the argument that gig work is nothing new, remains marginal, and is actually nothing else than independent contracting more generally. Therefore, the economic impact of gig work is nothing to worry about.

The *WSJ* repeatedly suggests that unions and Democrats are condemning and attacking platform businesses for no reason other than that they do not fit their worldview, which consists of regulating the market in any way possible. The *WSJ* advocates in favor of self-regulation of the platforms and does not see the need for further policy changes. Ideas like the UBI are not discussed in the context of the *sharing* or *gig economy* to any great extent and other policies such as the Affordable Care Act (and the support it gets from Silicon Valley actors) are rejected.

References

Brezina V (2018) Statistics in corpus linguistics. a practical guide. Cambridge University Press, Cambridge, UK. https://doi.org/10.1017/9781316410899

Farrell D, Greig F, Hamoudi A (2018) The online platform economy in 2018: drivers, workers, sellers, and lessors. JPMorgan Chase & Co Institute. https://www.jpmorganchase.com/institute/research/labor-markets/report-ope-2018.htm. Accessed 10 May 2021

Pew-Research-Center (2019) Defining generations: where millennials end and generation Z begins. Pew Research Center. https://www.pewresearch.org/fact-tank/2019/01/17/where-millennials-end-and-generation-z-begins/. Accessed 4 July 2020

Sperling G (2015) How Airbnb combats middle class income stagnation. Airbnb

Thompson D (2015) A world without work. The Atlantic, July/August 2015 Issue

Chapter 7
The Discourse Around Technological Progress and the Future of Work

7.1 Summary of Findings

The political and public sphere reflects on the ongoing restructuring process of the American economy in many ways including direct political debates in Congress such as committee hearings or public debates that are reflected in media discourses. The issues of automation, the future of work, and the sharing economy platforms are three more specific areas that are discussed in the political and public realm in this regard. Examining these discourses is significant because they contribute to technological progress. The way certain subjects are treated in discourses, for example in political institutions such as Congress, influences areas such as research or adoption of technology and public policy, and it influences acceptance of technology in many ways. The public discourses reflect these issues likewise and contribute to the virality of knowledge around technology which can lead to enthusiasm, acceptance, concerns, or fears about technological progress. The public and the political discourses on these subjects influence and reinforce each other. Through a quantitative and qualitative analysis of specific terms, themes, and contexts, this book illustrates how certain aspects of technological progress are reflected in political and public debates and contributes to our knowledge of how political actors and the public view and respond to technological developments of recent years such as further automation, digitization, or the rise of the sharing economy. These developments and the discourses treating these subjects contribute to the assessment of the future of work in the USA, including which issues and policies are of interest to the public and are addressed by political stakeholders.

The discourse around technological progress and the future of work is concerned with many different issues. In this book, two major terms around technological progress were investigated first through the corpus analysis of political and public sources, namely *digitization* and *automation*.

Although digitization could be considered a new "layer" of automation with the rise of digital technology, the use of the term is not very common in this regard.

N. Rauscher, *The Future of Work in the United States*, Contributions to Economics,
https://doi.org/10.1007/978-3-030-82307-8_7

There are some areas such as specific business-related discourses where the term refers to digital strategies of specific business actors or innovation in fields such as manufacturing, health care, or AI. This is especially clear in sources from the WSJ where the term is more common than in any of the other sources investigated. In general, however, the term is not used in this context to a great extent. In most of the sources investigated, the term *digitization* is used to refer to the method of preserving certain artifacts or data in digital form. There are different subject matters related to this such as copyright issues, intellectual property, or Big Data that are discussed in the context of digitization. This points to a cultural difference in the use of the term in the English-speaking world and in Germany, for example, where "Digitalisierung" is used very intensively (but not exclusively) to refer to the most recent wave of automation. The term is especially prevalent when discussing innovations in sectors such as manufacturing where AI and smart robotics are used intensively ("Industrie 4.0").

Generally, the term *automation* is used much more frequently throughout all the sources investigated in this work. In the context of automation, new technologies are discussed such as the self-driving car, smart robotics, and AI more generally. In the political discourse, automation is most often associated with disruptive innovation in various fields from aviation, self-driving cars, and AI to robotics. There are surprisingly detailed discussions of certain specific digital technologies in Congress (especially in House hearings) that point to the awareness of political actors that some of the disruptive innovations will have a profound impact on the future of the US economy in the coming decades. It is clear that political actors of all affiliations see automation as a driver for progress, growth, and productivity that has benefitted consumers greatly, but that will also have enormous unforeseen and complex consequences in the future.

Taking the sheer number of instances into account, public discourses are very engaged in discussing automation and its impact. The media sources investigated here feature many discussions around actual economic actors and their automation and digitization strategies as well the products and services they offer. In the public discourses, the business-friendly side focuses on the innovations and welfare effects that automation has had and will have on the economy as a whole. This is considered consistent with historical developments from the Luddites to today and into the future. This can be considered the more "traditional" narrative of technological progress, stressing the historical advances of technology that have always rendered some jobs obsolete, but that have brought about much more significant welfare effects overall. The Luddites surface quite often in the discourses around technological progress, in both the liberal and the more conservative outlets investigated here. The references to the Luddites seem to serve the purpose of establishing a narrative around automation that emphasizes the futileness of concerns and fears over technological progress. The Luddites tried to fight the machines but ended up defeated. This aims to show that technological progress cannot and should not be stopped. Luddite thinking is then either used to refer to misguided fears and techno-criticism per se (more often on the business-friendly side) or to allude to the painful restructuring processes that technological progress also initiates (on the liberal side). These processes are especially painful for those workers who might be replaced by technology and cannot move easily into other employment.

Both the political and the public discourses are engaged in debating the more painful and problematic consequences of technological progress through automation, but to different degrees. The liberal media sources are more committed in assessing the impact of automation critically, especially when it comes to the pressure on (middle-skill) jobs that could disappear in greater numbers while demand for high- and low-skill work could grow. Apart from this polarization of the labor market, the ongoing decoupling of productivity growth on the one hand and job and income growth on the other is a ubiquitous topic throughout the political and public discourses. Additionally, the lack in adequate responses to these issues is discussed, such as a lack in adequate skills training and poor access to higher education. This can lead to growing inequality and even more polarization in the labor market with growth at the higher and lower end of the skills spectrum. In Congress, infrastructure reform is continuously discussed in order to support more workers' transition into better jobs, on both political sides.

On the business-friendly side of the public debate (WSJ), the concerns over a more automated economy are mostly dismissed. The historical pattern of automation is stressed overall, which has brought about safer and more desirable work and higher pay, while some jobs and industries will always have to go down. In this narrative, the "creative" part of the creative destruction process is stressed, not the destructive one. Government should only engage in market-strengthening policies if necessary (infrastructure, education). Other policy proposals such as higher minimum wages, strengthening of the social benefits structure (health care), or a universal basic income are largely and openly rejected. In contrast to this, the more liberal-oriented public discourse is more concerned about the "destructive" part of creative destruction and technological progress. In order to counter the more undesirable effects of the restructuring process, rather traditional policies are discussed such as a higher minimum wage, the earned income tax credit, or infrastructure and education reform, but also more radical ideas such as the UBI. The liberal media outlets are also more engaged in showing that new work arrangements that are facilitated through technology such as sharing economy platforms are leaving their mark on the American labor force.

Overall, the political and public discourse around technological progress in the USA has been quite engaged with the rise of the platform economy. Not only academics and experts are talking about the nature and the impact of digital platforms, but ever since its beginning both the political and public realm have been committed to discussing the "so-called sharing economy." It has inspired idealism and hope for a fairer and more sustainable way of life, has spurred large venture capital investment, and the growth of some of the biggest names of Silicon Valley today. Eventually it has created concerns over everything from taxation, regulation, crowding-out effects, and congestion of inner cities to pressure on labor standards.

As indicated earlier in this book, the term *platform economy* is actually not used to any great extent in any discourse other than technical or academic. In the political and public realm, the two terms *sharing* and *gig economy* dominate. Although the two terms are often used interchangeably, they still indicate a certain attitude toward this new sector. Especially in the liberal discourse and to a certain extent in the political discourse investigated, the term *sharing economy* indicates the initial positive and hopeful outlook of these new economic activities. The sharing economy was seen as the "right thing to do": A more sustainable and collaborative way to use resources and skill sets that would lead the economy into a new age of alternative consumption and mindfulness. Although there are some examples of local, small-scale sharing economy efforts, this romanticized notion of the early days has largely disappeared, especially when it comes to ecological considerations.

Today, the sharing economy platforms are often presented through the lens of economic opportunity, especially for small-scale businesses and the individual worker. The platforms themselves also often portray themselves as a much better option for workers than actual employment. Workers are free to work where and when they choose, to the extent they need. This notion is strongly reflected in the political discourse as well as in the business-oriented side of the public discourse. The sharing economy platforms are presented as the epitome of the American entrepreneurial spirit where anyone can be their own boss and start their own (micro) business. Especially consumers have benefitted from these developments as new platforms have improved the access, quality, and affordability of consumer goods. This view refers to disruption through the platforms as a good thing that only happens in sectors that are "ripe for disruption," plagued by overregulation and slow productivity growth. Especially on the business-friendly side of the public discourse, this narrative is prevalent. Moreover, platform or gig work is not seen as anything worth worrying about. It is portrayed as overall marginal and much the same as regular independent contracting. The business-friendly discourse puts an emphasis on the innovative power of the platforms which should not be stifled by tighter rules or an extension of labor laws in this sector. In fact, allowing platform workers to organize or qualifying them as employees rather than independents is presented as an existential threat to the platform business model as a whole, which would have negative consequences for both workers and the growth of the economy.

In contrast to this, the more intensive use of the term *gig economy* indicates the more problematic side of the sharing economy platforms. When the term *gig economy* is used in the different discourses, it often refers to the overall changing nature of the American labor force that becomes more diverse and independent. Especially in the liberal discourse in Congress and the media, the use of the term indicates that progressives now see the more problematic side of these new work arrangements facilitated through digital platforms and have largely abandoned the earlier more romanticized notion of the sharing idea. The empowerment of the individual has not materialized, at least not for most workers, and platforms have also not led to more sustainability. Individual consumption has become more readily available which explains a lot of the success of platforms but has, for the most part, not become more sustainable.

The liberal discourse spends more time assessing the consequences of the rise of the platform economy when it comes to labor. Generally, there are fewer good jobs available and the platform jobs are not seen as a good alternative. They only serve as a convenient way to supplement your income if you need to. But this points to the fact that many people today are looking for ways to supplement their wages in order to keep up with living expenses. The quality of jobs is in decline overall and the future of work will be problematic for many members of the labor force, especially when things like gig work become even more common and wages remain low. Apart from emphasizing the need to look at the quality of jobs overall, there are other policies discussed in Congress and in the liberal media discourse. These include the call for a portable social safety net and a possible reform of the classification of workers.

In fact, worker (mis)classification is an issue that is quite extensively debated, both in the political and in the public realm. Are workers in the platform economy employees or independents? This is especially often debated in regard to Uber. Over and over, Uber is facing lawsuits over the status of drivers, which is both debated in Congress and extensively covered in the media sources. In the public debate, the opinions are rather clear: The business-friendly side (WSJ) does not see an issue with the independent contractor status of drivers and paints the ongoing challenges as an organized attack by labor unions and the Democrats to stifle innovation and overhaul the whole business model of the platform economy because it does not fit the liberal worldview.

The liberal media outlets seem to present a more nuanced picture. There is no general argument to make all platform workers employees. Yet, there are those platforms that should be more heavily scrutinized because they exert more control over workers than others. This is an issue for ride-hailing platforms like Uber, and less of an issue for marketplace or renting platforms like Etsy or Airbnb. In some cases, the liberal media outlets take a look at the "dark sides" of platform work, emphasizing that the gig aspect can be problematic. Although some workers value the flexibility and easy access, the rise of the gig economy points to an insecure workforce overall that suffers from stagnant wages and high living costs. Supplementing the income through a "side hustle" is then not an opportunity but a necessity to counter growing living expenses and to maintain a middle-class lifestyle in a society that has witnessed growing inequality overall. This points to a general issue in the American labor market: The lack of good jobs for many groups of workers that give them access to sustainable wage growth and career paths.

In the debates in Congress, both the opportunity and the more critical narrative around the sharing or gig economy can be found. Platforms are seen as an innovative opportunity and easy access to extra income, as well as part of worrisome developments in the labor market that is becoming more diverse and challenging for many Americans. The younger generation of millennials is especially affected by these developments. Yet, no politician regardless of party wants to really overhaul the whole platform business model by outlawing their business practice (of hiring contractors) especially because platforms have garnered enormous consumer welfare effects. Additionally, platforms have already established themselves to such a great extent that it becomes even more challenging to find the right policy response. Policies that are discussed are suspended in between the will to regulate the market to maintain competition and fair labor standards on the one hand and to support the innovative power, the entrepreneurial spirit, opportunities, and consumer benefits associated with many digital platforms on the other hand.

All these discussions in the public and political realm show that technological progress through automation and the rise of the platform economy are going to change the future of work in profound ways. Although the term *future of work* is not a big part of the political or public discourses when it comes to frequency, the overall discussions around automation and the sharing economy platforms are very much engaged with the future of the American labor force as a whole. The discourses include allusions to technological change and the still relevant dynamism of the American economy that has led to cutting-edge innovations in the fields of software, AI, or robotics. The rise of the sharing economy platforms can also be counted among the innovations of recent years.

At the same time, many of these innovations have led to more complicated developments such as the growth of the independent workforce and a changing demand for skill sets. Overall, the political and public discourses do not reflect the notion that large-scale technological unemployment is around the corner or will come true at any point in time. In light of recent mainstream discussions around the topic, emphasizing the threat of imminent large-scale job loss, this might be somewhat surprising. By looking closer at the actual political and public discourses around the future of work, it is relatively clear that a more nuanced but eventually unclear picture is painted of the future of work. Especially the liberal discourse addresses several issues that are of concern in the future. Again, the growth of the independent workforce is seen as a challenge. On the one hand, it points to changing attitudes toward work that values more flexibility, individualism, and a work–life balance. On the other hand, a more flexible workforce will become a challenge for income, career sustainability, and social benefit provision. Additionally, the growing independent workforce seems to point to the absence of enough high-quality stable jobs when it comes to pay, security, and career paths (job training and development).

In relation to Silicon Valley, especially Democratic lawmakers are ambiguous and lack a coherent way to address its innovations. On the one hand, they recognize and acknowledge the need for technical innovations. But at the same time, Democrats are uneasy about their impact. Unresolved issues around Silicon Valley tech firms include their taxation, data protection, market size, competition, their impact on existing laws and regulation such as labor laws, or net neutrality. At the same time, Silicon Valley leaders and high-tech workers are in line with progressives culturally and on many social reform projects and represent a rather loyal voter base for Democrats. So far, progressives seem to remain internally divided on how best to deal with the digital market and its largest actors. For Republicans, the new platforms do not pose such an ambiguous issue when it comes to regulation. Their pro-market attitudes could have made them a stronger ally in Silicon Valley. Here, the differences seem to be cultural and political rather than interest-based.

Generally, the discourses around automation, the sharing economy platforms, and the future of work reflect the innovative potential of technological progress with disruptive innovations shaping the American economy and society as a whole. This will have an enormous impact on businesses, consumers, and workers in the future. In the different discourses, there are some common opinions about how this future will play out, as well as more diverging views.

On the one hand, it is stressed that there are enormous welfare effects for consumers being created. Innovations like digital platforms have benefitted consumers greatly and have made many high-quality goods and services affordable and more readily available. Additionally, there will certainly be certain groups of workers who will immensely benefit from more technological progress. This will especially be true for the highly skilled portion of the labor market that will continue to be in demand. Others might face (gradual) replacement in the future, yet other jobs will be created as well. In the discourses investigated, there is a large emphasis on the rather traditional narrative around automation that stresses that automation has always had a replacement effect but that, ultimately, technological progress is nothing to really worry about. This narrative around technological progress remains a strong component in the public and political debate. In Congress, but also in the more business-friendly discourse, this narrative is strongly stressed. But also the more liberal discourse reflects this notion to a certain extent.

Nevertheless, there are also more nuanced pictures concerning this development toward the future of work, especially concerning the consequences of the restructuring processes for workers. Both political actors and the more liberal public discourse spent some time assessing the consequences of more technological progress on the future of work. A more challenging labor market is likely to arise: Middle-skill jobs are disappearing while low- and high-skill jobs are in demand. Yet, many Americans either lack the skills to move to better employment or will not be able to sustain their lifestyle with a low-wage job. Additionally, it is not at all clear which skills and tasks will truly be "safe" from further automation in the future. A truly coherent policy plan in response to this development is hard to find in the discourses investigated here. Rather, all actors mention certain proposals such as improving infrastructure or strengthening education here and there, as well as subsidizing low-wage income through the earned income tax credit. Yet, these efforts remain somewhat vague and often lack a path toward actual implementation through Congress.

The same is true for a response to the rise of the sharing economy platforms. Differing and ambiguous attitudes toward the platforms remain among all political and public actors, ranging from clear antipathy due to their unchallenged market power and negative influence on labor standards to true appraisal as the epitome of entrepreneurism, opportunity, and liberty in the market. What seems to be clear is that the more romanticized notion of the beginning of the sharing economy that stressed alternative consumption and sustainability has almost completely disappeared from the discourse over the years. For proponents of the sharing economy, it has become more common to stress the narrative of the sharing economy as a hub for economic opportunity rather than ecological or alternative considerations. This can be said for all political and public discourses investigated. Yet, business-friendly political and public actors seem to be more likely to portray the economic opportunity aspect of platforms in especially positive terms. But even more liberal political actors and media outlets see the platforms as an opportunity for some workers or small-scale businesses. Yet, in contrast to business-friendly actors, liberal outlets and progressive political actors are much more engaged in also looking at the more problematic side of the platforms. They stress the poor health of the American economy and labor market as a whole as one key aspect in the rise and success of platforms in recent years. In a slow economy with few good and stable jobs available, people have to look elsewhere for further income. But platform work is a poor alternative, in this view, to traditional steady employment.

In this context, certain policies are discussed to alleviate some of the issues surrounding digital platforms. Most conservative or business-friendly actors largely dismiss any calls for further strengthening or changing any (labor) laws as long as the platforms deliver inexpensive and safe consumer goods. Rather, platforms should be free to self-regulate in the market and their business model should not be artificially stifled by overregulation. For many liberal actors, there are, however, problematic aspects such as the degree of independent contracting, the lack of collective bargaining rights, a lack of security or social benefits such as health care, a lack of minimum pay, or other labor standards that should be addressed. Yet, although many of the sharing economy platforms have now established themselves in many sectors, the initial problems that have surrounded the platforms from the beginning have largely not been solved. This includes the status of workers (misclassification), taxation issues, congestion of inner cities, compliance with standards and (local) rules such as licensing or zoning, security issues, etc. These issues remain and are discussed again and again. This also shows that the digital platform structure of many Silicon Valley businesses including sharing economy companies or other new economy firms such as social media companies still poses a major issue for lawmakers and the public that remains unresolved. Although it has become clear that many platform businesses are not the mere platform intermediaries that they portray themselves as, politics has still not found a coherent answer to the issues arising through the structure and impact of digital (platform) businesses. Therefore, in many instances, local legal authorities are asked to address and solve issues surrounding platform businesses.

All in all, both the public and the political discourses around the future of work investigated in this work paint a picture of a likely new relationship of humans and machines—rather one of more cooperation than replacement. This holds enormous potential for economic and productivity growth in the future and will produce superior products that many Americans will benefit from as consumers. Most discourses reflect this notion. Yet, more specific training and access to education across the board will be necessary so that more Americans can participate in this future as workers. This is also an agreed point throughout the discourses examined here. Yet, as said before, concrete proposals to make this happen were rarely discussed.

Apart from the overall allusions to better education access and training programs, the UBI is discussed on several occasions, especially in the liberal discourse in the media. It is a topic that is pushed by several members of the business community in Silicon Valley and is presented as a solution to insecure times for the American workforce in the future. In the WSJ, although a very business-friendly outlet, the UBI is rarely discussed, if at all, and is usually discarded as an outlandish idea by some tech entrepreneurs. However, the virality of this topic indicates that there is no other agreed path that shows how to truly alleviate issues that a more technologically advanced future could hold for many Americans. The discussion around the UBI also shows that there are concerns that this wave of automation could be different from the past, breaking with historical patterns. Yet, it is unclear how much a UBI would be accepted in a society that values hard work as a profound part of life and how it could lead to more (economic) participation among Americans.

Apart from the expansion of the earned income tax credit that both parties seem to agree on, a consistent debate about the role of a more activating welfare state is largely missing from the debate. Neither the political nor the liberal public discourse examined in this work engages in coherent debates about a new welfare reform. Conservative and business-friendly actors usually outright reject any new welfare provisions. The last welfare reform in the 1990s has slashed large parts of the welfare system, which could also be a factor in the debate around the UBI. Long-term basic welfare payments are absent in the American welfare system. Additionally, the plans to make the welfare state more responsive and supportive of workers who face pressures from globalized trade and technology by introducing stronger active labor market policies have largely failed. More recent national debates to improve and open up social security programs such as Medicare for All or the discussion around forgiving student debts are important to highlight the struggles many Americans face today. Yet, it seems that coherent reforms to tackle the root of these struggles is not up for debate.

It might thus be up to the local and state level to introduce policies to support workers and open up ways for their continued economic participation in the future. There are signs that some local reforms and programs go in that direction by enacting stronger bargaining rights (for independents and platform workers for example) or introducing free community college (Tennessee Promise Program; Wermund 2019). These policies, however, are fragmented and small-scale attempts to address the profound restructuring processes in the American economy through globalization and technological progress and will once again lead to a very uneven picture throughout the USA with many regions missing out on the opportunities of the new economy in the future. Political action is needed so that everyone can participate in the future, especially because: "Neither the market nor technology has an internal moral compass; thus, any attempts to secure a more just world order will require social and political decisions" (Bader-Saye 2015: 96).

7.2 Outlook: Discourse on Technological Progress After 2017

This book looks at the political and public discourses around technological progress in the USA by examining material from the years 2013–2017 in detail. But of course these discourses are ongoing, both in the political and the public realm. These discourses have a profound effect on how technological progress advances as they reflect on positive or negative notions toward technology, funding of research areas and institutions, the adoption processes, public policy around technology and its impact, and the acceptance of technology in the workplace or in everyday life. As argued throughout this book, discourses influence how we feel about technology, fueling our enthusiasm and belief in the good of technology, or spiking concerns and fears toward certain future scenarios. In general, the tendencies and arguments identified in the political and public discourses in this work continue after 2017 as can be seen in the following short outlook into the years 2018 and 2019.[1]

In Congress, the years 2018 and 2019 saw hearings in different committees on various topics related to the ongoing restructuring processes and technological progress in the US economy. An additional search on the Government Publishing Office's website showed that the search terms *automation, digitization,* and *sharing economy* produced over 200 separate hearings in the years 2018–2019.[2] Interestingly, the term *sharing economy* produced only 4 hearings in this time frame, whereas the term *gig economy* produced 30 hearings. This again points to the changing use of these terms that has been indicated in the analysis of this book. The use of *gig economy* becomes more common, especially in regard to labor aspects of platforms, whereas the use of *sharing economy* becomes less common.

Hearings concerned with the three subjects could again be found throughout many different committees such as the Committee on Energy and Commerce, the Committee on Transportation and Infrastructure, the Committee on Science, Space and Technology, the Committee on Education and Labor, the Committee on Education and the Workforce, the Committee on Small Business and Entrepreneurship, the Joint Economic Committee, and many more. Different topics were discussed in

[1]This is a brief assessment of the political and public discourses around the three key terms (automation, digitization, sharing economy) that was accomplished through a search on the GPO website (Congress hearings), NexisUni database (articles from the *New York Times* and *Washington Post*), and the Wall Street Journal Website. All of the sites were searched between January 1, 2018, and November 30, 2019, using the three key terms. The journalistic articles were assessed based on the headlines. Congress hearings were also scanned through headlines. Additionally, some Congress hearings were looked at in more detail because of their connection to the issues addressed in this book. No quantitative analysis was conducted with material from 2018 to 2019; therefore, results described here are based on a qualitative assessment and not a strictly comprehensive analysis of the discourses.

[2]The search was conducted between January 1, 2018, and November 30, 2019. The number was not checked for duplicates. Irrelevant committees were not removed, which was the case in the corpus analysis in this book.

these hearings, such as Fintech, the blockchain, cloud computing, automotive innovation, social media, infrastructure, minimum wage, "Agritech," digital currencies, intellectual property, climate change, multi-employer pension systems, and many other things. This again shows that technological progress is not limited to a specific area but makes inroads in all economic sectors.

In the years 2018–2019, there were several hearings on artificial intelligence specifically, such as *Artificial Intelligence: With Great Power Comes Great Responsibility* in a Joint Hearing before the Subcommittee on Research and Technology and the Subcommittee on Energy, Committee on Science, Space, and Technology in the House of Representatives (2018), or *Game Changers: Artificial Intelligence Part I-III* in the Subcommittee on Information Technology, Committee on Oversight and Government Reform, House of Representatives (2018), which were concerned with AI in regard to the federal government or public policy. *Artificial Intelligence: Societal and Ethical Implications* in the Committee on Science, Space, and Technology, House of Representatives (2019), and *Artificial Intelligence and the Future of Work*, Subcommittee on Research and Technology, Committee on Science, Space, and Technology, House of Representatives (2019), were also specifically concerned with the impact of AI. The latter hearing talks about the issue of the future of work in regard to the "impact of machine learning and artificial intelligence on the workforce, including issues related to worker displacement, retraining of the current workforce, and developing a skilled technical workforce of the future that can thrive in an economy in which AI increasingly plays a role" (Congress 2019a: 2). The hearing is also concerned with AI's impact on existing economic inequalities. Witnesses include Erik Brynjolfsson from the MIT Initiative on the Digital Economy who has worked extensively on the topic with his colleague Andrew McAfee. It seems that artificial intelligence is increasingly seen as the biggest disrupter for the economy in the future, both for the business side and for the labor force that could see profound changes in the quantity and nature of work. The *Disrupter Series* in the House of Representatives that is concerned with state-of-the-art technological innovations has also continued after 2017 for example with hearings on the Internet of Things and quantum computing.

Some of the hearings from 2018 and 2019 stood out in regard to the main components of this book, such as *Millennials and the Gig Economy* in the Committee on Small Business, House of Representatives (2018). Holding a specific hearing on the gig economy and the millennial generation points to the significance and virality of the topic. It emphasizes again, as this work shows, that the gig economy is often associated with millennial lifestyle. Additionally, the term *gig economy* is used rather than *sharing economy* when it comes to working independently and flexibly. In the hearing, the so-called gig economy is discussed in regard to who participates in it, what working in it looks like, and how its growth affects small business. Most of these issues have been discussed in various hearings before. The gig economy is equated with short-term contract work that has always existed but is now "re-envisioned" through technology and the platform infrastructure. Thus, the part of the economy that has been using contracting for a long time has become more efficient through technology. It has become more common to work in this way, with possibly one in three workers engaging in nonstandard work and millennials being especially engaged in this part of the economy. Representative Velazquez (Dem) argues that "Technology has always been a catalyst for entrepreneurship" (Congress 2018: 2), and the gig economy has created new channels for entrepreneurs. "Millennials are establishing new digital platforms and markets to share everything from apartment space to transportation to artisan goods" (Congress 2018: 2). This leads to the blurring of business and employee status. Although millennials value the independence, autonomy, and flexibility of this kind of work, the root of success of the gig economy can also be found in larger economic struggles after the Great Recession, which is a notion she previously expressed about the sharing economy as well. Again, the changing use of the term can be seen here. Yet, it is also apparent that the "sharing idea" lives on despite the change of name, alluding here to millennials "sharing everything." The balance between economic opportunity and labor standards also remains a debated issue: "As this technological revolution advances, government policy must keep pace. It is, therefore, important this committee deepen its understanding of what is happening in the gig economy and has a grasp on how we can minimize risk for millennial employees while maximizing growth and productivity for small business" (Congress 2018: 2). In this statement, it again becomes clear that both concerns for workers and the narrative of opportunity in this sector exist side by side.

In the light of the gig economy, another hearing called *The History and Structure of the Multiemployer Pension System* in Joint Select Committee on Solvency of Multiemployer Pension Plans (2018) is significant as it discusses multi-employer pension plans in the USA that have existed since the 1940s and are very diverse. With the rise of independent work, several experts have suggested multi-employer plans for the general allocation of social benefits. The existing plans include options for employees of one specific firm, but also for those who have multiple employers throughout their careers. There are over 1000 such plans and quite a few face bankruptcy (and employees the loss of pensions) because of general shifts in the economy and financial troubles after the Great Recession. On the one hand, this shows that multi-employer plans are not uncommon in the USA. On the other hand, their structures and overall financial health are in trouble, which makes it questionable if these schemes can be enlarged to include more workers without significant structural changes.

After the switch of the House in the midterm election 2018 from Republican to a Democratic majority, more hearings can be found on issues that Democrats are concerned about such as the minimum wage or labor organization. It is very apparent in these hearings that the partisan divide is unlikely to be bridged on these issues. For example, the hearing *Gradually Raising the Minimum Wage to 15: Good for Workers, Good for Business, and Good for the Economy*, held in the Committee on Education and Labor, House of Representatives (2019), starkly contrasts the two partisan sides. Democrats advocate in favor of a (gradual) increase of the minimum wage to $15 to make it possible to earn a living wage. The federal minimum wage has not increased in over 10 years and was designed to help low-wage families. Republicans continue to denounce an increase of the minimum wage as part of extreme social policy proposals of the left such as free college or universal health care that are portrayed as unworkable and headline-grabbing. Republicans argue that a high minimum wage will increase poverty because it will eliminate jobs and hurt (small) business.

The partisan divide is also very apparent when it comes to bargaining power. In the hearing *Protecting Worker's Right to Organize: The Need for Labor Law Reform*, held in the Subcommittee on Health, Employment, Labor, and Pensions, Committee on Education and Labor, House of Representatives (2019), Democrats argue that unions have ensured workers' rights and have fueled prosperity and growth of the middle class throughout American history. They have protected benefits and have also played an important political role. As unionization continues to decline, there are negative consequences for working families. Decline in unionization is seen as the missing link between productivity growth and rising pay. Inequality and stagnant wages are seen in relation to a lack in unionization and a government that has sided too much with big corporations. Unsurprisingly, the Republican side argues that workers' rights to organize are not under attack at all. Moreover, unions are not solely in the interest of workers but pursue their own interests. Republicans argue that giving unions more power is not the same as giving workers more power. Unions are pressuring workers even though they might reject union representation. Overall, Republicans argue that the economy is doing well and there is no need for any reform that would enforce union power.

Another interesting hearing from the Senate (*Small Business and the American Worker*, Committee on Small Business and Entrepreneurship, 2019) seems to show a somewhat more nuanced picture when it comes to Republicans and labor, both arguing in line with the Trump administration but also in favor of some reforms. Marco Rubio (Rep) argues that policymakers have focused exclusively on consumer welfare and have paid too little attention to the "welfare of workers." Yet, he does not want to expand the government social safety net because such a move ignores the role and dignity of work in the lives of Americans. Rather, economic growth needs to create "good and dignified jobs, not just good statistics" (Congress 2019b: 1). He admits that many Americans have been left behind despite GDP growth (labor force participation rates are low and incomes of the high-school educated have fallen). Rubio argues that the labor market has to become more dynamic, while not disregarding the power of the free market and competition. More in line with what the Trump administration would argue concerning regulation and taxes, the USA needs to strengthen its productive capacity and businesses should invest in physical capital and workers' skills to become more productive. Government should provide infrastructure, education, and research, while "aligning regulation with labor market needs" (Congress 2019b: 2). This would include deregulation such as cutting restrictions in licensing, non-compete agreements, lowering the tax burden on middle-income families, and a parental leave program.

These examples show that the partisan divide in the USA is only becoming wider. Democrats and Republicans might see similar problems in the future for the American workforce, but they will most likely not be able to agree on a coherent, bipartisan strategy to tackle this future. The growth of the independent workforce, the rise of AI in all sectors, and the ongoing wage stagnation that many workers face are crucial developments, which both sides seem to agree on. Yet, the partisan views on how to respond to these developments seem to be far apart with many Democrats arguing in favor of strengthening the social safety net, increasing bargaining power, and the minimum wage, while Republicans argue in favor of deregulation, tax cuts, and the free market that will bring opportunities for the American worker through the trickle-down effect. With these opposing views, it seems very unlikely that bipartisan reforms will happen any time soon.

Looking at the discourse in the liberal media, one can see that the topics of *automation*, *digitization,* and the *sharing economy* continue to be covered extensively. For the period of 2018–2019[3] there were about 1291 articles on the topics. After scanning most of the headlines of that period, it is clear that many topics investigated in this work are still part of the debate in the liberal media discourse. For example, there are articles on transportation innovation, the self-driving car (e.g., in development by GM), robots and their possible capacity to replace jobs, Silicon Valley (business-making, Tech Unicorns, ethical concerns), or future education and access to higher education. Job training and (community) college education come up as specific themes, as well as articles about the right college and skills choice that are decisive for future success in the labor market. Robots and their impact on jobs in all kinds of branches are covered extensively. The self-driving car or truck is also a topic that comes up repeatedly, for example in relation to safety concerns. Technology in all branches and sectors is debated throughout the articles. Specific technologies that are discussed are AI algorithms, for example in self-driving vehicles, the blockchain, and smart robotics. There are also articles on archives, libraries, and museums engaging in digitization. Other articles talk about specific businesses (like Amazon) that engage in training efforts for their workers.

The *sharing economy* as a term seems to be less and less common, as was indicated in the analysis of this book, and the term *gig economy* is becoming more prevalent. There are some specific articles on the *gig economy* in this time period, for example on the fact that platform work does not pay sustainable wages and is not a good replacement for stable jobs. There are also several allusions to delivery jobs that are part of the gig economy. The *sharing economy* appears more in the context of renting. Platforms like Airbnb and their negative impact on inner cities are discussed, as well as other platforms such as Uber or Lyft that started public trading in 2019. Uber is again mentioned quite extensively throughout the time period, for example when talking about its efforts to establish self-driving cars and trucks in the

[3]The search was last conducted on April 20, 2020, on Nexis Uni for the period of January 1, 2018, to November 30, 2019, in the Washington Post Blogs, Washingtonpost.com, *The Washington Post*, The New York Times Blogs, and *The New York Times*. Terms were used as follows: “automation,” “digitization,” and “sharing economy.” Duplicates were not removed from the sample. The articles were concerned with the following branches: automotive, computing and information, technology, consumer, products, electronics, manufacturing, media and telecommunications, and transportation and warehousing. Articles in entertainment and arts were excluded.

future. Other platforms like social media (Facebook, Twitter) or Amazon are also covered to a great extent.

Apart from that, there are larger assessments of the rise of populism and the economy under the Trump administration that include the trade war with China, NAFTA, Russian interferences, or tax cuts. The Democratic presidential candidate race also plays a role in this time frame. In general, there are also corporate and market news that report on the success and troubles of some specific companies such as GM, Siemens, Boeing, Uber, Lyft, FedEx, or Airbnb at home and abroad.

Artificial intelligence is a topic that comes up quite often in the form of driverless vehicles (Tesla) or cockpit automation, but also in smart robotics in other sectors such as retail or high-skilled workplaces. AI, algorithms, and robotics are three factors that are continuously discussed because they have so much influence on the workplace and on many sectors like manufacturing, retail, farmwork, or the hotel industry. There are also allusions to more rural parts of the USA and smaller cities still being largely left behind in this more automated future (e.g., the Rust Belt). Additionally, there are allusions to the polarizing effect of technology on wages, leading to growth in high-wage and low-wage sectors.

The term *future of work* appears from time to time in the headlines, especially in relation to the presidential race where Andrew Yang ran his campaign talking quite extensively about the future of work under the influence of more automation and AI. He featured a specific plan for a UBI in his campaign proposal. The UBI is also covered in other articles throughout this time period, for example in allusions to (the end of) Finland's UBI experiment or new plans for such experiments in California. There are also associations with the Nordic model of the welfare state and social democracy as a solution to a more insecure future, as well as infrastructure spending as a source for employment. The minimum wage and other possible future policies like a robot tax also come up in the articles investigated here.

The *Wall Street Journal* (WSJ) was taken as an example of the more conservative, business-friendly side of public discourse. In the years 2018 and 2019, around 761 articles (only WSJ articles and press releases) could be found using the search terms *automation, digitization,* and *sharing economy—automation* delivered by far the most research results (over 590 of the articles).[4] From examining the headlines of these articles, one can see that the topics were largely similar to the ones investigated in this book before. Most of the articles were market and corporate news about performance, as well as mergers and acquisitions of specific firms. There were also specific sectors that were covered in the articles such as manufacturing, health care, and robotics more generally where automation plays a big role. Additionally, the digital or financial sector (cryptocurrency), social media, retail, and e-commerce

[4]The time frame of this search was January 1, 2018 to November 30, 2019 on wsj.com. The search was last conducted on April 20, 2020, with the search terms "automation," "digitization," and "sharing economy" separately. WSJ articles and press releases were searched. Duplicates were not removed from the sample. This search was conducted on the WSJ website and not on the database ABI/INFORM used to compile the data for the corpus analysis. As the articles were not downloaded, the website was enough to deliver article headlines over the last few years.

were sectors discussed in the WSJ. There were also specific allusions to the oil and gas industry, as well as the mining industry that sees more innovation due to new automation efforts. Siemens, IBM, Apple, Microsoft, Amazon, Honeywell, Tesla, Airbus and Boeing, or Walmart were some of the big players mentioned, but there was an extremely large number of other businesses mentioned, both small businesses and startups. The IPOs and initial trading efforts of some sharing economy platforms like Uber and Lyft were also mentioned. The years 2018–2019 also saw a lot of coverage of the troubles of WeWork and SoftBank that financed the startup.

Apart from that, the sharing economy was mentioned in the context of a new California law on the reclassification of gig workers which could mean a significant shift of employment structures in the gig economy (which in the meantime has been successfully challenged through a ballot initiative in 2020). It was also mentioned that many platforms only offer low wages. In general, there were few articles on the gig or sharing economy overall compared to articles on automation. There were about 98 articles that dealt with the sharing economy in more detail. Silicon Valley and more generally "big tech" was also mentioned several times in the article headlines, talking about the founders and culture of Silicon Valley, as well as technology more broadly.

Just like in the other sources, the topic of AI and its impact on all kinds of sectors from office work to manufacturing was quite intensively covered in the articles from the WSJ. AI is making inroads in all kinds of jobs, even white-collar ones. In the context of AI, robots and robotics were regularly covered in the WSJ articles. Their development even points to a "new industrial revolution" where humans and robots will go hand in hand. Additionally, cybersecurity is another concern with the growing impact of AI in all kinds of fields.

Automation more generally is discussed in relation to pressure on (middle class) wages and in relation to demographic changes of an aging society. Women and their growing presence in the (tech) labor market was also mentioned several times. Generally, there were allusions to new skills that are in demand in a more automated future where more AI and robots make an entry into the workplace. Interestingly, the UBI is more explicitly mentioned in the articles from 2018 and 2019. This can, for example, be seen in coverage of Andrew Yang's presidential bid and a basic income experiment in California.

In all of the aforementioned material, the topic of artificial intelligence and its impact in the future seems to be evident. As said before, the discourses around ongoing technological progress paint a picture of a new human-machine relationship that is marked by cohabitation rather than replacement. The subjects of AI and the future of work have already been important in the discourses examined previously, but more recently there seems to be an even more intense interest in these topics. Several hearings in Congress and a large amount of articles in both the liberal media outlets and the more business-friendly medium cover the field of AI, robotics, and algorithms. In this context, innovations like the self-driving vehicle are discussed, which could have a profound influence on the world of work, for example in the trucking industry. Yet, AI is also moving into other sectors because many new digital applications use some form of AI in their products. This way, AI moves into areas from retail to office work, the factory floor, and even agriculture.

The presidential race that started to be covered in the media in 2018 also enhanced the visibility of the topic of AI and automation as Andrew Yang launched a campaign to become the Democratic presidential nominee. His program included details on possible negative effects of automation and AI on the availability of jobs in the future, and he ran his campaign on the introduction of a universal basic income, which he called the "freedom dividend" (Yang 2020). After ending his bid to become the Democratic presidential candidate, Yang announced the launch of his own UBI experiment in New York (Ward 2020). The term *future of work* can also be found in some articles and hearings in the time frame 2018 to 2019, indicating that the term becomes more of a fixed expression when the implications of more technological progress on the world of work are discussed.

In the political realm, it is clear that the topics around technological progress and its impact on the American economy and workforce continue to be discussed in all kinds of contexts. Yet, the partisan divide that has become even deeper after the election of Donald Trump in 2016 and the midterm elections in 2018 is also apparent. Although there seems to be an agreement on the factors that will shape the American economy profoundly in the coming decades, there seems to be even less agreement to work together in alleviating some of the pressures and preparing Americans for the future of work. This is not due to a total lack of agreement on the challenges of the future, but seems to be an effect of deepening political polarization that paints every reach across the aisle as a political defeat. While Republicans continue to emphasize free market ideas and the trickle-down effect, Democrats have a harder time coming to grasp with technological innovations and its actors. Silicon Valley platforms are seen as innovators offering opportunities, while at the same time their power and influence is seen as problematic when it comes to data, communication, market power, or the influence on the workforce. Overall, the opposition of Silicon Valley to the Trump administration runs along cultural and political lines, rather than business interests, which could be more closely aligned with Republicans in theory. Therefore, the recent considerations to break up big tech by Republican lawmakers might be motivated by political opposition rather than any real concern for functioning market forces. For liberal Democrats, considerations for the breakup of big tech seem to be more in regard to their market power and size, as well as their mishandling of consumer data and political meddling of foreign powers that revealed the power of some platform when it comes to communication and data (Lohr 2019).

7.3 Conclusion: A Difficult Vision for Future Participation in the Face of Disruption

In conclusion of this book that is concerned with the future of work and discourses around technological progress in the USA, we can say that a more technologically advanced society and economy hold great potential but also pose enormous difficulties when it comes to the economic participation of the majority of workers who will face even more disruptions in the future. What can be done to improve their outlook? In line with what is argued throughout this book, education remains one of the key areas that will be able to give more Americans a chance to meaningfully participate in the economy of the future. In order to become part of the group that really benefits from technological progress, education needs to improve in the USA across the board. Ryan Avent argues, however, that the "low-hanging educational fruit have been picked" and what advanced economies really need is a small group of highly educated specialists. But not everyone is up to this skill level and there is no abundance of jobs in the high-tech sector. Additionally, those who will be replaced through technology and automated processes are not necessarily those who will go on to get a post-secondary degree. This will lead to disruption in the labor market and issues for the modern welfare state.

Ryan Avent is one of the more critical assessors of the digital age. He sees many possible issues awaiting us in a world where digital technology is even more advanced than today. He does see a possibility of new technologies creating new, good work. "But it will not be scalable mass employment" (Avent 2016: 64). The more probable future could be a scenario where technology creates new disruptive products with decreasing costs for consumers, but destroying many more jobs than it creates (Avent 2016: 76). In this world, income for many will remain low and they might opt out of work, which will strain social safety nets further and could lead to social division among those who work and finance the social welfare state and those who live off of it (Avent 2016: 77). Society will face a trade-off between accepting this situation and making it work most effectively, or intense conflict between haves and have-nots (Avent 2016: 77).

Today, it is clear that "the hardest part in finding utopia is not the figuring out of how to produce more. We've managed that. The hard part is the redistribution" (Avent 2016: 10). But if we do not find a feasible way to redistribute the wealth that is garnered by the rise of technology, then we will soon face even harsher political backlash to the ongoing rise of inequality, maybe even comparable to the political conflicts of the Industrial Revolution. The growth of radical populist tendencies throughout the West might point in that direction (Avent 2016: 12f). In the long run, the dissatisfaction of many Americans with failing economic integration and stagnation could fuel nationalist, "inward-looking political movements" that favor protectionism, identity politics, slamming established institutions, the 'corrupt elites,' and liberal democracy more broadly. As of now, "Faith in markets and their ability to generate broad-based growth has been shaken" (Avent 2016: 213).

The political and economic climate already seems to reflect the notion that faith in the liberal order has been fundamentally shaken and that many turn toward these "inward-looking political movements." Are we even approaching the end of the liberal era altogether? In his book *Why Liberalism Failed*, Patrick Deneen argues that the concept of liberalism as the basis for democracy in the West is in crisis, which can be seen in the skewed "distribution of wealth; decay in traditional institutions, from civic associations to labor unions to the family; a loss of trust in authority—political, religious, scientific, journalistic—and among citizens themselves; growing disillusionment with progress in effecting equal justice for all (...)" (Deneen 2019: Foreword, Pos. 110). In Deneen's view, the success of the logic of liberalism ultimately leads to its demise, which finds its manifestation in the populist "revolutions" in the transatlantic world in recent years. Liberalism as an ideology is focused on liberating the individual from any restraints that geography, history, nature, religion, or culture have posed (Deneen 2019: Introduction, Pos 233). Yet, such a notion seems to be untenable, and a "popular reaction to an increasingly oppressive liberal order might be forms of authoritarian illiberalism that would promise citizens power over those forces that no longer seemed under their control: government, economy, and the dissolution of social norms and unsettled ways of life" (Deneen 2019: Introduction, Pos 330). Nowadays, many Americans think that the "country is moving in the wrong direction" and that "its best days are behind it." Additionally, future generations will be worse off than their parent generations, something unthinkable to a society steadfastly aspiring to the American Dream (Deneen 2019: 2). It seems "evident to all that the political system is broken and social fabric is fraying, particularly as a growing gap increases between wealthy haves and left-behind have-nots (...)" (Deneen 2019: 2). This "Civic unhappiness is mirrored in economic discontent" (Deneen 2019: 9).

In this environment, globalization and technology are increasingly perceived as forces that are inevitable and unstoppable by "any individual or nation" (Deneen 2019: 15) and the mere thought of alternatives to the current economic integration, standardization, and homogenization is not even entertained. Although people are supposed to be free, even liberated from the limits of place and time through technology, they have the feeling that this technology and their future is increasingly out of their control. Technological devices are disrupting workplaces, "apparently granting us liberty but making us our technology's ward and helpmeet" (Deneen 2019: 15). These developments do very little to make people feel liberated. Many people rather feel pessimistic and frustrated about their future, "insecure, powerless, afraid, and alone" (Deneen 2019: 16), as Deneen puts it. The future remains unknown and thus technological progress is met with both "wild optimism" and "profound terror about the apocalypse" (Deneen 2019: 91) that this same technology could bring. Popular reflections of technological progress paint a picture of powerlessness toward coming innovation and a fear of technological "bondage," despite its aim to liberate us (Deneen 2019: 93): "Whether told as praise or lament, this narrative of inevitability tends to grant autonomy to technology itself, as if its advances occurred independently of human intention and thought" (Deneen 2019: 98).

Although technology does not exist without political and social norms, liberalism itself makes us believe that "technology develops independent of any norms and intentions, but rather shapes our norms, our polity, and even humanity, and inevitably escapes our control" (Deneen 2019: 102). Given this narrative, it is not surprising that many Americans feel frustrated and insecure. Deneen sees the recent backlash against liberal democracy as a culminating event fed by the realization that liberalism has not brought the desired liberating effect, especially if you are not part of the governing cosmopolitan political, cultural, and economic elite that has prospered in Western liberal democracies. Technological progress of recent years also plays a crucial role in this discontent because a large group of Americans has not profited from this development but has rather come under even more pressure economically.

The rise of populist leaders can thus be seen as an answer to an ongoing alienation people feel toward a system that does not seem to take into account their interest nor understand their frustration. The current elites are unable to really understand this backlash fed by deep economic and cultural frustration. Mere insistence on overall consumer welfare through technology or general benefits from trade are not enough to alleviate the frustrations of those groups who feel they are culturally, politically, and economically isolated and left behind with no positive vision for their future. Deneen does not offer a comprehensive strategy against these developments or a way forward, apart from allusions to smaller and local forms of resistance. This view rejects the homogenizing effect of globalization and technological progress and emphasizes local communities that should uphold their traditional values and identities. Whether such efforts can resist the far-reaching pull of liberal thought that seems to emphasize market value against anything else seems questionable, however.

Deneen's view on the recent backlash against the liberal order and frustrations among large groups of the American citizenry certainly rings true to a great extent. Yet, there are different views of what the future will look like under the influence of more and more advanced technology. Whether you are among the concerned "Luddite thinkers" who see machines becoming much too powerful for our own good, or you are among the group of "traditionalists" who argue that the historical pattern of creative destruction through technological innovation will benefit us all, or somewhere in between these two extremes, these perceptions and attitudes toward the future that are reflected in the discourses around technological change and the future of work certainly have a profound impact on our political and economic behavior.

Looking once again at the field of narrative economics, one cannot be sure which narratives will come to dominate our thinking. Unlike "the hypothesized business 'cycles,' narratives don't recur at regular time intervals" (Shiller 2018: 271). But this does not mean that they can or should be ignored in our assessment of society and the political and economic climate. Some narratives that were powerful in the past are forgotten, but some are rediscovered and become contagious once more in new context. This is true for narratives around technological development as well. Since the Industrial Revolution, people have both cherished and feared the outlook of a more automated future and every time narratives about advancing technology have influenced our (economic) behavior. Taking recent post-liberal thought into account, people today fundamentally fear that technology and their future is out of their own hands and the system does not work *for* them, but *against* their best interests, leaving everyone to fight on their own in a harsh capitalist system. It is a fear of becoming gradually obsolete and not being needed anymore that destroys the self-esteem of Americans who used to steadfastly believe in the American Dream (Shiller 2019: 18). Recent labor participation rates illustrate that many Americans have entirely stopped to participate in the USA economically (Uchitelle 2019). It is therefore crucial to be aware of the perceptions and notions toward these profound transformations in our economy and society in order to understand the current political and economic climate. This will improve our understanding of these developments and make it possible to evaluate answers to these changes, as well as predict likely future scenarios that will come out of proposed solutions.

People make sense of the world through narratives that shape the overall discourses around a certain subject. With the rise of social media as one of the most common means of communication, (economic) narratives and discourses become even more widespread. They are not spread randomly anymore, but they are reinforced through the algorithms of search engines and platforms (Shiller 2018: 273). This will also have a profound effect on how we understand the technological change that is going on around us and will likely shape our response to it. We already see that social media algorithms can be deeply problematic in distorting facts and spreading false claims, seemingly favoring the most absurd and gloomy stories over actual events. This could further emphasize the pessimistic and threatening stories around technological change that lead to increasing insecurity among citizens. In order to combat this development "Policymakers should try to create and disseminate counternarratives that establish more rational and more public-spirited economic behavior. Even if the counternarratives are slower to take effect than a more contagious destructive narrative, they can eventually be corrective" (Shiller 2018: 278).

More recent scapegoating narratives that paint a picture of a down-trodden America, unfairly treated by its allies and exploited through global trade, have been highly contagious, at least among certain groups. These scapegoating mechanisms offering easy solutions to complex processes such as globalization and technological development could successfully claim at least some electoral victories in the USA. Yet, this will do little to eventually help those groups of Americans who already feel the economic pinch and are fearing economic decline and further status loss in the future. Thus, solutions to tackle economic insecurity and frustration among the American public should not only include viable policy plans in response to the challenges of the future of work, but it is also crucial to convey these policies and future visions through narratives that people will understand and can relate to. Mere allusions to the overall benefits from trade and technological advancement, wait-and-see attitudes, and continuing partisan battles in the face of such profound changes as automation, digitization, and the rise of the sharing economy platforms seem inadequate to convey any unifying vision of a better future for all Americans.

References

Avent R (2016) The wealth of humans: work and its absence in the twenty-first century. Allen Lane/ Penguin, New York/London

Bader-Saye S (2015) Closing the gap: a social imaginary for the common good. Anglican Theol Rev 98(1):91–109. https://doi.org/10.1787/9789264235120-en

Congress (2018) Millennials and the gig economy. U.S. Government Publishing Office, Washington, DC

Congress (2019a) Artificial intelligence and the future of work. U.S. Government Publishing Office, Washington, DC

Congress (2019b) Small business and the American worker. U.S. Government Publishing Office, Washington, DC

Deneen PJ (2019) Why liberalism failed (Kindle version). Yale University Press, New Haven, CT

Lohr S (2019) New Google and Facebook inquiries show big tech scrutiny is rare bipartisan act. The New York Times. https://www.nytimes.com/2019/09/06/technology/attorney-generals-tech-antitrust-investigation.html. Accessed 15 July 2020

Shiller RJ (2018) Narrative economics: how stories go viral & drive major economic events. Princeton University Press, Princeton, NJ

Shiller RJ (2019) Narratives about technology-induced job degradations then and now. NBER Working paper no. 25536

Uchitelle L (2019) Unemployment is low, but that's only part of the story. The New York Times. https://www.nytimes.com/2019/07/11/business/low-unemployment-not-seeking-work.html. Accessed 15 July 2020 2020

Ward M (2020) Andrew Yang's nonprofit will give $500 to 20 New Yorkers every month for 5 years in his first big experiment with universal basic income. Business Insider. https://www.businessinsider.com/andrew-yang-universal-basic-income-cash-experiment-upstate-new-york-2020-5?r=DE&IR=T. Accessed 15 July 2020

Wermund B (2019) The red state that loves free college. Politico. https://www.politico.com/agenda/story/2019/01/16/tennessee-free-college-000867. Accessed 29 Nov 2019

Yang A (2020) The freedom dividend, defined. https://www.yang2020.com/what-is-freedom-dividend-faq/. Accessed 15 July 2020

The manufacturer's authorised representative in the EU is Springer Nature Customer Service Centre GmbH, Europaplatz 3, 69115 Heidelberg, Germany. If you have any concerns regarding our products, please contact ProductSafety@springernature.com

Printed and bound by CPI Group (UK) Ltd, Croydon, CR0 4YY
30/09/2026
02225692-0013